D0367417

The Editor

LEAH S. MARCUS is Edwin Mims Professor of English at Vanderbilt University. She is the author of *Childhood and Cultural Despair, The Politics of Mirth, Puzzling Shakespeare*, and *Unediting the Renaissance*. She has edited two volumes of the writings of Queen Elizabeth I (with Janel Mueller and Mary Beth Rose), a Norton Critical Edition of *The Merchant of Venice*, and an Arden Early Modern Drama text of John Webster's *The Duchess of Malfi*.

W. W. NORTON & COMPANY, INC.
Also Publishes

ENGLISH RENAISSANCE DRAMA: A NORTON ANTHOLOGY
edited by David Bevington et al.

THE NORTON ANTHOLOGY OF AFRICAN AMERICAN LITERATURE
edited by Henry Louis Gates Jr. and Nellie Y. McKay et al.

THE NORTON ANTHOLOGY OF AMERICAN LITERATURE
edited by Nina Baym et al.

THE NORTON ANTHOLOGY OF CHILDREN'S LITERATURE
edited by Jack Zipes et al.

THE NORTON ANTHOLOGY OF DRAMA
edited by J. Ellen Gainor, Stanton B. Garner Jr., and Martin Puchner

THE NORTON ANTHOLOGY OF ENGLISH LITERATURE
edited by M. H. Abrams and Stephen Greenblatt et al.

THE NORTON ANTHOLOGY OF LITERATURE BY WOMEN
edited by Sandra M. Gilbert and Susan Gubar

THE NORTON ANTHOLOGY OF MODERN AND CONTEMPORARY POETRY
edited by Jahan Ramazani, Richard Ellmann, and Robert O'Clair

THE NORTON ANTHOLOGY OF POETRY
edited by Margaret Ferguson, Mary Jo Salter, and Jon Stallworthy

THE NORTON ANTHOLOGY OF SHORT FICTION
edited by R. V. Cassill and Richard Bausch

THE NORTON ANTHOLOGY OF THEORY AND CRITICISM
edited by Vincent B. Leitch et al.

THE NORTON ANTHOLOGY OF WORLD LITERATURE
edited by Sarah Lawall et al.

THE NORTON FACSIMILE OF THE FIRST FOLIO OF SHAKESPEARE
prepared by Charlton Hinman

THE NORTON INTRODUCTION TO LITERATURE
edited by Alison Booth and Kelly J. Mays

THE NORTON READER
edited by Linda H. Peterson and John C. Brereton

THE NORTON SAMPLER
edited by Thomas Cooley

THE NORTON SHAKESPEARE, BASED ON THE OXFORD EDITION
edited by Stephen Greenblatt et al.

For a complete list of Norton Critical Editions, visit
www.wwnorton.com/college/English/nce_home.htm

A NORTON CRITICAL EDITION

William Shakespeare
AS YOU LIKE IT

AUTHORITATIVE TEXT
SOURCES AND CONTEXTS
CRITICISM

Edited by

LEAH S. MARCUS
VANDERBILT UNIVERSITY

W · W · NORTON & COMPANY · *New York* · *London*

W. W. Norton & Company has been independent since its founding in 1923, when William Warder Norton and Mary D. Herter Norton first published lectures delivered at the People's Institute, the adult education division of New York City's Cooper Union. The firm soon expanded its program beyond the Institute, publishing books by celebrated academics from America and abroad. By mid-century, the two major pillars of Norton's publishing program—trade books and college texts—were firmly established. In the 1950s, the Norton family transferred control of the company to its employees, and today—with a staff of four hundred and a comparable number of trade, college, and professional titles published each year—W. W. Norton & Company stands as the largest and oldest publishing house owned wholly by its employees.

Copyright © 2012 by W. W. Norton & Company, Inc.

All rights reserved
Printed in the United States of America
First Edition

Book design by Antonina Krass
Production manager: Sean Mintus

Library of Congress Cataloging-in-Publication Data

Shakespeare, William, 1564–1616.
    As you like it : authoritative text, sources and contexts, criticism / William Shakespeare ; edited by Leah S. Marcus. — 1st ed.
        p. cm. — (A Norton critical edition)
    Includes bibliographical references.
    ISBN 978-0-393-92762-7 (pbk.)
1. Shakespeare, William, 1564–1616. As you like it.   2. Fathers and daughters—Drama.   3. Exiles—Drama.   I. Marcus, Leah S. (Leah Sinanoglou)   II. Title.
    PR2803.A2M36   2012
    822.3'3—dc23

                                                            2011026207

W. W. Norton & Company, Inc., 500 Fifth Avenue, New York, NY 10110
www.wwnorton.com

W. W. Norton & Company Ltd., Castle House, 75/76 Wells Street, London
W1T 3QT

1 2 3 4 5 6 7 8 9 0

Contents

List of Illustrations vii

Preface ix

The Text of *As You Like It* 1

    A Note on the Text 87

Sources and Contexts 93

    Thomas Lodge • *Rosalynde* 95

    Richard Pace • [The Benefit of a Liberal Education] 196

    Keith Thomas • [Boundaries between Animal and Human] 197

    Michel de Montaigne • [Humans versus Animals] 201

    Sir Thomas More • [How Sheep Devour the English] 202

    William C. Carroll • Enclosure, Vagrancy, and Sedition in
the Tudor-Stuart Period 203

    Thomas Bastard • [Proto-ecological Epigrams] 209

    George Gascoygne • The Woeful Words of the Hart to
the Hunter 210

    William Prynne • [The Dangers of Theatrical
Cross-Dressing] 214

    Erica Fudge • Dressing Up as a Human 217

    Joseph W. Meeker • The Comic Mode 220

    Walter Benjamin • Gloves 234

Criticism 235

    William Hazlitt • *As You Like It* 237

    Mrs. Anna Jameson • Rosalind 240

    Edward Dowden • [*As You Like It* as Escape] 243

    Anne Barton • *As You Like It*: Shakespeare's 'Sense
of an Ending' 246

    Rosalie Colie • Perspectives on Pastoral 254

    Linda Woodbridge • Country Matters: *As You Like It* and
the Pastoral-Bashing Impulse 269

    Clara Claiborne Park • As We Like It: How a Girl Can Be
Smart and Still Popular 277

Louis Adrian Montrose • "The Place of a Brother"
  in *As You Like It*   281
Richard Wilson • "Like the Old Robin Hood":
  As You Like It and the Enclosure Riots   314
Jean E. Howard • Crossdressing, the Theatre, and
  Gender Struggle in Early Modern England   337
Marjorie Garber • Rosalind the Yeshiva Boy   355
James Shapiro • [The Play in 1599]   361
Juliet Dusinberre • Pancakes and a Date for *As You Like It*   370
Laurie Shannon • [Friendship in *As You Like It*]   377
Valerie Traub • [The Homoerotics of *As You Like It*]   380
Cynthia Marshall • Constructions of Negation in
  As You Like It   387
Jeffrey Masten • Ganymede's Hand in *As You Like It*   395
Robert N. Watson • [Likenesses: Jaques and the Deer]   404
Gabriel Egan • Food and Biological Nature [in]
  As You Like It   409
Michael Jamieson • *As You Like It*: Performance and
  Reception   423
Robert Smallwood • [Royal Shakespeare Company
  Stagings of the Final Scene]   440

Selected Bibliography   463

Illustrations

George Gascoygne, "The Woeful Words of
    the Hart to the Hunter"   210
Inigo Jones, Sketch for a Bird-Man   220
Rosalind   241
Nicholas Poussin, "Et in Arcadia ego," first version   251
Nicholas Poussin, "Et in Arcadia ego," second version   252
Thomas Morley, "It Was a Lover and His Lass"   369
A possible court epilogue to *As You Like It*   372
Excerpt from First Folio text of *As You Like It*   397
The final scene in Glen Byam Shaw's first
    Stratford production   443
The final dance in Glen Byam Shaw's second
    Stratford production   445
The entry of Vanessa Redgrave as Rosalind   447
Hymen descends in a rainbow   450
The paired lovers sing "Wedding is great Juno's crown"   453
A female Hymen in a modern pantsuit   456

Preface

The title of Shakespeare's *As You Like It* is brilliantly apt. We know very little about what audiences thought of it during Shakespeare's lifetime, but readers and viewers have mostly liked it, even loved it, from 1740, when the play was first brought back on stage in London, until the present. What's not to like? In addition to its perennial appeal as a light-hearted comedy of escape, it has many features that fascinate us now. Its heroine Rosalind is one of Shakespeare's greatest characters, not only witty and charming but also interestingly complicated in terms of her identity. Over the course of the play she is cross-dressed and multiply gendered—a boy playing a girl masquerading as a boy pretending to be a girl—the only case in Shakespeare where this extreme degree of layering in gender roles is brought to life on stage. *As You Like It* also offers other forms of complexity that we now find particularly intriguing. Most of the play takes place in the Forest of Arden, and it asks searching questions about its human characters in relation to the animals and plants around them: is Orlando abusing trees by carving his love poems on them? Is hunting wrong, given that deer have as much right to the forest as people do? Is there, in fact, a clear line dividing humans from animals? It would be historically reckless to suggest that Shakespeare's play is ecological in our modern sense of the term. But its focus on the relationship between things that occur as part of nature and things that are made by humans (which Shakespeare collectively terms "art") gives us access to debates in Renaissance England that relate in important ways to ecological issues in our own time.

One important feature of this edition is its inclusion of the full text of Shakespeare's primary source for *As You Like It*, Thomas Lodge's very popular prose romance *Rosalynde* (1590), which went through several editions in the 1590s and early 1600s. *Rosalynde* is very much worth reading as a literary masterpiece in its own right, though its highly wrought style, in the manner of John Lyly's earlier *Euphues*, requires a bit of adjustment for those not accustomed to the form. There are many similarities, large and small, between Lodge's romance and Shakespeare's play, which should give pause

to those who like to think of Shakespeare as a creative genius who
never deigned to borrow from others. But there are also fascinating
differences, such as Shakespeare's excision of most of the blood
and death from Lodge's *Rosalynde* and his decision (assuming that
it was his) not to name his own play *Rosalind* after its central character. Users of this volume should not deprive themselves of the
pleasure of reading the two texts with—and against—each other.
To do so is to come as close as we can ever reasonably expect to
understanding Shakespeare's artistic decisions, his practices in
transmitting his sources while also transforming them into something that feels entirely fresh and new.

In addition to Lodge's romance, this Norton Critical Edition
offers an array of readings that allow users to come closer to the
play as it would have resonated for Shakespeare's contemporaries
while also understanding how literary scholars have changed their
views of it over time. Particular emphasis is placed on two areas:
gender and ecology. The collection engages gender questions with
particular intensity in William Prynne's tirade against crossdressing on stage in the 1630s (p. 214), in Mrs. Anna Jameson's
early nineteenth-century reading of Rosalind (p. 240), and in interpretations by second- and third-wave feminists and queer theorists
(see in particular Park, Howard, Garber, Traub, and Masten). In his
essay (p. 395), Jeffrey Masten makes the point that modern editors
of the play almost always emend the 1623 First Folio text of *As You
Like It,* the earliest known printed edition of the play, in order to
clean up some troubling gender ambiguities in its language. This
Norton Critical Edition is, to my knowledge, the first to preserve
folio readings that occasionally, for example, refer to Rosalind as a
"he" rather than a "she": these anomalies should not be edited out
of existence in our texts of the play because they are important
clues to the malleability of gender categories for early readers and
probably also for Shakespeare's dramatic company, particularly in
relation to its central character.

A number of sixteenth- and seventeenth-century readings
included here explore the play's broad environmental contexts,
from Sir Thomas More's famous harangue against sheep who
devour men to Montaigne's defense of animals to William Prynne
(again), who thought humans masquerading as animals on stage
was nearly as bad as men playing the parts of women. In George
Gascoygne's oddly compelling "The Woeful Words of the Hart to
the Hunter," the author of a treatise about hunting allows the deer
an opportunity to save its own life by arguing its case against the
hunters (p. 210). There are also excerpts on pastoral in contemporary England (Colie, Woodbridge) and on the enclosure crisis (Carroll, Wilson), on literature and the environment generally (Meeker,

Fudge), and on the play as read from a twenty-first-century ecocritical perspective (Watson, Egan).

During the last century and a half, As You Like It has been one of the most popular of Shakespeare's plays on stage. Reading a Norton Critical Edition, or any other edition of the play, we are likely to lose sight of the fact that Shakespeare wrote his plays to be performed in the theater. This edition at least nods toward the long and distinguished performance history of As You Like It by including two essays (Jamieson, Smallwood) that engage the colorful world of performance and try to re-create some of the most lively and innovative ways the play has been staged over time. The Selected Bibliography also includes a section on adaptations that lists the best-known film and video versions of the play.

In creating this edition I have received help in finding and preparing texts from Jennifer Clement and Sarah White, and I would like to offer them both warm thanks. My husband David has been patient and nurturing, as always. My younger daughter Lauren read the manuscript from the perspective of a twenty-two-year-old and offered many helpful suggestions. The able Norton staff have performed their customary magic of turning a large and unruly stack of papers into a tidy and attractive book, and their labors are much appreciated. Any remaining errors are, of course, my own. My thanks also to Vanderbilt University, which has helped pay the fees for reproducing essays and photographs. Last but not least, I thank my sisters Esther May Powell and Mildred Ann Powell. One of the things to like about As You Like It is the play's portrayal of female friendship and the strong overlap between friendship and sisterhood. Rosalind and Celia are only cousins, but more than sisters. I'm quite sure that one of the reasons I love the play is because I myself have wonderful sisters whom I also count as friends, and this edition is dedicated to them.

The Text of
AS YOU LIKE IT

As You Like It

[The Persons of the Play

ROSALIND, daughter of the banished Duke Senior and later disguised as Ganymede.

CELIA, daughter of the present Duke Frederick and cousin of Rosalind; later disguised as Aliena.

ORLANDO, youngest son of Sir Rowland de Bois and suitor to Rosalind.

OLIVER, eldest son of Sir Rowland de Bois and later suitor to Celia.

ADAM, servant to Oliver, later to Orlando.

DENNIS, servant to Oliver.

DUKE SENIOR, banished ruler, now living in exile in the forest.

AMIENS
JAQUES
FIRST LORD } courtiers attending on Duke Senior in exile.
SECOND LORD
TWO PAGES

DUKE FREDERICK, usurping duke, younger brother of Duke Senior.

TOUCHSTONE, court jester to Duke Frederick.

CHARLES, wrestler attached to Duke Frederick's court.

LE BEAU
FIRST LORD } courtiers attending on Duke Frederick.
SECOND LORD

CORIN, an old shepherd.

SILVIUS, a young shepherd, in love with Phoebe.

PHOEBE, a shepherdess.

WILLIAM, a countryman, in love with Audrey.

AUDREY, a country wench, betrothed to Touchstone.

SIR OLIVER MARTEXT, a country vicar.

JAQUES DE BOIS, second son of Sir Rowland de Bois.

HYMEN, god of marriage.

Attendants, Musicians.]

Act 1 Scene 1

Enter ORLANDO *and* ADAM.

ORLANDO As I remember, Adam, it was upon this fashion
bequeathed me by will, but poor a thousand crowns and, as thou
say'st, charged my brother on his blessing to breed me well—
and there begins my sadness. My brother Jaques he keeps at
school and report speaks goldenly of his profit. For my part, he ⁵
keeps me rustically at home or, to speak more properly, stays me
here at home unkept. For call you that keeping for a gentleman
of my birth that differs not from the stalling of an ox? His horses
are bred better: for besides that they are fair with their feeding,
they are taught their manage, and to that end riders dearly hired. ¹⁰
But I, his brother, gain nothing under him but growth, for the
which his animals on his dunghills are as much bound to him as I.
Besides this nothing that he so plentifully gives me, the something
that nature gave me his countenance seems to take from me. He
lets me feed with his hinds, bars me the place of a brother, and as ¹⁵
much as in him lies, mines my gentility with my education. This is
it, Adam, that grieves me; and the spirit of my father, which I think
is within me, begins to mutiny against this servitude. I will no
longer endure it, though yet I know no wise remedy how to avoid it.

Enter OLIVER.

ADAM Yonder comes my master, your brother. ²⁰
ORLANDO Go apart, Adam, and thou shalt hear how he will shake
me up.
OLIVER Now, sir, what make you here?
ORLANDO Nothing. I am not taught to make anything.
OLIVER What mar you then, sir? ²⁵
ORLANDO Marry sir, I am helping you to mar that which God
made—a poor unworthy brother of yours with idleness.

1.1. **Location:** the orchard of Oliver de Bois's estate.
  2. **poor:** only.
  3. **charged:** i.e., my father charged.
  5. **profit:** success.
9–10. **for . . . hired:** Not only are they fed well, they are also trained, and for that purpose riders brought in at great expense.
  14. **countenance:** behavior.
  15. **hinds:** farm laborers.
  16. **mines:** undermines.
21–22. **shake me up:** treat me badly.
  23. **make you:** are you doing.
  25. **mar you:** are you damaging (opposite of "make," above).
  26. **Marry:** indeed.

OLIVER   Marry sir, be better employed and be naught awhile.

ORLANDO   Shall I keep your hogs and eat husks with them? What prodigal portion have I spent that I should come to such penury? 30

OLIVER   Know you where you are, sir?

ORLANDO   O sir, very well: here in your orchard.

OLIVER   Know you before whom, sir?

ORLANDO   Ay, better than him I am before knows me. I know you 35 are my eldest brother and, in the gentle condition of blood, you should so know me. The courtesy of nations allows you my better in that you are the first born, but the same tradition takes not away my blood, were there twenty brothers betwixt us. I have as much of my father in me as you, albeit I confess your coming 40 before me is nearer to his reverence.

OLIVER   What, boy? [*Attacks him.*]

ORLANDO   Come, come, elder brother—you are too young in this! [*Grabs him by the throat.*]

OLIVER   Wilt thou lay hands on me, villain?

ORLANDO   I am no villain. I am the youngest son of Sir Rowland de 45 Bois. He was my father, and he is thrice a villain that says such a father begot villains. Wert thou not my brother I would not take this hand from thy throat till this other had pulled out thy tongue for saying so: thou hast railed on thyself.

ADAM   Sweet masters, be patient! For your father's remembrance, 50 be at accord.

OLIVER   Let me go I say!

ORLANDO   I will not till I please. You shall hear me. My father charged you in his will to give me good education. You have trained me like a peasant, obscuring and hiding from me all gentleman- 55 like qualities. The spirit of my father grows strong in me and I will no longer endure it. Therefore allow me such exercises as may become a gentleman, or give me the poor allottery my father left me by testament. With that I will go buy my fortunes.

---

28. **be naught:** make yourself scarce.
29–31. **Shall . . . penury:** reference to the biblical **prodigal** son, who wasted the money given him by his father and starved to the point that he wanted to eat the grain husks used to feed swine (Luke 15:11–32).
36–37. **in . . . me:** Since we share the same distinguished blood you should treat me as a brother.
37–38. **my better:** having precedence.
41. **nearer . . . reverence:** more deserving of respect.
48. **this other:** my other hand.
49. **railed on thyself:** i.e., your rudeness (railing) says more about you than about me.
57. **exercises:** activity.
58. **allottery:** allotment (his inheritance of a thousand crowns).

OLIVER   And what wilt thou do—beg when that is spent? Well sir,   60
get you in. I will not long be troubled with you. You shall have
some part of your will. I pray you leave me.
ORLANDO   I will no further offend you than becomes me for my good.
OLIVER   Get you with him, you old dog.
ADAM   Is "old dog" my reward? Most true—I have lost my teeth in   65
your service. God be with my old master; he would not have
spoke such a word.   *Exeunt* ORLANDO [*and*] ADAM.
OLIVER   Is it even so? Begin you to grow upon me? I will physic
your rankness and yet give no thousand crowns neither. Holla,
Dennis!
                                                                   70

Enter DENNIS.

DENNIS   Calls your worship?
OLIVER   Was not Charles, the duke's wrestler, here to speak with me?
DENNIS   So please you, he is here at the door and importunes
access to you.
OLIVER   Call him in. 'Twill be a good way, and tomorrow the wres-   75
tling is.   [*Exit* DENNIS.]

Enter CHARLES.

CHARLES   Good morrow to your worship.
OLIVER   Good Monsieur Charles, what's the new news at the new
court?
CHARLES   There's no news at the court, sir, but the old news: that   80
is, the old duke is banished by his younger brother, the new duke;
and three or four loving lords have put themselves into voluntary
exile with him, whose lands and revenues enrich the new duke;
therefore he gives them good leave to wander.
OLIVER   Can you tell if Rosalind, the duke's daughter, be banished   85
with her father?
CHARLES   Oh no, for the duke's daughter, her cousin, so loves her,
being ever from their cradles bred together, that he would have
followed her exile or have died to stay behind her. She is at the

---

62. **some . . . will:** part of what you wish for (with a pun on **will** as inheritance).
63. **becomes . . . good:** is appropriate for bettering my situation.
68. **grow upon me:** encroach on my space.
68–69. **physic . . . rankness:** cure your disease.
75. **way:** "to accomplish my goal" left unstated.
84. **gives . . . leave:** is happy to give them permission.
88. **bred:** brought up.
88. **he:** Since this is a reference to Duke Ferdinand's daughter Celia, "she" would be
    expected; "he" relates to the underlying sex of the adolescent male actor who would
    have played the role on the Shakespearean stage, where female actors were not
    allowed.

court and no less beloved of her uncle than his own daughter, 90
and never two ladies loved as they do.

OLIVER   Where will the old duke live?

CHARLES   They say he is already in the Forest of Arden, and a many
merry men with him; and there they live like the old Robin Hood
of England. They say many young gentlemen flock to him every 95
day and fleet the time carelessly as they did in the golden world.

OLIVER   What, you wrestle tomorrow before the new duke?

CHARLES   Marry, do I, sir, and I came to acquaint you with a matter:
I am given, sir, secretly to understand that your younger brother
Orlando hath a disposition to come in disguised against me to 100
try a fall. Tomorrow, sir, I wrestle for my credit, and he that
escapes me without some broken limb shall acquit him well. Your
brother is but young and tender, and for your love I would be
loath to foil him, as I must for my own honor, if he come in.
Therefore, out of my love to you I came hither to acquaint you 105
withal, that either you might stay him from his intendment or
brook such disgrace well as he shall run into, in that it is a thing
of his own search and altogether against my will.

OLIVER   Charles, I thank thee for thy love to me, which thou shalt
find I will most kindly requite. I had myself notice of my brother's 110
purpose herein, and have by underhand means labored to dissuade him from it, but he is resolute. I'll tell thee, Charles, it is the
stubbornest young fellow of France: full of ambition, an envious
emulator of every man's good parts, a secret and villainous con-
triver against me, his natural brother. Therefore use thy discre- 115
tion: I had as lief thou didst break his neck as his finger. And thou
wert best look to't, for if thou dost him any slight disgrace, or if he
do not mightily grace himself on thee, he will practice against

93. **Forest of Arden:** Arden Forest, near Shakespeare's home in Stratford-upon-
Avon; or the Ardennes, a forest that straddles the border between France and
modern Belgium and is therefore appropriate to a play situated in France.
94–95. **Robin Hood of England:** legendary folk hero who lived in Sherwood Forest
and stole from the rich to give to the poor.
96. **golden world:** in classical myth, the first age of history, when humans were
still innocent, carefree, and rustic.
100. **hath a disposition:** intends.
101. **credit:** reputation.
102. **acquit him:** perform.
104. **foil:** defeat.
106. **withal:** with it.
106. **intendment:** intention.
106–108. **you . . . search:** You will stop him from following his plan (of wrestling with
Charles) or endure the disgrace that he will experience (in being defeated),
because he has brought this on himself.
111. **underhand:** secret.
114. **parts:** qualities.
116. **had as lief:** would like it as much.
118. **grace:** gain credit for.

thee by poison, entrap thee by some treacherous device, and never
leave thee till he hath ta'en thy life by some indirect means or 120
other. For I assure thee, and almost with tears I speak it, there is
not one so young and so villainous this day living. I speak but
brotherly of him, but should I anatomize him to thee as he is, I
must blush and weep and thou must look pale and wonder.

CHARLES   I am heartily glad I came hither to you. If he come tomor- 125
row I'll give him his payment. If ever he go alone again, I'll never
wrestle for prize more. And so God keep your worship!   *Exit.*

OLIVER   Farewell, good Charles. Now will I stir this gamester. I
hope I shall see an end of him, for my soul—yet I know not why—
hates nothing more than he. Yet he's gentle, never schooled and 130
yet learned, full of noble device, of all sorts enchantingly beloved,
and indeed so much in the heart of the world, and especially of
my own people, who best know him, that I am altogether misprized. But it shall not be so long—this wrestler shall clear all.
Nothing remains but that I kindle the boy thither, which now I'll 135
go about.   *Exit.*

Act 1 Scene 2

Enter ROSALIND *and* CELIA.

CELIA   I pray thee, Rosalind, sweet my coz, be merry.

ROSALIND   Dear Celia, I show more mirth than I am mistress of,
and would you yet were merrier? Unless you could teach me to
forget a banished father, you must not learn me how to remember any extraordinary pleasure.   5

CELIA   Herein I see thou lov'st me not with the full weight that
I love thee. If my uncle, thy banished father, had banished thy
uncle, the duke my father, so thou hadst been still with me I could
have taught my love to take thy father for mine. So wouldst thou
if the truth of thy love to me were so righteously tempered as 10
mine is to thee.

---

123. **anatomize:** dissect, analyze.
126. **go alone:** walk without a crutch (because Charles will have lamed him).
128. **stir this gamester:** stir up Orlando for the fight.
133–34. **misprized:** unvalued.
134. **clear all:** fix everything.
135. **kindle . . . thither:** inspire the boy (Orlando) to go there (to fight Charles).
1.2. **Location:** court of the usurping Duke Frederick.
1. **coz:** cousin.
4. **learn:** teach.
8. **so:** so long as.
9. **take . . . mine:** love your father as I do my own.
10. **righteously tempered:** properly managed.

ROSALIND   Well, I will forget the condition of my estate to rejoice in yours.

CELIA   You know my father hath no child but I, nor none is like to have. And truly, when he dies, thou shalt be his heir; for what he 15 hath taken away from thy father, perforce I will render thee again in affection. By mine honor I will, and when I break that oath let me turn monster. Therefore, my sweet Rose, my dear Rose, be merry.

ROSALIND   From henceforth I will, coz, and devise sports. Let me see—what think you of falling in love?   20

CELIA   Marry, I prithee do—to make sport withal. But love no man in good earnest, nor no further in sport neither than with safety of a pure blush thou mayst in honor come off again.

ROSALIND   What shall be our sport then?

CELIA   Let us sit and mock the good housewife Fortune from her 25 wheel, that her gifts may henceforth be bestowed equally.

ROSALIND   I would we could do so, for her benefits are mightily misplaced, and the bountiful blind woman doth most mistake in her gifts to women.

CELIA   'Tis true, for those that she makes fair she scarce makes 30 honest and those that she makes honest she makes very ill-favoredly.

ROSALIND   Nay, now thou goest from Fortune's office to Nature's: Fortune reigns in gifts of the world, not in the lineaments of Nature.   35

Enter [TOUCHSTONE, *the*] *Clown.*

CELIA   No, when Nature hath made a fair creature, may she not by Fortune fall into the fire? Though Nature hath given us wit to flout at Fortune, hath not Fortune sent in this fool to cut off the argument?

ROSALIND   Indeed, there is Fortune too hard for Nature when For- 40 tune makes Nature's natural the cutter-off of Nature's wit.

---

12. **estate:** circumstances.
15–17. **what . . . affection:** I will of necessity pay you back for my father's taking of your father's dukedom by giving you affection.
19. **devise sports:** think up amusing things to do.
21. **prithee:** pray thee.
22–23. **than . . . again:** than you can escape from with only a blush, and thus save your honor, if things threaten to get serious.
25–26. **good . . . wheel:** The goddess Fortune was imagined with a wheel used to throw her victims from good luck to bad. Celia compares her to a housewife with a spinning wheel.
28. **blind woman:** Fortune, imagined as blind because her benefits are not given according to need or worthiness.
31. **honest:** chaste.
31–32. **ill-favoredly:** ugly.
33. **office:** responsibility.
34–35. **lineaments of Nature:** one's natural features.
41. **natural:** fool, i.e., Touchstone.

CELIA   Peradventure this is not Fortune's work neither, but Nature's, who perceiveth our natural wits too dull to reason of such goddesses, hath sent this natural for our whetstone. For always the dullness of the fool is the whetstone of the wits. How now, wit,   45
whither wander you?

TOUCHSTONE   Mistress, you must come away to your father.

CELIA   Were you made the messenger?   ·

TOUCHSTONE   No, by mine honor, but I was bid to come for you.

ROSALIND   Where learned you that oath, fool?   50

TOUCHSTONE   Of a certain knight that swore by his honor they were good pancakes and swore by his honor the mustard was naught. Now I'll stand to it the pancakes were naught and the mustard was good, and yet was not the knight forsworn.

CELIA   How prove you that in the great heap of your knowledge?   55

ROSALIND   Ay marry, now unmuzzle your wisdom.

TOUCHSTONE   Stand you both forth now: stroke your chins and swear by your beards that I am a knave.

CELIA   By our beards, if we had them, thou art.

TOUCHSTONE   By my knavery, if I had it, then I were. But if you   60
swear by that that is not you are not forsworn. No more was this knight swearing by his honor, for he never had any; or if he had, he had sworn it away before ever he saw those pancakes or that mustard.

CELIA   Prithee, who is't that thou mean'st?   65

TOUCHSTONE   One that old Frederick, your father, loves.

ROSALIND   My father's love is enough to honor him enough. Speak no more of him: you'll be whipped for taxation one of these days.

TOUCHSTONE   The more pity that fools may not speak wisely what   70
wise men do foolishly.

CELIA   By my troth thou sayest true, for since the little wit that fools have was silenced, the little foolery that wise men have makes a great show. Here comes Monsieur the Beau.

42. **Peradventure:** perhaps.
44. **hath:** and has.
44. **whetstone:** stone used to sharpen knives (or metaphorically, wits).
53. **naught:** worthless.
54. **was . . . forsworn:** The knight did not break his oath.
58. **knave:** worthless fellow.
61. **not:** not true.
66. **One . . . loves:** a subtle insult against Duke Frederick, who, according to Touchstone, loves a dishonorable knight.
67. **My . . . enough:** If my father, who (unlike Celia's father) is honorable, loved him, the knight would be considered honorable. Some editors give this speech to Celia, who can then be understood to defend her father's honor against Touchstone's imputation.
68. **taxation:** slander.
72–73. **since . . . silenced:** suggesting that Duke Frederick censors fools; possibly also a contemporary reference to the suppression and public burning of satirical books in London in 1599.

Enter LE BEAU.

ROSALIND   With his mouth full of news.   75

CELIA   Which he will put on us as pigeons feed their young.

ROSALIND   Then shall we be news-crammed.

CELIA   All the better: we shall be the more marketable.—Bonjour,
Monsieur Le Beau, what's the news?

LE BEAU   Fair princess, you have lost much good sport.   80

CELIA   Sport? Of what color?

LE BEAU   What color, madam? How shall I answer you?

ROSALIND   As wit and fortune will.

TOUCHSTONE   Or as the destinies decrees.

CELIA   Well said—that was laid on with a trowel.   85

TOUCHSTONE   Nay, if I keep not my rank—

ROSALIND   Thou losest thy old smell.

LE BEAU   You amaze me, ladies. I would have told you of good
wrestling, which you have lost the sight of.

ROSALIND   Yet tell us the manner of the wrestling.   90

LE BEAU   I will tell you the beginning, and if it please your lady-
ships, you may see the end. For the best is yet to do, and here,
where you are, they are coming to perform it.

CELIA   Well, the beginning? That is dead and buried.

LE BEAU   There comes an old man and his three sons—   95

CELIA   I could match this beginning with an old tale.

LE BEAU   Three proper young men, of excellent growth and presence—

ROSALIND   With bills on their necks: "Be it known unto all men by
these presents"—

LE BEAU   The eldest of the three wrestled with Charles, the duke's   100
wrestler, which Charles in a moment threw him and broke three

---

76. **put:** impose.

78. **we . . . marketable:** If we are crammed like pigeons we'll weigh more and therefore bring a higher price; **Bonjour:** good day (French).

81. **color:** type.

82. Le Beau takes Celia literally and is at a loss to figure out what **color** can be attached
to the sport of wrestling.

84. **destinies decrees:** as fate wills. The lack of verb-subject agreement is standard in
Shakespearean English.

85. **laid . . . trowel:** applied like mortar to bricks; i.e., a bit heavy-handed.

86–87. **rank . . . smell:** Rosalind puns on two meanings of rank: social status (as Touchstone uses the term in his previous speech, meaning his standing as a jester) and
foul-smelling.

88. **amaze:** confuse (Le Beau fails to get the joke).

92. **to do:** to be done.

94. **Well . . . buried:** suggesting that Le Beau is so distractible that he has already
forgotten his promise to tell the beginning, which, however, he goes on to do.

96. **I could . . . old tale:** It sounds just like the beginning of a fairy tale (since they
often commenced with the motif of a man and his three sons).

98–99. Yet another comical attempt to throw off Le Beau: Rosalind puns on his use of
presence in the previous speech to mean "demeanor" and **presents** in the sense
of "in attendance" as part of a legal formula. The **bills on their necks** are evidently legal documents, like those worn by felons forced to appear in public wearing placards stating the nature of their crimes.

of his ribs, that there is little hope of life in him. So he served the
second and so the third. Yonder they lie, the poor old man, their
father, making such pitiful dole over them that all the beholders
take his part with weeping.   105
ROSALIND Alas!
TOUCHSTONE But what is the sport, monsieur, that the ladies have
lost?
LE BEAU Why, this that I speak of.
TOUCHSTONE Thus men may grow wiser every day. It is the first   110
time that ever I heard breaking of ribs was sport for ladies.
CELIA Or I, I promise thee.
ROSALIND But is there any else longs to see this broken music in
his sides? Is there yet another dotes upon rib-breaking? Shall we
see this wrestling, cousin?   115
LE BEAU You must if you stay here, for here is the place appointed
for the wrestling and they are ready to perform it.
CELIA Yonder, sure, they are coming. Let us now stay and see it.

Flourish. Enter DUKE [FREDERICK], LORDS, ORLANDO, CHARLES,
and Attendants.

DUKE FREDERICK Come on! Since the youth will not be entreated,
his own peril on his forwardness.   120
ROSALIND Is yonder the man?
LE BEAU Even he, madam.
CELIA Alas, he is too young! Yet he looks successfully.
DUKE FREDERICK How now, daughter and cousin—are you crept
hither to see the wrestling?   125
ROSALIND Ay, my liege, so please you give us leave.
DUKE FREDERICK You will take little delight in it, I can tell you:
there is such odds in the man. In pity of the challenger's youth I
would fain dissuade him, but he will not be entreated. Speak to
him, ladies; see if you can move him.   130
CELIA Call him hither, good Monsieur Le Beau.
DUKE FREDERICK Do so. I'll not be by.
LE BEAU Monsieur the Challenger, the princess calls for you.
ORLANDO I attend them with all respect and duty.

---

104. **dole:** lament, sadness.
113. **any:** anyone; **broken music:** lost harmony (i.e., broken ribs).
118. *Flourish:* trumpet fanfare.
120. **his . . . forwardness:** He is being too ambitious, and it is at his own peril.
123. **successfully:** as if he will succeed.
126. **liege:** lord.
128. **odds:** superiority (of strength).
129. **would fain:** wish I could.
132. **by:** at hand.

ROSALIND   Young man, have you challenged Charles the wrestler?   135
ORLANDO   No, fair princess. He is the general challenger. I come
but in, as others do, to try with him the strength of my youth.
CELIA   Young gentleman, your spirits are too bold for your years.
You have seen cruel proof of this man's strength: if you saw yourself with your eyes or knew yourself with your judgment, the   140
fear of your adventure would counsel you to a more equal enterprise. We pray you for your own sake to embrace your own safety
and give over this attempt.
ROSALIND   Do, young sir. Your reputation shall not therefore be
misprized. We will make it our suit to the duke that the wrestling   145
might not go forward.
ORLANDO   I beseech you, punish me not with your hard thoughts,
wherein I confess me much guilty to deny so fair and excellent
ladies anything. But let your fair eyes and gentle wishes go with
me to my trial, wherein if I be foiled there is but one shamed that   150
was never gracious; if killed, but one dead that is willing to be so.
I shall do my friends no wrong, for I have none to lament me; the
world no injury, for in it I have nothing. Only in the world I fill up
a place, which may be better supplied when I have made it empty.
ROSALIND   The little strength that I have, I would it were with you.   155
CELIA   And mine to eke out hers.
ROSALIND   Fare you well! Pray heaven I be deceived in you.
CELIA   Your heart's desires be with you.
CHARLES   Come, where is this young gallant that is so desirous to
lie with his mother earth?   160
ORLANDO   Ready, sir, but his will hath in it a more modest working.
DUKE FREDERICK   You shall try but one fall.
CHARLES   No, I warrant your grace, you shall not entreat him to a
second that have so mightily persuaded him from a first.
ORLANDO   You mean to mock me after. You should not have   165
mocked me before—but come your ways.
ROSALIND   Now Hercules be thy speed, young man!
CELIA   I would I were invisible, to catch the strong fellow by the
leg.

139–40. if . . . judgment: if you were actually using your eyes and your judgment.
   143. give over: give up.
   147. hard thoughts: displeasure (since I am about to deny your wishes).
   151. gracious: favored.
   156. eke out: add to.
   161. working: action (i.e., he doesn't plan to lose).
   162. but: only.
   165. after: after the fight.
   166. come your ways: Let's get on with it.
   167. Hercules . . . speed: May Hercules (a mythic hero so strong he won a wrestling
      match against the Nemean lion) come to your aid.
   168. would: wish.

[CHARLES *and* ORLANDO] *wrestle.*

ROSALIND   O excellent young man!   170
CELIA   If I had a thunderbolt in mine eye, I can tell who should down.

   Shout. [ORLANDO *throws* CHARLES.]

DUKE FREDERICK   No more, no more!
ORLANDO   Yes, I beseech your grace—I am not yet well breathed.
DUKE FREDERICK   How dost thou, Charles?
LE BEAU   He cannot speak, my lord.
DUKE FREDERICK   Bear him away.

   [*Attendants carry* CHARLES *off.*]

                                What is thy name, young man?   175
ORLANDO   Orlando, my liege, the youngest son of Sir Rowland de
   Bois.
DUKE FREDERICK   I would thou hadst been son to some man else.
   The world esteemed thy father honorable,
   But I did find him still mine enemy.   180
   Thou shouldst have better pleased me with this deed
   Hadst thou descended from another house.
   But fare thee well! Thou art a gallant youth.
   I would thou hadst told me of another father.
                        Exeunt DUKE [FREDERICK, LORDS, *and* LE BEAU.]
CELIA   Were I my father, coz, would I do this?   185
ORLANDO   I am more proud to be Sir Rowland's son,
   His youngest son, and would not change that calling
   To be adopted heir to Frederick.
ROSALIND   My father loved Sir Rowland as his soul,
   And all the world was of my father's mind.   190
   Had I before known this young man his son
   I should have given him tears unto entreaties
   Ere he should thus have ventured.
CELIA   Gentle cousin,
   Let us go thank him and encourage him.
   My father's rough and envious disposition   195
   Sticks me at heart.—Sir, you have well deserved.

---

171. **If I . . . should down:** If I could hurl a thunderbolt (like Jupiter), I would use it to
   help defeat Charles.
173. **well breathed:** short of breath.
180. **still:** always.
187. **calling:** status.
190. **of . . . mind:** agreed with my father.
192. **unto:** added to.
196. **Sticks . . . heart:** wounds me in the heart.

If you do keep your promises in love
But justly, as you have exceeded all promise,
Your mistress shall be happy.
ROSALIND   Gentleman,
    Wear this for me,
    [*Gives him a chain from her neck.*]
                one out of suits with fortune,   200
    That could give more but that her hand lacks means.
    —Shall we go, coz?
CELIA   Ay.—Fare you well, fair gentleman.
ORLANDO   Can I not say I thank you? My better parts
    Are all thrown down, and that which here stands up
    Is but a quintain, a mere lifeless block.   205
ROSALIND   He calls us back. My pride fell with my fortunes:
    I'll ask him what he would.—Did you call, sir?
    Sir, you have wrestled well and overthrown
    More than your enemies.
CELIA   Will you go, coz?
ROSALIND   Have with you—fare you well.   210
                Exeunt [CELIA, ROSALIND *and* TOUCHSTONE].
ORLANDO   What passion hangs these weights upon my tongue?
    I cannot speak to her, yet she urged conference.

    Enter LE BEAU.

    O poor Orlando, thou art overthrown!
    Or Charles or something weaker masters thee.
LE BEAU   Good sir, I do in friendship counsel you   215
    To leave this place. Albeit you have deserved
    High commendation, true applause, and love,
    Yet such is now the duke's condition
    That he misconsters all that you have done.
    The duke is humorous: what he is indeed   220
    More suits you to conceive than I to speak of.
ORLANDO   I thank you, sir, and pray you tell me this:
    Which of the two was daughter of the duke
    That here was at the wrestling?

201. **could:** would like to.
203. **better parts:** finer attributes.
205. **quintain:** wooden post.
207. **would:** wants.
210. **Have with you:** I'll go with you.
214. **Or:** either.
216. **Albeit:** although.
219. **misconsters:** misconstrues.
220. **humorous:** capricious, mentally unbalanced.

LE BEAU   Neither his daughter if we judge by manners,   225
But yet indeed, the taller is his daughter;
The other is daughter to the banished duke,
And here detained by her usurping uncle
To keep his daughter company, whose loves
Are dearer than the natural bond of sisters.   230
But I can tell you that of late this duke
Hath ta'en displeasure 'gainst his gentle niece
Grounded upon no other argument
But that the people praise her for her virtues
And pity her for her good father's sake.   235
And on my life, his malice 'gainst the lady
Will suddenly break forth. Sir, fare you well.
Hereafter, in a better world than this,
I shall desire more love and knowledge of you.
ORLANDO   I rest much bounden to you. Fare you well.   240
                                        [*Exit* LE BEAU.]
Thus must I from the smoke into the smother—
From tyrant duke unto a tyrant brother.
But heavenly Rosalind!   *Exit.*

Act 1 Scene 3

Enter CELIA *and* ROSALIND.

CELIA   Why cousin, why Rosalind—Cupid have mercy! Not a
word?
ROSALIND   Not one to throw at a dog.
CELIA   No, thy words are too precious to be cast away upon curs.
Throw some of them at me; come, lame me with reasons.   5
ROSALIND   Then there were two cousins laid up, when the one
should be lamed with reasons and the other mad without any.
CELIA   But is all this for your father?
ROSALIND   No, some of it is for my child's father. Oh, how full of
briars is this working-day world!   10

226. **taller is his daughter:** Le Beau is confused again: as we learn later, Rosalind is the
taller of the two.
231. **of late:** recently.
233. **argument:** reason.
240. **bounden:** obliged.
241. **from . . . smother:** i.e., from bad to worse; **smother** is suffocatingly dense smoke.
    1. **Cupid:** god of love (he is commonly depicted as an infant with a bow and arrow that
    Celia imagines may strike Rosalind in the heart and cause her to fall in love).
    4. **curs:** dogs.
    5. **lame:** injure (as a dog might be lamed by something thrown at it).
    7. **mad without any:** insane because she has lost her reason (through love).
    9. **child's father:** Orlando, whom she is already thinking of as marriage material.

CELIA They are but burs, cousin, thrown upon thee in holiday
foolery; if we walk not in the trodden paths our very petticoats
will catch them.

ROSALIND I could shake them off my coat; these burs are in my
heart.   15

CELIA Hem them away.

ROSALIND I would try if I could cry "hem" and have him.

CELIA Come, come—wrestle with thy affections.

ROSALIND Oh, they take the part of a better wrestler than myself.

CELIA Oh, a good wish upon you: you will try in time in despite of   20
a fall. But turning these jests out of service, let us talk in good
earnest. Is it possible on such a sudden you should fall into so
strong a liking with old Sir Rowland's youngest son?

ROSALIND The duke my father loved his father dearly.

CELIA Doth it therefore ensue that you should love his son dearly?   25
By this kind of chase I should hate him, for my father hated his
father dearly; yet I hate not Orlando.

ROSALIND No, faith, hate him not, for my sake.

CELIA Why should I not? Doth he not deserve well?

Enter Duke [FREDERICK] *with* LORDS.

ROSALIND Let me love him for that, and do you love him because   30
I do. Look, here comes the duke.

CELIA With his eyes full of anger.

DUKE FREDERICK Mistress, dispatch you with your safest haste
And get you from our court.

ROSALIND   Me, uncle?

DUKE FREDERICK   You, cousin.
Within these ten days if that thou beest found   35
So near our public court as twenty miles,
Thou diest for it.

ROSALIND   I do beseech your grace,
Let me the knowledge of my fault bear with me:
If with myself I hold intelligence
Or have acquaintance with mine own desires,   40

11–12. **burs . . . foolery:** sticky weed-flowers flung about as part of a holiday celebration
(as we might now throw confetti on a special occasion).

16. **Hem them away:** Say "ahem" to clear them out (as one might clear the throat,
with a pun on **hem**ming the petticoat).

20–21. **Oh, a good . . . fall:** Good luck to you: you will struggle through it eventually
although you **fall** (punning on wrestling and sexual intercourse).

21. **turning . . . service:** abandoning these jests (literally dismissing them from their job).

22. **on . . . sudden:** so suddenly.

26. **chase:** pursuit (of the argument).

39. **If . . . intelligence:** If I know myself.

If that I do not dream or be not frantic—
As I do trust I am not—then, dear uncle,
Never so much as in a thought unborn
Did I offend your highness.
DUKE FREDERICK   Thus do all traitors:
If their purgation did consist in words,   45
They are as innocent as grace itself.
Let it suffice thee that I trust thee not.
ROSALIND   Yet your mistrust cannot make me a traitor.
Tell me whereon the likelihood depends.
DUKE FREDERICK   Thou art thy father's daughter—there's enough.   50
ROSALIND   So was I when your highness took his dukedom;
So was I when your highness banished him.
Treason is not inherited, my lord;
Or if we did derive it from our friends,
What's that to me? My father was no traitor.   55
Then, good my liege, mistake me not so much
To think my poverty is treacherous.
CELIA   Dear sovereign, hear me speak.
DUKE FREDERICK   Ay, Celia, we stayed her for your sake;
Else had she with her father ranged along.   60
CELIA   I did not then entreat to have her stay:
It was your pleasure and your own remorse.
I was too young that time to value her,
But now I know her: if she be a traitor,
Why so am I. We still have slept together,   65
Rose at an instant, learned, played, eat together,
And wheresoe'er we went, like Juno's swans,
Still we went coupled and inseparable.
DUKE FREDERICK   She is too subtle for thee, and her smoothness,
Her very silence and her patience,   70
Speak to the people, and they pity her.
Thou art a fool. She robs thee of thy name,
And thou wilt show more bright and seem more virtuous
When she is gone. Then open not thy lips.
Firm and irrevocable is my doom,   75
Which I have passed upon her: she is banished.

41. **frantic:** out of my wits.
49. **Tell me . . . depends:** Tell me the basis for your accusation.
54. **friends:** relatives.
60. **ranged along:** wandered off.
61–62. **I . . . remorse:** I didn't beg you to keep Rosalind with me; you did it of your own wish out of a sense of guilt.
67. **Juno's swans:** inseparable because together they pulled the chariot of Juno, queen of the gods.
75. **doom:** sentence, judgment.

CELIA   Pronounce that sentence then on me, my liege.
I cannot live out of her company.
DUKE FREDERICK   You are a fool.—You, niece, provide yourself:
If you out-stay the time, upon mine honor   80
And in the greatness of my word, you die.
                    Exeunt DUKE [FREDERICK *and* LORDS.]
CELIA   O my poor Rosalind, whither wilt thou go?
Wilt thou change fathers? I will give thee mine.
I charge thee, be not thou more grieved than I am.
ROSALIND   I have more cause.
CELIA   Thou hast not, cousin.   85
Prithee be cheerful. Know'st thou not the duke
Hath banished me, his daughter?
ROSALIND   That he hath not.
CELIA   No, hath not? Rosalind lacks then the love
Which teacheth thee that thou and I am one.
Shall we be sundered? Shall we part, sweet girl?   90
No, let my father seek another heir.
Therefore devise with me how we may fly,
Whither to go and what to bear with us;
And do not seek to take your change upon you,
To bear your griefs yourself and leave me out.   95
For by this heaven, now at our sorrows pale,
Say what thou canst, I'll go along with thee.
ROSALIND   Why, whither shall we go?
CELIA   To seek my uncle in the Forest of Arden.
ROSALIND   Alas, what danger will it be to us,   100
Maids as we are, to travel forth so far!
Beauty provoketh thieves sooner than gold.
CELIA   I'll put myself in poor and mean attire
And with a kind of umber smirch my face;
The like do you. So shall we pass along   105
And never stir assailants.
ROSALIND   Were it not better
Because that I am more than common tall,
That I did suit me all points like a man:
A gallant curtal-ax upon my thigh,
A boar-spear in my hand, and—in my heart   110

83. change: exchange.
94. take . . . you: bear alone the burden of your altered circumstances.
96. now . . . pale: implying that the heavens have lost color out of shocked sympathy for
    the plight of Rosalind und Celia.
104. with . . . face: smear my face with dark pigment (so Celia will look like a suntanned
    peasant instead of a fair-skinned aristocrat).
108. all points: in every detail.
109. curtal-ax: short sword, cutlass.

Lie there what hidden woman's fear there will—
We'll have a swashing and a martial outside,
As many other mannish cowards have
That do outface it with their semblances.
CELIA What shall I call thee when thou art a man?   115
ROSALIND I'll have no worse a name than Jove's own page,
And therefore look you call me Ganymede.
But what will you be called?
CELIA Something that hath a reference to my state:
No longer Celia, but Aliena.   120
ROSALIND But cousin, what if we assayed to steal
The clownish fool out of your father's court—
Would he not be a comfort to our travel?
CELIA He'll go along o'er the wide world with me.
Leave me alone to woo him. Let's away   125
And get our jewels and our wealth together,
Devise the fittest time and safest way
To hide us from pursuit that will be made
After my flight. Now go in we content
To liberty and not to banishment.   *Exeunt.* 130

Act 2 Scene 1

Enter DUKE SENIOR, AMIENS, *and two or three* LORDS *like Foresters.*

DUKE SENIOR Now, my co-mates and brothers in exile,
Hath not old custom made this life more sweet
Than that of painted pomp? Are not these woods
More free from peril than the envious court?
Here feel we not the penalty of Adam—   5
The season's difference, as the icy fang

112. **swashing . . . outside:** the appearance of a swaggering, strutting soldier.
114. **outface . . . semblances:** cover up their actual cowardice with an appearance of courageous manhood.
116. **Jove's own page:** pageboy of Jupiter, king of the gods.
117. **Ganymede:** Jupiter's cup-bearer and, according to some mythological accounts, his sexual partner.
120. **Aliena:** a stranger (Latin).
121. **assayed:** tried.
123. **travel:** Here and throughout, the folio spelling "travail" is used for both "travel" and "travail," suffering, so that **travel** always implies "travail."
2.1. **Location:** the Forest of Arden (see n. 93, p. 7); **like:** dressed as.
2. **old custom:** long acquaintance.
3. **painted pomp:** artificial glory.
5. **penalty of Adam:** Adam's punishment in Genesis 3:17–19 for disobeying divine command and eating the fruit of the Tree of Knowledge. He suffered, among other things, from extremes in the weather, which the duke goes on to mention.
6. **fang:** bite, imagined as an actual tooth.

And churlish chiding of the winter's wind,
Which when it bites and blows upon my body
Even till I shrink with cold, I smile and say,
"This is no flattery: these are counselors   10
That feelingly persuade me what I am."
Sweet are the uses of adversity
Which like the toad, ugly and venomous,
Wears yet a precious jewel in his head.
And this our life exempt from public haunt   15
Finds tongues in trees, books in the running brooks,
Sermons in stones, and good in everything.
AMIENS   I would not change it. Happy is your grace
That can translate the stubbornness of fortune
Into so quiet and so sweet a style.   20
DUKE SENIOR   Come, shall we go and kill us venison?
And yet it irks me the poor, dappled fools,
Being native burghers of this desert city,
Should in their own confines, with forkèd· heads,
Have their round haunches gored.
FIRST LORD   Indeed my lord,   25
The melancholy Jaques grieves at that,
And in that kind swears you do more usurp
Than doth your brother that hath banished you.
Today my lord of Amiens and myself
Did steal behind him as he lay along   30
Under an oak, whose antic root peeps out
Upon the brook that brawls along this wood,
To the which place a poor sequestered stag
That from the hunter's aim had ta'en a hurt
Did come to languish. And indeed, my lord,   35
The wretched animal heaved forth such groans
That their discharge did stretch his leathern coat
Almost to bursting; and the big, round tears

11. **feelingly:** by means of the senses.
13–14. **like the toad . . . head:** Toads were popularly believed to be poisonous but also, in the duke's view at least, a source of unexpected value, like his life in the forest.
15. **public haunt:** crowds, publicity.
22. **dappled fools:** i.e., deer.
23. **burghers:** citizens.
24. **confines:** territory.
24. **forkèd:** horn-bearing (with intimations of cuckoldry).
26. **Jaques:** The French spelling of his name would be Jacques; Jaques suggests a pun on "jakes," latrine. At several points in the play, however, including this line, the rhythm suggests that his name is pronounced as two syllables—Ja-ques.
27. **kind:** vein, style.
30. **along:** stretched out.
31. **antic:** irregular, playfully wayward.
32. **brawls:** rushes noisily.
33. **sequestered:** separated from his companions.

Coursed one another down his innocent nose
In piteous chase. And thus the hairy fool,   40
Much markèd of the melancholy Jaques,
Stood on th'extremest verge of the swift brook,
Augmenting it with tears.
DUKE SENIOR   But what said Jaques?
Did he not moralize this spectacle?
FIRST LORD   Oh yes—into a thousand similes.   45
First, for his weeping into the needless stream,
"Poor deer," quoth he, "thou mak'st a testament
As worldlings do, giving thy sum of more
To that which had too much." Then, being there alone,
Left and abandoned of his velvet friend,   50
" 'Tis right," quoth he, "thus misery doth part
The flux of company." Anon a careless herd,
Full of the pasture, jumps along by him
And never stays to greet him. "Ay," quoth Jaques,
"Sweep on, you fat and greasy citizens!   55
'Tis just the fashion: wherefore do you look
Upon that poor and broken bankrupt there?"
Thus most invectively he pierceth through
The body of country, city, court—
Yea, and of this our life—swearing that we   60
Are mere usurpers, tyrants, and what's worse
To fright the animals and to kill them up
In their assigned and native dwelling place.
DUKE SENIOR   And did you leave him in this contemplation?
SECOND LORD   We did, my lord, weeping and commenting   65
Upon the sobbing deer.
DUKE SENIOR   Show me the place.
I love to cope him in these sullen fits,
For then he's full of matter.
FIRST LORD   I'll bring you to him straight.
                                              Exeunt.

    39. **Coursed:** pursued.
    41. **markèd of:** observed by.
    42. **verge:** edge.
    44. **moralize:** draw a lesson from.
    46. **needless:** not needing more water.
47–48. **mak'st . . . do:** make a will as people of the world do.
    48. **sum of more:** additional amount.
51–52. **part / The flux:** part from the flow.
52–53. **Anon . . . pasture:** then a carefree herd, well fed.
    56. **wherefore:** why.
    58. **invectively . . . through:** Jaques wounds with his words (that can pierce like a sword).
    61. **what's:** something.
    62. **up:** off.
    67. **cope:** contend with.
    68. **full of matter:** full of ideas, full of himself.

Act 2 Scene 2

Enter DUKE [FREDERICK] *with* LORDS.

DUKE FREDERICK   Can it be possible that no man saw them?
It cannot be! Some villains of my court
Are of consent and sufferance in this.
FIRST LORD   I cannot hear of any that did see her.
The ladies, her attendants of her chamber,   5
Saw her abed, and in the morning early
They found the bed untreasured of their mistress.
SECOND LORD   My lord, the roynish clown at whom so oft
Your grace was wont to laugh is also missing.
Hisperia, the princess' gentlewoman,   10
Confesses that she secretly o'erheard
Your daughter and her cousin much commend
The parts and graces of the wrestler
That did but lately foil the sinewy Charles;
And she believes, wherever they are gone,   15
That youth is surely in their company.
DUKE FREDERICK   Send to his brother. Fetch that gallant hither.
If he be absent, bring his brother to me.
I'll make him find him. Do this suddenly,
And let not search and inquisition quail   20
To bring again these foolish runaways.   *Exeunt.*

Act 2 Scene 3

Enter ORLANDO *and* ADAM [*from different doors*].

ORLANDO   Who's there?
ADAM   What, my young master? O my gentle master,
O my sweet master, O you memory
Of old Sir Rowland, why, what make you here?
Why are you virtuous? Why do people love you?   5
And wherefore are you gentle, strong, and valiant?

2.2. **Location:** the court of Duke Frederick.
  3. **Are of consent . . . this:** consented to this and tolerated it.
  6. **abed:** to bed.
  8. **roynish:** coarse, low.
  9. **wont:** accustomed.
 14. **did . . . Charles:** just defeated the well-built Charles.
 19. **him find him:** Oliver find Orlando.
 20. **quail:** fail.
 21. **again:** back.
2.3. **Location:** outside Oliver's house.

Why would you be so fond to overcome
The bonny prizer of the humorous duke?
Your praise is come too swiftly home before you.
Know you not, master, to some kind of men,   10
Their graces serve them but as enemies?
No more do yours: your virtues, gentle master,
Are sanctified and holy traitors to you.
Oh, what a world is this, when what is comely
Envenoms him that bears it?   15
ORLANDO   Why, what's the matter?
ADAM   O unhappy youth,
Come not within these doors. Within this roof
The enemy of all your graces lives.
Your brother—no, no brother, yet the son—
Yet not the son, I will not call him son—   20
Of him I was about to call his father—
Hath heard your praises and this night he means
To burn the lodging where you use to lie,
And you within it. If he fail of that
He will have other means to cut you off.   25
I overheard him and his practices.
This is no place; this house is but a butchery:
Abhor it, fear it, do not enter it!
ORLANDO   Why, whither, Adam, wouldst thou have me go?
ADAM   No matter whither, so you come not here.   30
ORLANDO   What, wouldst thou have me go and beg my food,
Or with a base and boisterous sword enforce
A thievish living on the common road?
This I must do or know not what to do.
Yet this I will not do, do how I can: 35
I rather will subject me to the malice
Of a diverted blood and bloody brother.
ADAM   But do not so. I have five hundred crowns,
The thrifty hire I saved under your father,

7. **fond to:** foolish as to.
8. **prizer:** prizefighter, wrestler.
10. **some:** emended from the folio's "seeme"
12. **No . . . yours:** That is true of yours (your virtues).
15. **Envenoms . . . bears it:** poisons him who has it as an attribute.
23. **use:** are accustomed to.
27. **butchery:** slaughterhouse.
32. **boisterous:** rough.
32–33. **enforce . . . road:** become a highwayman (the plight of many actual younger sons of the period).
36. **me:** myself.
37. **diverted blood:** family feeling gone wrong.
39. **thrifty hire:** wages I thriftily saved.

Which I did store to be my foster nurse   40
When service should in my old limbs lie lame
And unregarded age in corners thrown.
Take that, and he that doth the ravens feed,
Yea providently caters for the sparrow,
Be comfort to my age. Here is the gold.   45
All this I give you. Let me be your servant.
Though I look old, yet I am strong and lusty,
For in my youth I never did apply
Hot and rebellious liquors in my blood,
Nor did not with unbashful forehead woo   50
The means of weakness and debility.
Therefore my age is as a lusty winter:
Frosty but kindly. Let me go with you.
I'll do the service of a younger man
In all your business and necessities.   55
ORLANDO   O good old man, how well in thee appears
The constant service of the antique world,
When service sweat for duty, not for meed!
Thou art not for the fashion of these times,
Where none will sweat but for promotion   60
And having that, do choke their service up,
Even with the having. It is not so with thee.
But poor old man, thou prun'st a rotten tree
That cannot so much as a blossom yield
In lieu of all thy pains and husbandry.   65
But come thy ways; we'll go along together
And ere we have thy youthful wages spent,
We'll light upon some settled, low content.
ADAM   Master, go on and I will follow thee
To the last gasp with truth and loyalty.   70
From seventeen years till now almost fourscore
Here livèd I, but now live here no more.

40. **foster nurse:** caregiver (in an age when there were no pensions for the retired).
41–42. **When . . . thrown:** when I'm too old to work and am uncared for and discarded because of my age.
43. **he . . . feed:** God, who according to Luke 12:1–30 takes care of natural things— sparrows, ravens, the lilies of the field.
49. **rebellious:** harmful to the health.
50–51. **Nor . . . debility:** nor boldly seduce women who would give me venereal disease.
57. **antique:** ancient.
58. **When service . . . meed!:** when servants toiled out of duty, not for reward.
61. **choke . . . up:** stop working.
63–65. **thou . . . husbandry:** Your investment in me is like pruning a diseased tree that will never yield fruit no matter how diligent the effort.
66. **come thy ways:** come along.
68. **content:** contentment.
71. **seventeen:** emended from the folio text, which reads "seauentie."
71. **fourscore:** eighty.

At seventeen years many their fortunes seek,
But at fourscore it is too late a week.
Yet fortune cannot recompense me better   75
Than to die well and not my master's debtor.   *Exeunt.*

Act 2 Scene 4

Enter ROSALIND *for Ganymede,* CELIA *for Aliena, and Clown,
alias* TOUCHSTONE.

ROSALIND   O Jupiter, how merry are my spirits!
TOUCHSTONE   I care not for my spirits if my legs were not weary.
ROSALIND   I could find in my heart to disgrace my man's apparel
and to cry like a woman, but I must comfort the weaker vessel,
as doublet and hose ought to show itself courageous to petticoat;   5
therefore, courage, good Aliena!
CELIA   I pray you, bear with me; I cannot go no further.
TOUCHSTONE   For my part, I had rather bear with you than bear
you; yet I should bear no cross if I did bear you, for I think you
have no money in your purse.   10
ROSALIND   Well, this is the Forest of Arden.
TOUCHSTONE   Ay, now am I in Arden, the more fool I. When I was
at home I was in a better place, but travelers must be content.

Enter CORIN *and* SILVIUS.

ROSALIND   Ay, be so good, Touchstone. Look you, who comes
here—a young man and an old in solemn talk.   15
CORIN   That is the way to make her scorn you still.
SILVIUS   O Corin, that thou knew'st how I do love her!
CORIN   I partly guess, for I have loved ere now.
SILVIUS   No Corin, being old, thou canst not guess,
Though in thy youth thou wast as true a lover   20
As ever sighed upon a midnight pillow.
But if thy love were ever like to mine—

---

74. **week:** time.
2.4. **Location:** the Forest of Arden. *for:* disguised as.
1. **Jupiter:** king of the Roman gods.
4. **weaker vessel:** traditional phrase to denote a woman.
5. **doublet . . . petticoat:** Men, who wear jackets and stockings, should be brave in
the presence of **petticoats,** worn by women.
8–10. **I . . . purse:** Touchstone puns on **bear with** (take as a companion) and **bear**
(carry); and on bearing a **cross** (suffering) and carrying money, since many coins of
the period were stamped with a cross.
13. **CORIN and SILVIUS:** traditional shepherd names in pastoral poetry of the period.
14. **be so good:** i.e., be content.

As sure I think did never man love so—
How many actions most ridiculous
Hast thou been drawn to by thy fantasy?   25
CORIN   Into a thousand that I have forgotten.
SILVIUS   Oh, thou didst then never love so heartily.
If thou rememb'rest not the slightest folly
That ever love did make thee run into,
Thou hast not loved.   30
Or if thou hast not sat as I do now,
Wearing thy hearer in thy mistress' praise,
Thou hast not loved.
Or if thou hast not broke from company
Abruptly, as my passion now makes me,   35
Thou hast not loved.
O Phoebe, Phoebe, Phoebe!   *Exit.*
ROSALIND   Alas, poor shepherd! Searching of thy wound,
I have by hard adventure found mine own.
TOUCHSTONE   And I mine. I remember when I was in love I broke   40
my sword upon a stone and bid him take that for coming a-night
to Jane Smile; and I remember the kissing of her batler and the
cow's dugs that her pretty chapped hands had milked; and I
remember the wooing of a peascod instead of her, from whom I
took two cods and, giving her them again, said with weeping   45
tears, "Wear these for my sake." We that are true lovers run into
strange capers; but as all is mortal in nature, so is all nature in
love mortal in folly.
ROSALIND   Thou speak'st wiser than thou art ware of.
TOUCHSTONE   Nay, I shall ne'er be ware of mine own wit till I   50
break my shins against it.

---

32. **Wearing thy hearer:** boring your listener.
34. **broke:** run away.
38. **Searching:** examining.
39. **hard adventure:** unhappy accident.
40–42. **broke . . . Smile:** His beloved **Jane Smile** took a warm stone to bed with her to heat it up for comfort; Touchstone interpreted the transaction as a form of infidelity and took revenge on the **stone** by attacking it with his **sword**.
42. **batler:** wooden tool used for washing cloth by beating it clean.
43. **dugs:** udders.
44. **peascod:** pea pod, possibly with relation to the scrotum, since "codpiece," or covering for the scrotum, is **peascod** with the syllables in reverse order.
45. **cods:** should mean pods but the reference seems to be to peas, worn as jewelry instead of pearls; also suggests two testicles; **giving . . . again:** suggesting that the pea pod may have been Jane Smile's to begin with—a possibility that introduces a whole range of female anatomical references, since the opening pea pod is suggestive of labia and the peas, of pregnancy.
47–48. **all is . . . folly:** capable of multiple interpretations, one of which might be "Just as everything in nature eventually dies, so all humans who are in love show their mortality through their folly."
49. **ware:** aware.
50. **ware:** wary (punning on Rosalind's **ware** in the previous speech).

ROSALIND   Jove, Jove! This shepherd's passion
  Is much upon my fashion.
TOUCHSTONE   And mine, but it grows something stale with me.
CELIA   I pray you, one of you question yond man   55
  If he for gold will give us any food.
  I faint almost to death.
TOUCHSTONE   [to CORIN] Holla, you clown!
ROSALIND   Peace, fool—he's not thy kinsman.
CORIN   Who calls?
TOUCHSTONE   Your betters, sir.
CORIN   Else are they very wretched.   60
ROSALIND   Peace, I say!—Good even to you, friend.
CORIN   And to you, gentle sir, and to you all.
ROSALIND   I prithee, shepherd, if that love or gold
  Can in this desert place buy entertainment,
  Bring us where we may rest ourselves and feed.   65
  Here's a young maid with travel much oppressed,
  And faints for succor.
CORIN   Fair sir, I pity her
  And wish, for her sake more than for mine own,
  My fortunes were more able to relieve her.
  But I am shepherd to another man   70
  And do not shear the fleeces that I graze.
  My master is of churlish disposition
  And little recks to find the way to heaven
  By doing deeds of hospitality.
  Besides, his cot, his flocks, and bounds of feed   75
  Are now on sale; and at our sheep-cote now,
  By reason of his absence, there is nothing
  That you will feed on. But what is, come see,
  And in my voice most welcome shall you be.
ROSALIND   What is he that shall buy his flock and pasture?   80
CORIN   That young swain that you saw here but erewhile,

---

53. **upon my fashion:** like mine.
54. **something:** somewhat.
55. **yond:** yonder, i.e., Corin, who is standing on a different part of the stage.
58. **Peace:** Quiet!; **he's . . . kinsman:** He's not a clown like you. Evidently Touchstone
  hails Corin in an overfamiliar manner.
60. **Else . . . wretched:** They would have to be in terrible shape to be worse off than I am.
61. **even:** evening.
61. **you:** emended from the folio's "your."
67. **succor:** help.
70. **shepherd . . . man:** i.e., a hired laborer.
73. **recks:** reckons.
75. **cot:** cottage; **bounds of feed:** pastures.
76. **on:** for.
79. **in my voice:** for my part.
81. **swain . . . erewhile:** youth you saw here just a while ago.

That little cares for buying anything.
ROSALIND   I pray thee, if it stand with honesty,
  Buy thou the cottage, pasture, and the flock,
  And thou shalt have to pay for it of us.   85
CELIA   And we will mend thy wages. I like this place
  And willingly could waste my time in it.
CORIN   Assuredly the thing is to be sold.
  Go with me: if you like upon report
  The soil, the profit, and this kind of life,   90
  I will your very faithful feeder be
  And buy it with your gold right suddenly.   *Exeunt.*

Act 2 Scene 5

Enter AMIENS, JAQUES, [LORDS], *and others.*

Song.

AMIENS   Under the greenwood tree
                Who loves to lie with me
                And turn his merry note
                Unto the sweet bird's throat:
            Come hither, come hither, come hither.   5
                Here shall he see
                No enemy
            But winter and rough weather.

JAQUES   More, more—I prithee more!
AMIENS   It will make you melancholy, Monsieur Jaques.   10
JAQUES   I thank it. More I prithee, more! I can suck melancholy
  out of a song as a weasel sucks eggs. More I prithee, more!
AMIENS   My voice is ragged; I know I cannot please you.
JAQUES   I do not desire you to please me, I do desire you to sing.
  Come, more—another stanzo. Call you 'em stanzos?   15

---

83. **stand with honesty:** is honest (since Silvius has already planned to buy it).
85. **thou shalt . . . of us:** We'll give you the money to pay for it.
86. **mend:** improve.
91. **feeder:** supporter.
92. **right suddenly:** at once.
 1. **greenwood:** leafy forest.
 3. **turn:** tune.
 4. **throat:** voice, song.
13. **ragged:** hoarse.
15. **stanzo:** stanza (from Italian); i.e., verse of the song.

AMIENS   What you will, Monsieur Jaques.

JAQUES   Nay, I care not for their names; they owe me nothing. Will
you sing?

AMIENS   More at your request than to please myself.

JAQUES   Well then, if ever I thank any man I'll thank you. But that   20
they call compliment is like th'encounter of two dog-apes; and
when a man thanks me heartily, methinks I have given him a
penny and he renders me the beggarly thanks. Come, sing—and
you that will not, hold your tongues.

AMIENS   Well, I'll end the song.—Sirs, cover the while. The duke   25
will drink under this tree.—He hath been all this day to look
you.

JAQUES   And I have been all this day to avoid him. He is too
disputable for my company. I think of as many matters as he, but
I give heaven thanks and make no boast of them. Come, warble,   30
come!

Song [sung by] all together here.

Who doth ambition shun
And loves to live i'th' sun,
Seeking the food he eats
And pleased with what he gets: 35
Come hither, come hither, come hither.
Here shall he see etc.

JAQUES   I'll give you a verse to this note that I made yesterday in
despite of my invention.

AMIENS   And I'll sing it. Thus it goes: 40

If it do come to pass
That any man turn ass,
Leaving his wealth and ease
A stubborn will to please,
Ducdame, ducdame, ducdame: 45

17. **I . . . nothing:** I would only need to know their names if they owed me money.
20. **that:** what.
21. **dog-apes:** baboons.
25. **cover the while:** Meanwhile, set the table.
26. **look:** look for.
29. **disputable:** eager to argue.
38. **note:** tune (since it was common in the period to sing different songs to the same tunes).
38–39. **in . . . invention:** i.e., I made this song despite my creativity, not by using it.
45. **Ducdame:** deliberately mysterious phrase that has inspired much speculation about its possible meaning, drawn from languages as remote as Welsh, Gaelic, and Romany. The likeliest meaning is probably *duc* (Latin for "lead" in the imperative singular) plus *dama* or *damma* (Latin for "fallow deer," a species of small deer; or "venison," *Cassell's New Latin Dictionary*). The phrase could then mean "Deer, lead!"—appropriate for hunters in a forest, but with the play's usual suggestions of

> Here shall he see
> Gross fools as he
> An if he will come to me.

What's that "ducdame"?

JAQUES   'Tis a Greek invocation to call fools into a circle. I'll go   50
sleep if I can; if I cannot I'll rail against all the first-born of Egypt.
AMIENS   And I'll go seek the duke. His banquet is prepared.

Exeunt.

Act 2 Scene 6

Enter ORLANDO *and* ADAM.

ADAM   Dear master, I can go no further. Oh, I die for food! Here
lie I down and measure out my grave. Farewell, kind master.
ORLANDO   Why, how now, Adam? No greater heart in thee? Live a
little, comfort a little, cheer thyself a little. If this uncouth forest
yield anything savage I will either be food for it or bring it for   5
food to thee. Thy conceit is nearer death than thy powers. For my
sake, be comfortable: hold death awhile at the arm's end. I will
here be with thee presently, and if I bring thee not something to
eat, I will give thee leave to die; but if thou diest before I come
thou art a mocker of my labor. Well said—thou look'st cheerily   10
and I'll be with thee quickly. Yet thou liest in the bleak air. Come,
I will bear thee to some shelter, and thou shalt not die for lack of
a dinner if there live anything in this desert. Cheerily, good Adam!

Exeunt.

Act 2 Scene 7

Enter DUKE SENIOR *and* LORD[S], *like outlaws.*

DUKE SENIOR   I think he be transformed into a beast,
For I can nowhere find him like a man.

---

cuckoldry. But **dame** is also English and French for "woman," and given the play's preoccupation with women, horns, and cuckoldry, if we don't mind mixing languages, "Lead
the woman" or more ominously from Jaques's point of view "Woman, lead!" are also
possible readings of the phrase.
51. **rail . . . Egypt:** complain vehemently against the firstborn sons of the Egyptians in
the biblical story from Exodus 12. Not until God slew the firstborn sons were the Jews
allowed to leave Egypt—an event sufficiently distant in time that Jaques' degree of
emotional involvement is comical.
2. **measure . . . grave:** indicate by the length of my prone body the size of grave I'll need.
6. **conceit:** imagining.
9. **leave:** permission.

FIRST LORD   My lord, he is but even now gone hence.
Here was he merry, hearing of a song.
DUKE SENIOR   If he, compact of jars, grow musical   5
We shall have shortly discord in the spheres.
Go seek him; tell him I would speak with him.

    Enter JAQUES.

FIRST LORD   He saves my labor by his own approach.
DUKE SENIOR   Why how now, monsieur, what a life is this
That your poor friends must woo your company?   10
What? You look merrily.
JAQUES   A fool, a fool! I met a fool i'th' forest—
A motley fool (a miserable world).
As I do live by food, I met a fool,
Who laid him down and basked him in the sun,   15
And railed on Lady Fortune in good terms,
In good, set terms, and yet a motley fool.
"Good morrow, fool," quoth I. "No sir," quoth he,
"Call me not fool till heaven hath sent me fortune."
And then he drew a dial from his poke,   20
And looking on it with lack-luster eye,
Says very wisely, "It is ten o'clock.
Thus we may see," quoth he, "how the world wags.
'Tis but an hour ago since it was nine,
And after one hour more 'twill be eleven.   25
And so from hour to hour we ripe and ripe,
And then from hour to hour we rot and rot,
And thereby hangs a tale." When I did hear
The motley fool thus moral on the time,
My lungs began to crow like chanticleer   30
That fools should be so deep contemplative;
And I did laugh sans intermission

---

5. **compact of jars:** made out of dissonances, contradictions.
6. **We shall . . . spheres:** i.e., everything will turn topsy turvy. Ordinarily, the heavenly **spheres** that moved the stars and planets in the Ptolemaic universe were associated with harmony and earth with disharmony.
8. **saves my labor:** saves me the trouble of looking for him.
13. **motley:** traditional jester's garb of variegated, bright colors.
17. **set terms:** conventionally formal language.
18. **morrow:** day.
19. proverbial: "Fortune favors fools."
20. **dial . . . poke:** watch from his pouch.
23. **wags:** goes on.
26. **ripe:** ripen, gain in perfection.
28. **thereby . . . tale:** proverbial expression meaning something like "That's the way it goes," but with a pun on "tail," penis.
30. **chanticleer:** standard name for a rooster.
32. **sans:** without (French).

An hour by his dial. O noble fool,
A worthy fool! Motley's the only wear.

DUKE SENIOR   What fool is this?   35

JAQUES   O worthy fool! One that hath been a courtier
And says if ladies be but young and fair,
They have the gift to know it. And in his brain,
Which is as dry as the remainder biscuit
After a voyage, he hath strange places crammed   40
With observation, the which he vents
In mangled forms. Oh, that I were a fool!
I am ambitious for a motley coat.

DUKE SENIOR   Thou shalt have one.

JAQUES   It is my only suit,
Provided that you weed your better judgments   45
Of all opinion that grows rank in them
That I am wise. I must have liberty
Withal—as large a charter as the wind
To blow on whom I please—for so fools have.
And they that are most gallèd with my folly,   50
They most must laugh. And why, sir, must they so?
The why is plain as way to parish church:
He that a fool doth very wisely hit
Doth very foolishly, although he smart,
Seem senseless of the bob. If not,   55
The wise man's folly is anatomized
Even by the squandering glances of the fool.
Invest me in my motley. Give me leave
To speak my mind, and I will through and through
Cleanse the foul body of th'infected world   60
If they will patiently receive my medicine.

---

39. **remainder:** leftover (therefore very stale).
40. **places:** technical term from rhetoric that could be used for commonplaces and say-
    ings, or for the **places** used by rhetors to aid memory. They trained themselves to
    think of memory as a vast room or building and to associate its specific architectural
    features with specific topics so that to retrieve the material relating to the topic
    they needed only to recall its place in the imaginary building that structured their
    memory.
41. **vents:** utters forth.
44. **suit:** suit of clothes or **suit** in the sense of petition (Jaques's wish to be a fool).
46. **rank:** too thickly (like a weed).
48. **charter:** license.
50. **gallèd . . . folly:** tormented by my criticism.
52. **way . . . church:** The path to a village church would be evident because it was
    traveled so frequently.
53. **hit:** attack with his wit.
54–55. **Doth . . . bob:** foolishly appears, despite his pain, to be unaware of the insult (an
    action that may be foolish in that it denies him the ability to retaliate, but is wise
    in that it hides the truth of the insult from others).
57. **squandering glances:** random hits (implying that a fool's satire is general and
    only hits base if a hearer shows signs that he considers it particular to himself).
58. **Invest:** dress.

DUKE SENIOR   Fie on thee! I can tell what thou wouldst do.
JAQUES   What, for a counter, would I do but good?
DUKE SENIOR   Most mischievous, foul sin in chiding sin:
For thou thyself hast been a libertine,   65
As sensual as the brutish sting itself;
And all th'embossèd sores and headed evils
That thou with license of free foot hast caught
Wouldst thou disgorge into the general world.
JAQUES   Why, who cries out on pride   70
That can therein tax any private party?
Doth it not flow as hugely as the sea,
Till that the weary, very means do ebb?
What woman in the city do I name
When that I say the city woman bears   75
The cost of princes on unworthy shoulders?
Who can come in and say that I mean her,
When such a one as she, such is her neighbor?
Or what is he of basest function
That says his bravery is not on my cost,   80
Thinking that I mean him, but therein suits
His folly to the mettle of my speech?
There then, how then, what then—let me see wherein
My tongue hath wronged him. If it do him right,
Then he hath wronged himself. If he be free,   85
Why then my taxing like a wild goose flies—
Unclaimed of any man. But who come here?

Enter ORLANDO [with sword drawn].

62. Fie: shame.
63. counter: token with no inherent value that was used in calculations or wagers (like a poker chip).
66. brutish sting: lust, animal appetite.
67. embossèd . . . evils: pustules and boils (associated at the time with venereal disease).
68. thou . . . caught: that you, with your freedom to travel anywhere, have caught (like a disease brought home from some foreign land).
69. disgorge: vomit.
70. pride: first and chief of the seven deadly sins.
71. tax: criticize.
72–73. Doth . . . ebb: Pride flows with the magnitude of an ocean until the human frailty it feeds on is finally exhausted.
75–76. bears . . . shoulders: wears over-sumptuous attire (illegal for commoners).
78. When such . . . her neighbor?: when her neighbor is just like her.
79. basest function: lowest social rank.
80–82. That says . . . speech: that takes my criticism personally, saying "You didn't have to pay for my fine clothes (bravery) so what are you complaining about?" and thereby shows that my criticism indeed applies to him (with a pun on suits as both "matches" and "clothes").
85. free: perceives no relevance of my criticism to himself.

ORLANDO   Forbear and eat no more!

JAQUES   Why, I have eat none yet.

ORLANDO   Nor shalt not till necessity be served.   90

JAQUES   Of what kind should this cock come of?

DUKE SENIOR   Art thou thus boldened, man, by thy distress?
Or else a rude despiser of good manners,
That in civility thou seem'st so empty?

ORLANDO   You touched my vein at first—the thorny point   95
Of bare distress hath ta'en from me the show
Of smooth civility. Yet am I inland bred,
And know some nurture. But forbear, I say!
He dies that touches any of this fruit
Till I and my affairs are answerèd.   100

JAQUES   An you will not be answered with reason, I must die.

DUKE SENIOR   What would you have? Your gentleness shall force
More than your force move us to gentleness.

ORLANDO   I almost die for food, and let me have it.

DUKE SENIOR   Sit down and feed, and welcome to our table.   105

ORLANDO   Speak you so gently? Pardon me, I pray you.
I thought that all things had been savage here,
And therefore put I on the countenance
Of stern commandment. But whate'er you are
That in this desert inaccessible   110
Under the shade of melancholy boughs,
Lose and neglect the creeping hours of time:
If ever you have looked on better days,
If ever been where bells have knolled to church,
If ever sat at any good man's feast,   115
If ever from your eyelids wiped a tear,
And know what 'tis to pity and be pitied,
Let gentleness my strong enforcement be,
In the which hope I blush and hide my sword.

DUKE SENIOR   True it is that we have seen better days,   120
And have with holy bell been knolled to church,
And sat at good men's feasts and wiped our eyes
Of drops that sacred pity hath engendered;
And therefore, sit you down in gentleness

---

91. What manner of beast is this rooster? (with suggestion of "cocky," insolent, and a pun on **cock**, penis).
94. **empty:** lacking.
95. **touched my vein:** described my condition; **point:** prick, stabbing pain.
97. **inland bred:** bred in a civilized fashion (as opposed to the wild border areas).
101. **An:** if.
102. **gentleness:** civility.
114. **knolled:** chimed (to summon people to worship).

And take upon command what help we have   125
That to your wanting may be ministered.
ORLANDO   Then but forbear your food a little while
Whiles like a doe I go to find my fawn
And give it food. There is an old, poor man,
Who after me hath many a weary step   130
Limped in pure love; till he be first sufficed—
Oppressed with two weak evils, age and hunger—
I will not touch a bit.
DUKE SENIOR   Go find him out
And we will nothing waste till your return.
ORLANDO   I thank ye, and be blest for your good comfort!   [*Exit.*]   135
DUKE SENIOR   Thou seest we are not all alone unhappy:
This wide and universal theater
Presents more woeful pageants than the scene
Wherein we play in.
JAQUES   All the world's a stage,
And all the men and women, merely players.   140
They have their exits and their entrances,
And one man in his time plays many parts,
His acts being seven ages. At first the infant,
Mewling and puking in the nurse's arms;
Then the whining schoolboy with his satchel   145
And shining morning face, creeping like snail
Unwillingly to school. And then the lover,
Sighing like furnace, with a woeful ballad
Made to his mistress' eyebrow. Then a soldier,
Full of strange oaths and bearded like the pard,   150
Jealous in honor, sudden and quick in quarrel,
Seeking the bubble reputation
Even in the cannon's mouth. And then the justice,
In fair, round belly with good capon lined,
With eyes severe and beard of formal cut,   155
Full of wise saws and modern instances,
And so he plays his part. The sixth age shifts
Into the lean and slippered pantaloon,
With spectacles on nose and pouch on side,

125. **upon:** at your.
131. **sufficed:** satisfied.
144. **Mewling:** crying.
148. **Sighing like furnace:** with sighs hot from the heat of passion.
150. **pard:** panther.
152. **bubble:** symbol of vanity.
154. **with . . . lined:** full of **capon,** castrated chicken, served as a delicacy.
156. **Full of . . . instances:** Full of wise proverbs and up-to-date cases (in law).
158. **pantaloon:** stereotyped stage figure of an old man.

His youthful hose, well saved, a world too wide   160
For his shrunk shank; and his big, manly voice,
Turning again toward childish treble, pipes
And whistles in his sound. Last scene of all,
That ends this strange eventful history,
Is second childishness and mere oblivion,   165
Sans teeth, sans eyes, sans taste, sans everything.

Enter ORLANDO *[carrying]* ADAM.

DUKE SENIOR   Welcome! Set down your venerable burden
And let him feed.
ORLANDO   I thank you most for him.
ADAM   So had you need:
I scarce can speak to thank you for myself.   170
DUKE SENIOR   Welcome! Fall to; I will not trouble you
As yet to question you about your fortunes.—
Give us some music and, good cousin, sing.

Song.

AMIENS   Blow, blow, thou winter wind.
Thou art not so unkind   175
   As man's ingratitude.
Thy tooth is not so keen
Because thou art not seen,
   Although thy breath be rude.
Hey-ho, sing hey-ho unto the green holly.   180
Most friendship is feigning, most loving mere folly.
   The hey-ho, the holly:
   This life is most jolly.

Freeze, freeze thou bitter sky
That dost not bite so nigh   185
   As benefits forgot.
Though thou the waters warp,
Thy sting is not so sharp
   As friend remembered not.
Hey-ho, sing etc.   190

DUKE SENIOR   If that you were the good Sir Rowland's son,
As you have whispered faithfully you were,

160–161. **His . . . shank:** The stockings (**hose**) he has saved up from his youth are now
    too big for his shrunken calf (**shank**).
185. **nigh:** closely.
187. **warp:** freeze (and thereby cause to change shape).

And as mine eye doth his effigies witness
Most truly limned and living in your face,
Be truly welcome hither. I am the duke   195
That loved your father. The residue of your fortune
Go to my cave and tell me.—Good old man,
Thou art right welcome, as thy master is.—
Support him by the arm. Give me your hand,
And let me all your fortunes understand.   *Exeunt.*   200

Act 3 Scene 1

Enter DUKE [FREDERICK], LORDS, *and* OLIVER.

DUKE FREDERICK   Not see him since? Sir, sir, that cannot be.
But were I not the better part made mercy,
I should not seek an absent argument
Of my revenge, thou present. But look to it:
Find out thy brother, wheresoe'er he is.   5
Seek him with candle; bring him dead or living
Within this twelvemonth, or turn thou no more
To seek a living in our territory.
Thy lands and all things that thou dost call thine
Worth seizure do we seize into our hands   10
Till thou canst quit thee by thy brother's mouth
Of what we think against thee.
OLIVER   Oh, that your highness knew my heart in this!
I never loved my brother in my life.
DUKE FREDERICK   More villain thou.—Well, push him out of doors, 15
And let my officers of such a nature
Make an extent upon his house and lands.
Do this expediently and turn him going.   *Exeunt.*

---

193. **effigies:** image, likeness.
194. **limned:** painted.
196. **residue . . . fortune:** remainder of your life story.
3.1. **Location:** the court of Duke Frederick.
2–4. **But . . . present:** If I were not mostly composed of mercy, I would take my revenge
       on you (Oliver) in your brother's absence.
7. **twelvemonth:** year; **turn:** return.
11. **Till thou . . . mouth:** till you can acquit yourself through your brother's testi-
       mony (the duke evidently suspects Oliver of helping Orlando make off with Celia
       and Rosalind).
16–17. **let . . . extent:** Let my officers whose job it is draw up a legal document giving me
       the right to take his estate.
18. **going:** out.

Act 3 Scene 2

Enter ORLANDO [*holding a sheaf of papers*].

ORLANDO   Hang there, my verse, in witness of my love.
And thou, thrice-crownèd queen of night, survey
With thy chaste eye from thy <u>pale sphere</u> above
Thy huntress' name, that my full life doth sway.
O Rosalind, these trees shall be my books,   5
And in their barks my thoughts I'll character,
That every eye which in this forest looks
Shall see thy virtue witnessed everywhere.
Run, run, Orlando—carve on every tree
The fair, the chaste and unexpressive she!   *Exit.* 10

Enter CORIN *and* [TOUCHSTONE, *the*] *Clown.*

CORIN   And how like you this shepherd's life, Mr. Touchstone?
TOUCHSTONE   Truly, shepherd, in respect of itself, it is a good life;
but in respect that it is a shepherd's life, it is naught. In respect
that it is solitary, I like it very well; but in respect that it is private, it is a very vile life. Now in respect it is in the fields, it pleas- 15
eth me well; but in respect it is not in the court, it is tedious. As
it is a spare life, look you, it fits my humor well; but as there is no
more plenty in it, it goes much against my stomach. Hast any
philosophy in thee, shepherd?
CORIN   No more but that I know the more one sickens, the worse 20
at ease he is; and that he that wants money, means, and content,
is without three good friends; that the property of rain is to wet
and fire to burn; that good pasture makes fat sheep and that a
great cause of the night is lack of the sun; that he that hath
learned no wit by nature nor art may complain of good breeding, 25
or comes of a very dull kindred.
TOUCHSTONE   Such a one is a natural philosopher. Wast ever in
court, shepherd?

3.2. **Location:** the Forest of Arden.
   2. **thrice-crownèd . . . night:** the goddess Diana, **thrice-crownèd** because she ruled in
      the heavens as Cynthia, goddess of the moon; on earth as Diana, goddess of the hunt
      and of chastity; and in the underworld as Hecate or Proserpina.
   4. **Thy huntress' . . . sway:** the name of your tributary huntress, Rosalind, who rules
      my entire life.
   6. **character:** write.
   10. **unexpressive:** inexpressible.
   17. **spare:** spartan, lacking in amenities.
   18. **stomach:** with a pun on **stomach** as inclination.
   21. **wants:** lacks.
   25. **complain:** lament his lack.

simile (handwritten annotation)

exaggeration (handwritten annotation)

hyperbole (handwritten annotation)

CORIN   No, truly.

TOUCHSTONE   Then thou art damned.   30

CORIN   Nay, I hope.

TOUCHSTONE   Truly thou art damned, like an ill-roasted egg all on
one side.

CORIN   For not being at court? Your reason?

TOUCHSTONE   Why if thou never wast at court thou never saw'st   35
good manners. If thou never saw'st good manners, then thy manners must be wicked and wickedness is sin and sin is damnation.
Thou art in a parlous state, shepherd!

CORIN   Not a whit, Touchstone—those that are good manners at
the court are as ridiculous in the country as the behavior of the   40
country is most mockable at the court. You told me you salute not
at the court but you kiss your hands. That courtesy would be
uncleanly if courtiers were shepherds.

TOUCHSTONE   Instance, briefly; come, instance.

CORIN   Why, we are still handling our ewes, and their fells, you   45
know, are greasy.

TOUCHSTONE   Why, do not your courtiers' hands sweat? And is not
the grease of a mutton as wholesome as the sweat of a man?
Shallow, shallow! A better instance, I say—come!

CORIN   Besides, our hands are hard.   50

TOUCHSTONE   Your lips will feel them the sooner. Shallow again—a
more sounder instance, come!

CORIN   And they are often tarred over with the surgery of our
sheep, and would you have us kiss tar? The courtiers' hands are
perfumed with civet.   55

TOUCHSTONE   Most shallow man, thou worm's meat in respect of a
good piece of flesh, indeed! Learn of the wise and perpend:
civet is of a baser birth than tar—the very uncleanly flux of a cat.
Mend the instance, shepherd.

CORIN   You have too courtly a wit for me; I'll rest.   60

---

31. **Nay, I hope:** I hope not.
32–33. **like . . . side:** like an egg that has been ruined by being roasted on one side (and
is still raw on the other).
38. **parlous:** dangerous.
42. **you . . . hands:** i.e., the way you greet people at court is by kissing their hands.
43. **uncleanly:** unclean.
44. **Instance:** proof.
45. **fells:** fleeces.
48. **mutton:** sheep.
53. **tarred . . . surgery:** covered with tar used to treat sores.
55. **civet:** musky perfume base obtained from the anal glands of an African species
of cat.
56–57. **worm's . . . flesh:** i.e., you are to a proper man as a cadaver (food only for worms)
is to a wholesome piece of meat.
57. **perpend:** ponder.
58. **flux:** excretion.
59. **Mend:** improve.

TOUCHSTONE Wilt thou rest damned? God help thee, shallow
man! God make incision in thee: thou art raw.

CORIN Sir, I am a true laborer: I earn that I eat, get that I wear,
owe no man hate, envy no man's happiness, glad of other men's
good, content with my harm; and the greatest of my pride is to 65
see my ewes graze and my lambs suck.

TOUCHSTONE That is another simple sin in you: to bring the ewes
and the rams together and to offer to get your living by the copulation of cattle, to be bawd to a bellwether and to betray a she-
lamb of a twelvemonth to a crooked-pated old cuckoldy ram, out 70
of all reasonable match. If thou beest not damned for this, the
devil himself will have no shepherds. I cannot see else how thou
shouldst scape.

CORIN Here comes young Master Ganymede, my new mistress'
brother.   75

Enter ROSALIND, [reading a paper].

ROSALIND From the east to western Inde,
No jewel is like Rosalind.
Her worth, being mounted on the wind,
Through all the world bears Rosalind.
All the pictures fairest lined   80
Are but black to Rosalind.
Let no face be kept in mind
But the fair of Rosalind.

TOUCHSTONE I'll rhyme you so eight years together, dinners and
suppers and sleeping-hours excepted; it is the right butter-women's 85
rank to market.

ROSALIND Out, fool!

TOUCHSTONE For a taste:

> 62. **God make . . . raw:** May God test you for doneness (as one might make incision
> in a roast) because you need more "cooking," or education.
> 63. **that: what; get:** produce.
> 65. **content . . . harm:** am contented with the degree of affliction that I have endured
> (i.e., I've been fairly lucky).
> 69. **bawd . . . bellwether:** be a pimp to the lead sheep (who would be able to copulate
> with most of the ewes).
> 70–71. **out . . . match:** even though the pairing was totally unreasonable (using human
> standards to judge the "marriage" customs of sheep).
> 71–72. **If . . . shepherds:** If you are not damned for this, it will only be because the devil
> admits no shepherds to hell.
> 72. **else:** otherwise.
> 73. **scape:** escape.
> 76. **Inde:** India; both the East and West Indies were major sources of gold and jewels.
> 78. **mounted:** carried.
> 80. **lined:** drawn.
> 81. **to:** compared to.
> 84. **together:** continuously.
> 85–86. **it . . . market:** obscure insult that may liken Orlando's inept versification to

If a hart do lack a hind,
Let him seek out Rosalind.   90
If the cat will after kind,
So, be sure, will Rosalind.
Wintered garments must be lined,
So must slender Rosalind.
They that reap must sheaf and bind,   95
Then to cart with Rosalind.
Sweetest nut hath sourest rind:
Such a nut is Rosalind.
He that sweetest rose will find
Must find love's prick and Rosalind.   100

This is the very false gallop of verses. Why do you infect yourself
with them?

ROSALIND   Peace, you dull fool! I found them on a tree.

TOUCHSTONE   Truly, the tree yields bad fruit.

ROSALIND   I'll graff it with you and then I shall graff it with a   105
meddler: then it will be the earliest fruit i'th' country, for you'll
be rotten ere you be half ripe, and that's the right virtue of the
meddler.

TOUCHSTONE   You have said—but whether wisely or no, let the forest judge.   110

Enter CELIA *with a writing.*

ROSALIND   Peace! Here comes my sister reading—stand aside.

CELIA   Why should this a desert be—
For it is unpeopled? No.
Tongues I'll hang on every tree
That shall civil sayings show:
Some, how brief the life of man   115

---

butter-sellers' plodding on their way to market or to their repeated hawking of their
wares once they are there.

89.   **hart:** male deer; **hind:** female deer.
91.   **cat . . . kind:** seek another cat (for sexual purposes).
93.   **lined:** with a pun on sexual penetration, intercourse.
96.   **to cart:** suggesting that she should be harvested, like grain carried off the field in a
cart, but also punning on the **cart** with which scolds and sexually promiscuous
women were paraded about a community as a form of punishment.
100.   **prick:** rose thorn, penis.
101.   **false gallop:** i.e., the rhythm is off.
105.   **graff:** graft, grow one plant on another's stock to produce a new variety.
106.   **meddler:** busybody, with a pun on "medlar," a tree and its fruit that has to be half
rotten before it is fit to eat.
107.   **right virtue:** proper quality (in the sense of just deserts).
113.   **For:** because.
114.   **Tongues:** language.
115.   **civil sayings:** sentiments that are the common property of people (as opposed to the
"unpeopled" nature of the "desert" he is in).

Runs his erring pilgrimage,
That the stretching of a span
Buckles in his sum of age;
Some of violated vows   120
'Twixt the souls of friend and friend.
But upon the fairest boughs,
 Or at every sentence end,
Will I Rosalinda write,
 Teaching all that read to know   125
The quintessence of every sprite
Heaven would in little show.
Therefore heaven nature charged
 That one body should be filled
With all graces wide enlarged: 130
 Nature presently distilled
Helen's cheek but not his heart,
 Cleopatra's majesty,
Atalanta's better part,
 Sad Lucretia's modesty.   135
Thus Rosalind of many parts,
 By heavenly synod was devised
Of many faces, eyes, and hearts
 To have the touches dearest prized.
Heaven would that she these gifts should have, 140
And I to live and die her slave.

ROSALIND O most gentle Jupiter! What tedious homily of love
have you wearied your parishioners withal, and never cried,
"Have patience, good people."

117. **erring:** wandering.
118–19. **That . . . age:** that the length of a **span**—a hand stretched open wide—
encompasses a full lifetime.
126. **sprite:** spirit.
127. **little:** miniature (so that Rosalind is the distillation of all that is best in nature).
130. **wide enlarged:** widely scattered (among people).
132. **Helen:** Helen of Troy, who was beautiful but (according to some traditions)
unfaithful because she gave up her Greek husband Menelaus for Paris of Troy.
132. **his:** another example of the folio's using the male possessive where we would
expect "her."
133. **Cleopatra:** ancient queen of Egypt; cf. Shakespeare's tragedy *Antony and
Cleopatra.*
134. **Atalanta:** beautiful and swift-footed maiden from Ovid's *Metamorphoses* 8.317
ff. who was able to outrun all her suitors until one of them distracted her by
throwing golden apples in her path. Orlando commends her for her **better part**
of beauty, presumably, not for her swiftness in evading sexual pursuit.
135. **Lucretia:** Roman matron who killed herself rather than accept dishonor after
she had been raped by Tarquin.
137. **synod:** assembly.
140. **would:** wished.
142. **tedious homily:** sermon that is boring because simply read out from the Book of
Common Prayer rather than being the original composition of the preacher.
Some editors emend "Jupiter" earlier in the sentence to "pulpiter," preacher, to
go along with the idea of a sermon.

CELIA   How now?—Back, friends. Shepherd, go off a little; go with   145
him, sirrah.

TOUCHSTONE   Come, shepherd, let us make an honorable retreat,
though not with bag and baggage, yet with scrip and scrippage.
Exeunt [TOUCHSTONE *and* CORIN].

CELIA   Didst thou hear these verses?

ROSALIND   Oh, yes, I heard them all and more too, for some of   150
them had in them more feet than the verses would bear.

CELIA   That's no matter; the feet might bear the verses.

ROSALIND   Ay, but the feet were lame and could not bear themselves without the verse, and therefore stood lamely in the verse.

CELIA   But didst thou hear without wondering how thy name   155
should be hanged and carved upon these trees?

ROSALIND   I was seven of the nine days out of the wonder before
you came; for look here what I found on a palm tree. I was never
so be-rhymed since Pythagoras' time, that I was an Irish rat,
which I can hardly remember.   160

CELIA   Trow you who hath done this?

ROSALIND   Is it a man?

CELIA   And a chain, that you once wore, about his neck. Change
you color?

ROSALIND   I prithee, who?   165

CELIA   O Lord, Lord—it is a hard matter for friends to meet, but
mountains may be removed with earthquakes and so encounter.

ROSALIND   Nay, but who is it?

CELIA   Is it possible?

---

146. **sirrah:** sir (but with an element of contempt).
148. **not . . . scrippage:** Touchstone and Corin will not depart in the manner of a
    military retreat, with "bag and baggage," but in humbler fashion, carrying a
    shepherd's pouch and its contents.
151. **feet:** metrical units.
152. **feet . . . verses:** The feet (punning on the **feet** we walk on) could carry the
    verses.
154. **stood . . . verse:** unable to walk alone without the verse holding them up (with a
    pun on **lame** as poetically incompetent).
157. **seven . . . wonder:** A "nine days' wonder" was proverbial for something marvelous;
    by having made it through seven of the days, Rosalind is almost to the point of
    marveling.
158–60. **I . . . remember:** I have never had such rhymes made about me since the time of
    Pythagoras (a Greek philosopher who believed in transmigration of souls). At
    that almost forgotten time, Rosalind quips, her soul inhabited the body of an
    Irish rat. By making the rat **Irish** she suggests that she may be rhymed to death,
    since Irish poets were believed to have the power to kill rats through their
    verses.
161. **Trow you:** can you believe.
163–64. **Change you color:** Are you blushing (or turning pale)?
166–67. **it . . . encounter:** It is difficult for friends to get together but mountains can
    meet by being moved by earthquakes. (Celia uses the proverbial "moving of
    mountains" to describe the wild improbability that Orlando and Rosalind could
    encounter each other in a forest so far distant from home).

ROSALIND Nay, I prithee now with most petitionary vehemence, 170
tell me who it is.

CELIA Oh, wonderful, wonderful, and most wonderful—
wonderful and yet again wonderful, and after that out of all
hooping!

ROSALIND Good, my complexion! Dost thou think though I am 175
caparisoned like a man I have a doublet and hose in my disposition? One inch of delay more is a South Sea of discovery. I
prithee, tell me who is it quickly and speak apace. I would thou
couldst stammer, that thou might'st pour this concealed man out
of thy mouth as wine comes out of a narrow-mouthed bottle: 180
either too much at once or none at all. I prithee, take the cork out
of thy mouth that I may drink thy tidings.

CELIA So you may put a man in your belly.

ROSALIND Is he of God's making? What manner of man? Is his
head worth a hat or his chin worth a beard?   185

CELIA Nay, he hath but a little beard.

ROSALIND Why, God will send more if the man will be thankful.
Let me stay the growth of his beard if thou delay me not the
knowledge of his chin.

CELIA It is young Orlando, that tripped up the wrestler's heels and 190
your heart both in an instant.

ROSALIND Nay, but the devil take mocking: speak sad brow and
true maid.

CELIA I'faith, coz, 'tis he.

ROSALIND Orlando?   195

CELIA Orlando!

ROSALIND Alas the day! What shall I do with my doublet and
hose? What did he when thou saw'st him? What said he? How
looked he? Wherein went he? What makes he here? Did he ask
for me? Where remains he? How parted he with thee? And when 200
shalt thou see him again? Answer me in one word.

---

170. **most . . . vehemence:** all the forcefulness I can manage in asking the question.
173–74. **out . . . hooping:** impossible to be contained.
175. **Good my complexion:** Consider my nature (implying that women lack patience
  by nature).
176. **caparisoned:** dressed.
177. **South . . . discovery:** as long as a voyage to the (newly charted) South Seas.
178. **apace:** quickly.
181–82. **take . . . tidings:** Uncork yourself so I can drink up your news (continuing with
  the wine bottle metaphor).
183. **put . . . belly:** literally drink up the as yet unnamed man, or get pregnant.
185. **worth:** worthy of.
188–89. **Let . . . chin:** I'll wait to hear about his beard if you'll tell me about his chin
  (with a quip on waiting as long as it takes for his beard to grow in or "staying" it
  in the sense of preventing it from doing so).
192–93. **sad . . . maid:** in sober earnest and on your honor as a virgin.

CELIA You must borrow me Gargantua's mouth first: 'tis a word
too great for any mouth of this age's size. To say ay and no to
these particulars is more than to answer in a catechism.
ROSALIND But doth he know that I am in this forest and in man's   205
apparel? Looks he as freshly as he did the day he wrestled?
CELIA It is as easy to count atomies as to resolve the propositions
of a lover. But take a taste of my finding him and relish it with
good observance. I found him under a tree, like a dropped acorn—
ROSALIND It may well be called Jove's tree, when it drops forth   210
fruit.
CELIA Give me audience, good madam.
ROSALIND Proceed.
CELIA There lay he, stretched along like a wounded knight—
ROSALIND Though it be pity to see such a sight, it well becomes   215
the ground.
CELLIA Cry "holla" to the tongue, I prithee; it curvets unseason-
ably. He was furnished like a hunter—
ROSALIND Oh, ominous: he comes to kill my heart!
CELIA I would sing my song without a burden. Thou bring'st me   220
out of tune.
ROSALIND Do you not know I am a woman? When I think I must
speak. Sweet, say on.

Enter ORLANDO *and* JAQUES.

CELIA You bring me out. Soft, comes he not here?
ROSALIND 'Tis he! Slink by and note him.   225
JAQUES I thank you for your company, but good faith, I had as lief
have been myself alone.
ORLANDO And so had I; but yet, for fashion sake, I thank you too
for your society.
JAQUES God b'wi' you, let's meet as little as we can.   230
ORLANDO I do desire we may be better strangers.

---

202. **Gargantua:** famous Rabelaisian giant whose mouth and appetite were so large
that even as a newborn child he required the milk of 17,913 cows (*Gargantua and
Pantagruel* 1.7).
204. **more . . . catechism:** not a simple matter (like answering questions in a standardized Christian testament of belief, which had rote questions and answers).
206. **freshly:** appealing.
207. **atomies:** tiny specks of matter; **propositions:** matters proposed for discussion,
riddles.
208–09. **take . . . observance:** Here's a sample for you to taste and savor by paying
attention.
212. **Give me audience:** Pay attention.
214. **along:** out.
215. **well becomes:** is very flattering to.
217. **holla:** i.e., halt; **curvets:** leaps about (often used of animals).
220. **burden:** refrain (i.e., your interruptions).
224. **bring me out:** cause me to lose track of where I was in my speech.

Lt device [handwritten margin note]

JAQUES I pray you, mar no more trees with writing love songs in their barks.

ORLANDO I pray you, mar no mo of my verses with reading them ill-favoredly.   235

JAQUES Rosalind is your love's name?

ORLANDO Yes, just.

JAQUES I do not like her name.

ORLANDO There was no thought of pleasing you when she was christened.   240

JAQUES What stature is she of?

ORLANDO Just as high as my heart.

JAQUES You are full of pretty answers. Have you not been acquainted with goldsmiths' wives and conned them out of rings?

ORLANDO Not so. But I answer you right painted cloth, from   245
whence you have studied your questions. *exaggeration to prove* [handwritten margin note]

JAQUES You have a nimble wit: I think 'twas made of Atalanta's *the*
heels. Will you sit down with me, and we two will rail against our *point*
mistress, the world, and all our misery?

ORLANDO I will chide no breather in the world but myself, against 250
whom I know most faults.

JAQUES The worst fault you have is to be in love.

ORLANDO 'Tis a fault I will not change for your best virtue. I am weary of you.

JAQUES By my troth, I was seeking for a fool when I found you.   255

ORLANDO He is drowned in the brook. Look but in and you shall see him.

JAQUES There I shall see mine own figure.

ORLANDO Which I take to be either a fool or a cipher.

JAQUES I'll tarry no longer with you. Farewell, good Signor Love. 260

ORLANDO I am glad of your departure. Adieu, good Monsieur Melancholy.   [*Exit* JAQUES.]

ROSALIND I will speak to him like a saucy lackey, and under that habit play the knave with him.—Do you hear, forester?

234. **mo:** more.
235. **ill-favoredly:** in an unflattering manner.
237. **just:** exactly right.
243–44. **Have . . . rings:** implying that Orlando uses his charm to steal from or seduce city wives (who were reputed to be easy marks for young gallants).
245–46. **I . . . questions:** I am answering you from the same hackneyed place from which you derived your questions. **painted cloth:** the equivalent of tapestry in less affluent households; it hung on the wall and often bore commonplace sayings (like a more modern sampler, but painted rather than embroidered).
247–48. **Atalanta's heels:** known for swiftness. See p. 43, n. 134.
250. **no breather:** no one alive.
253. **change:** exchange.
255. **By my troth:** by my truth (mild oath).
256. **Look but:** only look.
259. **cipher:** meaningless sign.
263–64. **I . . . with him:** I will pretend to be an impertinent servant and under that disguise I'll trick him.

ORLANDO   Very well. What would you?   265
ROSALIND   I pray you, what is't o'clock?
ORLANDO   You should ask me what time o'day. There's no clock in
the forest.
ROSALIND   Then there is no true lover in the forest, else sighing
every minute and groaning every hour would detect the lazy foot   270
of time as well as a clock.
ORLANDO   And why not the swift foot of time? Had not that been
as proper?
ROSALIND   By no means, sir. Time travels in divers paces with divers persons. I'll tell you who Time ambles withal, who Time trots   275
withal, who Time gallops withal, and who he stands still withal.
ORLANDO   I prithee, who doth he trot withal?
ROSALIND   Marry, he trots hard with a young maid between the
contract of her marriage and the day it is solemnized. If the
interim be but a se'nnight Time's pace is so hard that it seems   280
the length of seven year.
ORLANDO   Who ambles Time withal? _easy pace_
ROSALIND   With a priest that lacks Latin and a rich man that hath
not the gout: for the one sleeps easily because he cannot study,
and the other lives merrily because he feels no pain—the one   285
lacking the burden of lean and wasteful learning, the other
knowing no burden of heavy, tedious penury. These Time ambles
withal.
ORLANDO   Who doth he gallop withal?
ROSALIND   With a thief to the gallows, for though he go as softly as   290
foot can fall he thinks himself too soon there.
ORLANDO   Who stays it still withal?
ROSALIND   With lawyers in the vacation, for they sleep between
term and term and then they perceive not how Time moves.
ORLANDO   Where dwell you, pretty youth?   295
ROSALIND   With this shepherdess, my sister, here in the skirts of
the forest like fringe upon a petticoat.
ORLANDO   Are you native of this place?
ROSALIND   As the cony that you see dwell where she is kindled.

269. **else:** or else.
270–71. **lazy . . . time:** slow passage of time, with a pun on **foot** as the hand of the clock,
    since many clocks at this period had only an hour hand, which moves very
    slowly.
279. **contract:** formal legal agreement between bride and groom.
280. **se'ennight:** week.
283. **lacks Latin:** understands no Latin (which was the commonest language for seri-
    ous scholarly writings at the period).
287. **penury:** poverty.
290. **softly:** slowly.
293. **vacation:** interim between law terms.
296. **skirts:** edge.
299. **cony:** rabbit; **kindled:** born.

ORLANDO   Your accent is something finer than you could purchase   300
in so removed a dwelling.

ROSALIND   I have been told so of many. But indeed, an old religious uncle of mine taught me to speak, who was in his youth an
inland man, one that knew courtship too well, for there he fell
in love. I have heard him read many lectures against it and I   305
thank God I am not a woman, to be touched with so many giddy
offences as he hath generally taxed their whole sex withal.

ORLANDO   Can you remember any of the principal evils that he
laid to the charge of women?

ROSALIND   There were none principal; they were all like one   310
another as halfpence are, every one fault seeming monstrous till
his fellow-fault came to match it.

ORLANDO   I prithee, recount some of them.

ROSALIND   No, I will not cast away my physic but on those that
are sick. There is a man haunts the forest that abuses our young   315
plants with carving "Rosalind" on their barks, hangs odes upon
hawthorns and elegies on brambles—all, forsooth, deifying the
name of Rosalind. If I could meet that fancy-monger, I would
give him some good counsel, for he seems to have the quotidian
of love upon him.   320

ORLANDO   I am he that is so love-shaked. I pray you tell me your
remedy.

ROSALIND   There is none of my uncle's marks upon you. He taught
me how to know a man in love, in which cage of rushes I am
sure you are not prisoner.   325

ORLANDO   What were his marks?

ROSALIND   A lean cheek, which you have not; a blue eye and
sunken, which you have not; an unquestionable spirit, which
you have not; a beard neglected, which you have not—but I pardon you for that, for simply your having in beard is a younger   330
brother's revenue. Then your hose should be ungartered, your

300. **purchase:** acquire.
302. **of:** by.
304. **courtship:** the behavior appropriate to a courtier, with a pun on courtship as
      "wooing."
306. **touched:** tainted.
314. **physic but:** medicine except.
316. **with:** by.
317. **forsooth:** in truth; **deifying:** folio reads "defying," which, if correct, could mean
      that Orlando's verses "defy" or disrespect Rosalind by associating her with the
      defacing of trees.
318. **fancy-monger:** seller of love.
319. **quotidian:** recurring fever.
321. **love-shaked:** shaking in the "fever" of his love.
324. **cage of rushes:** prison made of reeds, hence easy to escape.
328. **unquestionable spirit:** unwillingness to take part in social exchange.
330–31. **for . . . revenue:** simply because what you have in the way of beard is not much
      because of your youth.

bonnet unbanded, your sleeve unbuttoned, your shoe untied, and everything about you demonstrating a careless desolation. But you are no such man; you are rather point-device in your accoutrements, as loving yourself than seeming the lover of any other. 335

ORLANDO   Fair youth, I would I could make thee believe I love.

ROSALIND   Me believe it? You may as soon make her that you love believe it, which I warrant she is apter to do than to confess she does: that is one of the points in the which women still give the lie to their consciences. But in good sooth, are you he that hangs 340 the verses on the trees, wherein Rosalind is so admired?

ORLANDO   I swear to thee, youth, by the white hand of Rosalind, I am that he—that unfortunate he.

ROSALIND   But are you so much in love as your rhymes speak?

ORLANDO   Neither rhyme nor reason can express how much. 345

ROSALIND   Love is merely a madness and I tell you, deserves as well a dark house and a whip as madmen do; and the reason why they are not so punished and cured is that the lunacy is so ordinary that the whippers are in love too. Yet I profess curing it by counsel. 350

ORLANDO   Did you ever cure any so?

ROSALIND   Yes, one—and in this manner: he was to imagine me his love, his mistress, and I set him every day to woo me. At which time would I, being but a moonish youth, grieve, be effeminate, changeable, longing and liking, proud, fantastical, apish, shallow, 355 inconstant, full of tears, full of smiles; for every passion something and for no passion truly anything, as boys and women are for the most part cattle of this color; would now like him, now loathe him, then entertain him, then forswear him, now weep for him, then spit at him; that I drave my suitor from his mad 360 humor of love to a living humor of madness, which was to forswear the full stream of the world and to live in a nook merely monastic. And thus I cured him, and this way will I take upon

---

332. **bonnet unbanded:** hat lacking a band.
333. Cf. the image of Hamlet after he has been rejected by Ophelia (*Hamlet* 2.1.79–81): "with his douhlet all unbraced, / No hat upon his head, his stockings fouled, / Ungartered, and down-gyvèd to his ankle."
334–35. **point-device . . . accoutrements:** dressed very spiffily.
339–40. **give . . . consciences:** deny what their consciences (or hearts) are telling them.
340. **sooth:** truth.
347. **dark . . . whip:** standard treatment for madmen at the period.
354. **moonish:** changeable.
358. **cattle . . . color:** creatures of this type.
359. **entertain him:** be hospitable to him.
360. **drave:** drove.
362. **full stream:** rushing activity (like a stream almost over its banks).
363. **monastic:** like a hermit's.

me to wash your liver as clean as a sound sheep's heart, that there
shall not be one spot of love in't.   365
ORLANDO   I would not be cured, youth.
ROSALIND   I would cure you if you would but call me Rosalind and
come every day to my cot and woo me.
ORLANDO   Now, by the faith of my love, I will. Tell me where it is.
ROSALIND   Go with me to it and I'll show it you, and by the way you   370
shall tell me where in the forest you live. Will you go?
ORLANDO   With all my heart, good youth.
ROSALIND   Nay, you must call me Rosalind.—Come, sister, will
you go?   *Exeunt.*

Act 3 Scene 3

Enter [TOUCHSTONE, *the*] *Clown,* AUDREY, *and* JAQUES.

TOUCHSTONE   Come apace, good Audrey. I will fetch up your goats,
Audrey. And how, Audrey—am I the man yet? Doth my simple
feature content you?
AUDREY   Your features! Lord warrant us, what features?
TOUCHSTONE   I am here with thee and thy goats as the most capri-   5
cious poet honest Ovid was among the Goths.
JAQUES   O knowledge ill-inhabited—worse than Jove in a thatched
house!
TOUCHSTONE   When a man's verses cannot be understood nor a
man's good wit seconded with the forward child understanding,   10
it strikes a man more dead than a great reckoning in a little
room. Truly, I would the gods had made thee poetical.
AUDREY   I do not know what "poetical" is. Is it honest in deed and
word? Is it a true thing?

---

364. **liver:** believed to be the seat of the passion of love, which caused it to appear spot-
ted or diseased.
370. **by:** along.
3. **feature:** appearance.
4. **warrant:** defend; Not understanding his word **feature,** Audrey evidently fears
Touchstone is asking her to comment on his private parts.
6. **Ovid . . . Goths:** The Roman poet **Ovid** was exiled to live along the Black Sea
among the barbarous **Goths** because he wrote offensively licentious verses.
7–8. **thatched house:** house with a roof made of straw, now considered romantic but
then a sign of poverty.
10. **seconded . . . understanding:** encouraged through the comprehension of his
audience, like the cleverness of a precocious child.
11–12. **great . . . room:** huge bill for a small space.

TOUCHSTONE   No, truly—for the truest poetry is the most feigning 15
and lovers are given to poetry; and what they swear in poetry may
be said, as lovers, they do feign.⇒ decert
AUDREY   Do you wish then that the gods had made me poetical?
TOUCHSTONE   I do, truly. For thou swear'st to me thou are honest.
Now if thou wert a poet I might have some hope thou didst feign. 20
AUDREY   Would you not have me honest?
TOUCHSTONE   No, truly, unless thou wert hard-favored; for honesty
coupled to beauty is to have honey a sauce to sugar.
JAQUES   A material fool!
AUDREY   Well, I am not fair, and therefore I pray the gods make me 25
honest.
TOUCHSTONE   Truly, and to cast away honesty upon a foul slut were
to put good meat into an unclean dish.
AUDREY   I am not a slut, though I thank the gods I am foul.
TOUCHSTONE   Well, praised be the gods for thy foulness— 30
sluttishness may come hereafter. But be it as it may be, I will
marry thee; and to that end I have been with Sir Oliver Martext,
the vicar of the next village, who hath promised to meet me in
this place of the forest and to couple us.
JAQUES   I would fain see this meeting. 35
AUDREY   Well, the gods give us joy!
TOUCHSTONE   Amen. A man may, if he were of a fearful heart, stag-
ger in this attempt: for here we have no temple but the wood, no
assembly but horn-beasts. But what though? Courage! As horns
are odious they are necessary. It is said many a man knows no end 40
of his goods: right—many a man has good horns and knows no
end of them. Well that is the dowry of his wife: 'tis none of his
own getting. Horns? Even so. Poor men alone? No, no—the
noblest deer hath them as huge as the rascal. Is the single man
therefore blest? No, as a walled town is more worthier than a vil- 45
lage, so is the forehead of a married man more honorable than the

---

16–17. **what . . . feign:** echoing a strain of opinion, going back to Plato's *Republic*, that
    poets are liars.
  19. **honest:** sexually chaste, of good reputation.
  22. **hard-favored:** ugly.
  23. **honey . . . sugar:** i.e., too much of a good thing.
  24. **material:** full of matter, ideas.
  29. **I . . . foul:** i.e., I'd rather be ugly than a slut.
  34. **place:** part; **couple:** marry.
  39. **horn-beasts:** deer, with the usual connotation of "cuckolds."
41–42. **knows . . . them:** has no idea of the extent of his wife's infidelity.
  42. **dowry:** marriage portion supplied by the wife's family (usually money or property
    but in Touchstone's case, horns).
42–43. **none . . . getting:** not his own acquisition, with a pun on **getting** as begetting,
    since his children may not be his own.
  44. **rascal:** young deer.

bare brow of a bachelor. And by how much defense is better than no skill, by so much is a horn more precious than to want.

Enter SIR OLIVER MARTEXT.

Here comes Sir Oliver.—Sir Oliver Martext, you are well met. Will you dispatch us here under this tree or shall we go with you to your chapel? 50

SIR OLIVER Is there none here to give the woman?

TOUCHSTONE I will not take her on gift of any man.

SIR OLIVER Truly, she must be given or the marriage is not lawful.

JAQUES Proceed, proceed. I'll give her. 55

TOUCHSTONE Good even, good Master What-ye-call't. How do you, sir? You are very well met. God 'ield you for your last company. I am very glad to see you. Even a toy in hand here, sir. Nay, pray be covered.

JAQUES Will you be married, motley? 60

TOUCHSTONE As the ox hath his bow, sir, the horse his curb, and the falcon her bells, so man hath his desires; and as pigeons bill, so wedlock would be nibbling.

JAQUES And will you, being a man of your breeding, be married under a bush like a beggar? Get you to church and have a good 65 priest that can tell you what marriage is; this fellow will but join you together as they join wainscot. Then one of you will prove a shrunk panel and, like green timber, warp, warp.

45–47. **as . . . bachelor:** (Turning a negative to a positive:) just as a town walled for defense is considered more substantial than a mere undefended village, so a horn-bearing married man is better off than a bachelor with bare forehead and therefore no means of protecting himself.

47–48. **by how . . . want:** To the degree that it is better to have the ability to defend oneself than to lack that ability, it is better to have horns than to lack them.

49. **you . . . met:** It's good to see you.

51. **chapel:** The fact that Sir Oliver Martext has a **chapel** rather than a church suggests that he may be an irregular clergyman who is unlicensed by the bishop, one who "mars" or misinterprets biblical texts, as his name suggests.

53. **I . . . man:** Playing on the idea of "giving" a woman in marriage, Touchstone implies that any woman given him by another man will already be sexually experienced.

57–58. **God . . . company:** May God reward you for your companionship toward me last time we met (and now).

58. **Even . . . sir:** Touchstone introduces Audrey as a mere bauble to be played with.

59. **pray . . . covered:** Please put your hat back on.

61. **bow:** heavy collar; **curb:** yoke.

62. **bells:** attached to trained falcons so their masters would know their location and be able to keep them under control.

62–63. **as . . . nibbling:** As loving pigeons preen each other with their beaks, so couples planning marriage want to explore each other sexually.

67. **wainscot:** wood paneling (implying that Martext will not be able to join them in a valid union because he lacks the necessary commission from a bishop).

68. **like . . . warp:** bend out of shape like unseasoned wood, i.e., go astray.

TOUCHSTONE   I am not in the mind but I were better to be married
of him than of another; for he is not like to marry me well, and   70
not being well married it will be a good excuse for me hereafter
to leave my wife.
JAQUES   Go thou with me
   And let me counsel thee.

TOUCHSTONE   Come, sweet Audrey—   75
   We must be married, or we must live in bawdry.
Farewell, good Master Oliver—not
   "O sweet Oliver,
   O brave Oliver,
   Leave me not behind thee!"   80
but
   Wind away,
   Begone I say.
   I will not to wedding with thee.

SIR OLIVER   'Tis no matter. Ne'er a fantastical knave of them all   85
shall flout me out of my calling.   *Exeunt.*

Act 3 Scene 4

Enter ROSALIND *and* CELIA.

ROSALIND   Never talk to me—I will weep!
CELIA   Do, I prithee, <u>but yet have the grace to consider that tears
do not become a man.</u>
ROSALIND   But have I not cause to weep?
CELIA   As good cause as one would desire; therefore, weep.   5
ROSALIND   His very hair is of the dissembling color.
CELIA   Something browner than Judas's; marry, his kisses are
Judas's own children.

69–70. **I . . . him:** My view is that I will be better off being married by him.
  70. **he . . . well:** i.e., our marriage will not hold up in the courts and can therefore be
       dissolved (at a time when divorce was illegal).
  76. **bawdry:** sin, fornication.
  80. **O . . . thee:** fragments of an actual ballad of the period, titled "O Sweet Oliver,
       Leave Me Not behind Thee."
  81. **Wind:** go.
85–86. **Ne'er . . . calling:** The fact that Martext has contempt for the "lighter [more
       frivolous] people" and considers his ministry a **calling** suggests anti-Puritan sat-
       ire, like Shakespeare's portrayal of Malvolio in *Twelfth Night.*
   1. **Never:** do not.
   3. **do not become:** are not appropriate to.
   6. **dissembling color:** red.
 7–8. **Something browner . . . own children:** Judas, the apostle who betrayed Christ,
       was popularly believed to have had red hair. He betrayed Jesus with a kiss; hence
       Orlando's kisses are kisses of betrayal like Judas's.

ROSALIND I'faith, his hair is of a good color.

CELIA An excellent color: your chestnut was ever the only color.   10

ROSALIND And his kissing is as full of sanctity as the touch of holy bread.

CELIA He hath bought a pair of cast lips of Diana. A nun of winter's sisterhood kisses not more religiously: the very ice of chastity is in them.   15

ROSALIND But why did he swear he would come this morning and comes not?

CELIA Nay, certainly there is no truth in him.

ROSALIND Do you think so?

CELIA Yes, I think he is not a pick-purse nor a horse-stealer, but   20 for his <u>verity in love</u>—I do think him as concave as a covered goblet or a worm-eaten nut.

ROSALIND Not true in love?

CELIA Yes, when he is in, but I think he is not in.

ROSALIND You have heard him swear downright he was.   25

CELIA Was is not is. Besides, the oath of lover is no stronger than the word of a tapster: they are both the confirmer of false reckonings. He attends here in the forest on the duke your father.

ROSALIND I met the duke yesterday and had much question with him. He asked me of what parentage I was; I told him of as good   30 as he, so he laughed and let me go. But what talk we of fathers when there is such a man as Orlando?

CELIA Oh, that's a brave man: he writes brave verses, speaks brave words, swears brave oaths, and breaks them bravely— quite travers, athwart the heart of his lover, as a puny tilter that   35 spurs his horse but on one side breaks his staff like a noble goose. But all's brave that youth mounts and folly guides. Who comes here?

Enter CORIN.

---

10. **chestnut**: reddish brown.
11–12. **holy bread**: communion wafers, which in Catholic tradition were believed to confer physical and spiritual benefits.
13. **cast . . . Diana**: chaste, like the lips of the perpetual virgin Diana (but also suggesting **cast** in the sense of "cast iron"—cold and unyielding).
13–14. **winter's sisterhood**: an imaginary religious order whose nuns were particularly cold and chaste.
21. **concave**: hollow, duplicitous.
26–28. **oath . . . reckonings**: As a barman (**tapster**) keeping a tab will cheat by saying you have had more drinks than you have had, so the lover will cheat by promising a faithfulness he does not intend to honor.
29–30. **had . . . him**: He asked me a lot of questions; we had much conversation.
35–37. **traverse . . . goose**: in the wrong direction (**traverse**), going against (**athwart**) the heart of his lover, as an immature (**puny**) jouster who only uses his spurs on one side causes his horse to run crooked and therefore breaks his staff like a highborn idiot (**goose**) instead of hitting the target.

CORIN   Mistress and master, you have oft enquired
    After the shepherd that complained of love,   40
    Who you saw sitting by me on the turf,
    Praising the proud, disdainful shepherdess
    That was his mistress.
CELIA   Well, and what of him?
CORIN   If you will see a pageant truly played
    Between the pale complexion of true love   45
    And the red glow of scorn and proud disdain,
    Go hence a little and I shall conduct you,
    If you will mark it.
ROSALIND   Oh come, let us remove.
    The sight of lovers feedeth those in love.
    Bring us to this sight and you shall say   50
    I'll prove a busy actor in their play.   *Exeunt.*

Act 3 Scene 5

Enter SILVIUS *and* PHOEBE.

SILVIUS   Sweet Phoebe, do not scorn me; do not, Phoebe.
    Say that you love me not, but say not so
    In bitterness. The common executioner,
    Whose heart th'accustomed sight of death makes hard,
    Falls not the axe upon the humbled neck   5
    But first begs pardon. Will you sterner be
    Than he that dies and lives by bloody drops?

Enter ROSALIND, CELIA, *and* CORIN.

PHOEBE   I would not be thy executioner.
    I fly thee, for I would not injure thee.
    Thou tell'st me there is murder in mine eye.   10
    'Tis pretty, sure, and very probable
    That eyes, that are the frail'st and softest things,
    Who shut their coward gates on atomies,

44–46. **pageant . . . disdain:** skit enacted by the pallor of unrequited love (Silvius) and
    the red of angry scorn (Phoebe).
48. **will mark:** would like to watch.
4. whose heart is hardened by having seen so much death.
5. **Falls:** Lowers.
9. **fly:** run away from.
10. **murder in mine eye:** A version of the Petrarchan commonplace, much over-used
    in love poetry by Shakespeare's time, that the woman's eyes cast fatal beams upon
    her wooer.
13. **Who shut . . . atomies:** that blink shut to keep out dust (and are therefore cow-
    ardly because they are afraid to encounter something so unthreatening).

Should be called tyrants, butchers, murderers.
Now I do frown on thee with all my heart,   15
And if mine eyes can wound, now let them kill thee.
Now counterfeit to swoon: why now fall down;
Or if thou canst not, oh for shame, for shame,
Lie not to say mine eyes are murderers!
Now show the wound mine eye hath made in thee.   20
Scratch thee but with a pin and there remains
Some scar of it; lean upon a rush,
The cicatrice and capable impressure
Thy palm some moment keeps. But now mine eyes,
Which I have darted at thee, hurt thee not;   25
Nor, I am sure, there is no force in eyes
That can do hurt.
SILVIUS   O dear Phoebe,
If ever—as that ever may be near—
You meet in some fresh cheek the power of fancy,
Then shall you know the wounds invisible   30
That love's keen arrows make.
PHOEBE   But till that time
Come not thou near me. And when that time comes,
Afflict me with thy mocks; pity me not,
As till that time I shall not pity thee.
ROSALIND   And why, I pray you? Who might be your mother   35
That you insult, exult, and all at once
Over the wretched? What, though you have no beauty—
As, by my faith, I see no more in you
Than without candle may go dark to bed—
Must you be therefore proud and pitiless?   40
Why, what means this? Why do you look on me?
I see no more in you than in the ordinary
Of nature's sale-work.—'Ods my little life,
I think she means to tangle my eyes too!—

---

17. **counterfeit to swoon**: pretend to faint; here and throughout, **swoon** is spelled "swound" in the folio.
22–24. **lean . . . keeps**: If you lean your hand against a reed (or any irregular surface) your palm will briefly carry its imprint or scar (**cicatrice**).
29. You encounter someone whose beauty (**fresh cheek**) causes you to fall in love.
31. **love's keen arrows**: the darts or arrows shot by Cupid, god of love (another hackneyed image).
33. **mocks**: mockery, scorn.
35. **Who . . . mother**: i.e., who do you think you are?
38–39. Your beauty is not bright enough to light you to bed without the help of a candle.
41. **Why . . . this**: Phoebe has evidently given Rosalind a desiring look.
42–43. **ordinary . . . work**: i.e., you're just average looking, standard ware (as opposed to something unique and finely made).
43. **'Ods . . . life**: mild oath equivalent to "God save me."
44. **tangle**: entrap (in passion).

No, faith, proud mistress, hope not after it;　　45
'Tis not your inky brows, your black silk hair,
Your bugle eyeballs, nor your cheek of cream
That can entame my spirits to your worship.
You foolish shepherd, wherefore do you follow her
Like foggy south, puffing with wind and rain?　　50
You are a thousand times a properer man
Than she a woman. 'Tis such fools as you
That makes the world full of ill-favored children.
'Tis not her glass but you that flatters her,
And out of you she sees herself more proper　　55
Than any of her lineaments can show her.
But mistress, know yourself: down on your knees
And thank heaven, fasting, for a good man's love.
For I must tell you friendly in your ear,
Sell when you can; you are not for all markets.　　60
Cry the man mercy, love him, take his offer.
Foul is most foul being foul to be a scoffer.
So take her to thee, shepherd. Fare you well.

PHOEBE　Sweet youth, I pray you, chide a year together.
I had rather hear you chide than this man woo.　　65

ROSALIND　He's fallen in love with your foulness—and she'll fall in love with my anger. If it be so, as fast as she answers thee with frowning looks, I'll sauce her with bitter words.—Why look you so upon me?

PHOEBE　For no ill will I bear you.　　70

ROSALIND　I pray you, do not fall in love with me,
For I am falser than vows made in wine.
Besides, I like you not. If you will know my house,
'Tis at the tuft of olives, here hard by.
Will you go, sister? Shepherd, ply her hard.　　75

---

47. **bugle:** shining and black (like a type of glass bead, but possibly with a jest on the alleged power of her eyes since a **bugle** could also be a hunting horn, drawing men to the hunt as her eyes draw potential lovers).
48. **That can . . . worship:** that can subdue my emotions into worshiping you.
50. **wind and rain:** sighing and weeping.
51. **properer:** more handsome.
54. **glass:** mirror.
55–56. **out . . . her:** By seeing herself through your eyes she thinks she is more attractive than any of her actual features can give evidence.
60. **you . . . markets:** You're not such a great bargain.
61. **Cry . . . mercy:** Beg his pardon.
62. The ugly are ugliest when, despite their own ugliness, they make fun of others.
63. **take . . . thee:** Make her your own.
68. **sauce:** rebuke, taunt.
72. **in wine:** while drunk.
74. **tuft . . . by:** grove of olive trees near here.
75. **ply her:** Work on her.

Come, sister.—Shepherdess, look on him better
And be not proud: though all the world could see
None could be so abused in sight as he.
Come—to our flock.   *Exeunt* [ROSALIND, CELIA, *and* CORIN].
PHOEBE   Dead shepherd, now I find thy saw of might: 80
"Who ever loved that loved not at first sight?"
SILVIUS   Sweet Phoebe—
PHOEBE   Ha? What sayst thou, Silvius?
SILVIUS   Sweet Phoebe, pity me.
PHOEBE   Why, I am sorry for thee, gentle Silvius.
SILVIUS   Wherever sorrow is, relief would be.   85
If you do sorrow at my grief in love,
By giving love your sorrow and my grief
Were both extermined.
PHOEBE   Thou hast my love—is not that neighborly?
SILVIUS   I would have you.
PHOEBE   Why that were covetousness.   90
Silvius, the time was that I hated thee,
And yet it is not that I bear thee love.
But since that thou canst talk of love so well,
Thy company, which erst was irksome to me,
I will endure, and I'll employ thee too.   95
But do not look for further recompence
Than thine own gladness that thou art employed.
SILVIUS   So holy and so perfect is my love,
And I in such a poverty of grace,
That I shall think it a most plenteous crop   100
To glean the broken ears after the man
That the main harvest reaps. Loose now and then
A scattered smile, and that I'll live upon.
PHOEBE   Know'st thou the youth that spoke to me erewhile?
SILVIUS   Not very well, but I have met him oft,   105
And he hath bought the cottage and the bounds

77–78. **though . . . he:** If everyone in the world could look at you, none would be as blind as he is to your actual appearance.
80. **Dead . . . might:** Dead shepherd (a reference to Christopher Marlowe, who wrote widely popular pastoral verse and had died only recently, in 1593), now I understand the power of your maxim.
81. **"Who ever . . . sight?":** from Marlowe's *Hero and Leander* 1.176.
88. **extermined:** eradicated, got rid of.
91. **the time was:** there was a time.
92. **yet . . . that:** the time hasn't come that.
94. **erst:** at first.
99. **poverty of grace:** deprived of your mercy (parodies religious language about the absence of divine grace).
101–02. **To . . . reaps:** to gather up the broken husks after Ganymede (i.e., Ganymede gets Phoebe's love but I'll get at least a few kind looks that are left over).
106. **bounds:** holdings in land.

That the old Carlot once was master of.
PHOEBE   Think not I love him though I ask for him.
  'Tis but a peevish boy, yet he talks well.
  But what care I for words? Yet words do well   110
  When he that speaks them pleases those that hear.
  It is a pretty youth—not very pretty—
  But sure, he's proud, and yet his pride becomes him.
  He'll make a proper man. The best thing in him
  Is his complexion; and faster than his tongue   115
  Did make offense, his eye did heal it up.
  He is not very tall, yet for his years he's tall.
  His leg is but so-so, and yet 'tis well.
  There was a pretty redness in his lip—
  A little riper and more lusty red   120
  Than that mixed in his cheek; 'twas just the difference
  Betwixt the constant red and mingled damask.
  There be some women, Silvius, had they marked him
  In parcels as I did, would have gone near
  To fall in love with him. But for my part,   125
  I love him not nor hate him not, and yet
  Have more cause to hate him than to love him.
  For what had he to do to chide at me?
  He said mine eyes were black and my hair black
  And, now I am remembered, scorned at me.   130
  I marvel why I answered not again.
  But that's all one; omittance is no quittance.
  I'll write to him a very taunting letter,
  And thou shalt bear it. Wilt thou, Silvius?
SILVIUS   Phoebe, with all my heart.
PHOEBE   I'll write it straight.   135
  The matter's in my head and in my heart.
  I will be bitter with him and passing short.
  Go with me, Silvius.   *Exeunt.*

107. **Carlot:** Corin's former boss (or it could be a generic term for "peasant").
122. **constant . . . damask:** pure red and red mixed with white (as in damask roses).
124. **In parcels:** bit by bit (implying she eyed him up and down).
128. **what . . . do:** what business did he have.
129. **He said . . . hair black:** By objecting to the fact that Ganymede called her hair and
     eyes black, the rustic Phoebe shows she is not up to date. By the late sixteenth
     century in England black was highly fashionable, as in sonnets by Sidney and
     Shakespeare.
130. **remembered:** reminded.
131. **answered not again:** didn't answer back.
132. **that's . . . quittance:** that doesn't matter; a debt is not canceled simply because one
     fails to demand repayment. (proverbial: i.e., I still have a chance to get back at him.)
137. **passing short:** extremely rude.

Act 4 Scene 1

Enter ROSALIND, CELIA, *and* JAQUES.

JAQUES I prithee, pretty youth, let me be better acquainted with thee.

ROSALIND They say you are a melancholy fellow.

JAQUES I am so: I do love it better than laughing.

ROSALIND Those that are in extremity of either are abominable 5 fellows and betray themselves to every modern censure worse than drunkards.

JAQUES Why, 'tis good to be sad and say nothing.

ROSALIND Why then 'tis good to be a post.

JAQUES I have neither the scholar's melancholy, which is emula- 10 tion; nor the musician's, which is fantastical; nor the courtier's, which is proud; nor the soldier's, which is ambitious; nor the lawyer's, which is politic; nor the lady's, which is nice; nor the lover's, which is all these; but it is a melancholy of mine own, compounded of many simples, extracted from many objects, and 15 indeed the sundry contemplation of my travels, in which by often rumination wraps me in a most humorous sadness.

ROSALIND A traveler? By my faith, you have great reason to be sad! I fear you have sold your own lands to see other men's, then: to have seen much and to have nothing is to have rich eyes and poor 20 hands.

JAQUES Yes, I have gained my experience.

Enter ORLANDO.

ROSALIND And your experience makes you sad. I had rather have a fool to make me merry than experience to make me sad—and to travel for it too! 25

ORLANDO Good day and happiness, dear Rosalind.

JAQUES Nay then, God b'wi' you an you talk in blank verse.

---

5. **extremity:** great excess.
13. **politic:** strategic; **nice:** precise, fastidious.
15. **compounded . . . simples:** put together from many ingredients.
16–17. **sundry . . . sadness:** various (**sundry**) meditations on my travels (with a pun on "travails"), which, through my frequent thinking about them, fill me with a very moody sadness.
19. **sold . . men's:** sold your own property to earn money so you can go look at other people's (as profligate youths sometimes did, since foreign travel was much in fashion).
27. **an:** if; **blank verse:** unrhymed iambic pentameter (of which Orlando's speech in the previous line is a good example).

ROSALIND Farewell, Monsieur Traveller. Look you lisp and wear
strange suits, disable all the benefits of your own country, be out
of love with your nativity, and almost chide God for making you 30
that countenance you are; or I will scarce think you have swum in
a gundello.   [*Exit* JAQUES.]
Why, how now, Orlando, where have you been all this while? You,
a lover? An you serve me such another trick, never come in my
sight more.   35

ORLANDO My fair Rosalind, I come within an hour of my promise.

ROSALIND Break an hour's promise in love? He that will divide a
minute into a thousand parts and break but a part of the thousand part of a minute in the affairs of love, it may be said of him
that Cupid hath clapped him o'th' shoulder, but I'll warrant him 40
heart-whole.

ORLANDO Pardon me, dear Rosalind.

ROSALIND Nay, an you be so tardy, come no more in my sight. I
had as lief be wooed of a snail.

ORLANDO Of a snail?   45

ROSALIND Ay, of a snail: for though he comes slowly, he carries his
house on his head—a better jointure, I think, than you make a
woman. Besides, he brings his destiny with him.

ORLANDO What's that?

ROSALIND Why, horns, which such as you are fain to be beholding 50
to your wives for. But he comes armed in his fortune and prevents the slander of his wife.

ORLANDO Virtue is no horn-maker, and my Rosalind is virtuous.

ROSALIND And I am your Rosalind.

CELIA It pleases him to call you so. But he hath a Rosalind of a 55
better leer than you.

ROSALIND Come—woo me, woo me, for now I am in a holiday
humor and like enough to consent. What would you say to me
now an I were your very, very Rosalind?

28. **Look you:** be sure to.
29. **strange:** foreign; **disable:** disparage.
31–32. **swum . . . gundello:** rowed in a gondola (in Venice).
34. **An . . . trick:** if you play another trick like this one on me.
40–41. **Cupid . . . heart-whole:** Cupid may have slapped him on the shoulder, but I'll
        guarantee that he was not struck in the heart (by Cupid's arrows).
44–45. **I . . . snail:** I would like it just as well to be courted by a snail.
47. **house:** snail shell.
47. **jointure:** money or real estate set aside for the wife's maintenance (since other-
        wise all her property legally became her husband's upon marriage).
50–51. **such . . . for:** men like you are inclined to be obliged to your wife for (since it is
        the wife's infidelity that makes the cuckold).
51–52. **prevents:** keeps from happening (since the snail has horns even before he mar-
        ries), but **prevents** can also mean "anticipates": his horns forecast his destiny as a
        cuckold.
56. **leer:** face, appearance.
58. **like:** likely.

ORLANDO   I would kiss before I spoke.   60

ROSALIND   Nay, you were better speak first, and when you were
graveled for lack of matter, you might take occasion to kiss. Very
good orators, when they are out, they will spit; and for lovers
lacking (God warn us) matter, the cleanliest shift is to kiss.

ORLANDO   How if the kiss be denied?   65

ROSALIND   Then she puts you to entreaty, and there begins new
matter.

ORLANDO   Who could be out, being before his beloved mistress?

ROSALIND   Marry, that should you if I were your mistress, or I
should think my honesty ranker than my wit.   70

ORLANDO   What, of my suit?

ROSALIND   Not out of your apparel, and yet out of your suit. Am
not I your Rosalind?

ORLANDO   I take some joy to say you are because I would be talking of her.   75

ROSALIND   Well, in her person, I say I will not have you.

ORLANDO   Then in mine own person, I die.

ROSALIND   No, faith, die by attorney. The poor world is almost six
thousand years old and in all this time there was not any man
died in his own person, *videlicet* in a love cause: Troilus had his   80
brains dashed out with a Grecian club; yet he did what he could
to die before, and he is one of the patterns of love. Leander, he
would have lived many a fair year though Hero had turned nun,
if it had not been for a hot midsummer-night; for, good youth, he
went but forth to wash him in the Hellespont and, being taken   85
with the cramp, was drowned, and the foolish chroniclers of that
age found it was Hero of Sestos. But these are all lies: men have
died from time to time and worms have eaten them, but not for
love.

62. **graveled . . . matter:** confounded by a lack of anything to say.
63. **orators . . . spit:** Public speakers, when they are at a loss for words, will spit (to
give themselves time to think of something to say).
64. **cleanliest shift:** cleanest strategy (since kissing is less polluting than spitting).
66–67. **Then . . . matter:** Then she forces you to beg and that gives you a new subject to
talk about.
68. **be out:** be at a loss for words (but with a pun on "being in," sexual penetration).
69–70. (Continuing the sexual pun), if I were your beloved I would think my lack of chastity more offensive than my lack of intelligence if I did not keep you out.
71. **of my suit:** would I be out of my suit (i.e., fail in my attempt to woo you).
72. with a pun on **suit** in the sense of "suit of clothes."
78. **die by attorney:** die by proxy (and not in your own person).
78–79. **world . . . old:** age calculated by beginning with the biblical Adam and Eve.
80. *videlicet*: namely (legal language from Latin).
80–82. **Troilus . . . love:** Troilus, the famed Trojan lover of Cressida, was killed by the
Greeks in the Trojan War, even though he tried to die of love after she rejected him.
82–87. **Leander . . . Sestos:** another famous pair: Leander, the beloved of Hero of Sestos,
was believed by historians to have died of love because he drowned trying to reach
her by swimming across the narrow Turkish strait now called the Dardanelles. But
his actual motive, Rosalind quips, was simply to take a bath and he died of a cramp.

ORLANDO   I would not have my right Rosalind of this mind, for I   90
protest her frown might kill me.

ROSALIND   By this hand, it will not kill a fly. But come—now I will
be your Rosalind in a more coming-on disposition, and ask me
what you will, I will grant it.

ORLANDO   Then love me, Rosalind.   95

ROSALIND   Yes, faith, will I—Fridays and Saturdays and all.

ORLANDO   And wilt thou have me?

ROSALIND   Ay, and twenty such.

ORLANDO   What sayest thou?

ROSALIND   Are you not good?   100

ORLANDO   I hope so.

ROSALIND   Why then, can one desire too much of a good thing?
Come, sister—you shall be the priest and marry us. Give me your
hand, Orlando. What do you say, sister?

ORLANDO   Pray thee, marry us.   105

CELIA   I cannot say the words.

ROSALIND   You must begin, "Will you, Orlando,"—

CELIA   Go to! Will you, Orlando, have to wife this Rosalind?

ORLANDO   I will.

ROSALIND   Ay, but when?   110

ORLANDO   Why now, as fast as she can marry us.

ROSALIND   Then you must say, "I take thee, Rosalind, for wife."

ORLANDO   I take thee, Rosalind, for wife.

ROSALIND   I might ask you for your commission, but I do take thee,
Orlando, for my husband. There's a girl goes before the   115
priest, and certainly a woman's thought runs before her actions.

ORLANDO   So do all thoughts: they are winged.

ROSALIND   Now tell me how long you would have her after you
have possessed her.

ORLANDO   Forever and a day.   120

ROSALIND   Say "a day" without the "ever." No, no, Orlando: men
are April when they woo, December when they wed; maids are
May when they are maids, but the sky changes when they are
wives. I will be more jealous of thee than a Barbary cock-pigeon

---

90. **mind:** opinion.
93. **coming-on:** approachable.
98. **such:** like you.
108. **Go to:** equivalent to a reproachful "Come on!"
114. **commission:** legal right to marry us (said to Celia).
115. **goes before:** anticipates (but also hinting at Rosalind's female identity beneath her
disguise as Ganymede).
117. **they are winged:** Thoughts have wings (in the sense that they can move faster and
more freely than human bodies can).
124. **Barbary cock-pigeon:** North African bird emblematic of sexual jealousy.

over his hen, more clamorous than a parrot against rain, more   125
new-fangled than an ape, more giddy in my desires than a mon-
key. I will weep for nothing, like Diana in the fountain, and I
will do that when you are disposed to be merry. I will laugh like
a hyen, and that when thou art inclined to sleep.

ORLANDO   But will my Rosalind do so?   130

ROSALIND   By my life, she will do as I do.

ORLANDO   Oh, but she is wise.

ROSALIND   Or else she could not have the wit to do this: the wiser
the waywarder. Make the doors upon a woman's wit and it will
out at the casement; shut that and 'twill out at the keyhole; stop   135
that, 'twill fly with the smoke out at the chimney.

ORLANDO   A man that had a wife with such a wit, he might say,
"Wit, whither wilt?"

ROSALIND   Nay, you might keep that check for it, till you met your
wife's wit going to your neighbor's bed.   140

ORLANDO   And what wit could wit have to excuse that?

ROSALIND   Marry, to say she came to seek you there. You shall
never take her without her answer unless you take her without
her tongue. Oh, that woman that cannot make her fault her husband's occasion, let her never nurse her child herself, for she will   145
breed it like a fool.

ORLANDO   For these two hours, Rosalind, I will leave thee.

ROSALIND   Alas, dear love, I cannot lack thee two hours!

ORLANDO   I must attend the duke at dinner. By two o'clock I will
be with thee again.   150

ROSALIND   Ay, go your ways, go your ways! I knew what you would
prove: my friends told me as much, and I thought no less. That

---

125. **against:** sensing the coming of.
126. **new-fangled:** distracted by new things.
127. **for:** over; **Diana . . . fountain:** a fountain in which water flows from the goddess's
    eyes like tears. There was a similar fountain in West Cheap, London, which
    featured water from the Thames flowing from Diana's breasts.
129. **hyen:** hyena (an animal able, according to popular myth, to alternate between
    male and female sexual identities).
134. **Make:** lock.
135. **casement:** window.
138. **whither wilt:** Where are you headed? (The jest appears to be that Orlando
    twists a catch-phrase usually employed to suggest a lack of wit by using it liter-
    ally of a potentially wayward wife.)
139. **keep . . . it:** use it to attempt to curb your wife's sexual waywardness.
143. **take . . . answer:** catch her without a retort.
144–46. **that . . . fool:** Any woman who can't turn her own fault back on her husband
    should not be allowed to nurse her own child because she will infect it with her
    own folly. (It was widely believed that whoever nursed an infant could influence
    its character through her milk.)
152. **prove:** turn out to be.

flattering tongue of yours won me. 'Tis but one cast away and so, come, death! Two o'clock is your hour?

ORLANDO   Ay, sweet Rosalind.   155

ROSALIND   By my troth and in good earnest and so God mend me, and by all pretty oaths that are not dangerous—if you break one jot of your promise or come one minute behind your hour, I will think you the most pathetical break-promise and the most hollow lover and the most unworthy of her you call Rosalind that may be   160 chosen out of the gross band of the unfaithful. Therefore beware my censure and keep your promise!

ORLANDO   With no less religion than if thou wert indeed my Rosalind. So, adieu.

ROSALIND   Well, Time is the old justice that examines all such   165 offenders, and let Time try. Adieu.   *Exit* [ORLANDO.]

CELIA   You have simply misused our sex in your love-prate: we must have your doublet and hose plucked over your head and show the world what the bird hath done to her own nest.

ROSALIND   O coz, coz, coz, my pretty little coz, that thou didst know   170 how many fathom deep I am in love! But it cannot be sounded: my affection hath an unknown bottom, like the Bay of Portugal.

CELIA   Or rather bottomless, that as fast as you pour affection in, it runs out.

ROSALIND   No, that same wicked bastard of Venus that was begot   175 of thought, conceived of spleen, and born of madness—that blind, rascally boy that abuses everyone's eyes because his own are out—let him be judge how deep I am in love. I'll tell thee, Aliena, I cannot be out of the sight of Orlando. I'll go find a shadow and sigh till he come.   180

CELIA   And I'll sleep.   *Exeunt.*

---

153. **one cast away:** one beloved spurned (implying that there will be many others).
158. **behind:** past.
166. **let Time try:** i.e., time will tell (with a pun on **Time** as a judge who will **try** Orlando's case).
167. **love-prate:** prattling about love or prattling because you are in love.
169. **what . . . nest:** i.e., that you are a woman who has abused your own kind.
172. **unknown . . . Portugal:** extremely deep, like the water off the coast of Portugal between Oporto and the Cape of Cintra.
173. **that:** so that.
175. **wicked . . . Venus:** Cupid, son of Venus, goddess of love.
177–78. **abuses . . . out:** makes lovers blind because he is blind himself (playing on the commonplace that "Love is blind").

Act 4 Scene 2

Enter JAQUES *and* LORDS *[dressed as] foresters.*

JAQUES Which is he that killed the deer?
FIRST LORD Sir, it was I.
JAQUES Let's present him to the duke like a Roman conqueror.
And it would do well to set the deer's horns upon his head for a
branch of victory. Have you no song, forester, for this purpose? 5
SECOND LORD Yes, sir.
JAQUES Sing it. 'Tis no matter how it be in tune, so it make noise
enough.

Music.
Song.

SECOND LORD
What shall he have that killed the deer?
His leather skin and horns to wear. 10
Then sing him home. The rest shall bear
This burden:
Take thou no scorn to wear the horn.
It was a crest e'er thou wast born.
Thy father's father wore it, 15
And thy father bore it.
The horn, the horn, the lusty horn
Is not a thing to laugh to scorn. *Exeunt.*

3. like . . . conqueror: In ancient Rome, successful generals returning from the
field would be presented to the emperor in a victory parade or "triumph."
5. branch: like the garland that would have crowned a Roman conqueror (but with
the usual connotations of cuckoldry).
8. The fact that *Song* is preceded by *Music* may indicate that an instrumental introduction preceded the singing of the song.
11–12. bear . . . burden: sing this refrain (but also suggesting that they will bear the
burden of being cuckolds).
13. Take . . . scorn: Don't be ashamed.
14. crest: coat of arms (suggesting gentry status but also implying the opposite, since
a cuckold may not know who his children's father is); also head ornament (ironically, like those worn by many birds to attract mates).

Act 4 Scene 3

Enter ROSALIND *and* CELIA.

ROSALIND   How say you now, is it not past two o'clock? And here
much Orlando!

CELIA   I warrant you, with pure love and troubled brain, he hath
ta'en his bow and arrows and is gone forth to sleep.

Enter SILVIUS [*with a letter*].

Look who comes here.   5

SILVIUS   My errand is to you, fair youth.
My gentle Phoebe did bid me give you this.
I know not the contents, but as I guess
By the stern brow and waspish action
Which she did use as she was writing of it,   10
It bears an angry tenor. Pardon me.
I am but as a guiltless messenger.

ROSALIND   [*Reads.*] Patience herself would startle at this letter
And play the swaggerer. Bear this, bear all:
She says I am not fair, that I lack manners;   15
She calls me proud and that she could not love me,
Were man as rare as phoenix. 'Od's my will,
Her love is not the hare that I do hunt!
Why writes she so to me? Well, shepherd, well—
This is a letter of your own device.   20

SILVIUS   No, I protest I know not the contents.
Phoebe did write it.

ROSALIND   Come, come—you are a fool, — but she also
And turned into the extremity of love.   has
I saw her hand. She has a leathern hand,
A freestone-colored hand. I verily did think   25
That her old gloves were on, but 'twas her hands.
She has a housewife's hand. But that's no matter.

1–2. **here . . . Orlando:** i.e., where is he? (spoken in deep irony).
11. **tenor:** meaning, drift.
13–14. **startle . . . swaggerer:** be shocked by this letter and bristle in response.
14. **Bear . . . all:** proverbial: if you put up with this, you'll put up with anything.
17. **Were . . . phoenix:** if there were only one man left (since the phoenix is a mythical
bird of which there is only one in the world); **'Od's:** God's.
20. **device:** making.
23. **turned into:** brought to.
25. **freestone-colored:** the color of a brownish rock; **verily:** truly.
27. **housewife's hand:** a hand rough and discolored from household chores.

I say she never did invent this letter;
This is a man's invention and his hand.
SILVIUS   Sure, it is hers.   30
ROSALIND   Why, 'tis a boisterous and a cruel style—
A style for challengers. Why she defies me
Like Turk to Christian. Women's gentle brain
Could not drop forth such giant, rude invention,
Such Ethiope words, blacker in their effect   35
Than in their countenance! Will you hear the letter?
SILVIUS   So please you, for I never heard it yet—
Yet heard too much of Phoebe's cruelty.
ROSALIND   She "Phoebes" me. Mark how the tyrant writes:

Read[s].   "Art thou god to shepherd turned,   40
          That a maiden's heart hath burned?"
—Can a woman rail thus?
SILVIUS   Call you this railing?
ROSALIND   Read[s]. "Why, thy godhead laid apart,
          Warr'st thou with a woman's heart?"   45
—Did you ever hear such railing?
          "Whiles the eye of man did woo me,
          That could do no vengeance to me."
—Meaning me a beast.
          "If the scorn of your bright eyne   50
          Have power to raise such love in mine,
          Alack, in me what strange effect
          Would they work in mild aspect?
          Whiles you chid me I did love:
          How then might your prayers move?   55
          He that brings this love to thee
          Little knows this love in me;
          And by him seal up thy mind,

33. **Like . . . Christian:** At this time the Muslim Ottoman Turks posed a military
    threat to Christian Europe from the East.
35. **Ethiope:** Ethiopian, i.e., black (with the implication of evil at this period).
44–45. **Why . . . heart:** Why, if you are not a god (since the classical deities were known
    for being both amorous and arbitrary) are you making war on my heart (i.e., reject-
    ing my love)?
49. **Meaning . . . beast:** Phoebe's letter has just said that she was not influenced by
    the power of the eyes of any man attempting to woo her. Rosalind chooses to
    interpret Phoebe as calling her less than human.
50. **eyne:** eyes.
53. **in mild aspect:** if you looked upon me more kindly.
54. **chid:** chided.
58. **by . . . mind:** Let me know your thoughts in a sealed letter that he can deliver
    back to me.

Whether that thy youth and kind
Will the faithful offer take   60
Of me and all that I can make.
Or else by him my love deny,
And then I'll study how to die."

SILVIUS   Call you this chiding?
CELIA   Alas, poor shepherd!   65
ROSALIND   Do you pity him? No, he deserves no pity.—Wilt thou
  love such a woman? What, to make thee an instrument and play
  false strains upon thee? Not to be endured! Well, go your way to
  her, for I see love hath made thee a tame snake, and say this to
  her: that if she love me I charge her to love thee; if she will not I 70
  will never have her unless thou entreat for her. If you be a true
  lover, hence and not a word, for here comes more company.
                                                    Exit SILVIUS.

          Enter OLIVER.

OLIVER   Good morrow, fair ones. Pray you, if you know,
  Where in the purlieus of this forest stands
  A sheep-cote fenced about with olive trees?   75
CELIA   West of this place, down in the neighbor bottom:
  The rank of osiers by the murmuring stream,
  Left on your right hand, brings you to the place.
  But at this hour the house doth keep itself:
  There's none within.   80
OLIVER   If that an eye may profit by a tongue
  Then should I know you by description,
  Such garments and such years: "The boy is fair,
  Of female favor, and bestows himself
  Like a ripe sister; the woman low   85
  And browner than her brother." Are not you
  The owner of the house I did inquire for?
CELIA   It is no boast, being asked, to say we are.
OLIVER   Orlando doth commend him to you both,

    59. **kind:** nature.
    61. **make:** give.
  67–68. **make . . . thee:** Phoebe has made Silvius her **instrument** in that he has carried
         the letter, with pun on a musical instrument that plays musical phrases (**strains**) out
         of tune just as Phoebe has deceived Silvius about the actual tone of her letter.
    74. **purlieus:** edges.
    75. **fenced . . . with:** surrounded by.
    76. **neighbor bottom:** next valley.
    77. **rank of osiers:** row of willows.
    78. **hand:** side. (Celia's directions seem deliberately confusing.)
    84. **favor:** appearance.
  84–85. **bestows . . . sister:** behaves like her older sister.
    85. **low:** short.

And to that youth he calls his Rosalind   90
He sends this bloody napkin. Are you he?
ROSALIND   I am. What must we understand by this?
OLIVER   Some of my shame, if you will know of me
What man I am, and how and why and where
This handkercher was stained.
CELIA   I pray you, tell it.   95
OLIVER   When last the young Orlando parted from you
He left a promise to return again
Within an hour; and pacing through the forest,
Chewing the food of sweet and bitter fancy,
Lo what befell: he threw his eye aside   100
And marked what object did present itself.
Under an old oak, whose boughs were mossed with age
And high top bald with dry antiquity,
A wretched, ragged man, o'ergrown with hair,
Lay sleeping on his back. About his neck   105
A green and gilded snake had wreathed itself,
Who with her head, nimble in threats, approached
The opening of his mouth. But suddenly,
Seeing Orlando, it unlinked itself
And with indented glides did slip away   110
Into a bush, under which bush's shade
A lioness with udders all drawn dry
Lay couching, head on ground, with catlike watch
When that the sleeping man should stir. For 'tis
The royal disposition of that beast   115
To prey on nothing that doth seem as dead.
This seen, Orlando did approach the man,
And found it was his brother, his elder brother.
CELIA   Oh, I have heard him speak of that same brother,
And he did render him the most unnatural   120
That lived amongst men.
OLIVER   And well he might so do,
For well I know he was unnatural.
ROSALIND   But to Orlando: did he leave him there,
Food to the sucked and hungry lioness?

91. **napkin:** handkerchief.
95. **handkercher:** handkerchief.
99. **Chewing . . . fancy:** ruminating about sweet and bitter fantasies.
100. **Lo . . . aside:** Look what happened: he looked to the side.
103. **dry:** too dried out to bear leaves.
109. **unlinked:** uncoiled.
110. **indented:** undulating.
112. **drawn dry:** nursed dry (which would make the lioness ravenously hungry).
116. **as:** to be.
120. **render him:** portray him as.

OLIVER   Twice did he turn his back, and purposed so;   125
But kindness, nobler ever than revenge,
And nature, stronger than his just occasion,
Made him give battle to the lioness,
Who quickly fell before him, in which hurtling
From miserable slumber, I awaked.   130
CELIA   Are you his brother?
ROSALIND   Was't you he rescued?
CELIA   Was't you that did so oft contrive to kill him?
OLIVER   'Twas I but 'tis not I: I do not shame
To tell you what I was, since my conversion
So sweetly tastes being the thing I am.   135
ROSALIND   But for the bloody napkin?
OLIVER   By and by.
When from the first to last, betwixt us two,
Tears our recountments had most kindly bathed
—as how I came into that desert place—
I' brief, he led me to the gentle duke,   140
Who gave me fresh array and entertainment,
Committing me unto my brother's love,
Who led me instantly unto his cave,
There stripped himself; and here upon his arm
The lioness had torn some flesh away,   145
Which all this while had bled; and now he fainted
And cried in fainting upon Rosalind.
Brief, I recovered him, bound up his wound;
And after some small space, being strong at heart,
He sent me hither, stranger as I am,   150
To tell this story, that you might excuse
His broken promise, and to give this napkin,
Dyed in this blood, unto the shepherd youth
That he in sport doth call his Rosalind.

        [ROSALIND *faints*.]

CELIA   Why, how, now, Ganymede? Sweet Ganymede!   155
OLIVER   Many will swoon when they do look on blood.
CELIA   There is more in it.—Cousin Ganymede!
OLIVER   Look, he recovers.

---

125. **purposed**: intended.
127. **just occasion**: valid grounds (for revenge).
129. **hurtling**: could refer either to the violence of the battle itself or to Oliver's being
    thrown into awakeness by it.
134–35. **my . . . am**: My transformation allows me to appreciate my (new) identity.
138. **recountments**: stories, recountings.
148. **recovered**: revived.

ROSALIND   I would I were at home.

CELIA We'll lead you thither.—

I pray you, will you take him by the arm?   160

OLIVER   Be of good cheer, youth. You a man?

You lack a man's heart.

ROSALIND   I do so, I confess it.

Ah, sirrah, a body would think this was well counterfeited! I

pray you, tell your brother how well I counterfeited. Hey-ho!

OLIVER   This was not counterfeit: there is too great testimony in   165

your complexion that it was a passion of earnest.

ROSALIND   Counterfeit, I assure you.

OLIVER   Well then, take a good heart and counterfeit to be a man.

ROSALIND   So I do, but i'faith, I should have been a woman by right.

CELIA   Come, you look paler and paler. Pray you, draw homewards.—   170

Good sir, go with us.

OLIVER   That will I, for I must bear answer back

How you excuse my brother, Rosalind.

ROSALIND   I shall devise something; but I pray you, commend my

counterfeiting to him. Will you go?   *Exeunt.*   175

Act 5 Scene 1

Enter [TOUCHSTONE, *the*] *Clown and* AUDREY.

TOUCHSTONE   We shall find a time, Audrey. Patience, gentle Audrey!

AUDREY   Faith, the priest was good enough, for all the old gentle-

man's saying.

TOUCHSTONE   A most wicked Sir Oliver, Audrey, a most vile Mar-

text. But Audrey, there is a youth here in the forest lays claim to   5

you.

AUDREY   Ay, I know who 'tis: he hath no interest in me in the world.

Here comes the man you mean.

Enter WILLIAM.

TOUCHSTONE   It is meat and drink to me to see a clown, by my

troth. We that have good wits have much to answer for: we shall   10

be flouting; we cannot hold.

---

158. **would:** wish.
163. **body:** person.
166. **of earnest:** genuine.
  7. **interest in:** right to.
  9. **clown:** punning on the word's other meaning of rube, country fellow.
11. **hold:** restrain ourselves.

WILLIAM   Good ev'n, Audrey.

AUDREY   God ye good ev'n, William.

WILLIAM   And good ev'n to you, sir. [*Takes off his hat.*]

TOUCHSTONE   Good ev'n, gentle friend. Cover thy head, cover thy 15
head—nay prithee, be covered! How old are you, friend?

WILLIAM   Five and twenty, sir.

TOUCHSTONE   A ripe age. Is thy name William?

WILLIAM   William, sir.

TOUCHSTONE   A fair name. Wast born i'th' forest here?   20

WILLIAM   Ay, sir, I thank God.

TOUCHSTONE   "Thank God"—a good answer. Art rich?

WILLIAM   Faith, sir, so-so.

TOUCHSTONE   "So-so" is good, very good, very excellent good. And
yet it is not; it is but so-so. Art thou wise?   25

WILLIAM   Ay, sir. I have a pretty wit.

TOUCHSTONE   Why, thou sayst well. I do now remember a saying:
"The fool doth think he is wise, but the wise man knows himself
to be a fool." The heathen philosopher, when he had a desire to
eat a grape, would open his lips when he put it into his mouth, 30
meaning thereby that grapes were made to eat and lips to open.
You do love this maid?

WILLIAM   I do, sir.

TOUCHSTONE   Give me your hand. Art thou learned?

WILLIAM   No, sir.   35

TOUCHSTONE   Then learn this of me: to have is to have. For it is a
figure in rhetoric that drink, being poured out of a cup into
a glass, by filling the one doth empty the other. For all your
writers do consent that *ipse* is he. Now you are not *ipse*, for I
am he.   40

WILLIAM   Which "he," sir?

TOUCHSTONE   He, sir, that must marry this woman. Therefore, you
clown, abandon—which is in the vulgar "leave"—the society—
which in the boorish is "company"—of this female—which in the
common is "woman." Which together is, abandon the society of 45
this female or, clown, thou perishest—or to thy better understanding, diest—or, to wit, I kill thee: make thee away, translate
thy life into death, thy liberty into bondage. I will deal in poison

---

13. **God ye**: God give you.
22. **Art rich**: Are you wealthy?
29. **heathen philosopher**: a manufactured authority for the purpose of overawing
William, who appears to be standing with his mouth agape in astonishment.
37. **figure in rhetoric**: rhetorical commonplace.
39. *ipse*: he himself (Latin).
47. **translate**: turn, transform.

with thee or in bastinado or in steel. I will bandy with thee in
faction; I will o'errun thee with policy; I will kill thee a hundred   50
and fifty ways. Therefore tremble and depart!
AUDREY   Do, good William.
WILLIAM   God rest you merry, sir.   *Exit.*

        Enter CORIN.

CORIN   Our master and mistress seeks you. Come away, away!
TOUCHSTONE   Trip, Audrey, trip, Audrey! I attend, I attend.   55
                                                          Exeunt.

Act 5 Scene 2

        Enter ORLANDO *and* OLIVER.

ORLANDO   Is't possible that on so little acquaintance you should
    like her? That but seeing, you should love her? And loving, woo?
    And wooing, she should grant? And will you persevere to enjoy her?
OLIVER   Neither call the giddiness of it in question, the poverty of   5
    her, the small acquaintance, my sudden wooing, nor sudden con-
    senting, but say with me, "I love Aliena." Say with her that she
    loves me. Consent with both, that we may enjoy each other. It
    shall be to your good, for my father's house and all the revenue
    that was old Sir Rowland's will I estate upon you, and here live
    and die a shepherd.   10

        Enter ROSALIND.

ORLANDO   You have my consent. Let your wedding be tomorrow.
    Thither will I invite the duke and all's contented followers. Go
    you and prepare Aliena; for look you, here comes my Rosalind.
ROSALIND   God save you, brother.
OLIVER   And you, fair sister.   *Exit.* 15

---

49. **bastinado:** fighting with sticks.
49–50. **bandy . . . faction:** beat you back and forth in disputation.
50. **o'errun . . . policy:** defeat you with strategy.
55. Touchstone repeats every phrase to make fun of Corin's repeated "away" in the
    previous speech.
9. **estate:** settle (in a legal sense).
12. **all's:** all his.
15. **sister:** Many editors emend to "brother," since Rosalind is still disguised as Gany-
    mede, but this could be another of the cases in which the play toys with its own
    gender categories. Or perhaps Oliver calls her "sister" to go along with the cha-
    rade by which she pretends to be Orlando's beloved.

ROSALIND   O my dear Orlando, how it grieves me to see thee wear
thy heart in a scarf!

ORLANDO   It is my arm.

ROSALIND   I thought thy heart had been wounded with the claws
of a lion.   20

ORLANDO   Wounded it is, but with the eyes of a lady.

ROSALIND   Did your brother tell you how I counterfeited to swoon
when he showed me your handkercher?

ORLANDO   Ay, and greater wonders than that.

ROSALIND   Oh, I know where you are. Nay, 'tis true. There was   25
never anything so sudden but the fight of two rams and Caesar's
thrasonical brag of "I came, saw, and overcome." For your brother
and my sister no sooner met but they looked, no sooner looked but
they loved, no sooner loved but they sighed, no sooner sighed but
they asked one another the reason, no sooner knew the reason   30
but they sought the remedy. And in these degrees have they made
a pair of stairs to marriage, which they will climb incontinent or
else be incontinent before marriage. They are in the very wrath
of love and they will together. Clubs cannot part them.

ORLANDO   They shall be married tomorrow, and I will bid the duke 35
to the nuptial. But oh, how bitter a thing it is to look into happiness through another man's eyes! By so much the more shall I
tomorrow be at the height of heart-heaviness by how much I shall
think my brother happy in having what he wishes for.

ROSALIND   Why then, tomorrow I cannot serve your turn for   40
Rosalind?

ORLANDO   I can live no longer by thinking.

ROSALIND   I will weary you, then, no longer with idle talking.
Know of me then, for now I speak to some purpose, that I know
you are a gentleman of good conceit. I speak not this that you   45
should bear a good opinion of my knowledge, insomuch I say I

----

17. **scarf:** sling.
19. **with:** by.
25. **where you are:** what you're getting at.
27. **thrasonical:** boasting (like that of Thraso, a braggart soldier in Terence's comedy
     Eunuchus); **overcome:** usually translated as "overcame," but the passive form of
     the verb can be interpreted to refer jestingly to the lack of agency of the lovers.
31. **in:** by.
32. **incontinent:** in haste (with a pun on sexual incontinence).
33. **wrath:** heated passion.
34. **they . . . them:** They must be together. Even if we were to beat them with clubs
     (as one might try to stop a dog fight), they will not separate.
37–39. **By . . . for:** The more I recognize my brother's happiness at his marriage the more
     I feel my own despair.
40. **serve your turn:** substitute (with sexual implications).
45. **conceit:** understanding.
46. **insomuch:** in that.

know you are. Neither do I labor for a greater esteem than may in
some little measure draw a belief from you, to do yourself good
and not to grace me. Believe then, if you please, that I can do
strange things: I have since I was three year old conversed with a   50
magician most profound in his art, and yet not damnable. If you
do love Rosalind so near the heart as your gesture cries it out,
when your brother marries Aliena shall you marry her. I know
into what straits of fortune she is driven, and it is not impossible
to me, if it appear not inconvenient to you, to set her before your   55
eyes tomorrow—human as she is and without any danger.

ORLANDO   Speak'st thou in sober meanings?

ROSALIND   By my life, I do—which I tender dearly, though I say I
am a magician. Therefore put you in your best array; bid your
friends. For if you will be married tomorrow you shall, and to   60
Rosalind if you will.

Enter SILVIUS *and* PHOEBE.

Look, here comes a lover of mine and a lover of hers.

PHOEBE   Youth, you have done me much ungentleness
To show the letter that I writ to you.

ROSALIND   I care not if I have. It is my study   65
To seem despiteful and ungentle to you.
You are there followed by a faithful shepherd.
Look upon him, love him; he worships you.

PHOEBE   Good shepherd, tell this youth what 'tis to love.

SILVIUS   It is to be all made of sighs and tears,   70
And so am I for Phoebe.

PHOEBE   And I for Ganymede.

ORLANDO   And I for Rosalind.

ROSALIND   And I for no woman.

SILVIUS   It is to be all made of faith and service,   75
And so am I for Phoebe.

PHOEBE   And I for Ganymede.

ORLANDO   And I for Rosalind.

ROSALIND   And I for no woman.

SILVIUS   It is to be all made of fantasy,   80

47–49. **Neither . . . me:** I'm not telling you this to gain more respect from you except
   insofar as it causes you to believe me and therefore leads to something that will be
   good for you.
51. **not damnable:** i.e., he practices white magic, not black magic, which would be
   cause for damnation.
52. **gesture . . . out:** behavior makes evident.
57. **Speak'st . . . meanings?:** Are you serious?
58. **tender dearly:** value greatly.
59. **bid:** invite.

All made of passion and all made of wishes,
All adoration, duty, and observance,
All humbleness, all patience and impatience,
All purity, all trial, all observance,
And so am I for Phoebe.   85
PHOEBE   And so am I for Ganymede.
ORLANDO   And so am I for Rosalind.
ROSALIND   And so am I for no woman.
PHOEBE   If this be so, why blame you me to love you?
SILVIUS   If this be so, why blame you me to love you?   90
ORLANDO   If this be so, why blame you me to love you?
ROSALIND   Why do you speak too, "Why blame you me to love
you?"
ORLANDO   To her that is not here, nor doth not hear.
ROSALIND   Pray you, no more of this—'tis like the howling of Irish   95
wolves against the moon. [To SILVIUS.] I will help you if I can.
[To PHOEBE.] I would love you if I could. Tomorrow meet me all
together. I will marry you if ever I marry woman, and I'll be mar-
ried tomorrow. [To ORLANDO.] I will satisfy you if ever I satisfied
man, and you shall be married tomorrow. [To SILVIUS.] I will con-   100
tent you if what pleases you contents you, and you shall be married tomorrow. [To ORLANDO.] As you love Rosalind, meet. [To
SILVIUS.] As you love Phoebe, meet. And as I love no woman, I'll
meet. So fare you well. I have left you commands.
SILVIUS   I'll not fail, if I live.   105
PHOEBE   Nor I.
ORLANDO   Nor I.   *Exeunt.*

Act 5 Scene 3

Enter [TOUCHSTONE, *the*] *Clown and* AUDREY.

TOUCHSTONE   Tomorrow is the joyful day, Audrey; tomorrow will
we be married.
AUDREY   I do desire it with all my heart, and I hope it is no dishon-
est desire to desire to be a woman of the world. Here come two of
the banished duke's pages.   5

Enter two PAGES.

95–96. **like . . . moon:** mournfully repetitive, like wolves howling at the moon (Irish
because all the wolves in England had been exterminated by the early sixteenth
century and because many in England believed Ireland to be a wild and desolate
place).

FIRST PAGE   Well met, honest gentleman!

TOUCHSTONE   By my troth, well met! Come, sit, sit—and a song.

SECOND PAGE   We are for you. Sit i'th' middle.

FIRST PAGE   Shall we clap into't roundly, without hawking or spitting or saying we are hoarse—which are the only prologues to a   10
bad voice?

SECOND PAGE   I'faith, i'faith—and both in a tune like two gypsies
on a horse.

[PAGES *sing the*] *song.*

It was a lover and his lass,
    With a hey and a ho and a hey nonny-no,   15
That o'er the green corn field did pass
    In the spring time, the only pretty ring time,
When birds do sing, hey ding-a ding, ding,
    Sweet lovers love the Spring.

And therefore take the present time,   20
    With a hey and a ho and a hey nonny-no,
For love is crownèd with the prime
    In spring time, etc.

Between the acres of the rye,
    With a hey and a ho and a hey nonny-no,   25
These pretty country folks would lie
    In spring time, etc.

This carol they began that hour,
    With a hey and a ho and a hey nonny-no,
How that a life was but a flower   30
    In spring time, etc.

TOUCHSTONE   Truly, young gentlemen, though there was no great
matter in the ditty, yet the note was very untunable.

---

8. **We . . . you:** fine with us.
9. **clap . . . roundly:** get into it right away; **hawking:** clearing our throats.
10. **the only:** only the.
12. **in a tune:** in unison.
16. **corn:** grain.
20. **take . . . time:** Seize the day (traditional message of *carpe diem*).
22. **crownèd . . . prime:** perfected by youth, or by the "youth" of the year, springtime.
28. **carol:** joyous song (often accompanied by a circling dance).
30. **How . . . flower:** Cf. James 1: 9–11: "Let the brother of low degree rejoice in that he is
    exalted: But the rich, in that he is made low: because as the flower of the grass he
    shall pass away. For the sun is no sooner risen with a burning heat, but it withereth
    the grass, and the flower thereof falleth, and the grace of the fashion of it per-
    isheth . . . ," one of the lessens proper for May Day in the Book of Common Prayer.
33. **ditty:** song lyrics.

FIRST PAGE   You are deceived, sir. We kept time; we lost not our time.
TOUCHSTONE   By my troth, yes. I count it but time lost to hear such   35
a foolish song. God b'wi' you and God mend your voices. Come,
Audrey.   *Exeunt.*

Act 5 Scene 4

Enter DUKE SENIOR, AMIENS, JAQUES, ORLANDO, OLIVER, [*and*]
CELIA.

DUKE SENIOR   Dost thou believe, Orlando, that the boy
Can do all this that he hath promisèd?
ORLANDO   I sometimes do believe and sometimes do not,
As those that fear they hope and know they fear.

Enter ROSALIND, SILVIUS, *and* PHOEBE.

ROSALIND   Patience once more whiles our compact is urged.   5
You say if I bring in your Rosalind,
You will bestow her on Orlando here?
DUKE SENIOR   That would I had I kingdoms to give with her.
ROSALIND   And you say you will have her when I bring her?
ORLANDO   That would I were I of all kingdoms king.   10
ROSALIND   You say you'll marry me if I be willing?
PHOEBE   That will I, should I die the hour after.
ROSALIND   But if you do refuse to marry me,
You'll give yourself to this most faithful shepherd?
PHOEBE   So is the bargain.   15
ROSALIND   You say that you'll have Phoebe if she will?
SILVIUS   Though to have her and death were both one thing.
ROSALIND   I have promised to make all this matter even:
Keep you your word, O duke, to give your daughter;
You yours, Orlando, to receive his daughter.   20
Keep you your word, Phoebe, that you'll marry me
Or else, refusing me, to wed this shepherd.
Keep your word, Silvius, that you'll marry her
If she refuse me; and from hence I go
To make these doubts all even.   *Exeunt* ROSALIND *and* CELIA.   25
DUKE SENIOR   I do remember in this shepherd boy
Some lively touches of my daughter's favor.

---

5. **compact is urged:** bargain is declared.
18. **make . . . even:** straighten this whole situation out (with a suggestion of "make equal").
27. **favor:** appearance.

ORLANDO My lord, the first time that I ever saw him
Methought he was a brother to your daughter.
But my good lord, this boy is forest-born   30
And hath been tutored in the rudiments
Of many desperate studies by his uncle,
Whom he reports to be a great magician
Obscurèd in the circle of this forest.

Enter [TOUCHSTONE, *the*] *Clown and* AUDREY.

JAQUES There is, sure, another flood toward, and these couples   35
are coming to the ark. Here comes a pair of very strange beasts,
which in all tongues are called fools.
TOUCHSTONE Salutation and greeting to you all!
JAQUES Good my lord, bid him welcome. This is the motley-
minded gentleman that I have so often met in the forest. He hath   40
been a courtier, he swears.
TOUCHSTONE If any man doubt that, let him put me to my purgation. I have trod a measure, I have flattered a lady, I have been
politic with my friend, smooth with mine enemy. I have undone
three tailors, I have had four quarrels, and like to have fought one. 45
JAQUES And how was that ta'en up?
TOUCHSTONE Faith, we met and found the quarrel was upon the
seventh cause.
JAQUES How seventh cause? Good my lord, like this fellow!
DUKE SENIOR I like him very well.   50
TOUCHSTONE God 'ield you, sir, I desire you of the like. I press in
here, sir, amongst the rest of the country copulatives to swear and
to forswear, according as marriage binds and blood breaks: a poor
virgin, sir, an ill-favored thing, sir, but mine own; a poor humor of
mine, sir, to take that that no man else will. Rich honesty dwells   55
like a miser, sir, in a poor house as your pearl in your foul oyster.
DUKE SENIOR By my faith, he is very swift and sententious.

29. **Methought:** I thought.
32. **desperate:** dangerous.
35. **sure:** surely; **toward:** coming.
36. **ark:** as in the story of Noah and the ark in Genesis 7:2. Noah built a ship large
       enough to hold one pair of every species of animal to save them from the flood
       that God sent to cover the earth.
42–43. **purgation:** confession.
43. **trod a measure:** danced.
44. **undone:** bankrupted.
45. **like . . . fought:** came close to fighting.
46. **ta'en up:** decided.
51. **desire . . . like:** wish the same to you.
52. **copulatives:** those who are about to copulate, have sex.
53. **blood breaks:** passion undoes (the marriage).
55–56. **Rich . . . oyster:** i.e., you can't judge a person's true worth from outward
       appearances.

TOUCHSTONE According to the fool's bolt, sir, and such dulcet
diseases.

JAQUES But for the seventh cause—how did you find the quarrel 60
on the seventh cause?

TOUCHSTONE Upon a lie seven times removed—bear your body
more seeming, Audrey—as thus, sir: I did dislike the cut of a
certain courtier's beard; he sent me word if I said his beard was
not cut well, he was in the mind it was. This is called the Retort 65
Courteous. If I sent him word again it was not well cut, he would
send me word he cut it to please himself. This is called the Quip
Modest. If again it was not well cut, he disabled my judgment.
This is called the Reply Churlish. If again it was not well cut, he
would answer I spake not true. This is called the Reproof Valiant. 70
If again it was not well cut, he would say I lie. This is called the
Countercheck Quarrelsome, and so to Lie Circumstantial and
the Lie Direct.

JAQUES And how oft did you say his beard was not well cut?

TOUCHSTONE I durst go no further than the Lie Circumstantial; 75
nor he durst not give me the Lie Direct, and so we measured
swords and parted.

JAQUES Can you nominate in order, now, the degrees of the lie?

TOUCHSTONE Oh, sir, we quarrel in print, by the book, as you have
books for good manners. I will name you the degrees: the first, 80
the Retort Courteous; the second, the Quip Modest; the third, the
Reply Churlish; the fourth, the Reproof Valiant; the fifth, the
Countercheck Quarrelsome; the sixth, the Lie with Circumstance;
the seventh, the Lie Direct. All these you may avoid but the Lie
Direct, and you may avoid that too with an "if." I knew when seven 85
justices could not take up a quarrel; but when the parties were
met themselves, one of them thought but of an "if"—as "if you
said so then I said so"—and they shook hands and swore brothers.
Your "if" is the only peace-maker: much virtue in "if."

---

58. **fool's bolt:** proverbial: "The fool's bolt, or arrow, is soon shot," i.e., the fool's wit
    doesn't last long; **dulcet:** sweet.
62–63. **bear . . . seeming:** Carry yourself more appropriately.
65. **in the mind:** of the opinion.
68. **again it was:** again I said it was.
72. **Countercheck:** rebuke.
73. **Lie Direct:** direct assertion "You lie," which was considered grounds for a duel in
    the courtly ethos of the time.
75. **durst:** dared.
76–77. **measured swords:** drew our swords and made sure they were of equal length, as
    if at the start of a duel.
78. **nominate:** name.
80. **books for good manners:** courtesy manuals, which taught proper behavior and
    were very popular during the period; Touchstone parodies them in his comically
    over-elaborate discussion of degrees of insult.
86. **take up:** patch up, arbitrate.
88. **swore brothers:** swore that they were brothers.

JAQUES   Is not this a rare fellow, my lord? He's as good at anything,   90
and yet a fool.
DUKE SENIOR   He uses his folly like a stalking-horse, and under
the presentation of that he shoots his wit.

Enter HYMEN, [*god of marriage,*] ROSALIND, *and* CELIA [*as
themselves*].

Still music.

HYMEN   Then is there mirth in heaven
When earthly things, made even,   95
Atone together.
Good duke, receive thy daughter;
Hymen from heaven brought her—
Yea, brought her hither
That thou might'st join his hand with his,   100
Whose heart within his bosom is.

ROSALIND   [*To* DUKE SENIOR.] To you I give myself, for I am yours.
[*To* ORLANDO.] To you I give myself, for I am yours.
DUKE SENIOR   If there be truth in sight, you are my daughter.
ORLANDO   If there be truth in sight, you are my Rosalind.   105
PHOEBE   If sight and shape be true,
Why then my love adieu!
ROSALIND   I'll have no father if you be not he.—
I'll have no husband if you be not he,—
Nor ne'er wed woman if you be not she.   110
HYMEN   Peace, ho! I bar confusion.
'Tis I must make conclusion
Of these most strange events.
Here's eight that must take hands
To join in Hymen's bands   115
If truth hold true contents.

92. **stalking-horse:** horse (which could be real or an imitation) used to conceal the
hunter in pursuit of game.
93. HYMEN . . . *marriage:* classical deity who may have carried a torch, as in Ben Jonson's masque *Hymenaei* (1606), where he was splendidly dressed in saffron and
white silk and wore a crown of roses; *as themselves:* no longer disguised as Ganymede and Aliena; **Still:** quiet but could also mean "continuing" (in which case it may
have played at least through Hymen's speech, and possibly through to accompany
Hymen's song at 1. 126).
96. **Atone:** seek forgiveness, are as one.
100. **his . . . his:** with reference to the underlying sexual identity of the actors.
111. **bar:** forbid.
116. **If . . . contents:** i.e., if your vows hold true.

[*To* ROSALIND *and* ORLANDO.] You and you no cross shall part.
[*To* CELIA *and* OLIVER.] You and you are heart in heart.
[*To* PHOEBE.] You to his love must accord,
Or have a woman to your lord.   120
[*To* TOUCHSTONE *and* AUDREY.] You and you are sure together,
As the winter to foul weather.
Whiles a wedlock hymn we sing,
Feed yourselves with questioning,
That reason wonder may diminish   125
How thus we met, and these things finish.

                    Song.

        Wedding is great Juno's crown.
        O blessèd bond of board and bed!
        'Tis Hymen peoples every town;
            High wedlock then be honorèd.   130
        Honor, high honor, and renown
        To Hymen, god of every town.

DUKE SENIOR   O my dear niece, welcome thou art to me!
Even daughter, welcome in no less degree.
PHOEBE   I will not eat my word: now thou art mine,   135
Thy faith my fancy to thee doth combine.

    Enter [JAQUES DE BOIS, *the*] *second brother.*

JAQUES DE BOIS   Let me have audience for a word or two.
I am the second son of old Sir Rowland,
That bring these tidings to this fair assembly.
Duke Frederick, hearing how that every day   140
Men of great worth resorted to this forest,
Addressed a mighty power, which were on foot
In his own conduct, purposely to take
His brother here and put him to the sword.
And to the skirts of this wild wood he came,   145
Where, meeting with an old religious man,
After some question with him, was converted

---

117. **cross:** disagreement, adversity.
124. **Feed:** nourish.
127. **Juno:** wife of Jupiter and associated with marriage and childbirth.
129. **peoples:** populates.
130. **High wedlock:** marriage imagined as a noble state.
134. **Even:** also.
142. **Addressed . . . power:** assembled a formidable fighting force.
143. **In . . . conduct:** under his own command.

Both from his enterprise and from the world,
His crown bequeathing to his banished brother
And all their lands restored to him again   150
That were with him exiled. This to be true
I do engage my life.
DUKE SENIOR   Welcome, young man.
Thou offer'st fairly to thy brothers' wedding:
To one his lands withheld and to the other
A land itself at large, a potent dukedom.   155
First in this forest let us do those ends
That here were well begun and well begot;
And after, every of this happy number
That have endured shrewd days and nights with us
Shall share the good of our returnèd fortune,   160
According to the measure of their states.
Meantime, forget this new-fall'n dignity
And fall into our rustic revelry.
Play music, and you brides and bridegrooms all,
With measure heaped in joy to th'measures fall.   165
JAQUES   Sir, by your patience, if I heard you rightly,
The duke hath put on a religious life
And thrown into neglect the pompous court?
JAQUES DE BOIS   He hath.
JAQUES   To him will I: out of these convertites   170
There is much matter to be heard and learned.
[To DUKE SENIOR.] You to your former honor I bequeath—
Your patience and your virtue well deserves it;
[To ORLANDO and ROSALIND.] You to a love that your true faith
    doth merit,

---

149. **bequeathing:** assigning, transferring.
150–51. **all . . . exiled:** According to the feudal system, Duke Senior held formal title to
    all of his lords' lands, which he presumably proceeded to regrant to them once
    his power had been restored to him.
153. **offer'st fairly:** bring beautiful gifts.
154. **To . . . withheld:** to Oliver the estate that had been confiscated by Duke
    Frederick.
154–55. **to . . . dukedom:** to Orlando the powerful dukedom of Duke Senior (since
    Orlando is marrying the duke's daughter and heiress).
156. **do those ends:** accomplish those purposes.
158. **every:** each.
159. **shrewd:** harsh.
161. **According . . . states:** as is appropriate to their social positions.
163. **rustic revelry:** country celebration.
165. With joyous moderation, fall to dancing (with a pun on **measure** as a bar of
    music).
167. **put on:** adopted.
170. **convertites:** converts.

[*To* OLIVER *and* CELIA.] You to your land and love and great allies,   175
[*To* SILVIUS *and* PHOEBE.]   You to a long and well-deservèd bed,
[*To* TOUCHSTONE *and* AUDREY.] And you to wrangling, for thy
   loving voyage
Is but for two months victualed. So—to your pleasures!
I am for other than for dancing measures.
DUKE SENIOR   Stay, Jaques, stay!   180
JAQUES   To see no pastime, I! What you would have
  I'll stay to know at your abandoned cave.   *Exit.*
DUKE SENIOR   Proceed, proceed! We'll begin these rites,
  As we do trust they'll end in true delights.
                  [*Dancing, then exeunt all but* ROSALIND].

[*Epilogue.*]

ROSALIND   It is not the fashion to see the lady the epilogue, but it
is no more unhandsome than to see the lord the prologue. If it be
true that good wine needs no bush, 'tis true that a good play needs
no epilogue; yet to good wine they do use good bushes, and good
plays prove the better by the help of good epilogues.   5
   What a case am I in, then, that am neither a good epilogue nor
cannot insinuate with you in the behalf of a good play? I am not
furnished like a beggar; therefore to beg will not become me. My
way is to conjure you, and I'll begin with the women: I charge you,
O women, for the love you bear to men, to like as much of this   10
play as please you. And I charge you, O men, for the love you bear
to women—as I perceive by your simpering, none of you hates
them—that between you and the women, the play may please. If
I were a woman I would kiss as many of you as had beards that
pleased me, complexions that liked me, and breaths that I defied   15
not. And I am sure, as many as have good beards or good faces or
sweet breaths will for my kind offer, when I make curtsey, bid me
farewell.   *Exit.*

FINIS

178. **victualed:** stocked with provisions.
181. **What . . . have:** your wishes.
  1. **lady:** lady as.
  3. **bush:** advertisement. (A sign with a bush painted on it was a traditional indication
     of a wine-merchant.)
  7. **in the:** on.
 12. **simpering:** smiling self-consciously.
13–14. **If . . . woman:** play's final reference to the underlying sexual identity of the
     actors.
 15. **liked:** pleased.
 15. **defied:** rejected with disdain.

A Note on the Text

The texts of many Shakespeare plays are highly problematic, existing in multiple versions that represent different staged versions and/or textual revisions of the work over time. There are, for example, three different early printed versions of *Hamlet*: two early quarto (small-format) editions and the version published in the First Folio edition, *Mr. William Shakespeare's Comedies, Histories, and Tragedies*, in 1623. Sorting out the three early texts of *Hamlet* has been a perplexing and controversial matter. Unlike the quartos, the First Folio was a large and impressive volume, but that does not guarantee that its texts of Shakespeare's plays are more authoritative than the earlier quartos. Even almost four hundred years later, editors still disagree over whether the second quarto of *Hamlet* is more reliable than the folio version and precisely what "reliable" means: closer to the play as written? as revised by Shakespeare himself? as performed by his company, the King's Men, either with or without his approval of changes that were made in the play as staged?

The text of *As You Like It* presents many fewer difficulties. There are no early quarto versions of the play—at least none that are known to have survived—and as a result we have only one authoritative early text, that preserved in the First Folio. Unlike many other plays in the First Folio, *As You Like It* is quite well printed by the standards of its time. It has a full set of act and scene divisions that most editors follow precisely. It is fairly reliable when it comes to speech prefixes and lineation that signals the difference between verse and prose. It has a full set of stage directions that are spare but for the most part not problematic. One major difference, beyond modernization of spelling and punctuation, between the First Folio text and modern editions is that with one exception, throughout the Folio text in entrances, exits, and speech prefixes, Shakespeare's memorable clown Touchstone is called only "Clown," a generic label that tends to emphasize his role as the play's official fool-figure rather than his individuality. Even in the one entrance that does give his name (at the beginning of 2.4), he is referred to in the First Folio as "*Clowne*, alias *Touchstone*." Aside from that brief mention, the only way we know his name in the First Folio is that he is addressed as "Touchstone" three times by other characters (2.4.14, 3.2.11, and 3.2.39). In this Norton Critical Edition, I have followed previous editors in replacing "Clown" with "Touchstone" for all mentions of his name in the speech prefixes.

There are other small difficulties with questions of casting, since the First Folio does not include lists of "The Persons of the Play" as modern editions do. How many attendant Lords are there on Duke Senior in the forest, or on the usurping Duke Frederick back at court? The answer would, no doubt, depend on the availability of extra actors for any given performance. I have tidied up the fluidity of the First Folio rendering of attendants by including "First Lord" and "Second Lord" as characters in addition to named courtiers like Amiens and Jaques. This decision reflects the likelihood that the anonymous "Lords" attending on Duke Senior were played by the same actors who attended upon Duke Frederick in early productions of the play. The servants of the exiled duke doubled as servants of the evil duke, his brother, who had overthrown his rule! So much for the loyalty of courtiers: the doubling of characters reflects a cynicism about loyalty toward princes that the play does not otherwise embrace. But readers need to bear in mind that this cynicism is constructed by a set of editorial decisions that are not fully supported by the Folio text of the play.

Although I have followed traditional editing practices in relation to speech prefixes and in sorting out the courtiers, there is one area in which this Norton Critical Edition of As You Like It breaks from most previous editions—that is, in the handling of personal pronouns in relation to Rosalind and other characters (as discussed briefly in the Preface, p. x). There are several points at which Rosalind is referred to as the "wrong" gender—most notably, in the final scene. Hymen in the First Folio seems to construct a tableau of same-sex marriage by inviting the duke to "receive thy daughter" and Orlando so that he can "join his hand with his" (5.4.100) where we would expect "her hand with his." Since in Shakespeare's company women's parts were all played by men or boys, Hymen's speech gestures toward the underlying sexual identity of the boy actor playing the part of Rosalind. In a play so rife with gender confusion, the mistake is perhaps not surprising, and most editors have emended one of the occurrences of "his" to "her."[1] If this were the only case of pronoun gender confusion in the play, we could perhaps chalk it up to error on the part of someone involved in its printing, but similar errors, most of them in connection with Rosalind, occur at several other points in the text (see 1.1.88, 3.2.132, 5.2.15, and as a confirmation to the audience of the male identity of the youth playing her part, Rosalind's "Epilogue"). As You Like It plays with gender confusion in hilarious, outrageously excessive ways, such as having a heroine who is a boy actor playing the part of a young woman who goes on to play the part of a young man who then enacts the part of the woman, Rosalind, he really "is" beneath his disguise. In such a dizzying array of possibilities for gender confusion, we should not be surprised to see a similar confusion in the play's language relating to

1. For discussion, see the Masten reading, pp. 395–404 and Richard Knowles, ed., *New Variorum Edition of As You Like It*, pp. 5–6.

gender identity, and we should not assume that it is error on Shakespeare or someone else's part. By keeping the original readings of passages in which stereotypical gender associations are challenged, this edition keeps before its readers some of the dazzling gender complexity of the play on stage—particularly as acted by an all-male company like the King's Men. The confusions in the text point to a creative undecideability of gender categories in Shakespearean culture that scholars had until recently lost sight of; the confusions also helps us understand more clearly why moralists like William Prynne (see selection, pp. 214–17) found the early modern theater so profoundly threatening to social norms.

My additions to the playtext are given in square brackets; by taking away that material readers can arrive at a fair approximation of the language of the Folio text. At a few points I have added stage directions, but these are usually implied by the language of the play. For example, in 1.1.43, when Orlando responds to Oliver's attack, I add [*Grabs him by the throat*] because Orlando states in his next speech, "Wert thou not my brother I would not take this hand from thy throat till this other [hand] had pulled out thy tongue . . ." At points where the Folio has two speakers share an iambic pentameter line, I arrange it on the page as two half lines of poetry rather than two independent lines. These alterations are not recorded in the list of emendations below. I have emended the Folio's language only if I could not make sense of it. But no amount of explaining can really substitute for the experience of encountering an early printing of Shakespeare firsthand, and interested users of this edition are encouraged to delve into the Folio for themselves. Originals are to be found only in major research libraries, particularly the Folger Shakespeare Library in Washington, D.C., which owns seventy-nine copies, but facsimiles are much easier to find, either in print versions such as the Charlton Hinman edition (1968; rpt. 1996), or online, via *Early English Books Online* or a number of websites. A listing of free online editions of the First Folio is available from the University of Virginia at http:www.2.lib.virginia.edu/digitalcuration/etext_shakespeare.html. In the following list of emendations, only significant deviations from the First Folio are recorded. A full listing of variants is beyond the scope of Norton Critical Editions. I have therefore not included minor alterations to spelling and punctuation that are a routine part of the process of modernizing the text to make it more comprehensible for modern users. I have also omitted the references to Touchstone as "Clown," as discussed above, from the list because both the First Folio and this Norton Critical text are consistent: except in the stage direction at the beginning of 2.4, where he is referred to by both names, the First Folio entrances and speech prefixes consistently call him "Clown" and this edition consistently calls him "Touchstone." In what follows, the reading adopted in this Norton Critical Edition is listed to the left of the square bracket and the First Folio reading in its original spelling is given to the right.

1.1
p. 5, line 35 and ff. ay] I.
p. 6, line 75–76 and ff. wrestling] wrastling.
p. 8, line 128 OLIVER] (no speech prefix).

1.2
p. 16, line 243 and ff. Rosalind] *Rosaline.*

1.3
p. 20, line 118 be] by.
p. 20, line 123 and ff. travel] trauaile.

2.1
p. 20, line 3 and ff. Than] Then
p. 22, line 49 much] must.
p. 22, line 68 and ff. straight] strait.

2.3
p. 24, line 10 some] seeme.
p. 24, line 16 ORLANDO] (no speech prefix).
p. 24, line 29 ORLANDO] *Ad.*
p. 24, line 29 and ff. whither] whether.
p. 25, line 50 and ff. woo] woe.
p. 25, line 71 seventeen] seauentie.

2.4
p. 27, line 38 thy wound] they would.
p. 27, line 43 chapped] chopd.
p. 28, line 61 you] your.
p. 29, lines 86–87 And we will mend thy wages. I like this place. / And willingly could waste my time in it.] (line breaks after "wages / . . . willingly / . . . it." /)

2.5
p. 29, lines 6–7 Here shall he see / No enemy] (all one line).
p. 30, line 31 *all together*] *Altogether.*

2.7
p. 33, line 38 brain] braiue.
p. 35, line 101 and ff. An] And.
p. 35, line 112 Lose] Loose.

p. 36, line 157 sixth] sixt.
p. 37, line 174 AMIENS] (no speech prefix).
p. 38, line 198 master] masters.

3.2
p. 39, line 15 vile] vild.
p. 39, line 23 good] pood.
p. 42, line 112 this a desert] this desert.
p. 46, line 219 heart] Hart.
p. 46, line 230 and ff. b'wi'] buy.
p. 49, line 305 lectures] Lectors.
p. 49, line 317 deifying] defying.
p. 49, line 325 are] art.
p. 51, line 368 cot] Coat.

3.3
p. 53, line 57 God 'ied] goddild.

3.4
p. 55, line 35 puny] puisny.

3.5
p. 57, line 17 and ff. swoon] swound.
p. 57, line 30 wounds] wouuds.
p. 59, line 104 erewhile] yere-while.
p. 60, line 133 taunting] tanting.

4.1
p. 61, line 1 me be better] me better.
p. 62, line 41 heart-whole] heart hole.
p. 66, line 174 it] in.

4.2
p. 67, line 2 FIRST LORD] *Lord*.
p. 67, line 6 SECOND LORD] *Lord*.
p. 67, lines 11–12 Then sing him home. The rest shall bear / This burden] (all one line).

5.1
p. 75, line 50 policy] police.

5.3
p. 79, line 17 ring] rang.

5.4
p. 84, line 136 and ff. JAQUES DE BOIS] 2. *Bro*.

SOURCES AND CONTEXTS

THOMAS LODGE

Rosalynde[†]

There dwelled adjoining to the city of Bordeaux a knight of most honourable parentage, whom fortune had graced with many favours, and nature honoured with sundry exquisite qualities, so beautified with the excellence of both, as it was a question whether fortune or nature were more prodigal in deciphering the riches of their bounties. Wise he was, as holding in his head a supreme conceit of policy, reaching with Nestor[1] into the depth of all civil government; and to make his wisdom more gracious, he had that *salem ingenii* and pleasant eloquence that was so highly commended in Ulysses:[2] his valour was no less than his wit, nor the stroke of his lance no less forcible than the sweetness of his tongue was persuasive; for he was for his courage chosen the principal of all the Knights of Malta. This hardy knight, thus enriched with virtue and honour, surnamed Sir John of Bordeaux, having passed the prime of his youth in sundry battles against the Turks, at last, as the date of time hath his course, grew aged. His hairs were silver-hued, and the map of age was figured on his forehead: honour sat in the furrows of his face, and many years were portrayed in his wrinkled lineaments, that all men might perceive his glass was run, and that nature of necessity challenged her due. Sir John, that with the Phoenix knew the term of his life was now expired, and could, with the swan, discover his end by her songs,[3] having three sons by his wife Lynida, the very pride of all his forepassed years, thought now, seeing death by constraint would compel him to leave them, to bestow upon them such a legacy as might bewray his love, and increase their ensuing amity. Calling, therefore, these young gentlemen before him, in the presence of all his fellow Knights of Malta, he resolved to leave them a memorial of all his fatherly care in setting down a method of their brotherly duties. Having, therefore, death in his looks to move them to pity, and tears in his eyes to paint out the depth of his passions, taking his eldest son by the hand, he began thus:

'O my sons, you see that fate hath set a period of my years, and destinies have determined the final end of my days: the palm tree

---

† Reprinted with added notes from W. W. Greg, ed., *Lodge's 'Rosalynde' Being the Original of Shakespeare's 'As You Like It'* (London: Chatto and Windus, 1907), pp. 1–164.
1. **Nestor:** wise advisor to the Greeks in *The Iliad*. [This and all the notes to *Rosalynde* that follow are the editor's.]
2. *salem ingenii* . . . **Ulysses:** shrewd wit (Latin) like that of **Ulysses** (Odysseus), Greek hero in the *Iliad* and *Odyssey*.
3. **Phoenix** . . . **songs:** The **Phoenix** was a unique, mythical bird that built its own funeral pyre; the **swan** sang to signal the end of its life.

waxeth away-ward, for he stoopeth in his height, and my plumes are full of sick feathers touched with age. I must to my grave that dischargeth all cares, and leave you to the world that increaseth many sorrows: my silver hairs containeth great experience, and in the number of my years are penned down the subtleties of fortune. Therefore, as I leave you some fading pelf[4] countercheck poverty, so I will bequeath you infallible precepts that shall lead you unto virtue. First, therefore, unto thee Saladyne, the eldest, and therefore the chiefest pillar of my house, wherein should be engraven as well the excellence of thy father's qualities, as the essential form of his proportion, to thee I give fourteen ploughlands, with all my manor houses and richest plate. Next, unto Fernandyne I bequeath twelve ploughlands. But, unto Rosader, the youngest, I give my horse, my armour, and my lance, with sixteen plough-lands; for if the inward thoughts be discovered by outward shadows, Rosader will exceed you all in bounty and honour. Thus, my sons, have I parted in your portions the substance of my wealth, wherein if you be as prodigal to spend as I have been careful to get, your friends will grieve to see you more wasteful than I was bountiful, and your foes smile that my fall did begin in your excess. Let mine honour be the glass of your actions, and the fame of my virtues the lodestar to direct the course of your pilgrimage. Aim your deeds by my honourable endeavours, and show yourselves scions worthy of so flourishing a tree, lest, as the birds Halcyones[5] which exceed in whiteness, I hatch young ones that surpass in blackness. Climb not, my sons: aspiring pride is a vapour that ascendeth high, but soon turneth to a smoke; they which stare at the stars stumble upon stones, and such as gaze at the sun, unless they be eagle-eyed, fall blind. Soar not with the hobby, lest you fall with the lark, nor attempt not with Phaeton, lest you drown with Icarus.[6] Fortune, when she wills you to fly, tempers your plumes with wax; and therefore either sit still and make no wing, or else beware the sun, and hold Daedalus' axiom authentical, *medium tenere tutissimum.*[7] Low shrubs have deep roots, and poor cottages great patience. Fortune looks ever upward, and envy aspireth to nestle with dignity. Take heed, my sons, the mean is sweetest melody; where strings high stretched, either soon crack, or quickly grow out of tune. Let your country's care be your heart's content, and think that you are not born for yourselves, but to level your thoughts to be loyal to your prince, careful for the common weal,

---

4. **pelf:** riches.
5. **Halcyones:** kingfishers, who are white as adults but dark as chicks.
6. **hobby . . . Icarus:** The **hobby** is a small falcon; **Phaeton** tried to drive the chariot of the sun but wrecked it and was killed; **Icarus** was provided with wings but flew too close to the sun and perished when the wax that attached the wings melted.
7. Keep the mean in all things (Latin).

and faithful to your friends; so shall France say, "These men are as excellent in virtues as they be exquisite in features." O my sons, a friend is a precious jewel, within whose bosom you may unload your sorrows and unfold your secrets, and he either will relieve with counsel, or persuade with reason; but take heed in the choice: the outward show makes not the inward man, nor are the dimples in the face the calendars of truth. When the liquorice leaf looketh most dry, then it is most wet: when the shores of Lepanthus[8] are most quiet, then they forepoint a storm. The Baaran[9] leaf the more fair it looks, the more infectious it is, and in the sweetest words is oft hid the most treachery. Therefore, my sons, choose a friend as the Hyperborei[1] do the metals, sever them from the ore with fire, and let them not bide the stamp before they be current: so try and then trust, let time be touch-stone of friendship, and then friends faithful lay them up for jewels. Be valiant, my sons, for cowardice is the enemy to honour; but not too rash, for that is an extreme. Fortitude is the mean, and that is limited within bonds, and prescribed with circumstance. But above all,' and with that he fetched a deep sigh, 'beware of love, for it is far more perilous than pleasant, and yet, I tell you, it allureth as ill as the Sirens.[2] O my sons, fancy is a fickle thing, and beauty's paintings are tricked up with time's colours, which, being set to dry in the sun, perish with the same. Venus[3] is a wanton, and though her laws pretend liberty, yet there is nothing but loss and glistering misery. Cupid's wings are plumed with the feathers of vanity, and his arrows, where they pierce, enforce nothing but deadly desires: a woman's eye, as it is precious to behold, so is it prejudicial to gaze upon; for as it affordeth delight, so it snareth unto death. Trust not their fawning favours, for their loves are like the breath of a man upon steel, which no sooner lighteth on but it leapeth off, and their passions are as momentary as the colours of a polype, which changeth at the sight of every object. My breath waxeth short, and mine eyes dim: the hour is come, and I must away; therefore let this suffice: women are wantons, and yet men cannot want one: and therefore, if you love, choose her that hath eyes of adamant, that will turn only to one point; her heart of a diamond, that will receive but one form; her tongue of a Sethin[4] leaf, that never wags but with a south-east wind: and yet, my sons, if she have all these qualities, to be chaste, obedient, and silent, yet for that she is a woman, shalt thou find in her sufficient vanities to countervail

8. **Lepanthus:** body of water noted for its changeable winds.
9. **Baaran:** plant whose leaves are poisonous or prickly.
1. **Hyperborei:** ancient people of central Asia.
2. **Sirens:** temptresses in the *Odyssey* whose song lured sailors to their doom.
3. **Venus:** goddess of love.
4. **Sethin:** white cedar.

her virtues. Oh now, my sons, even now take these my last words as my latest legacy, for my thread is spun, and my foot is in the grave. Keep my precepts as memorials of your father's counsels, and let them be lodged in the secret of your hearts; for wisdom is better than wealth, and a golden sentence worth a world of treasure. In my fall see and mark, my sons, the folly of man, that being dust climbeth with Biares to reach at the heavens, and ready every minute to die, yet hopeth for an age of pleasures. Oh, man's life is like lightning that is but a flash, and the longest date of his years but as a bavin's blaze.[5] Seeing then man is so mortal, be careful that thy life be virtuous, that thy death may be full of admirable honours: so shalt thou challenge fame to be thy fautor, and put oblivion to exile with thine honourable actions. But, my sons, lest you should forget your father's axioms, take this scroll, wherein read what your father dying wills you to execute living.' At this he shrunk down in his bed, and gave up the ghost.

John of Bordeaux being thus dead was greatly lamented of his sons, and bewailed of his friends, especially of his fellow Knights of Malta, who attended on his funerals, which were performed with great solemnity. His obsequies done, Saladyne caused, next his epitaph, the contents of the scroll to be portrayed out, which were to this effect:

The Contents of the Schedule which Sir John of Bordeaux gave to his Sons

My sons, behold what portion I do give:
  I leave you goods, but they are quickly lost;
I leave advice, to school you how to live;
  I leave you wit, but won with little cost;
But keep it well, for counsel still is one,
When father, friends, and worldly goods are gone.

In choice of thrift let honour be thy gain,
  Win it by virtue and by manly might;
In doing good esteem thy toil no pain;
  Protect the fatherless and widow's right:
Fight for thy faith, thy country, and thy king,
For why? this thrift will prove a blessed thing.

In choice of wife, prefer the modest-chaste;
  Lilies are fair in show, but foul in smell:
The sweetest looks by age are soon defaced;
  Then choose thy wife by wit and living well.

5. **bavin's blaze:** fire made from light kindling and therefore quickly extinguished.

Who brings thee wealth and many faults withal,
Presents thee honey mixed with bitter gall.

In choice of friends, beware of light belief;
    A painted tongue may shroud a subtle heart;
The Siren's tears do threaten mickle grief;
    Foresee, my sons, for fear of sudden smart:
Choose in thy wants, and he that friends thee then,
When richer grown, befriend thou him agen.

Learn with the ant in summer to provide;
    Drive with the bee the drone from out thy hive:
Build like the swallow in the summer tide;
    Spare not too much, my sons, but sparing thrive:
Be poor in folly, rich in all but sin:
So by thy death thy glory shall begin.

Saladyne having thus set up the schedule, and hanged about his father's hearse many passionate poems, that France might suppose him to be passing sorrowful, he clad himself and his brothers all in black, and in such sable suits discoursed his grief: but as the hyena when she mourns is then most guileful, so Saladyne under this show of grief shadowed a heart full of contented thoughts. The tiger, though he hide his claws, will at last discover his rapine: the lion's looks are not the maps of his meaning, nor a man's physnomy is not the display of his secrets. Fire cannot be hid in the straw, nor the nature of man so concealed, but at last it will have his course: nurture and art may do much, but that *natura naturans*,[6] which by propagation is ingrafted in the heart, will be at last perforce predominant according to the old verse:

Naturam expellas furca, tamen usque recurret.[7]

So fared it with Saladyne, for after a month's mourning was passed, he fell to consideration of his father's testament; how he had bequeathed more to his younger brothers than himself, that Rosader was his father's darling, but now under his tuition, that as yet they were not come to years, and he being their guardian, might, if not defraud them of their due, yet make such havoc of their legacies and lands, as they should be a great deal the lighter: whereupon he began thus to meditate with himself:

'Saladyne, how art thou disquieted in thy thoughts, and perplexed with a world of restless passions, having thy mind troubled with the tenor of thy father's testament, and thy heart fired with the hope of

---

6. *natura naturans*: nature as active generator of life (Latin).
7. You can drive nature out with a pitchfork but she always comes back (Latin).

present preferment! By the one thou art counselled to content thee with thy fortunes, by the other persuaded to aspire to higher wealth. Riches, Saladyne, is a great royalty, and there is no sweeter physic than store. Avicen,[8] like a fool, forgot in his Aphorisms to say that gold was the most precious restorative, and that treasure was the most excellent medicine of the mind. O Saladyne, what, were thy father's precepts breathed into the wind? hast thou so soon forgotten his principles? did he not warn thee from coveting without honour, and climbing without virtue? did he not forbid thee to aim at any action that should not be honourable? and what will be more prejudicial to thy credit, than the careless ruin of thy brothers' welfare? why, shouldst not thou be the pillar of thy brothers' prosperity? and wilt thou become the subversion of their fortunes? is there any sweeter thing than concord, or a more precious jewel than amity? are you not sons of one father, scions[9] of one tree, birds of one nest, and wilt thou become so unnatural as to rob them, whom thou shouldst relieve? No, Saladyne, entreat them with favours, and entertain them with love, so shalt thou have thy conscience clear and thy renown excellent. Tush, what words are these, base fool, far unfit, if thou be wise, for thy humour? What though thy father at his death talked of many frivolous matters, as one that doated for age and raved in his sickness; shall his words be axioms, and his talk be so authentical, that thou wilt, to observe them, prejudice thyself? No no, Saladyne, sick men's wills that are parole and have neither hand nor seal, are like the laws of a city written in dust, which are broken with the blast of every wind. What, man, thy father is dead, and he can neither help thy fortunes, nor measure thy actions; therefore bury his words with his carcase, and be wise for thyself. What, 'tis not so old as true,

Non sapit, qui sibi non sapit.[1]

Thy brother is young, keep him now in awe; make him not checkmate with thyself, for

Nimia familiaritas contemptum parit.[2]

Let him know little, so shall he not be able to execute much: suppress his wits with a base estate, and though he be a gentleman by nature, yet form him anew, and make him a peasant by nurture: so shalt thou keep him as a slave, and reign thyself sole lord over all thy father's possessions. As for Fernandyne, thy middle brother, he

---

8. **Avicen:** Avicenna, early Islamic scientist and philosopher whose works were very influential in early modern Europe.
9. **scions:** branches.
1. He is not wise who is not wise for himself (Latin).
2. Too much familiarity breeds contempt (Latin).

is a scholar and hath no mind but on Aristotle: let him read on Galen[3] while thou riflest with gold, and pore on his book till thou dost purchase lands: wit is great wealth; if he have learning it is enough: and so let all rest.'

In this humour was Saladyne, making his brother Rosader his foot-boy, for the space of two or three years, keeping him in such servile subjection, as if he had been the son of any country vassal. The young gentleman bore all with patience, till on a day, walking in the garden by himself, he began to consider how he was the son of John of Bordeaux, a knight renowmed for many victories, and a gentleman famosed for his virtues; how, contrary to the testament of his father, he was not only kept from his land and entreated as a servant, but smothered in such secret slavery, as he might not attain to any honourable actions.

'Ah,' quoth he to himself, nature working these effectual passions, 'why should I, that am a gentleman born, pass my time in such unnatural drudgery? were it not better either in Paris to become a scholar, or in the court a courtier, or in the field a soldier, than to live a foot-boy to my own brother? Nature hath lent me wit to conceive, but my brother denied me art to contemplate: I have strength to perform any honourable exploit, but no liberty to accomplish my virtuous endeavours: those good parts that God hath bestowed upon me, the envy of my brother doth smother in obscurity; the harder is my fortune, and the more his frowardness.'[4]

With that casting up his hand he felt hair on his face, and perceiving his beard to bud, for choler he began to blush, and swore to himself he would be no more subject to such slavery. As thus he was ruminating of his melancholy passions in came Saladyne with his men, and seeing his brother in a brown study, and to forget his wonted reverence, thought to shake him out of his dumps thus:

'Sirrah,' quoth he, 'what is your heart on your halfpenny, or are you saying a dirge for your father's soul? What, is my dinner ready?'

At this question Rosader, turning his head askance, and bending his brows as if anger there had ploughed the furrows of her wrath, with his eyes full of fire, he made this reply:

'Dost thou ask me, Saladyne, for thy cates?[5] ask some of thy churls who are fit for such an office: I am thine equal by nature, though not by birth, and though thou hast more cards in the bunch, I have as many trumps in my hands as thyself. Let me question with thee, why thou hast felled my woods, spoiled my manor houses, and made havoc of such utensils as my father bequeathed unto me? I

3. **Aristotle . . . Galen:** key classical authorities in philosophy and medicine, respectively.
4. **frowardness:** backwardness.
5. **cates:** food.

tell thee, Saladyne, either answer me as a brother, or I will trouble thee as an enemy.'

At this reply of Rosader's Saladyne smiled as laughing at his presumption, and frowned as checking his folly: he therefore took him up thus shortly:

'What, sirrah! well I see early pricks the tree that will prove a thorn: hath my familiar conversing with you made you coy, or my good looks drawn you to be thus contemptuous? I can quickly remedy such a fault, and I will bend the tree while it is a wand. In faith, sir boy, I have a snaffle[6] for such a headstrong colt. You, sirs, lay hold on him and bind him, and then I will give him a cooling card for his choler.'

This made Rosader half mad, that stepping to a great rake that stood in the garden, he laid such load upon his brother's men that he hurt some of them, and made the rest of them run away. Saladyne, seeing Rosader so resolute and with his resolution so valiant, thought his heels his best safety, and took him to a loft adjoining to the garden, whither Rosader pursued him hotly. Saladyne, afraid of his brother's fury, cried out to him thus:

'Rosader, be not so rash: I am thy brother and thine elder, and if I have done thee wrong I'll make thee amends: revenge not anger in blood, for so shalt thou stain the virtue of old Sir John of Bordeaux. Say wherein thou art discontent and thou shalt be satisfied. Brothers' frowns ought not to be periods of wrath: what, man, look not so sourly; I know we shall be friends, and better friends than we have been, for, *Amantium ira amoris redintegratio est.*'[7]

These words appeased the choler of Rosader, for he was of a mild and courteous nature, so that he laid down his weapons, and upon the faith of a gentleman assured his brother he would offer him no prejudice: whereupon Saladyne came down, and after a little parley they embraced each other and became friends; and Saladyne promising Rosader the restitution of all his lands, 'and what favour else,' quoth he, 'any ways my ability or the nature of a brother may perform.' Upon these sugared reconciliations they went into the house arm in arm together, to the great content of all the old servants of Sir John of Bordeaux.

Thus continued the pad hidden in the straw,[8] till it chanced that Torismond, king of France, had appointed for his pleasure a day of wrastling and of tournament to busy his commons' heads, lest, being idle, their thoughts should run upon more serious matters, and call to remembrance their old banished king. A champion there

---

6. **snaffle**: bridle.
7. The anger of lovers is what brings them back together (Latin).
8. **pad . . . straw**: problem kept under wraps (literally toad hidden in the straw).

was to stand against all comers, a Norman, a man of tall stature and of great strength; so valiant, that in many such conflicts he always bare away the victory, not only overthrowing them which he encountered, but often with the weight of his body killing them outright. Saladyne hearing of this, thinking now not to let the ball fall to the ground, but to take opportunity by the forehead, first by secret means convented with the Norman, and procured him with rich rewards to swear that if Rosader came within his claws he should never more return to quarrel with Saladyne for his possessions. The Norman desirous of pelf—as *Quis nisi mentis inops oblatum respuit aurum?*[9] taking great gifts for little gods, took the crowns of Saladyne to perform the stratagem.

Having thus the champion tied to his villainous determination by oath, he prosecuted the intent of his purpose thus. He went to young Rosader, who in all his thoughts reached at honour, and gazed no lower than virtue commanded him, and began to tell him of this tournament and wrastling, how the king should be there, and all the chief peers of France, with all the beautiful damosels of the country.

'Now, brother,' quoth he, 'for the honour of Sir John of Bordeaux, our renowmed father, to famous that house that never hath been found without men approved in chivalry, show thy resolution to be peremptory. For myself thou knowest, though I am eldest by birth, yet never having attempted any deeds of arms, I am youngest to perform any martial exploits, knowing better how to survey my lands than to charge my lance: my brother Fernandyne he is at Paris poring on a few papers, having more insight into sophistry and principles of philosophy, than any warlike endeavours; but thou, Rosader, the youngest in years but the eldest in valour, art a man of strength, and darest do what honour allows thee. Take thou my father's lance, his sword, and his horse, and hie thee to the tournament, and either there valiantly crack a spear, or try with the Norman for the palm of activity.'

The words of Saladyne were but spurs to a free horse, for he had scarce uttered them, ere Rosader took him in his arms, taking his proffer so kindly, that he promised in what he might to requite his courtesy. The next morrow was the day of the tournament, and Rosader was so desirous to show his heroical thoughts that he passed the night with little sleep; but as soon as Phoebus had vailed the curtain of the night, and made Aurora blush with giving her the *bezo les labres*[1] in her silver couch, he gat him up, and taking his

---

9. Who other than the mentally deficient refuses proffered gold? (Latin).
1. **Phoebus . . . *labres*: Phoebus,** the sun god, kissed the lips of blushing **Aurora,** dawn; i.e., it was morning.

leave of his brother, mounted himself towards the place appointed, thinking every mile ten leagues till he came there.

But leaving him so desirous of the journey, to Torismond, the king of France, who having by force banished Gerismond, their lawful king, that lived as an outlaw in the forest of Arden, sought now by all means to keep the French busied with all sports that might breed their content. Amongst the rest he had appointed this solemn tournament, whereunto he in most solemn manner resorted, accompanied with the twelve peers of France, who, rather for fear than love, graced him with the show of their dutiful favours. To feed their eyes, and to make the beholders pleased with the sight of most rare and glistering objects, he had appointed his own daughter Alinda to be there, and the fair Rosalynde, daughter unto Gerismond, with all the beautiful damosels that were famous for their features in all France. Thus in that place did love and war triumph in a sympathy; for such as were martial might use their lance to be renowned for the excellence of their chivalry, and such as were amorous might glut themselves with gazing on the beauties of most heavenly creatures. As every man's eye had his several survey, and fancy was partial in their looks, yet all in general applauded the admirable riches that nature bestowed on the face of Rosalynde; for upon her cheeks there seemed a battle between the Graces, who should bestow most favours to make her excellent. The blush that gloried Luna, when she kissed the shepherd on the hills of Latmos,[2] was not tainted with such a pleasant dye as the vermilion flourished on the silver hue of Rosalynde's countenance: her eyes were like those lamps that make the wealthy covert of the heavens more gorgeous, sparkling favour and disdain, courteous and yet coy, as if in them Venus had placed all her amorets, and Diana[3] all her chastity. The trammels of her hair, folded in a caul of gold, so far surpassed the burnished glister of the metal, as the sun doth the meanest star in brightness: the tresses that folds in the brows of Apollo[4] were not half so rich to the sight, for in her hairs it seemed love had laid herself in ambush, to entrap the proudest eye that durst gaze upon their excellence. What should I need to decipher her particular beauties, when by the censure of all she was the paragon of all earthly perfection? This Rosalynde sat, I say, with Alinda as a beholder of these sports, and made the cavaliers crack their lances with more courage: many deeds of knighthood that day were performed, and many prizes were given according to their several deserts.

---

2. **Luna . . . Latmos: Luna,** goddess of the moon, kissed the sleeping Endymion, a shepherd on Mount **Latmos** she had fallen in love with.
3. **amorets . . . Diana: amorets** are little loves, offspring of Venus; **Diana** is goddess of the opposite idea, chastity.
4. **Apollo:** god associated with the arts, medicine, and the sun.

At last, when the tournament ceased, the wrastling began, and the Norman presented himself as a challenger against all comers, but he looked like Hercules when he advanced himself against Achelous,[5] so that the fury of his countenance amazed all that durst attempt to encounter with him in any deed of activity: till at last a lusty franklin[6] of the country came with two tall men that were his sons, of good lineaments and comely personage. The eldest of these doing his obeisance to the king entered the list, and presented himself to the Norman, who straight coped with him, and as a man that would triumph in the glory of his strength, roused himself with such fury, that not only he gave him the fall, but killed him with the weight of his corpulent personage: which the younger brother seeing, leaped presently into the place, and thirsty after the revenge, assailed the Norman with such valour, that at the first encounter he brought him to his knees; which repulsed so the Norman, that, recovering himself, fear of disgrace doubling his strength, he stepped so sternly to the young franklin, that taking him up in his arms he threw him against the ground so violently, that he broke his neck, and so ended his days with his brother. At this unlooked for massacre the people murmured, and were all in a deep passion of pity; but the franklin, father unto these, never changed his countenance, but as a man of a courageous resolution took up the bodies of his sons without show of outward discontent.

All this while stood Rosader and saw this tragedy; who, noting the undoubted virtue of the franklin's mind, alighted off from his horse, and presently sate down on the grass, and commanded his boy to pull off his boots, making him ready to try the strength of this champion. Being furnished as he would, he clapped the franklin on the shoulder and said thus:

'Bold yeoman, whose sons have ended the term of their years with honour, for that I see thou scornest fortune with patience, and thwartest the injury of fate with content in brooking the death of thy sons, stand awhile, and either see me make a third in their tragedy, or else revenge their fall with an honourable triumph.'

The franklin, seeing so goodly a gentleman to give him such courteous comfort, gave him hearty thanks, with promise to pray for his happy success. With that Rosader vailed bonnet[7] to the king, and lightly leaped within the lists, where noting more the company than the combatant, he cast his eye upon the troop of ladies that glistered there like the stars of heaven; but at last, Love, willing to make him as amorous as he was valiant, presented him with the sight of

---

5. **Hercules . . . Achelous:** Hercules was a hero so powerful that he could even defeat the river **Achelous** in a wrestling match.
6. **franklin:** landowner who was not of gentry status.
7. **vailed bonnet:** took off his hat.

Rosalynde, whose admirable beauty so inveigled the eye of Rosader, that forgetting himself, he stood and fed his looks on the favour of Rosalynde's face; which she perceiving blushed, which was such a doubling of her beauteous excellence, that the bashful red of Aurora at the sight of unacquainted Phaeton, was not half so glorious.

The Norman seeing this young gentleman fettered in the looks of the ladies drave him out of his *memento*[8] with a shake by the shoulder. Rosader looking back with an angry frown, as if he had been wakened from some pleasant dream, discovered to all by the fury of his countenance that he was a man of some high thoughts: but when they all noted his youth and the sweetness of his visage, with a general applause of favours, they grieved that so goodly a young man should venture in so base an action; but seeing it were to his dishonour to hinder him from his enterprise, they wished him to be graced with the palm of victory. After Rosader was thus called out of his *memento* by the Norman, he roughly clapped to him with so fierce an encounter, that they both fell to the ground, and with the violence of the fall were forced to breathe; in which space the Norman called to mind by all tokens, that this was he whom Saladyne had appointed him to kill; which conjecture made him stretch every limb, and try every sinew, that working his death he might recover the gold which so bountifully was promised him. On the contrary part, Rosader while he breathed was not idle, but still cast his eye upon Rosalynde, who to encourage him with a favour, lent him such an amorous look, as might have made the most coward desperate: which glance of Rosalynde so fired the passionate desires of Rosader, that turning to the Norman he ran upon him and braved him with a strong encounter. The Norman received him as valiantly, that there was a sore combat, hard to judge on whose side fortune would be prodigal. At last Rosader, calling to mind the beauty of his new mistress, the fame of his father's honours, and the disgrace that should fall to his house by his misfortune, roused himself and threw the Norman against the ground, falling upon his chest with so willing a weight, that the Norman yielded nature her due, and Rosader the victory.

The death of this champion, as it highly contented the franklin, as a man satisfied with revenge, so it drew the king and all the peers into a great admiration, that so young years and so beautiful a personage should contain such martial excellence; but when they knew him to be the youngest son of Sir John of Bordeaux, the king rose from his seat and embraced him, and the peers entreated him with all favourable courtesy, commending both his valour and his virtues, wishing him to go forward in such haughty deeds, that he might attain to the glory of his father's honourable fortunes.

8. *memento*: reverie.

As the king and lords graced him with embracing, so the ladies favoured him with their looks, especially Rosalynde, whom the beauty and valour of Rosader had already touched: but she accounted love a toy, and fancy a momentary passion, that as it was taken in with a gaze, might be shaken off with a wink, and therefore feared not to dally in the flame; and to make Rosader know she affected him, took from her neck a jewel, and sent it by a page to the young gentleman. The prize that Venus gave to Paris was not half so pleasing to the Troyan[9] as this gem was to Rosader; for if fortune had sworn to make him sole monarch of the world, he would rather have refused such dignity, than have lost the jewel sent him by Rosalynde. To return her with the like he was unfurnished, and yet that he might more than in his looks discover his affection, he stepped into a tent, and taking pen and paper wrote this fancy:

> Two suns at once from one fair heaven there shined,
>   Ten branches from two boughs, tipped all with roses,
> Pure locks more golden than is gold refined,
>   Two pearled rows that nature's pride encloses;
> Two mounts fair marble-white, down-soft and dainty,
>   A snow-dyed orb, where love increased by pleasure
> Full woeful makes my heart, and body fainty:
>   Her fair, my woe, exceeds all thought and measure.
> In lines confused my luckless harm appeareth,
> Whom sorrow clouds, whom pleasant smiling cleareth.

This sonnet he sent to Rosalynde, which when she read she blushed, but with a sweet content in that she perceived love had allotted her so amorous a servant.

Leaving her to her new entertained fancies, again to Rosader, who triumphing in the glory of this conquest, accompanied with a troop of young gentlemen that were desirous to be his familiars, went home to his brother Saladyne's, who was walking before the gates, to hear what success his brother Rosader should have, assuring himself of his death, and devising how with dissimuled sorrow to celebrate his funerals. As he was in his thought, he cast up his eye, and saw where Rosader returned with the garland on his head, as having won the prize, accompanied with a crew of boon companions. Grieved at this, he stepped in and shut the gate. Rosader seeing this, and not looking for such unkind entertainment, blushed at the disgrace, and yet smothering his grief with a smile, he turned to the gentlemen, and desired them to hold his brother excused, for he did not this upon any malicious intent or niggardize,[1] but being

---

9. **prize . . . Troyan:** Venus gave the Trojan **Paris** the beautiful Helen, thus setting in motion the Trojan War.
1. **niggardize:** cheapness.

brought up in the country, he absented himself as not finding his nature fit for such youthful company. Thus he sought to shadow abuses proffered him by his brother, but in vain, for he could by no means be suffered to enter: whereupon he ran his foot against the door, and broke it open, drawing his sword, and entering boldly into the hall, where he found none, for all were fled, but one Adam Spencer, an Englishman, who had been an old and trusty servant to Sir John of Bordeaux. He for the love he bare to his deceased master, favoured the part of Rosader, and gave him and his such entertainment as he could. Rosader gave him thanks, and looking about, seeing the hall empty, said:

'Gentlemen, you are welcome; frolic and be merry: you shall be sure to have wine enough, whatsoever your fare be. I tell you, cavaliers, my brother hath in his house five tun of wine, and as long as that lasteth, I beshrew him that spares his liquor.'[2]

With that he burst open the buttery door, and with the help of Adam Spencer covered the tables, and set down whatsoever he could find in the house; but what they wanted in meat, Rosader supplied with drink, yet had they royal cheer, and withal such hearty welcome as would have made the coarsest meats seem delicates. After they had feasted and frolicked it twice or thrice with an upsee freeze,[3] they all took their leaves of Rosader and departed. As soon as they were gone, Rosader growing impatient of the abuse, drew his sword, and swore to be revenged on the discourteous Saladyne; yet by the means of Adam Spencer, who sought to continue friendship and amity betwixt the brethren, and through the flattering submission of Saladyne, they were once again reconciled, and put up all forepassed injuries with a peaceable agreement, living together for a good space in such brotherly love, as did not only rejoice the servants, but made all the gentlemen and bordering neighbours glad of such friendly concord. Saladyne, hiding fire in the straw, and concealing a poisoned hate in a peaceable countenance, yet deferring the intent of his wrath till fitter oportunity, he showed himself a great favourer of his brother's virtuous endeavours: where leaving them in this happy league, let us return to Rosalynde.

Rosalynde returning home from the triumph, after she waxed[4] solitary love presented her with the idea of Rosader's perfection, and taking her at discovert[5] struck her so deep, as she felt herself grow passing passionate. She began to call to mind the comeliness of his person, the honour of his parents, and the virtues that, excelling both, made him so gracious in the eyes of every one. Sucking in thus

---

2. I . . . liquor: I curse anyone who fails to drink heartily.
3. upsee freeze: in the Dutch fashion and/or with Dutch beer.
4. waxed: became.
5. at discovert: off her guard.

the honey of love by imprinting in her thoughts his rare qualities, she began to surfeit with the contemplation of his virtuous conditions; but when she called to remembrance her present estate, and the hardness of her fortunes, desire began to shrink, and fancy to vail bonnet, that between a Chaos of confused thoughts she began to debate with herself in this manner:

'Infortunate Rosalynde, whose misfortunes are more than thy years, and whose passions are greater than thy patience! The blossoms of thy youth are mixed with the frosts of envy, and the hope of thy ensuing fruits perish in the bud. Thy father is by Torismond banished from the crown, and thou, the unhappy daughter of a king, detained captive, living as disquieted in thy thoughts as thy father discontented in his exile. Ah Rosalynde, what cares wait upon a crown! what griefs are incident to dignity! what sorrows haunt royal palaces! The greatest seas have the sorest storms, the highest birth subject to the most bale,[6] and of all trees the cedars soonest shake with the wind: small currents are ever calm, low valleys not scorched in any lightnings, nor base men tied to any baleful prejudice. Fortune flies, and if she touch poverty it is with her heel, rather disdaining their want with a frown, than envying their wealth with disparagement. O Rosalynde, hadst thou been born low, thou hadst not fallen so high, and yet being great of blood thine honour is more, if thou brookest misfortune with patience. Suppose I contrary fortune with content, yet fates unwilling to have me anyway happy, have forced love to set my thoughts on fire with fancy. Love, Rosalynde! becometh it women in distress to think of love? Tush, desire hath no respect of persons: Cupid is blind and shooteth at random, as soon hitting a rag as a robe, and piercing as soon the bosom of a captive as the breast of a libertine. Thou speakest it, poor Rosalynde, by experience; for being every way distressed, surcharged with cares, and overgrown with sorrows, yet amidst the heap of all these mishaps, love hath lodged in thy heart the perfection of young Rosader, a man every way absolute as well for his inward life, as for his outward lineaments, able to content the eye with beauty, and the ear with the report of his virtue. But consider, Rosalynde, his fortunes, and thy present estate: thou art poor and without patrimony, and yet the daughter of a prince; he a younger brother, and void of such possessions as either might maintain thy dignities or revenge thy father's injuries. And hast thou not learned this of other ladies, that lovers cannot live by looks, that women's ears are sooner content with a dram of *give me* than a pound of *hear me*, that gold is sweeter than eloquence, that love is a fire and wealth is the fuel, that Venus' coffers should be ever full?

6. **bale:** evil.

Then, Rosalynde, seeing Rosader is poor, think him less beautiful because he is in want, and account his virtues but qualities of course for that he is not endued with wealth. Doth not Horace tell thee what method is to be used in love?

Quaerenda pecunia primum, post nummos virtus.[7]

Tush, Rosalynde, be not over rash: leap not before thou look: either love such a one as may with his lands purchase thy liberty, or else love not at all. Choose not a fair face with an empty purse, but say as most women use to say:

Si nihil attuleris, ibis Homere foras.[8]

Why, Rosalynde! can such base thoughts harbour in such high beauties? can the degree of a princess, the daughter of Gerismond harbour such servile conceits, as to prize gold more than honour, or to measure a gentleman by his wealth, not by his virtues? No, Rosalynde, blush at thy base resolution, and say, if thou lovest, either Rosader or none. And why? because Rosader is both beautiful and virtuous.' Smiling to herself to think of her new-entertained passions, taking up her lute that lay by her, she warbled out this ditty:

Rosalynde's Madrigal

Love in my bosom like a bee
 Doth suck his sweet:
Now with his wings he plays with me,
 Now with his feet.
Within mine eyes he makes his nest,
His bed amidst my tender breast;
My kisses are his daily feast,
And yet he robs me of my rest.
 Ah, wanton, will ye?

And if I sleep, then percheth he
 With pretty flight,
And makes his pillow of my knee
 The livelong night.
Strike I my lute, he tunes the string,
He music plays if so I sing;
He lends me every lovely thing,
Yet cruel he my heart doth sting.
 Whist, wanton, still ye!

7. Money is to be sought first of all; virtue after wealth (Horace, *Epistles* 1.1.53–54).
8. If you bring nothing, O Homer, out you go! (Latin).

Else I with roses every day
        Will whip you hence,
And bind you, when you long to play,
        For your offence;
I'll shut mine eyes to keep you in,
I'll make you fast it for your sin,
I'll count your power not worth a pin.
        Alas, what hereby shall I win,
            If he gainsay⁹ me?

What if I beat the wanton boy
        With many a rod?
He will repay me with annoy,
        Because a God.
Then sit thou safely on my knee,
And let thy bower my bosom be;
Lurk in mine eyes, I like of thee.
        O Cupid, so thou pity me,
            Spare not but play thee.

Scarce had Rosalynde ended her madrigal, before Torismond
came in with his daughter Alinda and many of the peers of France,
who were enamoured of her beauty; which Torismond perceiving,
fearing lest her perfection might be the beginning of his prejudice,
and the hope of his fruit end in the beginning of her blossoms, he
thought to banish her from the court: 'for,' quoth he to himself, 'her
face is so full of favour, that it pleads pity in the eye of every man;
her beauty is so heavenly and divine, that she will prove to me as
Helen did to Priam;¹ some one of the peers will aim at her love, end
the marriage, and then in his wife's right attempt the kingdom. To
prevent therefore *had I wist*² in all these actions, she tarries not
about the court, but shall, as an exile, either wander to her father,
or else seek other fortunes.' In this humour, with a stern countenance full of wrath, he breathed out this censure unto her before
the peers, that charged her that that night she were not seen about
the court: 'for,' quoth he, 'I have heard of thy aspiring speeches,
and intended treasons.' This doom was strange unto Rosalynde,
and presently, covered with the shield of her innocence, she boldly
brake out in reverent terms to have cleared herself; but Torismond
would admit of no reason, nor durst his lords plead for Rosalynde,
although her beauty had made some of them passionate, seeing the
figure of wrath portrayed in his brow. Standing thus all mute, and
Rosalynde amazed, Alinda, who loved her more than herself, with

9. **gainsay:** deny.
1. **Helen . . . Priam:** Helen's beauty caused a long war for **Priam**, king of Troy.
2. *had I wist:* If only I had known.

grief in her heart and tears in her eyes, falling down on her knees, began to entreat her father thus:

'If, mighty Torismond, I offend in pleading for my friend, let the law of amity crave pardon for my boldness; for where there is depth of affection, there friendship alloweth a privilege. Rosalynde and I have been fostered up from our infancies, and nursed under the harbour of our conversing together with such private familiarities, that custom had wrought a union of our nature, and the sympathy of our affections such a secret love, that we have two bodies and one soul. Then marvel not, great Torismond, if, seeing my friend distressed, I find myself perplexed with a thousand sorrows; for her virtuous and honourable thoughts, which are the glories that maketh women excellent, they be such as may challenge love, and rase out suspicion. Her obedience to your majesty I refer to the censure of your own eye, that since her father's exile had smothered all griefs with patience, and in the absence of nature, hath honoured you with all duty, as her own father by nouriture,[3] not in word uttering any discontent, nor in thought, as far as conjecture may reach, hammering on revenge; only in all her actions seeking to please you, and to win my favour. Her wisdom, silence, chastity, and other such rich qualities, I need not decipher; only it rests for me to conclude in one word, that she is innocent. If then, fortune, who triumphs in a variety of miseries, hath presented some envious person, as minister of her intended stratagem, to taint Rosalynde with any surmise of treason, let him be brought to her face, and confirm his accusation by witnesses; which proved, let her die, and Alinda will execute the massacre. If none can avouch any confirmed relation of her intent, use justice, my lord, it is the glory of a king, and let her live in your wonted favour; for if you banish her, myself, as copartner of her hard fortunes, will participate in exile some part of her extremities.'

Torismond, at this speech of Alinda, covered his face with such a frown, as tyranny seemed to sit triumphant in his forehead, and checked her up with such taunts, as made the lords, that only were hearers, to tremble.

'Proud girl,' quoth he, 'hath my looks made thee so light of tongue, or my favours encouraged thee to be so forward, that thou darest presume to preach after thy father? Hath not my years more experience than thy youth, and the winter of mine age deeper insight into civil policy, than the prime of thy flourishing days? The old lion avoids the toils, where the young one leaps into the net: the care of age is provident and foresees much: suspicion is a virtue, where a man holds his enemy in his bosom. Thou, fond girl, measurest all by present affection, and as thy heart loves, thy thoughts censure; but

3. **nouriture:** sustenance.

if thou knowest that in liking Rosalynde thou hatchest up a bird to peck out thine own eyes, thou wouldst entreat as much for her absence as now thou delightest in her presence. But why do I allege policy to thee? Sit you down, housewife, and fall to your needle: if idleness make you so wanton, or liberty so malapert, I can quickly tie you to a sharper task. And you, maid, this night be packing, either into Arden to your father, or whither best it shall content your humour, but in the court you shall not abide.'

This rigorous reply of Torismond nothing amazed Alinda, for still she prosecuted her plea in the defence of Rosalynde, wishing her father, if his censure might not be reversed, that he would appoint her partner of her exile; which if he refused to do, either she would by some secret means steal out and follow her, or else end her days with some desperate kind of death. When Torismond heard his daughter so resolute, his heart was so hardened against her, that he set down a definite and peremptory sentence, that they should both be banished, which presently was done, the tyrant rather choosing to hazard the loss of his only child than anyways to put in question the state of his kingdom; so suspicious and fearful is the conscience of an usurper. Well, although his lords persuaded him to retain his own daughter, yet his resolution might not be reversed, but both of them must away from the court without either more company or delay. In he went with great melancholy, and left these two ladies alone. Rosalynde waxed very sad, and sate down and wept. Alinda she smiled, and sitting by her friend began thus to comfort her:

'Why, how now, Rosalynde, dismayed with a frown of contrary fortune? Have I not oft heard thee say, that high minds were discovered in fortune's contempt, and heroical scene in the depth of extremities? Thou wert wont to tell others that complained of distress, that the sweetest salve for misery was patience, and the only medicine for want that precious implaister[4] of content. Being such a good physician to others, wilt thou not minister receipts to thyself? But perchance thou wilt say:

Consulenti nunquam caput doluit.[5]

Why then, if the patients that are sick of this disease can find in themselves neither reason to persuade, nor art to cure, yet, Rosalynde, admit of the counsel of a friend, and apply the salves that may appease thy passions. If thou grievest that being the daughter of a prince, and envy thwarteth thee with such hard exigents, think that royalty is a fair mark, that crowns have crosses when mirth is in

---

4. **implaister** soothing substance.
5. Don't take advice from someone with a headache (Latin), i.e., suffering from the same ailment as you are.

cottages; that the fairer the rose is, the sooner it is bitten with cater-pillars; the more orient the pearl is, the more apt to take a blemish; and the greatest birth, as it hath most honour, so it hath much envy. If then fortune aimeth at the fairest, be patient Rosalynde, for first by thine exile thou goest to thy father: nature is higher prized than wealth, and the love of one's parents ought to be more precious than all dignities. Why then doth my, Rosalynde grieve at the frown of Torismond, who by offering her a prejudice proffers her a greater pleasure? and more, mad lass, to be melancholy, when thou hast with thee Alinda, a friend who will be a faithful copartner of all thy misfortunes, who hath left her father to follow thee, and chooseth rather to brook all extremities than to forsake thy presence. What, Rosalynde,

Solamen miseris socios habuisse doloris.[6]

Cheerly, woman: as we have been bed-fellows in royalty, we will be fellow-mates in poverty: I will ever be thy Alinda, and thou shalt ever rest to me Rosalynde; so shall the world canonize our friend-ship, and speak of Rosalynde and Alinda, as they did of Pylades and Orestes.[7] And if ever fortune smile, and we return to our former honour, then folding ourselves in the sweet of our friendship, we shall merrily say, calling to mind our forepassed miseries:

Olim haec meminisse juvabit.[8]

At this Rosalynde began to comfort her, and after she had wept a few kind tears in the bosom of her Alinda, she gave her hearty thanks, and then they sat them down to consult how they should travel. Alinda grieved at nothing but that they might have no man in their company, saying it would be their greatest prejudice in that two women went wandering without either guide or attendant.

'Tush,' quoth Rosalynde, 'art thou a woman, and hast not a sudden shift to prevent a misfortune? I, thou seest, am of a tall stature, and would very well become the person and apparel of a page; thou shalt be my mistress, and I will play the man so properly, that, trust me, in what company soever I come I will not be discovered. I will buy me a suit, and have my rapier very handsomely at my side, and if any knave offer wrong, your page will show him the point of his weapon.'

At this Alinda smiled, and upon this they agreed, and presently gathered up all their jewels, which they trussed up in a casket, and Rosalynde in all haste provided her of robes, and Alinda, from her royal weeds, put herself in more homelike attire. Thus fitted to the purpose, away go these two friends, having now changed their names,

6. Misery loves company (Latin).
7. **Pylades and Orestes:** famous friends in ancient Greece each of whom tried to die to save the other.
8 It will be a joy to remember even this (Latin).

Alinda being called Aliena, and Rosalynde Ganymede. They travelled along the vineyards, and by many by-ways at last got to the forest side, where they travelled by the space of two or three days without seeing any creature, being often in danger of wild beasts, and pained with many passionate sorrows. Now the black ox began to tread on their feet,[9] and Alinda thought of her wonted royalty; but when she cast her eyes on her Rosalynde, she thought every danger a step to honour. Passing thus on along, about midday they came to a fountain, compassed with a grove of cypress trees, so cunningly and curiously planted, as if some goddess had entreated nature in that place to make her an arbour. By this fountain sat Aliena and her Ganymede, and forth they pulled such victuals as they had, and fed as merrily as if they had been in Paris with all the king's delicates, Aliena only grieving that they could not so much as meet with a shepherd to discourse them the way to some place where they might make their abode. At last Ganymede casting up his eye espied where on a tree was engraven certain verses; which as soon as he espied, he cried out:

'Be of good cheer, mistress, I spy the figures of men; for here in these trees be engraven certain verses of shepherds, or some other swains that inhabit hereabout.'

With that Aliena start up joyful to hear these news, and looked, where they found carved in the bark of a pine tree this passion:

Montanus's Passion

Hadst, thou been born whereas perpetual cold
Makes Tanais[1] hard, and mountains silver old;
Had I complained unto a marble stone,
Or to the floods bewrayed my bitter moan,
    I then could bear the burthen of my grief:
But even the pride of countries at thy birth,
Whilst heavens did smile, did new array the earth
                With flowers chief;
Yet thou, the flower of beauty blessed born,
Hast pretty looks, but all attired in scorn.
Had I the power to weep sweet Mirrha's tears,
Or by my plaints to pierce repining ears;
Hadst thou the heart to smile at my complaint,
To scorn the woes that doth my heart attaint,
    I then could bear the burthen of my grief:
But not my tears, but truth with thee prevails,
And seeming sour my sorrows thee assails:
                Yet small relief;

---

9. ox . . . feet: They began to know what misfortune is.
1. Tanais: ancient name for the Russian River Don.

For if thou wilt thou art of marble hard,
And if thou please my suit shall soon be heard.

'No doubt,' quoth Aliena, 'this poesy is the passion of some perplexed shepherd, that being enamoured of some fair and beautiful shepherdess, suffered some sharp repulse, and therefore complained of the cruelty of his mistress.'

'You may see,' quoth Ganymede, 'what mad cattle you women be, whose hearts sometimes are made of adamant that will touch with no impression, and sometime of wax that is fit for every form: they delight to be courted, and then they glory to seem coy, and when they are most desired then they freeze with disdain: and this fault is so common to the sex, that you see it painted out in the shepherd's passions, who found his mistress as froward as he was enamoured.'

'And I pray you,' quoth Aliena, 'if your robes were off, what mettle are you made of that you are so satirical against women? Is it not a foul bird defiles the own nest? Beware, Ganymede, that Rosader hear you not, if he do, perchance you will make him leap so far from love, that he will anger every vein in your heart.'

'Thus,' quoth Ganymede, 'I keep decorum: I speak now as I am Aliena's page, not as I am Gerismond's daughter; for put me but into a petticoat, and I will stand in defiance to the uttermost, that women are courteous, constant, virtuous, and what not.'

'Stay there,' quoth Aliena, 'and no more words, for yonder be characters graven upon the bark of the tall beech tree.'

'Let us see,' quoth Ganymede; and with that they read a fancy written to this effect:

First shall the heavens want starry light,
    The seas be robbed of their waves,
The day want sun, and sun want bright,
    The night want shade, the dead men graves,
The April flowers and leaf and tree,
Before I false my faith to thee.

First shall the tops of highest hills
    By humble plains be overpried,
And poets scorn the Muses' quills,
    And fish forsake the water glide,
And Iris loose her coloured weed,
Before I fail thee at thy need.

First direful hate shall turn to peace,
    And love relent in deep disdain,
And death his fatal stroke shall cease,
    And envy pity every pain,

And pleasure mourn and sorrow smile,
Before I talk of any guile.

First time shall stay his stayless race,
  And winter bless his brows with corn,
And snow bemoisten July's face,
  And winter spring, and summer mourn,
Before my pen, by help of fame,
Cease to recite thy sacred name.

MONTANUS.

'No doubt,' quoth Ganymede, 'this protestation grew from one full of passions.'

'I am of that mind too,' quoth Aliena, 'but see, I pray, when poor women seek to keep themselves chaste, how men woo them with many feigned promises; alluring with sweet words as the Sirens, and after proving as trothless as Aeneas.[2] Thus promised Demophoon to his Phyllis,[3] but who at last grew more false?'

'The reason was,' quoth Ganymede, 'that they were women's sons, and took that fault of their mother, for if man had grown from man, as Adam did from the earth, men had never been troubled with inconstancy.'

'Leave off,' quoth Aliena, 'to taunt thus bitterly, or else I'll pull off your page's apparel, and whip you, as Venus doth her wantons, with nettles.'

'So you will,' quoth Ganymede, 'persuade me to flattery, and that needs not: but come, seeing we have found here by this fount the tract of shepherds by their madrigals and roundelays, let us forward; for either we shall find some folds, sheepcotes, or else some cottages wherein for a day or two to rest.'

'Content,' quoth Aliena, and with that they rose up, and marched forward till towards the even,[4] and then coming into a fair valley, compassed with mountains, whereon grew many pleasant shrubs, they might descry where two flocks of sheep did feed. Then, looking about, they might perceive where an old shepherd sat, and with him a young swaine, under a covert most pleasantly situated. The ground where they sat was diapered with Flora's riches, as if she meant to wrap Tellus[5] in the glory of her vestments: round about in the form of an amphitheatre were most curiously planted pine trees, interseamed with limons and citrons, which with the thickness of

---

2. **Aeneas:** hero from the *Aeneid* who abandoned Dido after promising love.
3. **Demophoon . . . Phyllis:** When **Domophoon** did not return on the appointed day to his wife **Phyllis**, she hanged herself.
4. **even:** evening.
5. **Flora's . . . Tellus: Flora**, goddess of flowers, wrapped **Tellus**, Mother Earth, in spring beauty.

their boughs so shadowed the place, that Phoebus could not pry
into the secret of that arbour; so united were the tops with so thick
a closure, that Venus might there in her jollity have dallied unseen
with her dearest paramour. Fast by, to make the place more gorgeous, was there a fount so crystalline and clear, that it seemed
Diana with her Dryades and Hamadryades[6] had that spring, as the
secret of all their bathings. In this glorious arbour sat these two
shepherds, seeing their sheep feed, playing on their pipes many
pleasant tunes, and from music and melody falling into much amorous chat. Drawing more nigh we might descry the countenance of
the one to be full of sorrow, his face to be the very portraiture of
discontent, and his eyes full of woes, that living he seemed to die:
we, to hear what these were, stole privily behind the thicket, where
we overheard this discourse:

A *Pleasant Eclogue between Montanus and Corydon*

CORYDON

Say, shepherd's boy, what makes thee greet so sore?
Why leaves thy pipe his pleasure and delight?
Young are thy years, thy cheeks with roses dight:
Then sing for joy, sweet swain, and sigh no more.

This milk-white poppy, and this climbing pine
Both promise shade; then sit thee down and sing,
And make these woods with pleasant notes to ring,
Till Phoebus deign all westward to decline.

MONTANUS

Ah, Corydon, unmeet is melody
To him whom proud contempt hath overborne:
Slain are my joys by Phoebe's bitter scorn;
Far hence my weal, and near my jeopardy.

Love's burning brand is couchèd in my breast,
Making a Phoenix of my faintful heart:
And though his fury do enforce my smart,
Ay blithe am I to honour his behest.

Prepared to woes, since so my Phoebe wills,
My looks dismayed, since Phoebe will disdain;
I banish bliss and welcome home my pain:
So stream my tears as showers from Alpine hills.

6. **Dryades and Hamadryades:** forest nymphs.

In error's mask I blindfold judgment's eye,
I fetter reason in the snares of lust,
I seem secure, yet know not how to trust;
I live by that which makes me living die.

Devoid of rest, companion of distress,
Plague to myself, consumèd by my thought,
How may my voice or pipe in tune be brought,
Since I am reft of solace and delight?

CORYDON

Ah, lorrel lad, what makes thee hery[7] love?
A sugared harm, a poison full of pleasure,
A painted shrine full filled with rotten treasure;
A heaven in show, a hell to them that prove.

A gain in seeming, shadowed still with want,
A broken staff which folly doth uphold,
A flower that fades with every frosty cold,
An orient rose sprung from a withered plant.

A minute's joy to gain a world of grief,
A subtle net to snare the idle mind,
A seeing scorpion, yet in seeming blind,
A poor rejoice, a plague without relief.

Forthy, Montanus, follow mine arede,[8]
Whom age hath taught the trains that fancy useth,
Leave foolish love, for beauty wit abuseth,
And drowns, by folly, virtue's springing seed.

MONTANUS

So blames the child the flame because it burns,
And bird the snare because it doth entrap,
And fools true love because of sorry hap,[9]
And sailors curse the ship that overturns.

But would the child forbear to play with flame,
And birds beware to trust the fowler's gin,[1]
And fools foresee before they fall and sin,
And masters guide their ships in better frame;

---

7. **lorrel:** worthless; **hery:** praise.
8. **Forthy:** unrestrainedly; **arede:** advice.
9. **hap:** mishap.
1. **fowler's gin:** bird catcher's trap.

The child would praise the fire because it warms,
And birds rejoice to see the fowler fail,
And fools prevent before their plagues prevail,
And sailors bless the barque that saves from harms.

Ah, Corydon, though many be thy years,
And crooked elde² hath some experience left,
Yet is thy mind of judgment quite bereft,
In view of love, whose power in me appears.

The ploughman little wots³ to turn the pen,
Or bookman skills to guide the ploughman's cart;
Nor can the cobbler count the terms of art,
Nor base men judge the thoughts of mighty men.

Nor withered age, unmeet for beauty's guide,
Uncapable of love's impression,
Discourse of that whose choice possession
May never to so base a man be tied.

But I, whom nature makes of tender mould,
And youth most pliant yields to fancy's fire,
Do build my haven and heaven on sweet desire,
On sweet desire, more dear to me than gold.

Think I of love, oh, how my lines aspire!
How haste the Muses to embrace my brows,
And hem my temples in with laurel boughs,
And fill my brains with chaste and holy fire!

Then leave my lines their homely equipage,
Mounted beyond the circle of the sun:
Amazed I read the stile when I have done,
And hery love that sent that heavenly rage.

Of Phoebe then, of Phoebe then I sing,
Drawing the purity of all the spheres,
The pride of earth, or what in heaven appears,
Her honoured face and fame to light to bring.

In fluent numbers, and in pleasant veins,
I rob both sea and earth of all their state,
To praise her parts: I charm both time and fate,
To bless the nymph that yields me lovesick pains.

2. **elde:** old age.
3. **wots:** knows.

My sheep are turned to thoughts, whom froward will
Guides in the restless labyrinth of love;
Fear lends them pasture wheresoe'er they move,
And by their death their life reneweth still.

My sheephook is my pen, mine oaten reed.[4]
My paper, where my many woes are written.
Thus silly swain, with love and fancy bitten,
I trace the plains of pain in woeful weed.[5]

Yet are my cares, my broken sleeps, my tears,
My dreams, my doubts, for Phoebe sweet to me:
Who waiteth heaven in sorrow's vale must be,
And glory shines where danger most appears.

Then, Corydon, although I blithe me not,
Blame me not, man, since sorrow is my sweet:
So willeth love, and Phoebe thinks it meet,
And kind Montanus liketh well his lot.

CORYDON

O stayless youth, by error so misguided,
Where will proscribeth laws to perfect wits,
Where reason mourns, and blame in triumph sits,
And folly poisoneth all that time provided!

With wilful blindness bleared, prepared to shame,
Prone to neglect Occasion when she smiles.
Alas, that love, by fond and froward guiles,
Should make thee tract[6] the path to endless blame!

Ah, my Montanus, cursed is the charm,
That hath bewitched so thy youthful eyes.
Leave off in time to like these vanities,
Be forward to thy good, and fly thy harm.

As many bees as Hybla[7] daily shields,
As many fry as fleet on ocean's face,
As many herds as on the earth do trace,
As many flowers as deck the fragrant fields,

As many stars as glorious heaven contains,
As many storms as wayward winter weeps,

4. **reed:** shepherd's pipe.
5. **I . . . weed:** I articulate my painful cries in doleful style.
6. **tract:** follow.
7. **Hybla:** site in ancient Sicily renowned for its honey.

As many plagues as hell enclosèd keeps,
So many griefs in love, so many pains.

Suspicions, thoughts, desires, opinions, prayers,
Mislikes, misdeeds, fond joys, and feignèd peace,
Illusions, dreams, great pains, and small increase,
Vows, hopes, acceptance, scorns, and deep despairs,

Truce, war, and woe do wait at beauty's gate;
Time lost, laments, reports, and privy[8] grudge,
And last, fierce love is but a partial judge,
Who yields for service shame, for friendship hate.

MONTANUS

All adder-like I stop mine ears, fond swain,
So charm no more, for I will never change.
Call home thy flocks in time that straggling range,
For lo, the sun declineth hence amain.

TERENTIUS

In amore haec omnia insunt vitia: induciae, inimicitiae, bellum, pax rursum: incerta haec si tu postules ratione certa fieri, nihilo plus agas, quam si des operam, ut cum ratione insanias.[9]

The shepherds having thus ended their eclogue, Aliena stepped with Ganymede from behind the thicket; at whose sudden sight the shepherds arose, and Aliena saluted them thus:

'Shepherds, all hail, for such we deem you by your flocks, and lovers, good luck, for such you seem by your passions, our eyes being witness of the one, and our ears of the other. Although not by love, yet by fortune, I am a distressed gentlewoman, as sorrowful as you are passionate, and as full of woes as you of perplexed thoughts. Wandering this way in a forest unknown, only I and my page, wearied with travel, would fain have some place of rest. May you appoint us any place of quiet harbour, be it never so mean, I shall be thankful to you, contented in myself, and grateful to whosoever shall be mine host.'

Corydon, hearing the gentlewoman speak so courteously, returned her mildly and reverently this answer:

---

8. **privy**: private.
9. Quotation is from Terence (Latin dramatist): In love all these problems are present: insults, suspicions, enmities, truces, breaking up, making up again. If you tried to deal with these uncertainties in a reasonable manner, you'd achieve no more than if you determined to go crazy in a logical way (*Eunuchus* 59–63).

'Fair mistress, we return you as hearty a welcome as you gave us a courteous salute. A shepherd I am, and this a lover, as watchful to please his wench as to feed his sheep: full of fancies, and therefore, say I, full of follies. Exhort him I may, but persuade him I cannot; for love admits neither of counsel nor reason. But leaving him to his passions, if you be distressed, I am sorrowful such a fair creature is crossed with calamity; pray for you I may, but relieve you I cannot. Marry,[1] if you want lodging, if you vouch to shroud yourselves in a shepherd's cottage, my house for this night shall be your harbour.'

Aliena thanked Corydon greatly, and presently sate her down and Ganymede by her. Corydon looking earnestly upon her, and with a curious survey viewing all her perfections, applauded in his thought her excellence, and pitying her distress was desirous to hear the cause of her misfortunes, began to question her thus:

'If I should not, fair damosel, occasion offence, or renew your griefs by rubbing the scar, I would fain crave so much favour as to know the cause of your misfortunes, and why, and whither you wander with your page in so dangerous a forest?'

Aliena, that was as courteous as she was fair, made this reply:

'Shepherd, a friendly demand ought never to be offensive, and questions of courtesy carry privileged pardons in their foreheads. Know, therefore, to discover my fortunes were to renew my sorrows, and I should, by discoursing my mishaps, but rake fire out of the cinders. Therefore let this suffice, gentle shepherd: my distress is as great as my travel is dangerous, and I wander in this forest to light on some cottage where I and my page may dwell: for I mean to buy some farm, and a flock of sheep, and so become a shepherdess, meaning to live low, and content me with a country life; for I have heard the swains say, that they drunk without suspicion, and slept without care.'

'Marry, mistress,' quoth Corydon, 'if you mean so you came in good time, for my landslord intends to sell both the farm I till, and the flock I keep, and cheap you may have them for ready money: and for a shepherd's life, O mistress, did you but live awhile in their content, you would say the court were rather a place of sorrow than of solace. Here, mistress, shall not fortune thwart you, but in mean misfortunes, as the loss of a few sheep, which, as it breeds no beggary, so it can be no extreme prejudice: the next year may mend all with a fresh increase. Envy stirs not us, we covet not to climb, our desires mount not above our degrees, nor our thoughts above our fortunes. Care cannot harbour in our cottages, nor do our homely couches know broken slumbers: as we exceed not in diet, so we

---

1. **Marry:** indeed.

have enough to satisfy: and, mistress, I have so much Latin, *Satis est quod sufficit.*[2]

'By my troth, shepherd,' quoth Aliena, 'thou makest me in love with your country life, and therefore send for thy landslord, and I will buy thy farm and thy flocks, and thou shalt still under me be overseer of them both: only for pleasure sake I and my page will serve you, lead the flocks to the field, and fold them. Thus will I live quiet, unknown, and contented.'

This news so gladded the heart of Corydon, that he should not be put out of his farm, that putting off his shepherd's bonnet, he did her all the reverence that he might. But all this while sate Montanus in a muse, thinking of the cruelty of his Phoebe, whom he wooed long, but was in no hope to win. Ganymede, who still had the remembrance of Rosader in his thoughts, took delight to see the poor shepherd passionate, laughing at Love, that in all his actions was so imperious. At last, when she had noted his tears that stole down his cheeks, and his sighs that broke from the centre of his heart, pitying his lament, she demanded of Corydon why the young shepherd looked so sorrowful.

'O sir,' quoth he, 'the boy is in love.'

'Why,' quoth Ganymede, 'can shepherds love?'

'Aye,' quoth Montanus, 'and overlove, else shouldst not thou see me so pensive. Love, I tell thee, is as precious in a shepherd's eye, as in the looks of a king, and we country swains entertain fancy with as great delight as the proudest courtier doth affection. Opportunity, that is the sweetest friend to Venus, harboureth in our cottages, and loyalty, the chiefest fealty that Cupid requires, is found more among shepherds than higher degrees. Then, ask not if such silly swains can love.'

'What is the cause then,' quoth Ganymede, 'that love being so sweet to thee, thou lookest so sorrowful?'

'Because,' quoth Montanus, 'the party beloved is froward, and having courtesy in her looks, holdeth disdain in her tongue's end.'

'What hath she, then,' quoth Aliena, 'in her heart?'

'Desire, I hope madam,' quoth he, 'or else, my hope lost, despair in love were death.'

As thus they chatted, the sun being ready to set, and they not having folded their sheep, Corydon requested she would sit there with her page, till Montanus and he lodged their sheep for that night.

'You shall go,' quoth Aliena, 'but first I will entreat Montanus to sing some amorous sonnet, that he made when he hath been deeply passionate.'

'That I will,' quoth Montanus, and with that he began thus:

---

2. Enough is as good as a feast.

Montanus's Sonnet

Phoebe sate,
Sweet she sate,
  Sweet sate Phoebe when I saw her;
White her brow,
Coy her eye:
  Brow and eye how much you please me!
Words I spent,
Sighs I sent:
  Sighs and words could never draw her.
O my love,
Thou art lost,
  Since no sight could ever ease thee.

Phoebe sat
By a fount;
  Sitting by a fount I spied her:
Sweet her touch,
Rare her voice:
  Touch and voice what may distain you?
As she sung
I did sigh,
  And by sighs whilst that I tried her,
O mine eyes!
You did lose
  Her first sight whose want did pain you.

Phoebe's flocks,
White as wool:
  Yet were Phoebe's locks more whiter.
Phoebe's eyes
Dovelike mild:
  Dovelike eyes, both mild and cruel.
Montan swears,
In your lamps
  He will die for to delight her.
Phoebe yield,
Or I die:
  Shall true hearts be fancy's fuel?

Montanus had no sooner ended his sonnet, but Corydon with a low courtesy rose up and went with his fellow, and shut their sheep in the folds; and after returning to Aliena and Ganymede, conducted them home weary to his poor cottage. By the way there was much good chat with Montanus about his loves, he resolving[3] Aliena

---

3. **resolving:** explaining to.

that Phoebe was the fairest shepherdess in all France, and that in his eye her beauty was equal with the nymphs.

'But,' quoth he, 'as of all stones the diamond is most clearest, and yet most hard for the lapidary[4] to cut: as of all flowers the rose is the fairest, and yet guarded with the sharpest prickles: so of all our country lasses Phoebe is the brightest, but the most coy of all to stoop unto desire. But let her take heed,' quoth he, 'I have heard of Narcissus,[5] who for his high disdain against Love, perished in the folly of his own love.'

With this they were at Corydon's cottage, where Montanus parted from them, and they went in to rest. Aliena and Ganymede glad of so contented a shelter, made merry with the poor swain; and though they had but country fare and coarse lodging, yet their welcome was so great, and their cares so little, that they counted their diet delicate, and slept as soundly as if they had been in the court of Torismond. The next morn they lay long in bed, as wearied with the toil of unaccustomed travel; but as soon as they got up, Aliena resolved there to set up her rest, and by the help of Corydon swept[6] a bargain with his landslord, and so became mistress of the farm and the flock, herself putting on the attire of a shepherdess, and Ganymede of a young swain: every day leading forth her flocks, with such delight, that she held her exile happy, and thought no content to the bliss of a country cottage. Leaving her thus famous amongst the shepherds of Arden, again to Saladyne.

When Saladyne had a long while concealed a secret resolution of revenge, and could no longer hide fire in the flax, nor oil in the flame, for envy is like lightning, that will appear in the darkest fog, it chanced on a morning very early he called up certain of his servants, and went with them to the chamber of Rosader, which being open, he entered with his crew, and surprised his brother being asleep, and bound him in fetters, and in the midst of his hall chained him to a post. Rosader, amazed at this strange chance, began to reason with his brother about the cause of this sudden extremity, wherein he had wronged, and what fault he had committed worthy so sharp a penance. Saladyne answered him only with a look of disdain, and went his way, leaving poor Rosader in a deep perplexity; who, thus abused, fell into sundry passions, but no means of relief could be had: whereupon for anger he grew into a discontented melancholy. In which humour he continued two or three days without meat, insomuch that seeing his brother would give him no food, he fell into despair of his life. Which Adam Spencer, the old servant of Sir

---

4. **lapidary:** jewel cutter.
5. **Narcissus:** youth who fell in love with his own reflection and eventually died of despair.
6. **swept:** concluded.

John of Bordeaux, seeing, touched with the duty and love he ought to his old master, felt a remorse in his conscience of his son's mishap; and therefore, although Saladyne had given a general charge to his servants that none of them upon pain of death should give either meat or drink to Rosader, yet Adam Spencer in the night rose secretly, and brought him such victuals as he could provide, and unlocked him, and set him at liberty. After Rosader had well feasted himself, and felt he was loose, straight his thoughts aimed at revenge, and now, all being asleep, he would have quit Saladyne with the method of his own mischief. But Adam Spencer did persuade him to the contrary with these reasons:

'Sir,' quoth he, 'be content, for this night go again into your old fetters, so shall you try the faith of friends, and save the life of an old servant. To-morrow hath your brother invited all your kindred and allies to a solemn breakfast, only to see you, telling them all that you are mad, and fain[7] to be tied to a post. As soon as they come, complain to them of the abuse proffered you by Saladyne. If they redress you, why so: but if they pass over your plaints *sicco pede*,[8] and hold with the violence of your brother before your innocence, then thus: I will leave you unlocked that you may break out at your pleasure, and at the end of the hall shall you see stand a couple of good pole-axes, one for you and another for me. When I give you a wink, shake off your chains, and let us play the men, and make havoc amongst them, drive them out of the house and maintain possession by force of arms, till the king hath made a redress of your abuses.'

These words of Adam Spencer so persuaded Rosader, that he went to the place of his punishment, and stood there while the next morning. About the time appointed, came all the guests bidden by Saladyne, whom he entreated with courteous and curious entertainment, as they all perceived their welcome to be great. The tables in the hall, where Rosader was tied, were covered, and Saladyne bringing in his guests together, showed them where his brother was bound, and was enchained as a man lunatic. Rosader made reply, and with some invectives made complaints of the wrongs proffered him by Saladyne, desiring they would in pity seek some means for his relief. But in vain, they had stopped their ears with Ulysses,[9] that were his words never so forceable, he breathed only his passions into the wind. They, careless, sat down with Saladyne to dinner, being very frolic and pleasant, washing their heads well with wine. At last, when the fume of the grape had entered peale-meale into their brains, they began in satirical speeches to rail against Rosader: which Adam

---

7. **fain**: wanting.
8. *sicco pede*: with dry foot; i.e., without getting into them (Latin).
9. **stopped . . . Ulysses**: In the *Odyssey* Ulysses covered his sailors' ears so they could not hear the tempting song of the Sirens.

Spencer no longer brooking,[1] gave the sign, and Rosader shaking off his chains got a poleaxe in his hand, and flew amongst them with such violence and fury, that he hurt many, slew some, and drave his brother and the rest quite out of the house. Seeing the coast clear, he shut the doors, and being sore anhungered, and seeing such good victuals, he sat him down with Adam Spencer, and such good fellows as he knew were honest men, and there feasted themselves with such provision as Saladyne had prepared for his friends. After they had taken their repast, Rosader rampired up[2] the house, lest upon a sudden his brother should raise some crew of his tenants, and surprise them unawares. But Saladyne took a contrary course, and went to the sheriff of the shire and made complaint of Rosader, who giving credit to Saladyne, in a determined resolution to revenge the gentleman's wrongs, took with him five-and-twenty tall men, and made a vow, either to break into the house and take Rosader, or else to coop him in till he made him yield by famine. In this determination, gathering a crew together, he went forward to set Saladyne in his former estate. News of this was brought unto Rosader, who smiling at the cowardice of his brother, brooked all the injuries of fortune with patience, expecting the coming of the sheriff. As he walked upon the battlements of the house, he descried where Saladyne and he drew near, with a troop of lusty gallants. At this he smiled, and called Adam Spencer, and showed him the envious treachery of his brother, and the folly of the sheriff to be so credulous.

'Now, Adam,' quoth he, 'what shall I do? It rests for me either to yield up the house to my brother and seek a reconcilement, or else issue out, and break through the company with courage, for cooped in like a coward I will not be. If I submit, ah Adam, I dishonour myself, and that is worse than death, for by such open disgraces, the fame of men grows odious. If I issue out amongst them, fortune may favour me, and I may escape with life. But suppose the worst; if I be slain, then my death shall be honourable to me, and so inequal a revenge infamous to Saladyne.'

'Why then, master, forward and fear not! Out amongst them; they be but faint-hearted losels,[3] and for Adam Spencer, if he die not at your foot, say he is a dastard.'

These words cheered up so the heart of young Rosader, that he thought himself sufficient for them all, and therefore prepared weapons for him and Adam Spencer, and were ready to entertain the sheriff; for no sooner came Saladyne and he to the gates, but

---

1. **brooking:** tolerating.
2. **rampired up:** fortified against an attack.
3. **losels:** scoundrels.

Rosader, unlooked for, leaped out and assailed them, wounded many of them, and caused the rest to give back, so that Adam and he broke through the prease in despite of them all, and took their way towards the forest of Arden. This repulse so set the sheriff's heart on fire to revenge, that he straight raised all the country, and made hue and cry after them. But Rosader and Adam, knowing full well the secret ways that led through the vineyards, stole away privily through the province of Bordeaux, and escaped safe to the forest of Arden. Being come thither, they were glad they had so good a harbour: but fortune, who is like the chameleon, variable with every object, and constant in nothing but inconstancy, thought to make them mirrors of her mutability, and therefore still crossed them thus contrarily. Thinking still to pass on by the by-ways to get to Lyons, they chanced on a path that led into the thick of the forest, where they wandered five or six days without meat, that they were almost famished finding neither shepherd nor cottage to relieve them; and hunger growing on so extreme, Adam Spencer, being old, began first to faint, and sitting him down on a hill, and looking about him, espied where Rosader lay as feeble and as ill perplexed: which sight made him shed tears, and to fall into these bitter terms:

'Oh, how the life of man may well be compared to the state of the ocean seas, that for every calm hath a thousand storms, resembling the rose tree, that for a few fair flowers hath a multitude of sharp prickles! All our pleasures end in pain, and our highest delights are crossed with deepest discontents. The joys of man, as they are few, so are they momentary, scarce ripe before they are rotten, and withering in the blossom, either parched with the heat of envy or fortune. Fortune, O inconstant friend, that in all thy deeds art froward and fickle, delighting, in the poverty of the lowest and the overthrow of the highest, to decipher thy inconstancy. Thou standest upon a globe, and thy wings are plumed with Time's feathers, that thou mayest ever be restless: thou art double-faced like Janus,[4] carrying frowns in the one to threaten, and smiles in the other to betray: thou profferest[5] an eel, and performest a scorpion, and where thy greatest favours be, there is the fear of the extremest misfortunes, so variable are all thy actions. But why, Adam, dost thou exclaim against Fortune? She laughs at the plaints of the distressed, and there is nothing more pleasing unto her, than to hear fools boast in her fading allurements, or sorrowful men to discover the sour of their passions. Glut her not, Adam, then with content, but

4. **Janus:** Roman god of the threshold who had two faces, one looking in and one looking out.
5. **profferest:** offer[est].

thwart her with brooking all mishaps with patience. For there is no greater check to the pride of Fortune, than with a resolute courage to pass over her crosses without care. Thou art old, Adam, and thy hairs wax white: the palm tree is already full of blooms, and in the furrows of thy face appears the calendars of death. Wert thou blessed by Fortune thy years could not be many, nor the date of thy life long: then sith[6] nature must have her due, what is it for thee to resign her debt a little before the day. Ah, it is not this which grieveth me, nor do I care what mishaps Fortune can wage against me, but the sight of Rosader that galleth unto the quick. When I remember the worships of his house, the honour of his fathers, and the virtues of himself, then do I say, that fortune and the fates are most injurious, to censure so hard extremes, against a youth of so great hope. O Rosader, thou art in the flower of thine age, and in the pride of thy years, buxom and full of May. Nature hath prodigally enriched thee with her favours, and virtue made thee the mirror of her excellence; and now, through the decree of the unjust stars, to have all these good parts nipped in the blade;[7] and blemished by the inconstancy of fortune! Ah, Rosader, could I help thee, my grief were the less, and happy should my death be, if it might be the beginning of thy relief: but seeing we perish both in one extreme, it is a double sorrow. What shall I do? prevent the sight of his farther misfortune with a present dispatch of mine own life? Ah, despair is a merciless sin!'

As he was ready to go forward in his passion, he looked earnestly on Rosader, and seeing him change colour, he rise up and went to him, and holding his temples, said:

'What cheer, master? though all fail, let not the heart faint: the courage of a man is showed in the resolution of his death.'

At these words Rosader lifted up his eye, and looking on Adam Spencer, began to weep.

'Ah, Adam,' quoth he, 'I sorrow not to die, but I grieve at the manner of my death. Might I with my lance encounter the enemy, and so die in the field, it were honour and content: might I, Adam, combate with some wild beast and perish as his prey, I were satisfied; but to die with hunger, O Adam, it is the extremest of all extremes!'

'Master,' quoth he, 'you see we are both in one predicament, and long I cannot live without meat; seeing therefore we can find no food, let the death of the one preserve the life of the other. I am old, and overworn with age, you are young, and are the hope of many honours: let me then die, I will presently cut my veins, and, master,

---

6. **sith:** since.
7. **nipped . . . blade:** cut off before they flowered.

with the warm blood relieve your fainting spirits: suck on that till I end, and you be comforted.'

With that Adam Spencer was ready to pull out his knife, when Rosader full of courage, though very faint, rose up, and wished Adam Spencer to sit there till his return; 'for my mind gives me,' quoth he, 'I shall bring thee meat.' With that, like a madman, he rose up, and ranged up and down the woods, seeking to encounter some wild beast with his rapier, that either he might carry his friend Adam food, or else pledge his life in pawn for his loyalty.

It chanced that day, that Gerismond, the lawful king of France banished by Torismond, who with a lusty crew of outlaws lived in that forest, that day in honour of his birth made a feast to all his bold yeomen, and frolicked it with store of wine and venison, sitting all at a long table under the shadow of limon trees. To that place by chance fortune conducted Rosader, who seeing such a crew of brave men, having store of that for want of which he and Adam perished, he stepped boldly to the board's end, and saluted the company thus:

'Whatsoever thou be that art master of these lusty squires, I salute thee as graciously as a man in extreme distress may: know that I and a fellow-friend of mine are here famished in the forest for want of food: perish we must, unless relieved by thy favours. Therefore, if thou be a gentleman, give meat to men, and to such men as are every way worthy of life. Let the proudest squire that sits at thy table rise and encounter with me in any honourable point of activity whatsoever, and if he and thou prove me not a man, send me away comfortless. If thou refuse this, as a niggard of thy cates, I will have amongst you with my sword; for rather will I die valiantly, than perish with so cowardly an extreme.'

Gerismond, looking him earnestly in the face, and seeing so proper a gentleman in so bitter a passion, was moved with so great pity, that rising from the table, he took him by the hand and bad him welcome, willing him to sit down in his place, and in his room not only to eat his fill, but be lord of the feast.

'Gramercy,[8] sir,' quoth Rosader, 'but I have a feeble friend that lies hereby famished almost for food, aged and therefore less able to abide the extremity of hunger than myself, and dishonour it were for me to taste one crumb, before I made him partner of my fortunes: therefore I will run and fetch him, and then I will gratefully accept of your proffer.'

Away hies[9] Rosader to Adam Spencer, and tells him the news, who was glad of so happy fortune, but so feeble he was that he could

8. **Gramercy:** thanks.
9. **hies:** goes.

not go; whereupon Rosader got him up on his back, and brought him to the place. Which when Gerismond and his men saw, they greatly applauded their league of friendship; and Rosader, having Gerismond's place assigned him, would not sit there himself, but set down Adam Spencer. Well, to be short, those hungry squires fell to their victuals, and feasted themselves with good delicates, and great store of wine. As soon as they had taken their repast, Gerismond, desirous to hear what hard fortune drave them into those bitter extremes, requested Rosader to discourse, if it were not any way prejudicial unto him, the cause of his travel. Rosader, desirous any way to satisfy the courtesy of his favourable host, first beginning his exordium[1] with a volley of sighs, and a few lukewarm tears, prosecuted[2] his discourse, and told him from point to point all his fortunes: how he was the youngest son of Sir John of Bordeaux, his name Rosader, how his brother sundry times had wronged him, and lastly how, for beating the sheriff and hurting his men, he fled.

'And this old man,' quoth he, 'whom I so much love and honour, is surnamed Adam Spencer, an old servant of my father's, and one, that for his love, never failed me in all my misfortunes.'

When Gerismond heard this, he fell on the neck of Rosader, and next discoursing unto him how he was Gerismond their lawful king exiled by Torismond, what familiarity had ever been betwixt his father, Sir John of Bordeaux, and him, how faithful a subject he lived, and how honourable he died, promising, for his sake, to give both him and his friend such courteous entertainment as his present estate could minister, and upon this made him one of his foresters. Rosader seeing it was the king, craved pardon for his boldness, in that he did not do him due reverence, and humbly gave him thanks for his favourable courtesy. Gerismond, not satisfied yet with news, began to inquire if he had been lately in the court of Torismond, and whether he had seen his daughter Rosalynde or no? At this Rosader fetched a deep sigh, and shedding many tears, could not answer: yet at last, gathering his spirits together, he revealed unto the king, how Rosalynde was banished, and how there was such a sympathy of affections between Alinda and her, that she chose rather to be partaker of her exile, than to part fellowship; whereupon the unnatural king banished them both: 'and now they are wandered none knows whither, neither could any learn since their departure, the place of their abode.' This news drave the king into a great melancholy, that presently he arose from all the company, and went into his privy chamber, so secret as the harbour of the woods would allow him. The company was all dashed at these tid-

1. **exordium:** the first part of a formal speech of persuasion.
2. **prosecuted:** continued.

ings, and Rosader and Adam Spencer, having such opportunity, went to take their rest. Where we leave them, and return again to Torismond.

The flight of Rosader came to the ears of Torismond, who hearing that Saladyne was sole heir of the lands of Sir John of Bordeaux, desirous to possess such fair revenues, found just occasion to quarrel with Saladyne about the wrongs he proffered to his brother: and therefore, dispatching a herehault,[3] he sent for Saladyne in all post-haste. Who marvelling what the matter should be, began to examine his own conscience, wherein he had offended his highness; but emboldened with his innocence, he boldly went with the here-hault unto the court; where, as soon as he came, he was not admitted into the presence of the king, but presently sent to prison. This greatly amazed Saladyne, chiefly in that the jailer had a straight[4] charge over him, to see that he should be close prisoner. Many passionate thoughts came in his head, till at last he began to fall into consideration of his former follies, and to meditate with himself. Leaning his head on his hand, and his elbow on his knee, full of sorrow, grief and disquieted passions, he resolved into these terms:

'Unhappy Saladyne! whom folly hath led to these misfortunes, and wanton desires wrapped within the labyrinth of these calamities! Are not the heavens doomers of men's deeds; and holds not God a balance in his fist, to reward with favour, and revenge with justice? O Saladyne, the faults of thy youth, as they were fond, so were they foul, and not only discovering little nurture, but blemishing the excellence of nature. Whelps[5] of one litter are ever most loving, and brothers that are sons of one father should live in friendship without jar. O Saladyne, so it should be; but thou hast with the deer fed against the wind, with the crab strove against the stream, and sought to pervert nature by unkindness. Rosader's wrongs, the wrongs of Rosader, Saladyne, cries for revenge; his youth pleads to God to inflict some penance upon thee; his virtues are pleas that enforce writs of displeasure to cross thee: thou hast highly abused thy kind and natural brother, and the heavens cannot spare to quite thee with punishment. There is no sting to the worm of conscience, no hell to a mind touched with guilt. Every wrong I offered him, called now to remembrance, wringeth a drop of blood from my heart, every bad look, every frown pincheth me at the quick, and says, "Saladyne thou hast sinned against Rosader." Be penitent, and assign thyself some penance to discover thy sorrow, and pacify his wrath.'

3. **herehault:** herald, messenger.
4. **straight:** strict.
5. **Whelps:** offspring.

In the depth of his passion, he was sent for to the king, who with a look that threatened death entertained him, and demanded of him where his brother was. Saladyne made answer, that upon some riot made against the sheriff of the shire, he was fled from Bordeaux, but he knew not whither.

'Nay, villain,' quoth he, 'I have heard of the wrongs thou hast proffered thy brother since the death of thy father, and by thy means have I lost a most brave and resolute chevalier. Therefore, in justice to punish thee, I spare thy life for thy father's sake, but banish thee for ever from the court and country of France; and see thy departure be within ten days, else trust me thou shalt lose thy head.'

And with that the king flew away in a rage, and left poor Saladyne greatly perplexed; who grieving at his exile, yet determined to bear it with patience, and in penance of his former follies to travel abroad in every coast till he had found out his brother Rosader. With whom now I begin.

Rosader, being thus preferred to the place of a forester by Gerismond, rooted out the remembrance of his brother's unkindness by continual exercise, traversing the groves and wild forests, partly to hear the melody of the sweet birds which recorded,[6] and partly to show his diligent endeavour in his master's behalf. Yet whatsoever he did, or howsoever he walked, the lively image of Rosalynde remained in memory: on her sweet perfections he fed his thoughts, proving himself like the eagle a true-born bird, since as the one is known by beholding the sun, so was he by regarding excellent beauty. One day among the rest, finding a fit opportunity and place convenient, desirous to discover his woes to the woods, he engraved with his knife on the bark of a myrtle tree, this pretty estimate of his mistress' perfection:

Sonetto

Of all chaste birds the Phoenix doth excell,
Of all strong beasts the lion bears the bell,
Of all sweet flowers the rose doth sweetest smell,
Of all fair maids my Rosalynde is fairest.

Of all pure metals gold is only purest,
Of all high trees the pine hath highest crest,
Of all soft sweets I like my mistress' breast,
Of all chaste thoughts my mistress' thoughts are rarest.

Of all proud birds the eagle pleaseth Jove,
Of pretty fowls kind Venus likes the dove,

6. **recorded:** sang.

Of trees Minerva doth the olive love,[7]
Of all sweet nymphs I honour Rosalynde.

Of all her gifts her wisdom pleaseth most,
Of all her graces virtue she doth boast:
For all these gifts my life and joy is lost,
If Rosalynde prove cruel and unkind.

In these and such like passions Rosader did every day eternize the name of his Rosalynde; and this day especially when Aliena and Ganymede, enforced by the heat of the sun to seek for shelter, by good fortune arrived in that place, where this amorous forester registered his melancholy passions. They saw the sudden change of his looks, his folded arms, his passionate sighs: they heard him often abruptly call on Rosalynde, who, poor soul, was as hotly burned as himself, but that she shrouded her pains in the cinders of honourable modesty. Whereupon, guessing him to be in love, and according to the nature of their sex being pitiful in that behalf, they suddenly brake off his melancholy by their approach, and Ganymede shook him out of his dumps thus:

'What news, forester? hast thou wounded some deer, and lost him in the fall?[8] Care not man for so small a loss: thy fees was but the skin, the shoulder, and the horns: 'tis hunter's luck to aim fair and miss; and a woodman's fortune to strike and yet go without the game.'

'Thou art beyond the mark, Ganymede,' quoth Aliena: 'his passions are greater, and his sighs discovers more loss: perhaps in traversing these thickets, he hath seen some beautiful nymph, and is grown amorous.'

'It may be so,' quoth Ganymede, 'for here he hath newly engraven some sonnet: come, and see the discourse of the forester's poems.'

Reading the sonnet over, and hearing him name Rosalynde, Aliena looked on Ganymede and laughed, and Ganymede looking back on the forester, and seeing it was Rosader, blushed; yet thinking to shroud all under her page's apparel, she boldly returned to Rosader, and began thus:

'I pray thee tell me, forester, what is this Rosalynde for whom thou pinest away in such passions? Is she some nymph that waits upon Diana's train, whose chastity thou hast deciphered in such epithets? Or is she some shepherdess that haunts these plains whose beauty hath so bewitched thy fancy, whose name thou shadowest in covert under the figure of Rosalynde, as Ovid did Julia

---

7. **eagle . . . love:** The **eagle, dove,** and **olive** tree were associated with **Jove** (Jupiter, king of the gods), **Venus,** and **Minerva** (goddess of wisdom), respectively.
8. **in the fall:** where he actually collapsed as a result of his injuries.

under the name of Corinna?[9] Or say me forsooth, is it that Rosalynde, of whom we shepherds have heard talk, she, forester, that is the daughter of Gerismond, that once was king, and now an outlaw in the forest of Arden?'

At this Rosader fetched a deep sigh, and said:

'It is she, O gentle swain, it is she; that saint it is whom I serve, that goddess at whose shrine I do bend all my devotions; the most fairest of all fairs, the phoenix of all that sex, and the purity of all earthly perfection.'

'And why, gentle forester, if she be so beautiful, and thou so amorous, is there such a disagreement in thy thoughts? Happily[1] she resembleth the rose, that is sweet but full of prickles? or the serpent Regius[2] that hath scales as glorious as the sun and a breath as infectious as the Aconitum[3] is deadly? So thy Rosalynde may be most amiable and yet unkind; full of favour and yet froward, coy without wit, and disdainful without reason.'

'O Shepherd,' quoth Rosader, 'knewest thou her personage, graced with the excellence of all perfection, being a harbour wherein the graces shroud their virtues, thou wouldest not breathe out such blasphemy against the beauteous Rosalynde. She is a diamond, bright but not hard, yet of most chaste operation; a pearl so orient, that it can be stained with no blemish; a rose without prickles, and a princess absolute as well in beauty as in virtue. But I, unhappy I, have let mine eye soar with the eagle against so bright a sun that I am quite blind: I have with Apollo enamoured myself of a Daphne, not, as she, disdainful, but far more chaste than Daphne: I have with Ixion laid my love on Juno, and shall, I fear, embrace nought but a cloud.[4] Ah, Shepherd, I have reached at a star: my desires have mounted above my degree, and my thoughts above my fortunes. I being a peasant, have ventured to gaze on a princess, whose honours are too high to vouchsafe[5] such base loves.'

'Why, forester,' quoth Ganymede, 'comfort thyself; be blithe and frolic man. Love souseth[6] as low as she soareth high: Cupid shoots at a rag as soon as at a robe; and Venus' eye that was so curious, sparkled favour on pole-footed Vulcan.[7] Fear not, man, women's looks are not

---

9. **Ovid . . . Corinna:** The classical Roman love poet **Ovid** wrote about his love **Julia** under the name of **Corinna.**
1. **Happily:** perhaps.
2. **Regius:** python.
3. **Aconitum:** flowering plant with a poisonous root.
4. **Apollo . . . cloud: Apollo** tried to seduce **Daphne** but she was turned into a laurel tree; **Ixion** tried to seduce **Juno,** queen of the gods, but embraced a **cloud** instead.
5. **vouchsafe:** bestow.
6. **souseth:** plunges.
7. **Venus' . . . Vulcan:** Venus, for all her fastidiousness, favored the club-footed **Vulcan,** god of fire.

tied to dignity's feathers, nor make they curious esteem where the stone is found, but what is the virtue. Fear not, forester; faint heart never won fair lady. But where lives Rosalynde now? at the court?'

'Oh no,' quoth Rosader, 'she lives I know not where, and that is my sorrow; banished by Torismond, and that is my hell: for might I but find her sacred personage, and plead before the bar of her pity the plaint of my passions, hope tells me she would grace me with some favour, and that would suffice as a recompense of all my former miseries.'

'Much have I heard of thy mistress' excellence, and I know, forester, thou canst describe her at the full, as one that hast surveyed all her parts with a curious eye; then do me that favour, to tell me what her perfections be.'

'That I will,' quoth Rosader, 'for I glory to make all ears wonder at my mistress' excellence.'

And with that he pulled a paper forth his bosom, wherein he read this:

Rosalynde's Description

Like to the clear in highest sphere
Where all imperial glory shines,
Of selfsame colour is her hair,
Whether unfolded or in twines:
     Heigh ho, fair Rosalynde.
Her eyes are sapphires set in snow,
Refining heaven by every wink:
The gods do fear whenas they glow,
And I do tremble when I think:
     Heigh ho, would she were mine.

Her cheeks are like the blushing cloud
That beautifies Aurora's face,
Or like the silver crimson shroud
That Phoebus' smiling looks doth grace:
     Heigh ho, fair Rosalynde.
Her lips are like two budded roses,
Whom ranks of lilies neighbour nigh,
Within which bounds she balm encloses,
Apt to entice a deity:
     Heigh ho, would she were mine,

Her neck, like to a stately tower
Where love himself imprisoned lies,
To watch for glances every hour

From her divine and sacred eyes:
          Heigh ho, fair Rosalynde.
Her paps[8] are centres of delight,
Her paps are orbs of heavenly frame,
Where nature moulds the dew of light,
To feed perfection with the same:
          Heigh ho, would she were mine.

With orient pearl, with ruby red,
With marble white, with sapphire blue,
Her body every way is fed,
Yet soft in touch, and sweet in view:
          Heigh ho, fair Rosalynde.
Nature herself her shape admires,
The gods are wounded in her sight,
And Love forsakes his heavenly fires
And at her eyes his brand doth light:
          Heigh ho, would she were mine.

Then muse not, nymphs, though I bemoan
The absence of fair Rosalynde,
Since for her fair there is fairer none,
Nor for her virtues so divine:
          Heigh ho, fair Rosalynde.
    Heigh ho, my heart, would God that she were mine!
                    Periit, quia deperibat.[9]

'Believe me,' quoth Ganymede, 'either the forester is an exquisite painter, or Rosalynde far above wonder; so it makes me blush to hear how women should be so excellent, and pages so unperfect.'

Rosader beholding her earnestly, answered thus:

'Truly, gentle page, thou hast cause to complain thee wert thou the substance, but resembling the shadow content thyself; for it is excellence enough to be like the excellence of nature.'

'He hath answered you, Ganymede,' quoth Aliena, 'it is enough for pages to wait on beautiful ladies, and not to be beautiful themselves.'

'O mistress,' quoth Ganymede, 'hold you your peace, for you are partial. Who knows not, but that all women have desire to tie sovereignty to their petticoats, and ascribe beauty to themselves, where, if boys might put on their garments, perhaps they would prove as comely; if not as comely, it may be more courteous. But tell me, forester,' and with that she turned to Rosader, 'under whom maintainest thou thy walk?'

---

8. **paps:** breasts.
9. He perished because he was desperately in love (Latin).

'Gentle swain, under the king of outlaws,' said he, 'the unfortunate Gerismond, who having lost his kingdom, crowneth his thoughts with content, accounting it better to govern among poor men in peace, than great men in danger.'

'But hast thou not,' said she, 'having so melancholy opportunities as this forest affordeth thee, written more sonnets in commendations of thy mistress?'

'I have, gentle swain,' quoth he, 'but they be not about me. To-morrow by dawn of day, if your flocks feed in these pastures, I will bring them you, wherein you shall read my passions whilst I feel them, judge my patience when you read it: till when I bid farewell.' So giving both Ganymede and Aliena a gentle good-night, he resorted to his lodge, leaving Aliena and Ganymede to their prittle-prattle.

'So Ganymede,' said Aliena, the forester being gone, 'you are mightily beloved; men make ditties in your praise, spend sighs for your sake, make an idol of your beauty. Believe me, it grieves me not a little to see the poor man so pensive, and you so pitiless.'

'All, Aliena,' quoth she, 'be not peremptory in your judgments. I hear Rosalynde praised as I am Ganymede, but were I Rosalynde, I could answer the forester: if he mourn for love, there are medicines for love: Rosalynde cannot be fair and unkind. And so, madam, you see it is time to fold our flocks, or else Corydon will frown and say you will never prove good housewife.'

With that they put their sheep into the cotes, and went home to her friend Corydon's cottage, Aliena as merry as might be that she was thus in the company of her Rosalynde; but she, poor soul, that had love her lodestar, and her thoughts set on fire with the flame of fancy, could take no rest, but being alone began to consider what passionate penance poor Rosader was enjoined to by love and fortune, that at last she fell into this humour with herself:

'Ah, Rosalynde, how the Fates have set down in their synod[1] to make thee unhappy: for when Fortune hath done her worst, then Love comes in to begin a new tragedy: she seeks to lodge her son in thine eyes, and to kindle her fires in thy bosom. Beware, fond girl, he is an unruly guest to harbour; for cutting in by entreats, he will not be thrust out by force, and her fires are fed with such fuel, as no water is able to quench. Seest thou not how Venus seeks to wrap thee in her labyrinth, wherein is pleasure at the entrance, but within, sorrows, cares, and discontent? She is a Siren, stop thine ears to her melody; she is a basilisk,[2] shut thy eyes and gaze not at her lest thou perish. Thou art now placed in the country content, where are heavenly thoughts and mean desires: in those lawns where thy

---

1. **set . . . synod**: decided in their council meeting.
2. **basilisk**: mythical reptile whose glance could kill anyone who looked at it.

flocks feed Diana haunts: be as her nymphs chaste, and enemy to
love, for there is no greater honour to a maid, than to account of
fancy as a mortal foe to their sex. Daphne, that bonny wench, was
not turned into a bay tree, as the poets feign: but for her chastity
her fame was immortal, resembling the laurel that is ever green.
Follow thou her steps, Rosalynde, and the rather, for that thou art
an exile, and banished from the court; whose distress, and it is
appeased with patience, so it would be renewed with amorous passions. Have mind on thy forepassed fortunes; fear the worst, and
entangle not thyself with present fancies, lest loving in haste, thou
repent thee at leisure. Ah, but yet, Rosalynde, it is Rosader that
courts thee; one who as he is beautiful, so he is virtuous, and harboureth in his mind as many good qualities as his face is shadowed
with gracious favours; and therefore, Rosalynde, stoop to love, lest,
being either too coy or too cruel, Venus wax wroth,[3] and plague thee
with the reward of disdain.'

Rosalynde, thus passionate, was wakened from her dumps by
Aliena, who said it was time to go to bed. Corydon swore that was
true, for Charles' Wain[4] was risen in the north. Whereupon each
taking leave of other, went to their rest, all but the poor Rosalynde,
who was so full of passions, that she could not possess any content.
Well, leaving her to her broken slumbers, expect what was performed by them the next morning.

The sun was no sooner stepped from the bed of Aurora, but Aliena was wakened by Ganymede, who, restless all night, had tossed
in her passions, saying it was then time to go to the field to unfold
their sheep. Aliena, that spied where the hare was by the hounds,
and could see day at a little hole,[5] thought to be pleasant with her
Ganymede, and therefore replied thus:

'What, wanton! the sun is but new up, and as yet Iris' riches lie
folded in the bosom of Flora: Phoebus hath not dried up the pearled
dew, and so long Corydon hath taught me, it is not fit to lead the
sheep abroad, lest, the dew being unwholesome, they get the rot:
but now see I the old proverb true, he is in haste whom the devil
drives, and where love pricks forward, there is no worse death than
delay. Ah, my good page, is there fancy in thine eye, and passions in
thy heart? What, hast thou wrapt love in thy looks, and set all thy
thoughts on fire by affection? I tell thee, it is a flame as hard to be
quenched as that of Aetna.[6] But nature must have her course: wom-
en's eyes have faculty attractive like the jet, and retentive like the
diamond: they dally in the delight of fair objects, till gazing on the

---

3. **wax wroth:** become angry.
4. **Charles' Wain:** the big dipper constellation.
5. **spied . . . hole:** "saw the light," i.e., could guess Rosalind's passion by her restlessness.
6. **Aetna:** active volcano in Sicily.

panther's beautiful skin, repenting experience tell them he hath a devouring paunch.'

'Come on,' quoth Ganymede, 'this sermon of yours is but a subtlety to lie still a-bed, because either you think the morning cold, or else I being gone, you would steal a nap: this shift carries no palm,[7] and therefore up and away. And for Love, let me alone; I'll whip him away with nettles, and set disdain as a charm to withstand his forces: and therefore look you to yourself; be not too bold, for Venus can make you bend, nor too coy, for Cupid hath a piercing dart, that will make you cry *Peccavi*.'[8]

'And that is it,' quoth Aliena, 'that hath raised you so early this morning.' And with that she slipped on her petticoat, and start up; and as soon as she had made her ready, and taken her breakfast, away go these two with their bag and bottles to the field, in more pleasant content of mind than ever they were in the court of Torismond.

They came no sooner nigh the folds, but they might see where their discontented forester was walking in his melancholy. As soon as Aliena saw him, she smiled and said to Ganymede:

'Wipe your eyes, sweeting, for yonder is your sweetheart this morning in deep prayers, no doubt, to Venus, that she may make you as pitiful as he is passionate. Come on, Ganymede, I pray thee, let's have a little sport with him.'

'Content,' quoth Ganymede, and with that, to waken him out of his deep *memento*, he began thus:

'Forester, good fortune to thy thoughts, and ease to thy passions. What makes you so early abroad this morn? in contemplation, no doubt, of your Rosalynde. Take heed, forester; step not too far, the ford may be deep, and you slip over the shoes.[9] I tell thee, flies have their spleen, the ants choler, the least hairs shadows, and the smallest loves great desires. 'Tis good, forester, to love, but not to overlove, lest in loving her that likes not thee, thou fold thyself in an endless labyrinth.'

Rosader, seeing the fair shepherdess and her pretty swain in whose company he felt the greatest ease of his care, he returned them a salute on this manner:

'Gentle shepherds, all hail, and as healthful be your flocks as you happy in content. Love is restless, and my bed is but the cell of my bane, in that there I find busy thoughts and broken slumbers: here, although everywhere passionate, yet I brook love with more patience, in that every object feeds mine eye with variety of fancies. When I

---

7. **shift . . . palm:** trick will not succeed.
8. *Peccavi:* I have sinned (Latin).
9. **slip . . . shoes:** get your feet wet.

look on Flora's beauteous tapestry, checked with the pride of all her treasure, I call to mind the fair face of Rosalynde, whose heavenly hue exceeds the rose and the lily in their highest excellence: the brightness of Phoebus' shine puts me in mind to think of the sparkling flames that flew from her eyes, and set my heart first on fire: the sweet harmony of the birds, puts me in remembrance of the rare melody of her voice, which like the Siren enchanteth the ears of the hearer. Thus in contemplation I salve my sorrows, with applying the perfection of every object to the excellence of her qualities.'

'She is much beholding unto you,' quoth Aliena, 'and so much, that I have oft wished with myself, that if I should ever prove as amorous as Oenone, I might find as faithful a Paris[1] as yourself.'

'How say you by this item, forester?' quoth Ganymede, 'the fair shepherdess favours you, who is mistress of so many flocks. Leave off, man, the supposition of Rosalynde's love, whenas watching at her you rove beyond the moon, and cast your looks upon my mistress, who no doubt is as fair though not so royal; one bird in the hand is worth two in the wood: better possess the love of Aliena than catch furiously at the shadow of Rosalynde.'

'I'll tell thee boy,' quoth Rosader, 'so is my fancy fixed on my Rosalynde, that were thy mistress as fair as Leda or Danaë, whom Jove courted in transformed shapes,[2] mine eyes would not vouch to entertain their beauties; and so hath love locked me in her perfections, that I had rather only contemplate in her beauties, than absolutely possess the excellence of any other.'

'Venus is to blame, forester, if having so true a servant of you, she reward you not with Rosalynde, if Rosalynde were more fairer than herself. But leaving this prattle, now I'll put you in mind of your promise about those sonnets, which you said were at home in your lodge.'

'I have them about me,' quoth Rosader, 'let us sit down, and then you shall hear what a poetical fury love will infuse into a man.' With that they sate down upon a green bank, shadowed with fig trees, and Rosader, fetching a deep sigh, read them this sonnet:

Rosader's Sonnet

> In sorrow's cell I laid me down to sleep,
>   But waking woes were jealous of mine eyes,
> They made them watch, and bend themselves to weep,
>   But weeping tears their want could not suffice:

1. **Oenone . . . Paris: Oenone** was the first wife of Trojan **Paris**; he abandoned her for Helen of Troy.
2. **Leda . . . shapes:** Jove raped **Leda** in the form of a swan and **Danaë** in the form of a shower of gold.

Yet since for her they wept who guides my heart,
They weeping smile, and triumph in their smart.[3]

Of these my tears a fountain fiercely springs,
    Where Venus bains[4] herself incensed with love,
Where Cupid bowseth[5] his fair feathered wings;
    But I behold what pains I must approve.
        Care drinks it dry; but when on her I think,
        Love makes me weep it full unto the brink.

Meanwhile my sighs yield truce unto my tears,
    By them the winds increased and fiercely blow:
Yet when I sigh the flame more plain appears,
    And by their force with greater power doth glow:
        Amid these pains, all phoenix-like I thrive
        Since love, that yields me death, may life revive.
                            Rosader en esperance.[6]

'Now, surely, forester,' quoth Aliena, 'when thou madest this sonnet, thou wert in some amorous quandary, neither too fearful as
despairing of thy mistress' favours, nor too gleesome[7] as hoping in
thy fortunes.'

'I can smile,' quoth Ganymede, 'at the sonettos, canzones, madrigals, rounds and roundelays, that these pensive patients pour out
when their eyes are more full of wantonness, than their hearts of
passions. Then, as the fishers put the sweetest bait to the fairest
fish, so these Ovidians, holding *amo* in their tongues, when their
thoughts come at haphazard, write that they be rapt in an endless
labyrinth of sorrow, when walking in the large lease of liberty, they
only have their humours in their inkpot. If they find women so fond,
that they will with such painted lures come to their lust, then they
triumph till they be full-gorged with pleasures; and then fly they
away, like ramage kites,[8] to their own content, leaving the tame fool,
their mistress, full of fancy, yet without even a feather. If they miss,
as dealing with some wary wanton, that wants not such a one as
themselves, but spies their subtlety, they end their amours with a
few feigned sighs; and so their excuse is, their mistress is cruel, and
they smother passions with patience. Such, gentle forester, we may
deem you to be, that rather pass away the time here in these woods
with writing amorets,[9] than to be deeply enamoured, as you say, of

3. **smart:** pain.
4. **bains:** bathes.
5. **bowseth:** drenches.
6. ***en esperance:*** in hope (French).
7. **gleesome:** gleeful.
8. **ramage kites:** unruly birds of prey.
9. **amorets:** love sonnets (literally, "little loves").

your Rosalynde. If you be such a one, then I pray God, when you think your fortunes at the highest, and your desires to be most excellent, then that you may with Ixion embrace Juno in a cloud, and have nothing but a marble mistress to release your martyrdom; but if you be true and trusty, eye-pained and heart-sick, then accursed be Rosalynde if she prove cruel: for, forester, I flatter not, thou art worthy of as fair as she.' Aliena, spying the storm by the wind, smiled to see how Ganymede flew to the fist without any call;[1] but Rosader, who took him flat for a shepherd's swain, made him this answer:

'Trust me, swain,' quoth Rosader, 'but my canzon was written in no such humour; for mine eye and my heart are relatives, the one drawing fancy by sight, the other entertaining her by sorrow. If thou sawest my Rosaylnde, with what beauties nature hath favoured her, with what perfection the heavens hath graced her, with what qualities the gods have endued her, then wouldst thou say, there is none so fickle that could be fleeting unto her. If she had been Aeneas' Dido, had Venus and Juno both scolded him from Carthage, yet her excellence, despite of them, would have detained him at Tyre.[2] If Phyllis had been as beauteous, or Ariadne as virtuous, or both as honourable and excellent as she, neither had the filbert tree sorrowed in the death of despairing Phyllis, nor the stars been graced with Ariadne, but Demophoon and Theseus had been trusty to their paragons.[3] I will tell thee, swain, if with a deep insight thou couldst pierce into the secret of my loves, and see what deep impressions of her idea affection hath made in my heart, then wouldst thou confess I were passing passionate, and no less endued with admirable patience.'

'Why,' quoth Aliena, 'needs there patience in love?'

'Or else in nothing,' quoth Rosader; 'for it is a restless sore that hath no ease, a canker that still frets, a disease that taketh away all hope of sleep. If then so many sorrows, sudden joys, momentary pleasures, continual fears, daily griefs, and nightly woes be found in love, then is not he to be accounted patient that smothers all these passions with silence?'

'Thou speaker by experience,' quoth Ganymede, 'and therefore we hold all thy words for axioms. But is love such a lingering malady?'

---

1. **flew . . . call:** responded without being prompted (from falconry).
2. **If . . . Tyre:** If **Dido** had been as attractive as Rosalynde, Aeneas would not only not have forsaken her in Carthage, prompted by Venus and Juno to move onward and found Rome, but he would have been drawn to her in her original home of **Tyre**.
3. **If . . . paragons:** If **Phyllis** and **Ariadne** had been as attractive as Rosalynde, they would never have been forsaken by their mates **Demophoon** and **Theseus**. **Phyllis** would not have hanged herself on a hazelnut tree and **Ariadne** would not have died and been transformed into a star.

'It is,' quoth he, 'either extreme or mean, according to the mind of the party that entertains it; for, as the weeds grow longer untouched than the pretty flowers, and the flint lies safe in the quarry when the emerald is suffering the lapidary's tool, so mean men are freed from Venus' injuries, when kings are environed[4] with a labyrinth of her cares. The whiter the lawn is, the deeper is the mole; the more purer the chrysolite, the sooner stained; and such as have their hearts full of honour, have their loves full of the greatest sorrows. But in whomsoever,' quoth Rosader, 'he fixeth his dart, he never leaveth to assault[5] him, till either he hath won him to folly or fancy; for as the moon never goes without the star Lunisequa,[6] so a lover never goeth without the unrest of his thoughts. For proof you shall hear another fancy of my making.'

'Now do, gentle forester,' quoth Ganymede; and with that he read over this sonetto:

Rosader's second Sonetto

Turn I my looks unto the skies,
Love with his arrows wounds mine eyes;
If so I gaze upon the ground,
Love then in every flower is found.
Search I the shade to fly my pain,
He meets me in the shade again;
Wend I to walk in secret grove,
Even there I meet with sacred Love.
If so I bain me in the spring,
Even on the brink I hear him sing·
If so I meditate alone,
He will be partner of my moan.
If so I mourn he weeps with me,
And where I am there will he be.
Whenas I talk of Rosalynde
The god from coyness waxeth kind,
And seems in selfsame flames to fry
Because he loves as well as I.
Sweet Rosalynde, for pity rue;
For why, than Love I am more true:
He, if he speed, will quickly fly,
But in thy love I live and die.

---

4. **environed**: surrounded.
5. **leaveth to assault**: stops assaulting.
6. **Lunisequa**: star believed to attend on the moon.

'How like you this sonnet?' quoth Rosader.

'Marry,' quoth Ganymede, 'for the pen well, for the passion ill; for as I praise the one, I pity the other, in that thou shouldst hunt after a cloud, and love either without reward or regard.'

''Tis not her frowardness,' quoth Rosader, 'but my hard fortunes, whose destinies have crossed me with her absence; for did she feel my loves, she would not let me linger in these sorrows. Women, as they are fair, so they respect faith, and estimate more, if they be honourable, the will than the wealth, having loyalty the object whereat they aim their fancies. But leaving off these interparleys,[7] you shall hear my last sonetto, and then you have heard all my poetry.' And with that he sighed out this:

Rosader's Third Sonnet

Of virtuous love myself may boast alone,
   Since no suspect my service may attaint:[8]
For perfect fair she is the only one,
   Whom I esteem for my beloved saint.
     Thus, for my faith I only bear the bell,
     And for her fair she only doth excel.
Then let fond Petrarch shroud his Laura's praise,
   And Tasso cease to publish his affect,[9]
Since mine the faith confirmed at all assays,
   And hers the fair, which all men do respect.
     My lines her fair, her fair my faith assures;
     Thus I by love, and love by me endures.

'Thus,' quoth Rosader, 'here is an end of my poems, but for all this no release of my passions; so that I resemble him that in the depth of his distress hath none but the echo to answer him.'

Ganymede, pitying her Rosader, thinking to drive him out of this amorous melancholy, said that now the sun was in his meridional heat and that it was high noon, 'therefore we shepherds say, 'tis time to go to dinner; for the sun and our stomachs are shepherds' dials.[1] Therefore, forester, if thou wilt take such fare as comes out of our homely scrips,[2] welcome shall answer whatsoever thou wantest in delicates.'

---

7. **interparleys:** conversation.
8. **attaint:** condemn.
9. **let . . . affect: Petrarch** (the famous Italian sonneteer) may as well stop praising his beloved **Laura**, and **Tasso** (his follower, also a famous poet) stop publishing his passions.
1. **dials:** clocks.
2. **scrips:** packs.

Aliena took the entertainment by the end, and told Rosader he should be her guest. He thanked them heartily, and sate with them down to dinner, where they had such cates as country state did allow them, sauced with such content, and such sweet prattle, as it seemed far more sweet than all their courtly junkets.[3]

As soon as they had taken their repast, Rosader, giving them thanks for his good cheer, would have been gone; but Ganymede, that was loath to let him pass out of her presence, began thus:

'Nay, forester,' quoth he, 'if thy business be not the greater, seeing thou sayest thou art so deeply in love, let me see how thou canst woo: I will represent Rosalynde, and thou shalt be as thou art, Rosader. See in some amorous eclogue,[4] how if Rosalynde were present, how thou couldst court her; and while we sing of love, Aliena shall tune her pipe and play us melody.'

'Content,' quoth Rosader, and Aliena, she, to show her willingness, drew forth a recorder, and began to wind[5] it. Then the loving forester began thus:

The wooing Eclogue betwixt Rosalynde and Rosader

ROSADER

I pray thee, nymph, by all the working words,
By all the tears and sighs that lovers know,
Or what or thoughts or faltering tongue affords,
I crave for mine in ripping up my woe.
Sweet Rosalynde, my love—would God, my love—
My life—would God, my life—aye, pity me!
Thy lips are kind, and humble like the dove,
And but with beauty pity will not be.
Look on mine eyes, made red with rueful tears,
From whence the rain of true remorse descendeth,
All pale in looks am I though young in years,
And nought but love or death my days befriendeth.
Oh let no stormy rigour knit thy brows,
Which love appointed for his mercy seat:
The tallest tree by Boreas'[6] breath it bows;
The iron yields with hammer, and to heat.
    O Rosalynde, then be thou pitiful,
    For Rosalynde is only beautiful.

---

3. **junkets:** sweet desserts.
4. **eclogue:** pastoral dialogue.
5. **wind:** tune.
6. **Boreas':** the North Wind's.

ROSALYNDE

Love's wantons arm their trait'rous suits with tears,
With vows, with oaths, with looks, with showers of gold;
But when the fruit of their affects appears,
The simple heart by subtle sleights[7] is sold.
Thus sucks the yielding ear the poisoned bait,
Thus feeds the heart upon his endless harms,
Thus glut the thoughts themselves on self-deceit,
Thus blind the eyes their sight by subtle charms.
The lovely looks, the sighs that storm so sore,
The dew of deep-dissembled doubleness,
These may attempt, but are of power no more
Where beauty leans to wit and soothfastness.
    O Rosader, then be thou wittiful,
    For Rosalynde scorns foolish pitiful.

ROSADER

I pray thee, Rosalynde, by those sweet eyes
That stain the sun in shine, the morn in clear,
By those sweet cheeks where Love encampèd lies
To kiss the roses of the springing year.
I tempt thee, Rosalynde, by ruthful plaints,
Not seasoned with deceit or fraudful guile,
But firm in pain, far more than tongue depaints,[8]
Sweet nymph, be kind, and grace me with a smile.
So may the heavens preserve from hurtful food
Thy harmless flocks; so may the summer yield
The pride of all her riches and her good,
To fat thy sheep, the citizens of field.
Oh, leave to arm thy lovely brows with scorn:
The birds their beak, the lion hath his tail,
And lovers nought but sighs and bitter mourn,
The spotless fort of fancy to assail.
    O Rosalynde, then be thou pitiful,
    For Rosalynde is only beautiful.

ROSALYNDE

The hardened steel by fire is brought in frame.[9]

ROSADER

And Rosalynde, my love, than any wool more softer;
And shall not sighs her tender heart inflame?

---

7. **sleights:** tricks.
8. **depaints:** expresses.
9. **in frame:** into shape.

ROSALYNDE

Were lovers true, maids would believe them ofter.

ROSADER

Truth, and regard, and honour, guide my love.

ROSALYNDE

Fain would I trust, but yet I dare not try.

ROSADER

Oh pity me, sweet nymph, and do but prove.[1]

ROSALYNDE

I would resist, but yet I know not why.

ROSADER

O Rosalynde, be *kind*, for times will change,
Thy looks ay nill[2] be fair as now they be;
Thine age from beauty may thy looks estrange:
Ah, yield in time, sweet nymph, and pity me.

ROSALYNDE

O Rasalynde, thou must be pitiful,
For Rosader is young and beautiful.

ROSADER

Oh, gain more great than kingdoms or a crown!

ROSALYNDE

Oh, trust betrayed if Rosader abuse me.

ROSADER

First let the heavens conspire to pull me down
And heaven and earth as abject quite refuse me.
Let sorrows stream about my hateful bower,
And restless horror hatch within my breast:
Let beauty's eye afflict me with a lour,
Let deep despair pursue me without rest,

---

1. **prove:** discover the genuineness (of my passion).
2. **ay nill:** will not always.

Ere Rosalynde my loyalty disprove,
Ere Rosalynde accuse me for unkind.

RASALYNDE

Then Rosalynde will grace thee with her love,
Then Rosalynde will have thee still in mind.

ROSADER

Then let me triumph more than Tithon's dear,[3]
Since Rosalynde will Rosader respect:
Then let my face exile his sorry cheer,
And frolic in the comfort of affect;
And say that Rosalynde is only pitiful,
Since Rosalynde is only beautiful.

When thus they had finished their courting eclogue in such a familiar clause, Ganymede, as augur[4] of some good fortunes to light upon their affections, began to be thus pleasant: 'How now, forester, have I not fitted your turn? have I not played the woman handsomely, and showed myself as coy in grants as courteous in desires, and been as full of suspicion as men of flattery? and yet to salve all, jumped I not all up with the sweet union of love? Did not Rosalynde content her Rosader?'

The forester at this smiling, shook his head, and folding his arms made this merry reply: 'Truth, gentle swain, Rosader hath his Rosalynde; but as Ixion had Juno, who, thinking to possess a goddess, only embraced a cloud: in these imaginary fruitions of fancy I resemble the birds that fed themselves with Zeuxis' painted grapes; but they grew so lean with pecking at shadows, that they were glad, with Aesop's cock, to scrape for a barley cornel.[5] So fareth it with me, who to feed myself with the hope of my mistress's favours, sooth myself in thy suits, and only in conceit reap a wished-for content; but if my food be no better than such amorous dreams, Venus at the year's end shall find me but a lean lover. Yet do I take these follies for high fortunes, and hope these feigned affections do divine[6] some unfeigned end of ensuing fancies.'

'And thereupon,' quoth Aliena, 'I'll play the priest: from this day forth Ganymede shall call thee husband, and thou shall call Ganymede wife, and so we'll have a marriage.'

3. **Tithon's dear:** the goddess of dawn, beloved by Tithon, a prince of Troy.
4. **augur:** prophet.
5. **birds . . . cornel:** The painter Zeuxis created **grapes** so realistic that **birds** almost starved trying to eat them; eventually, like the hungry **cock** in **Aesop's** fable who found an inedible precious jewel, they were happy to settle for **barley** corn.
6. **divine:** predict.

'Content,' quoth Rosader, and laughed.

'Content,' quoth Ganymede, and changed as red as a rose: and so with a smile and a blush, they made up this jesting match, that after proved to a marriage in earnest, Rosader full little thinking he had wooed and won his Rosalynde.

But all was well; hope is a sweet string to harp on, and therefore let the forester awhile shape himself to his shadow, and tarry fortune's leisure, till she may make a metamorphosis fit for his purpose. I digress; and therefore to Aliena, who said, the wedding was not worth a pin, unless there were some cheer, nor that bargain well made that was not stricken up[7] with a cup of wine: and therefore she willed Ganymede to set out such cates as they had, and to draw out her bottle, charging the forester, as he had imagined his loves, so to conceit[8] these cates to be a most sumptuous banquet, and to take a mazer[9] of wine and to drink to his Rosalynde; which Rosader did, and so they passed away the day in many pleasant devices. Till at last Aliena perceived time would tarry no man, and that the sun waxed very low, ready to set, which made her shorten their amorous prattle, and end the banquet with a fresh carouse: which done, they all three arose, and Aliena broke off thus:

'Now, forester, Phoebus that all this while hath been partaker of our sports, seeing every woodman more fortunate in his loves than he in his fancies, seeing then hast won Rosalynde when he could not woo Daphne,[1] hides his head for shame and bids us adieu in a cloud. Our sheep, they poor wantons, wander towards their folds, as taught by nature their due times of rest, which tells us, forester, we must depart. Marry, though there were a marriage, yet I must carry this night the bride with me, and to-morrow morning if you meet us here, I'll promise to deliver you her as good a maid as I find her.'

'Content,' quoth Rosader, ''tis enough for me in the night to dream on love, that in the day am so fond to doat on love: and so till to-morrow you to your folds, and I will to my lodge.' And thus the forester and they parted.

He was no sooner gone, but Aliena and Ganymede went and folded their flocks, and taking up their hooks, their bags, and their bottles, hied homeward. By the way Aliena, to make the time seem short, began to prattle with Ganymede thus:

'I have heard them say, that what the fates forepoint, that fortune pricketh down with a period;[2] that the stars are sticklers in Venus'

---

7. **stricken up:** concluded.
8. **conceit:** imagine.
9. **mazer:** wooden goblet.
1. **he . . . Daphne:** Apollo (**Phoebus**) could not have his beloved **Daphne** because she was turned into a laurel tree.
2. **pricketh . . . period:** writes down specifying an end point.

court, and desire hangs at the heel of destiny: if it be so, then by all probable conjectures, this match will be a marriage: for if augurism be authentical, or the divines' dooms[3] principles, it cannot be but such a shadow portends the issue of a substance, for to that end did the gods force the conceit of this eclogue, that they might discover the ensuing consent of your affections: so that ere it be long, I hope, in earnest, to dance at your wedding.'

'Tush,' quoth Ganymede, 'all is not malt that is cast on the kiln:[4] there goes more words to a bargain than one: Love feels no footing in the air, and fancy holds it slippery harbour to nestle in the tongue: the match is not yet so surely made, but he may miss of his market; but if fortune be his friend, I will not be his foe: and so I pray you, gentle mistress Aliena, take it.'

'I take all things well,' quoth she, 'that is your content, and am glad Rosader is yours; for now I hope your thoughts will be at quiet; your eye that ever looked at love, will now lend a glance on your lambs, and then they will prove more buxom and you more blithe, for the eyes of the master feeds the cattle.'

As thus they were in chat, they spied old Corydon where he came plodding to meet them, who told them supper was ready, which news made them speed them home. Where we will leave them to the next morrow, and return to Saladyne.

All this while did poor Saladyne, banished from Bordeaux and the court of France by Torismond, wander up and down in the forest of Arden, thinking to get to Lyons, and so travel through Germany into Italy: but the forest being full of by-paths, and he unskilful of the country coast, slipped out of the way, and chanced up into the desert, not far from the place where Gerismond was, and his brother Rosader. Saladyne, weary with wandering up and down and hungry with long fasting, finding a little cave by the side of a thicket, eating such fruit as the forest did afford and contenting himself with such drink as nature had provided and thirst made delicate, after his repast he fell in a dead sleep. As thus he lay, a hungry lion came hunting down the edge of the grove for prey, and espying Saladyne began to seize upon him: but seeing he lay still without any motion, he left to touch him, for that lions hate to prey on dead carcases; and yet desirous to have some food, the lion lay down and watched to see if he would stir. While thus Saladyne slept secure, fortune that was careful of her champion began to smile, and brought it so to pass, that Rosader, having stricken a deer that but lightly hurt fled through the

---

3. **dooms:** judgments.
4. **all . . . kiln:** Just because something happens doesn't mean it is a sign of something else (from beer brewing).

thicket, came pacing down by the grove with a boar-spear in his hand in great haste. He spied where a man lay asleep, and a lion fast by him: amazed at this sight, as he stood gazing, his nose on the sudden bled, which made him conjecture it was some friend of his. Whereupon drawing more nigh, he might easily discern his visage, perceived by his physnomy that it was his brother Saladyne, which drave Rosader into a deep passion, as a man perplexed at the sight of so unexpected a chance, marvelling what should drive his brother to traverse those secret deserts, without any company, in such distress and forlorn sort. But the present time craved no such doubting ambages,[5] for either he must resolve to hazard his life for his relief, or else steal away, and leave him to the cruelty of the lion. In which doubt he thus briefly debated with himself:

'Now, Rosader, fortune that long hath whipped thee with nettles, means to salve thee with roses, and having crossed thee with many frowns, now she presents thee with the brightness of her favours. Thou that didst count thyself the most distressed of all men, mayest account thyself the most fortunate amongst men, if Fortune can make men happy, or sweet revenge be wrapped in a pleasing content. Thou seest Saladyne thine enemy, the worker of thy misfortunes, and the efficient cause[6] of thine exile, subject to the cruelty of a merciless lion, brought into this misery by the gods, that they might seem just in revenging his rigour, and thy injuries. Seest thou not how the stars are in a favourable aspect, the planets in some pleasing conjunction, the fates agreeable to thy thoughts, and the destinies performers of thy desires, in that Saladyne shall die, and thou be free of his blood: he receive meed for his amiss,[7] and thou erect his tomb with innocent hands. Now, Rosader, shalt thou return unto Bordeaux and enjoy thy possessions by birth, and his revenues by inheritance: now mayest thou triumph in love, and hang fortune's altars with garlands. For when Rosalynde hears of thy wealth, it will make her love thee the more willingly: for women's eyes are made of Chrysocoll,[8] that is ever unperfect unless tempered with gold, and Jupiter soonest enjoyed Danaë, because he came to her in so rich a shower. Thus shall this lion, Rosader, end the life of a miserable man, and from distress raise thee to be most fortunate.' And with that, casting his boar-spear on his neck, away he began to trudge.

But he had not stepped back two or three paces, but a new motion stroke him to the very heart, that resting his boar-spear against his breast, he fell into this passionate humour:

5. **ambages:** ambiguities.
6. **efficient cause:** the primary source of a change (from Aristotle).
7. **meed . . . amiss:** punishment for his faults.
8. **Chrysocoll:** bluish-green stone.

'Ah, Rosader, wert thou the son of Sir John of Bordeaux, whose virtues exceeded his valour, and yet the most hardiest knight in all Europe? Should the honour of the father shine in the actions of the son, and wilt thou dishonour thy parentage, in forgetting the nature of a gentleman? Did not thy father at his last gasp breathe out this golden principle: Brothers' amity is like the drops of balsamum,[9] that salveth the most dangerous sores? Did he make a large exhort unto concord, and wilt thou show thyself careless? O Rosader, what though Saladyne hath wronged thee, and made thee live an exile in the forest, shall thy nature be so cruel, or thy nurture so crooked, or thy thoughts so savage, as to suffer so dismal a revenge? What, to let him be devoured by wild beasts! *Non sapit qui non sibi sapit*[1] is fondly spoken in such bitter extremes. Lose not his life, Rosader, to win a world of treasure; for in having him thou hast a brother, and by hazarding for his life, thou gettest a friend, and reconcilest an enemy: and more honour shalt thou purchase by pleasuring a foe, than revenging a thousand injuries.'

With that his brother began to stir, and the lion to rouse himself, whereupon Rosader suddenly charged him with the boar-spear, and wounded the lion very sore at the first stroke. The beast feeling himself to have a mortal hurt, leapt at Rosader, and with his paws gave him a sore pinch on the breast, that he had almost fallen; yet as a man most valiant, in whom the sparks of Sir John of Bordeaux remained, he recovered himself, and in short combat slew the lion, who at his death roared so loud that Saladyne awaked, and starting up, was amazed at the sudden sight of so monstrous a beast lying slain by him, and so sweet a gentleman wounded. He presently, as he was of a ripe conceit,[2] began to conjecture that the gentleman had slain him in his defence. Whereupon, as a man in a trance, he stood staring on them both a good while, not knowing his brother, being in that disguise. At last he burst into these terms:

'Sir, whatsoever thou be, as full of honour thou must needs be by the view of thy present valour, I perceive thou hast redressed my fortunes by thy courage, and saved my life with thine own loss, which ties me to be thine in all humble service. Thanks thou shalt have as thy due, and more thou canst not have, for my ability denies me to perform a deeper debt. But if anyways it please thee to command me, use me as far as the power of a poor gentleman may stretch.'

Rosader, seeing he was unknown to his brother, wondered to hear such courteous words come from his crabbed nature; but glad of such reformed nurture, he made this answer:

9. **balsamum:** aromatic balm.
1. See p. 100, n. 1.
2. **of . . . conceit:** mature in his judgment.

'I am, sir, whatsoever thou art, a forester and ranger of these walks, who, following my deer to the fall, was conducted hither by some assenting fate, that I might save thee, and disparage myself. For coming into this place, I saw thee asleep, and the lion watching thy awake, that at thy rising he might prey upon thy carcase. At the first sight I conjectured thee a gentleman, for all men's thoughts ought to be favourable in imagination, and I counted it the part of a resolute man to purchase a stranger's relief, though with the loss of his own blood; which I have performed, thou seest, to mine own prejudice. If, therefore, thou be a man of such worth as I value thee by thy exterior lineaments, make discourse unto me what is the cause of thy present fortunes. For by the furrows in thy face thou seemest to be crossed with her frowns: but whatsoever, or howsoever, let me crave that favour, to hear the tragic cause of thy estate.'

Saladyne sitting down, and fetching a deep sigh, began thus:

'Although the discourse of my fortunes be the renewing of my sorrows, and the rubbing of the scar will open a fresh wound, yet that I may not prove ingrateful to so courteous a gentleman, I will rather sit down and sigh out my estate, than give any offence by smothering my grief with silence. Know therefore, sir, that I am of Bordeaux, and the son and heir of Sir John of Bordeaux, a man for his virtues and valour so famous, that I cannot think but the fame of his honours hath reached farther than the knowledge of his personage. The infortunate son of so fortunate a knight am I; my name, Saladyne; who succeeding my father in possessions, but not in qualities, having two brethren committed by my father at his death to my charge, with such golden principles of brotherly concord, as might have pierced like the Sirens' melody into any human ear. But I, with Ulysses, became deaf against his philosophical harmony, and made more value of profit than of virtue, esteeming gold sufficient honour, and wealth the fittest title for a gentleman's dignity. I set my middle brother to the university to be a scholar, counting it enough if he might pore on a book while I fed upon his revenues; and for the youngest, which was my father's joy, young Rosader'—And with that, naming of Rosader, Saladyne sate him down and wept.

'Nay, forward man,' quoth the forester, 'tears are the unfittest salve that any man can apply for to cure sorrows, and therefore cease from such feminine follies, as should drop out of a woman's eye to deceive, not out of a gentleman's look to discover his thoughts, and forward with thy discourse.'

'O sir,' quoth Saladyne, 'this Rosader that wrings tears from mine eyes, and blood from my heart, was like my father in exterior personage and in inward qualities; for in the prime of his years he aimed all his acts at honour, and coveted rather to die than to brook any injury unworthy a gentleman's credit. I, whom envy had made blind, and covetousness masked with the veil of self-love, seeing the palm tree grow straight, thought to suppress it being a twig; but nature will have her course, the cedar will be tall, the diamond bright, the carbuncle[3] glistering, and virtue will shine though it be never so much obscured. For I kept Rosader as a slave, and used him as one of my servile hinds,[4] until age grew on, and a secret insight of my abuse entered into his mind; insomuch, that he could not brook it, but coveted to have what his father left him, and to live of himself. To be short, sir, I repined at his fortunes, and he counterchecked me, not with ability but valour, until at last, by my friends and aid of such as followed gold more than right or virtue, I banished him from Bordeaux, and he, poor gentleman, lives no man knows where, in some distressed discontent. The gods, not able to suffer such impiety unrevenged, so wrought, that the king picked a causeless quarrel against me in hope to have my lands, and so hath exiled me out of France for ever. Thus, thus, sir, am I the most miserable of all men, as having a blemish in my thoughts for the wrongs I proffered Rosader, and a touch in my state[5] to be thrown from my proper possessions by injustice. Passionate thus with many griefs, in penance of my former follies I go thus pilgrim-like to seek out my brother, that I may reconcile myself to him in all submission, and afterward wend to the Holy Land, to end my years in as many virtues as I have spent my youth in wicked vanities.'

Rosader, hearing the resolution of his brother Saladyne, began to compassionate his sorrows, and not able to smother the sparks of nature with feigned secrecy, he burst into these loving speeches:

'Then know, Saladyne,' quoth he, 'that thou hast met with Rosader, who grieves as much to see thy distress, as thyself to feel the burden of thy misery.' Saladyne, casting up his eye and noting well the physnomy[6] of the forester, knew, that it was his brother Rosader, which made him so bash and blush at the first meeting, that Rosader was fain to recomfort him, which he did in such sort, that he showed how highly he held revenge in scorn. Much ado there was between these two brethren, Saladyne in craving pardon, and Rosader in forgiving and forgetting all former injuries; the one submiss, the other courteous; Saladyne penitent and passionate, Rosader kind and loving, that at length nature working an union of their thoughts, they earnestly embraced, and fell from matters of unkindness, to talk of the country life, which Rosader so highly commended, that

3. **carbuncle:** garnet or ruby.
4. **hinds:** farm hands.
5. **touch . . . state:** damage to my position in life.
6. **physnomy:** features.

his brother began to have a desire to taste of that homely content. In this humour Rosader conducted him to Gerismond's lodge, and presented his brother to the king, discoursing the whole matter how all had happened betwixt them. The king looking upon Saladyne, found him a man of a most beautiful personage, and saw in his face sufficient sparks of ensuing honours, gave him great entertainment, and glad of their friendly reconcilement, promised such favour as the poverty of his estate might afford, which Saladyne gratefully accepted. And so Gerismond fell to question of Torismond's life. Saladyne briefly discoursed unto him his injustice and tyrannies, with such modesty, although he had wronged him, that Gerismond greatly praised the sparing speech of the young gentleman.

Many questions passed, but at last Gerismond began with a deep sigh to inquire if there were any news of the welfare of Alinda, or his daughter Rosalynde?

'None, sir,' quoth Saladyne, 'for since their departure they were never heard of.'

'Injurious fortune,' quoth the king, 'that to double the father's misery, wrongest the daughter with misfortunes!'

And with that, surcharged with sorrows, he went into his cell, and left Saladyne and Rosader, whom Rosader straight conducted to the sight of Adam Spencer. Who, seeing Saladyne in that estate, was in a brown study; but when he heard the whole matter, although he grieved for the exile of his master, yet he joyed that banishment had so reformed him, that from a lascivious youth he was proved a virtuous gentleman. Looking a longer while, and seeing what familiarity passed between them, and what favours were interchanged with brotherly affection, he said thus:

'Aye, marry, thus should it be; this was the concord that old Sir John of Bordeaux wished betwixt you. Now fulfil you those precepts he breathed out at his death, and in observing them, look to live fortunate and die honourable.'

'Well said, Adam Spencer,' quoth Rosader, 'but hast any victuals in store for us?'

'A piece of a red deer,' quoth he, 'and a bottle of wine.'

''Tis foresters' fare, brother,' quoth Rosader; and so they sate down and fell to their cates.

As soon as they had taken their repast, and had well dined, Rosader took his brother Saladyne by the hand, and showed him the pleasures of the forest, and what content they enjoyed in that mean estate. Thus for two or three days he walked up and down with his brother to show him all the commodities that belonged to his walk.

In which time he was missed of his Ganymede, who mused greatly, with Aliena, what should become of their forester. Somewhile they thought he had taken some word unkindly, and had taken the pet;[7] then they imagined some new love had withdrawn his fancy, or happily that he was sick, or detained by some great business of Gerismond's, or that he had made a reconcilement with his brother, and so returned to Bordeaux.

These conjectures did they cast in their heads, but specially Ganymede, who, having love in her heart, proved restless, and half without patience, that Rosader wronged her with so long absence; for Love measures every minute, and thinks hours to be days, and days to be months, till they feed their eyes with the sight of their desired object. Thus perplexed lived poor Ganymede, while on a day, sitting with Aliena in a great dump, she cast up her eye, and saw where Rosader came pacing towards them with his forest bill[8] on his neck. At that sight her colour changed, and she said to Aliena:

'See, mistress, where our jolly forester comes.'

'And you are not a little glad thereof,' quoth Aliena, 'your nose bewrays[9] what porridge you love: the wind cannot be tied within his quarter, the sun shadowed with a veil, oil hidden in water, nor love kept out of a woman's looks: but no more of that, *Lupus est in fabula.*'[1]

As soon as Rosader was come within the reach of her tongue's end, Aliena began thus:

'Why, how now, gentle forester, what wind hath kept you from hence? that being so newly married, you have no more care of your Rosalynde, but to absent yourself so many days? Are these the passions you painted out so in your sonnets and roundelays? I see well hot love is soon cold, and that the fancy of men is like to a loose feather that wandereth in the air with the blast of every wind.'

'You are deceived, mistress,' quoth Rosader; 'twas a copy of unkindness that kept me hence, in that, I being married, you carried away the bride; but if I have given any occasion of offence by absenting myself these three days, I humbly sue for pardon, which you must grant of course, in that the fault is so friendly confessed with penance. But to tell you the truth, fair mistress and my good Rosalynde, my eldest brother by the injury of Torismond is banished from Bordeaux, and by chance he and I met in the forest.'

And here Rosader discoursed unto them what had happened betwixt them, which reconcilement made them glad, especially

7. **taken the pet:** become offended.
8. **forest bill:** woodsman's knife.
9. **bewrays:** betrays, indicates.
1. The wolf is in the tale (Latin: said when there is a sudden silence).

Ganymede. But Aliena, hearing of the tyranny of her father, grieved inwardly, and yet smothered all things with such secrecy, that the concealing was more sorrow than the conceit; yet that her estate might be hid still, she made fair weather of it, and so let all pass.

Fortune, that saw how these parties valued not her deity, but held her power in scorn, thought to have a bout with them, and brought the matter to pass thus. Certain rascals that lived by prowling in the forest, who for fear of the provost marshal had caves in the groves and thickets to shroud themselves from his trains, hearing of the beauty of this fair shepherdess, Aliena, thought to steal her away, and to give her to the king for a present; hoping, because the king was a great lecher, by such a gift to purchase all their pardons, and therefore came to take her and her page away. Thus resolved, while Aliena and Ganymede were in this sad talk, they came rushing in, and laid violent hands upon Aliena and her page, which made them cry out to Rosader; who having the valour of his father stamped in his heart, thought rather to die in defence of his friends, than any way be touched with the least blemish of dishonour, and therefore dealt such blows amongst them with his weapon, as he did witness well upon their carcases that he was no coward. But as *Ne Hercules quidem contra duos*,[2] so Rosader could not resist a multitude, having none to back him; so that he was not only rebated,[3] but sore wounded, and Aliena and Ganymede had been quite carried away by these rascals, had not fortune, that meant to turn her frown into a favour, brought Saladyne that way by chance, who wandering to find out his brother's walk, encountered this crew: and seeing not only a shepherdess and her boy forced, but his brother wounded, he heaved up a forest bill he had on his neck, and the first he stroke had never after more need of the physician, redoubling his blows with such courage that the slaves were amazed at his valour. Rosader, espying his brother so fortunately arrived, and seeing how valiantly he behaved himself, though sore wounded rushed amongst them, and laid on such load, that some of the crew were slain, and the rest fled, leaving Aliena and Ganymede in the possession of Rosader and Saladyne.

Aliena after she had breathed awhile and was come to herself from this fear, looked about her, and saw where Ganymede was busy dressing up the wounds of the forester: but she cast her eye upon this courteous champion that had made so hot a rescue, and that with such affection, that she began to measure every part of him with favour, and in herself to commend his personage and his

2. Even Hercules can't win against two (Latin).
3. **rebated:** beaten back.

virtue, holding him for a resolute man, that durst assail such a troop of unbridled villains. At last, gathering her spirits together, she returned him these thanks:

'Gentle sir, whatsoever you be that have adventured your flesh to relieve our fortunes, as we hold you valiant so we esteem you courteous, and to have as many hidden virtues as you have manifest resolutions. We poor shepherds have no wealth but our flocks, and therefore can we not make requital with any great treasures; but our recompense is thanks, and our rewards to her friends without feigning. For ransom, therefore, of this our rescue, you must content yourself to take such a kind gramercy as a poor shepherdess and her page may give, with promise, in what we may, never to prove ingrateful. For this gentleman that is hurt, young Rosader, he is our good neighbour and familiar acquaintance; we'll pay him with smiles, and feed him with love-looks, and though he be never the fatter at the year's end, yet we'll so hamper[4] him that he shall hold himself satisfied.'

Saladyne, hearing this shepherdess speak so wisely, began more narrowly to pry into her perfection, and to survey all her lineaments with a curious insight; so long dallying in the flame of her beauty, that to his cost he found her to be most excellent. For love that lurked in all these broils to have a blow or two, seeing the parties at the gaze, encountered them both with such a veny,[5] that the stroke pierced to the heart so deep as it could never after be rased out. At last, after he had looked so long, till Aliena waxed red, he returned her this answer:

'Fair shepherdess, if Fortune graced me with such good hap as to do you any favour, I hold myself as contented as if I had gotten a great conquest; for the relief of distressed women is the special point that gentlemen are tied unto by honour. Seeing then my hazard to rescue your harms was rather duty than courtesy, thanks is more than belongs to the requital of such a favour. But lest I might seem either too coy or too careless of a gentlewoman's proffer, I will take your kind gramercy for a recompense.'

All this while that he spake, Ganymede looked earnestly upon him, and said:

'Truly, Rosader, this gentleman favours you much in the feature of your face.'

'No marvel,' quoth he, 'gentle swain, for 'tis my eldest brother Saladyne.'

'Your brother?' quoth Aliena, and with that she blushed, 'he is the more welcome, and I hold myself the more his debtor; and for

---

4. **hamper:** fill up.
5. **seeing . . . veny:** seeing the two looking at each other, struck them both with such a blow.

that he hath in my behalf done such a piece of service, if it please him to do me that honour, I will call him servant, and he shall call me mistress.'

'Content, sweet mistress,' quoth Saladyne, 'and when I forget to call you so, I will be unmindful of mine own self.'

'Away with these quirks and quiddities of love,' quoth Rosader, 'and give me some drink, for I am passing thirsty, and then will I home, for my wounds bleed sore, and I will have them dressed.'

Ganymede had tears in her eyes, and passions in her heart to see her Rosader so pained, and therefore stepped hastily to the bottle, and filling out some wine in a mazer, she spiced it with such comfortable drugs as she had about her, and gave it him, which did comfort Rosader, that rising, with the help of his brother, he took his leave of them, and went to his lodge. Ganymede, as soon as they were out of sight, led his flocks down to a vale, and there under the shadow of a beech tree sate down, and began to mourn the misfortunes of her sweetheart.

And Aliena, as a woman passing discontent, severing herself from her Ganymede, sitting under a limon tree, began to sigh out the passions of her new love, and to meditate with herself in this manner:

'Ay me! now I see, and sorrowing sigh to see, that Diana's laurels are harbours for Venus' doves; that there trace as well through the lawns wantons as chaste ones; that Calisto, be she never so chary, will cast one amorous eye at courting Jove,[6] that Diana herself will change her shape, but she will honour Love in a shadow; that maidens' eyes be they as hard as diamonds, yet Cupid hath drugs to make them more pliable than wax. See, Alinda, how Fortune and Love have interleagued themselves to be thy foes, and to make thee their subject, or else an abject, have inveigled thy sight with a most beautiful object. A-late thou didst hold Venus for a giglot,[7] not a goddess, and now thou shalt be forced to sue suppliant to her deity. Cupid was a boy and blind; but, alas, his eye had aim enough to pierce thee to the heart. While I lived in the court I held love in contempt, and in high seats I had small desires. I knew not affection while I lived in dignity, nor could Venus countercheck me, as long as my fortune was majesty, and my thoughts honour; and shall I now be high in desires, when I am made low by destiny? I have heard them say, that Love looks not at low cottages, that Venus jets[8] in robes not in rags,

---

6. **Diana's . . . Jove:** The goddess of chastity's trees provide shelter for the **doves** of the goddess of love; the sexually licentious pass through the lawns as well as the **chaste**; **Calisto** (a nymph associated with Diana and therefore with chastity), however reluctant she seemed, looked amorously upon **Jove** when he wooed her.

7. **A-late . . . giglot:** Recently you considered love a mere girl.

8. **jets:** swaggers about.

that Cupid flies so high, that he scorns to touch poverty with his heel. Tush, Alinda, these are but old wives' tales, and neither authentical precepts, nor infallible principles; for experience tells thee, that peasants have their passions as well as princes, that swains as they have their labours, so they have their amours, and Love lurks as soon about a sheepcote as a palace.

'Ah, Alinda, this day in avoiding a prejudice thou art fallen into a deeper mischief; being rescued from the robbers, thou art become captive to Saladyne: and what then? Women must love, or they must cease to live; and therefore did nature frame them fair, that they might be subjects to fancy. But perhaps Saladyne's eye is levelled upon a more seemlier saint. If it be so, bear thy passions with patience; say Love hath wronged thee, that hath not wrung him; and if he be proud in contempt, be thou rich in content, and rather die than discover any desire: for there is nothing more precious in a woman than to conceal love and to die modest. He is the son and heir of Sir John of Bordeaux, a youth comely enough. O Alinda, too comely, else hadst not thou been thus discontent; valiant, and that fettered thine eye; wise, else hadst thou not been now won; but for all these virtues banished by thy father, and therefore if he know thy parentage, he will hate the fruit for the tree, and condemn the young scion for the old stock.[9] Well, howsoever, I must love, and whomsoever, I will; and, whatsoever betide, Aliena will think well of Saladyne, suppose he of me as he please.'

And with that fetching a deep sigh, she rise up, and went to Ganymede, who all this while sate in a great dump, fearing the imminent danger of her friend Rosader; but now Aliena began to comfort her, herself being overgrown with sorrows, and to recall her from her melancholy with many pleasant persuasions. Ganymede took all in the best part, and so they went home together after they had folded their flocks, supping with old Corydon, who had provided their cates. He, after supper, to pass away the night while bedtime, began a long discourse, how Montanus, the young shepherd that was in love with Phoebe, could by no means obtain any favour at her hands, but, still pained in restless passions, remained a hopeless and perplexed lover.

'I would I might,' quoth Aliena, 'once see that Phoebe. Is she so fair that she thinks no shepherd worthy of her beauty? or so froward that no love nor loyalty will content her? or so coy that she requires a long time to be wooed? or so foolish that she forgets that like a fop she must have a large harvest for a little corn?'[1]

---

9. **condemn . . . stock:** condemn the young branch because of the **stock** from which it came.
1. **like . . . corn:** Like a fool she expects to have a large harvest after planting little corn.

'I cannot distinguish,' quoth Corydon, 'of these nice qualities; but one of these days I'll bring Montanus and her down, that you may both see their persons, and note their passions; and then where the blame is, there let it rest. But this I am sure,' quoth Corydon, 'if all maidens were of her mind, the world would grow to a mad pass; for there would be great store of wooing and little wedding, many words and little worship, much folly and no faith.'

At this sad sentence of Corydon, so solemnly brought forth, Aliena smiled, and because it waxed late, she and her page went to bed, both of them having fleas in their ears to keep them awake; Ganymede for the hurt of her Rosader, and Aliena for the affection she bore to Saladyne. In this discontented humour they passed away the time, till falling on sleep, their senses at rest, Love left them to their quiet slumbers, which were not long. For as soon as Phoebus rose from his Aurora, and began to mount him in the sky, summoning plough-swains to their handy labour, Aliena arose, and going to the couch where Ganymede lay, awakened her page, and said the morning was far spent, the dew small, and time called them away to their folds.

'Ah, ah!' quoth Ganymede, 'is the wind in that door? then in faith I perceive that there is no diamond so hard but will yield to the file, no cedar so strong but the wind will shake, nor any mind so chaste but love will change. Well, Aliena, must Saladyne be the man, and will it be a match? Trust me, he is fair and valiant, the son of a worthy knight, whom if he imitate in perfection, as he represents him in proportion, he is worthy of no less than Aliena. But he is an exile. What then? I hope my mistress respects the virtues not the wealth, and measures the qualities not the substance. Those dames that are like Danaë, that like love in no shape but in a shower of gold, I wish them husbands with much wealth and little wit, that the want of the one may blemish the abundance of the other. It should, my Aliena, stain the honour of a shepherd's life to set the end of passions upon pelf. Love's eyes looks not so low as gold; there is no fees to be paid in Cupid's courts; and in elder time, as Corydon hath told me, the shepherds' love-gifts were apples and chestnuts, and then their desires were loyal, and their thoughts constant. But now

Quaerenda pecunia primum, post nummos virtus.[2]

And the time is grown to that which Horace in his Satires wrote on:
omnis enim res
Virtus fama decus divina humanaque pulchris
Divitiis parent: quas qui construxerit ille

2. See p. 110, n. 7.

Clarus erit, fortis, justus. Sapiensne? Etiam et rex
Et quicquid volet—[3]

But, Aliena, let it not be so with thee in thy fancies, but respect his
faith and there an end.'

Aliena, hearing Ganymede thus forward to further Saladyne in
his affections, thought she kissed the child for the nurse's sake, and
wooed for him that she might please Rosader, made this reply:

'Why, Ganymede, whereof grows this persuasion? Hast thou seen
love in my looks, or are mine eyes grown so amorous, that they discover some new-entertained fancies? If thou measurest my thoughts
by my countenance, thou mayest prove as ill a physiognomer, as the
lapidary that aims at the secret virtues of the topaz by the exterior
shadow of the stone. The operation of the agate is not known by the
strakes,[4] nor the diamond prized by his brightness, but by his hardness. The carbuncle that shineth most is not ever the most precious;
and the apothecaries choose not flowers for their colours, but for
their virtues. Women's faces are not always calendars of fancy, nor do
their thoughts and their looks ever agree; for when their eyes are fullest of favours, then are they oft most empty of desire; and when they
seem to frown at disdain, then are they most forward to affection. If
I be melancholy, then, Ganymede, 'tis not a consequence that I am
entangled with the perfection of Saladyne. But seeing fire cannot be
hid in the straw, nor love kept so covert but it will be spied, what
should friends conceal fancies? Know, my Ganymede, the beauty
and valour, the wit and prowess of Saladyne hath fettered Aliena so
far, as there is no object pleasing to her eyes but the sight of Saladyne; and if Love have done me justice to wrap his thoughts in the
folds of my face, and that he be as deeply enamoured as I am passionate, I tell thee, Ganymede, there shall not be much wooing, for she is
already won, and what needs a longer battery.[5]

'I am glad,' quoth Ganymede, 'that it shall be thus proportioned,
you to match with Saladyne, and I with Rosader: thus have the
Destinies favoured us with some pleasing aspect, that have made
us as private in our loves, as familiar in our fortunes.'

With this Ganymede start up, made her ready, and went into the
fields with Aliena, where unfolding their flocks, they sate them
down under an olive tree, both of them amorous, and yet diversely
affected; Aliena joying in the excellence of Saladyne, and Gany-

---

3. For all things—worth, reputation, honor, things divine and human—are slaves to the
   beauty of wealth; and he who has made his fortune will be famous, brave and just. And
   wise too? Yes, wise, and a king, and anything else he pleases (Horace, *Satires* 2.3).
4. **strakes:** streaks.
5. **what . . . battery:** What would be the purpose of a longer pursuit?

mede sorrowing for the wounds of her Rosader, not quiet in thought till she might hear of his health. As thus both of them sate in their dumps, they might espy where Corydon came running towards them, almost out of breath with his haste.

'What news with you,' quoth Aliena, 'that you come in such post?'[6]

'Oh, mistress,' quoth Corydon, 'you have a long time desired to see Phoebe, the fair shepherdess whom Montanus loves; so now if you please, you and Ganymede, but to walk with me to yonder thicket, there shall you see Montanus and her sitting by a fountain, he courting with his country ditties, and she as coy as if she held love in disdain.'

The news were so welcome to the two lovers, that up they rose, and went with Corydon. As soon as they drew nigh the thicket, they might espy where Phoebe sate, the fairest shepherdess in all Arden, and he the frolickest swain in the whole forest, she in a petticoat of scarlet, covered with a green mantle, and to shroud her from the sun, a chaplet[7] of roses, from under which appeared a face full of nature's excellence, and two such eyes as might have amated[8] a greater man than Montanus. At gaze upon the gorgeous nymph sat the shepherd, feeding his eyes with her favours, wooing with such piteous looks, and courting with such deep-strained sighs, as would have made Diana herself to have been compassionate. At last, fixing his looks on the riches of her face, his head on his hand, and his elbow on his knee, he sung this mournful ditty:

Montanus' Sonnet

A turtle[9] sate upon a leaveless tree,
    Mourning her absent fere[1]
    With sad and sorry cheer:
    About her wondering stood
    The citizens of wood,
    And whilst her plumes she rents
    And for her love laments,
    The stately trees complain them,
    The birds with sorrow pain them.
    Each one that doth her view
    Her pain and sorrows rue;
    But were the sorrows known
    That me hath overthrown,

6. **post:** a hurry.
7. **chaplet:** wreath.
8. **amated:** defeated.
9. **turtle:** turtle dove.
1. **fere:** mate.

Oh how would Phoebe sigh if she did look on me!

The lovesick Polypheme, that could not see,
Who on the barren shore
His fortunes doth deplore,
And melteth all in moan
For Galatea gone,[2]
And with his piteous cries
Afflicts both earth and skies,
And to his woe betook
Doth break both pipe and hook,
For whom complains the morn,
For whom the sea-nymphs mourn,
Alas, his pain is nought;
For were my woe but thought,
Oh how would Phoebe sigh if she did look on me!

Beyond compare my pain;
Yet glad am I,
If gentle Phoebe deign
To see her Montan die.

After this, Montanus felt his passions so extreme, that he fell into this exclamation against the injustice of Love:

Hélas, tyran, plein de rigueur,
Modère un peu ta violence:
Que te sert si grande dépense?
C'est trop de flammes pour un cœur.
Épargnez en une étincelle,
Puis fais ton effort d'émouvoir,
La fière qui ne veut point voir,
En quel feu je brûle pour elle.
Exécute, Amour, ce dessein,
Et rabaisse un peu son audace:
Son cœur ne doit être de glace,
Bien qu'elle ait de neige le sein.[3]

Montanus ended his sonnet with such a volley of sighs, and such a stream of tears, as might have moved any but Phoebe to have granted him favour. But she, measuring all his passions with a coy

---

2. **Polypheme . . . gone:** Polyphemus, a monster who was blinded by Odysseus, mourned hopelessly because the nymph **Galatea** did not reciprocate his love.

3. Alas, strict tyrant, moderate your violence a little: what is the point of such a great expense? There are too many flames for one heart. Spare one spark, then do your best to move the proud one who refuses to see in what fire I burn for her. Execute, Love, this plan and reduce her pride a little. Her heart should not be ice even though her breast is snowy. (French: from Desportes, *Amours de Diane*, poem following sonnet 41).

disdain, and triumphing in the poor shepherd's pathetical humours, smiling at his martyrdom as though love had been no malady, scornfully warbled out this sonnet:

Phoebe's Sonnet, a Reply to Montanus' Passion

Down a down,
    Thus Phyllis sung,
      By fancy once distressed;
Whoso by foolish love are stung
    Are worthily oppressed.
      And so sing I. With a down, down, &c.

When Love was first begot,
    And by the mover's will
Did fall to human lot
    His solace to fulfil,
Devoid of all deceit,
    A chaste and holy fire
Did quicken man's conceit,
    And women's breast inspire.
The gods that saw the good
    That mortals did approve,
With kind and holy mood
    Began to talk of Love.

Down a down,
    Thus Phyllis sung
      By fancy once distressed, &c.

But during this accord,
    A wonder strange to hear,
Whilst Love in deed and word
    Most faithful did appear,
False-semblance came in place,
    By Jealousy attended,
And with a double face
    Both love and fancy blended;
Which made the gods forsake,
    And men from fancy fly,
And maidens scorn a make,[4]
    Forsooth, and so will I.

Down a down,
    Thus Phyllis sung,

4. **make:** mate.

By fancy once distressed;
Who so by foolish love are stung
Are worthily oppressed.
And so sing I.
With down a down, a down down, a down a.

Montanus, hearing the cruel resolution of Phoebe, was so over-grown with passions, that from amorous ditties he fell flat into these terms:

'Ah, Phoebe,' quoth he, 'whereof art thou made, that thou regardest not my malady? Am I so hateful an object that thine eyes condemn me for an abject? or so base, that thy desires cannot stoop so low as to lend me a gracious look? My passions are many, my loves more, my thoughts loyalty, and my fancy faith: all devoted in humble devoir[5] to the service of Phoebe; and shall I reap no reward for such fealties? The swain's daily labours is quit with the evening's hire,[6] the ploughman's toil is eased with the hope of corn, what the ox sweats out at the plough he fatteneth at the crib; but infortunate Montanus hath no salve for his sorrows, nor any hope of recompense for the hazard of his perplexed passions. If, Phoebe, time may plead the proof of my truth, twice seven winters have I loved fair Phoebe: if constancy be a cause to farther my suit, Montanus' thoughts have been sealed in the sweet of Phoebe's excellence, as far from change as she from love: if outward passions may discover inward affections, the furrows in my face may decipher the sorrows of my heart, and the map of my looks the griefs of my mind. Thou seest, Phoebe, the tears of despair have made my cheeks full of wrinkles, and my scalding sighs have made the air echo her pity conceived in my plaints: Philomele hearing my passions, hath left her mournful tunes to listen to the discourse of my miseries. I have portrayed in every tree the beauty of my mistress, and the despair of my loves. What is it in the woods cannot witness my woes? and who is it would not pity my plaints? Only Phoebe. And why? Because I am Montanus, and she Phoebe: I a worthless swain, and she the most excellent of all fairies. Beautiful Phoebe! oh, might I say pitiful, then happy were I, though I tasted but one minute of that good hap. Measure Montanus not by his fortunes but by his loves, and balance not his wealth but his desires, and lend but one gracious look to cure a heap of disquieted cares. If not, ah! if Phoebe cannot love, let a storm of frowns end the discontent of my thoughts, and so let me perish in my desires, because they are above my deserts:

5. **devoir:** duty.
6. **The . . . hire:** The countryman's daily labor is rewarded when he gets paid in the evening.

only at my death this favour cannot be denied me, that all shall say Montanus died for love of hard-hearted Phoebe.'

At these words she filled her face full of frowns, and made him this short and sharp reply:

'Importunate shepherd, whose loves are lawless, because restless, are thy passions so extreme that thou canst not conceal them with patience? or art thou so folly-sick, that thou must needs be fancy-sick, and in thy affection tied to such an exigent, as none serves but Phoebe? Well, sir, if your market may be made no where else, home again, for your mart is at the fairest.[7] Phoebe is no lettuce for your lips, and her grapes hangs so high, that gaze at them you may, but touch them you cannot. Yet, Montanus, I speak not this in pride, but in disdain; not that I scorn thee, but that I hate love; for I count it as great honour to triumph over fancy as over fortune. Rest thee content therefore, Montanus: cease from thy loves, and bridle thy looks, quench the sparkles before they grow to a further flame; for in loving me thou shalt live by loss, and what thou utterest in words are all written in the wind. Wert thou, Montanus, as fair as Paris, as hardy as Hector, as constant as Troilus, as loving as Leander,[8] Phoebe could not love, because she cannot love at all: and therefore if thou pursue me with Phoebus, I must fly with Daphne.'

Ganymede, overhearing all these passions of Montanus, could not brook the cruelty of Phoebe, but starting from behind the bush said:

'And if, damsel, you fled from me, I would transform you as Daphne to a bay, and then in contempt trample your branches under my feet.'

Phoebe at this sudden reply was amazed, especially when she saw so fair a swain as Ganymede; blushing therefore, she would have been gone, but that he held her by the hand, and prosecuted his reply thus:

'What, shepherdess, so fair and so cruel? Disdain beseems[9] not cottages, nor coyness maids; for either they be condemned to be too proud, or too froward. Take heed, fair nymph, that in despising love, you be not overreached with love, and in shaking off all, shape yourself to your own shadow, and so with Narcissus prove passionate and yet unpitied. Oft have I heard, and sometimes have I seen, high disdain turned to hot desires. Because thou art beautiful be not so coy: as there is nothing more fair, so there is nothing more fading; as momentary as the shadows which grows from a cloudy sun. Such,

---

7. **your . . . fairest:** This is the best "price" you are going to get.
8. **fair . . . Leander:** Paris was handsome enough to win Helen of Troy; **Hector** was the chief Trojan hero, **Troilus** was faithful to Cressida even after she forsook him, and **Leander** loved Hero so much that he drowned trying to swim to her.
9. **beseems:** is appropriate to.

my fair shepherdess, as disdain in youth desire in age, and then are they hated in the winter, that might have been loved in the prime. A wrinkled maid is like to a parched rose, that is cast up in coffers to please the smell,[1] not worn in the hand to content the eye. There is no folly in love to *had I wist*, and therefore be ruled by me. Love while thou art young, least thou be disdained when thou art old. Beauty nor time cannot be recalled, and if thou love, like of Montanus; for if his desires are many, so his deserts are great.'

Phœbe all this while gazed on the perfection of Ganymede, as deeply enamoured on his perfection as Montanus inveigled with hers; for her eye made survey of his excellent feature, which she found so rare, that she thought the ghost of Adonis had been leaped from Elysium in the shape of a swain.[2] When she blushed at her own folly to look so long on a stranger, she mildly made answer to Ganymede thus:

'I cannot deny, sir, but I have heard of Love, though I never felt love; and have read of such a goddess as Venus, though I never saw any but her picture; and, perhaps'—and with that she waxed red and bashful, and withal silent; which Ganymede perceiving, commended in herself the bashfulness of the maid, and desired her to go forward.

'And perhaps, sir,' quoth she, 'mine eye hath been more prodigal to-day than ever before'—and with that she stayed again, as one greatly passionate and perplexed.

Aliena seeing the hare through the maze, bade her forward with her prattle, but in vain; for at this abrupt period she broke off, and with her eyes full of tears, and her face covered with a vermilion dye, she sate down and sighed. Whereupon Aliena and Ganymede, seeing the shepherdess in such a strange plight, left Phoebe with her Montanus, wishing her friendly that she would be more pliant to Love, lest in penance Venus joined her to some sharp repentance. Phoebe made no reply, but fetched such a sigh, that Echo made relation of her plaint,[3] giving Ganymede such an adieu with a piercing glance, that the amorous girl-boy perceived Phoebe was pinched by the heel.[4]

But leaving Phoebe to the follies of her new fancy, and Montanus to attend upon her, to Saladyne, who all this last night could not rest for the remembrance of Aliena; insomuch that he framed a sweet conceited[5] sonnet to content his humour, which he put in his

---

1. **parched . . . smell:** sachet made of dried roses.
2. **Adonis . . . swain:** The ghost of **Adonis** (Venus's beloved who was killed in a hunting accident) had been brought back from the underworld in the form of a country youth.
3. **Echo . . . plaint:** **Echo** communicated her complaint (i.e., it echoed).
4. **pinched . . . heel:** i.e., in love.
5. **conceited:** ingenious.

bosom, being requested by his brother Rosader to go to Aliena and Ganymede, to signify unto them that his wounds were not dangerous. A more happy message could not happen to Saladyne, that taking his forest bill on his neck, he trudgeth in all haste towards the plains where Aliena's flocks did feed, coming just to the place when they returned from Montanus and Phoebe. Fortune so conducted this jolly forester, that he encountered them and Corydon, whom he presently saluted in this manner:

'Fair shepherdess, and too fair, unless your beauty be tempered with courtesy, and the lineaments of the face graced with the lowliness of mind, as many good fortunes to you and your page, as yourselves can desire or I imagine. My brother Rosader, in the grief of his green[6] wounds still mindful of his friends, hath sent me to you with a kind salute, to show that he brooks his pains with the more patience, in that he holds the parties precious in whose defence he received the prejudice. The report of your welfare will be a great comfort to his distempered body and distressed thoughts, and therefore he sent me with a strict charge to visit you.'

'And you,' quoth Aliena, 'are the more welcome in that you are messenger from so kind a gentleman, whose pains we compassionate with as great sorrow as he brooks them with grief; and his wounds breeds in us as many passions as in him extremities, so that what disquiet he feels in body we partake in heart, wishing, if we might, that our mishap might salve his malady. But seeing our wills yields him little ease, our orisons[7] are never idle to the gods for his recovery.'

'I pray, youth,' quoth Ganymede with tears in his eyes, 'when the surgeon searched[8] him, held he his wounds dangerous?'

'Dangerous,' quoth Saladyne, 'but, not mortal; and the sooner to be cured, in that his patient is not impatient of any pains: whereupon my brother hopes within these ten days to walk abroad and visit you himself.'

'In the meantime,' quoth Ganymede, 'say his Rosalynde commends her to him, and bids him be of good cheer.'

'I know not,' quoth Saladyne, 'who that Rosalynde is, but whatsoever she is, her name is never out of his mouth, but amidst the deepest of his passions he useth Rosalynde as a charm to appease all sorrows with patience; insomuch that I conjecture my brother is in love, and she some paragon that holds his heart perplexed, whose name he oft records with sighs, sometimes with tears, straight with joy, then with smiles; as if in one person love had lodged a Chaos of

6. **green:** fresh.
7. **orisons:** prayers.
8. **searched:** examined.

confused passions. Wherein I have noted the variable disposition of fancy, that like the polype[9] in colours, so it changeth into sundry humours, being, as it should seem, a combat mixed with disquiet and a bitter pleasure wrapped in a sweet prejudice, like to the Sinople[1] tree, whose blossoms delight the smell, and whose fruit infects the taste.'

'By my faith,' quoth Aliena, 'sir, you are deep read in love, or grows your insight into affection by experience? Howsoever, you are a great philosopher in Venus' principles, else could you not discover her secret aphorisms. But, sir, our country amours are not like your courtly fancies, nor is our wooing like your suing; for poor shepherds never plain them till love pain them, where the courtier's eyes is full of passions, when his heart is most free from affection; they court to discover their eloquence, we woo to ease our sorrows; every fair face with them must have a new fancy sealed with a forefinger kiss and a far-fetched sigh, we here love one and live to that one so long as life can maintain love, using few ceremonies because we know few subtleties, and little eloquence for that we lightly account of flattery; only faith and troth, that's shepherds' wooing; and, sir, how like you of this?'

'So,' quoth Saladyne, 'as I could tie myself to such love.'

'What, and look so low as a shepherdess, being the son of Sir John of Bordeaux? Such desires were a disgrace to your honours.' And with that surveying exquisitely every part of him, as uttering all these words in a deep passion, she espied the paper in his bosom; whereupon growing jealous that it was some amorous sonnet, she suddenly snatched it out of his bosom and asked if it were any secret. She was bashful, and Saladyne blushed, which she preceiving, said:

'Nay then, sir, if you wax red, my life for yours 'tis some love-matter. I will see your mistress' name, her praises, and your passions.' And with that she looked on it, which was written to this effect:

Saladyne's Sonnet

If it be true that heaven's eternal course
With restless sway and ceaseless turning glides;
If air inconstant be, and swelling source
Turn and returns with many fluent tides;
    If earth in winter summer's pride estrange,
    And nature seemeth only fair in change;

---

9. **polype:** many legged sea creature capable of changing color.
1. **Sinople:** green (from heraldry).

If it be true that our immortal spright,[2]
Derived from heavenly pure, in wand'ring still,
In novelty and strangeness doth delight,
And by discoverent power discerneth ill;
    And if the body for to work his best
    Doth with the seasons change his place of rest;

Whence comes it that, enforced by furious skies,
I change both place and soil, but not my heart,
Yet salve not in this change my maladies?
Whence grows it that each object works my smart?
    Alas, I see my faith procures my miss,
    And change in love against my nature is.
                                    Et florida pungunt.[3]

Aliena having read over his sonnet, began thus pleasantly to descant upon it:

'I see, Saladyne,' quoth she, 'that as the sun is no sun without his brightness, nor the diamond accounted for precious unless it be hard, so men are not men unless they be in love; and their honours are measured by their amours, not their labours, counting it more commendable for a gentleman to be full of fancy, than full of virtue. I had thought

> Otia si tollas, periere Cupidinis arcus,
> Contemptaeque jacent et sine luce faces.[4]

But I see Ovid's axiom is not authentical, for even labour hath her loves, and extremity is no pumice-stone to rase out fancy. Yourself exiled from your wealth, friends, and country by Torismond, sorrows enough to suppress affections, yet amidst the depth of these extremities, love will be lord, and show his power to be more predominant than fortune. But I pray you, sir, if without offence I may crave it, are they some new thoughts, or some old desires?'

Saladyne, that now saw opportunity pleasant, thought to strike while the iron was hot, and therefore taking Aliena by the hand, sate down by her; and Ganymede, to give them leave to their loves, found herself busy about the folds, whilst Saladyne fell into this prattle with Aliena:

'Fair mistress, if I be blunt in discovering my affections, and use little eloquence in levelling out my loves, I appeal for pardon to your own principles, that say, shepherds use few ceremonies, for

---

2. **spright**: spirit.
3. *Et . . . pungunt*: Even blossoms prick (Latin).
4. If you take away leisure Cupid's bow is lost and his torches lie mocked and extinguished (Ovid, *Remedia Amoris* 139–40).

that they acquaint themselves with few subtleties. To frame myself, therefore, to your country fashion with much faith and little flattery, know, beautiful shepherdess, that whilst I lived in the court I knew not love's cumber,[5] but I held affection as a toy, not as a malady; using fancy as the Hyperborei do their flowers, which they wear in their bosom all day, and cast them in the fire for fuel at night. I liked all, because I loved none, and who was most fair, on her I fed mine eye, but as charily[6] as the bee, that as soon as she hath sucked honey from the rose, flies straight to the next marigold. Living thus at mine own list,[7] I wondered at such as were in love, and when I read their passions, I took them only for poems that flowed from the quickness of the wit, not the sorrows of the heart. But now, fair nymph, since I became a forester, Love hath taught me such a lesson that I must confess his deity and dignity, and say as there is nothing so precious as beauty, so there is nothing more piercing than fancy. For since first I arrived at this place, and mine eye took a curious survey of your excellence, I have been so fettered with your beauty and virtue, as, sweet Aliena, Saladyne without further circumstance loves Aliena. I could paint out my desires with long ambages; but seeing in many words lies mistrust, and that truth is ever naked, let this suffice for a country wooing, Saladyne loves Aliena, and none but Aliena.'

Although these words were most heavenly harmony in the ears of the shepherdess, yet to seem coy at the first courting, and to disdain love howsoever she desired love, she made this reply:

'Ah, Saladyne, though I seem simple, yet I am more subtle than to swallow the hook because it hath a painted bait: as men are wily so women are wary, especially if they have that wit by others' harms to beware. Do we not know, Saladyne, men's tongues are like Mercury's pipe, that can enchant Argus with an hundred eyes, and their words as prejudicial as the charms of Circes, that transform men into monsters.[8] If such Sirens sing, we poor women had need stop our ears, lest in hearing we prove so foolish hardy as to believe them, and so perish in trusting much and suspecting little. Saladyne, *piscator ictus sapit*,[9] he that hath been once poisoned and afterwards fears not to bowse[1] of every potion, is worthy to suffer double penance. Give me leave then to mistrust, though I do not condemn. Saladyne is now in love with Aliena, he a gentleman of great parentage, she a shepherdess of mean parents; he honourable and she poor? Can love consist of

---

5. **cumber:** burden.
6. **charily:** warily.
7. **at . . . list:** as I liked.
8. **men's . . . monsters:** The god Mercury lulled the many-headed monster **Argus** asleep with his flute; **Circe** in the *Odyssey* used her magic to transform men into animals.
9. The fisherman learns from a sting (Latin).
1. **bowse:** drink.

contrarieties? Will the falcon perch with the kestrel,[2] the lion harbour with the wolf? Will Venus join robes and rags together, or can there be a sympathy between a king and a beggar? Then, Saladyne, how can I believe thee that love should unite our thoughts, when fortune hath set such a difference between our degrees? But suppose thou likest Aliena's beauty: men in their fancy resemble the wasp, which scorns that flower from which she hath fetched her wax; playing like the inhabitants of the island Tenerifa, who, when they have gathered the sweet spices, use the trees for fuel; so men, when they have glutted themselves with the fair of women's faces, hold them for necessary evils, and wearied with that which they seemed so much to love, cast away fancy as children do their rattles, and loathing that which so deeply before they liked; especially such as take love in a minute and have their eyes attractive, like jet,[3] apt to entertain any object, are as ready to let it slip again.'

Saladyne, hearing how Aliena harped still upon one string, which was the doubt of men's constancy, he broke off her sharp invective thus:

'I grant, Aliena,' quoth he, 'many men have done amiss in proving soon ripe and soon rotten; but particular instances infer no general conclusions, and therefore I hope what others have faulted in shall not prejudice my favours. I will not use sophistry to confirm my love, for that is subtlety; nor long discourses lest my words might be thought more than my faith: but if this will suffice, that by the honour of a gentleman I love Aliena, and woo Aliena, not to crop the blossoms and reject the tree, but to consummate my faithful desires in the honourable end of marriage.'

At the word marriage Aliena stood in a maze what to answer, fearing that if she were too coy, to drive him away with her disdain, and if she were too courteous, to discover the heat of her desires. In a dilemma thus what to do, at last this she said:

'Saladyne, ever since I saw thee, I favoured thee; I cannot dissemble my desires, because I see thou dost faithfully manifest thy thoughts, and in liking thee I love thee so far as mine honour holds fancy still in suspense; but if I knew thee as virtuous as thy father, or as well qualified as thy brother Rosader, the doubt should be quickly decided: but for this time to give thee an answer, assure thyself this, I will either marry with Saladyne, or still live a virgin.'

And with this they strained one another's hand; which Ganymede espying, thinking he had had his mistress long enough at shrift,[4] said:

---

2. **kestrel**: species of small hawk.
3. **have . . . jet**: have eyes that attract like jet, a form of hard, black coal with magnetic properties.
4. **shrift**: confession.

'What, a match or no?'

'A match,' quoth Aliena, 'or else it were an ill market.'

'I am glad,' quoth Ganymede. 'I would Rosader were well here to make up a mess.'[5]

'Well remembered,' quoth Saladyne; 'I forgot I left my brother Rosader alone, and therefore lest being solitary he should increase his sorrows, I will haste me to him. May it please you, then, to command me any service to him, I am ready to be a dutiful messenger.'

'Only at this time commend me to him,' quoth Aliena, 'and tell him, though we cannot pleasure him we pray for him.'

'And forget not,' quoth Ganymede, 'my commendations; but say to him that Rosalynde sheds as many tears from her heart as he drops of blood from his wounds, for the sorrow of his misfortunes, feathering all her thoughts with disquiet, till his welfare procure her content. Say thus, good Saladyne, and so farewell.'

He having his message, gave a courteous adieu to them both, especially to Aliena, and so playing loath to depart, went to his brother. But Aliena, she perplexed and yet joyful, passed away the day pleasantly, still praising the perfection of Saladyne, not ceasing to chat of her new love till evening drew on; and then they, folding their sheep, went home to bed. Where we leave them and return to Phoebe.

Phoebe, fired with the uncouth flame of love, returned to her father's house, so galled with restless passions, as now she began to acknowledge, that as there was no flower so fresh but might be parched with the sun, no tree so strong but might be shaken with a storm, so there was no thought so chaste, but time armed with love could make amorous; for she that held Diana for the goddess of her devotion, was now fain to fly to the altar of Venus, as suppliant now with prayers, as she was forward before with disdain. As she lay in her bed, she called to mind the several beauties of young Ganymede; first his locks, which being amber-hued, passeth the wreath that Phoebus puts on to make his front glorious; his brow of ivory was like the seat where love and majesty sits enthroned to enchain fancy; his eyes as bright as the burnishing of the heaven, darting forth frowns with disdain and smiles with favour, lightning such looks as would inflame desire, were she wrapped in the circle of the frozen zone;[6] in his cheeks the vermilion teinture of the rose flourished upon natural alabaster, the blush of the morn and Luna's silver show were so lively portrayed, that the Troyan that fills out wine to Jupiter[7] was not half so beautiful; his face was full of pleasance,

5. **make up a mess:** fill out the disorderly group.
6. **circle . . . zone:** Arctic circle.
7. **Troyan . . . Jupiter:** Ganymede, cupbearer to **Jupiter**.

and all the rest of his lineaments proportioned with such excellence, as Phoebe was fettered in the sweetness of his feature. The idea of these perfections tumbling in her mind made the poor shepherdess so perplexed, as feeling a pleasure tempered with intolerable pains, and yet a disquiet mixed with a content, she rather wished to die than to live in this amorous anguish. But wishing is little worth in such extremes, and therefore was she forced to pine in her malady, without any salve for her sorrows. Reveal it she durst not, as daring in such matters to make none her secretary,[8] and to conceal it, why, it doubled her grief; for as fire suppressed grows to the greater flame, and the current stopped to the more violent stream, so love smothered wrings the heart with the deeper passions.

Perplexed thus with sundry agonies, her food began to fail, and the disquiet of her mind began to work a distemperature of her body, that, to be short, Phoebe fell extreme sick, and so sick as there was almost left no recovery of health. Her father, seeing his fair Phoebe thus distressed, sent for his friends, who sought by medicine to cure, and by counsel to pacify, but all in vain; for although her body was feeble through long fasting, yet she did *magis aegrotare animo quam corpore.*[9] Which her friends perceived and sorrowed at, but salve it they could not.

The news of her sickness was bruited abroad through all the forest, which no sooner came to Montanus' ear, but he, like a madman, came to visit Phoebe. Where sitting by her bedside he began his exordium with so many tears and sighs, that she, perceiving the extremity of his sorrows, began now as a lover to pity them, although Ganymede held her from redressing them. Montanus craved to know the cause of her sickness, tempered with secret plaints, but she answered him, as the rest, with silence, having still the form of Ganymede in her mind, and conjecturing how she might reveal her loves. To utter it in words she found herself too bashful; to discourse by any friend she would not trust any in her amours; to remain thus perplexed still and conceal all, it was a double death. Whereupon, for her last refuge, she resolved to write unto Ganymede, and therefore desired Montanus to absent himself a while, but not to depart, for she would see if she could steal a nap. He was no sooner gone out of the chamber, but reaching to her standish,[1] she took pen and paper, and wrote a letter to this effect:

'Phoebe to Ganymede wisheth what she wants herself.

---

8. **secretary:** confidante.
9. fall ill more in mind than in body (Latin).
1. **standish:** ink stand.

Fair shepherd—and therefore is Phoebe infortunate, because thou art so fair—although hitherto mine eyes were adamants to resist love, yet I no sooner saw thy face, but they became amorous to entertain love; more devoted to fancy than before they were repugnant to affection, addicted to the one by nature and drawn to the other by beauty: which, being rare and made the more excellent by many virtues, hath so snared the freedom of Phoebe, as she rests at thy mercy, either to be made the most fortunate of all maidens, or the most miserable of all women. Measure not, Ganymede, my loves by my wealth, nor my desires by my degrees; but think my thoughts as full of faith, as thy face of amiable favours. Then, as thou knowest thyself most beautiful, suppose me most constant. If thou deemest me hard-hearted because I hated Montanus, think I was forced to it by fate; if thou sayest I am kind-hearted because so lightly I love thee at the first look, think I was driven to it by destiny, whose influence, as it is mighty, so is it not to be resisted. If my fortunes were anything but infortunate love, I would strive with fortune: but he that wrests against the will of Venus, seeks to quench fire with oil, and to thrust out one thorn by putting in another. If then, Ganymede, love enters at the eye, harbours in the heart, and will neither be driven out with physic nor reason, pity me, as one whose malady hath no salve but from thy sweet self, whose grief hath no ease but through thy grant; and think I am a virgin who is deeply wronged when I am forced to woo, and conjecture love to be strong, that is more forcible than nature. Thus distressed unless by thee eased, I expect either to live fortunate by thy favour, or die miserable by thy denial. Living in hope. Farewell.

She that must be thine,

or not be at all,

Phoebe.'

To this letter she annexed this sonnet:

Sonetto

My boat doth pass the straits
of seas incensed with fire,
Filled with forgetfulness;
amidst the winter's night,
A blind and careless boy,
brought up by fond desire,
Doth guide me in the sea
of sorrow and despite.

For every oar he sets
a rank of foolish thoughts,

And cuts, instead of wave,
   a hope without distress;
The winds of my deep sighs,
   that thunder still for noughts,
Have split my sails with fear,
   with care and heaviness.

A mighty storm of tears,
   a black and hideous cloud,
A thousand fierce disdains
   do slack the halyards[2] oft;
Till ignorance do pull,
   and error hale the shrouds,[3]
No star for safety shines,
   no Phoebe from aloft.

      Time hath subdued art,
         and joy is slave to woe:
      Alas, Love's guide, be kind!
         what, shall I perish so?

    This letter and the sonnet being ended, she could find no fit messenger to send it by, and therefore she called in Montanus, and entreated him to carry it to Ganymede. Although poor Montanus saw day at a little hole, and did perceive what passion pinched her, yet, that he might seem dutiful to his mistress in all service, he dissembled the matter, and became a willing messenger of his own martyrdom. And so, taking the letter, went the next morn very early to the plains where Aliena fed her flocks, and there he found Ganymede, sitting under a pomegranate tree, sorrowing for the hard fortunes of her Rosader. Montanus saluted him, and according to his charge delivered Ganymede the letters, which, he said, came from Phoebe. At this the wanton blushed, as being abashed to think what news should come from an unknown shepherdess; but taking the letters, unripped the seals, and read over the discourse of Phoebe's fancies. When she had read and over-read them Ganymede began to smile, and looking on Montanus, fell into a great laughter, and with that called Aliena, to whom she showed the writings. Who, having perused them, conceited them very pleasantly, and smiled to see how love had yoked her, who before would not stoop to the lure; Aliena whispering Ganymede in the ear, and saying, 'Knew Phoebe what want there were in thee to perform her will, and how unfit thy kind is to be kind to her, she would be more

---

2. **slack . . . halyards:** cause the ropes to slacken (from sailing).
3. **hale . . . shrouds:** pull the ropes that connect to the masthead.

wise, and less enamoured; but leaving that, I pray thee let us sport with this swain.' At that word Ganymede, turning to Montanus, began to glance at him thus:

'I pray thee, tell me, shepherd, by those sweet thoughts and pleasing sighs that grow from my mistress' favours, art thou in love with Phoebe?'

'Oh, my youth,' quoth Montanus, 'were Phoebe so far in love with me, my flocks would be more fat and their master more quiet; for through the sorrows of my discontent grows the leanness of my sheep.'

'Alas, poor swain,' quoth Ganymede, 'are thy passions so extreme or thy fancy so resolute, that no reason will blemish the pride of thy affection, and rase out that which thou strivest for without hope?'

'Nothing can make me forget Phoebe, while Montanus forget himself; for those characters which true love hath stamped, neither the envy of time nor fortune can wipe away.'

'Why but, Montanus,' quoth Ganymede, 'enter with a deep insight into the despair of thy fancies, and thou shalt see the depth of thine own follies; for, poor man, thy progress in love is a regress to loss, swimming against the stream with the crab, and flying with Apis Indica[4] against wind and weather. Thou seekest with Phoebus to win Daphne, and she flies faster than thou canst follow: thy desires soar with the hobby, but her disdain reacheth higher than thou canst make wing. I tell thee, Montanus, in courting Phoebe, thou barkest with the wolves of Syria against the moon, and rovest at such a mark, with thy thoughts, as is beyond the pitch[5] of thy bow, praying to Love, when Love is pitiless, and thy malady remediless. For proof, Montanus, read these letters, wherein thou shalt see thy great follies and little hope.'

With that Montanus took them and perused them, but with such sorrow in his looks, as they betrayed a source of confused passions in his heart; at every line his colour changed, and every sentence was ended with a period of sighs.

At last, noting Phoebe's extreme desire toward Ganymede and her disdain towards him, giving Ganymede the letter, the shepherd stood as though he had neither won nor lost. Which Ganymede perceiving wakened him out of his dream thus:

'Now, Montanus, dost thou see thou vowest great service and obtainest but little reward; but in lieu of thy loyalty, she maketh thee, as Bellerophon, carry thine own bane.[6] Then drink not willingly of that potion wherein thou knowest is poison; creep not to her that cares not for thee. What, Montanus, there are many as fair

---

4. **Apis Indica:** Asian honeybee, capable of long flight.
5. **pitch:** reach.
6. **Bellerophon . . . bane:** mythological figure who unknowingly carried a message stating that he himself should be killed.

as Phoebe, but most of all more courteous than Phoebe. I tell thee, shepherd, favour is love's fuel; then since thou canst not get that, let the flame vanish into smoke, and rather sorrow for a while than repent thee for ever.'

'I tell thee, Ganymede,' quoth Montanus, 'as they which are stung with the scorpion, cannot be recovered but by the scorpion, nor he that was wounded with Achilles'[7] lance be cured but with the same truncheon, so Apollo was fain to cry out that love was only eased with love, and fancy healed by no medicine but favour. Phoebus had herbs to heal all hurts but this passion; Circes had charms for all chances but for affection, and Mercury subtle reasons to refel all griefs but love. Persuasions are bootless,[8] reason lends no remedy, counsel no comfort, to such whom fancy hath made resolute; and therefore though Phoebe loves Ganymede, yet Montanus must honour none but Phoebe.'

'Then,' quoth Ganymede, 'may I rightly term thee a despairing lover, that livest without joy, and lovest without hope. But what shall I do, Montanus, to pleasure thee? Shall I despise Phoebe, as she disdains thee?'

'Oh,' quoth Montanus, 'that were to renew my griefs, and double my sorrows; for the sight of her discontent were the censure of my death.[9] Alas, Ganymede! though I perish in my thoughts, let not her die in her desires. Of all passions, love is most impatient: then let not so fair a creature as Phoebe sink under the burden of so deep a distress. Being lovesick, she is proved heartsick, and all for the beauty of Ganymede. Thy proportion hath entangled her affection, and she is snared in the beauty of thy excellence. Then, sith she loves thee so dear, mislike not her deadly. Be thou paramour to such a paragon: she hath beauty to content thine eye, and flocks to enrich thy store. Thou canst not wish for more than thou shalt win by her; for she is beautiful, virtuous and wealthy, three deep persuasions to make love frolic.'

Aliena seeing Montanus cut it against the hair,[1] and plead that Ganymede ought to love Phoebe, when his only life was the love of Phoebe, answered him thus:

'Why, Montanus, dost thou further this motion, seeing if Ganymede marry Phoebe thy market is clean marred?'

'Ah, mistress,' quoth he, 'so hath love taught me to honour Phoebe, that I would prejudice my life to pleasure her, and die in despair rather than she should perish for want. It shall suffice me to see her contented, and to feed mine eye on her favour. If she marry, though

---

7. **Achilles:** the best soldier on the Greek side in the Trojan war.
8. **bootless:** useless.
9. **were . . . death:** would be my death sentence.
1. **cut . . . hair:** i.e., go against his own interests.

it be my martyrdom, yet if she be pleased I will brook it with patience, and triumph in mine own stars to see her desires satisfied. Therefore, if Ganymede be as courteous as he is beautiful, let him show his virtues in redressing Phoebe's miseries.' And this Montanus pronounced with such an assured countenance, that it amazed both Aliena and Ganymede to see the resolution of his loves; so that they pitied his passions and commended his patience, devising how they might by any subtlety get Montanus the favour of Phoebe. Straight, as women's heads are full of wiles, Ganymede had a fetch[2] to force Phoebe to fancy the shepherd, malgrado[3] the resolution of her mind: he prosecuted his policy thus:

'Montanus,' quoth he, 'seeing Phoebe is so forlorn, lest I might be counted unkind in not salving so fair a creature, I will go with thee to Phoebe, and there hear herself in word utter that which she hath discoursed with her pen; and then, as love wills me, I will set down my censure. I will home by our house, and send Corydon to accompany Aliena.'

Montanus seemed glad of this determination and away they go towards the house of Phoebe.

When they drew nigh to the cottage, Montanus ran before, and went in and told Phoebe that Ganymede was at the door. This word 'Ganymede,' sounding in the ears of Phoebe, drave her into such an ecstasy for joy, that rising up in her bed, she was half revived, and her wan colour began to wax red; and with that came Ganymede in, who saluted Phoebe with such a courteous look, that it was half a salve to her sorrows. Sitting him down by her bedside, he questioned about her disease, and where the pain chiefly held her? Phoebe looking as lovely as Venus in her night-gear, tainting her face with as ruddy a blush as Clytia[4] did when she bewrayed her loves to Phoebus, taking Ganymede by the hand began thus:

'Fair shepherd, if love were not more strong than nature, or fancy the sharpest extreme, my immodesty were the more, and my virtues the less; for nature hath framed women's eyes bashful, their hearts full of fear, and their tongues full of silence; but love, that imperious love, where his power is predominant, then he perverts all, and wresteth the wealth of nature to his own will: an instance in myself, fair Ganymede, for such a fire hath he kindled in my thoughts, that to find ease for the flame, I was forced to pass the bounds of modesty, and seek a salve at thy hands for my harms. Blame me not if I be overbold for it is thy beauty, and if I be too forward it is fancy, and the deep insight into thy virtues that makes me thus fond; for

2. **fetch:** trick.
3. **malgrado:** in spite of.
4. **Clytia:** water nymph loved by Phoebus/Apollo.

let me say in a word what may be contained in a volume, Phoebe loves Ganymede.'

At this she held down her head and wept, and Ganymede rose as one that would suffer no fish to hang on his fingers,[5] made this reply:

'Water not thy plants, Phoebe, for I do pity thy plaints, nor seek not to discover thy loves in tears, for I conjecture thy truth by thy passions: sorrow is no salve for loves, nor sighs no remedy for affection. Therefore frolic, Phoebe; for if Ganymede can cure thee, doubt not of recovery. Yet this let me say without offence, that it grieves me to thwart Montanus in his fancies, seeing his desires have been so resolute, and his thoughts so loyal. But thou allegest that thou art forced from him by fate: so I tell thee, Phoebe, either some star or else some destiny fits my mind, rather with Adonis to die in chase than be counted a wanton on Venus' knee.[6] Although I pity thy martyrdom, yet I can grant no marriage; for though I held thee fair, yet mine eye is not fettered. Love grows not, like the herb Spattana,[7] to his perfection in one night, but creeps with the snail, and yet at last attains to the top. *Festina lente*,[8] especially in love, for momentary fancies are oft-times the fruits of follies. If, Phoebe, I should like thee as the Hyperborei do their dates, which banquet with them in the morning and throw them away at night, my folly should be great, and thy repentance more. Therefore I will have time to turn my thoughts, and my loves shall grow up as the watercresses, slowly, but with a deep root. Thus, Phoebe, thou mayest see I disdain not, though I desire not; remaining indifferent till time and love makes me resolute. Therefore, Phoebe, seek not to suppress affection, and with the love of Montanus quench the remembrance of Ganymede; strive thou to hate me as I seek to like of thee, and ever have the duties of Montanus in thy mind, for I promise thee thou mayest have one more wealthy, but not more loyal.' These words were corrosives to the perplexed Phoebe, that sobbing out sighs, and straining out tears, she blubbered out these words:

'And shall I then have no salve of Ganymede but suspense, no hope but a doubtful hazard, no comfort, but be posted off to the will of time? Justly have the gods balanced my fortunes, who, being cruel to Montanus, found Ganymede as unkind to myself; so in forcing him perish for love, I shall die myself with overmuch love.'

5. **would . . . fingers:** was in a hurry to be off.
6. **with . . . knee:** [I would] rather die actively during hunting like Venus' lover **Adonis** than be one of **Venus'** infant Cupids who never left her lap.
7. **Spattana:** (or spattania) a plant that grows and dies back very quickly.
8. Hasten slowly (Latin).

'I am glad,' quoth Ganymede, 'you look into your own faults, and see where your shoe wrings[9] you, measuring now the pains of Montanus by your own passions.'

'Truth,' quoth Phoebe, 'and so deeply I repent me of my frowardness toward the shepherd, that could I cease to love Ganymede, I would resolve to like Montanus.'

'What, if I can with reason persuade Phoebe to mislike of Ganymede, will she then favour Montanus?'

'When reason,' quoth she, 'doth quench that love I owe to thee, then will I fancy him; conditionally, that if my love can be suppressed with no reason, as being without reason Ganymede will only wed himself to Phoebe.'

'I grant it, fair shepherdess,' quoth he; 'and to feed thee with the sweetness of hope, this resolve on: I will never marry myself to woman but unto thyself.'

And with that Ganymede gave Phoebe a fruitless kiss, and such words of comfort, that before Ganymede departed she arose out of her bed, and made him and Montanus such cheer, as could be found in such a country cottage; Ganymede in the midst of their banquet rehearsing the promises of either in Montanus' favour, which highly pleased the shepherd. Thus, all three content, and soothed up in hope, Ganymede took his leave of his Phoebe and departed, leaving her a contented woman, and Montanus highly pleased. But poor Ganymede, who had her thoughts on her Rosader, when she called to remembrance his wounds, filled her eyes full of tears, and her heart full of sorrows, plodded to find Aliena at the folds, thinking with her presence to drive away her passions. As she came on the plains she might espy where Rosader and Saladyne sate with Aliena under the shade; which sight was a salve to her grief, and such a cordial unto her heart, that she tripped alongst the lawns full of joy.

At last Corydon, who was with them, spied Ganymede, and with that the clown[1] rose, and, running to meet him, cried:

'O sirrah, a match, a match! our mistress shall be married on Sunday.'

Thus the poor peasant frolicked it before Ganymede, who coming to the crew saluted them all, and especially Rosader, saying that he was glad to see him so well recovered of his wounds.

'I had not gone abroad so soon,' quoth Rosader, 'but that I am bidden to a marriage, which, on Sunday next, must be solemnized between my brother and Aliena. I see well where love leads delay is loathsome, and that small wooing serves where both the parties are willing.'

---

9. **wrings:** pinches.
1. **clown:** country fellow.

'Truth,' quoth Ganymede; 'but a happy day should it be, if Rosader that day might be married to Rosalynde.'

'Ah, good Ganymede,' quoth he, 'by naming Rosalynde, renew not my sorrows; for the thought of her perfections is the thrall of my miseries.'

'Tush, be of good cheer, man,' quoth Ganymede: 'I have a friend that is deeply experienced in negromancy[2] and magic; what art can do shall be acted for thine advantage. I will cause him to bring in Rosalynde, if either France or any bordering nation harbour her; and upon that take the faith of a young shepherd.'

Aliena smiled to see how Rosader frowned, thinking that Ganymede had jested with him. But, breaking off from those matters, the page, somewhat pleasant, began to discourse unto them what had passed between him and Phoebe; which, as they laughed, so they wondered at, all confessing that there is none so chaste but love will change. Thus they passed away the day in chat, and when the sun began to set they took their leaves and departed; Aliena providing for their marriage day such solemn cheer and handsome robes as fitted their country estate, and yet somewhat the better, in that Rosader had promised to bring Gerismond thither as a guest. Ganymede, who then meant to discover herself before her father, had made her a gown of green, and a kirtle of the finest sendal,[3] in such sort that she seemed some heavenly nymph harboured in country attire.

Saladyne was not behind in care to set out the nuptials, nor Rosader unmindful to bid guests, who invited Gerismond and all his followers to the feast, who willingly granted, so that there was nothing but the day wanting[4] to this marriage.

In the meanwhile, Phoebe being a bidden guest made herself as gorgeous as might be to please the eye of Ganymede; and Montanus suited himself with the cost of many of his flocks to be gallant against[5] the day, for then was Ganymede to give Phoebe an answer of her loves, and Montanus either to hear the doom of his misery, or the censure of his happiness. But while this gear was a-brewing, Phoebe passed not one day without visiting her Ganymede, so far was she wrapped in the beauties of this lovely swain. Much prattle they had, and the discourse of many passions, Phoebe wishing for the day, as she thought, of her welfare, and Ganymede smiling to think what unexpected events would fall out at the wedding. In these humours the week went away, that at last Sunday came.

No sooner did Phoebus' henchman[6] appear in the sky, to give warning that his master's horses should be trapped in his glorious

2. **negromancy:** enchantment.
3. **kirtle . . . sendal:** outer skirt of thin, silky fabric.
4. **wanting:** missing.
5. **against:** in anticipation of.
6. **Phoebus' henchman:** servant of Phoebus, the sun god.

coach, but Corydon, in his holiday suit, marvellous seemly, in a rus-
set jacket, welted with the same and faced with red worsted, having
a pair of blue chamlet[7] sleeves, bound at the wrists with four yellow
laces, closed before very richly with a dozen of pewter buttons; his
hose was of grey kersey,[8] with a large slop barred overthwart the
pocket-holes with three fair guards,[9] stitched of either side with red
thread; his stock was of the own, sewed close to his breech, and for
to beautify his hose, he had trussed himself round with a dozen of
new-threaden points of medley colour:[1] his bonnet was green,
whereon stood a copper brooch with the picture of Saint Denis;[2]
and to want nothing that might make him amorous in his old days,
he had a fair shirt-band of fine lockram, whipped over[3] with Coventry blue of no small cost. Thus attired, Corydon bestirred himself
as chief stickler[4] in these actions, and had strowed all the house
with flowers, that it seemed rather some of Flora's choice bowers
than any country cottage.

Thither repaired Phoebe with all the maids of the forest, to set
out the bride in the most seemliest sort that might be; but howsoever she helped to prank out Aliena, yet her eye was still on Ganymede, who was so neat in a suit of grey, that he seemed Endymion
when he won Luna with his looks, or Paris when he played the
swain to get the beauty of the nymph Oenone. Ganymede, like a
pretty page, waited on his mistress Aliena, and overlooked that all
was in a readiness against the bridegroom should come; who, attired
in a forester's suit, came accompanied with Gerismond and his
brother Rosader early in the morning; where arrived, they were solemnly entertained by Aliena and the rest of the country swains;
Gerismond very highly commending the fortunate choice of Saladyne, in that he had chosen a shepherdess, whose virtues appeared
in her outward beauties, being no less fair than seeming modest.
Ganymede coming in, and seeing her father, began to blush, nature
working affects by her secret effects. Scarce could she abstain from
tears to see her father in so low fortunes, he that was wont to sit in
his royal palace, attended on by twelve noble peers, now to be contented with a simple cottage, and a troop of revelling woodmen for
his train. The consideration of his fall made Ganymede full of sorrows; yet, that she might triumph over fortune with patience, and
not any way dash that merry day with her dumps, she smothered her

---

7. **chamlet:** fabric of wool and silk.
8. **kersey:** coarse cloth.
9. **slop . . . guards:** baggy breeches striped crosswise with three rows of decorative trim.
1. **new-threaden . . . colour:** multi-colored tags of new thread (used to attach the hose to the breeches).
2. **Saint Denis:** patron saint of France.
3. **lockram . . . over:** linen embroidered.
4. **stickler:** master of ceremonies.

melancholy with a shadow of mirth, and very reverently welcomed the king, not according to his former degree, but to his present estate, with such diligence as Gerismond began to commend the page for his exquisite person and excellent qualities.

As thus the king with his foresters frolicked it among the shepherds, Corydon came in with a fair mazer full of cider, and presented it to Gerismond with such a clownish salute that he began to smile, and took it of the old shepherd very kindly, drinking to Aliena and the rest of her fair maids, amongst whom Phoebe was the foremost. Aliena pledged the king, and drunk to Rosader; so the carouse went round from him to Phoebe, &c. As they were thus drinking and ready to go to church, came in Montanus, apparelled all in tawny, to signify that he was forsaken; on his head he wore a garland of willow, his bottle hanged by his side, whereon was painted despair, and on his sheep-hook hung two sonnets, as labels of his loves and fortunes.

Thus attired came Montanus in, with his face as full of grief as his heart was of sorrows, showing in his countenance the map of extremities. As soon as the shepherds saw him, they did him all the honour they could, as being the flower of all the swains in Arden; for a bonnier boy was there not seen since that wanton wag of Troy that kept sheep in Ida.[5] He, seeing the king, and guessing it to be Gerismond, did him all the reverence his country courtesy could afford; insomuch that the king, wondering at his attire, began to question what he was. Montanus overhearing him, made this reply:

'I am, sir,' quoth he, 'Love's swain, as full of inward discontents as I seem fraught with outward follies. Mine eyes like bees delight in sweet flowers, but sucking their full on the fair of beauty, they carry home to the hive of my heart far more gall than honey, and for one drop of pure dew, a ton full of deadly Aconiton. I hunt with the fly to pursue the eagle, that flying too nigh the sun, I perish with the sun; my thoughts are above my reach, and my desires more than my fortunes, yet neither greater than my loves. But daring with Phaëthon, I fall with Icarus, and seeking to pass the mean, I die for being so mean; my night-sleeps are waking slumbers, as full of sorrows as they be far from rest; and my days' labours are fruitless amours, staring at a star and stumbling at a straw, leaving reason to follow after repentance; yet every passion is a pleasure though it pinch, because love hides his wormseed in figs, his poisons in sweet potions, and shadows prejudice with the mask of pleasure. The wisest counsellors are my deep discontents, and I hate that which should salve my harm, like the patient which stung with the Tarantula loathes music, and yet the disease incurable but

5. **wanton . . . Ida:** Paris of **Troy**, who spent his early years as a shepherd on Mount **Ida**.

by melody.[6] Thus, sir, restless I hold myself remediless, as loving
without either reward or regard, and yet loving because there is none
worthy to be loved but the mistress of my thoughts. And that I am
as full of passions as I have discoursed in my plaints, sir, if you
please, see my sonnets, and by them censure of my sorrows.'
    These words of Montanus brought the king into a great wonder,
amazed as much at his wit as his attire, insomuch that he took the
papers off his hook, and read them to this effect:

Montanus' first Sonnet

Alas! how wander I amidst these woods
    Whereas no day-bright shine doth find access;
But where the melancholy fleeting floods,
    Dark as the night, my night of woes express.
Disarmed of reason, spoiled of nature's goods,
    Without redress to salve my heaviness
        I walk, whilst thought, too cruel to my harms,
        With endless grief my heedless judgment charms.

My silent tongue assailed by secret fear,
    My traitorous eyes imprisoned in their joy,
My fatal peace devoured in feignèd cheer,
    My heart enforced to harbour in annoy,
My reason robbed of power by yielding ear,
    My fond opinions slave to every toy.
        O Love! thou guide in my uncertain way,
        Woe to thy bow, thy fire, the cause of my decay.
                                    Et florida pungunt.

    When the king had read this sonnet he highly commended the
device of the shepherd, that could so wittily wrap his passions in
a shadow, and so covertly conceal that which bred his chiefest
discontent; affirming, that as the least shrubs have their tops, the
smallest hairs their shadows, so the meanest swains had their fancies, and in their kind were as chary of love as a king. Whetted on
with this device, he took the second and read it: the effects were
these:

Montanus' second Sonnet

When the Dog[7]
Full of rage,

---

6. **incurable . . . melody:** The bite of the tarantula was believed to be curable only by
dancing the tarantella.
7. **Dog:** Sirius, the dog star, associated with the heat of summer.

With his ireful eyes
Frowns amidst the skies,
The shepherd, to assuage
The fury of the heat,
Himself doth safely seat
By a fount
Full of fair,
Where a gentle breath,
Mounting from beneath,
Tempereth the air.
There his flocks
Drink their fill,
And with ease repose,
Whilst sweet sleep doth close
Eyes from toilsome ill.
But I burn
Without rest,
No defensive power
Shields from Phoebe's lour;
Sorrow is my best.
Gentle Love,
Lour no more;
If thou wilt invade
In the secret shade,
Labour not so sore.
I myself
And my flocks,
They their love to please,
I myself to ease,
Both leave the shady oaks;
Content to burn in fire,
Sith Love doth so desire.

Et florida pungunt.

Gerismond, seeing the pithy vein of those sonnets, began to make further inquiry what he was. Whereupon Rosader discoursed unto him the love of Montanus to Phoebe, his great loyalty and her deep cruelty, and how in revenge the gods had made the curious nymph amorous of young Ganymede. Upon this discourse the king was desirous to see Phoebe, who being brought before Gerismond by Rosader, shadowed the beauty of her face with such a vermilion teinture, that the king's eyes began to dazzle at the purity of her excellence. After Gerismond had fed his looks awhile upon her fair, he questioned with her why she rewarded Montanus' love with so little regard, seeing his deserts were many, and his passions extreme. Phoebe, to make reply to the king's demand, answered thus:

'Love, sir, is charity in his laws, and whatsoever he sets down for justice, be it never so unjust, the sentence cannot be reversed; women's fancies lend favours not ever by desert, but as they are enforced by their desires; for fancy is tied to the wings of fate, and what the stars decree, stands for an infallible doom. I know Montanus is wise, and women's ears are greatly delighted with wit, as hardly escaping the charm of a pleasant tongue, as Ulysses the melody of the Sirens. Montanus is beautiful, and women's eyes are snared in the excellence of objects, as desirous to feed their looks with a fair face, as the bee to suck on a sweet flower. Montanus is wealthy, and an ounce of *give me* persuades a woman more than a pound of *hear me*. Danaë was won with a golden shower, when she could not be gotten with all the entreaties of Jupiter. I tell you, sir, the string of a woman's heart reacheth to the pulse of her hand; and let a man rub that with gold, and 'tis hard but she will prove his heart's gold. Montanus is young, a great clause[8] in fancy's court; Montanus is virtuous, the richest argument that love yields; and yet knowing all these perfections, I praise them and wonder at them, loving the qualities, but not affecting the person, because the destinies have set down a contrary censure. Yet Venus, to add revenge, hath given me wine of the same grape, a sip of the same sauce, and firing me with the like passion, hath crossed me with as ill a penance; for I am in love with a shepherd's swain, as coy to me as I am cruel to Montanus, as peremptory in disdain as I was perverse in desire; and that is,' quoth she, 'Aliena's page, young Ganymede.'

Gerismond, desirous to prosecute the end of these passions, called in Ganymede, who, knowing the case, came in graced with such a blush, as beautified the crystal of his face with a ruddy brightness. The king noting well the physnomy of Ganymede, began by his favours to call to mind the face of his Rosalynde, and with that fetched a deep sigh. Rosader, that was passing familiar with Gerismond, demanded of him why he sighed so sore.

'Because Rosader,' quoth he, 'the favour of Ganymede puts me in mind of Rosalynde.'

At this word Rosader sighed so deeply, as though his heart would have burst.

'And what's the matter,' quoth Gerismond, 'that you quite[9] me with such a sigh?'

'Pardon me, sir,' quoth Rosader, 'because I love none but Rosalynde.'

'And upon that condition,' quoth Gerismond, 'that Rosalynde were here, I would this day make up a marriage betwixt her and thee.'

8. **clause:** member.
9. **quite:** requite.

At this Aliena turned her head and smiled upon Ganymede, and she could scarce keep countenance. Yet she salved all with secrecy; and Gerismond, to drive away his dumps, questioned with Ganymede, what the reason was he regarded not Phoebe's love, seeing she was as fair as the wanton that brought Troy to ruin.[1] Ganymede mildly answered:

'If I should affect the fair Phoebe, I should offer poor Montanus great wrong to win that from him in a moment, that he hath laboured for so many months. Yet have I promised to the beautiful shepherdess to wed myself never to woman except unto her; but with this promise, that if I can by reason suppress Phoebe's love towards me, she shall like of none but of Montanus.'

'To that,' quoth Phoebe, 'I stand; for my love is so far beyond reason, as will admit no persuasion of reason.'

'For justice,' quoth he, 'I appeal to Gerismond.'

'And to his censure will I stand,' quoth Phoebe.

'And in your victory,' quoth Montanus, 'stands the hazard of my fortunes; for if Ganymede go away with conquest, Montanus is in conceit love's monarch; if Phoebe win, then am I in effect most miserable.'

'We will see this controversy,' quoth Gerismond, 'and then we will to church. Therefore, Ganymede, let us hear your argument.'

'Nay, pardon my absence a while,' quoth she, 'and you shall see one in store.'[2]

In went Ganymede and dressed herself in woman's attire, having on a gown of green, with kirtle of rich sendal, so quaint, that she seemed Diana triumphing in the forest; upon her head she wore a chaplet of roses, which gave her such a grace that she looked like Flora perked in the pride of all her flowers. Thus attired came Rosalynde in, and presented herself at her father's feet, with her eyes full of tears, craving his blessing, and discoursing unto him all her fortunes, how she was banished by Torismond, and how ever since she lived in that country disguised.

Gerismond, seeing his daughter, rose from his seat and fell upon her neck, uttering the passions of his joy in watery plaints, driven into such an ecstasy of content, that he could not utter one word. At this sight, if Rosader was both amazed and joyful, I refer myself to the judgment of such as have experience in love, seeing his Rosalynde before his face whom so long and deeply he had affected. At last Gerismond recovered his spirits, and in most fatherly terms entertained his daughter Rosalynde, after many questions demanding of her what had passed between her and Rosader?

---

1. **wanton . . . ruin:** Helen of Troy.
2. **in store:** kept in reserve.

'So much, sir,' quoth she, 'as there wants nothing but your grace to make up the marriage.'

'Why, then,' quoth Gerismond, 'Rosader take her: she is thine, and let this day solemnize both thy brother's and thy nuptials.' Rosader beyond measure content, humbly thanked the king, and embraced his Rosalynde, who turning to Phoebe, demanded if she had shown sufficient reason to suppress the force of her loves.

'Yea,' quoth Phoebe, 'and so great a persuasive, that if it please you, madame, and Aliena to give us leave, Montanus and I will make this day the third couple in marriage.'

She had no sooner spake this word, but Montanus threw away his garland of willow, his bottle, where was painted despair, and cast his sonnets in the fire, showing himself as frolic as Paris when he hand-selled[3] his love with Helena. At this Gerismond and the rest smiled, and concluded that Montanus and Phoebe should keep their wedding with the two brethren. Aliena seeing Saladyne stand in a dump, to wake him from his dream began thus:

'Why how now, my Saladyne, all amort?[4] what melancholy, man, at the day of marriage? Perchance thou art sorrowful to think on thy brother's high fortunes, and thine own base desires to choose so mean a shepherdess. Cheer up thy heart, man; for this day thou shalt be married to the daughter of a king; for know, Saladyne, I am not Aliena, but Alinda, the daughter of thy mortal enemy Torismond.'

At this all the company was amazed, especially Gerismond, who rising up, took Alinda in his arms, and said to Rosalynde:

'Is this that fair Alinda famous for so many virtues, that forsook her father's court to live with thee exiled in the country?'

'The same,' quoth Rosalynde.

'Then,' quoth Gerismond, turning to Saladyne, 'jolly forester be frolic, for thy fortunes are great, and thy desires excellent; thou hast got a princess as famous for her perfection, as exceeding in proportion.'

'And she hath with her beauty won,' quoth Saladyne, 'an humble servant, as full of faith as she of amiable favour.'

While every one was amazed with these comical events, Corydon came skipping in, and told them that the priest was at church, and tarried for their coming. With that Gerismond led the way, and the rest followed; where to the admiration of all the country swains in Arden their marriages were solemnly solemnized. As soon as the priest had finished home they went with Alinda, where Corydon had made all things in readiness. Dinner was provided, and the tables

---

3. **handselled:** pledged.
4. **amort:** dejected.

being spread, and the brides set down by Gerismond, Rosader, Saladyne, and Montanus that day were servitors; homely cheer they had, such as their country could afford, but to mend their fare they had mickle[5] good chat, and many discourses of their loves and fortunes. About mid-dinner, to make them merry, Corydon came in with an old crowd,[6] and played them a fit of mirth, to which he sung this pleasant song:

Corydon's Song

A blithe and bonny country lass,
    heigh ho, the bonny lass!
Sate sighing on the tender grass
    and weeping said, will none come woo her.
A smicker[7] boy, a lither swain,
    heigh ho, a smicker swain!
That in his love was wanton fain,
    with smiling looks straight came unto her.

Whenas the wanton wench espied,
    heigh ho, when she espied!
The means to make herself a bride,
    she simpered smooth like Bonnybell:[8]
The swain, that saw her squint-eyed kind,
    heigh ho, squint-eyed kind!
His arms about her body twined,
    and: 'Fair lass, how fare ye, well?'

The country kit said: 'Well, forsooth,
    heigh ho, well forsooth!
But that I have a longing tooth,
    a longing tooth that makes me cry.'
'Alas!' said he, 'what gars[9] thy grief?
    heigh ho, what gars thy grief?'
'A wound,' quoth she, 'without relief,
    I fear a maid that I shall die.'
'If that be all,' the shepherd said,
    heigh ho, the shepherd said!
'Ile make thee wive it gentle maid,
    and so recure thy malady.'

---

5. **mickle:** much.
6. **crowd:** stringed instrument, ancestor of the fiddle.
7. **smicker:** handsome.
8. **Bonnybell:** ballad heroine.
9. **gars:** causes.

Hereon they kissed with many an oath,
   heigh ho, with many an oath!
And fore God Pan did plight their troth,
   and to the church they hied them fast.
And God send every pretty peat,[1]
   heigh ho, the pretty peat!
That fears to die of this conceit,
   so kind a friend to help at last.

Corydon having thus made them merry, as they were in the
midst of their jollity, word was brought in to Saladyne and Rosader
that a brother of theirs, one Fernandyne, was arrived, and desired
to speak with them. Gerismond overhearing this news, demanded
who it was.

'It is, sir,' quoth Rosader, 'our middle brother, that lives a scholar in
Paris; but what fortune hath driven him to seek us out I know not.'

With that Saladyne went and met his brother, whom he welcomed
with all courtesy, and Rosader gave him no less friendly entertainment; brought he was by his two brothers into the parlour where
they all sate at dinner. Fernandyne, as one that knew as many manners as he could points of sophistry, and was as well brought up as
well lettered, saluted them all. But when he espied Gerismond,
kneeling on his knee he did him what reverence belonged to his
estate, and with that burst forth into these speeches:

'Although, right mighty prince, this day of my brother's marriage
be a day of mirth, yet time craves another course; and therefore
from dainty cates rise to sharp weapons. And you, the sons of Sir
John of Bordeaux, leave off your amours and fall to arms; change
your loves into lances, and now this day show yourselves as valiant
as hitherto you have been passionate. For know, Gerismond, that
hard by at the edge of this forest the twelve peers of France are up
in arms to recover thy right; and Torismond, trooped with a crew of
desperate runagates,[2] is ready to bid them battle. The armies are
ready to join; therefore show thyself in the field to encourage thy
subjects. And you, Saladyne and Rosader, mount you, and show
yourselves as hardy soldiers as you have been hearty lovers; so shall
you, for the benefit of your country, discover the idea of your
father's virtues to be stamped in your thoughts, and prove children
worthy of so honourable a parent.'

At this alarm, given him by Fernandyne, Gerismond leaped from
the board, and Saladyne and Rosader betook themselves to their
weapons.

---

1. **peat:** girl.
2. **runagates:** renegades, outlaws.

'Nay,' quoth Gerismond, 'go with me; I have horse and armour for us all, and then, being well mounted, let us show that we carry revenge and honour at our falchions'[3] points.'

Thus they leave the brides full of sorrow, especially Alinda, who desired Gerismond to be good to her father. He, not returning a word because his haste was great, hied him home to his lodge, where he delivered Saladyne and Rosader horse and armour, and himself armed royally led the way; not having ridden two leagues before they discovered where in a valley both the battles were joined. Gerismond seeing the wing wherein the peers fought, thrust in there, and cried 'Saint Denis!' Gerismond laying on such load upon his enemies, that he showed how highly he did estimate of a crown. When the peers perceived that their lawful king was there, they grew more eager; and Saladyne and Rosader so behaved themselves, that none durst stand in their way, nor abide the fury of their weapons. To be short, the peers were conquerors, Torismond's army put to flight, and himself slain in battle. The peers then gathered themselves together, and saluted their king, conducted him royally into Paris, where he was received with great joy of all the citizens. As soon as all was quiet and he had received again the crown, he sent for Alinda and Rosalynde to the court, Alinda being very passionate for the death of her father, yet brooking it with the more patience, in that she was contented with the welfare of her Saladyne.

Well, as soon as they were come to Paris, Gerismond made a royal feast for the peers and lords of his land, which continued thirty days, in which time summoning a parliament, by the consent of his nobles he created Rosader heir apparent to the kingdom; he restored Saladyne to all his father's land and gave him the Dukedom of Nameurs; he made Fernandyne principal secretary to himself; and that fortune might every way seem frolic, he made Montanus lord over all the forest of Arden, Adam Spencer Captain of the King's Guard, and Corydon master of Alinda's flocks.

FINIS

---

3. **falchions:** broad swords with curved blades.

RICHARD PACE

[The Benefit of a Liberal Education]†

* * *

My little book is entitled, "The Benefit of a Liberal Education." If
the content is as good as the title, I almost think students should
read it first, before anything else. For people are usually willing to
take pains with something they can clearly see will benefit them. But
if my meager talent has deceived me, I leave it to you and to others to
imitate Vergil and gather gold from dung[1] and make a living face
from a mask. In fact, I'll be content with this thought alone, that I've
furnished you and them with an excellent subject for exercise (which
is certainly useful for all studious young men). It now remains for me
to explain to you why I wrote and published a book with this title.

About two years ago, more or less, when I returned to my country
from the city of Rome, I was at a banquet where I was unknown to
most of the guests. After we had drunk a sufficient amount, one of
them (I don't know who, but, as you could tell from his speech and
appearance, he was no fool) began to talk about the proper education for his children. He thought first of all that he should find them
a good teacher and that they should by all means attend school and
not have a tutor. Now there happened to be a certain person there, a
nobleman, or so we call them, who always carry horns hanging
down their backs as though they were going to hunt while they ate.
When he heard us praise learning, he became wild, overwhelmed
with an uncontrollable rage, and burst out, "What's all this stuff,
buddy? To hell with your stupid studies. Scholars are a bunch of
beggars. Even Erasmus[2] is a pauper, and I hear he's the smartest of
them all. In one of his letters he calls *tên kataraton penian*, that is,
goddamn poverty, his wife and complains bitterly that he's not able
to get her off his back and throw her in the ocean, *bathykêtea pon-
ton*. God damn it, I'd rather see my son hanged than be a student.
Sons of the nobility ought to blow the horn properly, hunt like
experts, and train and carry a hawk gracefully. Studies, by God,
ought to be left to country boys."

---

† Richard Pace, *De Fructu qui ex doctrina percipitur*. Ed. and trans. Frank Manley and
  Richard S. Sylvester (New York: Frederick Ungar, 1967), pp. 23–25. Reprinted by permission of *Renaissance Quarterly* and The Renaissance Society of America. Pace was
  an early English humanist and diplomat; his book was originally published in Latin in
  1517. Notes are the Norton editor's but adapted from Manley and Sylvester.
1. **Vergil . . . dung:** According to later writers, the Roman poet Virgil claimed that he
  sought to find gold in dung, i.e., artistic value in the humblest of substances.
2. **Erasmus:** famous Dutch humanist who made his living by writing and the patronage of
  his admirers.

At that point I wasn't able to keep myself from making some reply to the loudmouth in defense of learning. I said, "I don't think you're right, my good man. For if some foreigner came to the king, a royal ambassador, for example, and he had to be given an answer, your son, brought up as you suggest, would only blow on his horn, and the learned country boys would be called on to answer him. They would obviously be preferred to your son, the hunter or hawker, and using the freedom that learning gives, they would say to your face, 'We would rather be learned, and thanks to learning no fools, than to be proud of our stupid nobility.'"

Then, glancing about him on all sides, he said, "Who's this, talking to me like that? I don't know the man." And when someone whispered in his ear who I was, he mumbled something to himself—I don't know what—and finding a fool to listen to him, he snatched up a cup of wine. Since he had no answer to give, he started to drink, and the conversation passed on to other things. And so I was saved not by Apollo, who saved Horace from a blowhard, but by Bacchus,[3] who saved me from an argument with a madman, which I was afraid would go on a lot longer.

* * *

KEITH THOMAS

[Boundaries between Animal and Human][†]

* * *

Wherever we look in early modern England, we find anxiety, latent or explicit, about any form of behaviour which threatened to transgress the fragile boundaries between man and the animal creation. Physical cleanliness was necessary because, as John Stuart Mill would put it, its absence, 'more than of anything else, renders man bestial.'[1] Nakedness was bestial, for clothes, like cooking, were a distinctively human attribute.[2] It was bestial for men to have unduly long hair: 'Beasts are more hairy than men,' wrote Bacon,

---

3. **Apollo . . . blowhard:** According to the Roman poet Horace, the god Apollo, protector of poets and the arts, saved him from being trapped by an insufferable bore (*Satires* 1.9.78); **Bacchus:** god of wine.
† From Keith Thomas, *Man and the Natural World: Changing Attitudes in England 1500–1800* (London: Penguin, 1983), pp. 38–41. Reproduced by permission of Penguin Ltd.
1. John Stuart Mill, *Essays on Ethics, Religion and Society*, ed. J. M. Robson (1969), 394.
2. Michael McDonald, *Mystical Bedlam* (Cambridge, 1981), 130; Adam Hill, *The Crie of England* (1595), 38; John Block Friedman, *The Monstrous Races in Medieval Art and Thought* (1981), 31.

'and savage men more than civil.'[3] It was bestial to work at night, for the same reason that burglary was a worse crime than daylight robbery; the night, as Sir Edward Coke explained, was 'the time wherein man is to rest, and wherein beasts run about seeking their prey'.[4] It was even bestial to go swimming, for, apart from being in many Puritan eyes a dangerous form of semi-suicide, it was essentially a non-human method of progression. As a Cambridge divine observed in 1600: men walked; birds flew; only fish swam.[5] One commentator even thought that the reason some Red Indians coloured their teeth black was that they supposed it 'essential to men to differ from the brutes in every respect, and therefore it was necessary not even to have teeth of the same colour'.[6]

Even to pretend to be an animal for purposes of ritual or entertainment was unacceptable. William Prynne declared it immoral to dress as a beast on the stage because to do so obliterated man's glorious image. Many moralists shared his objection to animal disguises; and in the early seventeenth century the hobby horse seems to have largely disappeared from the morris dance. Other ways of dressing as animals also became uncommon until they were revived by folklorists in modern times. At the same time traditional tales about the metamorphosis of humans into animals were condemned as either poetical fancies or diabolical fictions.[7] One of the reasons that monstrous births caused such horror was that they threatened the firm dividing-line between men and animals.

Close relations with animals were also frowned upon. When in 1667 Dr. Edmund King planned the transfusion of a lamb's blood into the veins of a man, the experiment was at first held up because of 'some considerations of a moral nature'; and in the nineteenth century one of the great arguments against vaccination would be that inoculation with fluid from cows would result in the 'animalization' of human beings.[8] Bestiality, accordingly, was the worst of sexual crimes because, as one Stuart moralist put it, 'it turns man into a

3. Francis Bacon, *The Works of Francis Bacon*, ed. J. Spedding, R. L. Ellis and D. D. Heath (1857–9), ii. 550–1. Cf. J[ohn] B[ulwer], *Anthropometamorphosis* (1653), 474, and C. R. Hallpike, *The Foundations of Primitive Thought* (Oxford, 1979), 153.
4. John Weemse, *An Explication of the Iudiciall Laws of Moses* (1632), 98; Sir Edward Coke, *Institutes of the Laws of England* (1794–1817 edn), iii. 63.
5. George Abbot, *An Exposition upon the Prophet Ionah* (1600), 549. Cf. Henry Thomas Buckle, *History of Civilization in England* (World's Classics, 1903–4), iii. 265n; John E. Mason, *Gentlefolk in the Making* (1935; reprint, New York, 1971), 81–2; *Englishmen at Rest and Play*, ed. Reginald Lennard (Oxford, 1931), 68–9. For a contrary view see Christofer Middleton, *A Short Introduction for to Learne to Swimme* (1595), sig. A4.
6. G. Gregory, *The Economy of Nature* (1796), iii. 556.
7. William Prynne, *Histrio-Mastix* (1633), 892–3; E. C. Cawte, *Ritual Animal Disguise* (Cambridge and Ipswich, 1978), esp. 21, 79, 181, 209; Edward Topsell, *The Historie of Foure-Footed Beastes* (1607), 463.
8. *Philosophical Trans.*, i (1665 and 1666), 519; Richard D. French, *Antivivisection and Medical Science in Victorian Society* (1975), 387–8.

very beast, makes a man a member of a brute creature'.[9] The sin was the sin of confusion; it was immoral to mix the categories.[1] Injunctions against 'buggery with beasts' were standard in seventeenth-century moral literature, though occasionally the topic was passed over, 'the fact being more filthy than to be spoken of'.[2] Bestiality became a capital offence in 1534 and, with one brief interval, remained so until 1861. Incest, by contrast, was not a secular crime at all until the twentieth century.[3]

In early modern England even animal pets were morally suspect, especially if admitted to the table and fed better than the servants. It was against the rules of civility to handle dogs at the table, ruled Erasmus. 'Over-familiar usage of any brute creature is to be abhorred,' said a moralist in 1633.[4] An unconventional pet—a toad or a fly or weasel—could be identified as a witch's familiar, while for gentlewomen to cherish pet monkeys in their bosoms was, as Helkiah Crooke ruled in 1631, 'a very wicked and inhumane thing'. The godly remembered the story of the pious Elizabethan Katherine Stubbes, who, on her deathbed, caught sight of her favourite little puppy.

> She had no sooner espied her, but she beat her away, and calling her husband to her, said 'Good husband, you and I have offended God grievously in receiving many a time this bitch into our bed; we would have been loathe to have received a Christian soul . . . into our bed, and to have nourished him in our bosoms, and to have fed him at our table, as we have done this filthy cur many times. The Lord give us grace to repent it' . . . and afterwards she could not abide to look upon the bitch any more.[5]

It was during these centuries that most farmers finally moved the animals out of their houses into separate accommodation.

9. Richard Capel, *Tentations* (1633), 356.
1. It is revealing of the extent to which sensibilities on this point have changed that a learned modern commentator should find the legal prohibition of bestiality 'pointless'; Tony Honoré, *Sex Law* (1978), 176.
2. Gervase Babington, *Comfortable Notes upon the Bookes of Exodus and Leviticus* (1604), 342. Cf. Peter Barker, *A Iudicious and Painefull Exposition upon the Ten Commandements* (1624), 270; Andrew Willet, *Hexapla in Leviticum* (1631), 434; James Usher, *A Body of Divinity* (1645), 280.
3. 25 Hen. VIII, c. 6 (1533–4), renewed by 28 Hen. VIII, c. 6 (1536); 32 Hen. VIII, c. 3 (1540); 2 & 3 Edw. VI, c. 29 (1548), lapsing in 1553 and renewed by 5 Eliz., c. 17 (1562–3) until 24 & 25 Vic., c. 100 (1861). For incest see Victor Bailey and Sheila Blackburn, 'The Punishment of Incest Act 1908', *Criminal Law Rev.* (1979).
4. Desiderius Erasmus, *De Civilitate Morum Puerilium*, trans. Robert Whittinton (1540), sig. c2ᵛ; Capel, *Tentations*, 356.
5. Helkiah Crooke, *Microcosmographia, A Description of the Body of Man* (2nd edn, 1631) . . . George Lyman Kittredge, *Witchcraft in Old and New England* (1929; reprint, New York, 1956), 209; Philip Stubbes, *A Christall Glasse for Christian Women* (1618), sigs. A4ᵛ–BI. Cf. Topsell, 105–6; chap. x.

Sentiments about animals, say the anthropologists, are usually projections of attitudes to man.[6] In early modern England the official concept of the animal was a negative one, helping to define, by contrast, what was supposedly distinctive and admirable about the human species. By embodying the antithesis of all that was valued and esteemed, the idea of the brute was as indispensable a prop to established human values as were the equally unrealistic notions held by contemporaries about witches or Papists. 'The meaning of order,' it has been well said, 'could only be grasped by exploring its antithesis or "contrary".'[7] Animal analogies came particularly readily to the lips of those who saw more of animals, wild and domestic, than do most people today. The brute creation provided the most readily-available point of reference for the continuous process of human self-definition. Neither the same as humans, nor wholly dissimilar, the animals offered an almost inexhaustible fund of symbolic meaning.

Yet there was little objective justification for the way in which the beasts were perceived. 'As drunk as a dog,' the proverb said. But who has ever seen a drunken dog?[8] Men attributed to animals the natural impulses they most feared in themselves—ferocity, gluttony, sexuality—even though it was men, not beasts, who made war on their own species, ate more than was good for them and were sexually active all the year round. It was as a comment on *human* nature that the concept of 'animality' was devised. As S. T. Coleridge would observe, to call human vices 'bestial' was to libel the animals.[9]

*　*　*

6. Raymond Firth, *Elements of Social Organization* (1951), 199.
7. Stuart Clark, 'King James's *Daemonologie*', in *The Damned Art*, ed. Sydney Anglo (1977), 177.
8. *All the Workes of Iohn Taylor the Water-Poet* (1630), 232; Samuel Pepys, *The Diary of Samuel Pepys*, ed. Robert Latham and William Matthews (1970–), vi. 290. Cf. [Sir James Stewart], *Jus Populi Vindicatum* (1669), 239 ('drunk as a beast').
9. S. T. Coleridge, *Lay Sermons*, ed. R. J. White (1972), 183n. Cf. 'Phylotheus Physiologus' [Thomas Tryon], *Monthly Observations for the Preserving of Health* (1688), 7. For reflections on this theme see John Berger, 'Animal World', *New Soc.*, 25 Nov. 1971; Mary Midgley, 'The Concept of Beastliness', *Philosophy*, 48 (1973), and *id., Beast and Man* (Hassocks, 1979) (and review by John Benson in *The Listener*, 102 (2 Aug. 1979)).

MICHEL DE MONTAIGNE

[Humans versus Animals]†

* * *

Presumption is our natural and original infirmity. Of all creatures man is the most miserable and frail, and therewithal the proudest and disdainfulest: who perceiveth and seeth himself placed here amidst their filth and mire of the world, fast tied and nailed to the worst, most senseless and drooping part of the world in the vilest corner of the house and farthest from heaven's cope, with those creatures that are the worst of the three conditions[1]—and yet dareth imaginarily place himself above the circle of the moon and reduce heaven under his feet? It is through the vanity of the same imagination that he dare equal himself to God, that he ascribeth divine conditions unto himself, that he selecteth and separateth himself from out the rank of other creatures, to which, his fellow brethren and compeers, he cuts out and shareth their parts and allotteth them what portions of means or forces he thinks good. How knoweth he by the virtue of his understanding the inward and secret motions of beasts? By what comparison from them to us doth he conclude the brutishness he ascribeth unto them? When I am playing with my cat, who knows whether she have more sport in dallying with me than I have in gaming with her? We entertain one another with mutual apish tricks. If I have my hour to begin or to refuse, so hath she hers. Plato, in setting forth the Golden Age under Saturn,[2] amongst the chief advantages that man had then reporteth the communication he had with beasts, of whom inquiring and taking instruction he knew the true qualities and differences of every one of them, by and from whom he got an absolute understanding and perfect wisdom, whereby he led a happier life than we can do. Can we have a better proof to judge of man's impudency touching beasts?

* * *

---

† Michel de Montaigne, *Essays*, trans. John Florio (London, 1613), Book 2, "Apology of Raymond Sebond," p. 250.
1. **three conditions:** animals that walk, fly, and swim.
2. **Plato:** ancient Greek philosopher; **Golden Age:** the first and best of the four ages of man, under the benevolent reign of **Saturn**, according to classical thought.

SIR THOMAS MORE

[How Sheep Devour the English][†]

* * *

[The traveler Raphael Hythloday speaks of abuses in England.] "But I do not think that this necessity of stealing arises only from hence [the aftermath of war]; there is another cause of it more peculiar to England."

"What is that?" said the cardinal [John Morton, Archbishop of Canterbury].

"The increase of pasture," said I, "by which your sheep, that are naturally mild and easily kept in order, may be said now to devour men and unpeople not only villages but towns. For wherever it is found that the sheep of any soil yield a softer and richer wool than ordinary, there the nobility and gentry, and even those holy men the abbots, not contented with the old rents which their farms yielded, nor thinking it enough that they, living at their ease, do no good to the public, resolve to do it hurt instead of good. They stop the course of agriculture and destroy houses and towns, reserving only the churches, and enclosed grounds that they may lodge their sheep in them. And as if forests and parks had swallowed up too little soil, those worthy countrymen turn the best inhabited places into solitudes, for when any insatiable wretch who is a plague to his country resolves to enclose many thousand acres of ground, the owners as well as tenants are turned out of their possessions: by tricks or by main force or being wearied out with ill-usage, they are forced to sell them. So those miserable people, both men and women, married [and] unmarried, old and young, with their poor but numerous families (since country business requires many hands), are all forced to change their seats, not knowing whither to go; and they must sell for almost nothing their household stuff, which could not bring them much money even though they might stay for a buyer. When that little money is at an end, for it will be soon spent, what is left for them to do but either to steal and so to be hanged (God knows how justly), or to go about and beg? And if they do this, they are put in prison as idle vagabonds; whereas they would willingly work but can find none that will hire them; for there is no more occasion for country labor to which they have been bred when there is no arable ground left. One shepherd can look after a flock which will stock an extent of ground that would require many hands if it were to be

---

† Sir Thomas More, *Utopia* (1516), trans. Gilbert Burnet (London: for Richard Chiswell, 1684), pp. 20–24.

ploughed and reaped. This likewise the price of corn in many places raises.

"The price of wool is also so risen that the poor people who were wont to make cloth are no more able to buy it; and this likewise makes many of them idle. For since the increase of pasture, God has punished the avarice of the owners by a rot among the sheep, which has destroyed vast numbers of them; but had been more justly laid upon the owners themselves. But suppose the sheep should increase ever so much, their price is not like to fall; since though they cannot be called a monopoly, because they are not engrossed[1] by one person, yet they are in so few hands and these are so rich that as they are not pressed to sell them sooner than they have a mind to it, so they never do it till they have raised the price as high as possible.

"And on the same account it is that the other kinds of cattle are so dear, and so much the more because that many villages being pulled down and all country labor being much neglected, there are none that look after the breeding of them. The rich do not breed cattle as they do sheep, but buy them lean and at low prices; and after they have fattened them on their grounds sell them again at high rates. And I do not think that all the inconveniences that this will produce are yet observed, for as they sell the cattle dear, so if they are consumed faster than the breeding counties from which they are brought can afford them, then the stock must decrease and this must needs end in a great scarcity; and by these means this your island, that seemed as to this particular the happiest in the world, will suffer much by the cursed avarice of a few persons. Besides that, the rising of corn makes all people lessen their families as much as they can; and what can those who are dismissed by them do, but either beg or rob? And to this last, a man of a great mind is much sooner drawn than to the former."

* * *

WILLIAM C. CARROLL

Enclosure, Vagrancy, and Sedition in the Tudor-Stuart Period[†]

The central interpretive paradigm of the sixteenth-century movement of enclosure was lucidly set forth in 1516 by Sir Thomas More.

---

1. **engrossed:** controlled.
† From William C. Carroll, "'The Nursery of Beggary': Enclosure, Vagrancy, and Sedition in the Tudor-Stuart Period," in Richard Burt and John Michael Archer, eds., *Enclosure Acts: Sexuality, Property, and Culture in Early Modern England* (Ithaca: Cornell University Press, 1994), pp. 34–39. © 1994 by Cornell University. Used by permission of the publisher, Cornell University Press.

In the famous account in Book 1 of *Utopia*, Hythloday describes the sheep "that used to be so meek and eat so little. Now they are becoming so greedy and wild that they devour men themselves." Parasitical landowners have enclosed "every acre for pasture," leaving "no land free for the plow." A single "greedy, insatiable glutton . . . may enclose many thousand acres of land within a single hedge. The tenants are dismissed and . . . forced to move out." When their pittance of money is gone, he continues, "what remains for them but to steal, and so be hanged . . . or to wander and beg? And yet if they go tramping, they are jailed as sturdy beggars. They would be glad to work, but they can find no one who will hire them." What can such displaced men do, Hythloday asks, "but rob or beg? And a man of courage is more likely to rob than to beg." Thus a generation of thieves and beggars is created. The English lawyer is preparing a response to these accusations and promises, "I will demolish all your arguments and reduce them to rubble," when the Cardinal interrupts him.[1] This might be the only instance in literature, or life, when we would have wished to hear a lawyer speak more.

I would emphasize here these primary elements of More's, or Hythloday's, analysis:

1. Enclosures are initiated by "the nobility and gentry, yes, and even some abbots."
2. Their intention, spurred by parasitical greed, is to replace arable land with pasture for sheep.
3. Their tenants are always victimized by enclosure and cast into poverty.
4. The formerly honest and hardworking peasants are turned into thieves or sturdy beggars wandering the countryside.

These four assertions in More's paradigm inevitably lead to some version of a pastoral communism as an eminently reasonable response to an intolerable economic and political situation. Economic historians have described any number of individual case histories that fit More's paradigm exactly, Sir Thomas Tresham being one of the more notorious.[2] More's paradigm, moreover, is quoted approvingly and taken over in all its essentials by Marx in *Capital*,

1. Sir Thomas More, *Utopia*, ed. Robert M. Adams (New York: Norton, 1975), pp. 14–16. On the connections between enclosure and vagrancy, I have found these sources particularly helpful: E. M. Leonard, *The Early History of English Poor Relief* (1900; reprint New York: Barnes & Noble, 1965); R. H. Tawney, *The Agrarian Problem in the Sixteenth Century* (London: Longmans, 1912); John Pound, *Poverty and Vagrancy in Tudor England* (London: Longman, 1971); Joan Thirsk, "Tudor Enclosures," in *The Tudors*, ed. Joel Hurstfield (New York: St. Martin's, 1973); Roger B. Manning, *Village Revolts: Social Protest and Popular Disturbances in England, 1509–1640* (Oxford: Oxford University Press, 1988); and Paul Slack, *Poverty and Policy in Tudor and Stuart England* (London: Longman, 1988).
2. See the convenient account in Manning, *Village Revolts*, pp. 237–41.

where this social upheaval is analyzed as an element of the transition to capitalist production: "Thus were the agricultural people, first forcibly expropriated from the soil, driven from their homes, turned into vagabonds, and then whipped, branded, tortured by laws grotesquely terrible, into the discipline necessary for the wage system."[3]

We should remind ourselves, however, that each generalization in More's paradigm is contradicted, or at least complicated, by considerable historical evidence:

1. Enclosures were not always initiated by the nobility, gentry or church; indeed, in 1549 even the rebel Robert Kett proclaimed a wish to preserve some long-standing enclosures in the first article of his demands ("We pray your grace that where it is enacted for inclosyng that it be not hurtfull to suche as have enclosed saffren grounds for they be gretly chargeablye to them, and that from hensforth noman shall enclose any more").[4]

2. The reason for enclosure was often technical agricultural innovation and improved efficiency of tillage rather than the wish to pasture sheep; and some acts of enclosure, as Roger B. Manning has shown, were initiated by gentry against other gentry as part of more complex political, religious, or personal feuds.[5]

3. Tenants were not always victimized; indeed, many formally agreed to enclosure.[6]

4. Not all displaced tenants turned into thieves or beggars. Moreover, enclosure was far from the only cause of vagrancy, even in rural areas, but was rather one of several complex social conditions that led to vagrancy.

What continues to stand out nearly five centuries later is not the historical accuracy of More's paradigm, though his account certainly was frequently if not always the case, but rather the interpretive power of that paradigm, its nostalgic vision—one might almost say fantasy—of an always already lost communal perfection.

*   *   *

The Thomas More paradigm held that enclosure creates vagrancy through depopulation. One opponent of enclosure a century and a half later put the case exactly as More had seen it: "When these

3. Karl Marx, *Capital: A Critique of Political Economy*, ed. Frederick Engels (New York: Modern Library, 1906), pp. 808–9.
4. Quoted in *Tudor Rebellions*, ed. Anthony Fletcher (London: Longmans, 1968), p. 142.
5. Manning, *Village Revolts*, p. 93.
6. See Thirsk, "Tudor Enclosures," pp. 108–9; some "agreements" were clearly made under duress, however.

enclosures have made farmers cottagers, and cottagers beggars, no way of livelihood being left them, these poor with their families are forced into market towns and open fielded towns, hoping they may find some employment there." But the process merely snowballs, for the newly poor "lay such burthens upon open fields that they are not able to bear them," and so yet more wandering poor are created.[7] In addition to outright expulsion from newly enclosed commons, rising prices led to higher rents for the legitimate tenants, with the same results—the expulsion from the land of those who had always worked it. The hypocrisy and cruelty of the landowners is perfectly captured in John Taylor's 1621 vision of the country Lord who

> Ignobly did oppresse
> His Tenants, raising Rents to such excesse:
> That they their states not able to maintaine,
> They turn'd starke beggers in a yeare or twaine.
> Yet though this Lord were too too miserable,
> He in his House kept a well furnish'd Table:
> Great store of Beggers dayly at his Gate,
> Which he did feed, and much Compassionate.
> (For 'tis within the power of mighty men
> To make five hundred Beggers, and feed ten.)[8]

Taylor's description of rising rents leading to impoverishment and beggary reflects hundreds of archival depositions. John Bayker's well-known letter to Henry VIII, nearly a century earlier, told exactly the same story: "Ys yt not a petyfull cays: to come in to a lytyll vylage or towne wer that thayre haythe beyne twentye or thyrty howses and now are halfe off thayme nothynge but bayre walls standing: ys yt not a petyfull cays to se one man have yt in hys hands wyche dyd suffyse ij or iij men wen the habytatyons were standynge."[9] The consummate dramatic exemplar of the type is no doubt Philip Massinger's Sir Giles Overreach (c. 1624), who shrugs off accusations that he is a "grand encloser / Of what was common, to my private use," his ears "pierced with widow's cries," while "undone orphans wash with tears" his threshold. Overreach also unfolds plans of Machiavellian cleverness "to hedge in the manor / Of [his] neighbor, Master Frugal."[1] The enclosing landlord, as one

7. Joan Thirsk and J. P. Cooper, eds., *Seventeenth-Century Economic Documents* (Oxford: Clarendon Press, 1972), p. 150; hereafter cited in the text as *SCED*.
8. John Taylor, *The Praise, Antiquity, and Commodity, of Beggery, Beggers, and Begging* (London, 1621), G2r.
9. Quoted in Frank Aydelotte, *Elizabethan Rogues and Vagabonds* (1913; reprint New York: Barnes & Noble, 1967), pp. 145–47.
1. Philip Massinger, *A New Way To Pay Old Debts, in Drama of the English Renaissance: The Stuart Period*, ed. Russell A. Fraser and Norman Rabkin (New York: Macmillan, 1976), 4.1.124–27, 2.1.27–39.

writer in 1632 ironically put it, "loves to see the bounds of his boundlesse desires; hee is like the Divell, for they both compasse the earth about."[2]

＊　＊　＊

In the counterdiscourse of enclosure in this period, arguments were made against excessive common waste ground, and *for* enclosures because they were for "the general good of the commonwealth," as Sir Thomas Smyth said, "both in the breed of serviceable men and subjects, and of answerable estates and abilities."[3] Sir Anthony Fitzherbert argued for enclosures in 1539 because the value of any piece of land would be increased "by reason of the compostyng and dongyng of the catell, that shall go and lye upon it both day and nighte," and because enclosure would create "as many newe occupations that were not used before" as were lost.[4] In 1573 Thomas Tusser asked in rhyme,

> More plentie of mutton and biefe,
> corne, butter, and cheese of the best,
> More wealth any where (to be briefe)
> more people, more handsome and prest,
> Where find ye (go search any coast)
> than there, where enclosure is most?
>
> (*TED* 3:64)

An anonymous pamphleteer in the 1650s argued more philosophically on behalf of enclosure, in part because "husbandry is the fundamental prop and nutriment of the Commonwealth," and, less convincingly, because there was "no example of common fields in all the divine word, nor in any skilful author writing of husbandry, as Virgil, Tully, etc" (*SCED*, p. 146). More mystically, he announced, "God is the God of order, and order is the soul of things, the life of a Commonwealth; but common fields are the seat of disorder, the seed plot of contention, the nursery of beggary" (*SCED*, p. 144).

In More's paradigm, then, enclosure *causes* beggars, but in the counterdiscourse it is the *failure* to enclose that causes beggars. In the aftermath of the Midlands revolt of 1607, one member of the House of Lords argued, using a familiar metaphor, that "the nurseries of beggars are commons as appeareth by fens and forests," whereas "wealthy people [live in] the enclosed countries as Essex,

---

2. Donald Lupton, *London and the Country Carbonadoed and Quartred into Severall Characters* (London, 1632), p. 107.
3. Quoted in L. C. Knights, *Drama and Society in the Age of Jonson* (New York: Norton, 1968), p. 99.
4. R. H. Tawney and Eileen Power, eds., *Tudor Economic Documents* (London: Longmans, 1924), 3:23–24; hereafter cited in the text as *TED*.

Somerset, Devon, etc" (*SCED*, p. 107). The anonymous pamphleteer quoted earlier argued that "common fields are the seedplots of
contention" because "there is much unrighteous dealing," and
"every man being for himself, he that thrives on his farm thriveth
commonly by hurting his neighbor, and by his loss," because "tres-
passes are very frequent" (*SCED*, p. 145). "Common of pasture,"
argued one Elizabethan surveyor, was a "maintaining of the idlers
and beggary of the cottagers," and King James proposed in 1610
that the House of Commons move against the numerous cottages
on commons and in forests which were "nurseries and receptacles
of thieves, rogues and beggars."[5] Enclosure, as always, was in the
eye of the copyholder.

Whether one argued for or against enclosures as state policy,
however, the common specter of social discord was the nightmarish
vision of a new-created race of masterless men, of beggars and vagabonds wandering the roads, homesteading on the dwindling common wastes, poaching and fence breaking at will; ironically,
vagabonds had even been hired to participate in local enclosure
riots by the disputants.[6] As More noted, "A man of courage is more
likely to rob than to beg." One antienclosure writer put it in 1550:
"And now they have nothynge, but goeth about in England from
dore to dore, and axe theyr almose for Goddes sake. And because
they will not begge, some of them doeth steale, and then they be
hanged, and thus the Realme doeth decay" (*TED* 3:56). It was exactly
this state of affairs that concerned government authorities, for the
swarms (in the usual dehumanizing metaphor) of masterless men
were, like their city cousins, also thought to be ready material for
riot and insurrection. Enclosure, or the lack of enclosure, led to beggars and masterless men, and *they* certainly led to sedition.[7] And
sedition could never be tolerated.

* * *

---

5. Both passages quoted in Christopher Hill, *The World Turned Upside Down* (New York:
   Viking, 1972), p. 41.
6. See Manning, *Village Revolts*, p. 163.
7. On the development of the sedition laws, see John Bellamy, *The Tudor Law of Treason*
   (London: Routledge, 1979), and Roger B. Manning, "The Origins of the Doctrine of
   Sedition," *Albion* 12 (1980), 99–121. As Manning notes, "The enclosure riot remained
   the pre-eminent form of social protest during the period from 1530 to 1640" (*Village
   Revolts*, p. 27).

THOMAS BASTARD

[Proto-ecological Epigrams][†]

Book 4 Epigram 7

Our fathers did but use the world before
And, having used, did leave the same to us.
We spill whatever resteth of their store;
What can our heirs inherit but our curse?
For we have sucked the sweet and sap away
And sowed consumption in the fruitful ground;
The woods and forests clad in rich array
With nakedness and baldness we confound.
We have defaced the lasting monuments
And caused all honor to have end with us:
The holy temples feel our ravishments.
What can our heirs inherit but our curse?
The world must end for men are so accursed.
Unless God end it sooner, they will first.

Book 4 Epigram 20

Sheep have eat up our meadows and our downs,
Our corn, our wood, whole villages and towns.
Yea, they have eat up many wealthy men,
Besides widows and orphan childeren,[1]
Besides our statutes and our iron laws,
Which they have swallowed down into their maws.
    Till now I thought the proverb did but jest
    Which said a black sheep was a biting beast.

---

† Thomas Bastard, *Chrestoloros: Seven Books of Epigrams* (London, 1598), pp. 81, 90.
1. **childeren:** The spelling of this word suggests that it be pronounced as three syllables to make up the meter.

GEORGE GASCOYGNE

The Woeful Words of the Hart to the Hunter[†]

Since I in deepest dread do yield myself to man
And stand full still between his legs which erst full wildly ran;
     Since I to him appeal when hounds pursue me sore,
As who should[1] say, "Now save me, man, for else I may no more!"
     Why dost thou then, O man, O hunter, me pursue
With cry of hounds, with blast of horn, with hallow and with hue?[2]
     Or why dost thou devise such nets and instruments,
Such toils and toys as hunters use to bring me to their bents?[3]
     Since I, as erst was said, do so with humble cheer
Hold down my head as who should say, "Lo man, I yield me here."
     Why art thou not content, O murdering, cruel mind,
Thyself alone to hunt me so, which art my foe by kind,[4]
     But that thou must instruct with words in skillful writ
All other men to hunt me eke?[5] O wicked, wily wit!
     Thou here hast set to show within this busy book
A looking-glass of lessons lewd[6] wherein all hunts may look.
     And so whiles world doth last they may be taught to bring
The harmless hart unto his bane[7] with many a wily thing.
     Is it because thy mind doth seek thereby some gains?
Canst thou in death take such delight? Breeds pleasure so in pains?

---

† George Gascoygne, *The Noble Art of Venery or Hunting* (London, 1611), pp. 136–40.
  "The Hart's Complaint" follows a hundred pages of technical advice about how to hunt
  deer successfully. Illustration precedes poem in the original.
1. **who should:** if to.
2. **hallow . . . hue:** loud shouts and clamor.
3. **bents:** inclinations.
4. **kind:** nature.
5. **eke:** also.
6. **lewd:** vile.
7. **bane:** destruction.

O cruel, be content to take in worth my tears,
Which grow to gum and fall from me; content thee with my hairs.
        Content thee with my horns, which every year I mew,[8]
Since all these three make medicines some sickness to eschew.[9]
        My tears congealed to gum by pieces from me fall,
And thee preserve from pestilence in pomander or ball.
        Such wholesome tears shed I when thou pursuest me so;
Thou, not content, doest seek my death and then thou get'st no mo.[1]
        My hair is medicine burnt all venomous worms to kill;
The snake herself will yield thereto—such was my Maker's will.
        My horns, which ay[2] renew, as many medicines make
As there be troches[3] on their tops and all, man, for thy sake.
        As first they heal the head from turning of the brain:[4]
A dram thereof in powder drunk doth quickly ease the pain.
        They skin a kibed heel; they fret an agnail off;[5]
Lo thus I skip from top to toe yet neither scorn nor scoff.
        They comfort fevers faint and lingering long disease;
Distilled when they be tender buds they sundry griefs appease.
        They master and correct both humors hot and cold,
Which strive to conquer blood and breed diseases many fold.[6]
        They bring down women's terms and stop them too, for need,[7]
They keep the mean 'tween both extremes and serve both turns
        indeed.
        They clear the dimmy sight; they kill both web and pin;[8]
They soon restore the milt or spleen[9] which putrifies within.
        They ease an aching tooth; they break the rumbling wind
Which grips the womb[1] with colic's pains—such is their noble kind.
        They quench the scalding fire which scorcheth with his heat
And skin the skall[2] full clean again and heal it trim and neat.
        They poison do expel from Kaiser, king or queen,
When it by chance or deep deceit is swallowed up unseen.
        But wherefore spend I time in vain at large to praise

8. **mew:** moult, shed.
9. **eschew:** avoid.
1. **mo:** more.
2. **ay:** always.
3. **troches:** points.
4. **turnings . . . brain:** vertigo.
5. **fret . . . off:** rub away chilblains and corns.
6. **humors . . . many fold:** reference to the Galenic doctrine of humors that range from hot and moist to cold and dry and control the spread of diseases within an organism; **many fold:** by many times.
7. **bring . . . need:** They bring on women's menstruation and stop it as needed.
8. **clear . . . pin:** clear poor eyesight, cataracts and corneal opacity.
9. **milt or spleen:** spleen or heart.
1. **womb:** abdomen.
2. **skall:** scab, skin disease.

The virtues of my harmless horns which heap[3] my harm always?
And yet such horns, such hair, such tears as I have told
I mew and cast for man's avail, more worth to him than gold.
But he to quite[4] the same, O murdering man therewhiles,
Pursues me still and traps me oft with sundry snares and guiles.
Alas, lo now I feel cold fear within my bones,
Which hangs her wings upon my heels to hasten for the nones.[5]
By swiftest starting[6] steps methinks she bids me bide
In thickest tufts of coverts close and so myself to hide.
Ah, rueful remedy! So shall I, as it were,
Even tear my life out of the teeth of hounds which make me fear,
And from those cruel curs and brainsick bawling tykes[7]
Which vow, foot hot, to follow me both over hedge and dikes.
Methinks I hear the horn, which rends the restless air
With shrillest sound of bloody blast and makes me to despair;
Methinks I see the toil, the tanglings and the stall,[8]
Which are prepared and set full sure to compass me withal;
Methinks the foster[9] stands full close in bush or tree
And takes his level[1] straight and true; methinks he shoots at me;
And hits the harmless heart of me, unhappy hart,
Which must needs please him by my death: I may it not astart.[2]
Alas and welaway! Methinks I see the hunt,
Which takes the measure of my slots[3] where I to tread was wont;
Because I shall not miss at last to please his mind
Alas, I see him where he seeks my latest lair to find.
He takes my fewmets[4] up and puts them in his horn;
Alas, methinks he leaps for joy and laugheth me to scorn.
Hark, hark, alas, give ear: "This gear[5] goeth well," saith he,
"This hart bears dainty venison in prince's dish to be."
Lo now he blows his horn even at the kennel door;
Alas, alas, he blows a seek; alas, yet blows he more:
He jeopards and rechates; alas he blows the fall[6]
And sounds that deadly, doleful note which I must die withal.

3. **heap:** cause to accumulate.
4. **to quite:** in return for.
5. **fear . . . nones:** Fear gives wings to my heels so I can flee.
6. **starting:** startled.
7. **tykes:** churls.
8. **tanglings . . . stall:** ringing bells and decoy.
9. **foster:** forester (in charge of the hunt).
1. **level:** aim.
2. **astart:** escape.
3. **slots:** tracks.
4. **fewmets:** excrement.
5. **gear:** business.
6. **seek . . . fall:** a series of horn calls that signal various stages of the hunt, from the original call to the hounds to **seek** the deer until the **fall**, where the wounded dear falls to earth.

What should the cruel mean? Perhaps he hopes to find
As many medicines me within to satisfy his mind.
    Maybe he seeks to have my suet for himself
Which sooner heals a merrygald than 'pothecary's pelf.[7]
    Maybe his joints be numb, as sinews shrunk with cold,
And that he knows my suet will the same full soon unfold.[8]
    Maybe his wife doth fear to come[9] before her time
And in my maw he hopes to find, amongst the slut and slime,
    A stone to help his wife that she may bring to light
A bloody babe, like bloody sire, to put poor harts to flight.
    Maybe himself is weak and cannot please his make[1]
But must have some restorative and would my marrow take.
    Maybe his heart doth quake, and therefore seeks the bone
Which huntsmen find within my heart when I, poor hart, am gone.
    It may be that he means my flesh for to present
Unto his prince for delicates; such may be his intent.
    Yea, more than this—maybe he thinks such nourriture[2]
Will still prolong men's days on earth since mine so long endure.
    But oh, mischievous man, although I thee outlive
By due degrees of age unseen which nature doth me give,
    Must thou, therefore, procure my death for to prolong
Thy lingering life in lusty wise?[3] Alas, thou dost me wrong!
    Must I with mine own flesh his hateful flesh so feed
Which me disdains one bit of grass or corn in time of need?
    Alas, man, do not so! Some other beasts go kill,
Which work thy harm by sundry means, and so content thy will;
    Which yield thee no such gains in life as I renew
When from my head my stately horns to thy behoof[4] I mew.
    But since thou art unkind, ungracious, and unjust,
Lo here I crave of mighty gods, which are both good and just,
    That Mars[5] may reign with man; that strife and cruel war
May set man's murdering mind on work with many a bloody jar;[6]
    That drums with deadly dub may countervail the blast
Which they with horns have blown full loud to make my mind
    aghast.
    That shot as thick as hail may stand for cross-bow shoots;[7]

---

7. **suet . . . pelf:** Deer fat heals sores caused by chafing better than the expensive reme-
dies supplied by apothecaries.
8. **unfold:** loosen up.
9. **come:** give birth.
1. **make:** mate.
2. **nourriture:** nourishment.
3. **wise:** manner.
4. **behoof:** benefit.
5. **Mars:** Roman god of war.
6. **jar:** shock, discord.
7. i.e., that the bullets of war may replace the arrows of hunting.

That cuisses, greaves[8] and such may serve instead of hunters' boots;
 That girt with siege full sure they may their toils repent;
That embuscados[9] stand for nets which they against me bent;
 That when they see a spy, which watcheth them to trap,
They may remember ring walks made in harbor me to hap;[1]
 That when their busy brains are exercisèd so
Harts may lie safe within their lair and never fear their foe.
 But if so chance there be some dastard, dreadful Mome[2]
Whom trumpets cannot well entice nor call him once from home,
 And yet will play the man in killing harmless deer—
I crave of God that such a ghost and such a fearful fere[3]
 May see Diana nak'd,[4] and she to venge her scorns
May soon transform his harmful head into my harmless horns
 Until his hounds may tear that heart of his in twain
Which thus torments us harmless harts and puts our hearts to pain.

WILLIAM PRYNNE

[The Dangers of Theatrical Cross-Dressing]†

* * *

Witness Saint Cyprian, *De spectaculis lib.*[1] where he writes thus:
"To this vile, shameful deed another equal wickedness is super-
added: a man enfeebled in all his joints, resolved into a more than
womanish effeminacy, whose art it is to speak with his hands and
gestures, comes forth upon the stage and for this one—I know not
whom, neither man nor woman—the whole city flock together that
so the fabulous lusts of antiquity may be acted. Yea, men," writes he
in another place, "are unmanned on the stage; all the honor and
vigor of their sex is effeminated with the shame, the dishonesty, of an
unsinewed body. He who is most womanish and best resembles the
female sex gives best content. The more criminous[2] the more
applauded is he, and by how much the more obscene he is the more

---

8. **cuisses, greaves:** thigh and leg armor.
9. **embuscados:** ambushes.
1. **ring . . . hap:** walks made by the hunter before the hunt to seek out the best place of
 retreat to trap the deer.
2. **Mome:** Momus, classical deity associated with satire and cruel mockery.
3. **fere:** mate, companion.
4. **May . . . naked:** may, like the hunter Actaeon, spy **Diana**, goddess of the hunt and of
 chastity, naked; Diana in retaliation turned Actaeon into a stag and he was killed by
 his own hounds.
† William Prynne, *Histriomastix* (London, 1633), pp. 168–69, 179, 892, 134–35. For writing this mammoth condemnation of the theater, Prynne was sentenced to be fined,
 imprisoned, and lose both his ears.
1. *De spectaculis lib.*: book about plays.
2. **criminous:** guilty of crime.

skillful is he accounted. What cannot he persuade who is such a one," etc. And in another epistle of his he writes to Eucratius "to excommunicate a player who did train up boys for the stage for that he taught them against the express instruction of God himself how a male might be effeminated into a female, how their sex might be changed by art, that so the devil who defiles God's workmanship might be pleased by the offenses of a depraved and effeminated body. I think it will not stand with the majesty of God nor the discipline of the gospel that the modesty and honor of the church should be polluted with such a filthy and infamous contagion. For since men are prohibited in the law to put on a woman's garment and such who do it are adjudged accursed, how much more greater a sin is it not only to put on woman's apparel but likewise to express obscene, effeminate womanish gestures by the skill or tutorship of an unchaste art?"

* * *

"One, being a youth," writes Saint Chrysostom, "combs back his hair and effeminating nature with his visage, his apparel, his gesture, and the like, strives to represent the person of a tender virgin," which he condemns as a most abominable, effeminate act. "There is another sort of actors," writes Nazianzen,[3] "more unhappy than these, to wit those who lose the glory of men and by unchaste infections of their members effeminate their manly nature, being both effeminate men and women, yea being neither men nor women if we will speak truly."

* * *

Deuteronomy 22 verse 5: "The woman shall not wear that which pertaineth unto a man, neither shall a man put on a woman's garment, for all that do so are abomination to the Lord thy God." God himself doth here expressly inhibit men to put on woman's apparel because it is an abomination to him: therefore it must certainly be unlawful, yea abominable, for players to put on such apparel to act a woman's part.

* * *

For first it [Deuteronomy] condemns men's disguising of themselves like women and women's metamorphosing themselves into men, either in hair, apparel, offices or conditions, how much more then men's transfiguring of themselves into the shapes of idols, devils, monsters, beasts, etc. Between which and man there is no analogy or proportion as is between men and women. * * * [Scripture] commands men "not to be like to horse and mule, which have no

---

3. **Nazianzen:** Grigorios Nazianzenos, early Church authority.

understanding," therefore not to act their parts or to put on their skins or likeness. It was God's heavy judgment upon King Nebuchadnezar that "he was driven from men and did eat grass as oxen" and that "his body was wet with the dew of heaven till his hairs were grown like eagle's feathers and his nails like bird's claws" [Daniel 4:33]; yea it is man's greatest misery that being in honor he "became like to the beasts that perish." And must it not then be man's sin and shame to act a beast or bear his image, with which he hath no proportion? What is this but to obliterate that most glorious image which God himself hath stamped on us, to strip ourselves of all our excellency and to prove worse than brutes?

* * *

What Polycarp[4] once replied to Marcion the heretic, "I know thee to be the firstborn of Satan," may be fitly applicable to our common actors, the arch-agents, instruments, and apparitors[5] of their original founder and father the devil, their very profession being nothing else, as Bodin[6] well observes, but "an apprenticeship of sin, a way or trade of wickedness, which leads down to hell," and their lives (a badge of their profession) much like the life of Vortiger,[7] which "was tragically vicious in the beginning, miserable in the middest, filthy in the end." What the conditions, lives, and qualities of stage players have been in former ages let Cyprian, Nazianzen, Chrysostom, Augustine, Nicholas Cabasila, Cornelius Tacitus, Marcus Aurelius,[8] with others, testify. The first of these informs us that "stage players are the masters not of teaching but of destroying youth, insinuating that wickedness into others which themselves have sinfully learned." Whence he writes to Eucratius to excommunicate a player who trained up youths for the stage, affirming that "it could neither stand with the majesty of God nor the discipline of the gospel that the chastity and honor of the church should be defiled with so filthy, so infamous a contagion." The more than sodomitical uncleanness of players' lives he farther thus deciphers; "O," writes he, "that thou couldest in that sublime watch-tower insinuate thine eyes into these players' secrets or set open the closed doors of their bedchambers and bring all their innermost hidden cells unto the conscience of thine eyes. Thou shouldest then see that which is even a very sin to see; thou mightest behold that which these groaning under the bur-

---

4. **Polycarp:** early Christian saint and church father.
5. **apparitors:** servants.
6. **Bodin:** French humanist Jean Bodin.
7. **Vortiger:** (or Vortigern) early king of ancient Britain.
8. **Cyprian . . . Augustine:** early church fathers; **Nicholas Cabasila:** medieval Byzantine saint; **Cornelius Tacitus:** Roman historian; **Marcus Aurelius:** Roman emperor and stoic philosopher.

den of their vices deny that they have committed and yet hasten to commit—men rush on men with outrageous lusts."

*   *   *

ERICA FUDGE

Dressing Up as a Human[†]

In 1633 the puritanical critic of the theatre, William Prynne, launched an attack on cross-dressing. In a period in which women were not allowed onto the public stage, the women's parts were always played by boys, and this, Prynne argued, could cause moral danger to the spectator.[1] Cross-dressing, however, was not the end of his complaint. There was something worse, something even more dangerous than a boy dressing up as a woman. Prynne wrote, 'And must it not then be man's sin and shame to act a beast, or bear his image, with which he hath no proportion? What is this but to obliterate that most glorious image which God himself hath stamped on us, to strip us of our excellency, and to prove worse than brutes?' It is by dressing as animals that 'the shape of reasonable men [is changed] into the likeness of unreasonable beasts and creatures'. In dressing as animals we destroy our own status. What is revealed in Prynne's attack on the stage is a sense that human status, which we might assume to be absolute and unquestionable, was figured as dangerously fragile. If dress can upset species stability, it doesn't say a great deal about the strength of that stability.

Prynne was writing over 300 years ago, but his representation of human frailty remains present in different forms today. * * * Some of the ways in which we assert our difference from animals are breaking down. A new sense of animal intelligence, and of animals' physical similarity to humans, for example, go towards making the relation more and more complex, and if in addition to that we also recognize ourselves as unstable entities then the relation becomes even more complicated. We now have evolutionary theory rather than Prynne's somewhat mystical account of human decline to remind us of the inseparability of humans and animals, but we also have very different conceptions of the moral place of animals.

In the thirteenth century the theologian Thomas Aquinas argued that cruelty to animals was not wrong in itself, but that animals

† From Erica Fudge, *Animal* (London: Reaktion Books, 2002), pp. 61–65. Reprinted by permission.
1. William Prynne, *Histrio-Mastix: The Players Scourge, or Actors Tragedie* (London, 1633), p. 892.

should be 'loved from charity as good things we wish others to have, in that by charity we cherish this for God's honour and man's service'.[2] For Aquinas, a person who was cruel to animals was more likely to be cruel to humans, and treating animals with kindness was a preparation to treat humans well, and was a way of securing your own place in heaven; the animal itself was not important. Prynne seems to follow this logic. The sin in dressing up as an animal—which, in all likelihood, involved fur—was a sin because of its [effect] upon human status, not upon the animal. Since that time moral arguments about the welfare of animals have shifted their focus. It is the animal's right not to be abused that is central to our discussions, whether we see it as such or not: the RSPCA[3] does not prosecute offenders in order to help them lead blameless lives, it prosecutes in defence of the animals who are abused. But, despite this key shift, some of Prynne's argument remains relevant. During the sixteenth and seventeenth centuries the human was central to God's creation (a status given by the Bible); alongside this, new philosophical arguments emerged to offer further evidence for human power. Human status was reiterated in humanist thought and in the New Scientific philosophy of Francis Bacon and René Descartes * * *. Reason was once again established as the realm of the human: in fact, for Descartes, it was what made us distinct. In the late eighteenth century the American Declaration of Independence formulated the human in a slightly different way by arguing that 'man' had certain inalienable rights, such as 'life, liberty and the pursuit of happiness' (and in the mid-nineteenth century Harriet Taylor Mill was to question the limitation of these rights to men). To say that a right is inalienable is to say that without those rights human status cannot be; is to say that, if those rights are gone, so too is the human. The human here becomes a being with an essential status that is fixed, stable. Only when infringing the rights of another human (by, for example, assaulting them) do we forfeit our own inalienable rights, and lose our liberty. An animal, you may recall, cannot be a criminal, as a criminal must have intent. By extension, an animal does not have inalienable rights, for if they did all meat-eaters might find themselves behind bars.

This kind of thinking about the human is often labelled 'humanist'. The philosopher Kate Soper sees humanist ideas as appealing '(positively) to the notion of a core humanity or common essential feature in terms of which human beings can be defined and understood'.[4] More recent philosophical discussions have begun to

---

2. Thomas Aquinas, *Summa Theologiae*, trans. R. J. Batten (London, 1975), p. 91.
3. Royal Society for the Prevention of Cruelty to Animals [*Editor*].
4. Kate Soper, *Humanism and Anti-Humanism*, cited in Neil Badmington, ed., *Posthumanism* (Basingstoke, 2000), p. 2.

unravel this idea of the human, and what emerged in the late twentieth century is what has been termed 'posthumanism', a philosophical
crisis in the conceptualization of humanity. In 1997 Jacques Derrida
outlined one of the problems facing posthumanist humanity. What,
Derrida asks, is 'proper to man'? That is, what is it that defines the
human as human (as opposed to animal, machine and so on)? He
cites the conventional responses—'speech, reason, the logos, history,
laughing, mourning, burial, the gift, etc.'—but regards the proliferation of proofs, the fact that there is no one thing that makes us
human, as evidence that it is not in the possession of one thing—the
ability to speak, for example—but in the 'configuration' of all of
those traits that the property of the human can be found. 'For that
reason,' he writes, what is proper to man 'can never be limited to a
single trait and it is never closed; structurally speaking it can attract
a non-finite number of other concepts, beginning with the concept of
a concept.'[5] Such a recognition of the limitless properties of humanity is not regarded by Derrida as a positive outcome, rather, it shows
that proving ourselves to be different from animals can take on
comic proportions: it is everything and nothing simultaneously.

Later in the same essay Derrida does, however, offer one place
where the human is distinguished from the animal. But his definition carries with it, almost inevitably, an inherently destructive force.
Bestiality is one of the worst crimes that a human can commit—in
the seventeenth century it was regarded as 'a sin against God, nature
and the law' (three strikes in one, you might say).[6] It is the place
where the isolation of humanity is destroyed. And yet, for Derrida,
it is also truly the property of man: 'beasts', he writes, "are in any
case exempt by definition' from bestiality. 'One cannot speak . . . of
the bêtise or bestiality of an animal.'[7] An animal will always engage
in sexual intercourse with another animal; only a human, therefore, can be a bestialist. This is not quite the same as claiming that
only a human has the capacity to think. Prynne's fears for humans
dressed as animals offer, then, a historical and visual version of a
contemporary philosophical problem. What is it that makes us
human? Or, perhaps that question should be rephrased: what is it
that makes us not animal?

An image contemporary with Prynne's argument takes this even
further (and it may be that this kind of costuming was the real
source of Prynne's complaint). When, in the early seventeenth
century, Inigo Jones sketched a design for a costume for 'a bird'

5. Jacques Derrida, 'The Animal That Therefore I Am (More to Follow)', trans.
David Wills, Critical Inquiry 28 (2002), pp. 373–4.
6. Michael Dalton, The Countrey Justice (London, 1618), p. 242.
7. Derrida, 'The Animal That Therefore I Am', p. 409.

(see left) for a performance at the court of Charles I, he was creating a spectacle. But if we place his illustration within the frame of Prynne's argument we can perhaps begin to see something more threatening.

* * *

The sketchy quality of this image—Jones also created more detailed costumes for a lion, ape, fox, ass and hog—echoes the emerging sketchiness of the human. A few strokes of the pen and a transformation has taken place. From bird-man to ape-astronaut, from transformed humanity to fake fur, we have travelled over 300 years, but we can see that we are little further forward. In fact, in Jones's image the idea that we never look into a chicken's eyes and see ourselves seems to be undermined: a look in the mirror might reveal a contiguity that is terrifying.

* * *

JOSEPH W. MEEKER

The Comic Mode†

The Biology of Comedy

Literary criticism has asserted from its beginnings the idea that literature is essentially an imitation of the actions of men. Few have disputed the doctrine of mimesis first spelled out in ancient Greece in Plato's *Republic* and revised in Aristotle's *Poetics*, though subsequent critics have modified the interpretation of the term *mimesis*. Without going into the niceties of the argument, let me merely assume in a simpleminded way that literature does imitate human actions, and consider two examples of such imitation. Both seek to

---

† Joseph W. Meeker, "The Comic Mode," in Cheryll Glotfelty and Harold Fromm, eds., *The Ecocriticism Reader: Landmarks in Literary Ecology* (Athens: University of Georgia Press, 1996), pp. 155–69. Reprinted by permission of the author.

reproduce the same fictional action, but from different historical perspectives and using different literary modes.

The first example is *Oedipus the King*, written in the fifth century B.C. by the Greek dramatist Sophocles. Early in the play Teiresias, the blind seer, confronts the king with the suggestion that the murderer he is seeking is perhaps Oedipus himself.

TEIRESIAS
I say you are the murderer of the king
whose murderer you seek.

OEDIPUS
Not twice you shall
say calumnies like this and stay unpunished.

TEIRESIAS
Shall I say more to tempt your anger more?

OEDIPUS
As much as you desire; it will be said
in vain.

TEIRESIAS
I say that with those you love best
you live in foulest shame unconsciously
and do not see where you are in calamity.

OEDIPUS
Do you imagine you can always talk
like this, and live to laugh at it hereafter?

TEIRESIAS
Yes, if the truth has anything of strength.[1]

In *Giles Goat-Boy*, a novel by the contemporary American novelist John Barth, a central chapter is devoted to the translation of the Oedipus story into the idiom of comedy in a post-Freudian world. Barth's version follows Sophocles' closely, but with rather different effect. The Barth account of the meeting between Gynander (Teiresias) and Taliped Decanus (Oedipus) shows all the solemnity of a vaudeville routine.

GYNANDER
When this play's over you'll
regret you made that silly vow of yours.
You tragic-hero types are bloody bores.
. . . You're

---

1. David Grene and Richmond Lattimore, *The Complete Greek Tragedies* (Chicago: University of Chicago Press, 1959), 2:26.

the wretch you want. You'll see, when
    Scene Four's done
that you're your daughter's brother,
    your own stepson
and foster-father, uncle to your cousin,
your brother-in-law's nephew, and (as
    if that wasn't
enough) a parricide—and a matriphile!
Bye-bye now Taliped. You call *me* vile,
But your two crimes will have us all
    upchucking:
father-murdering and mother—

TALIPED

                              Ducking
out won't save you. You'll hear from me!

GYNANDER

    You killed your daddy!
    You shagged your mommy!
                    [He is taken away][2]

Both scenes are recognizable imitations of the actions of men, and in this case the action being imitated is the same: the revelation of Oedipus's crimes. But the purposes, the language, the moods, and the contexts of the two passages could hardly contrast more than they do. Sophocles and John Barth are imitating different aspects of human action, and the difference between them illustrates a basic distinction between the tragic and the comic views of human behavior. Sophocles' purpose is to imitate man insofar as he is a creature of suffering and greatness; through his characters he demonstrates the enormous human capacity for creating and for enduring pain, for following a passion to its ultimate end, for employing the power of mind and spirit to rise above the contradictions of matter and circumstance even though one is destroyed by them. Sophocles imitates man as a noble creature. Barth imitates man's absurdity. Barth's version emphasizes the ridiculousness of Oedipus's situation and suggests that the hero is slightly dense for not avoiding the mess he's made of his life. Barth's image shows man's innate stupidity and ignorance and emphasizes the triviality of human passions by reducing them to the level of street-corner disputes.

The tragic view of man has not often been achieved. Whole cultures have lived and died without producing tragedy or the philosophical views that tragedy depends upon. Both as a literary form

2. John Barth, *Giles Goat-Boy* (New York: Fawcett, 1967), 323.

and as a philosophical attitude, tragedy seems to have been an invention of Western culture, specifically of the Greeks. It is shared by those traditions influenced by Greek thought, though few of the cultures even in the direct line of that influence have produced a significant tragic literature rivaling that of ancient Greece. The intellectual presuppositions necessary to the creation of tragic literature have not been present in all civilizations. It is conspicuously absent, for instance, in Oriental, Middle Eastern, and primitive cultures. The tragic view assumes that man exists in a state of conflict with powers that are greater than he is. Such forces as nature, the gods, moral law, passionate love, the greatness of ideas and knowledge all seem enormously above mankind and in some way determine his welfare or his suffering. Tragic literature and philosophy, then, undertake to demonstrate that man is equal or superior to his conflict. The tragic man takes his conflict seriously, and feels compelled to affirm his mastery and his greatness in the face of his own destruction. He is a triumphant image of what man can be. Outside of ancient Greece and Elizabethan England, few playwrights have been able to produce this image in a convincing manner.

Comedy, on the other hand, is very nearly universal. Comic literature appears wherever human culture exists, and often where it doesn't. Comedy can be universal largely because it depends less upon particular ideologies or metaphysical systems than tragedy does. Rather, comedy grows from the biological circumstances of life. It is unconcerned with cultural systems of morality. As the contemporary American philosopher Susanne Langer has put it, comedy is truly amoral in that it has, literally, "no use" for morality—that is, moral insights play no significant role in the comic experience.[3] Similarly, comedy avoids strong emotions. Passionate love, hate, or patriotism generally appear ridiculous in a comic context, for comedy creates a psychological mood which is incompatible with deep emotions. Great ideas and ideals fare no better at the hands of comedy, which ordinarily treats them as if they were insignificant. When noble idealism does appear in comedy, its vehicle is commonly a Tartuffe (as in Moliere's *Tartuffe: or the Imposter*) or a Malvolio (as in Shakespeare's *Twelfth Night*), whose nobility turns out to be merely a sham to conceal selfish or ignoble motives. The comic view of man demonstrates that men behave irrationally, committing follies which reveal their essential ignorance and ridiculousness in relation to civilized systems of ethical and social behavior. As Aristotle puts it, comedy imitates the actions of men who are subnormal or inferior to the social norm and tragedy imitates the actions of superior men.

3. Susanne Langer, *Feeling and Form* (New York: Charles Scribner's Sons, 1953), 345.

It could thus be argued that comedy is basically pessimistic and tragedy basically optimistic, as tragedy shows man's potential strength and greatness. This is true only if it is assumed that the metaphysical morality that encourages man to rise above his natural environment and his animal origins is mankind's best hope for the future. That assumption is seriously in doubt in our time. There are good reasons to suspect the wisdom of the traditions of metaphysical idealism. Philosophy since Nietzsche has demonstrated the poverty of humanistic idealism, evolutionary biology has demonstrated the animality of mankind, and contemporary psychology has shown that the mind is guided by many forces stronger than great ideas. Political philosophies fail daily to meet mankind's simplest needs, and now the environmental crisis raises the possibility that the world itself and all its creatures are in jeopardy because humanity has thought too highly of itself. The tragic view of man, for all its flattering optimism, has led to cultural and biological disasters, and it is time to look for alternatives which might encourage better the survival of our own and other species.

Comedy demonstrates that man is durable even though he may be weak, stupid, and undignified. As the tragic hero suffers or dies for his ideals, the comic hero survives without them. At the end of his tale he manages to marry his girl, evade his enemies, slip by the oppressive authorities, avoid drastic punishment, and to stay alive. His victories are all small, but he lives in a world where only small victories are possible. His career demonstrates that weakness is a common condition of mankind that must be lived with, not one worth dying for. Comedy is careless of morality, goodness, truth, beauty, heroism, and all such abstract values men say they live by. Its only concern is to affirm man's capacity for survival and to celebrate the continuity of life itself, despite all moralities. Comedy is a celebration, a ritual renewal of biological welfare as it persists in spite of any reasons there may be for feeling metaphysical despair.

The Greek demigod Comus, whose name was probably the origin of the word comedy, was a god of fertility in a large but unpretentious sense. His concerns included the ordinary sexual fertility of plants, men, and animals, and also the general success of family and community life insofar as these depend upon biological processes. Comus was content to leave matters of great intellectual import to Apollo and gigantic passions to Dionysus while he busied himself with the maintenance of the commonplace conditions that are friendly to life. Maintaining equilibrium among living things, and restoring it once it has been lost, are Comus's special talents, and they are shared by the many comic heroes who follow the god's example.

Literary comedy depicts the loss of equilibrium and its recovery. Wherever the normal processes of life are obstructed unnecessarily, the comic mode seeks to return to normal. The point can be illustrated by a Greek comic drama from the fifth century B.C., Aristophanes' *Lysistrata:* When the young men all disappear from their wives' beds in order to fight a foolish foreign war, the comic heroine Lysistrata calls a sex strike of all women and bargains for an end to the war in exchange for a restoration of normal sexual activities. Lysistrata counts on her own wit and the natural lecherousness of men to solve her immediate problem. Lysistrata's motive is not peace with honor but peace with love—or at least with lovemaking. Honor belongs to the vocabulary of tragedy and warfare. At best it is irrelevant to peace, at worst destructive of it. As Americans have learned during the Vietnam decade, honor can be dangerous and disruptive when used as a principle of public policy. Lysistrata and her women puncture the inflated rhetoric of warriors and politicians to reassert the comic primacy of sex and its attendant social needs: mutual access of men and women to one another, family wholeness, and the maintenance of normal reproduction, child rearing, and nourishment.

Typical of comic action, *Lysistrata* demonstrates no discovery of a new truth and no permanent conquest over an evil force, but merely a return to a former normalcy. No enemy has been destroyed and no new victories have been won. Success is temporary, and it has been accomplished with the most modest of weapons: wit, luck, persuasion, and a bit of fanciful inventiveness. The antagonists are momentarily reconciled, the killing ceases, the men make love to their wives, and the wives raise children and keep house, which is exactly what they were doing before the heroics of warfare interfered with their lives. Like most significant comedy, *Lysistrata* pretends only to show how mankind can hold its own and survive in a world where both real and artificial threats to survival abound. Comedy is concerned with muddling through, not with progress or perfection.

To people disposed in favor of heroism and idealistic ethics, comedy may seem trivial in its insistence that the commonplace is worth maintaining. The comic point of view is that man's high moral ideals and glorified heroic poses are themselves largely based upon fantasy and are likely to lead to misery or death for those who hold them. In the world as revealed by comedy, the important thing is to live and to encourage life even though it is probably meaningless to do so. If the survival of our species is trivial, then so is comedy.

The Comedy of Biology

If comedy is essentially biological, it is possible that biology is also comic. Some animal ethologists argue that humor is not only a deterrent to aggression, but also an essential ingredient in the formation of intraspecific bonds. It appears to have a phylogenetic basis in many animals as well as in man.[4] Beyond this behavioral level, structures in nature also reveal organizational principles and processes which closely resemble the patterns found in comedy. Productive and stable ecosystems are those which minimize destructive aggression, encourage maximum diversity, and seek to establish equilibrium among their participants—which is essentially what happens in literary comedy. Biological evolution itself shows all the flexibility of comic drama, and little of the monolithic passion peculiar to tragedy.

Ecology is to a large extent the study of plant and animal succession. Ecologists seek to understand the processes through which interactions among species over long periods of time produce the various biological communities and environments found in the natural world. At an early stage in any given environment, pioneering or invading species dominate the scene. These are highly generalized, flexible, and adaptable creatures capable of surviving despite the inhospitable nature of their environments. Pioneers must be aggressive, competitive, and tough. On an evolutionary time scale, their careers are brief but dramatic episodes, but they make possible the more stable ecosystems which follow them. Many weeds that grow on newly cleared land following fires, volcanic eruptions, or construction projects are pioneer plants such as dandelions and crabgrass. Weekend gardeners know well their tenacity and durability. Rats, too, are pioneers capable of thriving against terrible odds by exploiting the meager resources available, as are starlings and several varieties of eels and carp. Many of the species that men find objectionable—the "weeds," "trash fish," and "nuisance" mammals and birds—are pioneering or invading species whose life styles resemble behavior that men have admired most when they have seen it in other men. We celebrate the qualities in human pioneers that we despise in the pioneers of other plant and animal species.

Ecological pioneering species, like human pioneers, are creatures capable of living without some of the normal needs felt by others of their kind: They are heroic individuals who make their homes where no one else wants to live, and their lives lead the way toward challenging and dangerous horizons. They risk death in order to conquer new territory, and their survival depends on their individual qualities of strength, aggressiveness, and often ruthlessness. Pioneer species are the loners of the natural world, the tragic heroes who sacrifice themselves in satisfaction of mysterious inner commands which they alone can hear.

---

4. Konrad Lorenz, *On Aggression* (New York: Bantam Books, 1967), 171–73, 284–87.

This may sound like anthropomorphism but it is not. I am not suggesting at all that plants and animals possess human qualities but that much elaborate philosophizing about human behavior has been mere rationalization of relatively common natural patterns of behavior which are to be found in many species of plants and animals. The tragic attitude assumes remarkable behavior to be the result of a remarkable personality and an exclusively human prerogative. But Achilles does no more or less for human posterity than a fireweed growing on a glacial moraine does for the plants that will succeed it. The major difference, perhaps, is that the fireweed will indeed be succeeded by different kinds of plants until ultimately a complex forest emerges, while Achilles will be reincarnated by imitators from among his own species for many centuries, to the grief of many Troys and many Hectors.

The process of ecological succession begun by the pioneer species, if left alone, results in a climax ecosystem. Climax communities of plants and animals are extremely diverse and complicated groupings of living things which exist in a relatively balanced state with one another and with their nonliving environment. A climax ecosystem is much more complicated than any human social organization, if only because it integrates the diverse needs and activities of a very large number of *different* species. Human social systems have only one animal to deal with, man, plus minor adjustments to keep alive the few domesticated plants and animals enslaved to man. But a natural ecosystem accommodates not only the complete life of every species within it, but also provides for relatively harmonious relationships among all its constituent species. In a mature ponderosa pine forest, for instance, thousands of highly specialized types of bacteria maintain stable soil chemistry as each type plays its particular role in the processes of decomposition; insects live upon plants and bacteria and are eaten by birds; small mammals breed in the complex vegetation; larger mammals eat certain specific kinds of plants or prey upon smaller animals; the many highly specialized plants, from small ferns to enormous pines, make up the setting for all other life, provide food and shelter, and in turn depend upon the environmental determinants of weather and geography. It is an unbelievably complicated community in which no individual and no species can survive well unless all other species survive, for all are ultimately dependent upon the completeness of the environment as a whole. The diversity of a climax ecosystem is one of the secrets of its durability.

Life is dangerous for any individual in such a system, for there is always some other individual who needs to eat him. The welfare of individuals is generally subordinated to the welfare of the group. No individuals and no particular species stand out as overwhelmingly dominant, but each performs unique and specialized functions which play a part in the overall stability of the community. It is the community itself that really matters, and it is likely to be an extremely durable community so long as balance is maintained among its many elements.

No human has ever known what it means to live in a climax ecosystem, at least not since the emergence of consciousness which has made us human. We have generally acted the role of the pioneer species, dedicating ourselves to survival through the destruction of all our competitors and to achieving effective dominance over other forms of life. Civilization, at least in the West, has developed as a tragedy does, through the actions of pioneering leaders who break new ground and surmount huge obstacles. Religion and philosophy have usually affirmed the pioneer's faith that only his own kind really counts, and that he has a right—perhaps even an obligation—to destroy or subjugate whatever seems to obstruct his hopes of conquest. Some relatively benevolent societies have provided for wide diversification among men, but none has extended *e pluribus unum* to include other species.

Like comedy, mature ecosystems are cosmopolitan. Whatever life forms may exist seem to have an equal right to existence, and no individual needs, prejudices, or passions give sufficient cause to threaten the welfare of the ecosystem structure as a whole. Necessity, of course, is real. All must eat and in turn be eaten, storms must come and go, and injustices must occur when so many rightful claimants contend. But that is just the point: comedy and ecology are systems designed to accommodate necessity and to encourage acceptance of it, while tragedy is concerned with avoiding or transcending the necessary in order to accomplish the impossible.

One of the tenets of the humanistic tradition is that human beings should try to accomplish whatever the human mind can imagine. Many of our imaginings have been directed toward making ourselves more perfect. The human brain makes it possible to modify human behavior according to conceptual plans which may or may not agree with established natural processes or with human instinctual needs. Unlike other animals, humans can select from a large number of conceptual possibilities the behavior that they prefer for mating, social organization, aggression and defense, rearing of offspring, and the maintenance of food supply.

The capacity to choose one's behavior includes the possibility of choosing erroneously, and many of the environmental problems facing mankind today seem to be the products of mistaken human choices. But what does "mistaken" mean, and how it is possible to know the difference between ecological wisdom and ecological insanity? It is depressing to realize that such questions have been asked seriously only in recent years. Human behavior has generally been guided by presumed metaphysical principles which have neglected to recognize that man is a species of animal whose welfare depends upon successful integration with the plants, animals, and land that make up his environment.

Because they do not have such a wide choice, other animals have more successfully maintained the behavioral patterns which make their own survival possible while contributing to the long-term maintenance of their environments. The recent growth of ethology, the study of animal behavior, is a sign that humans are now beginning to see animals as significant sources of information about living well. Ethologists have consistently discovered that even the simplest of creatures follow exceedingly complicated and often highly sophisticated patterns of behavior, many of which continue to defy human understanding. Animal rituals of reproduction and rearing, defense of territory, maintenance of social systems, nest-building, migrations, and food-gathering are quite as intricate as comparable human activities. The simplest migratory bird has a guidance system that is more subtle and far more reliable than the most sophisticated ICBM, and any pair of whooping cranes has a courtship and sex life at least as complicated as Romeo and Juliet's. We are slowly beginning to realize that we have grossly underestimated the animals.

The truth may be that civilized human life is much simpler than most animal life. We seem to have used our enlarged brain in order to reduce the number of choices facing us, and we have sought the simple way of destroying or ignoring our competition rather than the more demanding task of accommodating ourselves to the forces that surround us. We establish artificial polarities like good and evil, truth and falsehood, pain and pleasure, and demand that a choice be made which will elevate one and destroy the other. We transform complicated wilderness environments into ecologically simple farmlands. We seek unity and we fear diversity. We demand that one species, our own, achieve unchallenged dominance where hundreds of species lived in complex equilibrium before our arrival. In the present environmental dilemma, humanity stands like a pioneer species facing heroically the consequences of its own tragic behavior, with a growing need to learn from the more stable comic heroes of nature, the animals.

Tragedy demands that choices be made among alternatives; comedy assumes that all choice is likely to be in error and that survival depends upon finding accommodations that will permit all parties to endure. Evolution itself is a gigantic comic drama, not the bloody tragic spectacle imagined by the sentimental humanists of early Darwinism. Nature is not "red in tooth and claw" as the nineteenth-century English poet Alfred, Lord Tennyson characterized it, for evolution does not proceed through battles fought among animals to see who is fit enough to survive and who is not. Rather, the evolutionary process is one of adaptation and accommodation, with the various species exploring opportunistically their environments in search of a means to maintain their existence. Like comedy, evolution is a matter of muddling through.

Literary comedy and biological evolution share in common the view that all change is conservative.[5] Organisms and comic heroes change their structure or behavior only in order to preserve an accustomed way of life which has been threatened by changes in the environment. The ancient fish that developed lungs when his home in the sea became untenable was not a radical revolutionary, but a public-spirited preserver of his genetic heritage. The famous peppered moth of Birmingham who changed his color from light gray to black when smoke from the industrial revolution discolored the bark on his native trees may have denied thousands of years of moth tradition, but his adaptation made it possible to preserve moth existence. If there were moral philosophers among the lungfishes and peppered moths, these innovations would very likely have been condemned as threats to the continuity of tradition, or perhaps as shameful immorality. All admiration would no doubt have been reserved for the heroic fish who would rather die than give up his gills and for the moth who nobly faced his end wearing customary gray. Fossilized remains attest to the many extinct animals who insisted upon the propriety of their traditions in the face of a changing world. Of the estimated one billion different species produced so far by evolution, ninety-nine percent have become extinct in such a manner.

To say that change is conservative may confuse anyone who thinks the term is the antonym of liberal and that it describes a mental attitude in favor of traditional social values and customs. The conservative principle in biology is evolutionary; it refers to those variations in structure and behavior which adapt an organism more perfectly to a changing environment, thus conserving its genetic continuity despite changes in form. Whatever may threaten the continuity of life itself is considered by evolution to be expendable and subject to modification, whether it be gills or social rituals. To evolution and to comedy, nothing is sacred but life itself.

The old Italian whoremaster in Joseph Heller's contemporary American novel, Catch-22, teaches a similar lesson:

> I was a fascist when Mussolini was on top, and I am an antifascist now that he has been deposed. I was fanatically pro-German when the Germans were here to protect us against

5. Charles F. Hockett and Robert Ascher, "The Human Revolution," Current Anthropology 5, no. 3 (1964): 140.

the Americans, and now that the Americans are here to protect us against the Germans I am fanatically pro-American.[6]

Nately, the naively idealistic American soldier to whom he is talking, sputters in dismay that he is a shameful, unscrupulous opportunist, and the old man replies only: "I am a hundred and seven years old." Young Nately, committed to the idealism of keeping the world safe for democracy, dies in combat before his twentieth birthday. The old man's morality rests upon the comic imperative of preserving life itself at all costs, a principle which overrides all other moral commitments.

Evolution is just such a shameful, unscrupulous, opportunistic comedy, the object of which appears to be the proliferation and preservation of as many life forms as possible without regard for anyone's moral ideas. Successful participants in it are those who remain alive when circumstances change, not those who are best able to destroy competitors and enemies. Its ground rules for participants (including man) are those which also govern literary comedy: organisms must adapt themselves to their circumstances in every possible way, must studiously avoid all-or-nothing choices, must prefer any alternative to death, must accept and encourage maximum diversity, must accommodate themselves to the accidental limitations of birth and environment, and must always prefer love to war—though if warfare is inevitable, it should be prosecuted so as to humble the enemy without destroying him. The events depicted in tragic literature *cannot* occur if these principles are observed. Comic action follows naturally from them.

Comic Survival

Oscar Wilde, the nineteenth-century British playwright, offered an important amendment to Aristotle when he observed that life imitates art at least as much as art imitates life. Artists and thinkers, he argued, create images of what life might be like and so provide models for human behavior which men may imitate. Don Quixote was not born a knight-errant, but discovered his profession by reading tales of adventure. People can choose to some extent the roles they wish to play from among the many models preserved by literature and cultural traditions. If people generally see themselves in the tragic mode, it is perhaps because it satisfies their vanity and makes their actions seem important. It is gratifying to think of oneself as a hero, a great sufferer, a martyr, or an oppressed idealist. Oedipus and Hamlet might not have been admired all these centuries if they had not offered illustrious images showing how to bear pain

6. Joseph Heller, *Catch*-22 (New York: Dell, 1961), 251–52.

magnificently. But unfortunately, the tragic heroes preserved in literature are the products of metaphysical presuppositions which most people can no longer honestly share, any more than Don Quixote could live up to the requirements of medieval chivalry while living in Renaissance Spain. A post-Freudian world no longer sees incest as an offense against the universe as Oedipus did, nor can we share Hamlet's view that revenge will give peace to the ghost of his slain father. The philosophical props and settings for genuine tragic experience have disappeared. Moderns can only pretend to tragic heroism, and that pretense is painfully hollow and melodramatic in the absence of the beliefs that tragedy depends upon.

Prerequisite to tragedy is the belief that the universe cares about the lives of human beings. There must be a faith that some superior order exists, and that man will be punished if he transgresses against it. It matters little whether this principle takes the form of fate, the gods, or impersonal moral law, for all are symbols of the world's interest in human actions and evidence that the welfare of all creation somehow depends upon what humans do. Corollary to this is the assumption that man is essentially superior to animal, vegetable, and mineral nature and is destined to exercise mastery over all natural processes, including those of his own body. The most respected tragedy further assumes that some truth exists in the universe which is more valuable than life itself. There must be abstract ideas and values which are worth dying and suffering for, otherwise the hero's painful quest for spiritual purity and enlightenment becomes absurd.

"Absurd" is the proper adjective to describe these assumptions, in the rather technical sense in which existential philosophy uses the term. The world has never cared about man, nature has never shown itself to be inferior to humanity, and truth has never been revealed in its awesome majesty except perhaps in the creations of tragic literature. Tragedy does not imitate the conditions of life, but creates artificial conditions which men mimic in their attempts to attain the flattering illusions of dignity and honor. In an age which perceives dignity, honor, truth, law, and the gods as the inventions of egocentric man and not as given facts of the universe, tragedy can only parody itself.

More appropriate to our time are the relatively modest assumptions made by the comic spirit. Man is a part of nature and subject to all natural limitations and flaws. Morality is a matter of getting along with one's fellow creatures as well as possible. All beliefs are provisional, subject to change when they fail to produce harmonious consequences. Life itself is the most important force there is: the proper study of mankind is survival. When the existence of many species, including the human, and the continuity of the biological environment are threatened as they are now, mankind can no longer afford the wasteful and destructive luxuries of a tragic view of life.

As patterns of behavior, both tragedy and comedy are strategies for the resolution of conflicts. From the tragic perspective, the world is a battleground where good and evil, man and nature, truth and falsehood make war, each with the goal of destroying its polar opposite. Warfare is the basic metaphor of tragedy, and its strategy is a battle plan designed to eliminate the enemy. That is why tragedy ends with a funeral or its equivalent. Comic strategy, on the other hand, sees life as a game. Its basic metaphors are sporting events and the courtship of lovers, and its conclusion is generally a wedding rather than a funeral. When faced with polar opposites, the problem of comedy is always how to resolve conflict without destroying the participants. Comedy is the art of accommodation and reconciliation.

Though the comic, ecological view of life may be modest and unheroic, it is anything but simple. Some superrationalists reject the current interest in ecology by arguing that a "return to nature" would be a denial of the mental capacities of mankind, and impossible in a world as complicated and populous as it is today. Their assumption that nature is simple while civilization is complex is one of the sad legacies of romantic thought. Nature is neither an idyll of simplicity and peace populated by noble savages (as pictured by the eighteenth-century French philosopher Jean Jacques Rousseau) nor a bloody battlefield where only the most brutal can survive (as defined by the seventeenth-century British philosopher Thomas Hobbes, and later elaborated by nineteenth-century social Darwinism). Both views drastically oversimplify the intricate processes of nature because they reflect the methods and values of a pioneer species, man, rather than the complexity of the more highly developed species of an ecological climax.

If a "return to nature" were to be based upon the model of a climax ecosystem, civilization would have to become far more complex than anything man has yet produced. Human values could no longer be based on the assumption that man is alone at the center of creation; allowance would have to be made for the welfare of all the plants, animals, and land of the natural environment. Mankind would have to cultivate a new and more elaborate mentality capable of understanding intricate processes without destroying them. Ecology challenges mankind to vigorous complexity, not passive simplicity.

If the lesson of ecology is balance and equilibrium, the lesson of comedy is humility and endurance. The comic mode of human behavior represented in literature is the closest art has come to describing man as an adaptive animal. Comedy illustrates that survival depends upon man's ability to change himself rather than his environment, and upon his ability to accept limitations rather than to curse fate for limiting him. It is a strategy for living which agrees well with the demands of ecological wisdom, and it cannot be ignored as a model for human behavior if man hopes to keep a place for himself among the animals who live according to the comic mode.

WALTER BENJAMIN

Gloves†

In an aversion to animals the predominant feeling is fear of being recognized by them through contact. The horror that stirs deep in man is an obscure awareness that in him something lives so akin to the animal that it might be recognized. All disgust is originally disgust at touching. Even when the feeling is mastered, it is only by a drastic gesture that overleaps its mark: the nauseous is violently engulfed, eaten, while the zone of finest epidermal contact remains taboo. Only in this way is the paradox of the moral demand to be met, exacting simultaneously the overcoming and the subtlest elaboration of man's sense of disgust. He may not deny his bestial relationship with animals, the invocation of which revolts him: he must make himself its master.

† From Walter Benjamin, *One-Way Street and Other Writings*, trans. Edmund Jephcott and Kingsley Shorter (London: NLB, 1979), pp. 50–51. Reprinted by permission.

CRITICISM

WILLIAM HAZLITT

As You Like It[†]

Shakspeare has here converted the forest of Arden into another Arcadia, where they "fleet the time carelessly, as they did in the golden world." It is the most ideal of any of this author's plays. It is a pastoral drama, in which the interest arises more out of the sentiments and characters than out of the actions or situations. It is not what is done, but what is said, that claims our attention. Nursed in solitude, "under the shade of melancholy boughs," the imagination grows soft and delicate, and the wit runs riot in idleness, like a spoiled child, that is never sent to school. Caprice and fancy reign and revel here, and stern necessity is banished to the court. The mild sentiments of humanity are strengthened with thought and leisure; the echo of the cares and noise of the world strikes upon the ear of those "who have felt them knowingly," softened by time and distance. "They hear the tumult, and are still." The very air of the place seems to breathe a spirit of philosophical poetry; to stir the thoughts, to touch the heart with pity, as the drowsy forest rustles to the sighing gale. Never was there such beautiful moralising, equally free from pedantry or petulance.

> "And this their life, exempt from public haunts,
> Finds tongues in trees, books in the running brooks,
> Sermons in stones, and good in everything."

Jaques is the only purely contemplative character in Shakspeare. He thinks and does, nothing. His whole occupation is to amuse his mind, and he is totally regardless of his body and his fortunes. He is the prince of philosophical idlers; his only passion is thought; he sets no value upon anything, but as it serves as food for reflection. He can "suck melancholy out of a song, as a weasel sucks eggs"; the motley fool, "who morals on the time," is the greatest prize he meets with in the forest. He resents Orlando's passion for Rosalind as some disparagement of his own passion for abstract truth; and leaves the Duke as soon as he is restored to his sovereignty, to seek his brother out who has quitted it, and turned hermit.

> —"Out of these convertites
> There is much matter to be heard and learnt."

† From William Hazlitt, *Lectures on the Dramatic Literature of the Age of Elizabeth* (New York: Derby & Jackson, 1860), pp. 198–201.

Within the sequestered and romantic glades of the forest of Arden, they find leisure to be good and wise, or to play the fool and fall in love. Rosalind's character is made up of sportive gaiety and natural tenderness: her tongue runs the faster to conceal the pressure at her heart. She talks herself out of breath, only to get deeper in love. The coquetry with which she plays with her lover in the double character which she has to support is managed with the nicest address. How full of voluble, laughing grace is all her conversation with Orlando—

> —"In heedless mazes running
> With wanton haste and giddy cunning."

How full of real fondness and pretended cruelty is her answer to him when he promises to love her "For ever and a day!"

> "Say a day without the ever: no, no, Orlando, men are April when they woo, December when they wed; maids are May when they are maids, but the sky changes when they are wives: I will be more jealous of thee than a Barbary cock-pigeon over his hen; more clamorous than a parrot against rain; more new-fangled than an ape; more giddy in my desires than a monkey; I will weep for nothing, like Diana in the fountain, and I will do that when you are disposed to be merry; I will laugh like a hyen and that when you are inclined to sleep.

> ORLANDO.   But will my Rosalind do so?
> ROSALIND.   By my life she will do as I do."

The silent and retired character of Celia is a necessary relief to the provoking loquacity of Rosalind, nor can anything be better conceived or more beautifully described than the mutual affection between the two cousins.

> —"We still have slept together,
> Rose at an instant, learn'd, play'd, eat together,
> And wheresoe'er we went, like Juno's swans,
> Still we went coupled and inseparable."

The unrequited love of Silvius for Phebe shows the perversity of this passion in the commonest scenes of life, and the rubs and stops which nature throws in its way, where fortune has placed none. Touchstone is not in love, but he will have a mistress as a subject for the exercise of his grotesque humor, and to show his contempt for the passion, by his indifference about the person. He is a rare fellow. He is a mixture of the ancient cynic philosopher with the modern buffoon, and turns folly into wit, and wit into folly, just as the fit takes him. His courtship of Aubrey not only throws a degree of ridicule on the state of wedlock itself, but he is equally an enemy to the prejudices of opinion in other respects. The lofty tone of enthusiasm which the Duke and his companion in exile spread over the stillness and solitude of a country life, receives a pleasant shock from Touchstone's skeptical determination of the question.

"CORIN.　And how like you this shepherd's life, Mr. Touchstone?

CLOWN.　Truly, shepherd, in respect of itself, it is a good life; but in respect that it is a shepherd's life, it is naught. In respect that it is solitary, I like it very well; but in respect that it is private, it is a very vile life. In respect it is in the fields, it pleaseth me well; but in respect it is not in the court, it is tedious. As it is a spare life, look you it fits my humor; but as there is no more plenty in it, it goes much against my stomach."

Zimmerman's celebrated work on Solitude discovers only one *half* the sense of this passage.

There is hardly any of Shakspeare's plays that contains a greater number of passages that have been quoted in books of extracts, or a greater number of phrases that have become in a manner proverbial. If we were to give all the striking passages, we should give half the play. We will only recall a few of the most delightful to the reader's recollection. Such are the meeting between Orlando and Adam, the exquisite appeal of Orlando to the humanity of the Duke and his company to supply him with food for the old man, and their answer, the Duke's description of a country life, and the account of Jaques moralising on the wounded deer, his meeting with Touchstone in the forest, his apology for his own melancholy and his satirical vein, and the well-known speech on the stages of human life, the old song of "Blow, blow, thou winter's wind," Rosalind's description of the marks of a lover and of the progress of time with different persons, the picture of the snake wreathed round Oliver's neck while the lioness watches her sleeping prey, and Touchstone's lecture to the shepherd, his defence of cuckolds, and panegyric on the virtues of "an If."—All of these are familiar to the reader: there is one passage of equal delicacy and beauty which may have escaped him, and with it we shall close our account of As you like it. It is Phebe's description of Ganimed, at the end of the third act.

"Think not I love him, tho' I ask for him;
'Tis but a peevish boy, yet he talks well;—
But what care I for words! yet words do well,
When he that speaks them pleases those that hear
It is a pretty youth; not very pretty;
But sure he's proud, and yet his pride becomes him;

He'll make a proper man; the best thing in him
Is his complexion; and faster than his tongue
Did make offence, his eye did heal it up:
He is not very tall, yet for his years he's tall;
His leg is but so so, and yet 'tis well;
There was a pretty redness in his lip,
A little riper, and more lusty red
Than that mix'd in his cheek; 'twas just the difference
Betwixt the constant red and mingled damask.
There be some women, Silvius, had they mark'd him
In parcels as I did, would have gone near
To fall in love with him: but for my part
I love him not, nor hate him not; and yet
I have more cause to hate him than to love him:
For what had he to do to chide at me?"

MRS. ANNA JAMESON
Rosalind[†]

* * *

The first introduction of Rosalind is less striking than interesting;
we see her a dependant, almost a captive, in the house of her usurping uncle; her genial spirits are subdued by her situation, and the
remembrance of her banished father: her playfulness is under a
temporary eclipse.

> I pray thee, Rosalind, sweet my coz, be merry

is an adjuration which Rosalind needed not when once at liberty
and sporting "under the greenwood tree." The sensibility and even
pensiveness of her demeanor in the first instance, render her arch-
ness and gaiety afterwards, more graceful, and more fascinating.

Though Rosalind is a princess, she is a princess of Arcady; and
notwithstanding the charming effect produced by her first scenes,
we scarcely ever think of her with a reference to them, or associate
her with a court, and the artificial appendages of her rank. She
was not made to "lord it o'er a fair mansion," and take state upon
her like the all-accomplished Portia; but to breathe the free air of
heaven and frolic among green leaves. She was not made to stand
the siege of daring profligacy, and oppose high action and high pas-

---

† From *The Heroines of Shakespeare* (1832; rpt. Philadelphia: John F. Potter, 1898), pp.
  82–86.

Rosalind. From Mrs. Anna Jameson, *The Heroines of Shakespeare.*

sion to the assaults of adverse fortune, like Isabel; but to "fleet the time carelessly as they did i' the golden age." She was not made to bandy wit with lords, and tread courtly measures with plumed and warlike cavaliers, like Beatrice; but to dance on the green sward, and "murmur among living brooks a music sweeter than their own."

* * *

Everything about Rosalind breathes of "youth and youth's sweet prime." She is fresh as the morning, sweet as the dew-awakened blossoms, and light as the breeze that plays among them. She is as witty, as voluble, as sprightly as Beatrice; but in a style altogether distinct. In both, the wit is equally unconscious; but in Beatrice it plays about us like the lightning, dazzling but also alarming; while the wit of Rosalind bubbles up and sparkles like the living fountain, refreshing all around. Her volubility is like the bird's song; it is the outpouring of a heart filled to overflowing with life, love, and joy, and all sweet and affectionate impulses. She has as much tenderness as mirth, and in her most petulant raillery there is a touch of softness—"By this hand it will not hurt a fly!" As her vivacity never lessens our impression of her sensibility, so she wears her masculine attire without the slightest impugnment of her delicacy. Shakspeare did not make the modesty of his women depend on their dress, as we shall see further when we come to Viola and Imogen. Rosalind has in truth "no doublet and hose in her disposition." How her heart seems to throb and flutter under her page's vest! What depth of love in her passion for Orlando! whether disguised beneath a saucy playfulness, or breaking forth with a fond impatience, or half betrayed in that beautiful scene where she faints at the sight of his 'kerchief stained with his blood! Here her recovery of her self-possession—her fears lest she should have revealed her sex—her presence of mind, and quick-witted excuse—

I pray you, tell your brother how well I counterfeited—

and the characteristic playfulness which seems to return so naturally with her recovered senses,—are all as amusing as consistent. Then how beautifully is the dialogue managed between herself and Orlando! how well she assumes the airs of a saucy page, without throwing off her feminine sweetness! How her wit flutters free as air over every subject! With what a careless grace, yet with what exquisite propriety!

> For innocence hath a privilege in her
> To dignify arch jests and laughing eyes.

And if the freedom of some of the expressions used by Rosalind or Beatrice be objected to, let it be remembered that this was not the fault of Shakspeare or the women, but generally of the age. Portia, Beatrice, Rosalind, and the rest, lived in times when more importance was attached to things than to words; now we think more of words than of things; and happy are we in these later days of super-refinement, if we are to be saved by our verbal morality. But this is meddling with the province of the melancholy Jaques, and our argument is Rosalind.

*   *   *

EDWARD DOWDEN

[*As You Like It* as Escape]†

* * *

Shakspere, when he had completed his English historical plays, needed rest for his imagination; and in such a mood, craving refreshment and recreation, he wrote his play of As You Like It. To understand the spirit of this play, we must bear in mind that it was written immediately after Shakspere's great series of histories, ending with Henry V. (1599), and before he began the great series of tragedies. Shakspere turned with a sense of relief, and a long easeful sigh, from the oppressive subjects of history, so grave, so real, so massive, and found rest and freedom and pleasure in escape from courts and camps to the Forest of Arden:

> Who doth ambition shun,
> And loves to live i' the sun,
> Come hither, come hither, come hither.

In somewhat the same spirit needing relief for an overstrained imagination he wrote his other pastoral drama, The Winter's Tale, immediately or almost immediately after Timon of Athens. In each case he chose a graceful story in great part made ready to his hand, from among the prose writings of his early contemporaries, Thomas Lodge and Robert Greene. Like the banished Duke, Shakspere himself found the forest life of Arden more sweet than that of painted pomp; a life "exempt from public haunt," in a quiet retreat, where for turbulent citizens, the deer, "poor dappled fools," are the only native burghers.

The play has been represented by one of its recent editors as an early attempt made by the poet to control the dark spirit of melancholy in himself "by thinking it away." The character of the banished Duke, of Orlando, of Rosalind are described as three gradations of cheerfulness in adversity, with Jacques placed over against them in designed contrast.[1] But no real adversity has come to any one of them. Shakspere, when he put into the Duke's mouth the words, "Sweet are the uses of adversity," knew something of deeper affliction than a life in the golden leisure of Arden. Of real melancholy there is none in the play; for the melancholy of Jacques is not grave and earnest, but sentimental, a self-indulgent humour, a petted foible

---

† From Edward Dowden, *Shakspere: A Critical Study of His Mind and Art* (London: Henry S. King, 1875), pp. 76–81.
1. As you Like it, edited by the Rev. C. E. Moberly (1872), pp. 7–9.

of character, melancholy prepense and cultivated; "it is a melancholy of mine own, compounded of many simples, extracted from many objects; and indeed the sundry contemplation of my travels, in which my often rumination wraps me in a most humorous sadness." The Duke declares that Jacques has been "a libertine as sensual as the brutish sting itself;" but the Duke is unable to understand such a character as that of Jacques.[2] Jacques has been no more than a curious experimenter in libertinism, for the sake of adding an experience of madness and folly to the store of various superficial experiences which constitute his unpractical foolery of wisdom. The haunts of sin have been visited as a part of his travel. By and by he will go to the usurping Duke who has put on a religious life, because

Out of these convertites
There is much matter to be heard and learned.

Jacques died, we know not how, or when, or where; but he came to life again a century later, and appeared in the world as an English clergyman; we need stand in no doubt as to his character, for we all know him under his later name of Lawrence Sterne. Mr Yorick[3] made a mistake about his family tree; he came not out of the play of Hamlet, but out of As You Like It. In Arden he wept and moralised over the wounded deer; and at Namport his tears and sentiment gushed forth for the dead donkey. Jacques knows no bonds that unite him to any living thing. He lives upon novel, curious, and delicate sensations. He seeks the delicious *imprévu* so loved and studiously sought for by that perfected French egoist, Henri Beyle.[4] "A fool! a fool! I met a fool i' the forest!"—and in the delight of coming upon this exquisite surprise, Jacques laughs like chanticleer,

Sans intermission
An hour by his dial.

His whole life is unsubstantial and unreal; a curiosity of dainty mockery. To him "all the world's a stage, and all the men and women merely players;" to him sentiment stands in place of passion; an æsthetic, amateurish experience of various modes of life stands in place of practical wisdom; and words, in place of deeds.

"He fatigues me," wrote our earnest and sensitive Thackeray[5] of the Jacques of English literature, "with his perpetual disquiet and his uneasy appeals to my risible or sentimental faculties. He is

2. Spelled "Jaques" in most modern editions of the play [*Editor*].
3. Sterne is the author of the comic novel *Tristram Shandy* (1759–67); Yorick is the dead jester in *Hamlet* and also the name of the quirky village parson in Sterne's novel [*Editor*].
4. Nineteenth-century French novelist better known as Stendahl [*Editor*].
5. Nineteenth-century British novelist William Thackeray, commenting on Sterne in "Sterne and Goldsmith," lectures on "The English Humourists of the Eighteenth Cen-

always looking in my face, watching his effect, uncertain whether I think him an impostor or not; posture-making, coaxing, and imploring me. 'See what sensibility I have—own now that I'm very clever—do cry now, you can't resist this.'" Yes; for Jacques was at his best in the Forest of Arden, and was a little spoiled by preaching weekly sermons, and by writing so long a caprice as his Tristram Shandy. Shakspere has given us just enough of Jacques; and not too much; and in his undogmatic, artistic, tender, playful, and yet earnest manner upon. Jacques Shakspere has pronounced judgment. Falstaff[6] supposed that by infinite play of wit, and inexhaustible resource of a genius creative of splendid mendacity, he could coruscate away the facts of life, and always remain master of the situation by giving it a clever turn in the idea, or by playing over it with an arabesque of arch waggery.

> I know thee not, old man; fall to thy prayers;
> How ill white hairs become a fool and jester!

That was the terrible incursion of fact; such words as these, coming from the lips of a man who had an unerring perception, and an unfaltering grasp of the fact, were more than words,—they were a deed, which Falstaff the unsubduable, with all his wit, could not coruscate away. "By my troth, he'll yield the crow a pudding one of these days; the king has kill'd his heart." Jacques in his own way supposes that he can dispense with realities. The world, not as it is, but as it mirrors itself in his own mind, which gives to each object a humorous distortion, this is what alone interests Jacques. Shakspere would say to us, "This egoistic, contemplative, unreal manner of treating life is only a delicate kind of foolery. Real knowledge of life can never be acquired by the curious seeker for experiences." But this Shakspere says in his non-hortatory, undogmatic way.

Upon the whole, As You Like It is the sweetest and happiest of all Shakspere's comedies. No one suffers; no one lives an eager intense life; there is no tragic interest in it as there is in The Merchant of Venice, as there is in Much Ado About Nothing. It is mirthful, but the mirth is sprightly, graceful, exquisite; there is none of the rollicking fun of a Sir Toby here; the songs are not "coziers' catches" shouted in the night time, "without any mitigation or remorse of voice," but the solos and duets of pages in the wild-wood, or the noisier chorus of foresters. The wit of Touchstone is not mere clownage, nor has it any indirect serious significances; it is a dainty kind of absurdity worthy to hold comparison with the melancholy of

---

tury," *The Works of William Makepeace Thackeray*, vol. 7, ed. Anne Richie (1898), p. 596 [*Editor*].
6. Character appearing in Shakespeare's *Henry IV, Parts 1* and *2*; Prince Hal repudiates Falstaff once he has ascended the throne as Henry V [*Editor*].

Jacques. And Orlando in the beauty and strength of early manhood, and Rosalind,

> A gallant curtle-axe upon her thigh,
> A boar-spear in her hand.

and the bright, tender, loyal womanhood within—are figures which quicken and restore our spirits, as music does, which is neither noisy nor superficial, and yet which knows little of the deep passion and sorrow of the world.

Shakspere, when he wrote this idyllic play, was himself in his Forest of Arden. He had ended one great ambition—the historical plays—and not yet commenced his tragedies. It was a resting-place. He sends his imagination into the woods to find repose. Instead of the courts and camps of England, and the embattled plains of France, here was this woodland scene, where the palm-tree, the lioness, and the serpent are to be found; possessed of a flora and fauna that flourish in spite of physical geographers. There is an open-air feeling throughout the play. The dialogue, as has been observed, catches freedom and freshness from the atmosphere. "Never is the scene within-doors, except when something discordant is introduced to heighten as it were the harmony."[7] After the trumpet-tones of Henry V. comes the sweet pastoral strain, so bright, so tender. Must it not be all in keeping? Shakspere was not trying to control his melancholy. When he needed to do that, Shakspere confronted his melancholy very passionately, and looked it full in the face. Here he needed refreshment, a sunlight tempered by forest-boughs, a breeze upon his forehead, a stream murmuring in his ears.

※ ※ ※

ANNE BARTON

As You Like It: Shakespeare's 'Sense of an Ending'[†]

I

Henri Focillon has argued that the word *classicism*, rightly understood, has nothing to do with academicism nor even necessarily with our formal legacy from Greece and Rome. Correctly, it refers to a condition of poise: 'a brief, perfectly balanced instant of com-

---

7. C. A. Brown. Shakespeare's Autobiographical Poems, p. 283.
† From Anne Barton, *Essays, Mainly Shakespearean* (Cambridge: Cambridge University Press, 1994), pp. 91–100. Reprinted with the permission of Cambridge University Press.

plete possession of forms' occurring at certain crucial moments in artistic styles which may otherwise have nothing in common.

Classicism consists of the greatest propriety of the parts one to the other. It is stability, security, following upon experimental unrest. It confers, so to speak, a solidity on the unstable aspects of experimentation (because of which it is also, in its way, a renunciation) . . . But classicism is not the result of a conformist attitude. On the contrary, it has been created out of one final, ultimate experiment, the audacity and vitality of which it has never lost . . . Classicism: a brief, perfectly balanced instant of complete possession of forms; not a slow and monotonous application of 'rules', but a pure, quick delight, like the ἀκμή of the Greeks, so delicate that the pointer of the scale scarcely trembles. I look at this scale not to see whether the pointer will presently dip down again, or even come to a moment of absolute rest. I look at it instead to see, within the miracle of that hesitant immobility, the slight, inappreciable tremor that indicates life.[1]

Focillon was writing about the visual arts, but there is surely a *classicism* of the kind he describes in literary styles as well. Dramatists too may achieve a 'perfectly balanced instant of complete possession of forms', the very stillness of which will, in the next moment, seem to imply limitation and invite its own destruction.

As You Like It is, in Focillon's sense, Shakespeare's classical comedy. It confers solidity upon the dazzling experimentation of eight comedies written before it, stands as the fullest and most stable realization of Shakespearean comic form.[2] Critics, aware now of the 'social' nature of the comedies, of their complex structure of silently juxtaposed scenes, tend to take this form more seriously than they once did. C. L. Barber and Northrop Frye in particular have argued for the essential unity of Shakespearean comedy in ways that reach far beyond shared plot devices, or the old spotting of resemblances among the clowns and witty heroines of different plays. It has become possible to agree that the comedies, from *The Two Gentlemen of Verona* and *The Comedy of Errors* to *Twelfth Night*, are plays concerned primarily with transformation, with the clarification and renewal attained, paradoxically, through a submission to some kind of disorder, whether festive or not. We have learned to notice as typically Shakespearean the way characters move between two contrasted locales—one of them heightened and more spacious than the other—and we regard that 'new society' which makes its way back

1. Henri Focillon, *The Life of Forms in Art*, 2nd edn, trans. C. B. Hogan and George Kubler (New York, 1948), pp. 11–12.
2. I am assuming that *The Merry Wives of Windsor* preceded *As You Like It*.

to the normal world at the end of the play as a subtler and more consequential achievement than older critics did.

The exceptionally full participation of *As You Like It* in this (after all) startlingly innovatory comic form built up through preceding plays is obvious. The comedy opposes its two environments, Arden and the court of Duke Frederick, with particular clarity and richness. This greenwood, even more strikingly than the ones in *The Two Gentlemen of Verona* and *A Midsummer Night's Dream*, is a place where people yield themselves for a time to the extraordinary, and emerge transformed. Realism is interwoven with romance, truth to life with certain fairy-tale conventions frankly exploited as such. To a greater extent than Julia and Portia, Rosaline and Beatrice before her, Rosalind in her boy's disguise is the central consciousness of it all: a heroine both involved and dispassionate who seems largely responsible for the structure of that new social order which leaves Arden so hopefully at the end. Most important of all, *As You Like It* tests against each other a great variety of love relationships and possible attitudes towards experience, by means of a technique of contrast and parallel which Shakespeare may have learned originally from Lyly, but which he had refined in the course of writing his earlier comedies to the point where it could, here, actually take the place of plot.

Except as a convenient excuse for getting characters into Arden, and out again at the end, intrigue scarcely seems to matter in this play. *As You Like It* derives much of its classical stability and poise from the fact that its plot barely exists. The comedy moves forward, not through a complex story line of the kind Shakespeare had spun out in *The Comedy of Errors*, or in the Hero/Claudio plot of *Much Ado About Nothing*, but simply through shifts in the grouping of characters. Their verbal encounters, their varying assessments of each other assume the status of events in this pastoral landscape where the gifts of Fortune are bestowed so equally as to throw a new and searching light on what people really are. Shakespeare's customary generosity to his characters, his reluctance to legislate, his faith in romantic love and in the ability of human beings to transform their own natures make *As You Like It* a richer and far more dramatic play than Jonson's *Every Man Out of His Humour* (1599). These two comedies, written perhaps in the same year, are nevertheless alike in their subordination of plot in the traditional sense to an intricate structure of meetings between characters, a concentration upon attitudes rather than action. The normal functions of plot are fulfilled almost entirely by form and, in both cases, a curious stillness at the heart of the play is the result.

Shakespeare had once before composed a comedy singularly devoid of intrigue. *Love's Labour's Lost*, too, unfolds principally by

way of echo and antithesis, through thematic juxtapositions suggesting relationships and judgements which Shakespeare often
does not care to make explicit in his text. There is a sense in which
the only thing that 'happens' in *Love's Labour's Lost*, after the
arrival in Navarre of the Princess and her ladies in Act II, is the
death of the King of France as reported in the fifth act by Mercade.
Yet the effect produced by this second event, geographically distant
though it is, is nothing less than the annihilation of the entire world
of the comedy. In the moments following the entrance of Mercade,
the sheltered, uneventful and thoughtlessly cruel life of the royal
park comes in retrospect to seem not only frivolous but unnatural
and false. The comedy turns and rends its own former preoccupation with words and attitudes as opposed to actions. Sadly, Navarre
and his companions prepare to leave their retreat for an altogether
less comfortable, if ultimately more rewarding, world in which things
happen and death and time cannot be sidestepped. Only by deeds as
opposed to vows, by dearly-bought and tangible 'deserts' (v.2.805),
can love's labours, grossly misconceived by the men for most of the
play, at last be won.

The plotlessness of *As You Like It* is not like this. In no sense
does it represent a criticism of the characters who flee into Arden,
nor of the life they lead there. Although it will be necessary for
most of them to return to an urban civilization at the end, to leave
the greenwood, this return does not imply a rejection of the values
of the forest. They have not been idle, nor is death a fact which the
inhabitants of Arden have ever tried, fraudulently, to evade. *Love's
Labour's Lost* is extreme in the suddenness with which it introduces
its reminder of mortality in Act V. Yet it is surely significant that all
but two of the comedies Shakespeare wrote before *As You Like It*
achieve their comic catharsis by way of some kind of confrontation
with the idea of death.

* * *

Even as Shakespearean tragedy usually makes some delusive gesture towards a happy ending just before the catastrophe, providing
us with a tantalizing glimpse of Lear re-united with Cordelia, Antony successful, or Hamlet reprieved, so the comedies tend to win
through to their happy endings by way of some kind of victory over
the opposite possibility. In doing so, they assure the theatre audience that the facts of the world as it is have not been forgotten.
Like the moment of false hope which animates the fourth acts of
tragedy, the encounter with death which precedes the comedy resolution demonstrates a saving awareness that this story might well
have ended differently. Comedy pauses to look disaster squarely in
the face, but is still able to proceed honestly towards a conclusion

flattering to our optimism. The manoeuvre is designed to shore up the happy ending, to allow us to surrender ourselves, at least temporarily, to a pleasing fiction.

II

In all the comedies which Shakespeare wrote before *As You Like It* (*The Taming of the Shrew* and *The Merry Wives of Windsor* excepted) this emphasis upon death towards the end of the play is strident and momentarily disorientating. The effect produced is not unlike the one achieved by Nicolas Poussin in the earlier of his two paintings on the theme 'Et in Arcadia ego'. In the version at Chatsworth (figure 1), painted about 1630, two shepherds and a shepherdess discover, in a pastoral landscape, a tomb which is the spokesman of death: 'I am here, even in Arcadia.' Poussin was influenced at the time by Titian (and also, as Erwin Panofsky has pointed out, by Guercino's treatment of the same subject[3]), but it is not simply an interest in Baroque diagonals which governs the rush of the three figures towards the sarcophagus. The movement contains within itself a sense of recoil: of sudden horror and dismay. Neither emotionally nor in terms of the composition do the two shepherds and the girl accept the object before them. They react against it with gestures full of disorder. Some twenty years after the Chatsworth *Et in Arcadia ego*, Poussin returned to the subject. The painting he produced, now in the Louvre (figure 2), is classical both in terms of specific stylistic indebtedness and, more importantly, in the sense of Focillon's definition. It stands in something of the same relationship to the Chatsworth painting as does *As You Like It* to Shakespeare's earlier comedies. Here, the tomb stands solidly and uncompromisingly in the midst of a sunlit landscape. The words carved on it now seem to emanate both from Death personified and from the regret of the dead man himself that he too once lived in Arcadia but does so no longer. The three shepherds and the shepherdess grouped about the monument are serious, but they are in no way discomposed by this reminder of their own mortality which they have come upon so suddenly in the midst of the Golden World, in no way frightened or thrown off balance. Indeed, they have contrived to use the rectangular mass of the tomb in the centre of the composition as a kind of support, or focal point, for the achieved harmony of their own attitudes and gestures. They have made it part of their own order, accommodated it perfectly within a pattern of line and movement which both emotionally and

---

3. Erwin Panofsky, '*Et in Arcadia ego*: Poussin and the elegiac tradition', in *Meaning in the Visual Arts* (New York, 1955), pp. 295–320. The Latin phrase means 'and I am in Arcadia' [*Editor*].

Figure 1 'Et in Arcadia ego', by Nicholas Poussin. The first version, in the Devonshire Collection, Chatsworth. Reproduced by permission of Chatsworth Settlement Trustees / The Bridgeman Art Library.

technically has been able to accept this potentially awkward fact of death and even to build upon it.

In *As You Like It* too, death is something faced steadily and with due consideration, but it has almost no power whatever over the balance, the poise of a comedy which has quietly assimilated this factor from the start. A comparison between *As You Like It* and its source, Thomas Lodge's *Rosalynde* (1590), reveals Shakespeare's desire at almost every point to mitigate the violence inherent in the original story. Lodge had moved from one explosive moment of time, one

Figure 2 'Et in Arcadia ego', by Nicholas Poussin. The second version, in the Louvre. Louvre, Paris, France / Giraudon / The Bridgeman Art Library.

crisis, to another. Shakespeare refused to do this. In his reworking of the tale, Charles the wrestler injures the old man's sons but does not kill them, and he himself is not killed. The episode of the robbers in *Rosalynde*, their attempt to abduct the heroine and her companion, is omitted and so is the battle at the end in which Lodge's usurping prince had been defeated and slain. Instead, Shakespeare's Duke Frederick is peacefully converted to goodness through the agency of an old religious man palpably invented for that purpose. The protracted scenes of enmity and struggle between Lodge's hero and his elder brother are made perfunctory, almost abstract, in the comedy. It is true that both Rosalind and Orlando incur a threat of death early in the comedy, but this threat is in both cases a transparent device for sending them into the forest rather than a possibility seriously explored. The wrestling match, Oliver's intention to burn the lodging where Orlando lies, the spite of Duke Frederick, are all treated in the manner of fairy-tale. Not for an instant do they endanger the comic tone. Lodge had described his hero's rescue of his unworthy brother in rousing and basically realistic terms. Shakespeare distances it into the most static and heraldic of pictures: an emblem of lioness and serpent sketched at secondhand. Old Adam may imagine that he is going to die in Arden for lack of food; Orlando rushes into the banquet with drawn sword. These images are no sooner presented than they are corrected. The crisis was false. Calmly, even a little mockingly, the play rights itself. It assimilates the intrusion. Harmonious, balanced, and tonally even, *As You Like It* harbours a stillness at the centre which no turn of the plot, apparently, can affect.

Although a consciousness that 'men have died from time to time, and worms have eaten them' (IV.i.106–7), that human life is 'but a flower' (V.3.28) is spread throughout the comedy, this consciousness is never allowed to sharpen into a dramatic or even into a genuine emotional climax. Reminders of mortality flicker everywhere through the language of the play. Most of the characters seem to carry with them, as visibly as the shepherds painted by Poussin, an awareness of death and time. Rosalind's high spirits, Orlando's love, Duke Senior's contentment in adversity, and Touchstone's wit all flower out of it. Yet when the melancholy Jaques, in his meditation on the wounded deer, his delighted account of Touchstone's platitudes—'from hour to hour, we ripe and ripe, / And then from hour to hour, we rot and rot' (II.7.26–7)—or in his dismal chronology of the ages of man, tries to argue that life must necessarily be trivial and pointless because it ends in the grave, his attitude is amended or put aside. It is as important to the classical equilibrium of the play that Jaques' pessimism should be qualified in this fashion, firmly displaced from the centre of the composition, as it is that the violence built into the story as Lodge had told it should be smoothed away.

In his encounters with the Duke and Touchstone, with Orlando and (above all) with Rosalind, Jaques fares badly. He stumbles from one discomfiture to another. Only in the closing moments of the play when Shakespeare, without warning, allows him to speak the valediction of the entire comedy does his voice go uncontradicted. Formally, in a speech which considerations of rank ought to have assigned to Duke Senior, and symbolism to the god Hymen, Jaques estimates the futures and, by the way, the basic natures of all the other main characters. He puts the seal on the weddings, sets in motion the dance he himself declines to join. As he does so, he becomes something that he was not when he wished for a suit of motley, when he destroyed the harmony of Amiens' song, begged Orlando to rail with him against the world, or when he sentimentalized over the herd-abandoned deer. A figure of sudden dignity, his judgements are both generous and just. Although his decision to seek out Duke Frederick, separating himself firmly from that new society embodied in the dance, may be regretted, it cannot really be criticized. Moreover, his absence from the dance sets up reverberations, asks questions more disturbing than any that were roused earlier by his twice-told tales of transience and decay. This new attitude towards Jaques is important in determining the character of *As You Like It* at its ending. It represents, in Focillon's terms, that 'slight, inappreciable tremor' within the immobility of the classical moment, a tremor which guarantees the vitality of the moment itself but which also prefigures its imminent destruction.

*   *   *

ROSALIE COLIE

Perspectives on Pastoral†

By the end of the sixteenth century, the pastoral mode embraced many particular genres, offered rich options to writers interested in literary experimentation, particularly in mixed genres, and, furthermore, had become embroiled in one of the great literary quarrels which characterized Renaissance literary theory. The pastoral permitted and encouraged opportunities for mixing in one work "imi-

† Rosalie Colie, "Perspectives on Pastoral: Romance, Comic and Tragic," 1974; rpt. in Harold Bloom, ed., *William Shakespeare's As You Like It* (New York: Chelsea House, 1988), pp. 47–62. Colie, Rosalie.; *Shakespeare's Living Ant.* © 1974 Princeton University Press, 2002 renewed PUP. Reprinted by permission of Princeton University Press.

tation" with "invention," art with artifice, the artless with the artful—and generated discussions of such mixes. Eclogues were the principal pastoral form, hallowed by antiquity, but other pastoral lyrics flourished: the love-lyric, the dialogue, the song. Pastoral episodes regularly offered relief in poems largely devoted to epic gests; an English poet wrote a heroic epic in prose entitled, in spite of its relatively scant preoccupation with shepherds, *Arcadia*, and set into this prose-epic a series of pastoral poems which are themselves a self-sufficient anthology of pastoral forms and themes. Following hints from Italian eclogue-writers and fulfilling medieval Latin literary traditions, Marot and Spenser presented unabashed models of Christian pastoral, enriching the imaginative possibilities for their successors; both poets also experimented successfully with satirical poems within the pastoral mode. Indeed, one can recognize anthologies of pastoral work—Sannazaro's *Arcadia* is one example; *The Shepheardes Calender* offers a survey of pastoral themes and topics, and Sidney's shepherds in the *Arcadia* offer a magnificent epideictic display of the eclogue's range of possibilities, formal and topical.

From commedia dell'arte and other popular forms to the grand productions of Tasso and Guarini, drama exploited pastoral scenes, pastoral characters, and what might be called (in the Renaissance anyway) the lyric pastoral *pathétique*. The way in which the pastoral locale was taken as an official site for love-play and for love-poetry can be illustrated by a late anthology of pastoral lyrics published in 1600, *England's Helicon*; that an English Arcadian rhetoric and a mildly Arcadian logic were produced at the turn of the century shows how powerfully the literary notion of Arcadia had come to operate across the spectrum of literary possibility in England's green and pleasant land. From one end to the other of the social and literary scale, pastoral myths and patterns were available: in Whitsun pastorals, pastoral interludes, pastoral romances, in narrative books and on the stage, pastoral masques and (even more common) pastoral episodes within masques, spectators could take their pastoral experience. The ways of pastoral, then, were many and varied; the mixtures of forms, conventions, devices in pastoral allowed in very wide range of decorums.

The richness of the mixture is not really surprising: the literary critical quarrel over the pastoral as *the* mixed dramatic genre, thus as the official locus of tragicomedy, broke out over Guarini's *Il pastor fido* and culminated in the establishment of the pastoral play as the official mixture of comedy with tragedy (sometimes with satire as well), exemplified in such devices as double-plotting, mixed styles, and even interludes from the non-literary arts, such as music, dancing, and the visual arts. Wherever one looked, one could find pastoral—and once-found, twice-found, for the generous, nearly

boundless forms of pastoral offered immense opportunities for craft
and for imagination.

From such a background, Shakespeare's sophisticated traffic
with pastoral is hardly surprising; typically, he experimented with
the mode in various ways, in both early and late plays. In *As You Like
It*, a play with a remarkably tight thematic construction, he worked
with many pastoral themes and motifs, to say nothing of pastoral
types in the dramatis personae, in what is primarily a romantic
love-story derived from a prose narrative. Although "romance" and
its proper subject, love, dominate this play, with the shepherding
and versifying rather its decoration than its psychological locus,
nonetheless the skeletal structure of this romantic comedy *is* the
standard dramatic pastoral pattern—a pattern of extrusion or exile,
recreative sojourn in a natural setting, with ultimate return "homeward" from the exile, a return in moral strength reinforced by the
country experience of kind and kindness.

As You Like It is, for once, about sheep, but this plot-form, from
academic drama to commedia dell'arte, was so thoroughly identified
with the pastoral that as a formula it could imply without overtly stating a great deal of standard pastoral thematics. Sheep, for instance,
were often quite absent from such plays, which sometimes lacked
even the pasture environment. But the *themes* associated with pastoral (court-country, art-nature, nature-nurture) could be counted
on to inform plays with this plot-pattern. A plot on this plan, thus,
was a recognizable vehicle for discourse on the pastoral themes, an
abstraction designed to interpret problems of nature and nurture
originally associated with more overtly pastoral topics.

Though it follows the pastoral dramatic plot and has to do with
sheep and shepherds, *As You Like It* is by no means "officially" pastoral. It ignores, certainly, some of the major cruces of Italian pastoral
dramatic theory: it has no double-plot, for instance, in the pure
sense. Though the De Boys story is separate from the ducal story,
nonetheless Orlando is early displayed at court, catching the attention of Rosalind; throughout, his situation is seen as a counterpart to
hers. Although the country lovers overlap with their courtly parallel
figures, they are in the play rather to round out the range of pastoral
alternatives than to divert into a "plot" of their own. Nor are there
radical shifts of locale and of genre in *As You Like It*; the ducal and
gentlemanly affairs, so to speak, are conveniently focused in one
place, the forest, by means of the exile-device; though the breath
of tragedy blows through the forest, the dominant tone is always,
through Duke Senior's and Rosalind's efforts, kept lucidly "comic."

Duke Senior, Rosalind, Orlando: all are exiled, and in their company come the spiritual exiles who will not part from them, Celia,
Touchstone, the Duke's men, Adam. In the forest these exiles, val-

iantly seeking some cheer, meet that symbolic, alienated, self-exiled figure, the melancholy Jaques, already located in the wood. All these victims—Jaques too—of the world find renewal in the simple culture of the Forest of Arden, and all, save Jaques and Touchstone, return triumphantly to reconstruct the social world from which they had been driven out. Against this basic construction, the play is rich in additional pastoral themes and motifs, many of them ultimately Theocritan and Vergilian, reworked throughout the Latin Middle Ages, reconceived in the Renaissance.

The play makes much of the dialogue and dialectic which so inform pastoral: the love-debates of Silvius and Corin, Silvius and Phebe; the discussion of court and country between Corin and Touchstone; the styles of courtship of Orlando and Rosalind; the dialogue on nature and nurture between Orlando and Oliver; and, as in Spenser's wonderful array of pastoral debates, *The Shepheardes Calender*, the themes so dialectically handled provide an enriching counterpoint to one another. Both the pastoral agon (Corin-Silvius) and the pastoral paragone of real sheep-herding versus literary sheep-keeping (Corin-Touchstone) are part of the play's thematic structure. Among the many things this play is, it is a comparative work about competing life-styles, among these the competition of shepherdly lives, with real shepherds who dip their sheep and lambs, whose hands smell of tar and of the oil from the sheep's wool, and others who live "poetically." We are asked to measure the real and literary shepherds against each other, not once but several times. Behind the prating of the shepherd's life, important thematically as it is in the play, lies a grander anthropological conception, the (pastoral) myth of the Golden World, "the antique world" in which there was perfect commerce and mutual service among men naturally well-disposed to one another, the myth, then, of the Golden Age. In antiquity, the pastoral life had been assigned to the Age of Gold, when men lived in commutual confidence and kept their flocks and herds together, their natural characters attuned to the gentle world they inhabited, their goods held comfortably and easily in common. Such a world had no need for war and was therefore an ideologically pacifist community; such discomfitures as men suffered were not caused by human agency but by natural hazards (winter and rough weather) and by creatures not yet enrolled in the peaceable kingdom (wolves and snakes, in ancient pastoral; snakes and lions in *As You Like It*; metaphorical kites and wolves and real bears in *The Winter's Tale*). Insofar as this ideal theme bears upon the dialectic of pastoral, it implies the corruption of an imperfect world of men—*urbs*, the court—against which its perfections could be fully felt.

With the development of a pastoral *pathétique* by which men identified with the gentler creatures and, in the Renaissance, allowed themselves the luxury of self-cultivation, even of emotional self-exploitation, love officially became the major pastoral occupation, taking precedence even over keeping sheep real or poetical. That is, the shepherd was naturally a poet in the pastoral genres, but before long was also a poet-lover. At first, the pastoral world was pleasant, natural, easy, and so was its love—although the shepherd's complaint about his cold, coy, or faithless mistress (with a corresponding saddening of his landscape to match his emotional situation) was the celebration of another kind of love troublesome, upsetting, potentially destructive of the mutuality of pastoral society. Gradually shepherds and, later, shepherdesses began to die of love— even the pastoral landscape was not always sufficient to nourish the love-struck pastoralist through his emotional afflictions. Though the pastoral world with its celebration of timelessness and harmony would seem to have been created precisely to deny the efficacy of death, nevertheless death's shadow lay across even its green perfections to chill its warm airs.

The pastoral elegy offers a marvelous rationale for death, with its classic expression of the wonderful comforts and assuagements for personal loss; it provides the pattern for the pastoral relation of man to nature, of creation to inspiration: there, the shepherd-singer, the shepherd-maker, is gathered into the pastoral artifice of nature's eternity, these two fused into one. At one with this imaginative and nutritive nature, the dead shepherd-poet becomes a part of the inspiration he had himself once drawn from nature's store. In life poetically competitive—shepherd, goatherd, and cowherd continually sang in agon, each praising his own particular life-style, ritualized into poetic activity—and in death tradition-preserving, the pastoralist invented a world of the imagination in which, depending on his temperament, he could live as he would. He might, then, live sparingly, in simple opposition to urban luxury, confident of nature's power to provide for him; or he might live richly, feasting from nature's endless store, recreating himself and his art thereby. Whichever "nature" he chose as his setting, that entity was expected to provide sufficiently for his aesthetic and emotional needs—in other words, to nurture him.

Theocritus, with whom this all began, was less concerned with the relative values of city and country than with the positive recreations in the country: what court-country agon we find in him, we bring with us from reading subsequent pastoral writers. Vergil, however, made overt the paragone of city and country life; certainly implied in his eclogues and subsequently in the pastoral psychology is the sense of relief from the pressure of daily concerns (*negotium*) in a "liberty" and "freedom" (*otium*) consciously contrasted to the workaday round, a praise of simplicity (and, therefore, of "nature") as contrasted with the artificiality of urban life. As needs no reminder, the inventors and practitioners of literary pastoral were not professional shepherds, but highly sophisticated city-dwellers, whose country life of the imagination was quite different from that enjoyed by the inhabitants of the real Arcadia or, after erosion, of the real Sicily. Thomas Rosenmeyer has put it well: Theocritus' Sicily is not so much a geographical place as a cartographical fiction. Even the country of Vergil's *Eclogues* is a mixed scene, by no means the recognizable North Italian locality of the *Georgics*, for instance. To call such a locale "Arcadia," Rosenmeyer tells us, is precisely to rob it of its "real" geographical implications, to insist that, as a natural spot, it is a mental artifact, a concept, an image in itself.

The encroachments of the city on the green world—of *negotium* upon *otium*—are destructive not only of a simpler form of society, but also of the psychological symbol the pastoral world is. For the literary pastoral celebrates the glorious unrealities of the imagination, its necessary furlough from its assignment of work, obligation, and duty. The iron, or at best brazen, world is man's normal portion: as Sidney put it, "poets only deliver a golden." In the literature with which we have here to deal, the literary opposition between *urbs* and *rus* shifted to become in the Renaissance a *topos* in itself, but with a particular fit to Renaissance literature and socio-economic notions—that is, it shifted its formulation from "city" to "court," and the court-country paradigm became one major focus of pastoral organization. The naturalness, freedom, delightfulness of the pastoral ethos often criticized, overtly or by implication, the self-seeking, self-aggrandizing materialistic artificiality of any court—"court" a synecdoche for any artificial, programed social organization. "Sicily" and "Arcadia" were not measured merely against (as Poggioli believed) the megalopolis, Alexandria, Rome, Paris, but against *any* strict program of social forms, formalities, polite fictions, or flatteries. At Versailles, later, queen and courtiers carried crooks and passed their time as shepherdesses and dairymaids; consciously or not, they acted out the extreme solipsism of the pastoral fiction, so delicately self-referential that only the most sophisticated can comprehend its significations. In the ambivalent symbiosis of court and country, at least in Renaissance pastoral writing, it was the courtier who came for instruction or confirmation to the shepherd, from whom the courtier, an apprentice shepherd, could learn what natural "courtesy" was.

Since the poet's world could be reshaped according to the imagination, could reject conventional decorum to set queens in the dairy, eating bread and honey, poetic imagination could work what miracles it would with its pastoral situation. If queens are dairymaids, shepherdesses can just as well be queens, or at least princesses—and so they turned out to be, over and over again, in the wish-fulfilling satisfactions of pastoral myths. The "marvelous," that subject for endless discussion among Italian critics, was commonplace in the pastoral environment, with social miracle one of pastoral's chief donations. Not least of these was the reestablishment in the pastoral environment of Golden Ageness ("poets only deliver a golden"), or (better) Golden Agelessness: in this generic country, there was no season's difference, in the forest no clock. The landscape stood, at its best, at a perpetual spring, fruiting, and harvest; at worst, the season's round was characteristically benevolent. When the landscape was not at its rich mellowness, the pastoral *pathétique* was generally to blame—the landscape had fallen off to mirror its shepherd's disappointments or depression. In this fiction, then, a poet's triumph was complete: by its means, he could create a nature whose sole poetic obligation was to identify with his emotional state. Such a nature is entirely dependent upon imaginative art, is a nature openly, proudly artificial, a nature which inverts the usual system of imitation, by which art conventionally looks to nature as its model, to offer an art form on which nature might model itself for its own improvement. The pastoral, then, offered a paradigm for the creative imagination in which the doctrine of mimesis is questioned or rejected—and so, really, is the idea of decorum. Not that the pastoral has not its own rules, conditions, and decorum—but its decorum is a conscious reversal of worldly decorus standards.

For these reasons, the art-nature question, another major critical topic of the period, was deeply tied to the pastoral mode, which became the debate's normal habitat. Poets played with the notion of pastoral nature, used as a stalking-horse against the artifices of another ethos—itself a magnificent, self-conscious artifact. From pastoral writing (often mixed with notions of education and cultivation generally classed as georgic), men took a major metaphor, that of the "improvement" of natural things, especially the improvement of breeds by crossing or grafting. "Breeding," that most natural of procedures, became an area where art counted most. The question was delightfully debated: was a man entitled to use his wit to perfect nature, or did he, by interfering in natural processes ("The Mower against Gardens"), degrade and adulterate natural patterns and products?

For agriculturalists as well as for poets speaking metaphorically, this is at once an aesthetic and a moral problem—involving, among other things, the right of the arts (all the arts, not just poetry, certainly not just pastoral poetry) to do what art does: that is, to "improve" the nature it imitates. In the simplified and rigid scheme of styles and topics inherited by Renaissance theorists ("systematized" is surely the better word), shepherds are honest people, as George Herbert put it: they speak in a simple, or low, style befitting the life they lead and the landscape in which they dwell. Should, then, kings and princesses masquerading as shepherds and shepherdesses undertake a simple style of life and of speech? What does such disguise do to a literary decorum based upon a hierarchy of values, which strict relations observed between social rank and level of style? Should those nobles who opt for the country learn, like Berowne, an uncourtly speech, doff, like Kent, the latinate orotundities of rank? Should they not, in short, suit their words to their new actions? Within the artifice of the pastoral frame, all this is made problematical, to be interestingly explored in many works. If, as countless Renaissance pastoralists demonstrate, the pastoral natural world is a complex imaginative artifice, why should not princes and princesses, with their sophisticated and finespun speech, be welcome in Arcadia, where their rhetorical finesse simply adds to the imaginative beauties in the pastoral ecology? And welcome they were—which meant that another mixture of decorums was made in this already most mixed of modes.

Such *genera mixta* bring their own contradictions. For instance, in this literary ethos so deceptively simple, the best of everything is selected: the best of genres, the best of styles, the best of solutions to human problems. No wonder then, when we seem to lose a major figure in Tasso's *Aminta* by suicide, we yet recover that figure alive by love's magic power and the accident of a convenient bush: Aminta is too valuable to be spared, and the landscape's marvels are sufficient to save even the most despairing shepherd. Art rescues men from the trials of their lives, and the pastoral makes no bones about it. No wonder, then, that as Guarini laboriously insisted against his fierce opponents and as Fletcher so gracefully observed, comedy and tragedy came so easily to dwell together in the nurturing environment of literary pastoral. Fletcher's comment on his own *Faithful Shepherdess*, written after *As You Like It* and well after the major documents of the Guarini quarrel, states the plain case for the mixture of comic and tragic modes:

> A tragie-comedie is not so called in respect of mirth and killing, but in respect it wants deaths, which is inough to make it no tragedie, yet brings some neere it, which is inough to make it no comedie: which must be a representation of familier people with such kinde of trouble as no life be questiond, so that a God is as lawfull in this case as in a tragedie, and meane people as in a comedie.

Part of the reason for the tragicomic mix, then, is in the nature of the action; another reason lies in the mixture of ranks involved in most pastoral romances and plays, where disguise of great ones is a principal plot-device.

With these literary or generic and social mixes, comes also moral mixture, a mixture of ways of life set in actual or implied contradistinction or even contradiction. Looking back to Theocritus, we can see that some cultural distinction underlies the agonistic presentation of pastoral eclogues, in the competitions between singers judged for their skill in singing—or, to say it another way, between singers judged for their success in defending their particular variant upon the pastoral life. Neatherd, goatherd, shepherd challenged one another, to be challenged in turn by fishermen and mowers, sometimes even by huntsmen—and, given such a thoroughly country mixture, why not by a courtier as well, especially a courtier disguised as a countryman? Of course, by the time we arrive at this particular elaboration of pastoral agon, a radical discharge of original pastoral democracy has been effected: when court invades country, rank, however understressed, intrudes upon such egalitarian commutuality as countrymen enjoy, alters the condition in which, as the Golden Age myth had it, social class was irrelevant. Once the mixture of class is accepted in the pastoral system, then alienation may become a conscious topic, too: perhaps this is Vergil's point in the First Eclogue. So the melancholy Jaques may not be all that out of place in the Forest of Arden, even though he is "Monsieur Traveler" and, it would seem, at the very least a university wit. He has, presumably, become disgusted and worn out by the conflicting sophistications he has seen and is, at least, true to the Arden be criticizes, when alone of the cast he declines to return to court. Celia's choice of pseudonym, Aliena, honors the reason for her voluntary exile and is one token of her courtier-status within the forest. The pastoral world is not for the disappointed and victimized alone, to relearn their integrity; it exists also for those more seriously estranged from society, as the early reference in As You Like It to Robin Hood suggests.

II

As You Like It miraculously collects the major themes of the pastoral, manipulating and juxtaposing them so as to bring that rich mix under critical scrutiny. Not only is the classic pastoral dramatic pattern its basic fiction—exile from court; country restoration; triumphant return to court—but so also are the themes of nature and nurture, of art and nature, of art and artifice, of court and country debated in eclogue-like exchanges uttered by representatives of pastoral and non-pastoral (sometimes even anti-pastoral) positions. The "parallel and parody" of the play, so well analyzed by Jay Halio and others, works beautifully to undermine doctrinaire attitudes, social, moral, or literary. The play's perspectivism is sufficient exposure of the implications of the *vie sentimentale* for which pastoral had come so masterfully to stand.

Even satire and folly, embodied in Jaques and Touchstone, in turn set into agon, come to challenge and to reinforce the values of this pastoral. The love at the center of the play is not a particularly pastoral love, save in that the playwright works toward eliminating the artificial and nonnatural aspects and elements of love; but the pastoral tradition, with its exquisite concentrations upon the emotional nuances and values of love, offered a superb literary opportunity for examining the love-subject.

Nor is love the only topic so scrutinized: Corin speaks of his content in the life he leads, in open contrast to Touchstone's obvious dependency upon his ladies, yet we know from his own mouth that Corin is shepherd to another man and not, in Fletcher's sense, one of the true literary shepherds who are "owners of flockes and not hyerlings." Corin qualifies his own position: so does Touchstone who, praising the court above the shepherd's life, by his witty choplogic lays open the shabbiness of the court's customs. Shepherd and jester are brothers, after all, under the skin: Touchstone, remembering Jane Smile, recalls that early love in the generic language of the peasant Corin. The "country copulatives" comment on each other, and on the courtiers: Orlando, courtly mock-shepherd genuinely disinherited, dotes on Rosalind; Silvius, a real shepherd who has learned his love-role as thoroughly as Orlando has his, dotes upon Phebe; Phebe, a real shepherdess struck by the *coup de foudre* prescribed by Marlowe (to whom they refer as "the dead shepherd," in pure literary idiom), dotes upon Ganymede; and Ganymede dotes, as he insists, upon no woman.

All of them, even the trim Ganymede, smugly apart from their encirclement, show some aspects of pastoral loving; all of them, in turn, have been called (like all fools) into a circle. Ganymede assumes with his disguise (Shakespeare's one-upmanship is manifest in this boy-actor-disguised-as-a-girl-disguised-as-a-boy-acting-the-part-of-a-girl) one proper pastoral love-attitude, that conventionally assigned the shepherdess, of coolness to the lover. Orlando may not have been given a gentleman's education by his hard-hearted brother, but he knows all the same that proper pastoral lovers hang poems on trees. Silvius loves his lady totally, as if she were perfectly beautiful, in spite of Rosalind's rebuke to Phebe; and Phebe illustrates, before our very eyes how totally love can wipe out all other considerations, particularly those of common sense.

Yet all shall be changed: though in the beginning each loves the wrong person, we see Phebe settle for Silvius; we see Touchstone,

clad in his courtly aura as well as in motley, win the goatgirl Audrey
from the well-to-do rural William—win her, then, by his courtly
"rank." We see Aliena paired with the repentant Oliver, both of
them struck as finally as Phebe by Marlovian love at first sight. And
we see, by a magic attributable to her forest-character, Ganymede-
Rosalind claim her lover Orlando. Only Silvius and Phebe, of the
whole crowd, are what they seem and no more: the others, one way
or another, have been disguised from others and from themselves.
And all of them, save Silvius and Phebe, must cope with the undis-
guising: Audrey must be either taken to the court by her fool or
brutally abandoned: Aliena-become-Celia at once threatens her
lover's recent vow of shepherdhood, that sign of his reconciliation
with kind nature; Orlando must learn what his beloved is to inherit.

Desengaño[1] does not rob the pastoral of its sweetness in *As You
Like It*. These considerations do not intrude upon the play itself, in
which, however much pastoral love is mocked, its sweet fidelities are
rewarded, too. By making fun of Orlando's language, Rosalind jokes
him into ever-increasing avowals of his love for her. She may seem
to mock all lovers, but at the news of Orlando's hurt by the lion faints
like a green girl. Touchstone does not want to be in Arden and contrasts Corin's life unfavorably with what he had known at the court,
but he makes the best of his forest opportunities, and his logic actually recoils on him, to endorse the simplicities Corin embodies. The
melancholy-satiric Jaques comes to scoff at pastoral sentimentalism,
but he is scoffed at in his turn—and for pastoral sentimentalism at
that. The data of various literary modes are mocked and yet, through
all the mockery, reaffirmed: questioned, teased, tested, found
wanting—and found valuable in spite of manifest weaknesses.

In this way, perspectivism is built into the play; it is the play's
method, but it relies on traditional implications within the mode,
by developing an inherent dialectical tendency in pastoral eclogues
to an astonishing degree. Many contests question the traditions
which ultimately they endorse: the lovers' fourfold catch suggests
the merry-go-round illusion of the experience of loving; Corin and
Silvius speak not just about love, but about the kinds of love appropriate to the different ages of man, and Jaques deals with love as
developmental folly in his far more total indictment of man's ages
and the illusions of each age. Touchstone and Corin debate the life
of court and country to demonstrate the limitations of both. Jaques
marches through the play, in his melancholy isolation a challenge
to everyone's social assumptions and conclusions: like Philisides,
Sidney's name for his symbolic self in the *Arcadia*, Jaques has
retired to the forest in disappointment with the world's offerings.

---

1. Disillusionment (Spanish) [*Editor*].

Though established in Arden, Jaques is characterized as a traveler, a continentalized Englishman who (as the character-books assure us) can never find aught at home good again. He is also—a bit unexpectedly—the superpastoralist of the play, speaking out for the pathetic identification of creatural suffering with human unhappiness. He it is who criticizes the Robin Hood band of gentlemen around Duke Senior for their unbrotherly attacks upon the deer-commonwealth, whose "fat burghers" are slaughtered for men's whims and pleasure; but all this while he is also unpastorally melancholy, unpastorally antisocial. As we look at him more narrowly, of course, we see the social role his melancholy fulfills, and how consistently Jaques acts the part of the Duke's men expect of him. It is he who recognizes a freedom even greater than that of the forest in his cry, "Motley's the only wear!" He knows how to call all fools into a circle; he, in short, reminds us by most unpastoral means that Arden is a pleasaunce, that for all its rough weather, the forest is also Cockayne, where all is upside down to be set aright. He knows what his fellow-fool recognizes at sight: "Ay, now I am in Arden; the more fool I; when I was at home I was in a better place; but travellers must be content." And yet Arden is his home, as he chooses to remain in the forest now solitary enough for his nature.

What the forest is, is never made entirely clear, although it *is* obvious that, even with the season's difference, the forest is a better place than the usurper's court. In the forest there is no need for "new news o' the new court"; fashionable gossip is irrelevant to the fundamental constants of courtesy, civility, and humanity. And yet, for all the talk of the golden world, Arden is never "really" that—Corin's master was of churlish disposition and inhospitable, ready to sell his sheepfarm for gold. Unprofessional cleric that he is, Sir Oliver Martext is nonetheless at home in Arden; Duke Senior's fellow exiles do not hesitate to comment on the bitter wind, painful to them if less "unkind" than man's ingratitude. The moral arrangements of the golden world are, come wind come weather, scrupulously observed, together with the pastoral delusions. The melancholy Jaques is courteously received, his idiosyncrasies are respected, enjoyed, and even admired; when Orlando, assuming the role of salvage man, bursts in upon the *fête champêtre*, he is welcomed, not repulsed, in spite of his words and his sword; the country lovers ultimately accept each other with grace. The Duke lives, "the Robin Hood of England" to whom young gentlemen flock "every day, and fleet the time carelessly," so that such rank as he has is, like Robin Hood's, only first among equals. To the forest come Rosalind and Celia, Touchstone faithfully in attendance; to the forest comes Jaques; to the forest comes the outlawed Orlando, with old Adam on his back. In the forest Oliver de Boys and Duke Frederick make their moral recoveries and find their various rewards. In the forest, the fairy-tale world rules: a serpent and a lion, hitherto inconceivable, threaten the only newcomer distinguished for his savagery: in token of his recognition of the beast within, Oliver had become a hairy man. In Arden, an untaught innocent younger-brother-hero can save that newcomer from these creatures by the "kindness" of his "nature," which marks him as trueborn in spite of his deprivation of nurture. In the forest, whatever nature's natural drawbacks, nature makes written calendars irrelevant: there are no clocks in the forest, and there is time enough for everyone's inner and social needs: the forest, as C. L. Barber reassuringly claims, induces and confirms holiday humor.

Time does not pass, theoretically at least, in the golden world—but this rule does not hold for our play, where we are endlessly made aware, both in earnest and in jest, of the passage of time: in the confrontation of generations (Silvius and Corin, dukes and daughters, Sir Rowland's sons and his aged servant Adam); Orlando comes late to his appointments with Ganymede, who rates him for that—because she is a younger girl in love, as she tells us in her psychological typology of time, time trots hard with her. A living emblem of the last age of man, the nearly dying Adam is brought in to emphasize Jaques's classic oration. In other words, this forest is at once ideal and real; the inhabitants of Arden insist that their life is unvaried, as in the Golden Age; but the play works in the rhythms of experience's human actuality. On one side, Arden *is* holiday, and thus timeless; it offers a chance for recovery and redemption, a parodic, exalted imitation of the real world, now corrected and purged. In Arden, fools are visibly in circles, men feast graciously on venison and wine—but time passes as they do so, as we are continually reminded, and men ripen and rot in spite of the lack of clocks.

What the forest offers is its liberties: love finds what it seeks; Jaques is allowed to criticize as he likes; Touchstone may mock, Corin may be threatened with impoverishment. But nothing untoward happens; the forest offers restitution to the dispossessed as well as the far more important imaginative freedom in which the natural spirits of men and women may expand. Duke Senior, Rosalind, and Orlando know that this forest is their goal; there they find a world where even real brothers can be brothers. For with the psychological flowering favored in Arden, we are reminded that all life is not so free: Cain and Abel patterns recur in the play, in each generation. Even in *that* pattern, indeed, one can find a pastoral analogue: the pastoral Abel is the contemplative man, Cain the cultivator, the active man, the man of violence prepared to defend the value of his way of life and its produce. In his underpopulated world, Cain felt he had to savage his brother, as Duke Frederick and Oliver seek to savage their brothers. When these romance-brothers enter the forest, however, reformation strikes at once; the virtuous maintain and corroborate their gentility and their gentleness, and the evil recover or discover the gentleness in themselves they had denied. Orlando's lapse into savagery, so clearly motivated by his concern for old Adam, is immediately reversed by the gentleness with which his threat of violence is received. As is usual in these discussions of pastoral nature, we find throughout the play the terms which form its structure: nature, natural, kind, kindness, civil, civility, gentle, and gentleness. For nature is kind, and kindness: a recognition of one's kind, a response designed to protect and to strengthen whatever is mutually human.

Against this background, Orlando's complaint against his unnatural nurture makes fell sense. His brother owed him, as kin, to raise him as the gentleman he is, but chose instead to rob him of his rights and to cast him, if he could, as a type of Prodigal Son. Finally, Oliver even tried to kill the boy, in an unmotivated gesture of the supreme unkindness. Oliver is presented, as Iago was to be, as simply evil—"simply" evil. The question of nature and nurture running through so much of the play is nowhere debated outright, but from the start the debaters are given real parts in the play. In contrast to his brother, Orlando is, as his behavior consistently confirms, preternaturally "gentle," even though he is also preternaturally strong. Actually, as he and we come to recognize, he has no need of that mysterious education he laments, and grows into a symbolic portion far grander than his inheritance would have been. Orlando assumes responsibility for Adam, grown old in his father's service, to the extent that he violates his own nature by attempting to steal for his sake. He cannot pass by on the other side and let the lion attack his sleeping brother, for all that his brother has done against him. His natural qualities caused him to fall in love with Rosalind, and her to fall in love with him. He speaks of his own gentility ("Yet am I inland bred") and recognizes the same "inland" quality in Ganymede's speech, anomalously cultured for the child of the forest he claims to be. Folk hero that he is, Orlando, the youngest of three sons, is eminently suited to take his place at the head of his family and to marry the Duke's daughter at the end of the play, to return with daughter and Duke to the court, confident of exhibiting the courtliness he has always naturally displayed.

The debate between nature and nurture overlaps the problem of nature and art: nurture is education, altering, improving, grafting, conventionally taken as "good." In Orlando's case, it turns out that the art of which he laments the lack is in fact superfluous. He is what he is "by nature"—and when he assumes various stylized, courtly poses, such as in his role of pastoral lover, Rosalind makes fun of his efforts. As often happens in Shakespeare's versions of pastoral, the nature-nurture debate is skewed and ultimately denied, as received dialectical opposites are shown to be fused in the person (Orlando, Perdita, Arviragus, Guiderius) whose gentle birth marches with his courteous nature. Nurture is not necessary for such as these: all the education in the world had failed to improve Oliver, until he experienced his brother's miraculous assertion of kindness. In Jaques, we see that education has even weakened his feelings for his kind. Rosalind is not the nutbrown boy she pretends she is; her cultivated ancestry of magicians is a fiction to account for the cultivation of her nature and her breeding. In her case, indeed, the disguise which makes it possible for her to take her place in Arden is a fiction in itself. Though she is spokeswoman for what is natural, real, and psychologically sincere, and persuades Orlando to natural and unstylized love, she is of course always neither simple nor boy.

The forest, then, shelters a countersociety, idyllic and playful, offering a model of possibility to the real world, a countersociety made up on the one hand by the fictions of a literary convention and on the other by the types of that convention, determined to express the goodness of their natures. The pastoral second chance offered by the Forest of Arden is not just a second chance for the people in the play; it is equally a second chance for the larger society of which the *dramatis personae* are representatives. As the procession troops courtward, men with antlers on their heads, girls dressed as country brother and sister, nutbrown from sun or dye, dukes and reconciled brothers, we believe in the escapade and in their unlikely return, believe in their capacity to maintain reform, because of the upright good sense they have demonstrated or learned in the forest, because of their natural courtesy, kindness, and radiant moral strength. But we believe in them also because the pastoral refuge has acknowledged the flawed realities of the working day world; the holiday has recognized real experience. Touchstone is not the only character on whom the truth of experience can be proved: all of them try, assay, essay the pastoral myth, each from his own perspective, and all of them find at its heart the recreative values of nature, kind, and kindness promised by the tradition. The play's perspectivism insists also upon the convergence of all views at its central and controlling point, the symbolic, simple truth of this most artificial of literary constructs.

LINDA WOODBRIDGE

Country Matters: *As You Like It* and the Pastoral-Bashing Impulse[†]

Audiences delight in *As You Like It*, but critics often get twitchy about it, which seems odd. The play after all features cross-dressing, the biggest female speaking role in all of Shakespeare, an intriguingly intimate friendship between two women, an exploited agricultural laborer, and a set speech on animal rights—one would think that this comedy offered satisfactions for gender theorists, feminists, queer theorists, Marxists, and ecocritics alike. What's not to like in *As You Like It*?

The answer, I think, is fairly straightforward: what's not to like is the pastoralism. For a couple of centuries now but especially in recent decades, a wide spectrum of critics has heaped scorn upon the bucolic realm of pastoral, and Shakespeare's most pastoral play has come in for its share of scorn. Shakespeare being who he is, critics are seldom as hard on him as on other writers of pastoral, and some exonerate him entirely by recasting *As You Like It* as itself a sneer at pastoral: Shakespeare is not himself conventional, but uses conventions playfully, self-consciously, mockingly. He writes not pastoral but antipastoral. This move in itself, of course, drives another nail into pastoral's coffin. Excavating the cultural meanings of the critical vendetta against pastoral, and exploring how it plays out in *As You Like It*, may give us not only a fresh perspective on the play, but a route into the enigma of pastoral bashing and what it says about our culture.

Critics often complain of a lack of action in *As You Like It*, beginning in act 2. It's not so much that they get bored when the wrestling match is over as that they feel uneasy being invited to share in a pastoral life that seems, well, lazy. In this relaxed world, exiled lords entertain each other with songs or gaze thoughtfully into brooks, lovers pin poetry to trees, and Jaques and Celia go off to take naps—troubling evidence of a lack of purposeful action in Arden. Peter Lindenbaum excoriates pastoral in general for its "life of leisure and freedom from the cares and responsibilities of the normal world," sternly averring that responsible Renaissance writers recognized that "in this world of ours man simply has no time for relaxation or even momentary escape from the pressing activity of day-to-day living";

[†] Linda Woodbridge, "Country Matters: *As You Like It* and the Pastoral-Bashing Impulse," in Evelyn Gajowski, ed., *Re-Visions of Shakespeare: Essays in Honor of Robert Ornstein* (Newark: University of Delaware Press, 2004), pp. 189–214. Reprinted by permission.

Sidney in *Arcadia* and Shakespeare in *As You Like It* "lodge an objection to the whole prospect of life in a pastoral setting, to a cast of mind that either seeks an easy, carefree existence anywhere in our present world or indulges overmuch in dreams of better times and better places, thereby avoiding full concentration upon the facts of man's present existence."[1] The shepherd's reprehensible life of ease has offended so many critics that A. Stuart Daley feels he must explain the habits of sheep to excuse all the slacking that goes on in an early Arden afternoon: "At midday, after a long morning of nibbling on the herbage, the animals needed complete rest, and lay down to ruminate. At noon, a shepherd such as those in *As You Like It* could expect two or three hours of comparative freedom. Indeed all English workers had the right to a midday rest, according to a statute of 1563."[2] The play's adjournment from the court into a rural world of ease is often belittled as an escapist fantasy. To avoid being charged with advocating escapism, a responsible author must "insist upon the need to leave Arcadia," Lindenbaum dictates;[3] Richard Helgerson insists, "the pastoral world is meant to be left behind."[4] Critics assume that characters in Arden scramble to get back to the court: Daley writes, "With the zeal of a reformed sinner, Celia's fiancé resolves to 'live and die a shepherd'; but his aristocratic calling obviously forbids the abandonment of his lands and great allies to the detriment of the commonweal."[5] Critics seem untroubled that *As You Like It* nowhere articulates this ideal of public service, or that the play not only leaves open the question of whether Oliver and Celia will stay in the country, but insists that Duke Frederick and Jaques opt to stay in Arden—Jaques's decision to stay is given an emphatic position at the very end of the play. Ignoring all this and focusing on characters who do leave the pastoral world, Lindenbaum, who is pretty hard on Duke Senior for using banishment as an excuse for lolling around in the woods, readmits him to favor when he makes the crucial decision "to leave Arcadia":

> His pastoral dream proves by the end to have been that of a basically good man on vacation. His essential moral health is affirmed at the play's end by his unhesitating willingness to return to court and take up responsible active life in the political world again. This final act reflects the whole play's anti-pastoral

---

1. Peter Lindenbaum, *Changing Landscapes: Anti-Pastoral Sentiment in the English Renaissance* (Athens: University of Georgia Press, 1986), 1, 3, 17.
2. A. Stuart Daley, "Where Are the Woods in *As You Like It?*" *Shakespeare Quarterly* 34 (1983): 176–77.
3. Lindenbaum, *Changing Landscapes*, 96.
4. Richard Helgerson, "The New Poet Presents Himself: Spenser and the Idea of a Literary Career," *PMLA* 93 (1978): 906.
5. A. Stuart Daley, "The Dispraise of the Country In *As You Like It*," *Shakespeare Quarterly* 36 (1985): 307.

argument. The forest is initially a place of ease, idleness, and escape from normal cares and responsibilities, but that view provides the stimulus for Shakespeare's eventual insistence upon a more active stance.[6]

Albert Cirillo expresses approval that once characters have straightened out their lives, "they can return to the court"; far from pastoral's challenging court values, he sees it the other way around: "the Forest needs the contrast with the court and worldly values to clarify the consciousness of the audience as to the essential illusory quality of the pastoral world."[7]

Renato Poggioli's belief that "the psychological root of the pastoral is a double longing after innocence and happiness, to be recovered not through conversion or regeneration, but merely through a retreat" rings false in *As You Like It*, where Frederick is converted, Oliver regenerated.[8] You'd think the discomfort of Arden, with its wintry wind, would obviate charges of escapism, but critics instead read this as Shakespearean contempt for pastoral. Daley notes that "characters who express an opinion about the Forest of Arden utter mostly dispraise"; taking at face value Touchstone's gripes and Rosalind's "saucy lackey" impertinences, he pronounces "the local women . . . vain and foul and the backwoods dialect lacking in grace and beauty"; the "consistent dispraise of the country" shows that Shakespeare did not intend "a traditional contrast between court and country."[9] But *did* such dispraise indicate that Shakespeare disdained the country? Traditionally, pastoral figures gain moral authority through asceticism; in pastoral, country harshness obviates charges of hedonism that would undermine pastoral's ability to critique the corruptions of a world of power. Lindenbaum reads dispraise of the country as unhappiness with pastoral, born of frustrated golden-world expectations, of finding country life "no different from life at court or in the city."[1] Svetlana Makurenkova generalizes about Shakespeare's career, "one may trace throughout the corpus of Shakespeare's work a certain dethroning of idyllic pastoral imagery."[2]

Taking the play's realism for antipastoralism, critics create a no-win situation. Pastorals *do* speak of rural harshness—Meliboeus's dispossession from his farm in Virgil's first eclogue or, in *As You Like*

6. Lindenbaum, *Changing Landscapes*, 110.
7. Albert Cirillo, "*As You Like It*: Pastoralism Gone Awry," *ELH* 38 (1971): 24.
8. Renato Poggioli, *The Oaten Flute: Essays on Pastoral Poetry and the Pastoral Ideal* (Cambridge: Harvard University Press, 1975), 1.
9. Daley, "Dispraise," 306–7, 311–12.
1. Lindenbaum, *Changing Landscapes*, 1.
2. Svetlana Makurenkova, "Intertextual Correspondences: The Pastoral in Marlowe, Raleigh, Shakespeare, and Donne," in *Russian Essays on Shakespeare and His Contemporaries*, ed. Alexandr Parfenov and Joseph G. Price (Newark: University of Delaware Press, 1998), 194.

It, Corin's low wages from a churlish absentee master (2.4.75–8) and description of shepherds' hands as greasy, work-hardened, and "tarr'd over with the surgery of our sheep" (3.2.50–51, 59–60).[3] But such details don't make critics revise their belief that pastoral ignores "real difficulties and hardships" and shuns "realistic description of the actual conditions of country life"; instead, critics consider such realism as "anti-pastoral sentiment" attributable to frustration at the genre's artificiality and escapism. Cirillo says "every force which would lead to the acceptance of life in Arden as a perfect world is negated by the intrusion of a harsher reality";[4] but the idea of Arden as a perfect world comes only from Cirillo's stereotype that pastorals deal in escapist golden worlds. For such critics, when a pastoral doesn't fit the stereotype, it doesn't negate stereotype but becomes evidence of the author's unhappiness with pastoral. This resembles the way that the Renaissance decried as unnatural women who didn't fit its stereotypes, thus preserving the stereotypes intact.

Touchstone finds shepherding "a very vile life" (3.2.16) and many think that his name, implying a test of genuineness, declares him the play's voice of truth. Yet his plans to wriggle out of his marriage discredit him; and anyway, a clown's-eye view of the action is never the whole story in Shakespeare. Against Touchstone's view we have Corin's sensible cultural relativism: "Those that are good manners at the court are as ridiculous in the country as the behavior of the country is most mockable at the court" (3.2.43–46). Touchstone's witty equivocation on "manners" shows how anti-rural prejudice works: "If thou never wast at court, thou never saw'st good manners; if thou never saw'st good manners; then thy manners must be wicked; and wickedness is sin, and sin is damnation. Thou art in a parlous state, shepherd" (3.2.38–42). The pun has lost its force, since "manners" now means only "etiquette"; in Shakespeare's day it also meant "morals." Considering country etiquette uncouth, courtiers assume that country morals are loose too. Touchstone discovers this untrue of country wench Audrey, who declares (to his disappointment) "I am not a slut" (3.3.35). Orlando too mistakes country manners, expecting violent inhospitality: "I thought that all things had been savage here" (2.7.71). Orlando, says Rawdon Wilson, "fails to understand the nature of Arden"; exiled courtiers need "a period of adjustment to Arden"[5]—a time to revise prejudices about country life?

---

3. William Shakespeare, *Complete Works*, ed. David Bevington, 4th ed. (Glenview, Ill.: Scott, Foresman, 1992), 292–325. All references to Shakespeare plays are to this edition.
4. Cirillo, "*As You Like it*," 27.
5. Rawdon Wilson, "The Way to Arden: Attitudes Toward Time in *As You Like It*," *Shakespeare Quarterly* 26 (1975): 22, 18.

The play has sometimes been attacked on aesthetic grounds, with complaints that the satiric and the bucolic are awkwardly joined and tonally disjunctive, especially in the person of Jaques, whom critics virulently attack, often on the assumption that a satiric voice doesn't belong in a choir making mellow pastoral music. But satiric voices have always spoken in Arcadia—satire is one thing pastoral is all about. Unwillingness to stomach Jaques echoes criticism of Spenser and Milton for letting sharp attacks on abuses intrude into a pastoral setting. Shakespeare is not alone in being scorned for writing pastoral or praised for allegedly resisting pastoral: the whole pastoral mode has been inimical to our general cultural climate for a good many years now.

It's hard to think of another genre that has been described so patronizingly, attacked so virulently, dismissed so contemptuously over many years. Samuel Johnson called *Lycidas* "a pastoral, easy, vulgar, and therefore disgusting." [6]

* * *

Sermons in Stones and Good in Every Thing

Pastoral's challenge—sometimes overt, sometimes implicit in its withdrawal from the frantic world—is to the assumption that power, public life, hard work, and success are everything. *As You Like It* represents the world of power in Frederick's court as literally repulsive: having banished Duke Senior and his followers, Frederick now banishes Rosalind and sends away Oliver. Through that great tool of patriarchy, male competitive sport, the Duke enacts a public semiotics of power in a scenario of invader-repulsion: the populace is invited to combat Charles the wrestler. The Duke's tyranny betrays paranoia: he banishes Rosalind because her "silence and her patience / Speak to the people, and they pity her," seemingly fearful that "the people" might rise up on behalf of Rosalind and her father (1.3.79–81). Do those who come to wrestle Charles represent for the Duke the challenge he fears? Does he invite it precisely to demonstrate that he can defeat such challenges? Frederick and Le Beau call Orlando "the challenger," though when asked "have you challenged Charles the wrestler?" Orlando answers "No, he is the general challenger" (1.2.169–78). That the court issues a challenge and then feels *it* is being challenged betrays a paranoid insecurity that it tries to assuage by violence.

A pivot between the court and Oliver's household, Charles the wrestler flags the sibling competition that is festering in each place.

6. Samuel Johnson, "Milton," in *Lives of the English Poets*, ed. Arthur Waugh (Oxford: Oxford University Press, 1906), 1:116.

Both paranoid tyrants, Duke Frederick and Oliver, project onto powerless siblings their own murderous impulses. Both keep the brother/competitor at bay by rustication—pushing him into a countryside that prejudice has encoded loathsome. Duke Frederick has pushed his brother Duke Senior into forest banishment, and Oliver has pushed his brother Orlando into a neglected life in a country home. Our initial view of the country is resentful: in the play's opening speech Orlando complains, "my brother keeps me rustically at home, or stays me here at home unkept; for call you that keeping for a gentleman of my birth, that differs not from the stalling of an ox? His horses are bred better. He lets me feed with his hinds" (1.1.3–18). A hind was a farm hand; it is appropriate that the word later occurs in its other meaning, "deer," for this passage superimposes peasant life on animal life. The servant Adam is pushed into the animal kingdom, called "old dog" (1.1.86). Frederick too has pushed his brother/competitor into the countryside, where he sleeps outside like an animal. Challengers must not rise; they are pushed out into the country, down among animals. The despised realm is that of peasants and animals, the world of shepherds: pastoral.

Rustication was a Tudor political punishment: noblemen fallen from grace often retreated to a country estate, remaining there under house arrest, an echo of the way pastoral poets were pushed out of the upper canon's polite society into a rustic underworld, for challenging the world of power. But Duke Senior's first speech defends country living and attacks the court, with its artificiality, danger, and competitiveness: "Hath not old custom made this life more sweet / Than that of *painted pomp*? Are not these woods / More free from *peril* than the *envious* court?" (2.1.2–4; emphasis mine). Any fear that his forest society might merely reproduce structures of authority, dominance, and competition of Frederick's court are immediately allayed by Duke Senior's style, a striking departure from Frederick's. By the time we meet Duke Senior in act 2, we are accustomed to Frederick's mode of communication, which like the speech of the early King Lear is performative, his speeches curt and peppered with commands: "Bear him away" (1.2.211); "Dispatch you with your safest haste / And get you from our court" (1.3.39–40); "Open not thy lips" (1.3.80); "You, niece, provide yourself" (1.3.85); "Push him out of doors" (3.1.15). In act 1, the average length of Frederick's speeches is less than three lines, mainly short sentences of staccato monosyllables. His longest flight, a twelve-line speech in act 3, is clogged with curt imperatives: "*Look* to it: / *Find* out thy brother. / *Seek* him with candle; *bring* him dead or living / or *turn* thou no more / To seek a living in our territory" (3.1.4–8). Frederick's curt, choppy, commanding language recreates the haste and arbitrariness of his acts—banishing Rosalind, turning Orlando out of favor, dispatching Oliver and seizing his lands. In contrast, Duke Senior's first words are egalitarian: "Now, my co-mates and brothers in exile" (2.1.1). Where Frederick's typical utterances are commands, Duke Senior's are questions: "Hath not old custom made this life more sweet? . . . Are not these woods / More free from peril?" (2.1.2–4); "Shall we go and kill us venison?" (2.1.21); "What said Jaques? / Did he not moralize this spectacle?" (2.1.43–44); "Did you leave him in this contemplation?" (2.1.64); "What would you have?" (2.7.101). Further, Duke Senior listens to the answers. Inquiring rather than commanding, he listens attentively to people, replacing Frederick's banishments and repulsions with hospitable welcomes: "Sit down and feed, and welcome to our table" (2.7.104). Speeches are longer than at court: Duke Senior's first is seventeen lines long, and his courteous questions elicit two unhurried nineteen-line answers. The verse grows relaxed and flowing, its complex sentences and run-on lines a relief after Frederick's tense verbal jabbings. The anthropomorphosed deer, prominent in this first forest scene, is an important reversal: in act 1 humans were pushed down into the animal kingdom, but in Arden, animals rise to the human level.

The exiles, suffering "the icy fang / of the winter's wind" (2.1.6–7), are not luxuriating in sloth; but their life is wholesomely easeful. It is simply not the case that the court is presented as the brisk, responsible world of action, the country as an irresponsible life of ease: the court is paranoid, twitchy, a world of hasty political decisions, its frenetic pace neurotic, born of the knowledge that its power is illegitimate. Its pace is so brisk as to abrogate both justice and courtesy. The relaxed movement, language, and song in the play's pastoral world have the rhythm of a livable environment.

Pastoral, always the wealth-eschewing genre, was well placed to be oppositional to the new capitalism; in the early scenes, set in "a commercial world of exchange and transaction," even good characters speak its language: "Orlando's initial lines (1.1.1–27) are strewn with references to types of change and exchange; and some of the same terminology is repeated in Celia's protestation of love to Rosalind . . . (1.2.17–25). Such words as 'bequeathed,' 'will,' 'profit,' 'hired,' and 'gain' are particularly suggestive."[7] In Arden, such language ebbs.

One of Arden's lessons is how little the world of power matters once it is out of sight. A bracing effect of the time-honored human strategy of running away from trouble—escapism—is that nobody in the new land has *heard* of our local tyrant, which shows the

---

7. Wilson, "The Way to Arden," 20.

world of power striving in a whole new light. Our exiles have arrived where nobody has heard of Duke Frederick's power grab. Corin never speaks of Frederick's usurpation, and the fact that Duke Senior, presumably his former ruler, is living in exile in the immediate neighborhood is something Corin never mentions. Before his exile, was Duke Senior too a tense, paranoid, competitive ruler? Was it rustication that taught him patience, courtesy, humaneness, relaxation—a conversion as stunning as Frederick's later conversion? We can't know—the play doesn't say what he was like before. If the Duke hasn't changed, if he was always a good, humane man, it might make us uneasy about the vulnerability of patient, courteous, humane, relaxed rulers—but the play doesn't invite us to worry about this, as *The Tempest* does. It doesn't matter what kind of ruler Duke Senior was and will be: the play loses interest in that, and directs our attention elsewhere.

The segregation of *As You Like It*'s twelve pastureland scenes from its four forest scenes makes it possible to drop Duke Senior after act 2—he reappears only in the last scene. The play moves from the real court to the forest court, to a pastureland with no court. As the play progresses, politics, which comes on strong at first, is entirely replaced by love. Interest is deflected from public to private. Was Shakespeare's pretended interest in the lesser spheres of politics, power, and authority all along a sublimation of his real interest, love and women? To paraphrase Montrose, political motives here displace or subsume forms of desire, frustration, and resentment other than the merely political.

Strongly approving Rosalind's and Orlando's return to court, Lindenbaum declares, "the pastoral sojourn was not strictly necessary; the love of Rosalind and Orlando was well under way even at the troubled court,"[8] but their return to court isn't strictly necessary either. Theirs is a world-peopling comedic destiny; one can procreate anywhere. The move from court to country prefigures the shift in the play's center of gravity from politics to love. The exclusionary circle tyranny drew around itself when Frederick forbade Rosalind to come nearer than twenty miles (1.3.41–43) yields to an inclusive circle: Rosalind reigns in "the circle of this forest" (5.4.34). Though many will return to the court, the play doesn't stage the return but ends with *everyone* in Arden, Duke Frederick and all; the court as the play ends is entirely empty. The ending dwells not on resumption of power or return to responsible public service but on living happily ever after in a world of love. Country matters.

As Edward Said's Orientalist is outside the Orient, so most pastoral writers have been outside the country, assuming, like Orien-

---

8. Lindenbaum, *Changing Landscapes*, 127.

talists, that city writers must represent the country, since it cannot represent itself.[9] But where Orientalism projects onto the Orient the West's disowned qualities, creating a worse self against which the West defines itself, pastoral does the opposite. Its rustic is an antienemy, an antiscapegoat: one on whom to project not one's most loathed but one's best qualities, or desired qualities. Like Browning's Setebos, a city writer created in country folk "things worthier than himself," made them "what himself would fain, in a manner, be." Pastoral writers created a standard against which to measure the value of contemporary striving. The potent pastoral dream recurred amid the Industrial Revolution, where it helped spawn Romanticism, and amid the malaise of the industrialized, urban twentieth century—there was a good deal of pastoralism in 1960s counterculture. However we mock and condemn it, pastoralism will likely keep reemerging, disquietingly indicting the way we live by holding out an ideal more attractive than the world we have created.

* * *

CLARA CLAIBORNE PARK

As We Like It: How a Girl Can Be Smart and Still Popular[†]

* * *

As classics go, Shakespeare isn't bad reading for a girl. The conventions of tragedy and romance offer horizons considerably wider than those available in Fanny Burney and Jane Austen; the courts of Europe and the seacoasts of Bohemia provide backgrounds in which a girl can imagine herself doing far more interesting things than she could at home. It is true that, unlike those paradoxical dramatists of male-chauvinist Athens, Shakespeare never allows a woman a play of her own. He provides neither *Antigones* nor *Medeas*; no feminine name appears in his titles except as the second member of a male-female pair. Yet a girl can read Shakespeare without calling upon the defenses necessary for Milton or Hemingway, or Lawrence or Mailer—writers she must read calloused for survival, a black in Mr. Charlie's land. Shakespeare liked women

9. Edward Said, *Orientalism* (New York: Pantheon, 1978), 8.
† From Clara Claiborne Park, "As We Like It: How a Girl Can Be Smart and Still Popular," 1973; rpt. in Carolyn Ruth Swift Lenz, Gayle Greene, and Carol Thomas Neely, eds., *The Woman's Part: Feminist Criticism of Shakespeare* (Urbana: University of Illinois Press, 1983), pp. 100–109. Reprinted by permission.

and respected them; not everybody does. We do not find him, like Milton, luxuriating in the amoebic submissiveness of an Eve in Paradise, and we can surmise that he would have found little interest in the dim Marias and complaisant Catherines whom Hemingway found nonthreatening. He is not afraid of the kind of assertiveness and insistence on her own judgment that Eve displays when she gets busy bringing death into the world and all our woe; the evidence of the plays is that he positively enjoyed it.

From Mrs. Jameson on, critics, male and female, have praised Shakespeare's women. "The dignity of Portia, the energy of Beatrice, the radiant high spirits of Rosalind, the sweetness of Viola"[1]— William Allan Neilson's encomia can stand for thousands of others. Juliet, Cordelia, Rosalind, Beatrice; Cleopatra, Hermione, Emilia, Paulina—Shakespeare's girls and mature women are individualized, realized, fully enjoyed as human beings. His respect for women is evident in all the plays, but it is in the middle comedies that the most dazzling image recurs. It is an image significant for what it can tell us about the extent—and the limits—of acceptable feminine activity in the Shakespearean world, a world which in this as in other things remains, over time and change, disconcertingly like our own.

Limits? What limits? It would seem that no girl need feel herself diminished when she reads *As You Like It, The Merchant of Venice* or *Much Ado.* Rather, she is given a glittering sense of possibility. Who would not, if she could, be beautiful, energetic, active, verbally brilliant and still sought after by desirable men, like these Shakespearean heroines? Hebraic and Pauline tradition might subordinate the female; secular codes might make her, like Juliet and Portia, her father's to dispose of as he wished, to a man who, once her husband, could exercise over her the same absolute dominion. Yet Juliet and Portia, like Rosalind and the ladies of *Love's Labour's Lost,* clearly think of themselves as autonomous people. Submissive mildness is not lacking in Shakespare; Bianca and Hero and Mariana would content a Milton and reassure even a Mailer. But such characters are never central to the action—logically enough, because they do not act. Apparent exceptions are seen to prove the rule: beneath Cordelia's gentleness is a strain of iron stubbornness that Milton would probably have welcomed much as Lear did.

Bianca and her like do not interest Shakespeare. When he does bring this kind of woman to full individuality it is, significantly enough, not to present her as an effective human being but to offer her to our sympathies, as he does with Desdemona and Ophelia, as

---

1. William Allan Neilson and Charles Jarvis Hill, eds., *The Complete Plays and Poems of William Shakespeare* (Boston: Houghton Mifflin, 1942), p. 457. All subsequent Shakespeare citations are to this edition.

a helpless victim. What catches his imagination in *As You Like It*, *The Merchant of Venice*, and *Much Ado* is a young woman of an entirely different kind: one who, by her energy, wit, and combativeness, successfully demonstrates her ability to control events in the world around her, not excluding the world of men. Perhaps we should not be surprised that the greatest Elizabethan was attracted by the qualities of his sovereign, who told her lords that "though I be a woman, I have as good a courage answerable to my place as ever my father had. . . . I thank God I am endued with such qualities that were I turned out of the realm in my petticoat, I were able to live in any place in christendom."[2] But perhaps we should be surprised; there are no such women in Marlowe or Jonson or the other dramatists who could have been expected to remember the qualities of the Virgin Queen. In drama as elsewhere, men find such women hard to handle, and often hard to take. Shakespeare knew how to manage them—at least on stage. That he could create women who were spunky enough to be fun to be with, and still find ways to mediate their assertiveness so as to render them as nonthreatening as their softer sisters, is one of the secrets of his perennial appeal. His is one of the surer methods of keeping a love story from liquefying prematurely, durable enough to remain serviceable to Yale professors who write best-sellers.[3]

※　※　※

If Beatrice is delightful, Rosalind is even better. Neilson (who, as president of Smith College, occupied a privileged position for girl-watching) describes her as having "the wit of Portia and Beatrice softened by the gentleness of Viola"[4]—exactly as we like it. In *As You Like It*, however, Shakespeare does not hesitate to tip the equal balance that affords the fun of *Much Ado* in favor of the lady; in wit and energy, Rosalind has no male rival. Insofar as any other character is able to match her repartee, it is Celia, who although she is usually remembered as the gentle foil, the "other kind" of girl, turns out to have a surprising number of the snappy lines. Orlando, however, is merely a nice young man.

Rosalind, however, is more than witty. *As You Like It* is her play. This is, of course, unusual in Shakespeare. Heroes act, but heroines commonly do not, which is why, unlike Antigone and Lysistrata, none of them gets a Shakespearean title to herself. Neither does Rosalind—although Thomas Lodge had accorded her one—but

2. Quoted in G. M. Trevelyan, *History of England* (New York: Longmans, Green, 1926), p. 327.
3. Reference is to Erich Segal's novel *Love Story* (1970), very popular at the time [*Editor*].
4. Neilson and Hill, *Complete Plays*, p. 212.

nevertheless it is she who moves the play. She is energetic, effective, successful. She has the courage to accept exile; she decides to assume male dress, and, playing brother, she guides her friend to the Forest of Arden. The late comedies no longer present these forceful young women, and the faithful Imogen of *Cymbeline* retroactively exposes the extent of Rosalind's autonomy. It is not Imogen but her husband's servant who originates the idea of male disguise; the necessity for her journey originates not in her own position but in her relation to her husband, and as soon as she lacks a man to guide her, she gets lost. Her complaint at this point measures her distance from Rosalind: "I see a man's life is a tedious one" (III.vi.1). (Her previous remark to Cloten also bears thinking about: "You put me to forget a lady's manners / By being so verbal"—II.iii.110–11.) Through Imogen we can appreciate the unique position of Rosalind in her play. Rosalind's decisions control the progress of *As You Like It*, and it is by her agency that the four couples assemble in the concluding nuptial dance which, as in *The Boke of the Governor*, "betokeneth concord" and embodies for the audience the harmony restored that is the essence of Shakespearean comedy.

Yet Shakespeare arranges for her to do all this without making the ladies censorious or the gentlemen nervous. He has various methods of rendering her wit painless and her initiatives acceptable. The most obvious way is to confine them to love matters, a proper feminine sphere. Rosalind is a political exile, but she shows no disposition to meddle in politics; it is not through her agency that her father is restored to his rightful place. Her wit is not, like Portia's, exercised in the service of sensible men engaged in the serious business of the world, nor are her jokes made at their expense. Her satire is, in fact, narrowly directed at two classes of beings—sighing lovers, and women. In the course of the fun she works her way through most of the accusations already traditional in a large antifeminist literature (inconstancy, contrariness, jealousy, unfaithfulness, etc.)[5] to the point where Celia tells her, "We must have your doublet and hose pluck'd over your head, and show the world what the bird hath done to her own nest" (IV.i.206–8). Add that we know all along that she herself is the butt of her own jokes, being herself both lovesick and female, and it would be a fragile Benedick indeed who could feel himself stabbed by her poniard.

The most useful dramatic device for mediating the initiatives of the female, however, is the male disguise. Male garments immensely broaden the sphere in which female energy can manifest itself.

---

5. The survey of this tradition is one of the most valuable contributions of Professor Betty Bandel's dissertation, *Shakespeare's Treatment of the Social Position of Women* (Ann Arbor: University Dissertation Microfilms, 1975), Set No. 2793, pp. 174–97.

Dressed as a man, a nubile woman can go places and do things she couldn't do otherwise, thus getting the play out of the court and the closet and into interesting places like forests or Welsh mountains. Once Rosalind is disguised as a man, she can be as saucy and self-assertive as she likes. (We can observe a similar change come over sweet Viola of *Twelfth Night* as soon as she begins to play the clever page.) The characters, male and female, will accept her behavior because it does not offend their sense of propriety; the audience, male and female, because they know she's playing a role. With male dress we feel secure. In its absence, feminine assertiveness is viewed with hostility, as with Kate the Shrew, or at best, as with Beatrice, as less than totally positive. Male dress transforms what otherwise could be experienced as aggression into simple high spirits.

The temporary nature of the male disguise is of course essential, since the very nature of Shakespearean comedy is to affirm that disruption is temporary, that what has turned topsy-turvy will be restored. It is evident that Rosalind has enjoyed the flexibility and freedom that come with the assumption of the masculine role, but it is also evident that she will gladly and voluntarily relinquish it. "Down on your knees," she tells the proud shepherdess who scorns her faithful swain, "And thank heaven, fasting, for a good man's love" (III.v.57–58). Rosalind, clearly, is thankful for Orlando's, and although she is twice the person he is, we are willing to believe that they live happily ever after, since that's obviously what she wants.

* * *

LOUIS ADRIAN MONTROSE

"The Place of a Brother" in *As You Like It*†

I

As You Like It creates and resolves conflict by mixing what the characters call Fortune and Nature—the circumstances in which they find themselves, as opposed to the resources of playfulness and boldness, moral virtue and witty deception, with which they master adversity and fulfill their desires.

The romantic action is centered on the meeting, courtship, and successful pairing of Rosalind and Orlando. This action is complicated, as Leo Salingar reminds us, by "a cardinal social

---

† Louis Adrian Montrose, "'The Place of Brother' in *As You Like It*: Social Process and Comic Form," *Shakespeare Quarterly* 32.1 (1981): 28–54. © 1981 Folger Shakespeare Library. Reprinted with permission of The Johns Hopkins University Press.

assumption . . . (which would have been obvious to . . . Shakespeare's first audiences)—that Rosalind is a princess, while Orlando is no more than a gentleman. But for the misfortune of her father's exile, they might not have met in sympathy as at first; but for the second misfortune of her own exile, as well as his, they could not have met in apparent equality in the Forest.[1] The personal situations of Rosalind and Orlando affect, and are affected by, their relationship to each other. Rosalind's union with Orlando entails the weakening of her ties to her natural father and to a cousin who has been closer to her than a sister; Orlando's union with Rosalind entails the strengthening of his ties to his elder brother and to a lord who becomes his patron. Orlando's atonements with other men—a natural brother, a social father—precede his atonement with Rosalind. They confirm that the disadvantaged young country gentleman is worthy of the princess, by "nature" and by "fortune." The atonement of earthly things celebrated in Hymen's wedding song incorporates man and woman within a process that reunites man with man. This process is my subject.

As the play begins, Orlando and Adam are discussing the terms of a paternal will; the first scene quickly explodes into fraternal resentment and envy, hatred and violence. By the end of the second scene, the impoverished youngest son of Sir Rowland de Boys finds himself victimized by "a tyrant Duke" and "a tyrant brother" (I. iii.278).[2] The compact early scenes expose hostilities on the manor and in the court that threaten to destroy both the family and the state. Although modern productions have shown that these scenes can be powerful and effective in the theatre, modern criticism has repeatedly downplayed their seriousness and significance. They are often treated merely as Shakespeare's mechanism for propelling his characters—and us—into the forest as quickly and efficiently as possible. Thus Harold Jenkins, in his influential essay on the play, writes of "the inconsequential nature of the action" and of "Shakespeare's haste to get ahead"; for him, the plot's interest consists in Shakespeare's ability to get "most of it over in the first act."[3] If we *reverse* Jenkins' perspective, we will do justice to Shakespeare's

1. Leo Salingar, *Shakespeare and the Traditions of Comedy* (Cambridge: Cambridge Univ. Press, 1974), pp. 297–98. On the *topos*, see John Shaw, "Fortune and Nature in *As You Like It*," *Shakespeare Quarterly*, 6 (1955), 45–50; *A New Varioum Edition of Shakespeare: "As You Like It*," ed. Richard Knowles, with Evelyn Joseph Mattern (New York: MLA, 1977), pp. 533–37.
2. *As You Like It* is quoted from the new Arden edition, ed. Agnes Latham (London: Methuen, 1975); all other plays are quoted from *The Riverside Shakespeare*, gen. ed. G. Blakemore Evans (Boston: Houghton Mifflin, 1974).
3. Harold Jenkins, "*As You like It*," *Shakespeare Survey*, 8 (1955), 40–51; quotation from p. 41. There is an exception to this predominant view in Thomas McFarland, *Shakespeare's Pastoral Comedy* (Chapel Hill: Univ. of North Carolina Press, 1972), pp. 98–103.

dramaturgy and make better sense of the play. What happens to Orlando at home is not Shakespeare's contrivance to get him into the forest; what happens to Orlando in the forest is Shakespeare's contrivance to remedy what has happened to him at home. The form of *As You Like It* becomes comic in the process of resolving the conflicts that are generated within it; events unfold and relationships are transformed in accordance with a precise comic teleology.

II

Jaques sententiously observes that the world is a stage; the men and women, merely players; and one man's time, a sequence of acts in which he plays many parts. Shakespeare's plays reveal many traces of the older drama's intimate connection to the annual agrarian and ecclesiastical cycles. But more pervasive than these are the connections between Shakespearean comic and tragic forms and the human life cycle—the sequence of acts performed in several ages by Jaques' social player. Action in Shakespearean drama usually originates in combinations of a few basic kinds of human conflict: conflict among members of different families, generations, sexes, and social classes. Shakespeare tends to focus dramatic action precisely *between* the social "acts," between the sequential "ages," in the fictional lives of his characters. Many of the plays turn upon points of transition in the life cycle—birth, puberty, marriage, death—where discontinuities arise and where adjustments are necessary to basic interrelationships in the family and in society. Such dramatic actions are analogous to rites of passage. Transition rites symbolically impose markers upon the life cycle and safely conduct people from one stage of life to the next; they give a social shape, order, and sanction to personal existence.[4]

In *As You Like It*, the initial conflict arises from the circumstances of inheritance by primogeniture. The differential relationship between the first born and his younger brothers is profoundly augmented at their father's death: the eldest son assumes a paternal relationship to his siblings; and the potential for sibling conflict increases when the relationship between brother and brother becomes identified with the relationship between father and son.

---

4. The paradigm for transition rites—the triadic movement from separation through marginality to reincorporation—was formulated in Arnold Van Gennep's classic, *The Rites of Passage* (1909), trans. M. B. Vizedom and G. L. Caffee (Chicago: Univ. of Chicago Press, 1960). Among more recent discussions, see *Essays on the Ritual of Social Relations*, ed. Max Gluckman (Manchester: Manchester Univ. Press, 1962); Victor Turner, *Dramas, Fields, and Metaphors* (Ithaca: Cornell Univ. Press, 1974); and Edmund Leach, *Culture and Communication* (Cambridge: Cambridge Univ. Press, 1976). For further discussion of analogies to transition rites in Shakespearean drama and Elizabethan theatre, see Louis Adrian Montrose, "The Purpose of Playing: Reflections on a Shakespearean Anthropology," *Helios*, NS, 7 (Winter 1980), 51–74.

The transition of the father from life to death both fosters and obstructs the transition of his sons from childhood to manhood. In *As You Like It*, the process of comedy accomplishes successful passages between ages in the life cycle and ranks in the social hierarchy. By the end of the play, Orlando has been brought from an impoverished and powerless adolescence to the threshold of manhood and marriage, wealth and title.

A social anthropologist defines inheritance practices as "the way by which property is transmitted between the living and the dead, and especially between generations."

> Inheritance is not only the means by which the reproduction of the social system is carried out . . . it is also the way in which interpersonal relationships are structured. . . .
>
> The linking of patterns of inheritance with patterns of domestic organization is a matter not simply of numbers and formations but of attitudes and emotions. The manner of splitting property is a manner of splitting people; it creates (or in some cases reflects) a particular constellation of ties and cleavages between husband and wife, parents and children, sibling and sibling, as well as between wider kin.[5]

As Goody himself concedes, the politics of the family are most powerfully anatomized, not by historians or social scientists, but by playwrights. Parents and children in Shakespeare's plays are recurrently giving or withholding, receiving or returning, property and love. Material and spiritual motives, self-interest and self-sacrifice, are inextricably intertwined in Shakespearean drama as in life.

Lear's tragedy, for example, begins in his division of his kingdom among his daughters and their husbands. He makes a bequest of his property to his heirs before his death, so "that future strife / May be prevented now" (I.i.44–45). Gloucester's tragedy begins in the act of adultery that begets an "unpossessing bastard" (II.i.67). Edmund rails against "the plague of custom . . . the curiosity of nations" (I.ii.3–4); he sees himself as victimized by rules of legitimacy and primogeniture. *As You Like It* begins with Orlando remembering the poor bequest from a dead father and the unnaturalness of an elder brother; he is victimized by what he bitterly refers to as "the courtesy of nations" (I.i.45–46). Rosalind dejectedly remembers "a banished father" (I.ii.4) and the consequent loss of her own preeminent social place. Celia responds to her cousin with naive girlhood loyalty: "You know my father hath no child but I, nor none is like to have; and truly when he dies, thou shalt be his heir; for

---

5. Jack Goody, "Introduction," in *Family and Inheritance: Rural Society in Western Europe, 1200–1800,* ed. Jack Goody, Joan Thirsk, and E. P. Thompson (Cambridge: Cambridge Univ. Press, 1976), pp. 1, 3.

what he hath taken away from thy father perforce, I will render thee again in affection" (I.ii.14–19). The comic action of *As You Like It* works to atone elder and younger brothers, father and child, man and woman, lord and subject, master and servant. Within his play, Rosalind's magician-uncle recreates situations that are recurrent sources of ambiguity, anxiety, and conflict in the society of his audience; he explores and exacerbates them, and he resolves them by brilliant acts of theatrical prestidigitation.

The tense situation which begins *As You Like It* was a familiar and controversial fact of Elizabethan social life. Lawrence Stone emphasizes that "the prime factor affecting all families which owned property was . . . primogeniture"; that "the principle and practice of primogeniture . . . went far to determine the behaviour and character of both parents and children, and to govern the relationship between siblings."[6] In the sixteenth and seventeenth centuries, primogeniture was more widely and rigorously practiced in England—by the gentry and lesser landowners, as well as by the aristocracy—than anywhere else in Europe. The consequent hardships, frequent abuses, and inherent inequities of primogeniture generated a "literature of protest by and for younger sons" that has been characterized as "plentiful," "vehement" in tone, and "unanimous" in its sympathies.[7]

Jaques was not the only satirist to "rail against all the first-born of Egypt" (II.v.57–58). John Earle included the character of a "younger Brother" in his *Micro-Cosmographie* (1628):

> His father ha's done with him, as *Pharaoh* to the children of Israel, that would have them make brick, and give them no straw, so he taskes him to bee a Gentleman, and leaves him nothing to maintaine it. The pride of his house has undone him, which the elder Knighthood must sustaine, and his beggery that Knighthood. His birth and bringing up will not suffer him to descend to the meanes to get wealth: but hee stands at the mercy of the world, and which is worse of his brother. He is something better then the Servingmen; yet they more saucy with him, then hee bold with the master, who beholds him with a countenance of sterne awe, and checks him oftner then his Liveries. . . . Nature hath furnisht him with a little more wit upon compassion; for it is like to be his best revenew. . . . Hee

6. Lawrence Stone, *The Family, Sex and Marriage in England 1500–1800* (New York: Harper & Row, 1977), pp. 87–88.
7. Joan Thirsk, "Younger Sons in the Seventeenth Century," *History* (London), 54 (1969), 358–77; quotation from p. 359. Thirsk cites *As You Like It*, I.i, as part of that literature.

is commonly discontented, and desperate, and the forme of his exclamation is, that Churle my brother.[8]

As a class, the gentry experienced a relative rise in wealth and status during this period. But the rise was achieved by inheriting eldest sons at the expense of their younger brothers. As Earle and other contemporaries clearly recognized, the gentry's drive to aggrandize and perpetuate their estates led them to a ruthless application of primogeniture; this left them without the means adequately to provide for their other offspring. The psychological and socio-economic consequences of primogeniture for younger sons (and for daughters) seem to have been considerable: downward social mobility and relative impoverishment, inability to marry or late marriage, and fewer children.

In 1600, about the time *As You Like It* was first performed, Thomas Wilson wrote a valuable analysis of England's social structure. His description of gentlemen reveals a very personal involvement:

> Those which wee call Esquires are gentlemen whose ancestors are or have bin Knights, or else they are the heyres and eldest of their houses and of some competent quantity of revenue fitt to be called to office and authority in their Country. . . . These are the elder brothers.
>
> I cannot speak of the number of yonger brothers, albeit I be one of the number myselfe, but for their estate there is no man hath better cause to knowe it, nor less cause to praise it; their state is of all stations for gentlemen most miserable. . . . [A father] may demise as much as he thinkes good to his younger children, but such a fever hectick hath custome brought in and inured amongst fathers, and such fond desire they have to leave a great shewe of the stock of their house, though the branches be withered, that they will not doe it, but my elder brother forsooth must be my master. He must have all, and all the rest that which the catt left on the malt heape, perhaps some smale annuytye during his life or what please our elder brother's worship to bestowe upon us if wee please him.[9]

The foregoing texts characterize quite precisely the situation of Orlando and his relationship to Oliver at the beginning of *As You Like It*. They suggest that Shakespeare's audience may have responded with some intensity to Orlando's indictment of "the courtesy of nations."

---

8. Ed. Edward Arber (1869; rpt., New York: AMS Press, 1966), pp. 29–30. I have modernized obsolete typographical conventions in quotations from this and other Renaissance texts.
9. Thomas Wilson, *The State of England Anno Dom. 1600*, ed. F. J. Fisher, Camden Miscellany, 16 (London: Camden Society, 1936), pp. 1–43; quotation from pp. 23–24.

In his constitutional treatise, *De Republica Anglorum* (written ca. 1562; printed 1583), Sir Thomas Smith observes that "whosoever studies the laws of the realm, who studies at the universities, who professes liberal sciences and to be short, who can live idly and without manual labour, and will bear the port, charge and countenance of a gentleman . . . shall be taken for a gentleman."[1] The expected social fate of a gentleborn Elizabethan younger son was to lose the ease founded upon landed wealth that was the very hallmark of gentility. Joan Thirsk suggests that, although there were places to be had for those who were industrious and determined to make the best of their misfortune,

> the habit of working for a living was not ingrained in younger sons of this class, and no amount of argument could convince them of the justice of treating them so differently from their elder brothers. The contrast was too sharp between the life of an elder son, whose fortune was made for him by his father, and who had nothing to do but maintain, and perhaps augment it, and that of the younger sons who faced a life of hard and continuous effort, starting almost from nothing. Many persistently refused to accept their lot, and hung around at home, idle, bored, and increasingly resentful.[2]

At the beginning of *As You Like It*, Orlando accuses Oliver of enforcing his idleness and denying him the means to preserve the gentility which is his birthright: "My brother Jaques he keeps at school, and report speaks goldenly of his profit; for my part, he keeps me rustically at home, or, to speak more properly, stays me here at home unkept; for call you that keeping for a gentleman of my birth, that differs not from the stalling of an ox? . . . [He] mines my gentility with my education" (I.i.5–10, 20–21). Orlando is "not taught to make anything" (1.30); and his natural virtue is marred "with idleness" (ll. 33–34). When Adam urges him to leave the family estate, Orlando imagines his only prospects to be beggary and highway robbery (II.iii.29–34). He finally agrees to go off with Adam, spending the old laborer's "youthful wages" in order to gain "some settled low content" (II.iii.67–68).

Shakespeare's opening strategy is to plunge his characters and his audience into the controversy about a structural principle of Elizabethan personal, family, and social life. He is not merely using something topical to get his comedy off to a lively start: the expression and resolution of sibling conflict and its social implications are integral to the play's form and function. The process of comedy

---

1. Rpt. in *Social Change and Revolution in England 1540–1640*, ed. Lawrence Stone (New York: Barnes & Noble, 1965), p. 120.
2. Thirsk, "Younger Sons," p. 368.

works against the seemingly inevitable prospect of social degradation suggested at the play's beginning, and against its literary idealization in conventions of humble pastoral retirement. In the course
of *As You Like It*, Orlando's gentility is preserved and his material
well-being is enhanced. Shakespeare uses the machinery of pastoral romance to remedy the lack of fit between deserving and having,
between Nature and Fortune. Without actually violating the primary
Elizabethan social frontier separating the gentle from the base, the
play achieves an illusion of social leveling and of unions across class
boundaries. Thus, people of every rank in Shakespeare's socially
heterogeneous audience might construe the action as they liked it.

Primogeniture is rarely mentioned in modern commentaries on
As You Like It, despite its obvious prominence in the text and in the
action.[3] Shakespeare's treatment of primogeniture may very well
have been a vital—perhaps even the dominant—source of engagement for many in his Elizabethan audience. The public theatre
brought together people from all the status and occupational groups
to be found in Shakespeare's London (except, of course, for the
poorest laborers and the indigent). Alfred Harbage points out that
the two groups "mentioned again and again in contemporary allusions to the theatres" are "the students of the Inns of Court and the
apprentices of London."[4] In addition to these youthful groups, significant numbers of soldiers, professionals, merchants, shopkeepers,
artisans, and household servants were also regular playgoers. The
careers most available to the younger sons of gentlemen were in
the professions—most notably the law, but also medicine and
teaching—as well as in trade, the army, and the church.[5] Thus,
Shakespeare's audience must have included a high proportion of
gentleborn younger sons—adults, as well as the youths who were
students and apprentices. Among these gentleborn younger sons,
and among the baseborn youths who were themselves socially subordinate apprentices and servants, it is likely that Orlando's desperate situation was the focus of personal projections and a catalyst of
powerful feelings. "During the sixteenth century," Thirsk concludes, "to describe anyone as '*a younger son*' was a short-hand way
of summing up a host of grievances. . . . *Younger son* meant an
angry young man, bearing more than his share of injustice and
resentment, deprived of means by his father and elder brother,
often hanging around his elder brother's house as a servant, com-

3. An exception is John W. Draper, "Orlando, the Younger Brother," *Philological Quarterly*, 13 (1934), 72–77.
4. See Alfred Harbage, *Shakespeare's Audience* (New York: Columbia Univ. Press, 1941),
pp. 53–91; quotation from p. 80.
5. See Thirsk, "Younger Sons," pp. 363, 366–68.

pletely dependent on his grace and favour.[6] Youths, younger sons, and all Elizabethan playgoers who felt that Fortune's benefits had been "mightily misplaced" (II.i.33–34) could identify with Shakespeare's Orlando.

III

It is precisely in the details of inheritance that Shakespeare makes one of the most significant departures from his source. Sir John of Bordeaux is on his deathbed at the beginning of Lodge's *Rosalynde*; he divides his land and chattels among his three sons:

> Unto thee *Saladyne* the eldest, and therefore the chiefest piller of my house, wherein should be ingraven as well the excellence of thy fathers qualities, as the essentiall forme of his proportion, to thee I give foureteene ploughlands, with all my Mannor houses and richest plate. Next unto *Fernadyne* I bequeath twelve ploughlands. But unto *Rosader* the youngest I give my Horse, my Armour and my Launce, with sixteene ploughlands: for if inward thoughts be discovered by outward shadowes, *Rosader* will exceed you all in bountie and honour.[7]

The partible inheritance devised by Lodge's Sir John was an idiosyncratic variation on practices widespread in Elizabethan society among those outside the gentry.[8] Saladyne, the eldest born, inherits his father's authority. Rosader receives more land and love—he is his father's joy, although his last and least. Saladyne, who becomes Rosader's guardian, is deeply resentful and decides not to honor their father's will: "What man thy Father is dead, and hee can neither helpe thy fortunes, nor measure thy actions: therefore, burie his words with his carkasse, and bee wise for thy selfe" (p. 391).

Lodge's text, like Thomas Wilson's, reminds us that primogeniture was not a binding law but rather a flexible social custom in which the propertied sought to perpetuate themselves by preserving their estates intact through successive generations. Shakespeare

---

6. Thirsk, "Younger Sons," p. 360.
7. *New Variorum* ed. of *AYL*, p. 382; future page references will be to this text of *Rosalynde*, which follows the First Quarto (1590). On the relationship of *AYL* to *Rosalynde*, see *Narrative and Dramatic Sources of Shakespeare*, ed. Geoffrey Bullough (London: Routledge & Kegan Paul, 1958), II. 143–57; Marco Mincoff, "What Shakespeare Did to *Rosalynde*," *Shakespeare Jahrbuch*, 96 (1960), 78–89; *New Variorum* ed. of *As You Like It*, pp. 475–83.
8. See Joan Thirsk, "The European Debate on Customs of Inheritance, 1500–1700," in *Family and Inheritance*, pp. 177–91: "The inheritance customs of classes below the gentry did not give rise to controversy: practices were as varied as the circumstances of families. Primogeniture in the original sense of advancing the eldest son, but nevertheless providing for the others, was common, perhaps the commonest custom among yeoman and below, but it did not exercise a tyranny. Among the nobility primogeniture was most common. . . . In general it did not cause excessive hardship to younger sons because the nobility had the means to provide adequately for all" (p. 186).

alters the terms of the paternal will in Lodge's story so as to alienate
Orlando from the status of a landed gentleman. The effect is to inten-
sify the differences between the eldest son and his siblings, and to
identify the sibling conflict with the major division in the Elizabethan social fabric: that between the landed and the unlanded, the
gentle and the base. (Within half a century after Shakespeare wrote
As You Like It, radical pamphleteers were using "elder brother" and
"younger brother" as synonyms for the propertied, enfranchised
social classes and the unpropertied, unenfranchised social classes.)
Primogeniture complicates not only sibling and socio-economic
relationships but also relationships between generations: between a
father and the eldest son impatient for his inheritance; between a
father and the younger sons resentful against the "fever hectic" that
custom has inured among fathers.

Shakespeare's plays are thickly populated by subjects, sons, and
younger brothers who are ambivalently bound to their lords, genitors, and elder siblings—and by young women moving ambivalently
between the lordships of father and husband. If this dramatic proliferation of patriarchs suggests that Shakespeare had a neurotic
obsession, then it was one with a social context. To see father-figures
everywhere in Shakespeare's plays is not a psychoanalytic anach-
ronism, for Shakespeare's own contemporaries seem to have seen
father-figures everywhere. The period from the mid-sixteenth to the
mid-seventeenth century in England has been characterized by
Lawrence Stone as "the patriarchal stage in the evolution of the
nuclear family."[9] Writing of the early seventeenth-century family
as "a political symbol and a social institution," Gordon J. Schochet
documents that

> virtually all social relationships—not merely those between
> fathers and children and magistrates and subjects—were
> regarded as patriarchal or familial in essence. The family was
> looked upon as the basis of the entire social order. . . .
>
> So long as a person occupied an inferior status within a
> household—as a child, servant, apprentice, or even as a wife—
> and was subordinated to the head, his social identity was alto-
> gether vicarious. . . .

9. Stone, *Family, Sex and Marriage*, p. 218. *Contra* Stone, there is evidence to suggest that
the nuclear family was in fact the pervasive and traditional pattern in English society
outside the aristocracy; that the English family at this period was profoundly patriarchal remains, however, undisputed. The assumptions and conclusions of Stone's massive study have not found complete acceptance among his colleagues. See the
important review essays on Stone's book by Christopher Hill, in *The Economic History
Review*, 2nd. Ser., 31 (1978), 450–63; by Alan Macfarlane, in *History and Theory*, 18
(1979), 103–26; and by Richard T. Vann, in *The Journal of Family History*, 4 (1979),
308–14.

Before a man achieved social status—if he ever did—he would have spent a great many years in various positions of patriarchal subordination.[1]

This social context shaped Shakespeare's preoccupation with fathers; and it gave him the scope within which to reshape it into drama, satisfying his own needs and those of his paying audience. His plays explore the difficulty or impossibility of establishing or authenticating a self in a rigorously hierarchical and patriarchal society, a society in which full social identity tends to be limited to propertied adult males who are the heads of households.

Shakespeare's Sir Rowland de Boys is dead before the play begins. But the father endures in the power exerted by his memory and his will upon the men in the play—his sons, Adam, the dukes—and upon their attitudes toward each other. The play's very first words insinuate that Orlando's filial feeling is ambivalent "As I remember, Adam, it was upon this fashion bequeathed me by will but poor a thousand crowns, and, as thou sayst, charged my brother on his blessing to breed me well; and there begins my sadness" (I.i.1–4). Orlando's diction is curiously indirect; he conspicuously avoids naming his father. Absent from Shakespeare's play is any expression of the special, compensatory paternal affection shown to Lodge's Rosader. There is an implied resentment against an unnamed father, who has left his son a paltry inheritance and committed him to an indefinite and socially degrading dependence upon his own brother. Ironically, Orlando's first explicit acknowledgment of his filial bond is in a declaration of personal *independence*, a repudiation of his bondage to his eldest brother: "The spirit of my father, which I think is within me, begins to mutiny against this servitude" (I.i.21–23). Orlando's assertions of filial piety are actually self-assertions, directed against his father's eldest son. As Sir Rowland's inheritor, Oliver perpetuates Orlando's subordination within the patriarchal order; he usurps Orlando's selfhood.

In a private family and household, the eldest son succeeds the father as patriarch. In a royal or aristocratic family, the eldest son also succeeds to the father's title and political authority. Thus, when he has been crowned as King Henry V, Hal tells his uneasy siblings, "I'll be your father and your brother too. / Let me but bear your love, I'll bear your cares" (*2 Henry IV*, V.ii.57–58). Like Henry, Oliver is simultaneously a father and a brother to his own natural sibling; he is at once Orlando's master and his peer. Primogeniture conflates the generations in the person of the elder brother and blocks the generational passage of the younger brother. What

1. *Patriarchalism in Political Thought* (New York: Basic Books. 1975), pp. 65–66.

might be described dispassionately as a contradiction in social categories is incarnated in the play, as in English social life, in family conflicts and identity crises.[2]

Orlando gives bitter expression to his personal experience of this social contradiction: "The courtesy of nations allows you my better in that you are the firstborn, but that same tradition takes not away my blood, were there twenty brothers betwixt us. I have as much of my father in me as you, albeit I confess that your coming before me is nearer his reverence" (I.i.45–51). Here Orlando asserts that all brothers are equally their father's sons. Oliver might claim a special paternal relationship because he is the first born; but Orlando's own claim actually to incorporate their father renders insubstantial any argument based on age or birth order. Thus, Orlando can indict his brother and repudiate his authority: "You have trained me like a peasant, obscuring and hiding from me all gentlemanlike qualities. The spirit of my father grows strong in me, and I will no longer endure it" (I.i.68–71). Because the patriarchal family is the basic political unit of a patriarchal society, Orlando's protests suggest that primogeniture involves contradictions in the categories of social status as well as those of kinship. Orlando is subordinated to his sibling as a son to his father; and he is subordinated to a fellow gentleman as a peasant would be subordinated to his lord.

Orlando incorporates not only his father's likeness and name ("Rowland") but also his potent "spirit"—his personal genius, his manliness, and his moral virtue. To Adam, Orlando is "gentle, strong, and valiant" (II.iii.6). He is his father's gracious and virtuous reincarnation: "O you memory of old Sir Rowland!" (II.iii.3–4). Adam challenges the eldest son's legal claim to be his father's heir by asserting that Oliver is morally undeserving, that he is *spiritually* illegitimate:

> Your brother, no, no brother, yet the son—
> Yet not the son, I will not call him son—
> Of him I was about to call his father.
> (II.iii.19–21)

Orlando's claim to his spiritual inheritance leads immediately to physical coercion: Oliver calls him "boy" and strikes him. Orlando responds to this humiliating form of parental chastisement not with deference but with rebellion: he puts his hands to Oliver's

2. Orlando's predicament may be compared to Hamlet's: for each of these young Elizabethan heroes, the process of becoming himself involves a process of "remembering" the father for whom he is named. But the generational passage of each is blocked by a "usurper" of his spiritual inheritance, who mediates ambiguously between the father and the son: Oliver is a brother-father to Orlando; Claudius, himself the old King's younger brother, is an uncle-father to Hamlet.

throat. Orlando's assertion of a self which "remembers" their father is a threat to Oliver's patriarchal authority, a threat to his own social identity: "Begin you to grow upon me?" (I.i.85). The brothers' natural bond, in short, is contaminated by their ambiguous social relationship.

Because fraternity is confused with filiation—because the generations have, in effect, been collapsed together—the conflict of elder and younger brothers also projects an oedipal struggle between father and son. In the second scene, the private violence between the brothers is displaced into the public wrestling match. Oliver tells Charles, the Duke's wrestler, "I had as lief thou didst break [Orlando's] neck as his finger" (I.i.144–45). Sinewy Charles, the "general challenger" (I.ii.159), has already broken the bodies of "three proper young men" (l. 111) before Orlando comes in to try "the strength of [his] youth" (l. 161). In a sensational piece of stage business, Orlando and Charles enact a living emblem of the generational struggle. When Orlando throws Charles, youth is supplanting age, the son is supplanting the father. This contest is preceded by a remarkable exchange:

> CHA. Come, where is this young gallant that is so desirous to
> lie with his mother earth?
> ORL. Ready sir, but his will hath in it a more modest working.
>
> (I.ii.188–91)

Charles's challenge gives simultaneous expression to a filial threat of incest and a paternal threat of filicide. In this conspicuously motherless play, the social context of reciprocal father-son hostility is a male struggle for identify and power fought between elders and youths, first-born and younger brothers.[3]

Orlando's witty response to Charles suggests that he regards neither his fears nor his threats. Orlando's "will" is merely to come to man's estate and to preserve the status of a gentleman. At the beginning of *As You Like It*, then, Shakespeare sets himself the problem of resolving the consequences of a conflict between Orlando's powerful assertion of identity—his spiritual claim to be a true inheritor—and the social fact that he is a subordinated and disadvantaged younger son. In the forest, Oliver will be spiritually reborn

---

3. Thus, I am not suggesting that the text and action of *As You Like It* displace a core fantasy about mother-son incest. My perspective is socio-anthropological rather than psychoanalytic: allusions to incest amplify the confusion between older and younger generations, kin and non-kin; they exemplify the tension inherent in the power relations between male generations in a patriarchal society. Perhaps one reason for Shakespeare's fascination with kingship as a dramatic subject is that it provides a paradigm for patriarchy and succession. Prince Hal's destiny is to replace his father as King Henry; his father's death is the legal condition for the creation of his own identity. A major aspect of comic form in the *Henry IV* plays is Hal's process of projecting and mastering his patricidal impulse until he comes into his kingdom legitimately.

and confirmed in his original inheritance. Orlando will be socially reborn as heir apparent to the reinstated Duke. Orlando will regain a brother by "blood" and a father by "affinity."

IV

Orlando is not only a younger son but also a youth. And in its language, characterization, and plot, *As You Like It* emphasizes the significance of age categories. Most prominent, of course, is Jaques' disquisition on the seven ages of man. But the play's *dramatis personae* actually fall into the three functional age groups of Elizabethan society: youth, maturity, and old age. Orlando's youth is referred to by himself and by others some two dozen times in the first two scenes: he is young; a boy; a youth; the youngest son; a younger brother, a young fellow; a young gallant; a young man; a young gentleman. Social historians have discredited the notion that adolescence went unexperienced or unacknowledged in early modern England. Lawrence Stone, for example, emphasizes that in Shakespeare's time there was "a strong contemporary consciousness of adolescence (then called 'youth'), as a distinct stage of life between sexual maturity at about fifteen and marriage at about twenty-six."[4] Shakespeare's persistent epithets identify Orlando as a member of the group about which contemporary moralists and guardians of the social order were most obsessively concerned. The Statute of Artificers (1563) summarizes the official attitude: "Until a man grow unto the age of twenty-four years he . . . is wild, without judgment and not of sufficient experience to govern himself."[5] The youthful members of an Elizabethan household—children, servants, and apprentices— were all supposed to be kept under strict patriarchal control. Stone points out that "it was precisely because its junior members were under close supervision that the state had a very strong interest in encouraging and strengthening the household. . . . It helped to keep in check potentially the most unruly element in any society, the floating mass of young unmarried males."[6] Orlando is physically mature and powerful, but socially infantilized and weak.

That Shakespeare should focus so many of his plays on a sympathetic consideration of the problems of youth is not surprising when we consider that perhaps half the population was under twenty, and that the youthfulness of Shakespeare's society was reflected in the composition of his audience.[7] In his richly documented study, Keith Thomas demonstrates that

4. Stone, *Family, Sex and Marriage*, p. 108.
5. Quoted in Keith Thomas, "Age and Authority in Early Modern England," *Proceedings of the British Academy*, 62 (1976), 205–48; quotation from p. 217.
6. Stone, *Family. Sex and Marriage*, p. 27.
7. See Stone, *Family, Sex and Marriage*, p. 72; Thomas, "Age and Authority," p. 212; Harbage, *Shakespeare's Audience*, p. 79.

So far as the young were concerned, the sixteenth and seventeenth centuries are conspicuous for a sustained drive to subordinate persons in their teens and early twenties and to delay
their equal participation in the adult world. This drive is
reflected in the wider dissemination of apprenticeship; in the
involvement of many more children in formal education; and
in a variety of measures to prolong the period of legal and
social infancy.[8]

Elizabethan adolescence seems to have been characterized by a high
degree of geographical mobility: youths were sent off to school, to
search for work as living-in servants, or to be apprenticed in a
regional town or in London. Alan Macfarlane has suggested that, "at
the level of family life," this widespread and peculiarly English custom of farming out adolescent children was "a mechanism for separating the generations at a time when there might otherwise have
been considerable difficulty." "The changes in patterns of authority
as the children approached adulthood would . . . be diminished." He
speculates further that, at the collective level, "the whole process
was a form of age ritual, a way of demarcating off age-boundaries
by movement through space."[9]

The family was a source of social stability, but most families were
short-lived and unstable. Youth was geographically mobile, but
most youths were given no opportunity to enjoy their liberty. In
schools and in households, the masters of scholars, servants, and
apprentices were to be their surrogate fathers. Thomas stresses
that, "though many children left home early and child labour was
thought indispensable, there was total hostility to the early achievement of economic independence."[1] The material basis of that hostility was alarm about the increasing pressure of population on very
limited and unreliable resources. One of its most significant results
was delayed marriage: "Combined with strict prohibition on alternative forms of sexual activity, late marriage was the most obvious
way in which youth was prolonged. For marriage was the surest test
of adult status and on it hinged crucial differences in wages, dress,
and economic independence."[2] Most Elizabethan youths and maidens were in their mid or late twenties by the time they entered
Hymen's bands.[3] When Touchstone quips that "the forehead of a
married man [is] more honourable than the bare brow of a bachelor"

---

8. Thomas, "Age and Authority," p. 214.
9. Alan Macfarlane, *The Family Life of Ralph Josselin, A Seventeenth-Century Clergyman:
   An Essay in Historical Anthropology* (Cambridge: Cambridge Univ. Press, 1970),
   Appendix B: "Children and servants: the problem of adolescence," pp. 205, 210.
1. Thomas, "Age and Authority," p. 216.
2. Stone, *Family, Sex and Marriage*, p. 226.
3. See Peter Laslett, *The World We Have Lost*, 2nd ed. (New York: Charles Scribner's
   Sons, 1973), pp. 85–86; Stone, *Family, Sex and Marriage*, pp 46–54; Thomas, "Age and
   Authority," pp. 225–27.

(III.iii.53–55), he is giving a sarcastic twist to a fundamental mark of status. And when, late in his pseudo-mock-courtship of Ganymede, Orlando remarks ruefully that he "can live no longer by thinking" (V.ii.50), he is venting the constrained libido of Elizabethan youth. One of the critical facts about the Elizabethan life cycle—one not noted in Jaques' speech—was that a large and varied group of codes, customs, and institutions regulated "a separation between physiological puberty and social puberty."[4] "Youth," then, was the Elizabethan age category separating the end of childhood from the beginning of adulthood. It was a social threshold whose transitional nature was manifested in shifts of residence, activity, sexual feeling, and patriarchal authority.

The dialectic between Elizabethan dramatic form and social process is especially conspicuous in the triadic romance pattern of exile and return that underlies *As You Like It*. Here the characters' experience is a fictional analogue of both the theatrical and the social experiences of its audience. "The circle of this forest" (V.iv.34) is equivalent to Shakespeare's Wooden O. When they enter the special space-time of the theatre, the playgoers have voluntarily and temporarily withdrawn from "this working-day world" (I.iii.12) and put on "a holiday humour" (IV.i.65–66). When they have been wooed to an atonement by the comedy, the Epilogue conducts them back across the threshold between the world of the theatre and the theatre of the world. The dramatic form of the characters' experience corresponds, then, not only to the theatrical experience of the play's audience but also to the social process of youth in the world that playwright, players, and playgoers share. In a playworld of romance, Orlando and Rosalind experience separation from childhood, journeying, posing and disguising, altered and confused relationships to parental figures, sexual ambiguity, and tension. The fiction provides projections for the past or ongoing youthful experiences of most of the people in Shakespeare's Elizabethan audience. The forest sojourn conducts Orlando and Rosalind from an initial situation of oppression and frustration to the threshold of interdependent new identities. In one sense, then, the whole process of romantic pastoral comedy—the movement into and out of Arden— is what Macfarlane calls "a form of age ritual, a way of demarcating off age-boundaries by movement through space." The characters' fictive experience is congruent with the ambiguous and therefore dangerous period of the Elizabethan life cycle that is betwixt and between physical puberty and social puberty.

4. Thomas, "Age and Authority," p. 225.

V

Not only relationships between offspring and their genitors, or between youths and their elders, but any relationship between subordinate and superior males might take on an oedipal character in a patriarchal society. Orlando is perceived as a troublemaker by Oliver and Frederick; his conflicts are with the men who hold power in his world, with its insecure and ineffectual villains. "The old Duke is banished by his younger brother the new Duke" (I.i.99–100). Old Adam has served Orlando's family "from seventeen years, till now almost fourscore" (II.iii.71), but under Oliver he must endure "unregarded age in corners thrown" (1. 42). It is precisely the elders abused by Frederick and Oliver who ally themselves to Orlando's oppressed youth.[5] Adam gives to Orlando the life savings that were to have been the "foster-nurse" (II.iii.40) of his old age; he makes his "young master" (1. 2) his heir. The idealized relationship of Orlando and his old servant compensates for the loss or corruption of Orlando's affective ties to men of his own kin and class. But Adam's paternity is only a phase in the reconstitution of Orlando's social identity. In the process of revealing his lineage to the old Duke, Orlando exchanges the father-surrogate who was his own father's servant for the father-surrogate who was his own father's lord.

> If that you were the good Sir Rowland's son,
> As you have whisper'd faithfully you were,
> And as mine eye doth his effigies witness
> Most truly limn'd and living in your face,
> Be truly welcome hither. I am the duke
> That lov'd your father.
>
> (II.vii.194–99)

The living son replaces his dead father in the affections of their lord. The Duke, who has no natural son, assumes the role of Orlando's patron, his social father: "Give me your hand / And let me all your fortunes understand" (ll. 202–3). Orlando's previous paternal benefactor has been supplanted: Adam neither speaks nor is mentioned again.

The reunion of the de Boys brothers is blessed by "the old Duke"; the circumstance which makes that reunion possible is Oliver's

5. In his learned and suggestive study, Thomas shows that youths were regarded with suspicion and were subordinated, while the very old—unless they had wealth—were regarded with scorn and were ignored. (*King Lear* records the consequences of an old man's self-divestment.) Thomas notes that the trend to exclude the young and the aged from "full humanity" was "already implicit in the plea made to an Elizabethan archdeacon's court to disregard the evidence of two witnesses. One was a youth of eighteen, the other was a man of eighty. Both, it was urged, lacked discretion. The one was too young; the other too old" (p. 248).

expulsion by "the new Duke." In Lodge's *Rosalynde*, the two kings are not kin. Shakespeare's departure from his immediate source unifies and intensifies the conflicts in the family and the polity. The old Duke who adopts Orlando in the forest has been disinherited by his own younger brother in the court; Frederick has forcibly made himself his brother's heir. In the course of the play, fratricide is attempted, averted, and repudiated in each sibling relationship. Tensions in the nuclear family and in the body politic are miraculously assuaged within the forest. The Duke addresses his first words to his "co-mates and brothers in exile" (II.i.1). The courtly decorum of hierarchy and deference may be relaxed in the forest, but it has not been abrogated; the Duke's "brothers in exile" remain courtiers and servants attendant upon his grace. An atmosphere of charitable community has been created among those who have temporarily lost or abandoned their normal social context; the sources of conflict inherent in the social order are by no means genuinely dissolved in the forest, but rather are translated into a quiet and sweet style. In the forest, the old usurped Duke is a co-mate and brother to his loyal subjects and a benevolent father to Orlando. The comedy establishes *brotherhood* as an ideal of social as well as sibling male relationships; at the same time, it reaffirms a positive, nurturing image of *fatherhood*. And because family and society are a synecdoche, the comedy can also work to mediate the ideological contradiction between spiritual fraternity and political patriarchy, between social communion and social hierarchy.[6]

Like Richard of Gloucester, Claudius, Edmund, and Antonio, Frederick is a discontented younger brother whom Shakespeare makes the malevolent agent of his plot. Frederick generates action in *As You Like It* by banishing successively his elder brother, his niece, and his subject. Like his fellow villains, Frederick is the effective agent of a dramatic resolution which he himself does not intend; the tyrant's perverted will subserves the comic dramatist's providential irony. Frederick enforces the fraternal bond between Orlando and Oliver by holding Oliver responsible for Orlando on peril of his inheritance, forcing Oliver out to apprehend his brother. By placing Oliver in a social limbo akin to that suffered by Orlando, Frederick unwittingly creates the circumstances that lead to the brothers' reunion:

---

6. On pastoral form and social order in *As You Like It*, see Charles W. Hieatt, "The Quality of Pastoral in *As You Like It*," *Genre*, 7 (1974), 164–82; Harold Toliver, *Pastoral Forms and Attitudes* (Berkeley: Univ. of California Press, 1971), pp. 100–114; Judy Z. Kronenfeld, "Social Rank and the Pastoral Ideals of *As You Like It*," *SQ*, 29 (1978), 333–48. For an interesting discussion of the interplay between patriarchal and fraternal models of social relations in the sixteenth century, see Mary Ann Clawson, "Early Modern Fraternalism and the Patriarchal Family," *Feminist Studies*, 6 (1980), 368–91.

DUKE F. Thy lands and all things that thou dost call thine,
         Worth seizure, do we seize into our hands,
         Till thou canst quit thee by thy brother's mouth
         Of what we think against thee.
OLI.   O that your Highness knew my heart in this!
         I never lov'd my brother in my life.
DUKE F. More villain thou.
                                        (III.i.9–15)

Oliver has abused the letter and the spirit of Sir Rowland's will: "It was . . . charged my brother on his blessing to breed me well" (I.i.3–4). Frederick is Oliver's nemesis.

In the exchange I have just quoted, Frederick's attitude toward Oliver is one of *moral* as well as political superiority. His judgment of Oliver's villainy is sufficiently ironic to give us pause. Is the usurper in Frederick projecting onto Oliver his guilt for his own unbrotherliness? Or is the younger brother in him identifying with Orlando's domestic situation? In seizing Oliver's lands and all things that he calls his until Oliver's (younger) brother can absolve him, Frederick parodies his own earlier usurpation of his own elder brother. Frederick's initial seizure takes place before the play begins; its circumstances are never disclosed. We do better to observe Frederick's dramatic function than to search for his unconscious motives. Frederick actualizes the destructive consequences of younger brothers' deprivation and discontent, in the family and in society at large. The first scenes demonstrate that such a threat exists within Orlando himself. The threat is neutralized as soon as Orlando enters the good old Duke's comforting forest home; there his needs are immediately and bountifully gratified:

DUKE SEN. What would you have? Your gentleness shall force,
           More than your force move us to gentleness.
ORL.   I almost die for food, and let me have it.
DUKE SEN. Sit down and feed, and welcome to our table.
ORL.   Speak you so gently? Pardon me, I pray you.
           I thought that all things had been savage here,
              . . . . . .
           Let gentleness my strong enforcement be;
           In the which hope, I blush, and hide my sword.
                                        (II.vii.102–7, 118–19)

What is latent and potential within Orlando is displaced onto Frederick and realized in his violence and insecurity, his usurpation and tyranny.

Frederick sustains the role of villain until he too comes to Arden:

> Duke Frederick hearing how that every day
> Men of great worth resorted to this forest,
> Address'd a mighty power, which were on foot
> In his own conduct, purposely to take
> His brother here, and put him to the sword.
> And to the skirts of this wild wood he came,
> Where, meeting with an old religious man,
> After some question with him, was converted
> Both from his enterprise and from the world,
> His crown bequeathing to his banish'd brother
> And all their lands restor'd to them again
> That were with him exil'd.
>
> (V.iv.153–64)

Like Orlando, Frederick finds a loving father in the forest. And his conversion is the efficient cause of Orlando's elevation. In the denouement of Lodge's *Rosalynde*, the reunited brothers, Rosader and Saladyne, join the forces of the exiled King Gerismond; the army of the usurping King Torismond is defeated, and he is killed in the action. With striking formal and thematic economy, Shakespeare realizes his change of plot as a change *within* a character; he gets rid of Frederick not by killing him off but by morally transforming him. Frederick gives all his worldly goods to his natural brother and goes off to claim his spiritual inheritance from a heavenly father.

VI

The reunion of the de Boys brothers is narrated retrospectively by a reborn Oliver, in the alien style of an allegorical dream romance:

> . . . pacing through the forest,
> Chewing the food of sweet and bitter fancy,
> Lo what befell! He threw his eye aside,
> And mark what object did present itself.
> Under an old oak, whose boughs were moss'd with age
> And high top bald with dry antiquity,
> A wretched ragged man, o'ergrown with hair,
> Lay sleeping on his back.
>
> (IV.iii.100–107)

These images of infirm age and impotence, of regression to wildness and ruin through neglect, form a richly suggestive emblem. Expounded in the context of the present argument, the emblem represents the precarious condition into which fratricidal feeling provoked by primogeniture has brought these brothers and their house: "Such a fever hectic hath custome brought in and inured among fathers, and such fond desire they have to leave a great shewe

of the *stock* of their house, though the *branches* be *withered*, that . . .
my elder brother forsooth must be my master.[7] Orlando, whose
"having in beard is a younger brother's revenue" (III.ii.367–68),
confronts a hairy man asleep amidst icons of age and antiquity. The
description suggests that, in confronting "his brother, his elder
brother" (IV.iii.120), young Orlando is confronting a personification
of his patriline and of the patriarchal order itself. The brothers find
each other under an *arbor consanguinitatis*, at the de Boys "family
tree."[8]

Agnes Latham suggests that the snake and the lioness which men-
ace Oliver are metaphors for his own animosities: as the snake "slides
away, Oliver's envy melts, and his wrath goes with the lion."[9] The text
suggests that it is Orlando who undergoes such an allergorical purgation. When it sees Orlando, the snake slips under the bush where the
lioness couches.

> OLI.   This seen, Orlando did approach the man,
>   And found it was his brother, his elder brother.
>   . . . . . .
> ROS.   But to Orlando. Did he leave him there,
>   Food to the suck'd and hungry lioness?
> OLI.   Twice did he turn his back, and purpos'd so.
>   But kindness, nobler ever than revenge,
>   And nature, stronger than his just occasion,
>   Made him give battle to the lioness,

---

7. Wilson, *State of England, 1600*, p. 24; italics mine.
8. Orlando and Oliver are sons of Sir Rowland de Boys, whose surname is a play on "woods"
   and "boys." The tree is an heraldic emblem for Orlando, as well as for Oliver: in Arden,
   Celia tells Rosalind that she "found him under a tree like a dropped acorn. . . . There lay
   he stretched along like a wounded knight" (III.ii.230–31, 236–37); we find him carving
   Rosalind's name "on every tree" (1.9). If my interpretation of the emblematic reunion
   scene seems fanciful, the fancy is decidedly Elizabethan. Unprecedented social mobility
   created an obsessive concern with marks of status: "One of the most striking features of
   the age was a pride of ancestry which now reached new heights of fantasy and elaboration. . . . Genuine genealogy was cultivated by the older gentry to reassure themselves of
   their innate superiority over the upstarts; bogus genealogy was cultivated by the new
   gentry in an effort to clothe their social nakedness" (Lawrence Stone, *The Crisis of the
   Aristocracy 1558–1641* [Oxford: Clarendon Press, 1965], p. 23). In the passage on primogeniture I have quoted in my text, Thomas Wilson's arboreal metaphors have a naturalness in their context that suggests that such metaphors were an integral part of
   Elizabethan thought patterns. Stone notes that in the sixteenth century the lengthy
   genealogies of the "upper landed classes, the country gentry and nobility," tended "to
   pay only cursory attention to collateral branches, and are mainly concerned with tracing
   the male line backward in time. Similarly, the growing complexity of coats of arms
   recorded alliances in the male line of the heir by primogeniture of the nuclear family,
   not kin connections. . . . The family mausoleums of the period contain the remains of
   the male heirs of the nuclear family and their wives from generation to generation, but
   only rarely adult younger children or kin relatives. The rule of primogeniture is clearly
   reflected in the disposal of the bodies after death" (*Family, Sex and Marriage*, p. 135).
   Orlando is in danger of becoming merely a withered branch of the old "de Boys" stock.
9. Latham, Arden ed. of *As You Like It*, p. xliii.

> Who quickly fell before him; in which hurtling
> From miserable slumber I awak'd.
>
> (IV.iii.119–20, 125–32)

In killing the lioness which threatens to kill Oliver, Orlando kills the impediment to atonement within himself. Oliver's narrative implies a causal relationship between Orlando's act of self-mastery and purgation and Oliver's own "awakening." When the brothers have been "kindly bath'd" (IV.iii.140) in mutual tears, Oliver's "conversion" (1. 136) and his atonement with Orlando are consecrated by the Duke who loved their father. In the play's first words, Orlando remembered that Oliver had been charged, on his blessing, to breed him well. The Duke's bequest and injunction reformulate Sir Rowland's last will and testament:

> he led me to the gentle Duke,
> Who gave me fresh array and entertainment
> Committing me unto my brother's love.
>
> (IV.iii.142–44)

What has taken place offstage is a conversion of the crucial event that precipitated the fraternal conflict, the event "remembered" in the very first words of the play.

At this point in the atonement, paternity and fraternity are reaffirmed as spiritual bonds rather than as bonds of blood and property. Brotherhood can now come to mean friendship freed from the material conflicts of kinship. Some remarks by Julian Pitt-Rivers illuminate the point:

> Kinship's nature . . . is not free of jural considerations. Rights and duties are distributed differentially to kinsmen because kinship is a system, not a network of dyadic ties like friendship. Status within it is ascribed by birth. . . . Rules of succession and inheritance are required to order that which cannot be left to the manifestations of brotherly love. . . . A revealing assertion echoes through the literature on ritual kinship: 'Blood-brothers are like brothers,' it is said, then comes, 'in fact they are closer than real brothers.' The implication is troubling, for it would appear that true fraternity is found only between those who are not real brothers. Amity does not everywhere enjoin the same open-ended generosity, least of all between kinsmen, who quarrel only too often, in contrast to ritual kinsmen, who are bound by sacred duty not to do so.[1]

Before he goes to Arden, Orlando feels he has no alternative but to subject himself "to the malice / Of a diverted blood and bloody

---

1. See Julian Pitt-Rivers, "The Kith and the Kin," in *The Character of Kinship*, ed. Jack Goody (Cambridge Univ. Press, 1973), pp. 89–105; quotation from p. 101.

brother" (II.iii.36–37). Shakespeare's task is to bring the relationship of Orlando and Oliver under the auspices of Hymen:

> Then is there mirth in heaven,
> When earthly things made even
> Atone together.
> (V.iv.107–9)

In Touchstone's terms (V.iv.101–2), hostile siblings are brought to shake hands and swear their brotherhood by the virtue of comedy's If. The spiritual principle of "brotherly love" is reconciled to the jural principle of primogeniture; "real brothers" are made "blood brothers"—as the napkin borne by Oliver so graphically testifies.[2] Some commentators have seen the outlines of a Christian allegory of redemption in the play. They point to the presence of a character named Adam; the Duke's disquisition on "the penalty of Adam"; the iconography of the serpent, the tree, and the *vetus homo;* the heroic virtue of Orlando; the comic rite of atonement.[3] Perhaps we do better to think of Shakespeare as creating resonances between the situations in his play and the religious archetypes at the foundations of his culture; as invoking what Rosalie Colie, writing of *King Lear,* calls "Biblical echo." What echoes deeply through the scenes I have discussed is the fourth chapter of Genesis, the story of Cain and Abel and what another of Shakespeare's fratricides calls "the primal eldest curse . . . / A brother's murther" (*Hamlet,* III.iii.37–38). Adam's two sons made offerings to the Lord: "and the Lord had respect unto Habel, and to his offering,"

> But unto Kain and to his offring he had no regarde: wherefore Kain was exceding wroth, & his countenance fel downe.
> Then the Lord said unto Kain, Why art thou wroth? and why is thy countenence cast downe?
> If thou do wel, shalt thou not be accepted? and if thou doest not well, sinne lieth at the dore: also unto thee his desire *shal be subject,* and thou shalt rule over him.
> Then Kain spake to Habel his brother. And when they were in the field, Kain rose up against Habel his brother, and slewe him.

---

2. The histories of brotherhood and sisterhood follow opposite directions in the play. We are introduced to Rosalind and Celia as first cousins "whose loves / Are dearer than the natural bond of sisters" (I.ii.265–66); since childhood, they have been "coupled and inseparable" (I.iii.72). In the course of the play, they are uncoupled and separated from each other and from their girlhoods by the intervention of sexual desire and the new emotional and social demands of marriage. All four female characters in the play are maidens on the threshold of wedlock. The inverse relationship between brotherhood and sisterhood within the play and the conspicuous absence of matronly characters are reflections of the male and patriarchal bias of Elizabethan family and social structures.
3. See Richard Knowles, "Myth and Type in *As You Like It,*" *ELH,* 33 (1966), 1–22; René E. Fortin, "'Tongues in Trees': Symbolic Patterns in *As You Like It,*" *Texas Studies in Literature and Language,* 14 (1973), 569–82.

> Then the Lord said unto Kain, Where is Habel thy brother?
> Who answered, I canot tel. Am I my brothers keper?
> Againe he said, What hast thou done? the voyce of thy broth-
> ers blood cryeth unto me from the grounde.
> Now therefore thou art cursed from the earth, which hath
> opened her mouth to receive thy brothers blood from thine
> hand?[4]

The Geneva Bible glosses the italicized phrase in the seventh verse
as a reference to the foundations of primogeniture: "The dignitie of
ye first borne is given to Kain over Habel."

The wrath of Cain echoes in Oliver's fratricidal musings at the
end of the first scene: "I hope I shall see an end of him; for my
soul—yet I know not why—hates nothing more than he. Yet he's
gentle, never schooled and yet learned, full of noble device, of all
sorts enchantingly beloved, and indeed so much in the heart of the
world, and especially of my own people, that I am altogether mis-
prised. But it shall not be so long" (I.i.162–69). Oliver feels humanly
rather than divinely misprized; and it is his tyrannical secular lord to
whom he declares that he is not his brother's keeper. Orlando sheds
his own blood for his elder brother, which becomes the sign of Oliver's conversion rather than the mark of his fratricidal guilt. Oliver
finds acceptance in the old Duke, who commits him to his brother's
love. Shakespeare is creating a resonance between his romantic fiction and Biblical history, between the dramatic process of assuaging
family conflict in the atonements of comedy and the exegetical process of redeeming the primal fratricide of Genesis in the spiritual
fraternity of the Gospel:

> For brethren, ye have bene called unto libertie: onely use not
> *your* libertie as an occasion unto the flesh, but by love serve one
> another.
> For all the Law is fulfilled in one worde, which is this, Thou
> shalt love thy neighbour as thy self.
> If ye byte & devoure one another, take hede lest ye be con-
> sumed one of another.
> Then I say, walke in the Spirit, and ye shal not fulfil the lustes
> of the flesh.[5]
>
>   (Galatians v. 13–16)

The rivalry or conflict between elder and younger brothers is a
prominent motif in the fictions of cultures throughout the world.

---

4. Genesis iv. 4–11, in *The Geneva Bible* (1560), facsimile ed. (Madison: Univ. of Wisconsin Press, 1969). Italics in the original. All further references to the Bible from this source.
5. "The flesh lusteth against the Spirit" (Galatians v. 17) is glossed in the Geneva Bible: "That is, the natural man striveth against ye Spirit of regeneration." The spiritually regenerate Oliver marries the aptly named Celia; the socially regenerate Orlando marries a Rosalind brought "from heaven" (V.iv.111) by Hymen.

Its typical plot has been described as "the disadvantaged younger sibling or orphan child besting an unjust elder and gaining great fortune through the timely intercession of a benevolent supernatural being."[6] Cultural fictions of the triumphs of younger siblings offer psychological compensation for the social fact of the deprivation of younger siblings. Such fictions are symbolic mediations of discrepancies between the social categories of status and the claims of individual merit, in which the defeat and supplanting of the elder sibling by the younger reconciles ability with status: "The younger outwits, displaces, and becomes the elder; the senior position comes to be associated with superior ability."[7]

The folk-tale scenario of sibling rivalry is clear in the fourteenth-century tale of *Gamelyn*, to which Lodge's Rosader plot and Shakespeare's Orlando plot are indebted.[8] The disinherited Gamelyn and his outlaw cohorts sentence Gamelyn's eldest brother to death by hanging. Their topsy-turvy actions are sanctioned and absorbed by the social order: the King pardons Gamelyn, restores his inheritance, and makes him Chief Justice. In *As You Like It*, Shakespeare's characters emphasize the discrepancy between "the gifts of the world" and "the lineaments of Nature" (I.ii.40–41), between social place and personal merit. The comedy's task is to "mock the good hussif Fortune from her wheel, that her gifts may henceforth be bestowed equally" (I.ii.30–32). Shakespeare transcends *Gamelyn* and its folktale paradigm in a wholehearted concern not merely to eliminate social contradictions, but also to redeem and reconcile human beings.[9] Oliver is not defeated, eliminated, supplanted; he is converted, reintegrated, confirmed. In the subplot of *King Lear*, the unbrotherly struggle for mastery and possession is resolved by fratricide; the comic resolution of *As You Like It* depends instead upon an expansion of opportunities for mastery and possession.

VII

In Lodge's *Rosalynde*, the crude heroic theme of *Gamelyn* is already fused with the elegant love theme of Renaissance pastorals. In constructing a romantic comedy of familial and sexual tension resolved

6. Michael Jackson, "Ambivalence and the Last-Born: Birth-order position in convention and myth," *Man*, NS, 13 (1978), 341–61; quotation from p. 350. This anthropological essay, based on comparative ethnography of the Kuranko (Sierra Leone) and Maori (New Zealand), has clarified my thinking about the society of Arden.

7. Jackson, "Ambivalence and the Last-Born," p. 354.

8. *New Variorum* ed. of *As You Like It*, pp. 483–87, provides a synopsis of the plot of *Gamelyn* and a digest of opinions about its direct influence on *As You Like It*.

9. Compare Lodge's address to the reader at the end of *Rosalynde*: "Heere Gentlemen may you see . . . that vertue is not measured by birth but by action; that younger brethren though inferiour in yeares, yet may be superiour to honours; that concord is the sweetest conclusion, and amitie betwixt brothers more forceable than fortune" (pp. 474–75).

in brotherhood and marriage, Shakespeare gives new complexity and cohesiveness to his narrative source. The struggle of elder and younger brothers is not simply duplicated; it is inverted. In the younger generation, the elder brother abuses the younger; in the older generation, the younger abuses the elder. The range of experience and affect is thereby enlarged, and the protest against primogeniture is firmly balanced by its reaffirmation. Myth, Scripture, and Shakespearean drama record "the bond crack'd betwixt son and father" (*King Lear*, I.ii.113–14). Hostilities between elder and younger brothers and between fathers and sons are homologous: "Yea, and the brother shal deliver the brother to death, and the father the sonne, and the children shal rise against their parents, and shal cause them to dye" (Mark xiii. 14). Because in *As You Like It* the doubling and inversion of fraternal conflict links generations, the relationship of brother and brother can be linked to the relationship of father and son. In the process of atonement, the two families and two generations of men are doubly and symmetrically bound: the younger brother weds the daughter of the elder brother, and the elder brother weds the daughter of the younger brother. They create the figure of *chiasmus*. Whatever vicarious benefit *As You Like It* brings to younger brothers and to youths, it is not achieved by perverting or destroying the bonds between siblings and between generations, but by transforming and renewing them— *through marriage*.

In Arden, Orlando divides his time between courting Rosalind (who is played by Ganymede, who is played by Rosalind) and courting the old Duke who is Rosalind's father. Celia teases Rosalind about the sincerity of Orlando's passion, the truth of his feigning, by reminding her of his divided loyalties: "He attends here in the forest on the Duke your father" (III.iv.29–30). Rosalind, who clearly resents that she must share Orlando's attentions with her father, responds: "I met the Duke yesterday and had much question with him. He asked me of what parentage I was: I told him of as good as he, so he laughed and let me go. But what talk we of fathers, when there is such a man as Orlando?" (III.iv.31–35). Celia has already transferred her loyalties from her father to Rosalind; Rosalind is transferring hers from her father and from Celia to Orlando. But she withholds her identity from her lover in order to test and to taunt him. In the forest, while Orlando guilelessly improves his place in the patriarchal order, Rosalind wittily asserts her independence of it. Rosalind avoids her father's recognition and establishes her own household within the forest; Orlando desires the Duke's recognition and gladly serves him in his forest-court.

It is only after he has secured a place within the old Duke's benign all-male community that Orlando begins to play the lover and the poet: "Run, run Orlando, carve on every tree/The fair, the chaste, and unexpressive she" (III.ii.9–10):

> But upon the fairest boughs,
> Or at every sentence end,
> Will I Rosalinda write,
> Teaching all that read to know
> The quintessence of every sprite
> Heaven would in little show.
> Therefore Heaven Nature charg'd
> That one body should be fill'd
> With all graces wide-enlarg'd.
> Nature presently distill'd
> Helen's cheek, but not her heart,
> Cleopatra's majesty,
> Atalanta's better part,
> Sad Lucretia's modesty.
> Thus Rosalind of many parts
> By heavenly synod was devis'd,
> Of many faces, eyes, and hearts,
> To have the touches dearest priz'd.
> Heaven would that she these gifts should have,
> And I to live and die her slave.
>
> (ll. 132–51)

The Petrarchan lover "writes" his mistress or "carves" her in the image of his own desire, incorporating virtuous feminine stereotypes and scrupulously excluding what is sexually threatening. The lover masters his mistress by inscribing her within his own discourse; he worships a deity of his own making and under his control. When Rosalind-Ganymede confronts this "fancy-monger" (III.ii.354–55) who "haunts the forest . . . deifying the name of Rosalind" (ll. 350, 353–54), she puts a question to him: "But are you so much in love as your rhymes speak?" (l. 386). Rosalind and Touchstone interrogate and undermine self-deceiving amorous rhetoric with bawdy wordplay and relentless insistence upon the power and inconstancy of physical desire. All the love-talk in the play revolves around the issue of mastery in the shifting social relationship between the sexes: in courtship, maidens suspect the faithfulness of their suitors; in wedlock, husbands suspect the faithfulness of their wives. The poems of feigning lovers and the horns of cuckolded husbands are the complementary preoccupations of Arden's country copulatives.

Consider the crucially-placed brief scene (IV.ii) which is barely more than a song inserted between the betrothal scene of Orlando and Rosalind-Ganymede and the scene in which Oliver comes to Rosalind bearing the bloody napkin. In IV.i, Rosalind mocks her tardy lover with talk of an emblematic snail: "He brings his destiny with him. . . . Horns—which such as you fain to be beholding to your wives for" (ll. 54–55, 57–58). Touchstone has already resigned himself to the snail's destiny with his own misogynistic logic: "As horns are odious, they are necessary. It is said, many a man knows no end of his goods. Right. Many a man has good horns and knows no end of them. Well, that is the dowry of his wife, 'tis none of his own getting" (III.iii.45–49). Now, in IV.ii, Jaques transforms Rosalind's jibes into ironic male self-mockery: "He that killed the deer" is to have the horns set on his head "for a branch of victory" (ll. 1, 5). Jaques calls for a song—"'Tis no matter how it be in tune, so it makes noise enough" (ll. 8–9). The rowdy horn song is a kind of *charivari* or "rough music," traditionally the form of ridicule to which cuckolds and others who offended the community's moral standards were subjected.[1] This *charivari*, however, is also a song of consolation and good fellowship, for not only the present "victor" but all his companions "shall bear this burden" (ll. 12–13).

> *Take thou no scorn to wear the horn,*
> *It was a crest ere thou wast born.*
> *Thy father's father wore it,*
> *And thy father bore it.*
> *The horn, the horn, the lusty horn,*
> *Is not a thing to laugh to scorn.*
>   (ll. 14–19)

The play's concern with patriarchal lineage and the hallmarks of gentility is here transformed into an heraldic celebration of the horn—instrument of male potency and male degradation—which marks all men as kinsmen. Thus, although cuckoldry implies the uncertainty of paternity, the song celebrates the paradox that it is precisely the common destiny they share with the snail that binds men together—father to son, brother to brother. Through the metaphor of hunting (with its wordplays on "deer" and "horns") and the medium of song, the threat that the power of insubordinate women poses to the authority of men is transformed into an occasion for affirming and celebrating patriarchy and fraternity.

---

1. On *charivari* and cuckoldry, see the masterful 1976 Neale Lecture in English History by Keith Thomas, "The Place of Laughter in Tudor and Stuart England," published in *The Times Literary Supplement*, 21 January 1977, pp. 77–81. Students of Shakespearean comedy would do well to bear in mind Thomas' point that "laughter has a social dimension. Jokes are a pointer to joking situations, areas of structural ambiguity in society itself, and their subject-matter can be a revealing guide to past tensions and anxieties." From this perspective, "Tudor humour about shrewish and insatiable wives or lascivious widows was a means of confronting the anomalies of insubordinate female behaviour which constantly threatened the actual working of what was supposed to be a male-dominated marital system. Hence the . . . obsession with cuckoldry" (p. 77).

After the mock-marriage (IV.i) in which they have indeed plighted their troth, Rosalind-Ganymede exuberantly teases Orlando about the shrewishness and promiscuity he can expect from his wife. Naively romantic Orlando abruptly leaves his threatening Rosalind in order "to attend the Duke at dinner" (IV.i.170). On his way from his cruel mistress to his kind patron, Orlando encounters his own brother. It is hardly insignificant that Shakespeare changes the details of the fraternal recognition scene to include an aspect of sexual differentiation wholly absent from Lodge's romance. He adds the snake which wreathes itself around Oliver's neck; and he makes it into an insidious female, "who with her head, nimble in threats, approach'd / The opening of his mouth" (IV.iii.109–10). Furthermore, he changes Lodge's lion into a lioness whose nurturing and aggressive aspects are strongly and ambivalently stressed: "a lioness, with udders all drawn dry" (l. 114); "the suck'd and hungry lioness" (l. 126). Orlando has retreated in the face of Rosalind's verbal aggressiveness. He has wandered through the forest, "chewing the food of sweet and bitter fancy" (l. 101), to seek the paternal figure who has nurtured him. Instead, he has found Oliver in a dangerously passive condition, threatened by a double source of oral aggression.

Oliver's fantastic narrative suggests a transformation of the sexual conflict initiated by Rosalind when she teases Orlando in IV.i. Rosalind and the lioness are coyly linked in the exchange between the lovers at their next meeting:

ROS. O my dear Orlando, how it grieves me to see thee wear thy heart in a scarf!

ORL. It is my arm.

ROS. I thought thy heart had been wounded with the claws of a lion.

ORL. Wounded it is, but with the eyes of a lady.

(V.ii.19–23)

The chain which Rosalind bestows upon Orlando at their first meeting ("Wear this for me" [I.ii.236]) is the mark by which Celia identifies him in the forest ("And a chain, that you once wore, about his neck" [III.ii.178]). The "green and gilded snake" (IV.iii.108) encircling Oliver's neck is a demonic parody of the emblematic stage property worn by his brother throughout the play. The gynephobic response to Rosalind is split into the erotic serpent and the maternal lioness, while Orlando is split into his victimized brother and his heroic self. Orlando's mastery of the lioness ("Who quickly fell before him" [IV.iii.131]) is, then, a symbolic mastery of Rosalind's challenge to Orlando. But it is also a triumph of fraternal "kindness" (l. 128) over the fratricidal impulse. Relationships between elder and younger brothers and between fathers and sons are purified by what the text suggests is a kind of matricide, a triumph of men over female powers. Thus the killing of the lioness may also symbolize a repudiation of the consanguinity of Orlando and Oliver. If this powerful female—the carnal source of siblings—is destroyed, both fraternity and paternity can be reconceived as male relationships unmediated by woman, relationships of the spirit rather than of the flesh. Orlando's heroic act, distanced and framed in an allegorical narrative, condenses aspects of both the romantic plot and the sibling plot. And these plots are themselves the complementary aspects of a single social and dramatic process.

Before Orlando is formally married to Rosalind at the end of the play, he has reaffirmed his fraternal and filial bonds in communion with other men. Orlando's rescue of Oliver from the she-snake and the lioness frees the brothers' capacity to give and to receive love. Now Oliver can "fall in love" with Celia; and now Orlando "can live no longer by thinking" (V.ii.50) about Rosalind. Oliver asks his younger brother's consent to marry, and resigns to him his birthright: "My father's house and all the revenue that was old Sir Rowland's will I estate upon you, and here live and die a shepherd" (ll. 10–12).[2] Orlando agrees with understandable alacrity: "You have my consent Let your wedding be tomorrow" (ll. 13–14). Marriage, the social institution at the heart of comedy, serves to ease or eliminate fraternal strife. And fraternity, in turn, serves as a defense against the threat men feel from women.

Rosalind-as-Ganymede and Ganymede-as-Rosalind—the woman out of place—exerts an informal organizing and controlling power over affairs in the forest. But this power lapses when she relinquishes her male disguise and formally acknowledges her normal status as daughter and wife: "I'll have no father, if you be not he. / I'll have no husband, if you be not he" (V.iv.121–22). In a ritual gesture of surrender, she assumes the passive role of mediatrix between the Duke and Orlando:

> [*To the Duke.*]   To you I give myself, for I am yours.
> [*To Orl.*]   To you I give myself, for I am yours.
>   (V.iv.115–16)

The Duke's paternal bond to Orlando is not established through the natural fertility of a mother but through the supernatural virginity of a daughter: "Good Duke receive thy daughter, / Hymen from heaven brought her" (V.iv.110–11). The play is quite persis-

---

2. Of course, Oliver's gallant gesture of social and economic deference to his youngest brother (a spontaneous reversal of the primogeniture rule into the ultimogeniture rule) cannot be made good until there is a profound change in the society from which they have fled. Oliver's lands and revenues are no longer his to give to Orlando; it is because of Orlando that Frederick has confiscated them.

tent in creating strategies for subordinating the flesh to the spirit, and female powers to male controls. Hymen's marriage rite gives social sanction to the lovers' mutual desire. But the atonement of man and woman also implies the social subordination of wife to husband. Rosalind's exhilarating mastery of herself and others has been a compensatory "holiday humor," a temporary, inversionary rite of misrule, whose context is a transfer of authority, property, and title from the Duke to his prospective male heir. From the perspective of the present argument, the romantic love plot serves more than its own ends: it is also the means by which other actions are transformed and resolved. In his unions with the Duke and with Rosalind, Orlando's social elevation is confirmed. Such a perspective does not deny the comedy its festive magnanimity; it merely reaffirms that Shakespearean drama registers the form and pressure of Elizabethan experience. If *As You Like It* is a vehicle for Rosalind's exuberance, it is also a structure for her containment.[3]

Jaques de Boys, "the second son of old Sir Rowland" (V.iv.151), enters suddenly at the end of the play. This Shakespearean whimsy fits logically into the play's comic process. As the narrator of Frederick's strange eventful history, Jaques brings the miraculous news that resolves the conflict between his own brothers as well as the conflict between the brother-dukes. As Rosalind mediates the affinity of father and son, so Jaques—a brother, rather than a mother— mediates the kinship of eldest and youngest brothers; he is, in effect, the incarnate middle term between Oliver and Orlando. The Duke welcomes him:

> Thou offer'st fairly to thy brothers' wedding;
> To one his lands withheld, and to the other
> A land itself at large, a potent dukedom.
> (V.iv.166–68)

Jaques' gift celebrates the wedding of his brothers to their wives and to each other. Solutions to the play's initial conflicts are worked

3. Several generations of critics—most of them men, and quite infatuated with Rosalind themselves—have stressed the exuberance and ignored the containment. Much the same may be said of some recent feminist critics (see, for example, Juliet Dusinberre, *Shakespeare and the Nature of Women* [London: Macmillan, 1975]), although they approach the character in another spirit The "feminism" of Shakespearean comedy seems to me more ambivalent in tone and more ironic in form than such critics have wanted to believe. *Contra* Dusinberre, Linda T. Fitz emphasizes that "the English Renaissance institutionalized, where it did not invent, the restrictive marriage-oriented attitude toward women that feminists have been struggling against ever since. . . . The insistent demand for the right—nay, obligation—of women to be happpily married arose as much in reaction against women's intractable pursuit of independence as it did in reaction against Catholic ascetic philosophy" ("'What Says the Married Woman?' Marriage Theory and Feminism in the English Renaissance," *Mosaic*, 13, no. 2 [Winter 1980], 1–22; quotations from pp. 11, 18). A provocative Renaissance context for Shakespeare's Rosalind is to be found in the essay, "Women on Top," in Natalie Zemon Davis, *Society and Culture in Early Modern France* (Stanford: Stanford Univ. Press, 1975), pp. 124–51.

out between brother and brother, father and son—among men. Primogeniture is reaffirmed in public and private domains: the Duke, newly restored to his own authority and possessions, now restores the de Boys patrimony to Oliver. The aspirations and deserts of the youngest brother are rewarded when the Duke acknowledges Orlando as his own heir, the successor to property, power, and title that far exceed Oliver's birthright The eldest brother regains the authority due him by primogeniture at the same time that the youngest brother is freed from subordination to his sibling and validated in his claim to the perquisites of gentility.

With his patrimony restored and his marriage effected, Oliver legitimately assumes the place of a patriarch and emerges into full social adulthood; he is now worthy to be the son and heir of Sir Rowland de Boys. Orlando, on the other hand, has proved himself worthy to become son and heir to the Duke. Thomas Wilson, another Elizabethan younger brother, made the bitter misfortune of primogeniture the spur to personal achievement: "This I must confess doth us good someways, for it makes us industrious to apply ourselves to letters or to armes, whereby many time we become my master elder brothers' masters, or at least their betters in honour and reputation."[4] Unlike Thomas Wilson, Shakespeare's Orlando is spectacularly successful, and his success is won more by spontaneous virtue than by industry. But like Wilson's, Orlando's accomplishments are those of a gentleman and a courtier. Unlike most Elizabethan younger sons, Orlando is not forced to descend to commerce or to labor to make his way in the world. He succeeds by applying himself to the otiose courtship of his mistress and his prince. Although the perfection of his social identity is deferred during the Duke's lifetime, Orlando's new filial subordination is eminently beneficent. It grants him by affinity what he has been denied by kinship: the social advancement and sexual fulfillment of which youths and younger sons were so frequently deprived. The de Boys brothers atone together when the eldest replaces a father and the youngest recovers a father.

VIII

Social and dramatic decorum require that, "to work a comedy kindly, grave old men should instruct, young men should show the imperfections of youth."[5] London's city fathers, however, were forever accusing the theatres and the plays of corrupting rather than instructing youth: "We verely think plays and theatres to be the cheif cause . . . of . . . disorder, & lewd demeanours which appear

4. Wilson, State of England, 1600, p. 24.
5. George Whetstone, Epistle Dedicatory to Promos and Cassandra (1578), quoted in Madeleine Doran, Endeavors of Art (Madison: Univ. of Wisconsin Press, 1954), p. 220.

of late in young people of all degrees."[6] Shakespeare's play neither preaches to youths nor incites them to riot. In the world of its Elizabethan audience, the form of Orlando's experience may indeed have functioned as a collective compensation, a projection for the wish-fulfillment fantasies of younger brothers, youths, and all who felt themselves deprived by their fathers or their fortunes. But Orlando's mastery of adversity could also provide support and encouragement to the ambitious individuals who identified with his plight. The play may have fostered strength and perseverance as much as it facilitated pacification and escape. For the large number of youths in Shakespeare's audience—firstborn and younger siblings, gentle and base—the performance may have been analogous to a rite of passage, helping to ease their dangerous and prolonged journey from subordination to identity, their difficult transition from the child's part to the adult's.

My subject has been the complex interrelationship of brothers, fathers, and sons in *As You Like It*. But I have suggested that the play's concern with relationships among men is only artificially separable from its concern with relationships between men and women. The androgynous Rosalind—boy actor and princess—addresses Shakespeare's heterosexual audience in an epilogue: "My way is to conjure you, and I'll begin with the women. I charge you, O women, for the love you bear to men, to like as much of this play as please you. And I charge you, O men, for the love you bear to women—as I perceive by your simpering none of you hates them—that between you and the women the play may please" (V.iv.208–14). Through the subtle and flexible strategies of drama—in puns, jokes, games, disguises, songs, poems, fantasies—*As You Like It* expresses, contains, and discharges a measure of the strife between the men and the women. Shakespeare's comedy manipulates the differential social relationships between the sexes, between brothers, between father and son, master and servant, lord and subject. It is by the conjurer's art that Shakespeare manages to reconcile the social imperatives of hierarchy and difference with the festive urges toward leveling and atonement. The intense and ambivalent personal bonds upon which the play is focused—bonds between brothers and between lovers— affect each other reciprocally and become the means of each other's resolution. And as the actions within the play are dialectically related to each other, so the world of Shakespeare's characters is dialectically related to the world of his audience. *As You Like It* is both a theatrical *reflection* of social conflict and a theatrical *source* of social conciliation.

---

6. From a document (1595) in the "Dramatic Records of the City of London," quoted in Harbage, *Shakespeare's Audience*, p. 104.

RICHARD WILSON

"Like the Old Robin Hood":
As You Like It and the Enclosure Riots†

In September 1592, while plague and riot gripped London, Queen Elizabeth made a progress into the West Midlands and was welcomed with pageants devised by John Lyly as a prospectus of pastoral England. When she crossed the Thames at Bisham, a "wilde man" sprang from the woods to assure "the Queen of this Island" that in her presence "my untamed thoughts wax gentle, & I fed in my self civility. . . . Your Majesty on my knees will I followe, bearing this Club, not as a Salvage, but to beate down those that are."¹ Elizabeth had left London to the rioters' cry of "Clubs!"; now sylvan power was presented as a force of counter-insurgency. Prompted by the civic emergency, Lyly's wodewose brandished a weapon that was a reminder of the violence surrounding Elizabethan pastoralism and of the urgent need to secure its boundaries. For, as the text explained, it was only the queen's peace that exempted England from the general European crisis: "By her it is our carts are laden with corn, when in other countries they are filled with harness: our horses are led with a whip, theirs with a lance."² Banished to Oxfordshire as a princess, she had said that nothing would give her greater happiness than to be a milkmaid of Woodstock, and forty years later her itinerary was restorative. "Your Highness is come into uneven country," she was therefore reassured as she entered the Cotswolds, "but healthy and harmeles, where a black sheepe is a perilous beast," and there were "no monsters."³ Yet when its climax came on September 28 at Rycote—the fortified mansion of her erstwhile companion-in-exile, Lady Norris—the progress ended with the precautionary presentation of an arsenal of arms to Gloriana, for as the "Old Soldier" and Lord Lieutenant, Lord Norris, swore, Midlanders would show loyalty "by deeds," if necessary, "and make it good with our lives, . . . what words cannot effect, my sword shall."⁴

† Richard Wilson, "'Like the Old Robin Hood': As You Like It and the Enclosure Riots," *Shakespeare Quarterly*, 43.1 (1992): 1–19. © 2003 Folger Shakespeare Library. Reprinted with permission of the Johns Hopkins University Press.
1. All quotations of Lyly are from "Speeches Delivered to Her Majesty this last Progress" in *The Complete Works of John Lyly*, ed. R. Warwick Bond, 3 vols. (Oxford: Clarendon Press, 1967), Vol. I, pp. 471–90; for the passage quoted here, see page 473. All quotations from *As You Like It* are from the Arden Shakespeare, ed. Agnes Latham (London: Methuen, 1975). All other quotations from Shakespeare refer to *The Riverside Shakespeare*, ed. G. Blakemore Evans (Boston: Houghton Mifflin, 1974).
2. p. 475.
3. p. 477.
4. p. 488.

The 1592 progress was riven with the anxiety of its occasion; thus, although the queen was saluted as "one by whom shepherds have their flocks in safety, and their own lives, and all the country quietness," Pan was made to pledge her that "During your abode, no theft shall be in the woods: in the field no noise: in the valleys no spies, my self will keep all safe."[5] Ringed by foes, the security of even the Elizabethan heartland would depend, it seemed, on a net of paid informers. In Lyly's pageant, therefore, pastoral discourse is troubled with rumors, voiced by foresters like Pan, of sylvan outlawry. If Elizabethan pastoralism was keyed, as Louis Montrose suggests, to the hegemony of England's sheepfarming gentry,[6] by 1592 its imaginative ecology could not ignore the resistance of woodland commoners and squatters to enclosure. That the forest had become problematic was signalled that year with John Manwood's treatise *Of the Lawes of the Forest*, which, written from an absolutist perspective, decried the fact that "the greatest part of them are spoiled and decayed" and saw enclosure as a circumscription of prerogative.[7] A site of sanctuary, the forest was the frontier between common law and feudal rights such as pasturage; thus it was destined to be a battleground between the regulated and market economies, with their warring concepts of legality. Though John Aubrey supposed that, because of the decay of "petty Mannors," the "meane people" of the woods "lived lawlesse, nobody to govern them," they in fact had an archaic court of "Justices in Eyre," whose forest law theoretically safeguarded the rights of both royal hunter and grazing commoner. But the forest remained symbolically outside capitalist order, a concrete sign of communal justice and resistance, never more challenging to the state than at this moment when the English woodlands of the Middle Ages were ceasing to exist in reality.[8] When the queen journeyed into the Midlands, therefore, it was the allegiance of foresters that her hosts dramatized, but it was the woods beyond Rycote towards which they looked with apprehension.

The wariness of Elizabeth's reception was to be justified in the dearth of 1596, when "a greate companie" converged on Rycote at Michaelmas to petition Lord Norris for relief, threatening that "yf they Could not have remedie, they would seek remedie them-

5. p. 475.
6. "Of Gentlemen and Shepherds: The Politics of Elizabethan Pastoral Form," *English Literary History*, 50 (1983), 415–59.
7. *A Brefe Collection of the Lawes of the Forest* (London: Private edition, 1592); *A Treatise and Discourse of the Lawes of the Forrest* (London: Thomas Wright, 1615).
8. See Richard Marienstras, *New perspectives on the Shakespearean world* (Cambridge: Cambridge Univ. Press, 1985), pp. 11–39; John Aubrey, *Wiltshire: The Topographical Collections of John Aubrey*, ed. John Edward Jackson (London: Longman, 1862), p. 9; David Underdown, *Revel, Riot and Rebellion: Popular Politics and Culture in England, 1603–1660* (Oxford: Clarendon Press, 1985), p. 34.

selves, and Cast down hedges and dytches, and knocke down gentlemen."[9] Repeatedly pressed to intervene "for Relief for Corne, and for puttinge downe of enclosures," the Lord Lieutenant did nothing, and it was one of his own servants, named Bartholomew Steer, who incited rebellion. During the autumn, at fairs across the Midlands, Steer recruited for "a rising of the people," preaching that he "hoped before long to see some ditches thrown down, and it would never be merry till some of the gentlemen were knocked down," for "there be lusty fellowes abroade . . . and wee shall have a meryer world."[1] Lyly's 1592 pageant had depicted shepherds crowning "Kings and Queens to make mirth" at their September sheepshearing, and it was festive culture that gave the rebels a web of contacts and a politics of Cockaigne, when they heard how "The poore did once Rise in Spaine and Cutt down the gent[lemen] and sithens that tyme they have lyved merily."[2] The nucleus of the rising consisted of servants, who were reputed to be "kept so like doggs as they would be ready to Cutt their masters' Throates," and its targets were houses of enclosing gentry such as Elizabeth's favorite, Sir Henry Lee of Woodstock. Steer planned a people's progress eastward to Rycote, where arms would be seized for a march on London, in expectation that "when the prentices heare that wee bee upp, they will Come and Joine with us."[3] Sacked in 1549, Rycote had a history of depopulation and imparkment, its owners, according to the Imperial ambassador, being "loathed by the people." To storm it, the rebels would assemble in the woods on Enslow Hill, an ancient "Speech Hill" and the forest camp of the insurgents who had been "hanged like dogs" a generation earlier. The date fixed for the rising was November 17, Elizabeth's accession day. The "merry world" of popular action would drive out the hard world of the encloser.[4]

In his study of the rising, John Walter describes the establishment's panic as the years of dearth threatened to give rise to an English version of Continental disorders. Burghley's intelligence was that 1596 "wylbe the hardeste yeare for the poore people . . . in anie man's memory"; his agents foresaw a repetition of Kett's rebellion, and Justices of the Peace amassed warnings that "before the yeare went aboute ther wold be . . . Cuttynge of throatts" as "Necessity hath no law." The government responded by attempting to reactivate feudal obligation. On November 2 a royal proclamation

---

9. Quoted in John Walter, "A 'Rising of the People'? The Oxfordshire Rising of 1596," *Past and Present*, 107 (1985), 90–143, esp. p. 98.
1. p. 100.
2. p. 108.
3. pp. 106–7.
4. For the intended targets of the rising, see pages 112–14.

condemned "rich owners of corn [who] would keep their store from common markets, therby to increase the prices," and commanded "good householders" to reside on their estates "in charitable sort to keep hospitality." At this moment news of a new Spanish Armada raised the stakes incalculably for the regime, which mobilized "the lieutenants of every shire" for "the necessary defense of [the] realm."[5] Though his wife remained in London, Lord Norris returned to Rycote. And it was in this period of the sharpest social conflict of the Elizabethan era that another West Midlander—routinely familiar with the terrain—dramatized agrarian conflict in As You Like It. Ever since Montrose tied its form to early modern family politics, it has been impossible to read this comedy as, in Helen Gardner's phrase, "free of time" or place and transhistorical.[6] Its resemblance to King Lear has long been noticed; but it is within the context of the subsistence crisis of the 1590s that its violent plot and implausibly romantic ending have their material meaning. No Shakespearean text transmits more urgently the imminence of the social breakdown threatened by the conjuncture of famine and enclosure. Though Shakespeare had alluded to the contemporary crisis in A Midsummer Night's Dream, where "The ploughman lost his sweat, and the green corn / Hath rotted ere his youth attain'd a beard" (2.1.94–95), it is in As You Like It that the dire implications of the dearth are brought home immediately to Warwickshire and Stratford.

Idealist critics imagine that "As You Like It derives much of its classical stability and poise from the fact that its plot barely exists,"[7] but the play is powerfully inflected by narratives of popular resistance, while its plot, as Montrose points out, is the brutal story of Elizabethan social transformation. This comedy confounds its own title with a setting of "winter and rough weather" (2.5.8) to frame the harshness of its social climate. "I pray thee Rosalind," pleads Celia in her opening line, "be merry" (1.2.1); but the "holiday humour" (4.1.65–66) of customary culture is disintegrating in As You Like It under the stress of social mobility and competition. Rosalind retorts with a significant metaphor of aristocratic insolvency: "I show more mirth than I am mistress of, and would you yet I were merrier?" (1.2.2–3). The only way she can be "merry," she objects, will be to forget her father's fall from power and the discrepancy between

5. Walter, p. 91; Paul L. Hughes and James F. Larkin, eds., Tudor Royal Proclamations, 3 vols. (New Haven: Yale Univ. Press. 1964–69), Vol. 3, pp. 169–72.
6. Louis Adrian Montrose, "'The Place of a Brother' In As You Like It: Social Process and Comic Form," Shakespeare Quarterly, 32 (1981), 28–54; Helen Gardner, "As You Like It" in John Garrett, ed., More Talking Of Shakespeare (New York: Theatre Arts Books, 1959), pp. 17–32. In Gardner's representative evaluation, As You Like It is "Shakespeare's most Mozartian comedy . . . consistently played over by a delighted intelligence" (p. 18).
7. Anne Barton, "As You Like It and Twelfth Night: Shakespeare's Sense of an Ending," Shakespearian Comedy, Malcolm Bradbury and David Palmer, eds., Stratford-upon-Avon Studies 14 (London: Edward Arnold, 1972), pp. 160–80, esp. p. 162.

inherited status and material success, "the lineaments of Nature" and Fortune's "gifts" (ll. 40–41). Thus the social reality of the fiction is one where, by feudal standards, Fortune's "benefits are mightily misplaced" (ll. 33–34), and Duke Frederick's usurpation typifies a "working-day world" of struggle (1.3.12), as the Midland economy was epitomized in the 1590s by a vicious property feud between Lord Norris and his kinsman, the Earl of Lincoln.[8] "Care not for worke," Bartholomew Steer had exhorted his "good fellows," "for we shall have a meryer world shortly"; and the "merry men" (1.1.115) who sing in the snow of Shakespeare's yuletide agree that the "winter wind / . . . [is] not so unkind / As man's ingratitude," the "bitter sky, / . . . dost not bite so nigh / As benefits forgot" (2.7.174–93). If this is "Merrie England," the "merry note" of these carols is "ragged" from the start (2.5.3, 14), like the "merry note" of the owl that gives *Love's Labor's Lost* its chilling close. Here the proverbial lore that "it was never merry world in England since gentlemen came up" (*2 Henry VI*, 4.2.8–9) is intensified by Elizabethan hunger, enmity, and dispossession:

> Who doth ambition shun,
>   And loves to live i'th'sun,
> Seeking the food he eats,
>   And pleas'd with what he gets,
> Come hither, come hither, come hither,
>   Here shall he see
>   No enemy,
> But winter and rough weather.
>   (2.5.35–42)

The 1590s were years in which Stratford-upon-Avon endured a series of calamitous fires, plagues, and famines, culminating in the dearth of 1596–97, and the resulting social conflict sears the text of Shakespeare's pastoral comedy. The first words of the play—"My brother . . . keeps me rustically . . . or . . . stays me here . . . unkept; for call you that keeping . . . that differs not from the stalling of an ox? His horses are bred better . . . but I, his brother, gain nothing under him but growth, for the which his animals on his dunghills are as much bound to him as I"—plunge the action into the bitter contradictions of England's agricultural revolution. Orlando must feed his brother's hogs "and eat husks with them" or be "naught" on his land (1.1.35, 37); the servant Adam will be thrown out like an "old dog" (1. 81). The recurring situation of Shakespearean tragedy

---

8. For the bitter and occasionally bloody feud between Lord Norris and the Earl of Lincoln, paralleling the strife between the dukes in *As You Like It*, see Norreys Jephson O'Connor, *Godes Peace and the Queenes: Vicissitudes of a House, 1539–1615* (London: Oxford Univ. Press, 1934).

here has determinants that would be recognizable to Bartholomew Steer, as the language is his own: the breakup of the feudal household and extended family through the capitalization of English farming. Oliver's farm, with its mixed plough-teams and manure, is typical of the intensive cultivation of the Midland Plain, where, as Eric Kerridge notes, seed yield doubled by a ratio of twenty to one after introduction of convertible husbandry during Shakespeare's lifetime. And Oliver's commercial discourse, which will be heard again in the diatribes of the grain-hoarding Coriolanus, is that of an improving landowner of so-called Chalk (as opposed to Cheese) country, where, as David Underdown explains, nucleated villages, a strong squirearchy, and the rhythm of sheep-corn agriculture produced an ordered deference society.[9] "And what wilt thou do?" Oliver jeers when Orlando claims his "poor allottery" of a thousand crowns, "Beg when that is spent? Well sir, get you in. I will not long be troubled with you" (ll. 75–77). Oliver's is the Elizabethan success story of the rise of gentry by engrossing and enclosure at the expense of evicted relatives and tenants. The text locates his power on the cutting-edge of agrarian change as it exposes the danger to the social order he provokes with Orlando's savage reaction: "Wert thou not my brother, I would not take this hand from thy throat till this other had pulled out thy tongue" (ll. 59–61). In 1607 the Midland counties would indeed erupt in enclosure riots: Orlando's rhetoric of violence would be realized then by England's earliest Levellers.

From its beginning, then, when Oliver "bars" Orlando from "the place of a brother" to "feed [him] with his hinds" (ll. 18–19), and Duke Frederick banishes Rosalind from a zone "So near our public court as twenty miles" (1.3.40), As You Like It is a drama of enclosure and exclusion. So when at his disinheritance Orlando exclaims that "the spirit of my father . . . begins to mutiny" (1.1.21–23), his appeal to ancestry ties him to seigneurial tradition, and it is customary culture that provides his pretext for revolt, as it gives Steer and his companions theirs. The opening of As You Like It follows other comedies in presenting popular games as contests between rival groups that might be subject to political manipulation, when the new duke exploits Carnival, like Theseus, to "Stir up the . . . youth to merriments" to legitimate his succession (A Midsummer Night's Dream, 1.1.12), and Oliver fixes the Christmas wrestling to break his brother's neck (1.1.145). Yet "breaking of ribs" in games of ritual violence might have unexpected results (1.2.128). Seasonal sports were a safety valve for rural and artisanal violence, but they

---

9. For Stratford-upon-Avon in the crisis of the 1590s, see J. M. Martin, "A Warwickshire Market Town in Adversity: Stratford-upon-Avon in the Sixteenth and Seventeenth Centuries," *Midland History*, 7 (1982), 26–41; Eric Kerridge, *The Agricultural Revolution* (London: George Allen and Unwin, 1967), pp. 184–95; Underdown, pp. 4–8.

offered cover for the protests of the "lusty guts" whom Stubbes says led the "wildheads of the parish," like the gang who cut down the pales of Windsor Park to hunt the deer in 1607 "under colour of playing at football."[1] So here, the champion Orlando becomes a "gamester . . . of all sorts enchantingly beloved," a local hero too much "in the heart of the world" to be outfaced (1.1.162–67). To complete the agricultural clearance, therefore, Oliver will burn down the upstart's cottage with him in it or drive him off the land. In this way the Shakespearean text is unequivocal about the realities of enclosure: depopulation, arson, and, as Adam says, "butchery" of those who dare resist (2.3.22–27). It knows commercial farming will thrust the destitute into vagrancy and crime. Orlando will become the bogeyman of the Elizabethan rich. He will be a "masterless man," a vagabond or beggar. Or he will become a highwayman, the lawless "wild man" of the woods, perhaps "a pick-purse" or "a horse-stealer" (3.4.21–22):

> What, wouldst thou have me go and beg my food,
> Or with a base and boist'rous sword enforce
> A thievish living on the common road?
> This I must do, or know not what to do. . . .
>   (2.3.31–34)

Interrogating the Oxfordshire rebels, Sir Edward Coke was determined to discover "what gentlemen or others doe you knowe that doe favour the Comunaltie and that wold after you hadd bene upp have taken yor parts?"[2] Gentry leadership had been a backbone of revolts like Kett's and remained crucial in the folklore of resistance. Thus in *The Two Gentlemen of Verona* Shakespeare connected outlawry with social displacement when Valentine, "A man . . . cross'd with adversity," joins a "wild faction" of bandits in the woods. Outlaws, he discovers, "are gentlemen, / Such as the fury of ungovern'd youth / Thrust from the company of aweful men," and have a hierarchy of their own. There is honor among such thieves, who swear to "do no outrages / On silly women or poor passengers" (4.1.12, 37, 42–44, 69–71). These characteristics conform to Eric J. Hobsbawm's portrait of the primitive rebel and define the role of the "noble robber" or "gentleman of the road" as a focus of communal discontent As Hobsbawm writes:

---

1. Quoted in Charles Chenevix Trench, *The Poacher and the Squire: A History of Poaching and Game Preservation in England* (London: Longman, 1967), p. 101; see also C. Holmes, "Drainers and Fenmen: the Problem of Popular Political Consciousness in the Seventeenth Century" in *Order and Disorder in Early Modern England*, Anthony Fletcher and John Stevenson, eds. (Cambridge: Cambridge Univ. Press, 1985), pp. 166–95, esp. p. 171. For popular games as pretexts of protest in Shakespeare's drama, see Richard Wilson, "'Is this a holiday?': Shakespeare Roman Carnival," *ELH*, 54 (1987), 31–44.
2. Walter, p. 127.

His role is that of the champion, the righter of wrongs, the bringer of justice and social equity. His relation with the peasants is that of total solidarity and identity. . . . It may be summarized in nine points. First, the noble robber begins his career of outlawry . . . as the victim of injustice. . . . Second, he "rights wrongs". Third, he "takes from the rich to give to the poor". Fourth, he "never kills unless in self-defence or just revenge". Fifth, if he survives, he returns to his people. . . . Sixth, he is admired, helped and supported by his people. Seventh, he dies invariably and only through treason, since no decent member of the community would help the authorities against him. Eighth, he is . . . invisible and invulnerable. Ninth, he is not the enemy of the king . . . but only of the local gentry, clergy or other oppressors.[3]

This is, of course, an identikit picture of Orlando and explains his combination of rebelliousness and conservatism that ensures he never loses audience appeal. For the social bandit has a vital role to play, according to Hobsbawm, on the frontier between capitalism and peasant society. In modern Sicily, the American West, pre-Revolutionary France, or early modern England, the bandit upholds the collective values of the poor against the "ambition" of the rich. He is one who "ambition shun[s]" (*As You Like It*, 2.5.35), a stalwart of the "merry world" of popular justice in opposition to the official legal institutions; and as he helps the weak, so the weak help him. In *As You Like It*, therefore, Adam gives Orlando his savings, and Orlando protects the old man. Outlaw and peasant stand together for a world where social relations are constant and true. That is how Adam is honored in a tribute that has extra weight if, as theatrical hearsay has it, the part of the aged servant was acted by Shakespeare himself:

> O good old man, how well in thee appears
> The constant service of the antique world,
> When service sweat for duty, not for meed.
> Thou art not for the fashion of these times,
> Where none will sweat but for promotion,
> And having that, do choke their service up
> Even with the having; it is not so with thee.
> (2.3.55–62)

In peasant wisdom "when Adam delved," there was no "gentleman"; but in *As You Like It* such radical levellings are absent. "Why do people love you?" Adam asks Orlando rhetorically (l. 5), and the answer the text supplies is that the primitive rebel is no revolutionary; "service"—the clientage of master and servant—will be what

3. E. J. Hobsbawm, *Bandits* (Harmondsworth: Penguin, 1985), pp. 42–43.

he restores. So with Adam beside him, Orlando becomes, as Celia jokes, uncannily like the protagonist of "an old tale" (1.2.110). In the earlier outlaw play the renegades acclaimed Valentine king with an oath, "By the bare scalp of Robin Hood's fat friar" (*The Two Gentlemen of Verona*, 4.1.36). Now Orlando joins the same criminal fraternity as he follows the route taken by the exiled Duke Senior, who "They say . . . is already in the Forest of Arden, and a many merry men with him; and there they live like the old Robin Hood of England. They say many young gentlemen flock to him every day, and fleet the time carelessly as they did in the golden world" (1.1.114–19). Until the 1900s no one doubted the affinity of *As You Like It* with the Robin Hood legend,[4] but modern critics have effaced this earthy analogue and stressed instead the play's literary debt to the 1590 novel *Rosalynde* by Lyly's euphuistic colleague, Thomas Lodge. In fact the "old tale" mentioned by Celia is undoubtedly the common source: the pseudo-Chaucerian *Tale of Gamelyn*. Yet it is easy to see why this "low" inheritance has been suppressed, since *Gamelyn* is the most bloodcurdling of all the outlaw tales. It tells how Gamelyn is disinherited by his brother John, and how he defeats John's wrestler and kills his servant. With his faithful retainer Adam, Gamelyn flees to the forest and becomes the outlaw king. When John is made sheriff, a third brother pleads for Gamelyn but is clapped in chains. So Gamelyn storms the court, takes the judge's place, and orders that everyone in the courtroom be hanged. As Maurice Keen remarks, the *Tale of Gamelyn* thus presents in stark outline the carnivalesque principle of popular justice that, when law is topsy-turvy, to turn it upside down will be the way to set it right:

> The Iustice and sherreue bothe honged hye,
> To weyuen with the ropes and with the wynde drye;
> And the twelue sisours (sorwe haue that rekke!)
> Alle they were hanged faste by the nekke.[5]

The outlaw ballads of medieval England legitimated peasant protest, but *As You Like It* is one of a cluster of plays written in the late 1590s that exalt the rank of Robin Hood to make him a gentleman or even, as in Anthony Munday's serial *Earl of Huntington* (1598),

---

4. A significant connection between *As You Like It* and the Robin Hood tradition, a commonplace of eighteenth- and nineteenth-century Shakespeare criticism, was last proposed in 1902 by A. H. Thorndike, "The Relation of *As You Like It* to Robin Hood Plays," *Journal of English and Germanic Philology*, 4 (1902), 59–69. A rare modern endorsement comes from W. Gordon Zeeveld, *The Temper of Shakespeare's Thoughts* (New Haven: Yale Univ. Press, 1974), p. 219.
5. *The Tale of Gamelyn*, ed. Walter W. Skeat (Oxford: Clarendon Press, 1894), p. 33, ll. 879–82; Maurice Keen, *The Outlaws of Medieval Legend* (London: Routledge and Kegan Paul, 1961), p. 92.

an aristocrat. These are texts that adapt the legend to the contemporary crisis by dramatizing the divided loyalty of the propertied. So when Orlando crosses from Chalk to Cheese, from an arable to a pastoral economy, he traverses a symbolic boundary that defined the cultural politics of the Shakespearean Midlands, leaving the "static and subservient" society of the feldon region for the "free and mobile" one of the woodlands, and entering the world of popular resistance. For as the Elizabethan topographer William Harrison summarized it, the fundamental demarcation in English life was between arable country, with its orderly parishes, and the dairying and cattle-grazing areas, with their less governable settlements: "Our soil being divided into champaign ground and woodland, the houses of the first lie uniformly builded in every town together, with streets and lanes, whereas in the woodland countries . . . they stand scattered abroad, each one dwelling in the midst of his own occupying."[6] Beyond the pale of church and manor, Underdown confirms, woodland districts were vulnerable to immigration, price fluctuations, dearth, and social instability, and became as a result the strongholds of popular justice. It was wood-pasture communities that most commonly instituted cucking-stools and evolved the most elaborate public shaming rites, since "lacking the resources of informal mediation available in arable villages through squire, parson, and more closely-bonded neighbours, . . . the wood-pasture village enforced its social norms in its own way, by rituals" rather than by litigation.[7]

"Now am I in Arden," shudders Touchstone when he crosses from the feldon, "the more fool I" (2.4.13). If "old custom" gives a role to a clown in the forest (2.1.2), a townsman is less at home among "removed" hamlets (3.2.334) and "ill-inhabited" crofts (3.3.7). With its emphatic "dispraise of the country,"[8] As You Like It engages in the discursive revaluation of woodland that coincided with the sale and disafforestation (the legal alienation of royal forests) of the crown estates. In 1600 disposal of royal woods realized £150,000 for the Irish war, and this alienation was accomplished by propaganda to devalue the forests as unproductive wastes, the abode of "people of very lewd lives and conversations, leaving their own and other counties and taking the place for a shelter as a cloak to their villainies."[9] Thus the Londoner John Norden defamed their inhabitants as "given to little or no kind of labour, living very hardly

6. Joan Thirsk, The Agrarian History of England and Wales, 5 vols. (Cambridge: Cambridge Univ. Press, 1967), Vol. 4, p. 111; William Harrison, The Description of England, ed. Georges Edelen (Ithaca, N.Y.: Cornell Univ. Press. 1968), p. 217.
7. Underdown (cited on p. 315, n. 8), p. 103.
8. See A. Stuart Daley, "The Dispraise of the Country In As You Like It." SQ, 36 (1985), 300–14.
9. Quoted in Christopher Hill, The World Turned Upside Down: Radical Ideas during the English Revolution (New York: Viking, 1975), p. 41.

with oaten bread, sour whey, and goats' milk, dwelling far from any church or chapel, and as ignorant of God or of any civil course of life as the very savages amongst the infidels."[1] The author of *Observations on Land Revenue of the Crown* concluded that while "gentleness . . . is showed . . . to the bribers and stealers of woods and hedge-breakers" who inhabited them, the poor would "dwell in woods . . . like drones devoted to thievery," whereas "the forests, if inclosed, would be more secure for travellers, . . . and more beneficial for the Commonwealth."[2] Thus, far from echoing some Neoplatonist debate about court and country, Duke Senior's prospectus of forest life as "ugly and venomous" but "sweet" in uses chimes with actual projects to extract the "precious jewel" from "these woods" by coal mining or marketing of timber. The duke reads the forest like an improving "book" (2.1.1–17); if, however, the draining of its running brooks and felling of its trees were upheld by James I as "a religious work," this was because forests were now to be textualized as the "nurseries and receptacles of thieves, rogues and beggars."[3] The migration to the woods facilitated their enclosure. Under the treasurership of Robert Cecil and Lionel Cranfield, royal policy would turn from paternalism to exploitation, as the forest was surveyed and parceled out to developers, but not without the inscription of its trees within a rhetoric of property that is unintentionally but metonymically imitated by the squatter Orlando, "with carving 'Rosalind' on their barks" (3.2.351–52).

Shakespeare's drama of feuding dukes predicts that the struggle between the regulated and market economies will be decided in "the skirts of this wild wood" (5.4.158). And, as Victor Skipp's work on subsistence crisis in the Warwickshire Forest of Arden reminds us, the site of outlawry in *As You Like It* is far from fanciful. The comedy transports its displaced characters to a wood-pasture community where population influx had put intense pressure on customary culture. While Shakespeare wrote, Arden was experiencing acute demographic problems, as timber was cleared for mining, industry, and convertible farming, and squatters vied with commoners for land.[4] In Underdown's words, it is no coincidence that the foresters "were generally believed to be addicted to crime and violence—'all rogues',," or that "between 1590 and 1620 the Henley-in-Arden court leet regularly presented people for engaging in violent affrays, in numbers out of all proportion to the population."[5]

1. Norden, quoted in Thirsk, p. 411.
2. Quoted in Hill, p. 41; see also Philip Pettit, *The Royal Forests of Northamptonshire: A Study in their Economy, 1558–1714* (Gateshead: Northumberland Press, 1968), p. 133.
3. James I. quoted in Hill, p. 41.
4. Victor Skipp, *Crisis and Development: An Ecological Case Study of the Forest of Arden, 1570–1674* (Cambridge: Cambridge Univ. Press, 1978).
5. p. 34.

With such an explosive mix of commoners and vagrants—reflected in the *dramatis personae* of the play—the peril to the magistracy in the Malthusian crisis of 1596–97 was precisely the "wild justice" that Shakespeare stages in the saga of the three brothers, the wrestling, and the outlaw fraternity in the woods. For, as Christopher Hill observes, the actual Forest of Arden was a hotbed of sedition that "gave shelter to a shifting population of blacksmiths and nailers as well as to Shakespeare's artless countrymen; to Tinker Fox and his partisans as well as to Coventry Ranters." And if the forest was "the receptacle of all schism and rebellion," this was not because the "scythe-smiths and other iron-labourers" of this "continued village" were ignorant but because among them was "found more knowledge and religion than among the poor enslaved husbandmen" of the feldon.[6] As the Sabbatarian Nicholas Bownd complained in 1606, the Bible may have been "as strange unto them as any news that you can tell them," but they were not ignorant about Robin Hood.[7] And Arden's laureate, Michael Drayton, agreed that the politics of Robin Hood were only too familiar to his countrymen:

> I thinke there is not one,
> But he hath heard some talke of him and little *John*;
> And to the end of time, the Tales shall ne'r be done,
> Of *Scarlock, George a Greene*, and *Much* the Millers sonne,
> Of *Tuck* the merry Frier, which many a Sermon made,
> In praise of *Robin Hood*, his Out-lawes, and their Trade . . .
> Then taking them to rest, his merry men and hee
> Slept many a Summers night under the Greenewood tree.
> From wealthy Abbots chests, and Churles abundant store,
> What often times he tooke, he shar'd amongst the poore. . . .[8]

"Under the greenwood tree, / Who loves to lie with me . . ." (2.5.1–2); the "merry world" of popular politics surfaces in *As You Like It* in fragments of song; but all the elements of the folk scenario are latent in the play. Thus when Drayton describes Maid Marian, "chiefe Lady of the Game," with "Clothes tuck'd to the knee," braids, and "Bow and Quiver arm'd,"[9] he preserves a cultural key to Rosalind's crossdressing as Ganymede. In folk games "the woman's part" was acted by a "shemale," a man or boy in drag, and since "wood-pasture villagers were especially concerned about female

6. pp. 36, 38.
7. Quoted in Keith Thomas, *Religion and the Decline of Magic: Studies in popular beliefs in sixteenth- and seventeenth-century England* (New York: Charles Scribner's Sons, 1971), p. 164.
8. *Poly-Olbion*, XXVI, II. 311–44, in *The Works of Michael Drayton*, ed. J. William Hebel, 5 vols. (Oxford: Basil Blackwell, 1961), Vol. 4, pp. 529–30. This poem was first published in 1622.
9. II. 354–56.

challenges to patriarchal authority,"[1] enclosure riots frequently took the form of masked nighttime attacks by bearded "ladies" or by scolds, like the "troop of lewd women" who obstructed the enclosure of Rockingham Forest by Cecil in 1602.[2] John Walter suggests that the explanation for this gender inversion lies in the opinion of authorities such as William Lambarde that "if a number of women . . . do flocke together for their own cause, this is none assembly punishable by these statutes," a notion professed by female rioters at Maldon in 1629, who insisted that "women were lawlesse, and not subject to the lawes."[3] But the logic, Martin Ingram deduces in his survey of rough music, was that of "stylised representations of anarchy" to reinstate the customary moral economy.[4] As Natalie Zemon Davis records, Maid Marian had queened over May games long before Robin Hood joined her in the fifteenth century, and her rebelliousness would be perpetuated by Marianne in 1789, with bare breasts and worker's cap. Madge Wildfire, who directed tax riots in Edinburgh in 1736; the Whiteboys led by Ghostly Sally, who trampled Irish fences in the 1760s dressed in frocks; General Ludd's Wives, who smashed Lancashire looms in 1812; and Rebecca's Daughters, who destroyed Welsh tollgates in the 1840s: all invoked an Amazonian license harking back as far as 1450, when black-faced and white-gowned men claiming to be under orders of the Queen of the Fairies had raided the deer park of the duke of Buckingham.[5] So when Celia resolves to disguise herself "in poor and mean attire, / And with a kind of umber smirch my face," and Rosalind resolves to wear a "curtle-axe upon my thigh, / A boar-spear in my hand" (1.3.107–8, 113–14), the "black" and the "shemale" act out an impudent challenge to the keepers of the game.

For these class and gender trespassers, determined to "walk not in the trodden paths" (1.3.14), Arden means "liberty, and not . . . banishment" (1. 134). In an essay on Robin Hood, Peter Stallybrass

1. Underdown, p. 101. For the prevalence of charivari in wood-pasture regions, see Underdown's essay, "The Taming of the Scold: the Enforcement of Patriarchal Authority in Early Modern England" in Fletcher and Stevenson (cited on p. 320, n. 1), pp. 116–36.
2. Pettit. p. 172.
3. Lambarde, quoted in Walter's "Grain Riots and popular attitudes to the law: Maldon and the crisis of 1929" in *An Ungovernable People: The English and their law in the seventeenth and eighteenth centuries,*, John Brewer and John Styles, eds. (New Brunswick, N.J.: Rutgers Univ. Press, 1980), pp. 47–84, esp. p. 63.
4. "Ridings, Rough Music and Mocking Rhymes in Early Modern England" in *Popular Culture In Seventeenth-Century England*, Barry Reay, ed. (New York: St. Martin's Press, 1985), pp. 166–97, esp. p. 177.
5. Natalie Zemon Davis, "'Women on Top': Symbolic Sexual Inversion and Political Disorder in Early Modern Europe" in *The Reversible World: Symbolic Inversion in Art and Society*, Barbara A. Babcock, ed. (Ithaca. N.Y.: Cornell Univ. Press, 1978), pp. 147–90; George Rude, *The Crowd in History: A Study of Popular Disturbances in France and England, 1730–1848* (London: Lawrence and Wishart, 1981); David J. V. Jones, *Rebecca's Children: A Study of Rural Society, Crime, and Protest* (Oxford: Clarendon Press, 1989), passim.

has described the ballads as a symbolic system transgressing spatial, bodily, and linguistic bounds and inverting the hierarchies of gender, class, and church, but he also shows how Robin is "an ideological sign intersected by differently orientated social interests." In the age of enclosure, the outlaw legend became the semantic field where the liberties of the forest were symbolically fought out between gamekeeper and poachers.[6] Tudor authority therefore deplored the "playes of Robyn hoode, mayde Marian, freer Tuck, wherin besides the lewdenes and rewbawdry that ther is opened to the people, disobedience also to your officers, is tought," for "the reversible world" of Carnival gave protesters a quasi-legal status, like that of the Derbyshire rebels who in 1497 donned Robin Hood's clothing "and in manere of insurrection wente into the wodes," or the Nottinghamshire rioters of 1502 led by the "felowe, whych had reneued many of Robin Hode's pagentes, which named himself Grenelef." Since both the Pilgrimage of Grace and Kett's rebellion had been instigated at folk plays, Cecil was shrewd to call the Gunpowder Conspirators "Robin Hoods." Spenser likewise correctly detected the festive structure of resistance when he observed that every corner of Ireland contained a "Robin Hood."[7] And in Shakespeare's text it is a mocking game or "rough music" that authorizes the forest trespass and felony of poaching, when "he that killed the deer" has its "horns [set] upon his head," and the hunters chant their horn song of blood brotherhood:

> Take thou no scorn to wear the horn,
> It was a crest ere thou wast born,
>   Thy father's father wore it,
>   And thy father bore it.
> The horn, the horn, the lusty horn,
> Is not a thing to laugh to scorn.
>   (4.2.14–19)

As Justice Shallow states, when he accuses Falstaff of having "beaten my men, killed my deer, and broke open my lodge" (*The Merry Wives of Windsor*, 1.1.103–4), "blacking" or poaching in disguise was "a Star Chamber matter" (ll. 1–2), which the Privy Council would treat as "a riot" (l. 33) since an Act of 1485 had made

6. Peter Stallybrass, "'Drunk with the Cup of Liberty': Robin Hood, the carnivalesque, and the rhetoric of violence in early modern England" in *The Violence of Representation: Literature and the History of Violence*, Nancy Armstrong and Leonard Tennenhouse, eds. (London: Routledge, 1989), pp. 45–76.

7. R. B. Dobson and J. Taylor, *Rymes of Robin Hood: An Introduction to the English Outlaw* (London: Heinemann, 1989), p. 4; Richard Axton, "Folk play in Tudor interludes" in *English Drama: Farms and Development*, Marie Axton and Raymond Williams, eds. (Cambridge: Cambridge Univ. Press, 1977), pp. 1–23, esp. p. 3; Edmund Spenser, *A View of the Present State of Ireland*, ed. W. L. Renwick (Oxford: Clarendon Press, 1970), p. 144.

"tumultuous hunting at night by persons with painted faces or otherwise disguised" an offense against the royal prerogative. It did not require a run-in with Sir Thomas Lucy over deer-stealing in Charlecote Park for Shakespeare to know that "What were perquisites . . . for one group . . . were theft, embezzlement or crime for another," nor that in the Robin Hood tradition "the question of 'Who wins the game?' becomes an argument over 'Who owns the game?'.[8] For, as E. P. Thompson observes of these so-called "Blacks," poaching was never simply a casual country pastime but was "retributive and concerned less with venison as such than with deer as symbols of an authority which threatened their economy, their crops and their customary agrarian rights."[9] Blacking was part of the symbolic repertoire of popular politics in early modern England, so when poachers "entered into the park and enclosed ground of . . . Sir Edward Grivelle [Greville]," Stratford's lord of the manor, and "took sundry bucks [and] broke their necks," James I viewed it as a "contemptuous and exceeding . . . presumptuous" offense against himself.[1] According to Thompson, "There was an ancient enmity between democracy and these gentle creatures," and it should be no surprise that the outbreak of the Civil War was marked by the slaughter of the herd in Windsor Park by squatters who "defied the keepers with pike and musket, refusing to be expelled," while in 1642–43 huge crowds chased and killed the deer in Waltham Forest.[2] Jaques had addressed the herd as "fat and greasy citizens" (2.1.55). He rightly saw that "To fright the animals and to kill them up / In their assign'd and native dwelling-place" (ll. 61–62) would be construed by the law as an act of symbolic treason against "The body of country, city, court" itself (l. 59).

As You Like It introduces all the Sherwood outlaws (even Tuck is identifiable as Martext), but it is in this stag-night horn dance, when the hunted become hunters, that the play edges closest to those rites of misrule that, as Robert Weimann shows, linked Tudor village green with metropolitan stage. "'Tis no matter how it be in tune, so it make noise enough" (4.2.8–9). Climaxing with this riotous assembly in the woods, the action follows the program of a "riding" or "skimmington": a caterwauling ritual of the Cheese country, whereby customary society "knew by shame," according to Marvell,

8. Barry Reay, "Popular Culture in Early Modern England" in Reay, pp. 1–31, esp. p. 17; Roberta Kevelson, *Inlaws/Outlaws, A Semiotics of Systemic Interaction: "Robin Hood" and the "King's Law"*, Studies in Semiotics 9 (Bloomington: Indiana Univ. Press, 1977), p. 67. For the myth of Shakespeare as deerslayer, see S. Schoenbaum, *William Shakespeare: A Documentary Life* (Oxford: Oxford Univ. Press, 1975), pp. 78–87.
9. E. P. Thompson, *Whigs and Hunters: The Origin of the Black Act* (Harmondsworth: Penguin, 1977), p. 64.
1. Quoted in Trench (cited on p. 320, n. 1), p. 100.
2. Trench, p. 106; Thompson, pp. 55–56.

"Better than law, domestic crimes to tame."[3] Urged on by rebellious women chanting "the right butter-women's rank to market" (3.2.95–96), the "very false gallop" (1. 111) of their rhyme, sung "out of tune" (l. 244) to mock husbands with "horns" (4.1.56), the characters in the play form the classic "riding" that historians describe: a procession led by a man wearing horns, with a shemale acting as the "woman on top," and some deviant ritually beaten with a skimming ladle. This was "A punishment invented first to awe / Masculine wives transgressing Nature's law";[4] or to shame an "old cuckoldly ram" married "out of all reasonable match" (3.2.80–81). But, as Touchstone notices, a skimmington could be targeted as much against a "walled" enclosure as against "the forehead of a married man" (3.3.52, 53–54) in the Shakespearean period, and the estate of a "man [who] knows no end of his goods" (ll. 46–47) could be as much the mock of "horn-beasts" as a "man [who] has good horns and knows no end of them" (ll. 44, 46–48). "As horns are odious, they are necessary" (l. 45): customary justice, as the play stages it, was turning from sexual to economic uses. Thus the "Robin Hoods" who defended common rights in the Forest of Dean in 1612 typified those in wood pasture who turned rough music against enclosure at this time, bequeathing a symbolic action to the popular movements of the Civil War. For, as Underdown notes, the conjuncture of a riot, a forest community, the leadership of "Lady Skimmington," and a seasonal game marks the point at which custom exploded into political action in the early seventeenth century.[5] Oliver is "shame[d]" out of his "unnatural" life (4.3.96, 125), but his Jacobean counterparts would find their fences burned.

Poaching, damaging trees, sending letters in fictitious names, blacking, and crossdressing: As You like It parades all the felonies associated with forest rioters. Performed in the season of the silencing of satire in 1599 (as Latham notes at 1.2.83), this is a text apprehensive that it is playing symbolically with fire: that, as the banished satirist Jaques realizes, the "motley coat" of Carnival has "as large a charter as the wind" to license protest or revolt (2.7.42,48). Yet if the play includes the "broken music" of a festive rout (1.2.131), it does so to defuse this radical potential, since contrary to Jaques's professional plan to "tax" the rich with mockery (2.7.70–87), the

3. Robert Weimann, *Shakespeare and the Popular Tradition in the Theater: Studies in the Social Dimension of Dramatic Form and Function* (Baltimore: Johns Hopkins Univ. Press, 1978), pp. 25–30; "The Last Instructions to a Painter," ll. 387–88 in *Andrew Marvell: The Complete Poems*, ed. Elizabeth Story Donno (Harmondsworth: Penguin, 1976), p. 167.
4. Marvell, ll. 377–78; Underdown (cited on p. 315, n. 8), pp. 100–11; Buchanan Sharp, *In Contempt of All Authority: Rural Artisans and Riot in the West of England, 1586–1660* (Berkeley: Univ. of California Press, 1980), p. 104.
5. Underdown, pp. 106–45; for the social and economic background to skimmingtons, see Ingram (cited on p. 324, n. 4), pp. 166–97.

textual refrain is expressly that offenders should "Take no scorn." Substituting the patriarchy of "Thy father's father" for rebellion, its project seems instead to incorporate the energies of charivari in a reconstituted order, which it does from the moment Orlando bursts upon the exiled duke "with sword drawn" (1. 88 s.d.) demanding food. This is a confrontation that restages the action of the early modern food riot, with its limited aim of reasserting the normative economy, but the fact that it is perversely directed at the figurehead of the old order highlights the self-destructiveness of rural insurrection. For the duke shares Orlando's nostalgia for "better days," when paupers "have with holy bell been knoll'd to church, / And sat at good men's feasts" (ll. 120–22), even though he responds with the question posed by the 1597 Poor Law: is this beggar one of the "deserving poor" or some "sturdy rogue"? Orlando replies that he is "inland bred" and civil but driven by "distress" to violence:

> You touch'd my vein at first: the thorny point
> Of bare distress hath ta'en from me the show
> Of smooth civility. Yet am I inland bred,
> And know some nurture. But forbear, I say,
> He dies that touches any of this fruit,
> Till I and my affairs are answered.
>
> (2.7.95–100)

Orlando's claim to be "inland bred," glossed by editors to mean that he is "not rustic,"[6] in fact affiliates him with the Midland rioters and seems to vindicate their cause. For it had been Julius Caesar, with his "thrasonical brag of I came, saw, and overcame" (5.2.30), who reported that "the Inlanders or Midland inhabitants of this Island" had "their beginning in the soil where they inhabited," thereby perpetuating, as Sir Thomas Browne complained, the "vulgar error" that Midlanders were the seed of the Autochthon.[7] Shakespeare's usage reminds us, then, that Arden puns with Eden in popular lore and that "an inland man" is civilized (3.2.337) because his country is the heart of the English state, where Adam delved long before courtiers came on progress, and where now as "an old poor man" he awaits relief (2.7.129). Moreover, as the OED records, to be "inland bred" in the Shakespearean era was to stand in complex mutual dependence with the outlanders, whose ports were "a wall sufficient to defend / Our inland" (Henry V, 1.2.141–42), but whose imposts had

6. See, for example, the Arden edition, p. 54, where *inland* is contrasted with "outlandish" but without commentary on the precise Elizabethan connotation and in defiance of the OED, which cites Shakespeare's line under definition 2, "Interior of the country, parts remote from sea or frontiers."

7. *Gallic Wars,* Bk. V, 12. Quoted from the Loeb edition, trans. H. J. Edwards (London: Heinemann, 1917): *Sir Thomas Browne's Pseudodexia Epidemica*, 2 vols. (Oxford: Clarendon Press, 1981). Vol. 1, p. 441.

often to be weighed against the Midlanders' protests that "They cannot spare the corne of the innelonde growthe to be caryed out, for feare of a famyne in thiese partyes."[8] It was precisely because of its unique inland status that Warwickshire would prove the "most retarded" of all counties in payment of shipmoney.[9] And Orlando's localist assertion, in boasting of his roots, is likewise an appeal to the Tudor moral economy, which regulated the transportation of food through inland counties to London and the coast, but which broke down calamitously after 1595, when, as Buchanan Sharp shows, communities on shipment routes in the Midlands and the West were starved in order to supply the city and the European market.[1] Nothing relates *As You Like It* to Steer's rising more explicitly than Orlando's inland breeding, nor confronts the court more starkly with the dearth of food. Jaques, the London cynic, scoffs that "I have eat none yet," but the Midlander seems unanswerable when he retorts, "Nor shalt not till necessity be served" (ll. 89–90).

"What can rich men do if poor men rise together?" asked rioters of the 1590s, and *As You Like It* has no reply. Instead it voices the ambivalence of propertied opinion about the unregulated market, and the governmental resolve that, as Duke Senior assures Orlando when he gasps he "almost die[s] for food": "Your gentleness shall force, / More than your force move us to gentleness" (ll. 102–4). In *A Midsummer Night's Dream* of 1595, the "hungry lion" of revolt had roared and run away, being acted by the terrified city worker Snug. But by the time of the later comedy and in the stricken country, "the thorny point / Of bare distress" (2.7.95–96) is far more sharp; so "Now the hungry lion roars" in earnest, even as the contemporary Irish "wolf behowls the moon" (*Dream*, 5.1.371–72; *As You Like It*, 5.2.110). With an average holding of fifteen sheep, a dozen cows, and a few goats, "to get your living by the copulation of cattle" (3.2.77–78), in competition with the deer, was a hazardous business in Arden, as Skipp's statistics prove. Yet as the impoverished shepherd Corin testifies, the causes of distress lie in the market economy that is encroaching the forest. Aubrey dated the decay of manorial institutions in the woodlands from 1500, and Corin confirms that in Shakespeare country the manorial economy has succumbed to the engrosser, since "I am shepherd to another man," he bemoans, "And do not shear the fleeces that I graze" (2.4.76–77). In *Poly-Olbion* of 1612, Drayton's Arden likewise laments that her "overthrowe" has been caused by engrossing and enclosure: "For, when the world found out the fitnesse of my soyle, / The gripple wretch began

---

8. *OED*, quoting from the *State Papers of Henry VIII*, 1546, XI, 75.
9. Ann Hughes, *Politics, Society and Civil War in Warwickshire, 1620–60* (Cambridge: Cambridge Univ. Press, 1987), p. 107.
1. pp. 18–21.

immediatly to spoyle / My tall and goodly woods, and did my grounds
inclose: / By which, in little time my bounds I came to lose." Over-
populated with cottages that "dislodg'd the Hart" and overgrazed by
"the sundry kinds of beasts . . . / That men for profit breed," Drayton's Arden is the ravaged site of Britain's economic transformation:
"Her people wexing still, and wanting where to build."[2] Profit, evidently, is the new law of the forest, as Corin grieves:

> My master is of churlish disposition,
> And little recks to find the way to heaven
> By doing deeds of hospitality.
> Besides, his cote, his flocks, and bounds of feed
> Are now on sale, and at our sheepcote now
> By reason of his absence there is nothing
> That you will feed on.
>
> (2.4.78–84)

"Assuredly the thing is to be sold" (l. 94): the Shakespearean text
knows the fate of sylvan society will hang on London finance, as in
actual Midland forests it was the city's projectors and monopolists
who profited from improvement and enclosure. So the forest pasture in Arden is bought up by Celia with "gold right suddenly" (ll.
89–98). Like Queen Elizabeth and Lady Norris, Rosalind and Celia
will play at rustics and solve the agrarian crisis through *noblesse
oblige*, assuring the pauperized shepherd "we will mend thy wages"
(l. 92). So too Orlando is disarmed by the duke to "sit down and
feed . . . in gentleness" at an old-style "good man's feast" (2.7.105,
115, 124). In the paternalist spirit of King James's *Declaration of
Sports*, it is the nobility who must ameliorate the market through
rites of commensality. Rosalind and Celia always intended to "be
merry" and "devise sports" to "mock the good hussif Fortune from
her wheel, that her gifts may henceforth be bestowed equally"; and
spinning Fortune's wheel through counterrevolution, *As You Like It*
foretells the Stuart campaign to reunify agrarian society under aristocratic leadership by "making sport" with economic change (1.2.22,
23, 30–32). In the aftermath of the 1607 rising, the landowners of
the West Midlands would indeed recognize in country sports "a
sign / Of harmlesse mirth and honest neighbourhood, / Where all
the Parish did in one combine / To mount the rod of peace, and none
withstood." Reerecting the maypoles of "Merry England" to "feaste
in our Defense,"[3] nobility and gentry "came [from] 60 miles" around,
Anthony a Wood recorded, to Robert Dover's Cotswold games.

---

2. Victor Skipp, "Economic and Social Change in the Forest of Arden, 1530–1649," *Agricultural History Review,* 18 (1970), 84–111; Drayton, *Poly-Olbion*, XIII, ll. 20–38 (cited
on p. 325, n. 8). Vol. 4, pp. 275–76.
3. Quoted in Peter Stallybrass, "'Wee feaste in our Defense': Patrician Carnival in Early
Modern England and Robert Herrick's *Hesperides,*" *English Literary Renaissance*, 16
(1986), 234–52, esp. pp. 237, 239.

Where rioters had threatened enclosers' mansions, the "harmless merriment" of wrestling and racing taught the "Glad countrey," Ben Jonson enthused, to "advance true love and neighbourhood, / And doe both Church and Common-wealth the good."[4] Thus on the greensward of Dover's Hill, the Robin Hood tradition was sentimentalized during the seventeenth century into the innocuous athletics of Jonson's own pastoral The Sad Shepherd.[5]

"Who durst assemble such a troope as hee," Nicholas Wallington asked in a 1636 encomium to Robert Dover, "But might of insurrection charged bee?"[6] It was a question that laid bare the hegemonic work of Shakespearean culture, by that date virtually complete, in neutralizing the rites of collective action, grafting the old rural games (in the words of Dover's editor) "to classical mythology and Renaissance culture, whilst linking them with the throne and the King's Protestant Church."[7] In As You Like It this work is effected with the incorporation of Orlando's strength inside the enclosure, established within the licensed "purlieus of this forest," of Rosalind's "sheep-cote fenc'd about with olive-trees" (4.3.76–77). For far from valorizing the archaic greenwood as a locale of freedom and asylum, as critics suppose, the play breaks up "the skirts of this wild wood" (5.4.158) to reinscribe it within private ownership. Its action is a discursive rehearsal of the enclosure legislation, invoking the "royal disposition" of the wilderness (4.3.117) only to authorize its destruction. Rosalind's fence of olive trees circumscribing antique oaks is a fitting symbol for Crown policy, since it is within its bounds that deforestation and depopulation will occur. Pastoral discourse, which promises the Arden woodlanders "measure heap'd in joy" and "rustic revelry" (5.4.176, 178), will conceal the real revolution in the forest economy, which was invariably towards cereal production. If "improvers continued to be more worried about the numbers of masterless men . . . in sylvan regions," and "wished to impose gentry control on the more egalitarian societies that these economics spawned," this was because of implacable resistance to their schemes to clear pastoral areas for grain.[8] Subsequent improvers would realize that dairying could support a larger population, but in the Shakespearean era the olive branches of Lord Norris and the sheepmasters, intended to pacify the wood-pasture community, served merely to secure the commoners' consent to the extinction of their rights and the intrusion of Oliver's capital and corn.

4. Quoted in Christopher Whitfield, Robert Dover and the Cotswold Games: Annalia Dubrensia (Evesham: Journal Press, 1962), pp. 18, 134.
5. Dennis Brailsford, Sport and Society: Elizabeth to Anne (London: Routledge and Kegan Paul, 1969), pp. 103–16.
6. Quoted in Whitfield, p. 150.
7. Whitfield, p. 2.
8. Richard Manning. Village Revolts: Social Protest and Popular Disturbances in England, 1509–1640 (Cambridge: Clarendon Press, 1988), p. 15.

"Then is there mirth in heaven, / When earthly things made even / Atone together" (5.4.107–9): the marriage of the princess Rosalind to the yeoman Orlando at a classicized fete like Robert Dover's Cotswold games affirms the alliance of England's nobility and gentry and their appropriation of popular laughter. As Orlando jokes, "Clubs cannot part" such lovers, who unite against insurgency (5.2.40). Contrary to Bakhtin's idealization of Carnival, *As You Like It* thus reveals how discourses work through social change and are never indeterminate. In fact, the discursive function of Shakespearean comedy will be to depoliticize Carnival, just as "in every society discourse is controlled and redistributed," as Foucault observes, "to avert its dangers and evade its formidable materiality."[9] Orlando's strength was "overthrown," therefore, the instant he met Rosalind and sensed that "something weaker" mastered him (1.2.249–50). Throughout the play his violence is subdued by his master-mistress, as the sylvan discourse of Robin Hood is occluded by Lodge's pastoral and the real Arden is assimilated to the idealized Ardennes. The last song takes us into a landscape full of crops, yet so free of fences the poor can roam "between the acres of the rye" and "o'er the green corn-field" (5.3.20, 16), though never to graze them nor "To glean the broken ears after the man / That the main harvest reaps" (3.5.102–3). Despite Celia's vow to waste her time "By doing deeds of hospitality" (2.4.80), the text foretells the development of Arden, which in Leland's time had "plentifull of gres, but no great plenty of corn," yet by 1652 had "grown as gallant a corn country as any in England."[1] Arden will be improved from wood pasture to cereal farmland of the kind described by Iris in *The Tempest*, "Of wheat, rye, barley, fetches, oats, and pease" (4.1.61). This is the arable landscape of the eighteenth century, where the "pretty country-folks" will sport "In spring-time, the only pretty ring-time" (*As You Like It*, 5.3.22–23) as picturesquely as Dover's lads. Between the sowing and the harvest, these fields are their playground because English culture will bridle insurrection, as out of Orlando's strength comes sweetness when he kills the lioness menacing his brother. There is real blood on his napkin, because this lion fights more ferociously than Snug, but Orlando saves the engrosser, reduced to beggary himself, from the predatory jungle. Thus the "middling sort" strangle protest in *As You Like It* and desert the dispossessed. The forester William, deprived of Audrey at the end, is therefore told by Touchstone

9. Michel Foucault, "The Order of Discourse" in *Untying the Text*, trans. I. McLeod (London: Routledge, 1981), p. 52.
1. Quoted in J. A. Yelling, *Common Field and Enclosure in England, 1450–1850* (London: Macmillan, 1977), pp. 175, 186–90; see also Skipp, *Crisis and Development* (cited on p. 324, n. 4), p. 91.

to "Tremble and depart." William's final words to the new land-owner are historically ironic: "God rest you merry, sir" (5.1.56–58).

" 'Twas never merry world / Since lowly feigning was call'd com-pliment" (*Twelfth Night*, 3.1.98–99): Shakespearean comedy moves from the merry world of "service" to a world of servility and intimi-dation. Though burial registers record the gravity of the famine—worst in Arden, where the mortality rate is shadowed in the obscure demise of Adam—the Midland oligarchy emerged from the crisis so secure in its control of popular culture that it would ride out the 1607 rising. Thus the Old Shepherd of *The Winter's Tale*, "that from very nothing . . . is grown into an unspeakable estate" (4.2.38–40), legitimates his rise by "welcom[ing] all" to his sheep-shearing (4.4.57), just as Robert Dover's "merriment" was devised to advertise how well "Lords, knights, swains, shepherds, churls agree." Mean-while on Enslow Hill, Bartholomew Steer waited for his merry world to rise, hopeful of support from Warwickshire, where "very many have enclosed in every place,"[2] but on the night, just ten men came. Though Queen Elizabeth was never persuaded to revisit, Rycote was preserved. Without the lead of gentry, none dared risk their necks to attack it: as historians deduce, the withdrawal of the prop-ertied from collective action, figured in *As You Like It*, spelled the effective end of agrarian revolt in England.[3] Touchstone had warned William "I [will] kill thee, make thee away, translate thy life into death, thy liberty into bondage" (5.1.51–53), and his jesting was half earnest. For while Steer was hanged at Enslow Hill and Arden foresters starved, the "Rich men" of the Midlands, as Thomas Fuller lamented, were busy jostling "the poor people out of their commons." By the early seventeenth century, enclosers had "turn'd so much of woodland into tillage" in Arden, it was noted, "that they produce[d] corn to furnish other counties," while "the ironworks destroyed such prodigious quantities of wood, that they quickly laid the country open, and by degrees made room for the plough." A magnate such as Fulke Greville had "thrown to the ground the better oaks for tim-bering," the foresters protested, "by what right" was not known.[4] Had he deigned to reply, Greville would doubtless have answered as Touchstone does to William, that his entitlement was posses-sion, since, according to the English law of property, "To have is to have" (5.1.39).

2. For Warwickshire, see Walter, p. 125.

3. p. 125.

4. Thomas Fuller quoted in Underdown (cited on p. 315, n. 8), p. 19; Edmund Gibson, *Camden's Britannia, Newly Translated into English: with large Additions and Improve-ments* (London: 1695), p. 510; Gibson also quoted in Skipp, "Economic and Social Change . . ." (cited on p. 332, n. 2), pp. 91, 94. For local resistance to Fulke Greville's activities in Arden, see Skipp, p. 95.

On May Day in 1515, according to Edward Hall, Henry VIII and his court had ridden to Shooter's Hill, the ancient woodland outside London and a site for popular games. There they were "ambushed" by two hundred "yeoman, clothed all in green with bows and arrows," whose leader, Robin Hood,

> came to the king, desiring him to see his men shoot. Then he whistled and the archers shot at once, so that the noise was strange and great. . . . Then Robin Hood desired the king and queen to come into the greenwood and see how the outlaws lived. The king demanded of the ladies if they durst adventure to go into the wood with so many outlaws. The queen said she was content. Then horns blew till they came to the wood. . . . The king and queen sat down and were served venison by Robin Hood and his men, to their great content.

Soon after, Hall adds, Henry "took his progress Westwards and heard complaints of his poor commonality, and ever as he rode he hunted and liberally departed with venison."[5] This episode from the beginning of the early modern era, with its cooption of violence and deflection of privation into pastoral, can stand as a paradigm of the state's appropriation of English Carnival. Likewise, at Christmas 1603, *As You Like It* was performed for James I at Wilton House after a day's hunting in Gillingham Forest.[6] In 1625 this royal forest would be the first sold for disafforestation, when its enclosure by a Scottish courtier, Sir James Fullerton, ignited the Western Rising. Though William might restage the game of Robin Hood—as the ubiquitous "Williams *alias* Lady Skimmington" led the Western riots—the king would learn from the comedy how to "share the good of [his] returned fortune" with investors "According to the measure of their states" (5.4.173–74), by reviving forest law for profit.[7] Thus Shakespearean comedy made its contribution to the process detailed by John Walter and Keith Wrightson, whereby a society incapable of eliminating dearth preserved itself by "interpreting and resisting" the disorder that dearth caused.[8] And if the shemale of Shakespeare's Epilogue shocked the Jacobean courtiers by threatening to "kiss as many of you as [have] beards" (5.4.215–16), their descendants would preempt such subversiveness with the infamous Black Act, making it a capital offense for "any persons to appear in any forest, chase, park or grounds enclosed with their faces blacked or being otherwise disguised."[9]

5. *Hall's Chronicle* (1547; London: Printed for J. Johnson, 1809), p. 582.
6. Schoenbaum (cited on p. 328, n. 8), p. 126.
7. Sharp (cited on p. 329, n. 4), pp. 102–4.
8. "Dearth and the Social Order in Early Modern England," *Past and Present*, 71 (1976), 22–42, esp. p. 42.
9. Sharp, pp. 86–89, 100–104; Thompson (cited on p. 328, n. 9), p. 271.

JEAN E. HOWARD

Crossdressing, the Theatre, and Gender Struggle in Early Modern England[†]

How many people crossdressed in Renaissance England? There is probably no way empirically to answer such a question. Given Biblical prohibitions against the practice and their frequent repetition from the pulpit and in the prescriptive literature of the period, one would guess that the number of people who dared walk the streets of London in the clothes of the other sex was limited. Nonetheless, there *are* records of women, in particular, who did so, and who were punished for their audacity; and from at least 1580 to 1620 preachers and polemicists kept up a steady attack on the practice. I am going to argue that the polemics signal a sex-gender system under pressure and that crossdressing, as fact and as idea, threatened a normative social order based upon strict principles of hierarchy and subordination, of which women's subordination to man was a chief instance, trumpeted from pulpit, instantiated in law, and acted upon by monarch and commoner alike.[1] I will also argue, however, that the subversive or transgressive potential of this practice could be and was recuperated in a number of ways. As with any social practice, its meaning varied with the circumstances of its occurrence, with the particulars of the institutional or cultural sites of its enactment, and with the class position of the transgressor. As part of a stage action, for example, the ideological import of crossdressing was mediated by all the conventions of dramatic narrative and Renaissance dramatic production. It cannot simply be conflated with crossdressing on the London streets or as part of a disciplining ritual such as a charivari or skimington. In what follows I want to pay attention to the *differences* among various manifestations of crossdressing in Renaissance culture but at the same time to suggest the ways they form an interlocking grid through which we can read aspects of class and gender struggle in the period, struggles in which the theatre—as I hope to show—played a highly contradictory role.

Inevitably, such readings of the past as I am about to undertake are motivated by present concerns and involve taking a position

† From Jean E. Howard, "Crossdressing, the Theatre, and Gender Struggle in Early Modern England," *Shakespeare Quarterly* 39.4 (1988): 418–40. © 1988 Folger Shakespeare Library. Reprinted with permission of The Johns Hopkins University Press.

1. For the idea of the sex-gender system, see Gayle Rubin's important essay "The Traffic in Women: Notes on the 'Political Economy' of Sex," in *Toward an Anthropology of Women*, ed. Rayna R. Reiter (New York: Monthly Review Press, 1975), pp. 157–210.

within present critical debates.[2] Recently, discussions of crossdressing on the Renaissance stage have become an important site for talking about the Renaissance sex-gender system in general and about the possibilities of transgressing or subverting that system.[3] Several questions are at issue. First, was crossdressing by male actors merely an unremarkable convention within Renaissance dramatic practice; was it a scandal, a source of homoerotic attraction, or an inevitable extension of a sex-gender system in which there was only one sex and that one sex male? Second, were women who crossdressed—in life or in dramatic fables—successfully challenging patriarchal domination, or were they serving its ends? In this paper I will enter these debates in part by arguing against those readings of the Renaissance sex-gender system that erase signs of gender struggle, in part by arguing that one should not concede in advance the power of patri-

2. As Louis Montrose argues, speaking of new forms of historical inquiry: "Integral to this new project of historical criticism is . . . a recognition of the agency of criticism in constructing and delimiting the subject of study, and of the historical positioning of the critic vis-à-vis that subject" ("Renaissance Literary Studies and the Subject of History," *English Literary Renaissance*, 16 [1986], 5–12, esp. p. 7). Clearly, my investments in contemporary feminism have shaped the focus of the present essay, which is an attempt to contribute to the collective project of making intelligible a gender system in many ways quite different from our own and yet one in large measure having the similar political effect of women's subordination and exploitation.
3. In regard to boys playing women's roles, cf. Laura Levine ("Men in Women's Clothing: Anti-theatricality and Effeminization from 1579 to 1642," *Criticism*, 28 [1986], 121–43), who argues that this practice brought to the surface deepseated fears that the self was not stable and fixed but unstable and monstrous and infinitely malleable unless strictly controlled. Behind the repeated protestations that the boy actors will be made effeminate by wearing women's clothing, she argues, lies the fear they will be found to have no essential being. By contrast, Stephen Greenblatt argues that an all-male acting troupe was the natural and unremarkable product of a culture whose conception of gender was "teleologically male" ("Fiction and Friction," in *Shakespearean Negotiations* [Berkeley: Univ. of California Press, 1988], pp. 66–93, esp. p. 88). Lisa Jardine ("'As boys and women are for the most part cattle of this colour': Female Roles and Elizabethan Eroticism," *Still Harping on Daughters: Women and Drama in the Age of Shakespeare* [Totowa, N.J.: Barnes and Noble Books, 1983], pp. 9–36) sees the Renaissance public theatre as in large measure designed for the gratification of male spectators and argues that in many cases it was homoerotic passion that the boy actors aroused in their male audience. Kathleen McLuskie ("The Act, the Role, and the Actor: Boy Actresses on the Elizabethan Stage," *New Theatre Quarterly*, 3 [1987], 120–30) in effect critiques this position by arguing that it collapses theatrical practice with real life and that in performance the sex of the actor is irrelevant and, on the Renaissance stage, conventional. A similar divergence of opinion characterizes scholarship on the presence of crossdressing in dramatic works of the period. Juliet Dusinberre, for example, argues that plays of crossdressing were sites where the freedom of women to play with gender identity was explored (*Shakespeare and the Nature of Women* [New York: Macmillan, 1975], pp. 231–71), while Clara Claiborne Park suggests that women who crossdress in these scripts doff their disguises willingly, providing the—to men—gratifying spectacle of spunky women who voluntarily tame themselves to suit male expectations ("As We Like It: How a Girl Can Be Smart and Still Popular," *The Woman's Part: Feminist Criticism of Shakespeare* [Urbana: Univ. of Illinois Press, 1980], pp. 100–16). Phyllis Rackin and Catherine Belsey both argue that at least in some instances crossdressing on the stage opens up the possibility of revealing the plurality and fluidity and cultural-constructedness of gender, thus toppling the essentialist binarism that was used to hold women in an inferior place (Rackin, "Androgyny, Mimesis, and the Marriage of the Boy Heroine on the English Renaissance Stage," *PMLA*, 102 [1987], 29–41, and Belsey, "Disrupting Sexual Difference: Meaning and Gender in the Comedies," *Alternative Shakespeares*, ed. John Drakakis [London: Methuen, 1985], pp. 166–90).

archal structures to contain or recuperate threats to their authority. Positioning myself within materialist feminism, I suggest that contradictions within the social formation enabled opposition to and modification of certain forms of patriarchal domination, and that struggle, resistance, and subversive masquerade are terms as important as recuperation and containment in analyzing Renaissance gender relations and female crossdressing in particular.[4]

It is clear that crossdressing in the Elizabethan and Jacobean periods caused controversy. At the far end of the era I am going to examine—that is, around 1620—James I ordered the preachers of London to inveigh from the pulpit against the practice of women dressing mannishly in the streets of London. That year also saw the publication of the two polemical tracts *Hic Mulier* and *Haec-Vir*, which respectively attack and defend crossdressing and which suggest that it had become a practice taken up with special enthusiasm by the fashion-mongering wives of the City who are accused of transgressing both class and gender boundaries.[5] By wearing ever more ornate clothing, they encroached on the privileges of aristocratic women; by wearing men's clothing they encroached on the privileges of the advantaged sex. Much earlier, during the reign of Elizabeth, the antitheatrical tracts had attacked crossdressing by boy actors, and often these attacks spilled over, as I will discuss, into attacks on women who dressed mannishly. Social commentators such as William Harrison in his *The Description of England* regularly railed against the decline of modesty and decorum in dress, and Harrison ends his diatribe against improperly dressed women by remarking that "I have met with some of these trulls in London so disguised that it hath passed my skill to discern whether they were men or women."[6] The word "trull" is important. The *OED* defines "trull" as "a low prostitute, or concubine; a drab, strumpet, trollop." Harrison's diction links the mannish woman with prostitution, and

---

4. Materialist or socialist feminism, better known in Britain than in the United States, assumes that gender differences are culturally constructed and historically specific, rather than innate, and that the hierarchical gender systems based on these differences can therefore be changed. Materialist feminists also recognize the plural nature of woman, i.e., that factors such as class and race forbid women sharing an easy "sisterhood." This suggests the undesirability of analyzing the gender system in isolation from other systematic modalities of oppression. For a brief introduction to materialist feminism, see "Toward a Materialist-feminist Criticism," *Feminist Criticism and Social Change*, eds. Judith Newton and Deborah Rosenfelt (New York: Methuen, 1985), pp. xv–xxxix. For an indication of the usefulness of materialist feminism to the analysis of drama, see "Materialist Feminism and Theatre" in Sue-Ellen Case's *Feminism and Theatre* (New York: Methuen, 1988), pp. 82–94. For a more complicated account of the history of materialist feminism, its relation to other feminisms, and the conceptual problems it presently faces, see Gail Omvedt's "'Patriarchy': The Analysis of Women's Oppression," *The Insurgent Sociologist*, 13 (1986), 30–50.
5. *Hic Mulier or The Man-Woman* (London, 1620), esp. B4^v–C.
6. William Harrison, *The Description of England*, ed. Georges Edelen (1587; rpt. Ithaca, N.Y.: Cornell Univ. Press, 1968), p. 147.

there were strong discursive linkages throughout the period between female crossdressing and the threat of female sexual incontinence. By examining records from Bridewell and the Aldermen's Court between about 1565 and 1605, R. Mark Benbow has indeed found that many of the women apprehended in men's clothing during the period were accused of prostitution.[7] For example, on 3 July 1575, the Aldermen's Court records report that one Dorothy Clayton, spinster, "contrary to all honesty and womanhood commonly goes about the City apparelled in man's atire. She has abused her body with sundry persons and lived an incontinent life. On Friday she is to stand on the pillory for two hours in men's apparell and then to be sent to Bridewell until further order" (Repertory of the Aldermen's Court, no. 19, p. 93). Of Margaret Wakeley in 1601 the Bridewell Records read: "[She] had a bastard child and went in man's apparell" (Bridewell Court Minute Book 4, p. 207). Of other women it was simply said that they were apprehended dressed as men, though clearly the suspicion was that any woman so apprehended probably led a loose life. One woman, Johanna Goodman, was whipped and sent to Bridewell in 1569 simply for dressing as a male servant so that she could accompany her soldier-husband to war (Aldermen's Court, no. 16, p. 522). It is impossible to tell the "class" position of many of these women.[8] Most appear to be unmarried women of the serving class eking out a precarious living in London. Some are recorded as being "in service" to various London tavern-keepers and tradesmen; some may have worn male clothing for protection in travelling about in the city; some may have been driven to prostitution by economic necessity, with their crossdressed apparel becoming a demonized

7. I am extremely grateful to Professor Benbow for sharing his research with me. The following material is taken from his transcription of records from the Repertories of the Aldermen's Court in the London City Record Office and from the Bridewell Court Minute Books between approximately 1565 and 1605.
8. As Leonard Tennenhouse pointed out in an astute critique of this paper, class categories derived from nineteenth-century culture are in some degree anachronistically imposed on the Renaissance social formation, which was, in part, simply a two-class culture with a tiny but powerful privileged group composed of gentry and aristocracy poised above an undifferentiated mass of laboring "others." Yet social historians of the period increasingly speak of the clash in the late sixteenth and early seventeenth centuries between emergent capitalistic social relations and older modes of social organization based on status or degree. Especially in London, the emergence of an entrepreneurial middle class, "the middling sort," seems an established fact by 1600, and to some degree enclosure movements, the putting-out system of cloth manufacture, and changes in agricultural practice were creating a rural proletariat dependent on wage labor for subsistence and creating that pool of "vagabonds and masterless men" so feared by the Elizabethan authorities. For discussions of class and status structures in this period, see David Underdown, *Revel, Riot, and Rebellion: Popular Politics and Culture in England 1603–1660* (Oxford: Clarendon Press, 1985); Lawrence Stone, "Social Mobility in England, 1500–1700," *Past and Present*, 33 (1966), 16–55; Keith Wrightson, *English Society 1580–1680* (New Brunswick, N.J.: Rutgers Univ. Press, 1982); and Barry Reay, *Popular Culture in Seventeenth-Century England* (New York: St. Martin's, 1985). See also David Harris Sacks, "Searching for 'Culture' in the English Renaissance," in this issue of *Shakespeare Quarterly*.

"sign" of their enforced sexual availability. It is tempting to speculate that if citizen wives of the Jacobean period assumed men's clothes as a sign of their wealth and independence, lower-class women may well have assumed them from a sense of vulnerability, with an eventual turn to prostitution merely marking the extent of that vulnerability. That actual women of several social classes *did* crossdress in Renaissance England is an important fact, but equally important is how their behavior was ideologically processed or rendered intelligible in the discourses of the time. Specifically, what made adopting the dress of the other sex so transgressive that lower-class women were pilloried and whipped and merchant wives were harangued from the pulpit for doing it? For the most general answer, one can begin by stating that crossdressing, like other disruptions of the Renaissance semiotics of dress, opened a gap between the supposed reality of one's social station and sexual kind and the clothes that were to display that reality to the world. As is well known, the state regulated dress in early modern England, especially in urban settings, precisely to keep people in the social "places" to which they were born. Elizabethan sumptuary proclamations list those who could wear certain colors (such as purple), certain fabrics (such as silk), and certain adornments (such as spurs, daggers, jewels).[9] In myriad ways clothes distinguished one social group from those both above and below; they were precise indicators of status and degree. To transgress the codes governing dress was to disrupt an official view of the social order in which one's identity was largely determined by one's station or degree—and where that station was, in theory, providentially determined and immutable.

Of course, as social historians such as Lawrence Stone, Keith Wrightson, Barry Reay, and David Underdown have argued, this view of the social order was under enormous pressure (see p. 340, note 8). Social mobility was a fact, its effects strikingly clear in an urban center such as London, and economic and cultural changes were creating tensions between a social order based on hierarchy and deference and one increasingly based on entrepreneurship and the social relations attendant upon the emergence of early capitalism. In general, official social ideologies did not acknowledge such changes. Rather, enormous energy was devoted to revealing the "monstrous" nature of those who moved out of their places.[1]

Dress, as a highly regulated semiotic system, became a primary site where a struggle over the mutability of the social order was conducted. Thus, Phillip Stubbes begins his *Anatomie of Abuses* of

9. See Wilfred Hooper, "The Tudor Sumptuary Laws," *English Historical Review*, XXX (1915), 433–49.
1. Francis Barker, *The Tremulous Private Body: Essays on Subjection* (London: Methuen, 1984), pp. 31–33.

1583 with an analysis of apparel. For Stubbes transgressions of the dress code don't just *signal* social disruption; they constitute such disruption. That is, when common subjects wear the gold, silk, and diamonds that properly signify an aristocratic birth and calling (as apparently a number did), they demean the social place they have usurped and erase necessary social distinctions. As Stubbes writes in his famous attack on social climbers: "there is such a confuse mingle mangle of apparell in Ailgna, and such preposterous excesse therof, as every one is permitted to flaunt it out, in what apparell he lust himselfe, or can get by anie kind of meanes. So that it is verie hard to knowe, who is noble, who is worshipfull, who is a gentleman, who is not."[2] In short, when rules of apparel are violated, class distinctions break down.

Crucially for my argument, Stubbes also says that when women dress as men and when men dress effeminately, distinctions between sexual "kinds" are also obliterated. The stability of the social order depends as much on maintaining absolute distinctions between male and female as between aristocrat and yeoman. Stubbes says: "Our Apparell was given us as a signe distinctive to discern betwixt sex and sex, & therefore one to weare the Apparel of another sex, is to participate with the same, and to adulterate the veritie of his owne kinde" (F5ᵛ). In *Hic Mulier* the crossdressed woman is enjoined to "Remember how your Maker made for our first Parents coates, not one coat, but a coat for the man, and a coat for the woman; coates of seuerall fashions, seuerall formes, and for seuerall uses: the mans coat fit for his labour, the womans fit for her modestie" (B2ᵛ–B3). To switch coats is to undo the work of heaven.

Stephen Greenblatt has recently argued that modern notions of sexual difference originate later than the Renaissance and that in at least some Renaissance discourses there appears to be only one sex, women being but imperfectly formed or incomplete men. Greenblatt then goes on to argue that a transvestite theatre was a natural, indeed, almost an inevitable, product of such a culture.[3] In contrast, the writings of Stubbes and the other antitheatrical polemicists suggest that a transvestite theatre could also be read, in the Renaissance, as *un*natural, as a transgression of a divinely sanctioned social order. What are we to make of this seeming contradiction? First, it suggests the need to recognize the plurality of discourses about gender in the Renaissance. If dominant medical discourses such as those cited by Greenblatt saw only male genitalia in both men and women and so, in some sense, authorized the view that there was only one sex, the Bible provided authority, seized by Stubbes, for a two-sex gender system: "Male and female created He them" (Genesis

---

2. *The Anatomie of Abuses* (London: Richard Jones, 1583), C2ᵛ.
3. Greenblatt, *Shakespearean Negotiations*, p. 88.

1:27). In some discourses masculine and feminine identity *were* seen as points on a continuum, not separate essences, but in works such as the antitheatrical tracts the language of two kinds predominates, and the injunction from Deuteronomy against wearing the clothes of the other sex is repeated with tiresome frequency.

I think the real point is that the Renaissance needed the idea of two genders, one subordinate to the other, to provide a key element in its hierarchical view of the social order and to buttress its gendered division of labor. The interesting possibility raised by Greenblatt's work is that, in the Renaissance, gender differences may not always or necessarily have been built upon a self-evident notion of biological sexual difference as was to be true in the nineteenth century.[4] This simply means that gender difference and hierarchy had to be produced and secured—through ideological interpellation when possible, through force when necessary—on other grounds. If women were not invariably depicted as anatomically different from men in an essential way, they could still be seen as different merely by virtue of their lack of masculine perfection (softer, weaker, less hot), and their subordination could be justified on those grounds. Then, as now, gender relations, however eroticized, were relations of power, produced and held in place through enormous cultural labor in the interests of the dominant gender. In the early modern period the regulation of dress was part of this apparatus for producing and marking gender difference, though cultural shifts were occurring. As I will suggest later in this essay, with the emergence of the bourgeois subject, whose essence is defined by his or her interiority, less emphasis was to fall on inscribing gender difference solely on the outside of the body through apparel; rather, the marks of gender difference were to be worn inwardly and made manifest through a properly gendered subjectivity.

Catherine MacKinnon has argued that the modern emphasis on sexual difference—as used to justify separate and unequal spheres of work and experience—has obscured the political realities of domination and exploitation that have continued to regulate relations between the genders.[5] By contrast, writers and speakers in the Renaissance were forthright about man's proper domination of women. Discourses of gender in the Renaissance were overwhelmingly hierarchical, with men and women first and foremost described, respectively, as dominant and subservient, perfect and less perfect, fit for rule and unfit for rule. Behind general assertions of man's proper lordship over woman lay standard appeals to differences

---

4. Behind Greenblatt's essay stands the work of Thomas Laqueur, particularly his important essay, "Orgasm, Generation and the Politics of Reproductive Biology," *Representations*, 14 (1986), 1–41.
5. *Feminism Unmodified: Discourses on Life and Law* (Cambridge, Mass.: Harvard Univ. Press, 1987), esp. "Difference and Dominance: On Sex Discrimination," pp. 32–45.

between men and women's capacities to reason, to control passion, etc. In short, languages of difference—though not necessarily biological, anatomical difference—were useful for underpinning sexual hierarchy. Keeping that hierarchy in place was an ongoing struggle, and as with conflicts over social mobility, gender struggles were in part played out on the terrain of dress.

Disruptions of the semiotics of dress by men and by women were not, however, read in the same way. For a man, wearing women's dress undermined the authority inherently belonging to the superior sex and placed him in a position of shame. At the simplest level, wearing effeminately ornate clothes would, in Stubbes's words, make men "weake, tender and infirme, not able to abide such sharp conflicts and blustering stormes" as their forefathers had endured.[6] At a more serious level, men actually wearing women's clothes, and not just ornate apparel, are so thoroughly "out of place" that they become monstrous. And in the antitheatrical tracts, as in the polemical attacks on effeminate Catholic priests, whose vestments were seen as a kind of female clothing, this monstrosity is figured as sexual perversion.[7] Sodomy haunts the fringes of Stubbes's text.[8] A man, and especially a boy, who theatricalizes the self as female, invites playing the woman's part in sexual congress. For a man this is shameful, as is the carrying of the distaff and the wearing of female dress by defeated or women-mastered warriors from Artegal to Antony. In comic form we see this in *The Merry Wives of Windsor* when Falstaff assumes the clothes of the Wise Woman of Brainford and is roundly beaten by the misogynist Ford.

For women the significance of crossdressing is different. In the polemical literature women who crossdressed were less often accused of sexual perversion than of sexual incontinence, of being whores. This was in part because the discursive construction of woman in the Renaissance involved seeing her as a creature of strong sexual appetites needing strict regulation. Her sexual desire was both a mark of her inferiority and a justification for her control by men. As Peter Stallybrass has argued, discipline and control of woman's body were central patriarchal preoccupations.[9] The orifices of that body

---

6. *The Anatomie of Abuses*, E. As Norbert Elias and others have noted, here we witness the highly mediated repercussions of the transition from a feudal culture, in which military prowess was required of the ruling orders, to a courtier culture, in which the arts of civility and social negotiation are more urgent. See *The History of Manners*, Vol. I of *The Civilizing Process*, 2 vols. (1939; rpt. New York: Pantheon, 1978).

7. For a venomous attack on the theatricality of the Catholic Mass and the sexual perversions encouraged by the wearing of ornate vestments by lewd priests, see Thomas Becon, *The Displaying of the Popish Masse* (London, 1637), esp. pp. 73–75.

8. See Levine, pp. 134–35 (cited on p. 338, note 3).

9. "Patriarchal Territories: The Body Enclosed," in *Rewriting the Renaissance: The Discourses of Sexual Difference in Early Modern Europe*, eds. Margaret W. Ferguson, Maureen Quilligan, and Nancy J. Vickers (Chicago: Univ. of Chicago Press, 1986), pp. 123–42.

were to be policed, the body's actions circumscribed. Women who gadded about outside the home or who talked too much (by male standards) were suspected of being whores—both the open door and the open mouth signifying sexual incontinence. The good woman was closed off: silent, chaste, and immured within the home. As Edmund Tilney asserted in a piece of advice that quickly became a Renaissance commonplace, the best way for a woman to keep a good name was for her never to leave her house.[1] When women took men's clothes, they symbolically left their subordinate positions. They became masterless women, and this threatened overthrow of hierarchy was discursively read as the eruption of uncontrolled sexuality.

The *Hic Mulier* tract of 1620 presents most clearly this particular construction of the crossdressed woman and the kinds of repression it elicited. Predictably, crossdressed women are accused in the tract of excessive sexual appetite. With their short waists and French doublets "all unbutton'd to entice," they "give a most easie way to every luxurious action" (A4ᵛ). Along with giving over their long hair and their sewing needles, they have given over modesty, silence, and chastity. Moreover, such women signal not only the breakdown of the hierarchical gender system, but of the class system as well. The author calls them "bu[t] ragges of Gentry," "the adulterate branches of rich Stocks," and "this deformitie all base, all barbarous" (B). The mannish woman not only produces bastards but is one herself, and she threatens the collapse of the entire class system. The very state is represented as threatened by her behavior. The author writes: "If this [crossdressing] bee not barbarous, make the rude *Scithian*, the untamed *Moore*, the naked *Indian*, or the wilde *Irish*, Lords and Rulers of well gouerned Cities" (Bᵛ). In a stunning revelation of a racial and national chauvinism, the aspiration of women beyond their place is associated with the monstrous notion of the black in rulership over the white, the Irish over the English. Such consequences—though imagined only—invite reprisal. Predictably, what is evoked at the end is the power of the state and of the patriarch within the family to quell woman's unruliness. The author wants the "powerfull Statute of apparell [to] lift vp his Battle-Axe, and crush the offenders in pieces, so as euery one may bee knowne by the true badge of their bloud, or Fortune" (Cᵛ). For when women "catch the bridle in their teeth, and runne away with their Rulers, they care not into what dangers they plunge either their Fortunes or Reputations" (C2); consequently, those who are "Fathers, Husbands, or Sustainers of these new *Hermaphrodites*" (C2ᵛ) must keep them in order, forbid the buying of such outrageous apparel, and

1. *A briefe and pleasant discourse of duties in Mariage, called the Flower of Friendship* (London, 1587), E2ᵛ–E3.

instruct them in the virtues which are women's best ornaments. It is important to remember that for the lower-class woman who found herself in the Aldermen's Court, it was not just a husband's chastisement but the whip, pillory, and prisons of the state's repressive apparatuses that constituted her as a guilty subject and effected her punishment.

I suggest that these worries about the unruly crossdressed woman, as well as the various means of control devised to contain the threat she constituted, are signs—as Karen Newman, Catherine Belsey, and others have indicated—that early modern England was not only permeated by well-documented social mobility and unsettling economic change, but by considerable instability in the gender system as well.[2] Social historians have found that in some areas, particularly where economic change was most rapid and changes in family form most pronounced, the disciplining and restraint of women increased during this period, sometimes taking the form of an increased regulation of women's sexuality. Martin Ingram has argued, for example, that the period 1580–1620 witnessed an increase in the prosecution of prenuptial pregnancies and an increasing preoccupation with the strains that bastards placed on the commonweal.[3] By 1620 it was common, as it had not been before, for a woman who produced a bastard to be jailed for up to a year.[4]

But not all the disciplining of women went on through the ecclesiastical or civil courts. Charivaris, skimingtons, or rough ridings were communal rituals through which unruly women were disciplined and insufficiently dominating husbands reproved.[5] The charivari specifically punished a woman's violation of her place in the gender hierarchy. Sometimes she had merely "worn the breeches" in the sense of ordering her husband about; sometimes she was accused of beating her spouse, sometimes of having made him a cuckold. In the punishment of those guilty of female dominance, the couple's inversion of gender hierarchy was mirrored by having the husband

2. Newman, "Renaissance Family Politics and Shakespeare's The Taming of the Shrew," ELR, 16 (1986), 86–100, esp. pp. 91–92. Belsey, The Subject of Tragedy: Identity and Difference in Renaissance Drama (London: Methuen, 1985), esp. pp. 129–221.
3. "The Reform of Popular Culture? Sex and Marriage in Early Modern England," Popular Culture in Seventeenth-Century England, ed. Barry Reay (New York: St. Martin's, 1985), pp. 129–65, esp. p. 148.
4. Ingram, "The Reform of Popular Culture? Sex and Marriage in Early Modern England," p. 155.
5. For discussion of these disciplining rituals, see Martin Ingram, "Ridings, Rough Music and Mocking Rhymes in Early Modern England" in Popular Culture in Seventeenth-Century England, ed. Barry Reay, pp. 166–97; David Underdown, "The Taming of the Scold: the Enforcement of Patriarchal Authority in Early Modern England" in Order and Disorder in Early Modern England, eds. Anthony Fletcher and John Stevenson (Cambridge: Cambridge Univ. Press, 1985), pp. 116–36; and Natalie Zemon Davis, "Women on Top: Symbolic Sexual Inversion and Political Disorder in Early Modern Europe" in The Reversible World: Symbolic Inversion in Art and Society, ed. Barbara Babcock (Ithaca, N.Y.: Cornell Univ. Press, 1978), pp. 147–90.

ride backward on a horse through the town while neighbors played cacophonous music. Husband-beating was specifically punished by having the husband or his substitute hold a distaff while riding backward on a horse, while a woman figure, a Lady Skimington (often a man dressed as a woman), beat him with the ladle used for making butter and cheese. These ritual punishments were all ways of registering the fact that important cultural boundaries had been erased, important social hierarchies disrupted, by the offending parties. Similarly, women who talked too much, who were "scolds," were put upon a cucking stool and dunked in water to stop the incontinence of the mouth.

David Underdown has argued that there was a marked increase in the years immediately after 1600 in charivaris and uses of the cucking stool, especially in communities where traditional modes of ordering society along vertical lines of hierarchy, deference, and paternalism were being disrupted and displaced by what we associate with the more modern horizontal alignment of people within classes and with the rise of protocapitalist economic practices.[6] For example, the upland wood and pasture areas of the west counties, where there was a strong influx of migrant labor, where families were dispersed and where capitalism had penetrated in terms of the heavy reliance on the putting-out system of cloth manufacture, evidenced more occurrences of charivaries, etc., than did the more centralized village communities of the grain-growing valleys where the population was more stable, families less isolated, and the pace of social change less rapid. Cities were another site of gender tension, in part because they uprooted people from traditional social structures. As many have noted, in times of general social dislocation, fears about change are often displaced onto women.[7] Cities also created new and unsettling positions for women (middle-class women, in particular) to occupy: positions as consumers of urban pleasures such as theatregoing and of the commodities produced by English trade and manufacture, positions of economic power as widows of merchants or as visible workers in their husbands' shops.[8] A foreign visitor to London, Thomas Platter, noted in 1599 how much freedom English women had vis-à-vis their continental counterparts.[9] But this freedom, I have been arguing, was unsettling to the patriarchal order. The calls at the end of Hic Mulier for the

6. See Underdown, "The Taming of the Scold," esp. pp. 125–35; for the expanded version of his argument, see Revel, Riot, and Rebellion.
7. For a general statement of this argument in regard to the Renaissance, see Lisa Jardine, Still Harping on Daughters, esp. p. 162.
8. See Joan Thirsk, Economic Policy and Projects: The Development of a Consumer Society in Early Modern England (Oxford: Oxford Univ. Press, 1978).
9. Quoted in Alfred Harbage, Shakespeare's Audience (New York: Columbia Univ. Press, 1941), pp. 76–77.

reining in of women's freedom are but one sign of just how unsettling change in the sex-gender system had become.

Ironically, and this seems to me a chief point to remember, if the vast social changes of the period led to intensified pressures on women and a strengthening of patriarchal authority in the family and the state, these changes also produced sites of resistance and possibilities of new powers for women. I do not mean to contest the view, which I believe is essentially correct, that the English Renaissance was no real Renaissance for women—i.e., it was not for most women a time of increased freedom from patriarchal oppression and exploitation.[1] Yet I want to argue that a dialectical view of history may enable us to attend not only to the success of dominant groups in controlling the social field but also to their failures and to the myriad ways in which subaltern and marginal groups contest hegemonic impositions.[2] If every cultural site is a site of social struggle, attention to the specifics of that struggle may reveal the lapses and contradictions of power that produce social change. Thus, even if, as has been argued, the invention of printing and the admittedly slow increase in women's literacy in the early modern period in part simply increased the ways in which women could be controlled and interpellated as good subjects of a patriarchal order (witness the outpouring of books on housewifery and female piety after the 1580s

1. I think it is as yet impossible to give a definitive answer to Joan Kelly's famous question "Did Women Have a Renaissance?" (*Women, History, and Theory: The Essays of Joan Kelly* [Chicago: Univ. of Chicago Press, 1984], pp. 19–50. If Juliet Dusinberre's account (*Shakespeare and the Nature of Women*) of the freedoms opening up for middle-class women in the Renaissance seems to take too little account of the recuperative powers of patriarchal systems, Lawrence Stone's more sober account (*The Family, Sex and Marriage in England 1500–1800* [New York: Harper and Row, 1977]) of the intensification of patriarchy toward the end of the sixteenth century, especially among the upper classes, tends simply to assign to patriarchy the absolute power it claimed for itself and to ignore the possibilities for women's resistance, which it has been the work of feminist scholars such as Catherine Belsey (*The Subject of Tragedy*, esp. pp. 129–221) and others to explore. We know that the gender system *changed* in the Renaissance as new family structures emerged, as patterns of work and production changed, etc.; but change does not necessarily mean progress or the amelioration of oppression. Feminist scholarship is in the process of discovering where these changes enabled instances of resistance and female empowerment, as well as the many ways in which change simply meant the old oppression in new guises.
2. In the wake of Althusser's writings on ideology (see, for example, "Ideology and Ideological State Apparatuses" in *Lenin and Philosophy and Other Essays* [New York: Monthly Review Press, 1971], pp. 127–86) much emphasis in cultural analysis fell on the success of various apparatuses in interpellating subjects within dominant ideologies. Such an emphasis allowed little latitude for theorizing change or resistance. As a corrective it is important to emphasize what Althusser states but does not develop: namely, that "ideological state apparatuses" are not only the stake but the site of class struggle (p. 147) and that resistance occurs within them; and to make use of Gramsci's work on the way subaltern groups contest hegemonic ideological practices (see *Selections from the Prison Notebooks*, ed. Quinten Hoare and Geoffrey Smith [New York: International Publishers, 1971]). For a useful overview of contemporary views of ideology, see Terry E. Boswell et al., "Recent Developments in Marxist Theories of Ideology," *Insurgent Sociologist*, 13 (1986), 5–22.

as documented by Suzanne Hull[3]), nonetheless skills in reading and writing allowed some women access to some authorities (such as scripture) and to some technologies (such as print), which allowed them to begin to rewrite their inscriptions within patriarchy. Many scholars, following on the work of William and Malleville Haller, have noted the contradictions in Protestant marriage theory.[4] Chiefly a means for making the home the center of patriarchal control and for instantiating the wife within the domestic sphere, this theory nonetheless stresses the wife's importance within that sphere and her spiritual equality with her husband. This calls into question the inevitability of starkly hierarchical theories of gender and opens space for ideas of negotiation, mutuality, and contract between husband and wife, some of which mutuality we may sense being worked out in Shakespeare's romantic comedies.[5]

All of this, I think, bears on how we are to evaluate the various forms of crossdressing detailed earlier in this paper. In a period of social dislocation in which the sex-gender system was one of the major sites of anxiety and change, female crossdressing in any context had the *potential* to raise fears about women wearing the breeches and undermining the hierarchical social order. In the *Haec-Vir* tract the mannish woman declares that not nature but custom dictates women's dress and women's subservient place in society and that, moreover, "*Custome* is an idiot."[6] No matter that the tract changes direction and ends up with the familiar plea that if men would be more mannish, women would return to their accustomed role; the fact remains that through the discussion of women's dress has come an attack on the naturalness of the whole gender system.

The subversive potential of women dressed as men was self-consciously exploited in other cultural contexts as well. Natalie Davis has documented that crossdressed figures were prominent both in carnival—where gender and class boundaries were simultaneously tested and confirmed—and in food riots, demonstrations against enclosures, and other forms of lower-class protest.[7] Sometimes in such activities men performed as Lady Skimingtons, appropriating the powerful iconography of the unruly woman to protest the

3. *Chaste, Silent and Obedient: English Books for Women 1475–1640* (San Marino, Cal.: Huntington Library, 1982).
4. Cf. William and Malleville Haller, "The Puritan Art of Love," *Huntington Library Quarterly*, 5 (1941–42), 235–72.
5. For an important study of the juxtaposition of patriarchal absolutism and contractual theories of state and family relations, see Gordon Schochet's *Patriarchalism in Political Thought: The Authoritarian Family and Political Speculation and Attitudes, Especially in Seventeenth-Century England* (Oxford: Basil Blackwell, 1975). For a fascinating examination of how Restoration drama embodies these changing ideologies of marriage and authority, see Susan Staves's *Players' Scepters: Fictions of Authority in the Restoration* (Lincoln: Univ. of Nebraska Press, 1979).
6. *Haec-Vir or The Womanish-Man* (London, 1620), B2ᵛ.
7. Davis, "Women on Top," pp. 154–55 and 176–83.

unequal distribution of power and material goods within the social order.[8] Clearly, crossdressing had enormous symbolic significance, and the state had an interest in controlling it. Witness James I's injunction to the preachers of London that they preach against the practice. The question I want to address in the remainder of this essay concerns the role of the theatre in gender definition. Did the theatre, for example, with its many fables of crossdressing, also form part of the cultural apparatus for policing gender boundaries, or did it serve as a site for their further disturbance? If women off the stage seized the language of dress to act out transgressions of the sex-gender system, did the theatre effectively co-opt this transgression by transforming it into fictions that depoliticized the practice? Or was the theatre in some sense an agent of cultural transformation, helping to create new subject positions and gender relations for men and women in a period of rapid social change? And how did the all-male mode of dramatic production—the fact of crossdressing as a daily part of dramatic practice—affect the ideological import of these fictions of crossdressing?

* * *

As You Like It * * * explicitly invites, through its epilogue, a consideration of how secure even the most recuperative representations of crossdressing could be in a theatre in which male actors regularly played women's roles. Rosalind's crossdressing, of course, occurs in the holiday context of the pastoral forest, and, as Natalie Davis has argued, holiday inversions of order can spur social change or, in other instances, can merely reconfirm the existing order.[9] The representation of Rosalind's holiday humor has the primary effect, I think, of confirming the gender system and perfecting rather than dismantling it by making a space for mutuality within relations of dominance.[1] Temporarily lording it over Orlando, teaching him how to woo and appointing the times of his coming and going, she *could* be a threatening figure if she did not constantly, contrapuntally, reveal herself to the audience as the not-man, as in actuality a lovesick maid whose love "hath an unknown bottom, like the bay of Portugal" (IV.i.208) and who faints at the sight of blood. Crucially, like Viola, Rosalind retains a properly feminine subjectivity: "dost thou think, though I am caparison'd like a man, I have a doublet and hose in my disposition?" (III.ii.194–96). As Annette

8. Buchanan Sharp, *In Contempt of All Authority: Rural Artisans and Riot in the West of England, 1586–1660* (Berkeley: Univ. of California Press, 1980), p. 5.
9. Davis, "Women on Top," esp. pp. 153–54.
1. For the view that the romantic comedies champion mutuality between the sexes, see Marianne Novy's *Love's Argument: Gender Relations in Shakespeare* (Chapel Hill: Univ. of North Carolina Press, 1984), esp. Chapter 2, "'An You Smile Not, He's Gagged': Mutuality in Shakespearean Comedy," pp. 21–44.

Kuhn has argued, in certain circumstances crossdressing intensifies, rather than blurs, sexual difference, sometimes by calling attention to the woman's failure to perform the masculine role signified by her dress.[2] Rosalind's fainting constitutes such a reminder, endearing her to earlier generations of readers and audiences for her true "womanliness." And, as in *Twelfth Night*, the thrust of the narrative is toward that long-delayed moment of disclosure, orchestrated so elaborately in Act V, when the heroine will doff her masculine attire along with the saucy games of youth and accept the position of wife, when her biological identity, her gender identity, and the semiotics of dress will coincide.

Where this account of the consequences of Rosalind's crossdressing becomes too simple, however, is in a close consideration of the particular *way* in which Rosalind plays with her disguise. Somewhat like Portia, Rosalind uses her disguise to redefine (albeit in a limited way) the position of woman in a patriarchal society. The most unusual aspect of her behavior is that while dressed as a man, Rosalind impersonates a woman, and that woman is herself—or, rather, a self that is the logical conclusion of Orlando's romantic, Petrarchan construction of her. Saucy, imperious, and fickle by turns, Rosalind plays out masculine constructions of femininity, in the process showing Orlando their limitations. Marianne Doane has argued that "masquerade," the self-conscious staging, parody, exaggeration of cultural constructions of self, offers women a choice between simple identification with male selves—which is how she reads the meaning of crossdressing—or simple inscription within patriarchal constructions of the feminine.[3] In my view, the figure of Rosalind dressed as a boy engages in playful masquerade as, in playing Rosalind for Orlando, she acts out the parts scripted for women by her culture. Doing so does not release Rosalind from patriarchy but reveals the constructed nature of patriarchy's representations of the feminine and shows a woman manipulating those representations in her own interest, theatricalizing for her own purposes what is assumed to be innate, teaching her future mate how to get beyond certain ideologies of gender to more enabling ones.

Moreover, this play, more than other Shakespearean comedies, deliberately calls attention to the destabilizing fact that it is boy actors playing the roles of all the women in the play, including Rosalind. There is a permanent gap on the stage between the incipiently masculine identity of the boy actors and their appropriation of the "grace, / Voice, gait, and action of a gentlewoman"—to borrow a

---

2. "Sexual Disguise and Cinema," *The Power of the Image: Essays on Representation and Sexuality* (London: Routledge and Kegan Paul, 1985), pp. 48–73, esp. pp. 55–57.
3. "Film and the Masquerade: Theorizing the Female Spectator," *Screen*, 23 (1982), 74–89.

definition of the actor's task from the job assigned the Page in the Induction to *The Taming of the Shrew* (Ind., ll. 131–32). I agree with Kathleen McLuskie that at some level boy actors playing women must simply have been accepted in performance as a convention.[4] Otherwise, audience involvement with dramatic narratives premised on heterosexual love and masculine/feminine difference would have been minimal. It is also true, as McLuskie and others suggest, that the convention of the boy actor playing a girl can, at any moment, be unmasked *as* a convention and the reality (that the fictional woman is played by a boy) can be revealed. One of those moments occurs at the end of *As You Like It*. The play has achieved closure in part by reinscribing everyone into his or her "proper" social position. The duke is now again a duke and not a forest outlaw, Rosalind is now Rosalind and not Ganymede, and so forth. But when in the Epilogue the character playing Rosalind reminds us that she is played by a boy, the neat convergence of biological sex and culturally constructed gender is once more severed. If a boy can so successfully personate the voice, gait, and manner of a woman, how stable are those boundaries separating one sexual kind from another, and thus how secure are those powers and privileges assigned to the hierarchically superior sex, which depends upon notions of difference to justify its dominance?[5] The Epilogue playfully invites this question. That it does so suggests something about the contradictory nature of the theatre as a site of ideological production, an institution that can circulate recuperative fables of crossdressing, reinscribing sexual difference and gender hierarchy, and at the same time can make visible on the level of theatrical practice the contamination of sexual kinds.

* * *

What then can we say, in conclusion, about female crossdressing on the Renaissance stage? I think that, often, female crossdressing on the stage is not a strong site of resistance to the period's patriarchal sex-gender system. Ironically, rather than blurring gender difference or challenging male domination and exploitation of women, female crossdressing often strengthens notions of difference by stressing what the disguised woman *cannot* do, or by stressing those feelings held to constitute a "true" female subjectivity. While some plots *do* reveal women successfully wielding male power and male authority, they nearly invariably end with the female's willing doffing of male clothes and, presumably, male prerogatives. It is hard to avoid

---

4. "The Act, the Role, and the Actor: Boy Actresses on the Elizabethan Stage," esp. p. 121.
5. For good discussions of the disruptive effects of the Epilogue, see Catherine Belsey's "Disrupting Sexual Difference" and Phyllis Rackin's "Androgyny, Mimesis, and the Marriage of the Boy Heroine on the English Renaissance Stage" (cited on p. 338, note 3).

concluding that many crossdressing comedies have as their social function the recuperation of threats to the sex-gender system, sometimes by ameliorating the worst aspects of that system and opening a greater space for woman's speech and action. Yet this recuperation is never perfectly achieved. In a few plays, such as *The Roaring Girl*, the resistance to patriarchy and its marriage customs is clear and sweeping; in others, such as *The Merchant of Venice*, the heroine achieves a significant rewriting of her position within patriarchy even as she takes up the role of wife. Others, simply by having women successfully play male roles, however temporarily, or by making women's roles the objects of self-conscious masquerade, put in question the naturalness, the inevitability, of dominant constructions of men's and women's natures and positions in the gender hierarchy.

Moreover, I think it is a mistake to restrict our considerations of the ideological import of Renaissance theatre to an analysis of the scripts, even an analysis of the scripts in relation to extradramatic practices and texts. Ideology is enacted through all the theatre's practices, from its pricing structures for admission to the times of its performances. As we have seen, the fact of an all-male acting company complicates the ideological import of these crossdressing plays in ways that simply don't obtain when, as is generally true today, women play women's parts on the stage. Moreover, whatever the conservative import of certain crossdressing fables, the very fact that women went to the theatre to see them attests to the contradictions surrounding this social institution. Women at the public theatre were doing many of the very things that the polemicists who attacked crossdressing railed against. They were gadding about outside the walls of their own houses, spending money on a new consumer pleasure, allowing themselves to become a spectacle to the male gaze.

Andrew Gurr has concluded in his exhaustive new study of Shakespeare's audience that women were indeed at the public theatres, and that many of them were probably citizen's wives—wives of the shopkeepers and merchants increasingly playing a leading part in the life of urban London.[6] These were the very women whose enhanced freedoms made them threats to the patriarchal order, and who were heavily recruited to the banner of chastity, silence, obedience, and domesticity. This is, in fact, the group—the gentlewomen citizens of London—to whom, as early as 1579, Stephen Gosson spoke in his warnings against the pollutions of the playhouse, enjoining them to

---

6. *Playgoing in Shakespeare's London* (Cambridge: Cambridge Univ. Press, 1987), esp. pp. 61–64.

"Keep home, and shun all occasions of ill speech."[7] His argument was that women who went to the theatre made themselves spectacles and therefore vulnerable to the suspicion of being whores. "Thought is free; you can forbidd no man, that vieweth you, to noute you and that noateth you, to judge you, for entring to places of suspition" (F2). It might be all right for court ladies to put themselves on public display, to occupy a box at the private theatres, for example, but not middle-class wives. Massinger ends *The City Madam* by warning city dames "to move / In their spheres, and willingly to confess / In their habits, manners, and their highest port, / A distance 'twixt the city and the court" (V.iii.153–56).[8] One of the most transgressive acts the real Moll Firth performed was to sit, in her masculine attire, on the stage of the Fortune and to sing a song upon the lute. She did what only court ladies and gallants were allowed to do: she made a spectacle of herself.

Of course, the average woman playgoer did not claim the clothes of the male gallant or his place upon the stage; nonetheless, to be at the theatre, especially without a male companion, was to transgress the physical and symbolic boundaries of the middle-class woman's domestic containment. Perhaps unwittingly, these women were altering gender relations. The public theatre was not a ritual space, but a commercial venture. Citizens' wives who went to this theatre might, at one extreme, be invited by its fictions to take up positions of chastity, silence, and obedience, but at another extreme by its commercial practices they were positioned as consumers, critics, spectators, and spectacles. The theatre as a social institution signified change. It blurred the boundaries between degrees and genders by having men of low estate wear the clothes of noblemen and of women, and by having one's money, not one's blood or title, decide how high and how well one sat, or whether, indeed, one stood. To go to the theatre was, in short, to be positioned at the crossroads of cultural change and contradiction—and this seems to me especially true for the middle-class female playgoer, who by her practices was calling into question the "place" of woman, perhaps more radically than did Shakespeare's fictions of crossdressing.

7. Stephen Gosson, *The School of Abuse* (1579; rpt. New York: Garland, 1973), F^v–F4^v, esp. F4.
8. Phillip Massinger, *The City Madam*, ed. Cyrus Hoy (Lincoln: Univ. of Nebraska Press, 1964), p. 100.

MARJORIE GARBER

Rosalind the Yeshiva Boy[†]

* * *

We are accustomed to Shakespeare's being fetishized in Western culture, made the touchstone of issues literary, philosophical, and social, the surety and verification of the issues of our—or any—time. But it is striking to note that of all Shakespeare's cross-dressed heroines it is Rosalind who is almost always chosen as the normative case by nineteenth- and twentieth-century authors. When, for example, Oscar Wilde's Dorian Gray falls in love, it is with an actress playing the part of Rosalind—or rather, the part of Ganymede: "You should have seen her! When she came on in her boy's clothes she was perfectly wonderful. She wore a moss-coloured velvet jerkin with cinnamon sleeves, slim brown cross-gartered hose, a dainty little green cap with a hawk's feather caught in a jewel, and a hooded cloak lined with dull red. She had never seemed to me more beautiful."[1]

"Rosalind" appears, in fact, in a surprising number of modern texts as a kind of shorthand for the cross-dressed woman, or the enigma that she represents. Why Rosalind rather than Viola, or Portia, or Julia, or Imogen? Why is it so often Rosalind who is singled out as the exemplary early modern cross-dresser, the Katharine Hepburn (if not the Marlene Dietrich or the Annie Lennox) of her time? To approach this question, which has some larger implications for the cultural construction of transvestism, let us look at a few diverse and fascinating examples.

Théophile Gautier's 1835 novel, *Mademoiselle de Maupin*, is a remarkable text about gender undecidability in which the sexually enigmatic Théodore de Serannes is beloved by both the narrator d'Albert and his mistress, Rosette. The dramatic and the psychological plots of *Mademoiselle de Maupin* turn on a production of *As You Like It* in which Théodore appears in the part of Rosalind.

D'Albert the narrator, it is almost needless to say, is cast as Orlando. When he first sees Théodore dressed as Rosalind, he is enchanted: this is the answer to his prayers. "You would think he had never worn any other costume in his life! He is not in the very least awkward in his movements, he walks very well and he doesn't get caught up in his train; he uses his eyes and his fan to admiration; and what a slim waist he has! . . . Oh, lovely Rosalind! Who

† From Marjorie Garber, *Vested Interests: Cross-Dressing & Cultural Anxiety* (New York: Routledge, 1992), pp. 72–77. Reprinted by permission.
1. Oscar Wilde, *The Picture of Dorian Gray* (London: Penguin Books, 1985; orig. pub. 1891), 103.

would not want to be her Orlando?"[2] Bear in mind that d'Albert at
least thinks of himself as heterosexual; his desire is for Théodore to
turn out to *be* a woman, so that he can safely love her. Thus his
consternation when, in the third act, Rosalind cross-dresses, and
appears as Ganymede.

> I grew all sombre when Théodore reappeared in masculine
> dress, more sombre than I had been before; for happiness only
> serves to make one more aware of grief. . . .
> And yet he was dressed in a way which suggested that this
> masculine attire had a feminine lining; something broader
> about the hips and fuller in the chest, some sort of flow which
> materials don't have on a man's body, left little doubt of the
> person's sex. . . .
> My serenity began to return, and I persuaded myself again
> that it was quite definitely a woman. (Gautier, 249)

Playing out the scene, in which Orlando tries to persuade the
"fair youth" that he is really in love, and "Ganymede" reproves him
for this mode of address, saying, "Nay, you must call me Rosalind,"
d'Albert feels that the play has been written for the express purpose
of verbalizing his own situation. "No doubt there is some important
reason, which I cannot know, which obliges this beautiful woman
to adopt this accursed disguise" (Gautier, 252).

As for his rival in love, his mistress Rosette, *she* is also—again,
needless to say—a member of the play's cast. Having refused the
part of Rosalind for herself because she was reluctant to dress up as
a man (a fact that surprises the self-absorbed and narcissistic
d'Albert: "prudery is hardly one of her failings. If I had not been
sure of the contrary, I would have thought that she had ugly legs"
[Gautier, 235]), Rosette has accepted the role of Phebe, who falls
hopelessly and fruitlessly in love with the fictive "Ganymede." As
d'Albert observes complacently,

> the history of Phebe is her own, as that of Orlando is mine
> with this difference, that everything ends happily for Orlando,
> and that Phebe, disappointed in love, is reduced to marrying
> Sylvius [sic] instead of the delightful ideal she wanted to
> embrace. Life is like that: one person's happiness is bound to
> be someone else's misfortune. It is very fortunate for me that
> Théodore is a woman; it is very unfortunate for Rosette that
> Théodore isn't a man, and that she now finds herself cast into
> the amorous impossibilities in which I went astray not long
> ago. (Gautier, 257)

---

2. Théophile Gautier, *Mademoiselle de Maupin*, trans. Joanna Richardson (Harmondsworth: Penguin Books, 1981), 246–47.

There is much more in this vein. Shakespeare's play serves as a *mise en abîme* into which Gautier's characters avidly hurl themselves, and the conundrum of gender undecidability is given a local habitation and a name. D'Albert's assertion, "I have no proofs, and I cannot remain in this state of uncertainty any longer" (Gautier, 257), mirrors Orlando's decisive "I can live no longer by thinking" (*AYLI* 5.2.50) and is equally self-delusive about the possibility of "proof" in matters of gender, identity, and role. "Théodore—Rosalind—for I don't know what name to call you by" (Gautier, 294). "Rosalind, you who have so many prescriptions for curing the malady of love, cure me, for I am very ill. Play your part to the end, cast off the clothes of the beautiful page Ganymede, and hold out your white hand to the youngest son of the brave Sir Rowland de Boys" (Gautier, 301).

So ends d'Albert's narrative. But this is not the end of the novel. Théodore now picks up the narration (this is very near the end of the book, Chapter 14 of 17) and "explains" the subterfuge. "Her" plan is in fact a "real life" version of the story of *As You Like It*:

> This was my plan. In my male attire I should make the acquaintance of some young man whose appearance pleased me; I should live familiarly with him; by skilful questions and by false, confidences which elicited true ones, I should soon acquire a complete understanding of his feelings and his thoughts. . . . I should make a pretext of some journey, and . . . come back in my women's clothes . . . then I should so arrange things that he met me and wooed me. (Gautier, 315)

The mystery would seem to be solved. Théodore, like "Rosalind" in the play, is a woman. Yet in the next moment she puts that identification, and the binarism of gender, in question.

> I was imperceptibly losing the idea of my sex, and I hardly remembered, at long intervals, that I was a woman; at the beginning, I'd often let slip some phrase or other which didn't fit in with the male attire that I was wearing. . . . If ever the fancy takes me to go and find my skirts again in the drawer where I left them, which I very much doubt, unless I fall in love with some young beau, I shall find it hard to lose this habit, and, instead of a woman disguised as a man, I shall look like a man disguised as a a woman. In truth, neither sex is really mine . . . I belong to a third sex, a sex apart, which has as yet no name. . . .
> My dream would be to have each sex in turn, and to satisfy my dual nature: man today, woman tomorrow. (Gautier 329–30)

At the close of the novel, however, even this certainty about transvestism and the third kind is undermined. A new narrative voice takes over in the sixteenth chapter, recording visits by Théodore to the rooms of d'Albert and Rosette, and Théodore's departure the next morning. The novel's last chapter takes the form of a letter from Théodore to d'Albert, offered as a substitute and an "explanation": a letter which establishes Théodore as the locus of desire. "Your unassuaged desire will still open its wings to fly to me; I shall always be for you something desirable, to which your fancy loves to return" (Gautier, 347).

The transvestite here articulates herself/himself as *that which escapes*, what Lacan describes in his essay on "The Signification of the Phallus" as "desire":

> desire is neither the appetite for satisfaction, nor the demand for love, but the difference that result from the subtraction of the first from the second, the phenomenon of their splitting (*Spaltung*).[3]

Thus desire is by definition that which cannot be satisfied: it is what is left of absolute demand when all possible satisfaction has been subtracted from it. And this is another definition of the transvestite, exemplified in Shakespeare as in Gautier. The transvestite is the space of desire.

In a way this space is denied by readings of Shakespearean transvestism like that of Stephen Greenblatt, who writes that "the unique qualities of [Rosalind's] identity—those that give Rosalind her independence, her sharply etched individuality—will not, as Shakespeare conceives the play, endure: they are bound up with exile, disguise, and freedom from ordinary constraint, and they will vanish, along with the playful chafing, when the play is done.[4] But "vanishing" here is the converse of escaping. Greenblatt describes this as "an improvisational self-fashioning that longs for self-effacement and reabsorption in the community," and attributes that "longing" to "a social system that marks out singularity, particularly in women, as prodigious." But whose longing is it, really, that is being described here under the cover of a social and cultural constraint? If Rosalind's "unique qualities"—which is to say, her capacity for becoming or constructing Ganymede—will not endure, will "vanish" when the play is done, so too will Rosalind and Orlando and all the rest of the dramatis personae who are part of how "Shakespeare conceives the play." But in fact what lingers, like the smile of the Cheshire Cat, is precisely that residue, that supplement: Ganymede.

---

3. Jacques Lacan, "The Signification of the Phallus," in *Ecrits: A Selection*, trans. Alan Sheridan (New York: W.W. Norton, 1977), 287.

4. Stephen Greenblatt, "Fiction and Friction," *Shakespearean Negotiations* (Berkeley: University of California Press, 1988), 90–91. For an excellent treatment of the relation of the boy actor to fears and assumptions about women in the Renaissance, and in these plays, see Stephen Orgel, "Call Me Ganymede: Shakespeare's Apprentices and the Representation of Women" (forthcoming in *Why Did the English Stage Take Boys for Women?* Routledge, 1992).

The "longing" for self-effacement and reabsorption is a domesticated and, I would suggest, finally once again patriarchal or masculinist longing, which is transferred onto the figure of the transvestite
in a gesture of denial or fending off. Not to endure, to vanish—these
are the negative reformulations of desire, which instead *escapes*, goes
everywhere rather than nowhere, for the transvestite is the space of
desire.

Let us look now at another recent fictional appropriation of Rosalind, this time from the twentieth rather than the nineteenth century: Angela Carter's novel *The Passion of New Eve*. First published
in 1977, Carter's postmodern novel tells the story of Evelyn, a young
Englishman who undergoes transsexual surgery to become Eve, and
the woman of his dreams, Tristessa, a former Hollywood star who
turns out to be literally a phallic woman, a male-to-female transvestite. The plot is intricate and unnecessary to summarize here, but
the wedding scene between Eve and Tristessa is one that finds both
participants cross-dressed. Tristessa wears "the white satin bridal
gown he'd last worn thirty years before in. . . . *Wuthering Heights*,"
and Eve appears in a costume once intended for an actor playing
Frédéric Chopin in the story of George Sand. (Sand was herself
a famous cross-dresser, and Chopin, her lover, was notoriously
described by his critics not only as "effeminate" but also as "the
only female musician,"[5] so that Carter's plot of inverted inversion
has yet further refractions, a cultural ripple effect.)

Here is Eve—formerly Evelyn—reflecting on her own reflection
in the mirror:

> the transformation that an endless series of reflections showed
> me was a double drag. This young buck, this Baudelairean
> dandy so elegant and trim in his evening clothes—it seemed at
> first glance, I had become my old self again in the inverted world
> of the mirrors. But this masquerade was more than skin deep.
> Under the mask of maleness I wore another mask of female-
> ness but a mask that now I never would be able to remove, no
> matter how hard I tried, although I was a boy disguised as a
> girl and now disguised as a boy again, like Rosalind in Elizabe-
> than Arden.[6]

The evocation of Rosalind, so similar, in a way, to that of Gautier's Théodore, produces similar ruminations on the questions
of constructed and essential gender identity. "Rosalind" becomes
here a sign word for that reflecting mirror, that infinite regress of

5. Otto Weininger, *Sex and Character* (London: William Heinemann, 1906), 67.
6. Angela Carter, *The Passion of New Eve*. (London: Victor Gollancz, 1977; rpt. Virago
Press, 1987), 132.

representation, of which the transvestite (*always*, in one sense, "in double drag") is a powerful and inescapable reminder.

Why, then, is Rosalind the favorite among Shakespeare's cross-dressers, the shorthand term for benign female-to-male cross-dressing in literature and culture?

Rosalind differs from Viola in a crucial way: she returns to the stage dressed as a woman. In the last scene of the play she leaves the stage as Ganymede and returns, led by Hymen, in a "sight and shape" so unmistakably female as to give joy to Orlando and con-sternation to Phebe. In the Epilogue that follows "she" deliberately breaks the frame to acknowledge the "real" gender of the actor ("If I were a woman, I would kiss as many of you as had beards that pleased me, complexions that liked me, and breaths that I defied not" [*AYLI* 5.4.214–17]), and by calling attention to her underlying male "identity" as an actor ("*if* I were a woman") Rosalind opens up the possibility of a male/male homoeroticism between male audience member and male actor that is the counterpart of the male/"male" homoeroticism animating Orlando's conversations with Ganymede, as well as the converse of the female/female homoeroticism figured in the play by Phebe's infatuation.

But in returning dressed as a woman she also allows for the pos-sibility of a recuperative interpretation (of which Greenblatt's is a very subtle and powerful version) that suggests a transformed woman now "reabsorbed" into the community and thus capable of "vanishing." Rosalind, according to this recuperative fantasy, has finished her job of education and self-instruction (Greenblatt calls it "improvisation," but it is clearly very temporary indeed), and can now take up her wifely role. There is no more need for Ganymede, who would have been very inconvenient if he had stayed around. As for the male Rosalind of the Epilogue, he doesn't need or want Gany-mede either, except as an Ovidian reminder that gods and boys often go well together. ("Ganymede" was also Elizabethan slang, usually pejorative in tone, for a male prostitute or a servant kept for sexual purposes.[7]) Neither ending—that of the onstage pairs in marital ranks, nor that of the Epilogue and its wink to certain members of the audience—acknowledges the "other" transvestite, the one who is *not* there in either final scene or Epilogue. Yet it is "Ganymede" who is the play's locus of desire, "Ganymede," not Rosalind, with whom Phebe falls so hopelessly in love, "Ganymede" who enchants the audience. How are we to account for "Ganymede"? For the erotic?

Here, then, is the paradox. Only by looking at the transvestite on the stage, in the literary text, can we see clearly that he or she is not

---

7. Alan Bray, *Homosexuality in Renaissance England* (London: Gay Men's Press, 1982; 2nd ed. Boston: Gay Men's Press, 1988), 65.

there. Only by regarding Ganymede, and Cesario and Dorothy Michaels in *Tootsie* as instated presences—not as other versions of Rosalind, or Viola, or Michael Dorsey, or Dustin Hoffman, but as constructs that have a subjectivity and an agency—can we understand something of their relation to narcissism, desire, and possibility. To appropriate them to a social and historical discourse is to understand their politics and their history, but not their power. For that power resides elsewhere.

JAMES SHAPIRO

[The Play in 1599][†]

* * *

In *Shakespeare's Language*, Frank Kermode rightly calls *As You Like It* "the most topical of the comedies." It's not topical, though, in the transparent way that *Henry the Fifth* (and its allusion to Essex and Ireland) or *Julius Caesar* (and its concern with holiday and republicanism) had been. From its casual allusions to Ireland to its mention of the celebrated new fountain of Diana in West Cheap (4.1.145)—the one that was "for the most part naked," John Stow writes, "with Thames-water pilling from her breasts"—there's no mistaking that *As You Like It* is rooted in its place and time. But its real topicality resides elsewhere, in its attentiveness to evolving notions of Elizabethan comedy and pastoral. Comedy tends to have a briefer shelf life than other genres even as it's more popular (there were, for example, as many comedies staged as histories and tragedies combined in 1599). What's funny or delightful to one generation often feels pointless and strained to the next. When conventions and social expectations change, comedy must, too. Shakespeare didn't need Marston or Jonson to remind him that it was no longer possible to write the kind of comedy that he had been writing for most of the past decade. In *As You Like It*, we can feel that a cultural page had turned, even if that page is no longer fully legible to us, and that Shakespeare knows it and moves to act on this knowledge.

Frank Kermode is also on the mark when he concludes that the play "has too much to say about what was once intimately interesting and now is not," for there "is no play by Shakespeare, apart perhaps from *Love's Labor's Lost*, that requires of the reader or spectator more knowledge of Elizabethan culture and especially of its styles of literature." Even the play's most devoted admirers must

† From James Shapiro, *A Year in the Life of William Shakespeare: 1599* (New York: Harper Collins, 2005), pp. 216–25. Reprinted by permission of Harper Collins Publishers.

admit that Shakespeare's often opaque reflections on literary matters are distracting. Few today read or see *As You Like It* for the pleasure of immersing themselves in literary issues that only matter now because they once mattered to Shakespeare. But this liability turns out to be a godsend for the literary biographer, for whom Shakespeare has left all too few clues about how and why he wrote what he did. That having been said, what clues there are often feel like riddles. When he does allude to another writer in *As You Like It*, it is to one who was no longer alive:

> Dead Shepherd, now I find thy saw of might,
> "Who ever loved that loved not at first sight?"
> (3.5.80–81)

The lines are spoken by Phoebe, a young shepherdess desperately in love with "Ganymede," who quotes from Christopher Marlowe's masterpiece *Hero and Leander*, posthumously published in 1598. It's the word "now" in the first line that carries particular emphasis for Phoebe, dumbstruck in love, and for Shakespeare as well. The line recalls the time back then in the early 1590s when he was working on *Venus and Adonis* and Marlowe on *Hero and Leander*. Poetry would never be quite so simple or pure as that again. Shakespeare also goes out of his way to recall Marlowe as "Dead Shepherd," the celebrated author of the pastoral lyric "The Passionate Shepherd to His Love." That the misattribution of this poem in *The Passionate Pilgrim* is still on his mind appears likely from another passage in the play, though this one is so obscure that it's unclear who would have caught the allusion. Shakespeare seems to be speaking to himself when he has Touchstone say: "When a man's verses cannot be understood, nor a man's good wit seconded with the forward child, understanding, it strikes a man more dead than a great reckoning in a little room" (3.3.10–13). This oblique allusion to Marlowe's violent death (stabbed over the "reckoning" or bill) and the echo of his famous line in *The Jew of Malta* about "infinite riches in a little room" seem to be linked here to how deadly it is to a writer's reputation—Marlowe's but undoubtedly Shakespeare's as well—to be misunderstood. It's hard not to feel that these recollections are but the tip of the iceberg. Lurking beneath the surface of the play is a decadelong struggle on Shakespeare's part to absorb and move beyond his greatest rival's work, an engagement that is at its most intense in 1598 to 1599 in *The Merry Wives of Windsor, Henry the Fifth, As You Like It*, and, finally, *Hamlet*. After that, the battle won, and Marlowe's innovations and "mighty line" thoroughly absorbed, Shakespeare was troubled no longer.

But Marlowe's ghost still visited Shakespeare as he turned to pastoral in *As You Like It*—for Marlowe had been there before him, both in refashioning and debunking the genre. One of the lessons Shakespeare learned from Marlowe, which he puts to good use in *As You Like It*, is that the most effective way to talk about love without sounding clichéd is to turn what others have written into cliché. Rosalind does this in dismissing Marlowe's tale of tragic lovers as a fiction. Leander didn't die for love, as Marlowe had it, in a desperate attempt to swim the Hellespont to reach his beloved Hero, but drowned while bathing, victim of a cramp:

> Leander, he would have lived many a fair year though Hero had turned nun, if it had not been for a hot midsummer night; for, good youth, he went but forth to wash him in the Hellespont and being taken with the cramp was drowned; and the foolish chroniclers of that age found it was—Hero of Sestos. (4.1.94–99)

What Marlowe's characters experienced was invented; what Rosalind feels in this most artificial of plays is real.

As Shakespeare was caught up in writing *As You Like It*, pretty clearly by late summer 1599, he was more concerned with living rivals than dead ones, including those with a strongly satiric bent, like Jonson. Jonson was collaborating on plays at the Rose and working by himself on his best play yet, a comical satire called *Every Man Out of His Humour*. Espousing a coolly critical form of comedy devoted to exposing human foibles, Jonson offered Londoners a dazzling alternative to Shakespearean romantic comedy. Shakespeare would have had advance notice, having heard the gist of it when Jonson read or pitched the play to him and his fellow sharers, for the Chamberlain's Men purchased it and staged it that autumn. Jonson took some clever swipes at Shakespeare in his play (at everything from his coat of arms to his recent *Julius Caesar*), but, for the Chamberlain's Men, profits mattered more than personal slights. This was Jonson's breakthrough play, and they were glad to have it.

Jonson's timing couldn't have been better. The banning and burning of verse satire in early June had done nothing to sate the public's hunger for this caustic stuff. Satire quickly found an outlet on the stage. Shakespeare, alert to the shift, offers a rare piece of editorializing about the ban and its aftermath in *As You Like It*: "Since the little wit that fools have was silenced, the little foolery that wise men have makes a great show" (1.2.85–87). Whatever misgiving he may have had about the genre, Shakespeare, who would soon write the trenchantly satiric *Troilus and Cressida*, was motivated to try his hand at satire for the first time in *As You Like It*, in the person of Jaques.

Jaques is something of an enigma. He has a significant presence in the play (speaking almost a tenth of its lines), but no effect on it.

He changes nothing, fails to persuade or reform anyone. Mostly, he likes to watch. He's melancholy, brooding, and sentimental, and some have seen in him a rough sketch for Hamlet; others find him little more than a self-deluding, jaundiced, onetime libertine. Shakespeare himself is careful to suspend judgment. For audiences at the Globe, whether or not they found Jaques sympathetic, his insistence that his aim was to "Cleanse the foul body of th' infected world, / If they will patiently receive my medicine" (2.7.60–61), signaled unambiguously that he was cut from the same cloth as the satiric types popularized by Jonson. Shakespeare even does his best to turn the type into a cliché, and other characters refer to Jaques generically as "Monsieur Melancholy" and "Monsieur Traveler" (3.2.290, 4.1.30).

Jaques's obsession with purging society helps explain the name Shakespeare gives him—pronounced like "jakes," the Elizabethan word for privy or water closet, with a nod here at John Harington's *The Metamorphosis of Ajax* (pronounced "a-jakes"). In case we miss Shakespeare's joke, Touchstone is there to remind us, calling Jaques not by his distasteful name, but rather, out of a dignified politeness, "Master What-ye-call't" (3.3.68). In portraying Jaques, Shakespeare manages to have it both ways, which wasn't easy to do. He creates a memorable satirist who nonetheless finds himself trumped at every turn. Touchstone gets the better of him, as does Rosalind. Even Orlando vanquishes him in their verbal sparring. These encounters also make Rosalind and Orlando feel more human and believable.

Jaques's finest moment is his famous speech on the seven ages of man, the one that begins "All the world's a stage, / And all the men and women merely players" (2.7.138–39). It ends with a grim portrait of old age:

> Last scene of all,
> That ends this strange, eventful history,
> Is second childishness and mere oblivion,
> Sans teeth, sans eyes, sans taste, sans everything.
>   (2.7.162–65)

Just as we find ourselves nodding in agreement, Shakespeare reverses course, repudiating Jaques's cynicism with the dramatic entrance of "Orlando with Adam." What we witness at this moment—Orlando bearing his ancient servant Adam on his back—is no portrait of a toothless second childhood, or of the inevitability of isolation as we age, but an emblem of devotion between old and young.

For Shakespeare, this undermining of the grim vision of Jonsonian comical satire was personal, and there's a good chance that he wrote himself into this scene. An anecdote set down in the late eighteenth century records how a "very old man" of Stratford-upon-Avon, "of weak intellects, but yet related to Shakespeare—being asked by

some of his neighbors what he remembered about him, answered—
that he saw him once brought on the stage upon another man's
back." Another independent and fuller version of this tradition from
around this time provides more corroborating details, recalling
how Shakespeare played the part of "a decrepit old man" in which
"he appeared so weak and drooping and unable to walk, that he
was forced to be supported and carried by another person to a table,
at which he was seated among some company, who were eating, and
one of them sung a song." The descriptions bear a close resemblance
to Adam's role. Scholars have long surmised that Shakespeare, not
the finest actor in his company, may have taken "old man" parts for
himself. There aren't any other anecdotes quite like this that describe
which roles Shakespeare created for himself, and, while there's no
way of authenticating this tradition, it sounds plausible.

Jaques's most poignant moment comes at the very end of the play.
Though the Duke begs him to "stay, Jaques, stay" for the imminent
wedding festivities, Jaques cannot find it in himself to join in the
dance, that timeless symbol of communal harmony: "I am for other
than for dancing measures" (5.4.192–93). Unable to change society,
Jaques turns his back on it. While the others leave Arden and return
to court, Jaques remains behind. Like Shylock before him and Malvolio not long after, he is an outsider whose isolation reminds us that
Shakespearean comedy, too, can be harsh, and draws a sharp line
between those it includes and those who remain outside its charmed
circle.

Shakespeare faced other challenges in this comedy, not least of
which was satisfying his audience's desire for a clown. *As You Like
It* accommodates both clown and satirist, though their roles—
exposing the foolishness of others—overlap considerably. As disappointed playgoers at the Globe had already discovered, Kemp was
no longer with the company. However personally relieved Shakespeare may have been, he and his fellow sharers still needed to find
a suitable replacement. By the time Shakespeare wrote *As You Like
It*, Kemp's successor, Robert Armin, had at last been found.

The Chamberlain's Men would have known Armin by reputation
as a goldsmith turned ballad writer and pamphleteer who had then
turned playwright and comedian. They may have seen him perform
as a member of Chandos's Men or attended one of his performances
for private, aristocratic audiences (Armin seemed to do a good bit of
freelancing). Had they seen an early version of *Two Maids of More-
Clack*, they would have been impressed by his intellect and versatil-
ity, for Armin not only wrote it, he also starred in two comic roles.
Armin may even have allowed the Chamberlain's Men a look at his
works in progress, a pair of books about the art of the clown, *Fool
upon Fool* and *Quips upon Questions*, both about to be published. If

he read the latter, Shakespeare would have seen that Armin was gifted at riddling and engaging others in witty, catechizing dialogue. It wasn't long before Shakespeare was drawing on this particular skill, creating for him the memorable role of the riddling Gravedigger in *Hamlet.* Armin was everything Kemp was not. He couldn't dance but he was a fine singer and mimic. Though a veteran performer, he was still young, having just turned thirty. He didn't do jigs. He didn't insist on being the center of attention. And he was physically unintimidating; a contemporary woodcut portrait suggests that he was almost dwarfish. He was someone Shakespeare could work with and learn from. Armin was more of a witty fool than a clown, though when called upon, he had no problem stepping into a role like *Much Ado's* Dogberry, which Shakespeare had written specifically for Kemp. All told, Armin's talents fit neatly with the trajectory of Shakespeare's art and had a liberating effect on it, culminating in Armin's role as the Fool in *King Lear.* It proved to be a good match. In the short term, however, it remained to be seen if audiences would embrace him as they had Kemp. It had taken several years for Shakespeare to write parts that fully capitalized on Kemp's strengths; he would not have the same luxury in Armin's case and must have felt considerable pressure to make Armin's debut a success.

The first role he would create for Armin would be Touchstone. Touchstones are literally objects that take the measure of things, tell us if they are real or fraudulent, which is very much Armin's role in the play (there's also a bit of a private joke here, given Armin's training as a goldsmith, for London's goldsmiths had a touchstone as their emblem). Breaking with the tradition of Kemp's country fellows, Armin is cast as a court or professional fool, dressed in motley. He loyally accompanies Celia and Rosalind into the woods, though he misses life at court. Once in Arden, he's a fish out of water, a situation that provides ample opportunity to show off Armin's dry wit. He has an unusually large part for a fool; excepting Feste in *Twelfth Night,* his three hundred lines in *As You Like It* are the longest part Shakespeare wrote for any fool. Surprisingly, Shakespeare didn't take advantage of Armin's singing ability (unless, that is, Armin also doubled the part of the play's professional adult singer, Amiens). Like any professional clown, Armin also had his set routines, and, when the play needs to stall for time near the end, he launched into one of them about the "Seven Degrees of the Lie" in act 5. Written specifically for Armin, it now feels dead on the page as well as in performance. Without his touch, its magic has evaporated.

In contrast to Jaques, his opposite number and self-appointed commentator, Touchstone finds himself becoming more of a participant in Arden than an observer. The fool who holds his nose and announces upon entering the pastoral world ("Ay, now am I in Arden; the more fool I" [2.4.14]), eventually surrenders to the impulses he has ridiculed and at the end of the play marries a country wench, Audrey. How long this marriage will last is anyone's guess (Jaques gives it two months, and he may be right). This, too, marked a signal change from Kemp, who consistently steered clear of romantic entanglements in his stage roles. Spectators still missed the charismatic Kemp, but from the perspective of the Chamberlain's Men, and surely from Shakespeare's, Armin was a welcome addition.

Shakespeare had more to worry about than clowns and fools. He knew that children's companies were about to start attracting more privileged audiences in London. In early May a new choirmaster, Edward Pearce, had taken over at St. Paul's, and it was under his tenure that the boys resumed playing for the first time in nearly a decade. Paul's Boys had a great advantage, for they performed on the grounds of the centrally located cathedral, in the city itself, an area off limits to adult players. And their advertised "private" performances, limited to two hundred or so spectators, allowed them to operate independent of the licensing control of the master of the revels. They were therefore free to put on plays that were more daringly satiric and topical. They also had some powerful backers: Rowland Whyte would report in November that William Stanley, the sixth Earl of Derby "hath put up the plays of the children in Paul's to his great pains and charge." The success of Paul's Boys soon led to creation of the Children of the Chapel, who began playing at the indoor Second Blackfriars by 1600.

The boys' pint-size appearance was perfect for parodying their rivals. And their uncracked voices were a strong selling point in so musically attuned a culture (Elizabethan England produced only a few painters of note, such as Isaac Oliver and Nicholas Hilliard, but the talent in musical composition was deep). Adult players could sword fight, dance, and carry a tune, but only a handful, including Armin, could compete musically with the children, who were after all trained choristers. The Chamberlain's Men would find themselves caught between the popular fare of rival adult companies and the intimate offerings of the boys.

If the children's companies highlighted boys and song, the Chamberlain's Men could, too. *As You Like It* includes an unprecedented six boy actors (as opposed to the usual pair). A lesser dramatist might have simply responded to the vogue for boys and their singing by adding a tune or two. Shakespeare chose to write more songs—five in all, three sung by adults, two by boys—than he would in any other play. Thinking of *As You Like It* as an embryonic musical may help explain why critics have had such a hard time with its meager, episodic plot, its rich vein of contemporary satire, its over-the-top climax where the god Hymen enters, and all its song and dance. The same ingredients, viewed from the perspective of musical comedy, make perfect sense. It's as if Shakespeare was feeling his way toward something not yet imaginable, for over a century would pass before the first English musical, John Gay's *The Beggar's Opera*, was staged in 1728. It's not entirely clear whether Shakespeare was fully aware of where his art was leading him, and in retrospect, this turns out to be one of the paths not taken, its tracks almost fully covered over.

But that wasn't the case in the years after the English musical became a sensation. Producers immediately recognized how little reworking it took to turn *As You Like It* into a fully fledged musical. When it was revived in 1740, for example, it was padded out with a song lifted from *Love's Labors Lost*. And by the time it was put on at the Theatre Royal at York in 1789, Celia, Phoebe, and Amiens all had singing parts, and more music—including a hornpipe solo at the end of act 1—was added as well. By 1824, at Drury Lane, you couldn't call it anything else but a musical, with a slew of songs added from *A Midsummer Night's Dream*, *Twelfth Night*, *The Passionate Pilgrim*, and *Venus and Adonis*, and a new finale—"An Allegorical Dance and Chorus of Aeriel Spirits"—brought in to replace the older and tired one starring Hymen.

Some of the songs Shakespeare wrote for *As You Like It* have a thematic function; others seem to be included simply to satisfy the audience's desire to hear good singing. The most accomplished of these songs is "It Was a Lover and His Lass," which appears in act 5, scene 3—a scene with no other purpose than to introduce it. It's sung by two boys, introduced as the "Duke's pages," who go out of their way to remind us that they're professionals who sing without making excuses, "without hawking or spitting or saying we are hoarse, which are the only prologues to a bad voice":

> It was a lover and his lass,
> With a hey, and a ho, and a hey-nonny-no,
> That o'er the green cornfield did pass
> In the springtime, the only pretty ring-time.
> When birds do sing, hey ding a ding, ding.
> Sweet lovers love the spring,
> And therefore take the present time,
> With a hey, and a ho, and a hey-nonny-no.
> For love is crowned with the prime.
> In springtime, etc.
>
> (5.3.16 ff.)

Original music for "It was a lover and his lass" survives, set for voice, lute, and bass viol, and was published shortly after it was first

"It Was a Lover and His Lass," from Thomas Morley's *First Book of Ayres* (London, 1600), item 6.

staged in Thomas Morley's *The First Book of Ayres* in 1600. Morley was one of the leading musicians and composers of the day and until recently had been Shakespeare's neighbor in Bishopsgate Ward. The best explanation for why the same song appears in both Shakespeare's and Morley's published work is that Shakespeare had sought out Morley as a collaborator. Lyrics in musical theater don't count for much unless they are accompanied by first-rate tunes. It looks like the two artists worked on this song together, Shakespeare providing the words, Morley the music, leaving both free to publish the joint venture independently. If so, audiences at the Globe would have been treated to an inspired collaboration between England's leading lyricist and one of its finest composers. If there are any lost Shakespearean lyrics still to be discovered, it's likely that they will be found in the anonymous songs in collections like Morley's *Book of Ayres*.

* * *

JULIET DUSINBERRE

Pancakes and a Date for *As You Like It*†

* * *

In the 1960s a document was discovered by Steven May and William Ringler which has received even less attention than the Public Record Office list of Blackfriars plays. It consists of nine verse lines titled "to ye Q. by ye players 1598" copied into the manuscript commonplace book of Henry Stanford, who was attached as chaplain and tutor to the household of George Carey, second Baron Hunsdon, and Lord Chamberlain from 1597.[1] May demonstrates that Stanford's book uses old-style dating with the new year beginning on 25 March.[2] Since the lines declare the occasion to be Shrovetide, which occurs earlier than 25 March, 1598 would here mean 1599 in modern dating.

Ringler and May published the original verse lines in a 1972 article in *Modern Philology* and suggested that they formed an epilogue probably by Shakespeare.[3] Their article was subsequently reprinted in the documents section of the 1974 *Riverside Shakespeare* with the title "An Epilogue by Shakespeare?" and is included in the second edition of 1997 with an affirmation of its likely connection to Shakespeare and the Chamberlains Men, but with still no suggestion about which play the epilogue might have followed. There the matter has rested until revived by Brian Vickers, who

---

† From Juliet Dusinberre, "Pancakes and a Date for *As You Like It*," *Shakespeare Quarterly* 4.4 (2003): 375–82. © 2003 Folger Shakespeare Library. Reprinted with permission of The Johns Hopkins University Press.
1. Stanford's commonplace book is preserved in Cambridge University Library as Cambridge MS Dd.5.75, and the nine-line epilogue appears on folio 46. Steven W. May reproduces the epilogue in his *Henry Stanford's Anthology: An Edition of Cambridge University Library Manuscript Dd.5.75* (New York and London: Garland Publishing, 1988), 162 (item 228), annotated on 373; the epilogue is also reproduced in this essay as Figure 1.
2. See May, xi–xv.
3. William A. Ringler and Steven W. May, "An Epilogue Possibly by Shakespeare," *Modern Philology* 70 (1972): 138–39; reprinted as "An Epilogue by Shakespeare?" in G. Blakemore Evans, ed., *The Riverside Shakespeare* (Boston: Houghton Mifflin, 1974), Appendix B, 1851–52; and 2d ed. (1997), Appendix C, 1978.

supports the claim of Shakespearean authorship of the epilogue, arguing that, in this age of media hype, Ringler and May's original modest scholarly presentation of the document contributed to its being overlooked.[4] A reconsideration of the epilogue, reproduced on p. 372, is long overdue.

The following lines were spoken after a performance before the queen at Shrove 1599:

As the diall hand tells ore / ye same howers yt had before
still beginning in ye ending / circuler accompt still lending
So most mightie Q. we pray / like ye Dyall day by day
you may lead ye seasons on / making new when old are gon
that the babe wch now is yong / & hathe yet no vse of tongue
many a Shrovetyde here may bow / to y^t Empresse I doe now
that the children of these lordes / sitting at your Counsell Bourdes
may be graue & aeged seene / of her y^t was ther father Quene
Once I wishe this wishe again / heauen subscribe yt wth amen.

The nine double lines, each divided with a virgule, are in rhymed trochaic couplets, as in Puck's epilogue to *A Midsummer Night's Dream* and Prospero's to *The Tempest*. The trochaic form, which was part of Sidney's poetic legacy, was used only by Shakespeare, Jonson, and Dekker, and twice as often by Shakespeare as by the other two playwrights combined. May points out that Shakespeare employs it in "more than twenty songs and poems in his plays, from the earliest to the latest."[5] Ringler and May note the uninflected genitive ("father Quene"), which also occurs in *Antony and Cleopatra*, "Oh *Anthony*, you haue my Father house" (TLN 1483 [2.7.127–28]). They find the syntax and vocabulary consistent with Shakespeare's normal practice, with the exception of the word "circuler," which occurs nowhere else in his work. However, it is not remarkable for Shakespeare to use a word on only one occasion.

Ringler and May argue that the Stanford epilogue is most likely to be connected with the Chamberlain's Men because of Henry Stanford's relation to the Lord Chamberlain's family. Stanford had been employed in the 1580s as a tutor by the Pagets, a well-known recusant family, and had moved with his pupil, William Paget, to the Carey household when Sir Thomas Paget died in 1587 and William became George Carey's ward. Sir George Carey (Lord Hunsdon), who succeeded his father Henry as Lord Chamberlain in 1597, was at court for the Shrovetide festivities of 1599: "On February 17 of that year he attended a meeting of the Privy Council at

4. See Brian Vickers, *'Counterfeiting' Shakespeare: Evidence, Authorship, and John Ford's Funerall Elegye* (Cambridge: Cambridge UP, 2002), 427–29.
5. Ringler and May, 139; Steven W. May, *Bibliography & First Line Index of English Verse, 1559–1603* (London: Continuum, 2004).

A possible court epilogue to *As You Like It*

Richmond, and on February 20 he signed a letter along with eight other Lords of the Council."[6] Hunsdon as Lord Chamberlain presided officially over court entertainment, and an epilogue for a particular performance discarded by the players might easily have come into his hands, especially if it was recited by one of his own players. Besides being the family's tutor, Stanford was also a poet, who subsequently developed a long-term friendship with Sir George Carey's daughter, Elizabeth (called "Bess"), whom he helped to translate two sonnets by Petrarch.[7] It would have been natural for the epilogue to have reached his hands either from the Lord Chamberlain or even from the players themselves. But what was the play? One of the most frustrating aspects of Elizabethan court records is their specificity about date and their failure except in a handful of cases to name the plays performed. Can that anonymity ever be cracked?

The epilogue's specific mention of performance at Shrovetide in 1598 (1599 new dating) limits the choice of available dramas. In 1599 Shrove was late, with Shrove Sunday (Quinquagesima) on 18 February and Shrove Tuesday on 20 February. The Admiral's Men performed at court on Shrove Sunday, and the Chamberlain's Men (Shakespeare's company) on Shrove Tuesday. The entry for the Chamberlain's Men in the Declared Accounts of the Treasurer of the Chamber records payments made on 2 October 1599:

> To John Heminges and Thomas Pope servants vnto the Lorde Chamberleyne vppon the Councells warraunt dated at the Courte at Nonesuche sc̄do die Ottobris 1599 for three Enterludes or playes played before her Matie vppon St Stephens daye at nighte, Newyeares daye at night and Shrovetuesday at nighte laste paste xx^li [£20] and to them more by waye of her Matie rewarde x^li [£10]. In all amounting to xxx^li [£30].[8]

The payment—including the queen's reward, a regularly granted extra for court performance—works out to £10 per play. At Shrovetide the court was at Richmond Palace, where they had removed on Saturday, 10 February, to mark the liturgical festival with suitable entertainment.[9]

The non-Shakespearean plays for which the Stanford epilogue might have been written can be quickly eliminated from debate.

6. Ringler and May, 138–39, citing *Acts of the Privy Council of England AD 1542–1631*, ed. J. R. Dasent et al., 46 vols. (London: His Majesty's Stationery Office, 1890–), 30:96.
7. See Katherine Duncan-Jones, "Bess Carey's Petrarch: Newly Discovered Elizabethan Sonnets," *Review of English Studies* 50 (1999): 304–19.
8. PRO E351/543, fol. 55; see also John H. Astington, *English Court Theatre 1558—1642* (Cambridge: Cambridge UP, 1999), 236. PRO is Public Record Office [*Editor*].
9. PRO E351/543, fol. 38. See also John Chamberlain, *Letters Written by John Chamberlain during the Reign of Queen Elizabeth*, ed. Sarah Williams ([Westminster:] Camden Society, 1861), 45; and Astington, 236.

Dekker's two plays *Old Fortunatus* and *The Shoemaker's Holiday* were performed by the Admiral's Men on 27 December 1599 and 1 January 1600 when the court was at Richmond. These dates are too late for the new epilogue. Nor, for the same reason, could the anonymous authors of *A Warning for Fair Women* (1599) or *A Larum for London* (1600), both performed by the Chamberlain's Men, have written the epilogue. The other possible author is Jonson. But *Every Man In His Humour* is too early, as it was seen by Tobie Matthew on 20 September 1598;[1] *Every Man Out of His Humour* is too late, being performed in the autumn of 1599 at the Globe.[2]

The Shakespeare play that the epilogue fits best is *As You Like It*. I want to argue that Shakespeare did, in fact, write the epilogue for a performance of this play at court in February 1599. The argument remains a hypothesis but one that, unlike other attempts to date the play, bears scrutiny, even though it seems surprising that Shakespeare would have written Rosalind's epilogue and then have decided to replace it for court performance with the epilogue in Stanford's book. However elegant and graceful the Stanford epilogue may be, it doesn't begin to approach the panache and audacity of Rosalind's final address to the audience.

Prologues and epilogues, as Tiffany Stern has demonstrated, were occasional pieces, often detached physically from the main body of the play and considered disposable when no longer useful; they did not always reach print.[3] The epilogue to *2 Henry IV* in the First Folio clearly combines a court epilogue, ending with homage to the queen, with a public-performance address to the audience. Dekker's *Shoemaker's Holiday* has a prologue that was spoken only at court. Rosalind's racy appeal at the end of *As You Like It* to men and women (not gentlemen and ladies) and saucy offering of kisses all round is arguably not deferential enough for queen and court. Lyly's Gallathea, the only other woman to speak an epilogue in an extant play of this period, addresses her patterned rhetoric emphatically to "Ladies."[4] Rosalind's epilogue could easily have been either specially written or—since cuts for court performance were standard practice—reinstated for performance at the Globe.

What follows is an account of a growing conviction—once it appeared that there could have been more than one epilogue to *As You Like It*—that the Stanford epilogue was written for a court performance of the play and specifically for the Shrovetide performance

1. See *Ben Jonson*, ed. C. H. Herford and Percy Simpson, 11 vols. (Oxford: Clarendon Press, 1925–52), 1:331.
2. See Ringler and May, 139.
3. Tiffany Stern, "'A Small-beer Health to his Second Day': Playwrights, Prologues, and First Performances in the Early Modern Theatre," *Studies in Philology* (forthcoming in 2004). Tiffany Stern generously allowed me to read her essay in manuscript.
4. John Lyly, *Gallathea 1592* (Oxford: The Malone Society, 1998), 55 (sig. H2ʳ).

at Richmond on 20 February 1599. The appropriateness of the Stanford epilogue to *As You Like It* can be demonstrated in a number of ways. But it casts its most startling light on one of Touchstone's worst jokes. Jesting about the oath "by mine honour," the Clown declares that he learned it

Of a certain knight, that swore by his honour they were good pancakes, and swore by his honour the mustard was naught. Now I'll stand to it, the pancakes were naught and the mustard was good, and yet was not the knight forsworn.

(1.2.60–65)

Pancakes. Queen and court were eating pancakes in the Great Hall at Richmond for Shrove Tuesday night when, according to the Declared Accounts, the Chamberlain's Men performed a play. That's why Touchstone's joke is funny. It was pancake day.[5] The Clown in *All's Well That Ends Well* remarks on the fitness of "a pancake for Shrove Tuesday" (2.2.22–23).[6] The Elizabethans ate pancakes stuffed with powdered beef (like a modern fritter)—hence the mustard. The Office of Works accounts, where the palace accounts are set out, record that in 1598–99 workmen at Richmond Palace were paid "for makeinge a larder to sett powdered meate in."[7] The larder must have been a cold safe for meat, ready for the pancakes.

Who, then, would have acted Touchstone? A performance of *As You Like It* as early as 20 February 1599 would settle the question. It would have been Will Kemp, not Robert Armin as is usually assumed (although no doubt Armin succeeded Kemp in the role, as he almost certainly did in the role of Dogberry).[8] Kemp was among the actors who signed the lease for the Globe the next day. Since he sold his share shortly afterwards, it has been thought that Kemp left the company before it moved to the Globe, although this is by no means certain.[9] But if the earlier date is accepted, then the part of Touchstone must have been written originally for Kemp.

---

5. Anne Owens connects Touchstone's pancakes to Shrove, although not in terms of performance; see "*As You Like It* or, The Anatomy of Melancholy," Q-W-E-R-T-Y 7 (1997): 15–26, esp. 20.
6. The court was summoned to eat pancakes by the "pancake bell" in Dekker's *The Shoemaker's Holiday*, 5.1.50, quoted here from François Laroque, *Shakespeare's Festive World*, trans. Janet Lloyd (Cambridge: Cambridge UP, 1991), 101. Laroque points out that the only other play which mentions Shrove is *2 Henry IV* (367n), where Silence breaks out in tipsy song: "And welcome merry Shrove-tide. / Be merry, be merry" (5.3.35–36). This play is too early for February 1599 performance, however, and *All's Well* is too late.
7. PRO E351/3234, fol. 6^r.
8. For Armin's playing of Dogberry, see Emma Marshall Denkinger, "Actors' Names in Registers of St. Bodolph Aldgate," *PMLA* 41 (1926): 91–109, esp. 95.
9. James Nielson argues that Kemp was still acting at the Globe in 1600; see "William Kemp at the Globe," *SQ* 44 (1993): 466–68.

While the part of Touchstone, the Clown, has never perfectly fitted scholarly preconceptions about Robert Armin,[1] it has nevertheless often seemed too courtly for Will Kemp's mode of clowning. This may be due to an underestimating of the extent to which Kemp belonged to a world of court music and performance. He had been taken to Flanders with the earl of Leicester's players in the mid-1580s, although more as a guest *artiste* than as a regular player, and he made his reputation in that context. His presence in *As You Like It* would have reminded the audience of a moment in the past with special poignancy through memories of Leicester. Moreover, Touchstone's jests that rout the hedge-priest Sir Oliver Mar-text would have recalled Kemp's long engagement in the Marprelate controversy, which raged throughout the 1580s and was revived at the turn of the century.[2] A date of early 1599 for *As You Like It* would confirm Kemp in the role of Touchstone.

Finally, the name *Ganymede*—for all its daring evocation of the homoerotic (in Jove's passion for the beautiful boy whom he seized and made his cupbearer)—has special implications for Shrovetide performance. Shrovetide, the Continental Mardi Gras, the days immediately preceding the forty days of fasting for Lent, is traditionally a time of carnival: feasts and carousings, plays and sports. Ganymede was especially associated with the zodiac sign of Aquarius (the water-bearer) within which Shrove usually fell.[3] In Nicholas Breton's *Vox Graculi* the figure of Carnival on Shrove Tuesday is described as "chiefe Ganimede to the Guts . . . Protector of Pancakes."[4] In John Withals's *Shorte Dictionarie in Latine and English*, the entry for varieties of sweet wine under "Colours and the Names of Wines" reads:

> *Misceri decet hoc a Ganimede merum:*
> You mingle delicate Wine and principall honie together, which delicate wine ought to be tempered and made of none but Ganymedes.[5]

---

1. As Gary Taylor, on behalf of the Oxford editors, writes: "It does not seem to us at all clear that Shakespeare wrote Touchstone's part for Robert Armin" (Stanley Wells and Gary Taylor with John Jowett and William Montgomery, *William Shakespeare: A Textual Companion* [Oxford: Clarendon Press, 1987], 121).

2. Julier Dusinberre, "Topical forest: Kemp and Mar-text in Arden" in *In Arden: Editing Shakespeare*, Ann Thompson and Gordon McMullan, eds. (London: Thomson Learning, 2003), 239–51; see also Juliet Dusinberre, "Kemp and Touchstone," *The Shakespeare Newsletter* 54.4 (2002/2003): 93–94, 106, 110, and 126.

3. See Owens, 26n. Shrovetide may fall at any date between 3 February and 9 March (depending on the date of Easter) and thus crosses two signs of the zodiac, Aquarius (the water-bearer), which ends on 19 February, and Pisces (the fish), which begins on 20 February.

4. Quoted here from Laroque, 102.

5. John Withals, *A Shorte Dictionarie in Latine and English, verie profitable for yong beginners* (London, 1586), sig. D7ᵛ. The literal translation of the Latin is: "It is fitting to mix this wine in the manner of Ganymede."

Rosalind as Ganymede can be seen as the high priest of Shrovetide merriment, warning Phoebe: "I pray you do not fall in love with me, / For I am falser than vows made in wine" (3.5.72–73). Drinking images are as natural to her as are appeals to Jupiter: "I would thou couldst stammer," she cries to Celia, "that thou mightst pour this concealed man out of thy mouth, as wine comes out of a narrow-mouthed bottle; either too much at once or none at all. I prithee take the cork out of thy mouth, that I may drink thy tidings" (3.2.195–200). The name *Ganymede* might have reminded the Elizabethans of their own special drink of mead. Ganymede is cupbearer to both Jove (a prototype of Elizabeth) and Shrove.

How well does the new epilogue splice on to the end of *As You Like It?* If Rosalind's epilogue were removed, the final lines of Shakespeare's play would then be: "Proceed, proceed. We'll begin these rites, / As we do trust they'll end, in true delights" (5.4.195–96). The epilogue in Stanford's book begins: "As the diall hand tells ore / ye same howers yt had before / still beginning in ye ending / circuler accompt still lending." Being rites, end in delights; still beginning in the ending. The epilogue joins seamlessly to Shakespeare's text. The play ends, but the wedding rites being. The motif of beginning and ending picks up the circular movement of the play from court to country and back to court again. The circularity noted in the epilogue is present both in the seasonal celebration and in the play itself.

* * *

LAURIE SHANNON

[Friendship in *As You Like It*]†

* * *

Scholars have long observed the special emphasis on likeness between friends, noting its rhetorical flourish as a poetic conceit.[1] But this conceit is not merely ornamental. The radical likeness of sex and station that friendship doctrines require singly enables a vision of parity, a virtually civic parity not modeled anywhere else in contemporary social structures. Further, the insistent emphasis on sexual and social sameness is a systematic response to that most

---

† From Laurie Shannon, *Sovereign Amity: Figures of Friendship in Shakespearean Contexts* (Chicago: University of Chicago Press, 2002), pp. 2–5. Reprinted by permission.
1. See Laurens Mills's encyclopedic account of ideal friendship's literary appearances, *One Soul in Bodies Twain: Friendship in Tudor and Stuart Literature* (Bloomington, Ind.: The Principia Press, 1937).

acute form of early modern difference: the hierarchical difference of degree, especially the categorical difference between rulers and the ruled (which, in friendship, becomes a difference in "kind"). A discourse of degree separates sovereign and subject through a quasi-legal differentiation of "private persons" from those of "public estate," and complex dispensations of agency and powers result. While for the subject the exalted discourses of amity radically figure a fantasy of agency that I term private sovereignty, the monarch's situation is sharply distinguished. The precondition of the king's function as an emblem of public sovereignty is his emphatic and comprehensive preclusion from exercising the very gestures and capacities friendship celebrates. Heroic, "true" friends, flatterers, counselors, monarchs, tyrants and their minions, and the tales of consent and counsel they enact all join to embody a mythography of the political institution before liberalism. Their early modern life enables these friendship figures to become familiars of the political imagination.

Classically derived figures of friendship at the center of the humanist curriculum held out a discourse of more than self-fashioning to readers when they cast the friend as "another self" and merged a pair of friends as "one soul in two bodies." Referencing an insistently same-sex friendship with complex relations to eroticism, these two phrasings appear across a remarkable range of cultural locations in the English Renaissance. Together, the two notions enable a sixteenth-century inquiry into the hypothetical workings of what must have seemed implausible on its face: volitional polity. Likeness in both sex and status *is* (the only) political equality in period terms; on the basis of this likeness, writers stress the making of a consensual social bond or body that is not inherently subordinating.[2] In the first English translation of Cicero's *De amicitia* (an incunable from William Caxton's press), humanist John Tiptoft terms the friend "another . . . the same" and recommends to his reader in 1481 "that of tho[se] tweyne he shold make wel nygh one.[3]

Through the sixteenth century, friendship's phrases make their way across increasingly popular materials. Erasmus's *Adagia* (1536) offers as economical a formulation as one could hope to find: "Amicitia aequalitas. Amicus alter ipse" ("friendship is equality" and "the friend is another self"). This adage appears as the second entry in a collection of more than four thousand adages (the first is "between friends all is common").[4] Thomas Elyot improvises on the *alter ipse*

2. For a discussion of "voluntary submission," see François Rigolot, "Reviving Harmodius and Aristogiton in the Renaissance: Friendship and Tyranny as Voluntary Servitude," *Montaigne Studies* 11 (1999): 107–19.

3. Cicero, *De amicitia,* trans. John Tiptoft (London: William Caxton, 1481), fols. 22r–22v.

4. Erasmus of Rotterdam, *Adagia,* trans. Margaret Mann Phillips, in *The Collected Works of Erasmus* (Toronto: University of Toronto Press, 1982), 31:31 (bk. 1, sec. 1, adage 2).

notion, informing readers of *The Bake Named the Governour* (1531) that "a frende is proprely named of Philosophers the other I."[5] Richard Taverner's gathering of "proper wytty and quycke sayenges," *The Garden of Wysdom* (1539), asserts that when Aristotle was "demau[n]ded, what a frend is, One soule, [quothe] he, in two bodyes."[6] Translating Erasmus's popular *Apophthegmes* through the 1540s and 1550s, Nicolas Udall further trades on these phrasings by referring to one of the most famous pairs of exemplary friends in friendship's archive: "Alexander estemed Hephestion a second Alexander, according to the prouerbe *amicus alter ipse* that is, two frendes are one soul and one [sic] body."[7] The errors here, glossing one proverb as the other and substituting "one" body for "two bodies," make no mistake: two equal corporeal bodies bound in friendship constitute a single corporate or juridical body, a legal fiction creating an operative unity.

From this basis in the broadly pedagogical texts of diverse social strata, the tropes of friendship make their way into even wider contexts in the latter part of the century. The poem "Of Frendship" appears in *Tottel's Miscellany*, condensing the much-circulated sentiments in a couplet: "Behold thy frend, and of thy self the pattern see: / One soull, a wonder shall it seem, in bodies twain to be."[8] Michel de Montaigne, in an essay plundered by English writers, affirms that such friends constitute "no other than one soule in two bodies, according to the fit definition of *Aristotle*."[9] Shakespearean instances abound: in *As You Like It*, for example, Celia chides Rosalind for not realizing that any misfortune is a shared one, saying she lacks "the love / That teaches thee that thou and I *am* one" (1.3. 92–3). The plural subject attaches to a singular verb, according to a friendship doctrine that schools its pupil-subjects about themselves and the specific rules governing their engaged unity, their assembled condition as they become "one."

* * *

5. Thomas Elyot, *The Boke Named the Governour*, ed. Foster Watson (New York: Everyman, 1907), p. 164.
6. Richard Taverner, *The Garden of Wysdom* (London: Richard Bankes, 1539), no pagination; quotations are from the second page of the section on Aristotelian sayings.
7. *Apophthegmes, that is to saie, prompte, quicke, wittie and sentencious sayinges, of certain emperours, kynges, capitaines, philosophiers and orators . . . First gathered and compiled in Latin by the ryght famous clerke Maister Erasmus of Roterodame*, trans. Nicolas Udall (London: Richard Grafton, 1542; John Kingston, 1564; reprint, ed. Robert Roberts, Boston: Lincolnshire, 1877), p. 233.
8. *Tottel's Miscellany (1557–1587)*, ed. Hyder Edward Rollins (Cambridge, Mass.: Harvard University Press, 1965), p. 106. The poem is attributed to Nicolas Grimald.
9. Michel de Montaigne, *The Essayes of Montaigne: John Florio's Translation*, ed. J. I. M. Stewart (New York: Modern Library, 1933), pp. 150–51.

380

VALERIE TRAUB

[The Homoerotics of *As You Like It*]†

* * *

The homoeroticism of *As You Like It* is playful in its ability to transcend binary oppositions, to break into a dual mode, a simultaneity, of desire. In so far as Rosalind/Ganymede is a multiply sexual object (simultaneously heterosexual and homoerotic), Orlando's effusion of desire toward her/him prevents the stable reinstitution of heterosexuality, upon which the marriage plot depends. By interrupting the arbitrary binarism of the heterosexual contract, male homoeroticism, even as it affirms particular masculine bonds, transgresses the erotic imperative of the Law of the Father. The proceedings of Hymen that conclude the play, once read in terms of the 'mock' marriage which precedes them, enact only an ambivalent closure. The reinstitution of gender role (and Rosalind's political subordination under her husband's rule) is incommensurate with a rigidification of sexuality.

* * *

In '"The Place of a Brother" in *As You Like It*: Social Process and Comic Form', Louis Adrian Montrose began the pathbreaking work of placing women's subordination in Shakespearean drama within the context of male homosocial bonds.[1] In a historicisation and politicisation of C. L. Barber's analysis of Rosalind in *Shakespeare's Festive Comedy*, Montrose argued that

> Rosalind's exhilarating mastery of herself and others has been a compensatory 'holiday humor', a temporary, inversionary rite of misrule, whose context is a transfer of authority, property and title from the Duke to his prospective male heir.[2]

More recently, Jean Howard continues within the Barber–Montrose lineage:

> The representation of Rosalind's holiday humor has the primary effect, I think, of confirming the gender system and perfecting rather than dismantling it by making a space for mutuality within relations of dominance.[3]

† From Valerie Traub, "The Homoerotics of Shakespearean Comedy," in *New Casebooks: Shakespeare, Feminism and Gender*, ed. Kate Chedgzoy (New York: Palgrave, 2001), pp. 135–43. Reprinted by permission.
1. Louis Adrian Montrose, '"The Place of a Brother" in *As You Like It*: Social Process and Comic Form', *Shakespeare Quarterly*, 32:1 (1981), 28–54.
2. Ibid., 51.
3. Jean Howard, 'Crossdressing, the Theatre and Gender Struggle in Early Modern England', *Shakespeare Quarterly*, 39:4 (1988), 434.

However, she complicates the analysis of Rosalind's subordination through reference to the French feminist analytic of female
'masquerade':

> the figure of Rosalind dressed as a boy engages in playful mas-
> querade as, in playing Rosalind for Orlando, she acts out the
> parts scripted for women by her culture. Doing so does not
> release Rosalind from patriarchy but reveals the constructed
> nature of patriarchy's representation of the feminine and shows
> a woman manipulating those representations in her own inter-
> est, theatricalising for her own purposes what is assumed to be
> innate, teaching her future mate how to get beyond certain
> ideologies of gender to more enabling ones.[4]

The distance traversed in the progression from Barber to Montrose to Howard indicates a corresponding movement from an
essentialist view of gender, to an emphasis on social structure as
determining gender, to an assertion of the limited possibilities of
subversive manipulation within dominant cultural codes. The sub-
jective if constrained agency conferred by Howard upon Rosalind
as a woman can be extended as well to Rosalind as erotic subject.
In excess of the dominant ideology of monogamous heterosexuality,
to which Rosalind is symbolically wed at the end of the play, exist
desires unsanctioned by institutional favour. By means of her male
improvisation, Rosalind leads the play into a mode of desire neither
heterosexual nor homoerotic, but both heterosexual *and* homoerotic. As much as she displays her desire for Orlando, she also
enjoys her position as male object of Phebe's desire and, more importantly, of Orlando's. S/he thus instigates a deconstruction of the
binary system by which desire in subsequent centuries came to be
organised, regulated and disciplined.

That homoerotic significations will play a part in *As You Like It* is
first intimated by Rosalind's adoption of the name Ganymede when
she imagines donning doublet and hose. Of all the male names
available to her, she chooses that of the young lover of Zeus, familiar
to educated Britons through Greek and Latin literature and European painting, and to less privileged persons as a colloquial term
used to describe the male object of male love. As James Saslow, who

---

4. Ibid., 435. Terms can be confusing here, in part due to translation. In Luce Irigaray's
formulation, *la mascarade* is 'An alienated or false version of femininity arising from
the woman's awareness of the man's desire for her to be his other, the masquerade
permits woman to experience desire not in her own right but as the man's desire situ-
ates her.' Masquerade is the role (playing) required by 'femininity'. Thus, Rosalind's
improvisation is really closer to *mimétisme* (mimicry) which, in Irigaray's terms, is 'An
interim strategy for dealing with the realm of discourse (where the speaking subject is
posited as masculine), in which the woman deliberately assumes the feminine style and
posture assigned to her within this discourse in order to uncover the mechanisms by
which it exploits her' (*This Sex which is not One*, trans. Catherine Porter [Ithaca, NY:
Cornell University Press, 1985], p. 220).

traces the artistic representation of Ganymede in Western culture
from the fifteenth to the seventeenth centuries, argues, 'the very
word *ganymede* was used from medieval times well into the seventeenth century to mean an object of homosexual desire'.[5] Saslow's
argument is seconded by Orgel: 'the name Ganymede [could not] be
used in the Renaissance without this connotation'.[6]

That Rosalind-cum-Ganymede becomes the object of another
woman's desire is obvious. Consciously, of course, Phebe believes
Ganymede to be a man, and is thus merely following the dominant
heterosexual course. And yet, what attracts Phebe to Ganymede
are precisely those qualities that could be termed 'feminine'. Notice
the progression of the following speech:

> It is a pretty youth—not very pretty. . . .
> He'll make a proper man. The best thing in him
> Is his complexion. . . .
> He is not very tall; yet for his years he's tall.
> His leg is but so so; and yet 'tis well.
> There was a pretty redness in his lip,
> A little riper and more lusty red
> Than that mix'd in his cheek; 'twas just the difference
> Betwixt the constant red and mingled damask.
>
> (III.v.113–23)

During the first half of her recollection, as she measures Ganymede
against the standard of common male attributes—height, leg—
Phebe fights her attraction, syntactically oscillating between affirmation and denial: he is; he is not. In the last four lines, as she
'feminises' Ganymede's lip and cheek, she capitulates to her desire
altogether.

Many critics acknowledge the underlying homoeroticism of
Phebe's attraction; however, they tend to undermine its thematic
importance by relegating it to the status of a temporary psychosex-
ual stage. C. L. Barber, for instance, remarks: 'She has, in effect,
a girlish crush on the femininity which shows through Rosalind's
disguise; the aberrant affection is happily got over when Rosalind
reveals her identity and makes it manifest that Phebe has been loving a woman.'[7] When Barber says that Phebe's 'aberrant' affection is
'happily got over' he reveals the extent to which homophobic anxiety

---

5. James Saslow, *Ganymede in the Renaissance: Homosexuality in Art and Society* (New
   Haven, CT: Yale University Press, 1986), p. 2.
6. Stephen Orgel, 'Nobody's Perfect: Or, Why did the English Stage Take Boys for
   Women?', *South Atlantic Quarterly*, 88 (1989), 7–29 (p. 22).
7. C. L. Barber, *Shakespeare's Festive Comedy: A Study of Dramatic Form and its Relation
   to Social Custom* (New York: Princeton University Press, 1963), p. 231. See also W.
   Thomas MacCary, *Friends and Lovers: The Phenomenology of Desire in Shakespearean
   Comedy* (New York: Columbia University Press, 1985).

structures the developmental logic of his response. But if a 'girlish crush' is outgrown or overcome, what are we to make of Rosalind's desire to 'prove a busy actor' in the 'pageant truly play'd' of Phebe and Silvius? (III.iv.50–8). Although her ostensible motivation is her belief that 'the sight of lovers feedeth those in love' (56), s/he soon interjects in order to correct the literal-mindedness that feeds Phebe's 'proud disdain' (III.iv.52). And yet the pleasure Rosalind/Ganymede takes in this task seems in excess of her putative function. Significantly, it is s/he who first mentions the possibility of Phebe's attraction, interpreting and then glorying in Phebe's changed demeanor:

> Why, what means this? Why do you look on me?
> I see no more in you than in the ordinary
> Of nature's sale-work. 'Od's my little life
> I think she means to tangle my eyes too!
> (III.v.41–4)

Is there not a sense in which Rosalind/Ganymede *elicits* Phebe's desire, constructing it even as she refuses it? Indeed, in these lines the conflict between discourses of gender and of sexuality are intensely manifested: at the level of gender, Rosalind restates compulsory heterosexuality; at the level of sexuality, Ganymede elicits a desire for that which falls outside (or on the cusp) of the binarism of gender. At any rate, s/he is represented as delighting in her role of the rejecting male:

> Down on your knees,
> And thank heaven, fasting, for a good man's love;
> For I must tell you friendly in your ear,
> Sell when you can, you are not for all markets.
> (III.v.57–60)

And why does s/he put Silvius through the exquisite torment of hearing Phebe's love letter to Ganymede read aloud, if not to aggrandise her own victorious position as male rival? (IV.iii.14–64). Indeed, as a male, her sense of power is so complete that s/he presumes to tell Silvius to tell Phebe, 'that if she love *me*, I charge her to love *thee*' (IV.iii.71–2, my emphasis).

Homoerotic desire in *As You Like It* thus circulates from Phebe's desire for the 'feminine' in Rosalind/Ganymede to Rosalind/Ganymede's desire to be the 'masculine' object of Phebe's desire. Even more suggestive of the text's investment in homoerotic pleasure is Orlando's willingness to engage in love-play with a young shepherd. Throughout his 'courtship' of Ganymede (who is now impersonating Rosalind), Orlando accepts and treats Ganymede as his beloved. To do so requires less his willing suspension of disbelief than the ability to hold in suspension a dual sexuality that feels no compulsion to make arbitrary distinction between kinds of objects. That Rosalind-cum-Ganymede takes the lead in their courtship has been noted by countless critics; that there is a certain homoerotic irony in that fact has yet to be noted. As a 'ganymede', Rosalind would be expected to play the part of a younger, more receptive partner in an erotic exchange. S/he thus not only inverts gender roles; s/he disrupts alleged homoerotic roles as well.

What began as a game culminates in the 'mock' marriage, when Orlando takes for his wife the boy he believes to be fictionalising as Rosalind. It is Celia, not Orlando, who hesitates in playing her part in the ceremony—'I cannot say the words', she responds to Orlando's request that she play the priest (IV.i.121)—in part because those words possess a ritualistic power to *enact* what is spoken. In so far as ritual was still popularly believed to be imbued with sacred or magical power, the fact that Orlando does not hesitate, but eagerly responds in the precise form of the Anglican marriage ceremony—'I take thee, Rosalind, for wife' (IV.i.129)—suggests the degree to which the play legitimises the multiple desires it represents. The point is not that Orlando and Ganymede formalise a homosexual marriage, but rather that as the distance between Rosalind and Ganymede collapses, distinctions between homoerotic and heterosexual collapse as well. As the woman and the shepherd boy merge, Orlando's words resound with the conviction that, for the moment, he (as much as Rosalind and the audience) is engaged in the ceremony as if it were real. As both a performative speech act and a theatricalisation of desire, the marriage is both true and fictional at once. The subversiveness of this dramatic gesture lies in the dual motion of first, appropriating the meaning of matrimony for deviant desires; and second, exposing the heterosexual imperative of matrimony as a reduction of the plurality of desire into the singularity of monogamy. The 'mock' marriage is not a desecration but a deconstruction—a displacement and subversion of the terms by which desire is encoded—of the ritual by which two are made one.

When Hymen in Act V symbolically reintroduces the logic of heterosexual marriage, the text's devotion to simultaneity would appear to be negated. The terms in which Hymen performs the quartet of marriages make the ideological function of the ritual clear: 'Peace, ho! I bar confusion. / 'Tis I must make conclusion / Of these most strange events' (V.iv.124–6). 'Hymen's bands' (V.iv.128) are called forth to 'make conclusion' not only of erotic 'confusion' but of the play. And yet the play does not end with Hymen's bars and bands, but with a renewed attack on the pretensions of erotic certitude. In a repetition of her previous gender and erotic mobility, Rosalind-cum-boy actor, still wearing female attire, leaps the frame of the play in order to address the audience in a distinctly erotic manner: 'If I were a woman I would kiss as many of you as had beards that pleas'd me, complexions that lik'd me, and breaths that I defied not' (Epilogue 16–19). As Orgel, Howard, Phyllis Rackin and Catherine Belsey all intimate, the effect of this statement is to highlight the constructedness of gender and the flexibility of erotic attraction at precisely the point when the formal impulse of comedy would be to essentialise and fix both gender and eroticism. Throughout the play, what makes erotic contingency possible is a simple conjunction: 'if'. Indeed, Touchstone's discourse on the virtues of 'if' can serve as an index of the play's entire erotic strategy: 'If you said so, then I said so' (V.iv.99–100). The dependence on the conditional structures the possibility of erotic exploration without necessitating a commitment to it. Orlando can woo and even wed Ganymede as '*if* thou wert indeed my Rosalind' and as *if* the marriage were real (IV.i.189–90, my emphasis). Through the magic of 'if', the boy actor playing Rosalind can offer and elicit erotic attraction to and from each gender in the audience. 'If' not only creates multiple erotic possibilities and positions, it also conditionally resolves the dramatic confusion that the play cannot sustain. As Rosalind says to Silvius, Phebe and Orlando, respectively: 'I would love you, if I could'; 'I will marry you, if ever I marry a woman, and I'll be married tomorrow'; and 'I will satisfy you, if ever I satisfied man, and you shall be married tomorrow' (V.ii.108–12). Even Hymen's mandate is qualified; 'Here's eight that must take hands / To join in Hymen's bands / If truth hold true contents' (V.iv.127–9, my emphasis).

My own reliance on 'if' should make it clear that I am not arguing that Rosalind or Orlando or Phebe 'is' 'a' 'homosexual'. Rather, at various moments in the play, these characters temporarily inhabit a homoerotic position of desire. To insist on a mode of desire as a position taken up also differs from formulating these characters as 'bisexual': as Phyllis Rackin reminds us, bisexuality implicitly defines the desiring subject as divided in order to maintain the ideologically motivated categories of homo- and hetero- as inviolate.[8] The entire logic of *As You Like It* works against such categorisation, against fixing upon and reifying any one mode of desire.

Simultaneity and flexibility, however, are not without their costs. In so far as the text circulates homoerotic desire, it displaces the anxieties so generated in the following tableau described by Oliver, Orlando's brother.

A wretched ragged man, o'ergrown with hair,
Lay sleeping on his back. About his neck
A green and gilded snake had wreath'd itself,

8. Phyllis Rackin, 'Historical Difference/Sexual Difference', in *Privileging Gender in Early Modern England*, ed. Jean R. Brink (Kirksville: 16th Century Journal Publisher, 1992).

Who with her head nimble in threats approach'd
The opening of his mouth. . . .
A lioness, with udders all drawn dry,
Lay couching, head on ground, with catlike watch,
When that the sleeping man should stir. . . .
                                        (IV.iii.107–17)

The dual dangers to which the sleeping Oliver is susceptible are, on
the face of it, female: the lioness an aged maternal figure ('with
udders all drawn dry'), the female snake seductively encircling Oliver's neck. Let us first give this passage a conventional psychoanalytic reading: the virile and virtuous Orlando banishes the snake
and battles with the lion while his evil 'emasculated' brother, unconscious of his position as damsel in distress, sleeps on—their sibling
rivalry displaced onto and mediated by gender conflict. Yet at the
same time as the snake encircles her prey, she approaches and
almost penetrates the vulnerable opening of Oliver's mouth. Rather
than posit the snake, in this aspect, as a representation of the 'phallic mother', I want to argue that in the snake's figure are concentrated
the anxieties generated by the text's simultaneous commitment to
homoeroticism and heterosexuality. If Oliver is endangered by the
snake's 'feminine' sexual powers, he is equally threatened by her
phallic ones. He becomes both the feminised object of male aggression and the *ef*feminised object of female desire. The snake thus
represents the erotic other of the text, the reservoir of the fears elicited by homoerotic exchanges—fears, I want to insist, that are not
inherent in the experience of homoerotic desire, but that are produced by those ideologies that position homoeroticism as unnatural,
criminal and heretical.

Indeed the relations represented in this tableau suggest that no
desire, male or female, heterosexual or homoerotic, is free of anxiety. As Touchstone says in a lighter vein, 'as all is mortal in nature,
so is all nature in love mortal in folly' (II.iv.52–3). But what is most
interesting is that in this play sexual danger is encoded as feminis-
ing to the object persistently figured as male. Consistently, the text
seems less interested in the threat of a particular mode of desire
(hetero/homo) than in the dangers desire *as such* poses to men. It is,
in this sense, thoroughly patriarchal, positing man as the centre of,
and vulnerable to, desire. That the text marginalises this expression
of vulnerability by not dramatising it on stage but reporting it only
in retrospect suggests the extent to which the anxiety is repressed in
the interests of achieving comic, heterosexual closure, however partially or problematically.

My highlighting of the affirmative possibilities of multiple pleasures is not meant to imply that *As You Like It* represents a paradisia-

cal erotic economy, a utopian return to a polymorphously perverse body unmediated by cultural restraints. As the penultimate gesture toward the institution of marriage clearly indicates, endless erotic mobility is difficult to sustain. But just as clearly, *As You Like It* registers its lack of commitment to the binary logic that dominates the organisation of desire. If *As You Like It* suggests that 'folly' of desire, part of that folly is the discipline to which it is subject.

CYNTHIA MARSHALL

Constructions of Negation in As You Like It†

* * *

The melancholy Jaques makes his living, we might say, by cheerfully lampooning what he could be but is not. The linguistic principle he practices is by no means particular to him. The very nature of language, as Lacan and others have unfolded it, is to cloak a meaning that may or may not exist. Building on the work of Ferdinand de Saussure, Lacan refers to the "incessant sliding of the signified under the signifier" as an effect creating a "chain of discourse." The chainlike structure of language in turn allows the possibility "to use it in order to signify *something quite other* than what it says."[1] Or, in Joan Copjec's words, *"Since signifiers are not transparent, they cannot demonstrate that they are not hiding something behind what they say—they cannot prove that they do not lie.* Language can only present itself to the subject as a veil that cuts off from view a reality that is other than what we are allowed to see."[2] For Lacan, language acquisition introduces a split within the subject; as "the discourse of the Other," the unconscious functions linguistically but inaccessibly.[3] *As You Like It* returns again and again to the ability or propensity of language, and in particular of names, to veil an inaccessible zone, a "reality that is other than what we are allowed to see" and is taken for reality precisely because we are unable to see it.

Consider, for instance, the "new news at the new court" in Act 1, which is nothing "but the old news," specifically that "the old Duke is banished by his younger brother the new Duke" (1.1.96–100). The wordplay unsettles the political structure whose machinations it

† From Cynthia Marshall, "The Doubled Jaques and Constructions of Negation in *As You Like It*," *Shakespeare Quarterly* 49.4 (1998): 378–84, 386, 388–89, 391. © 1998 Folger Shakespeare Library. Reprinted with permission of The Johns Hopkins University Press.
1. Jacques Lacan, *Ecrits: A Selection*, trans. Alan Sheridan (New York: W. W. Norton, 1977), 154 and 155.
2. Joan Copjec, *Read My Desire: Lacan against the Historicists* (Cambridge, MA: MIT Press, 1994), 54.
3. Lacan, *Ecrits*, 172.

documents: there is a certain obvious equivalency between old and new news, between old and new dukes, but the placement of Duke Senior away from court, outside of power, underlines his authority as the "real" duke. The keen nostalgia that inspires Charles's comparison of the old duke to "the old Robin Hood of England," fleeting the time "as they did in the golden world" (1.1.116, 118–19), furthers the image of an authoritative, originary, but utterly inaccessible reality. The play's world becomes one of substitutions, where duke replaces duke, brother challenges brother, cousin threatens to unseat cousin, fool topples oaf in the affections of Audrey, Ganymede supplants Silvius in those of Phebe; in the midst of all this, the old duke's namelessness testifies to his unique place outside the linguistic chain of replacements. That he, moreover, embraces pain for its capacity to "feelingly persuade me what I am" (2.1.11) seems to indicate further that he is one character (and the only one, it seems to me, other than Touchstone and the melancholy Jaques) not at least intermittently in the grip of repression.

In contrast to the duke's placement outside the linguistic turnstile, Rosalind fully occupies it. Ganymede's success at standing in for Rosalind is the showpiece of the play's set of substitutions. "Nay, you must call me Rosalind" (3.2.422): what is the love-cure but a glorification of the symbol's substitutive power, an intoxicating revelry in the capacity of language to construct a character, a relationship, a love affair? Ganymede's reiterated claim "And I am your Rosalind" (4.1.62) is accepted on a linguistic basis by Orlando: "I take some joy to say you are, because I would be talking of her" (ll. 85–86). But the claim underscores a sense that Ganymede's Rosalind is *only* a creation of words. In contrast to Rosalind's transformation into Ganymede, which requires a costume and altered behavior, Ganymede adopts the Rosalind role simply and only through conversation with Orlando. Such a demonstration of the character's purely linguistic reality is gravely taxing to theatrical mimesis. In the face of the dissolution threatened by Ganymede as reminder that all the characters are but verbal artifice, the play emphasizes instead the gendered frisson, the apparently stubborn presence of the male Ganymede rather than the female Rosalind enacting amorous play with Orlando. Ganymede indeed protests too much that "he" is really "she," highlighting for viewers the gendered gap between Orlando's actual and virtual love partners. Even Orlando's late signal that he is weary of the game—"I can live no longer by thinking" (5.2.50)—offers no certain escape from the dilemma of equivocal gender: where, and how, might one live without thinking? How can he opt out of the social arrangements born of cognitive ordering? If Orlando's comment does suggest a preference for the physical reality of Rosalind over that of Ganymede, and if the wedding with which the play closes seems to grant his wish, the theatrical condition of the original performance by an all-male cast nevertheless works to undermine this heterosexual ordering. Ganymede's masquerade as Rosalind opens up the equivocacy of Orlando's desire: it is apparent during the loveplay in Arden that Orlando desires both of them. The compression of male and female personae into one character functions like the symbol of negation, allowing Orlando to acknowledge a repressed idea—"I desire him"— on condition that the idea is negated—"I desire her, not him." Orlando's increased vividness testifies to his enrichment through this symbol of negation. Whereas his first encounter with Rosalind at Duke Frederick's court strikes him dumb, Orlando's interaction with Ganymede/Rosalind shows how, to quote Freud again, his "thinking frees itself from the restrictions of repression and enriches itself with material that is indispensable." But, perhaps because of the arrival of Oliver and his immediate assertion of a heterosexual claim on Celia, Orlando quails from continued "thinking" of this free and enriched sort. His demand of a settled arrangement of heterosexual coupling reinstates the repression of his desire for Ganymede.[4]

Desire, as Freud was well aware, involves identificatory wishes as well as possessive ones; it can take the form of wishing to be the object or wishing to have it. Not only are Orlando and those readers or viewers who primarily identify with him allowed to acknowledge the titillating possibility of a boy lover, but Rosalind and those who identify with her are likewise allowed the fantasy of being male. This wish seems, to most viewers, not at all surprising: in a masculinist society, who wouldn't choose to be male? Yet I think it's not enough to read the politics of gendered privilege in the Ganymede disguise; we also need to see how erotic play is pressured and manipulated. Rosalind's decision to maintain the Ganymede persona in her interactions with Orlando suggests that she does not wish to participate only as a female in a heterosexual couple. She also wishes to be a boy interacting with Orlando; perhaps she wishes to be, or at least to be *like*, Orlando himself. Recognizing this erotic tendency allows us to see desire as something other than lack. The Ganymede disguise, once again, lifts the barrier of repression, allowing temporary acknowledgment of illicit erotic desires that are safely veiled by the symbol of negation: not Rosalind but Ganymede; not Ganymede

4. For discussion of how the play's acknowledgment of multiple and shifting erotic desires works against the concluding image of heterosexual marriage, see Valerie Traub, *Desire and Anxiety: Circulations of Sexuality in Shakespearean Drama* (New York: Routledge, 1992), 122–30, esp. 123. For the argument that Rosalind/Ganymede's doubled gender is necessary for the play's happy ending, see Susanne L. Wofford, "'To You I Give Myself, For I Am Yours': Erotic Performance and Theatrical Performatives in *As You Like It*" in *Shakespeare Reread: The Texts in Mew Contexts*, Russ McDonald, ed. (Ithaca, NY: Cornell UP, 1994), 147–69.

but the pretended Rosalind; and, most encompassingly, not us but Shakespeare's fiction.

In spite of the contrast between Rosalind and her father, between her subordination to linguistic order and her father's placement outside it, there is a sense that what is banished in both their cases takes on greater reality. The old duke is the real duke, and the disguised Rosalind is, or more precisely becomes, the real Rosalind. Rosalind's low spirits in the opening act of the play, that is, make her seem less "herself"—the exuberant, inventive character whom viewers cherish—when she appears before us as a girl than during her lengthy period in drag. Celia's pleading tones suggest that her cousin's gloom is uncharacteristic: "I pray thee Rosalind, sweet my coz, be merry" (1.2.1); "my sweet Rose, my dear Rose, be merry" (ll. 21–22). Melancholy has displaced Rosalind from herself. By means of her banishment and subsequent disguise, she recovers her spirits. The trip to Arden and the entry into male dress constitute an adventure, of course, but we should also notice that disguise and substitution—veiling her identity—allow Rosalind's return to happiness. Viewers, along with Orlando, know Rosalind better when she is hidden beneath Ganymede than when she appears as herself. Displacement is shown to be the key to characterological recognition, even though all such recognition is bracketed: the tantalizing promise of a reality hidden by the veiling signifier cannot be confirmed; the signifier cannot prove that it does not lie.

This bracketing of linguistically constructed reality means that banishments, displacements, and disguises are never totally realized in *As You Like It*. Inevitably some trace of what they repress remains behind. I here use *trace* as both noun and verb, as a suggestive bit left behind and as the action of following the outline or shape of something. Understanding the emotional logic of *As You Like It* requires attending to such traces, because the play achieves its much-admired balance by covering up with one hand what it reveals with the other. Thus Rosalind's first-act sadness re-emerges momentarily when as Ganymede she sighs that "men have died from time to time and worms have eaten them, but not for love" (4.1.101–3). While she is disguised, her feminine excitability comes to the fore during private exchange with Celia (3.2.215–220; 3.4.1–35; 4.1.195–207). By the same token, Ganymede's ambivalent gender and rhetorical cleverness re-emerge in the Epilogue. *As You Like It* is unlike a lighter comedy such as *A Midsummer Night's Dream*, which simply banishes melancholy ("Turn melancholy forth to funerals: / The pale companion is not for our pomp" [1.1.14–15]), and unlike a heavier one such as *Measure for Measure*, which takes account of the cost of repression on both individual and societal levels. *As You Like It* achieves its vaunted balance by admitting troubling ideas but cloaking them so as to limit their impact. Joseph

Westlund says the play "is sane and wonderful, and it makes us feel that we are too."[5] This complexly satisfying effect may suggest a triumphalist plot in which evil is overcome, but *As You Like It* is not a heavily plotted play. As Jenkins observes, it contains a "minimum of action" and most of it occurs in the first act.[6] Instead, what *As You Like It* offers are symbolic conversions of troubling material. The process starts early, with the mutation of Orlando's fratricidal anger into the recreational rhythm of the wrestling match.[7] It includes Duke Senior's conversion of exile into sabbatical and Rosalind's interpretation of banishment as adventure. Repeatedly, painful events are mastered through their symbolic reorganization. As Touchstone says, "when I was at home I was in a better place, but travellers must be content" (2.4.13–14).

Most important to note, the rhythm at work in these repeated instances of painful emotion converted to positive gain is that of the Freudian *Fort/Da*. Observing his grandson cast a toy away (*Fort* ["gone"]) only to drag it back (*Da* ["there"]) by an attached string, Freud found an emblem of the compensatory psyche.[8] He partially answered the problem of why the child would repeat a painful experience of loss by noting the mastery achieved in the game and hence, by implication, over the painful departures of his mother that the game supposedly symbolized. But the triumphant ego is ultimately less significant in Freud's analysis of the game than the vexing fact of repetition; and by the end of "Beyond the Pleasure Principle," Freud is led to propose both a death instinct and primary masochism.[9]

The problem with Freud's *Fort/Da* formulation, as Lacan allows us to see, is that he overlooks the step of converting actual loss (the mother's departure) into symbolic loss (casting away the toy and assigning words to the enactment). Reading the two as equivalent, Freud proposes a mechanical repetition of emotions on the part of the little boy. Lacan, however, places the crucial step in the process of symbolizing loss, for the positions of absence and presence are reversed through "the introduction of the symbol." "[D]on't forget," Lacan writes, "when he says *Fort*, it is because the object is here, and when he says *Da* the object is absent." Language thus effects not a simple repetition but an inversion, so that "absence is evoked

---

5. Joseph Westlund, *Shakespeare's Reparative Comedies: A Psychoanalytic View of the Middle Plays* (Chicago: U of Chicago P, 1984), 69.
6. Harold Jenkins, "As You Like It," *Shakespeare Survey* 8 (1955): 40–51, esp. 42 and 41. Anne Barton similarly observes that "the play's plot barely exists" ("'As You Like It' and 'Twelfth Night': Shakespeare's Sense of an Ending" in *Shakespearian Comedy*, David Palmer and Malcom Bradbury, eds. [London: Edward Arnold, 1972], 160–80, esp. 162).
7. See Cynthia Marshall, "Wrestling as Play and Game in *As You Like It*," *Studies in English Literature* 33 (1993): 265–87.
8. Sigmund Freud, "Beyond the Pleasure Principle," in *The Standard Edition of the Complete Psychological Works of Sigmund Freud*, trans. James Strachey, 24 vols. (London: Hogarth Press and the Institute of Psychoanalysis, 1961), 18:1–64, esp. 15.
9. Freud, "Beyond the Pleasure Principle," *Standard Edition*, 18:38 and 54–55.

in presence, and presence in absence." Far from understanding this as accident or coincidence, Lacan labels it the essence of human discourse; the introduction of the symbol "opens up the world of negativity, which constitutes both the discourse of the human subject and the reality of his world in so far as it is human."[1] Where a mechanistic reading of the *Fort/Da* scenario finds only compulsion to repeat and master, Lacan sees a symbolic conversion that opens up a world of negativity, a linguistic reality in which "the thing" accords imperfectly with "the symbol." If under this order nothing is ever quite what it seems, if reality is displaced by language, a world is nevertheless opened up by the symbolic process. As Lacan puts it, the "*subject does not just in this master his privation . . . but he also raises his desire to a second power.*"[2]

Lacan goes on to link the "primal masochism" Freud had mentioned in "Beyond the Pleasure Principle" with "this initial negativation . . . this original murder of the thing."[3] Freud found masochism an intensely troubling concept because it contradicted his fundamental premise of an essentially self-protective (and pre-linguistic) psychic economy; over the course of his career he changed his mind several times about the existence and status of primary masochism.[4] Lacan's recognition of language as a fundamental third term of psychic reality complicates the idea of primary masochism. Rather than simply implying self-destructiveness, Lacan's sense of an "initial negativation" founded in the symbol develops, and takes us back to, Freud's recognition that "the symbol of negation" proves "indispensable" for thinking. Lacan views the *Fort/Da* episode, I am suggesting, not in terms of mastery but as an instance of Freudian negation. The synchronic structure of language complicates the diachronic order of events.

Now, *As You Like It's* Arden, that impossible realm of pastoral possibility, is itself "a world of negativity." This "golden world," with its "tongues in trees, books in the running brooks, / Sermons in stones, and good in everything" (2.1.16–17), is the universe of discourse opened up by symbolic conversion.[5] Here language in its

1. Jacques Lacan, *The Seminar of Jacques Lacan: Book I: Freud's Papers on Technique 1953–1954*, ed. Jacques Alain Miller, trans. John Forrester (New York: W. W. Norton, 1988), 173–74.
2. Lacan, *Seminar I*, 173.
3. Lacan, *Seminar I*, 174.
4. In "Three Essays on the Theory of Sexuality" (1905) Freud views sadism and masochism as congruent; in "Instincts and Their Vicissitudes" (1915) he questions the existence of primary masochism, but his claim that sadists identify with their victims essentially posits a hidden masochism; in "The Economic Problem of Masochism" (1924) Freud theorizes that a conjunction of the death instinct with the libido produces the various forms of masochism.
5. William Kerrigan similarly observes that "Arden is a text. . . . a forest of literacy, teeming with heteroglossia" ("Female Friends and Fraternal Enemies in *As You Like It*" in *Desire in the Renaissance: Psychoanalysis and Literature*, Valeria Finucci and Regina Schwartz, eds. [Princeton, NJ: Princeton UP, 1994], 184–203, esp. 194).

various forms proliferates: Corin counsels Silvius and debates with Touchstone; Orlando becomes a poet, "character[ing]" his thoughts in the bark of trees; Jaques orates his view of the "seven ages of man"; and Rosalind/Ganymede uses verbal pretense to engage in courtship with Orlando. All this is predicated on an initial Lacanian "murder of the thing," a willingness to sacrifice a sure reality for the linguistic *If* whose powers Touchstone documents late in the play (5.4.102). I have discussed already the erotic expansion and possibility enabled by the replacement of Rosalind with Ganymede's personified "Rosalind." The border-crossing "conversion" of Oliver from villain to lover is another signal instance of symbolic inversion. Viewers complain that Oliver's transformation is unrealistic because unmotivated, but his is only the most abrupt of a sheaf of similar changes. He, moreover, narrates his own alteration:

> CELIA   Was't you that did so oft contrive to kill him?
> OLIVER 'Twas I. But 'tis not I. I do not shame
>   To tell you what I was, since my conversion
>   So sweetly tastes, being the thing I am.
>   (4.3.134–37)

The point is not that Oliver's essence has been miraculously altered, any more than Rosalind's feminine nature has been replaced by Ganymede's boyish one. Instead it is a matter in each case of new symbolic or linguistic possibilities being opened up through the process of negation: "'Twas I. But 'tis not I.'"

What of the part of the melancholy Jaques in this world of negativity? I am arguing that Jaques, even more than Ganymede's Rosalind, exemplifies the power of a symbol to hold at bay a repressed and troubling idea. The melancholy affect of Rosalind is overdetermined in Act 1: her father's banishment has left her unable and unwilling "to remember any extraordinary pleasure" (1.2.5–6); her sudden passion for Orlando produces "burs . . . in [her] heart" (1.3.16–17); the duke banishes her, on pain of death, for the simply stated reason "that I trust thee not" (1.3.51). Orlando, too, grieves for multiple causes; not only has he been barred from "the place of a brother" (1.1.19), but his successful wrestling is "misconster[ed]" by the duke (1.2.255) and Oliver treacherously plots to kill him. All this, together with the old duke's banishment in Arden, constitutes a weighty burden of gloom at the play's start, a weight that must somehow be acknowledged despite the changed conditions of Orlando and Rosalind when they reappear in Arden. The absent Jaques de Boys becomes the emblem of the severing of family that troubles both Orlando and Rosalind, merging with the melancholy Jaques, who thereby takes on the melancholic burden set down by the other characters upon their entry into Arden.

* * *

With the melancholy Jaques serving as the symbol for melancholia, the other characters are freed to practice the proliferating substitutions of happy linguistic function. Yet Jaques will eventually depart, and as if in preparation for his exit, Rosalind, with her final words in the play, gives herself to the duke ("I'll have no father, if you be not he") and to Orlando ("I'll have no husband, if you be not he") and announces to Phebe that she will "ne'er wed woman, if you be not she" (5.4.121–23). Positioning herself in relation to father and husband, Rosalind enters the culturally mandated silence of femininity. The line with which she bars herself from ever "wed[ding] woman" is ordinarily played with a comic turn, but it signals that the descent of prescribed gender roles entails prohibition as well as partnership. The easy erotic attractions that proliferate earlier in the play cease with the movement into organized, marriageable couples. The presiding figure for this nuptial ceremony is Hymen, god of marriage and hence of conjunction, but also, through irreducible linguistic association, evoking virginity and hence obstacle or limit. Marriage involves loss as well as gain, and "virginity" names only part of what is lost; Rosalind also leaves behind the Ganymede persona, the affiliated habit of linguistic ease, and the possibility of a primary bond with a(nother) woman.

* * *

Anna Barton observes that Jaques's "withdrawal at the end impoverishes the comic society. . . . Like a ship which has suddenly jettisoned its ballast, the play no longer rides quite evenly in the waves."[6] Certainly I agree that Jaques's presence is crucial to the balance of the play, but I see his departure as disruptive because of what he leaves behind rather than what he takes away with him. Before his departure Jaques announces an inheritance to each of the male characters on stage: his "former honour" to the duke, "love" to Orlando and Oliver, "a long and well-deserved bed" to Silvius, "wrangling" to Touchstone (5.4.185–90). Jaques's bequest here returns the play to the issues of inheritance with which it began but does so within a more overtly gendered arrangement, since four of the five inheritors stand as part of a newly married couple. It is an odd speech, not only because "considerations of rank ought to have assigned" it to the duke,[7] but because it is difficult to know what Jaques could have to "bequeath" (1. 185)—other than his melancholy. Melancholy is what I understand him to be redistributing over the four couples, in the strongly prescribed gender formations in which Hymen has left them.

* * *

6. Barton, 171.
7. Barton, 166.

At the end of *As You Like It*, then, when Orlando has tired of "thinking" (both in his own sense and in the one Freud indicates as a benefit of negation) and invited the reassertion of gendered order and heterosexual coupling, the melancholic truth of gender emerges with Ganymede's disappearance and Hymen's arrival. Both Orlando and Rosalind must disavow an aspect of desire that has emerged in Arden so that a proper marriage can occur. Significantly, the melancholy Jaques here departs, replaced by the Second Brother, who appears as through a revolving door. We miss the point if we suppose that the melancholy Jaques leaves because he finds the concluding happiness inimical to his interests. The doubling of the two Jaqueses should make us suspicious of just such an emphasis on character at the expense of symbolic patterning. Rather, by serving as the placeholder for melancholy, the melancholy Jaques has helped to keep gender questions open; more broadly, he has allowed an opening-up of discourse, an enriched thinking. By enabling the function of negation, he has made the play a comedy.

* * *

JEFFREY MASTEN

Ganymede's Hand in *As You Like It*†

[Shaw] might have been churlish about the knowing giggles of an audience all too ready to read more into the cross-dressing than Shakespeare ever imagined. [T]he night I saw the production, a lot of the laughs seemed to have less to do with the text than with the double-entendres sought out by the audience.
— Vincent Canby in *The New York Times*, reviewing the October 1994, all-male Cheek-By-Jowl production of *As You Like It*[1]

The habits of Compositor D with respect to [the spelling of] other words than "do," "go," and "here"—both his preferences and his *tolerances*—are yet to be thoroughly studied. So too are such non-spelling peculiarities as may be discovered in his work.
— Charlton Hinman on the typesetting of the 1623 First Folio collection of Shakespeare's plays[2]

Taking my cue from the binary question that heads this section of the volume,[3] I want to assert that it's time for "the most conservative

† Jeffrey Masten, "Textual Deviance: Ganymede's Hand in *As You Like It*," in Marjorie Garber, Paul B. Franklin, and Rebecca L. Walkowitz, eds., *Field Work: Sites in Literary and Cultural Studies* (New York: Routledge, 1996), pp. 153–63. Reprinted by permission.
1. Vincent Canby, 'As You Like It,' "Sunday View," *New York Times*, October 16, 1994.
2. Charlton Hinman, *The Printing and Proofreading of the First Folio of Shakespeare*, 2 vols. (Oxford: Clarendon, 1963) 1: 199, Hinman's italics. Subsequent references to these volumes will appear parenthetically in the text.
3. "Textual Editing: The Most Conservative Practice, or the Most Radical?"

practice" in the editing of early modern texts. If you're not in the field of Renaissance literature, and possibly even if you are, you have, I'm guessing, no sense of how radical our editions of Shakespeare and others from this period have become. Editors and publishers, intent on undermining our shared cultural heritage, the very foundations of Western Culture, have changed (or, as they euphemistically say, "emended") whole words and lines of the very texts that are most important to us; even when purporting to represent to us the texts as written, they have given us what are essentially *translations* from the early modern English, simplifying and reinterpreting (or again, as they would have it, "modernizing") the complexities of a language spoken and written before the advent of standardization. They have, furthermore, given us editions of Shakespeare that, in their very monumentality, or in their paperback slickness, bear no resemblance either to the original staged productions at the Globe and the Blackfriars, or to the editions of his texts printed during his lifetime. As surely as judicial activism subverts the intent of the Framers of the Constitution, current editorial practice is subversion, and editors are outside agitators imposing their own agendas on the relics of Western Culture. The only possible response is an avowed conservatism. *We must reclaim what Shakespeare wrote.*

You don't think I'm going to let that stand, do you? Take that as an example, at least, of one direction in which a conservative practice might proceed. I do mean to disavow this rhetoric, and I've attached it to Shakespeare in order to raise the pitch and the stakes, though many of the same points could be made of early modern texts in general; at the same time, I nevertheless want to argue, for reasons I have at least hinted at above, for a conservative editorial practice. By *conservative* I mean a practice that will, to the greatest extent possible, conserve the documents, and the texts inscribed in those documents, in the forms in which they initially were written, and/or performed, and/or read, and/or circulated, in early modern England. I will argue this from what I take to be a historicist perspective, though I do so while remarking that many of the practitioners of new historicism, whatever the historical attentiveness of their arguments in general, have continued to quote Shakespeare and others from modern, emended, reformatted, modernized, repunctuated editions.

There isn't space in this brief essay to discuss all of this, particularly the questions of modernization as translation I've raised above.[4]

4. The commentary to my edition of *The Old Law*, a collaborative play-text included in *The Collected Works of Thomas Middleton*, general ed. Gary Taylor (Oxford: Oxford University Press, forthcoming) suggests some of the problematics of simultaneously modernizing a text and reading historically. See also the preface and commentary to Stephen Booth's edition of *Shakespeare's Sonnets* (New Haven: Yale University

I'll restrict my task here to finding an example of editing so inflam-
matory in its radicalness that you will be convinced that you should
care about editorial matters—matters we've been taught institution-
ally to devalue as pedantic and largely inconsequential, the tedious
work that happens prior to the real business of literary and cultural
studies today. With the caveat that I know I'm participating in a
certain canonical hegemony, I'll examine *As You Like It*, or rather,
one page of *As You Like It*, since the play may (for whatever reasons,
including the *New York Times* coverage of the controversial 1994
production) retain some interest and accessibility for those outside
the field. My intention, however, is to make an argument that speaks
about early modern English texts and culture more generally.

In the final moments of *As You Like It*, with a number of weddings seemingly both imminent and impossible, and with Rosalind
(disguised as the young man Ganymede) having promised to return,
sort out the marriage plots, and "make all this matter euen" (TLN
2594),[5] the following text appears in the 1623 First Folio edition, the
only early printed text of this play:

> *Enter Hymen, Rosalind, and Celia.*
> *Still Muficke.*
> Hymen. *Then is there mirth in heauen,*
> *When earthly things made euen*
> *attone together.*
> *Good Duke receiue thy daughter,*
> *Hymen from Heauen brought her,*
> *Yea brought her hither.*
> *That thou mightft ioyne his hand with his,*
> *Whofe heart within his bofome is.*

(TLN 2681-90)[6]

The radicalism of the editorial tradition is clear and virtually
univocal; to my knowledge there is no recent edition that conserves

Press, 1977); Margreta de Grazia, "Homonyms Before and After Lexical Standardization," *Shakespeare Jahrbuch* (1990): 143–56. For a more quietistic view of historicism's
relation to the "unchanging" "basic issues" of textual criticism, see G. Thomas Tanselle,
"Historicism and Critical Editing," *Studies in Bibliography* 39 (1986): 1–46, especially
45–46.

5. Except in the photoquotation below, *As You Like It* is cited from *Mr. William Shakespeares Comedies, Histories & Tragedies* (London: by Isaac Iaggard, and Ed. Blount,
1623), as reproduced in *The Norton Facsimile: The First Folio of Shakespeare*, prepared
by Charlton Hinman (New York: Norton, 1968). Parenthetical citations refer to that
edition's through-line numbering (TLN).

6. *Mr. William Shakespeares Comedies, Histories & Tragedies* (London: by Isaac Iaggard,
and Ed. Blount, 1623), page 206 of the Comedies; the photoquotation is from one of the
Houghton Library copies, Harvard University. Photo courtesy of the Houghton Library.

the Folio text joining "his hand with his,"[7] and as the 1977 Shakespeare Variorum edition notes in its survey of previous editions:

> 2689–90 *his hand . . . his bosome*] The editors are almost
> unanimous in finding *his hand* an error *for her hand . . .* —
> COLLIER (ed. 1842) notes that *his* is an easy misreading of
> *hir*—but are deeply divided over whose bosom is the repository
> of whose heart.[8]

The note proceeds to quote a number of the "deeply divided" editors, but notice that they are deeply divided on this second issue
only once one has decided that the first (men holding hands in the
last scene of a Shakespearean comedy) is simply "an error" or "an
easy misreading"—deeply divided, that is, within a heterosexualiz-
ing paradigm. (We can call this "the radical heterosexual agenda.")
By the time the note gets around to quoting an editor who conserva-
tively retains the Folio reading "his hand with his," that reading is
already on the defensive, already a defendant: the Folio's reading "is
defended by CALDECOTT (ed. 1820) on the ground that *his* in both
places refers to Rosalind as Ganymede, whose costume he thinks
she still wears."

But if you were reading the Variorum carefully, you might have
seen this coming in the much earlier note on Rosalind's chosen
male name, Ganymede:

> *Ganimed*] SMITH (ed. 1894) "A beautiful boy, beloved by Jupiter,
> who (in the form of the eagle) carried him off and made him his
> cup-bearer. (Ovid, *Met[amorphoses]* x. 155–161.)" WALTER (ed.
> 1965, p. 7): "[In the Renaissance,] Ganymede was thought to
> represent intelligence, or rational thought, more elaborately his
> name was thought to derive from two Greek words meaning to
> joy or rejoice, and advice or counsel, and this was extended to
> suggest that he led people to love of divine truth. So greatly is
> Rosalind composed of these qualities of intelligence, joy, wis-
> dom, and truth that it is difficult not to believe that Shake-
> speare deliberately clad her in the myth of Ganymede."[9]

Perhaps he did, and I'll have more to say about Shakespeare's delib-
erations in a moment, but, to say the absolute minimum, the Variorum's note suggests that the editorial tradition has privileged
abstraction and allegory over the erotic meanings of this myth,

---

7. The Folio reading has been advocated most recently by Maura Slattery Kuhn, "Much
Virtue in *If*," *Shakespeare Quarterly* 28 (1977): 40–50. For Kuhn, the importance of the
Folio reading lies in its raising of the theatrical question of whether Rosalind resumes
women's clothes for her final entrance in 5.4; Kuhn is largely uninterested in the issues
of homoeroticism that concern me in this essay.
8. Richard Knowles, ed., *As You Like It*, A New Variorum Edition of Shakespeare (New
York: MLA, 1977), 293.
9. Knowles, Variorum *As You Like It* 64 (italics and brackets in the original).

meanings that were widely available in Renaissance culture and not necessarily separate from those celebrated in the note.[1] There remains, of course, the possibility that the interpretation I am about to suggest is, in the words of the Variorum editor's handbook, "mere nonsense of course to be excluded."[2] Critics skeptical of the Folio's reading will remark that Rosalind and Celia have returned to the stage dressed "as themselves,"[3] and Rosalind has been referred to as "her" in the lines that directly precede "his hand with his."[4] Of course, those critics are probably reading out of the radical editorial tradition that has routinely inserted a stage direction indicating for Rosalind a return to women's dress, and, if Rosalind in this speech is referenced as both female and male, it is neither the first nor the last time in the play that this occurs, as those familiar with the play's epilogue will already have anticipated. In any event—and here I'm relying on recent work on Renaissance homoeroticism by social and cultural historians, theorists, and literary critics[5]—I wouldn't want to exclude too quickly the possibility

1. There is widespread evidence for the erotic meanings of *Ganymede* in early modern England. Here for example is John's Minsheu's; definition of the word: "*a Ganimede or Ganymede, a boy hired to be used contrary to nature, to commit the detestable sinne of Sodomie.* Vi. Ingle"; Iohn Minsheu, *Ductor in Linguas, The Guide into the tongue.* (London: Iohn Browne, 1617), 211. On the convergence of the idealizing and homoerotic meanings of this myth, see in particular Leonard Barkan, *Transuming Passion: Ganymede and the Erotics of Humanism* (Stanford: Stanford University Press, 1991). On Renaissance representations and contextualizations of Ganymede more generally, see: Gregory W. Bredbeck, *Sodomy and Interpretation* (Ithaca: Cornell University Press, 1991); James Saslow, *Ganymede in the Renaissance: Homosexuality in Art and Society* (New Haven: Yale University Press, 1986); Bruce Smith, *Homosexual Desire in Shakespeare's England: A Cultural Poetics* (Chicago: University of Chicago Press, 1991). Mario DiGangi observes an important class dynamic in the Ganymede myth and its early modern appropriations, including *As You Like It*; he remarks that the story "concerns the disruption by a male servant and lover of the family of Jupiter, Juno, and their daughter Hebe"; "Queer Outsiders Inside the Renaissance Family" (paper delivered at MLA 1993), 8.
2. *Shakespeare Variorum Handbook* (New York: MLA, 1971).
3. This is the stage direction of the new Oxford edition at 5.4.105; William Shakespeare, *The Complete Works*, Stanley Wells and Gary Taylor, gen. eds. (Oxford: Clarendon, 1986), 732.
4. This Norton Critical Edition retains the folio reading [*Editor*].
5. Alan Bray, *Homosexuality in Renaissance England* (London: Gay Men's Press, 1982); Bray, "Homosexuality and the Signs of Male Friendship in Elizabethan England," in *Queering the Renaissance*, ed. Jonathan Goldberg, (Durham: Duke University Press, 1993), 40–61; Jonathan Goldberg, *Sodometries: Renaissance Texts, Modern Sexualities* (Stanford: Stanford University Press, 1992); Bredbeck; DiGangi; Smith. Discussions of gender and cross-dressing in the period and in this play have also been formative for this reading; see Catherine Belsey, "Disrupting Sexual Difference: Meaning and Gender in the Comedies," in John Drakakis, ed., *Alternative Shakespeares* (London: Methuen, 1985), 166–90; Marjorie Garber, *Vested Interests: Cross Dressing and Cultural Anxiety* (New York: HarperCollins, 1993); Goldberg, *Sodometries*; Jean E. Howard, "Crossdressing, the Theatre, and Gender Struggle in Early Modern England," *Shakespeare Quarterly* 39 (1988): 418–40; Laura Levine, "Men in Women's Clothing: Anti-theatricality and Effeminization from 1579–1642," *Criticism* 28 (1986): 121–43; Stephen Orgel, "Nobody's Perfect: Or, Why Did the English Stage Take Boys for Women," in *Displacing Homophobia*, ed. Ronald R. Butters, John M. Clum, and Michael Moon (Durham: Duke University Press, 1989), 7–29; Phyllis Rackin, "Androgyny, Mimesis, and the Marriage of the Boy Heroine on the English Renaissance Stage," *PMLA* 102 (1987): 29–41; Mary Beth Rose, "Sexual Disguise and Social Mobility in Jacobean City Comedy," chapter 2

of two male hands joined in the last scene of a play that repeatedly directs attention to the boy actor playing the part of Rosalind, has emphasized the choice of the name "Ganymede," and has earlier, in Act 4, Scene 1, staged the rehearsal of this same marriage between two men: "Come sister," Rosalind-as-Ganymede says, "you shall be the Priest, and marrie vs: giue me your hand *Orlando*" (TLN 2033-34).[6]

The radical tradition of editing would settle this question by asking whose hand is responsible for these joined hands; if the hand is Shakespeare's, or a hand near Shakespeare's—and the Folio text of *As You Like It* is often said to derive from a copy of Shakespeare's manuscript—then the reading "ioyne his hand with his" should stand. If not—if the hand is said to be that of a transcriber, or the Folio collectors, or the publisher, or the compositor who set the type—then the reading is said to be a corruption (an "error" or "easy misreading") and should be changed.[7] Editors have avoided this first possibility (that Shakespeare wrote "his" and the compositor then set this word), either because they have thought the line nonsensical, and therefore non-Shakespearean, or (and?) because the line as printed may raise uncomfortable questions about Shakespeare's "preferences," "habits," "tolerances," or views on the subject of early modern boys' relations with men—what we might call, appropriating Hinman, Shakespeare's "non-spelling peculiarities."[8]

I don't mean to save Shakespeare from the perceived threat of homoeroticism by suggesting some other possible agencies for this

---

of *The Expense of Spirit: Love and Sexuality in English Renaissance Drama* (Ithaca: Cornell University Press, 1988), 43–92.

6. Kuhn also quotes this line in support of her interpretation: "The final stage picture of these two boys holding hands should mirror the earlier scene" (43). But Kuhn's larger argument suggests, in fact, that the idea of male-male marriage that she too sees figured in the play is part of the larger "unreal condition of the play itself," figured and facilitated by "if."

7. In the context of another emendation of *his* to *hir/her*, Gary Taylor writes: "In an Elizabethan secretary hand, terminal *s* was often almost impossible to distinguish from *r*, and in contemporary orthography *her* could be spelled with a medial *i*; in such circumstances, a "hir" and a "his" are materially identical, and can only be differentiated by cultural context" (217); "Textual and Sexual Criticism: A Crux in *The Comedy of Errors*," *Renaissance Drama* 19 (1988): 195–225. Part of the argument of the present essay, of course, is that the cultural context does not easily settle the question in this instance. That this "exceptionally easy misreading, well attested elsewhere" seems to occur in other plays (223 n17) does not guarantee the correctness of this correction in the context of *As You Like It*; that Taylor cites this instance in *As You Like It* as a transparent case suggests that we need to return to the other instances of presumed his/her confusion.

8. I don't mean to imply that Hinman believes that sexual preferences or behaviors can be ascertained on the basis of spelling choices. On the other hand, I *do* mean to suggest that the language of twentieth-century compositorial study, in its search for stable essences/identities that can be read out from spelling behaviors, bears resemblance to, and is contemporaneous with, other twentieth-century attempts to discern identities—*sexual* identities—on the basis of visible physical signs and behaviors. On the detection of homosexuality in the 1950s and 1960s, see Lee Edelman, "Tearooms and Sympathy; or, The Epistemology of the Water Closet," in *Homographesis: Essays in Gay Literary and Cultural Theory* (New York: Routledge, 1994), 148–70.

reading; I think it's more than possible that "his with his" was initially written into the play by Shakespeare. But I also think that, lacking a manuscript in Shakespeare's hand, this is an unanswerable question, and even were we to possess such a manuscript, we would not know whether Shakespeare made an "error," or performed an "easy misreading" of his own intention, in writing "his for his." What we *do* possess is a text that was produced through the collaborative efforts and mediations of, yes, a playwright (and probably a later revising playwright who could be Shakespeare or someone else),[9] several songwriters, probably the actors of the King's company, the book holder of the company, who supervised the use of the script in performance, the publishers of the Folio volume produced in part from that script or a copy of it, the compositor or compositors who typeset the text, and the proofreaders who either failed to correct this "error" or didn't see it as such.[1] Each of these persons or groups of persons might have, to quote Hinman's terms again, "preferences and tolerances" that might lead him to retain or change the reading of this line. By these terms, Hinman means that a compositor has certain spellings he prefers and that he also "tolerates" certain spellings that go against those habits when they're present in the documents from which he's setting type. I want, in the space remaining, to speculate briefly about the hands and habits of the compositors.

Hinman says, on the basis of particular spellings and types that appear in the text, that the page on which "his with his" appears was set by Compositor B from typecase y (II: 448). I would argue that the idea of fixed spelling habits and preferences among compositors needs to be retheorized in the context of a language system without standardized spelling,[2] and, as Randall McLeod has shown,

9. I base this suggestion on G. E. Bentley's argument that "almost any play first printed more than ten years after composition and . . . kept in active repertory by the company that owned it is most likely to contain later revisions by the author or, in many cases, by another playwright"; *The Profession of Dramatist in Shakespeare's Time 1590–1642* (Princeton: Princeton University Press, 1971), 263.

1. There is the remote possibility that this line is the site of a press variant not yet observed/recorded. Hinman did not exhaustively collate all copies of the Folio for his study (or even all the Folger copies), and others have found further variants. For a discussion of additional variants and the utility of this pursuit, see Paul Werstine, "More Unrecorded States in the Folger Shakespeare Library's Collection of First Folios," *The Library*, 6th ser., 11 (1989): 47–51. Hinman's *Norton Facsimile*, it is important to recall, is "an ideal representation of the Folio" (xxii) that reproduces no single extant book, but rather brings together the "best" pages of a number of copies of the Folio that reside at the Folger Shakespeare Library. On Hinman's principles of selection, see xxxiii.

2. The assumption of compositor-identification studies would seem to be that, even if the language as a whole did not operate according to principles of standardized spelling, each individual writer/speaker/typesetter operated according to a personal, largely self-standardized, glossary. My term "standardized" is shorthand: in this period, as Juliet Fleming argues, "English appears to have been not unruled, but ruled differently—perhaps in accordance with a rhetorical rather than grammatical, lexical, and orthographic order"; "Dictionary English and the Female Tongue," in *Enclosure Acts: Sexuality, Property, and Culture in Early Modern England*, ed. Richard Burt and John Michael Archer (Ithaca: Cornell University Press, 1994), 301–302.

printed spellings seem to have been dependent as much on the local exigencies of printing as on ostensible, individually produced differences.[3] But even Hinman, who's deeply invested in the separability of compositors, admits that Compositor B's spellings are sometimes variable and that B's work is sometimes difficult to distinguish from that of Compositor E elsewhere in the folio (II: 512, I: 226).[4] Though he argues that "it is now quite plain that sins committed by E have been laid to the charge of B" (II: 512), Hinman further notes that the habits and preferences of E (who he thinks is an *inexperienced* compositor) actually change over the course of the pages of the Folio he works on—that early on he "follows copy" closely but quickly develops "strong spelling preferences" of his own (I: 213n2).[5] Such evidence might be said to undermine the separability of B and E, or the separation of E's work from that of the other compositors who helped in the composing of Shakespeare. In other words, by Hinman's own logic, there is the possibility that the reading that "ioyne[s] his hand with his" on page 206 of the Folio Comedies was produced by B, an experienced compositor, working with the younger, inexperienced E. Two hands joined, one of whom Hinman calls "The Prentice Hand" (I: 214).[6]

As I've been hinting, I think much of this evidence is highly tenuous, and I've emphasized the language of "preferences" and "toler-

3. McLeod shows, for example, that the name "Shakspeare" is typeset to take into account the fact that, in certain typefaces, certain letters of type (in this case, "k" and long "s") will collide with those around them, necessitating the medial *e* and/or hyphen to avoid type breakage; "Spellbound: Typography and the Concept of Old-Spelling Editions," *Renaissance and Reformation*, n.s., 3 (1979): 50–65.
4. Though *not* in the Comedies. Still, there has been a fair amount of work on this issue, and the evidence for B's ostensible consistency isn't nearly as stable as Hinman suggests. Hinman himself notes that "both A and B now and again used non-characteristic spellings, and sometimes without ascertainable reason" (I: 185). In a reconsideration of Hinman's and Alice Walker's work on Compositor B, Paul Werstine confronts this problem: "perhaps an editor must conclude that compositor variability is so high, as Compositor B's is between the comedies and *1 H4*, that compositor identification is a useless tool"; "Compositor B of the Shakespeare First Folio," *Analytical and Enumerative Bibliography* 2.4 (1978): 260. See also Andrew S. Cairncross's disputing of Hinman's and Howard-Hill's attributions to Compositor B in "Compositors E and F of the Shakespeare First Folio," *Papers of the Bibliographical Society of America* 66 (1972): 369–406.
5. Commenting on and revising Hinman's work, T. H. Howard-Hill concludes: "We can see more clearly than before the closeness of E's working relationship with compositor B, and, throughout the Tragedies, we can observe E's gradual acquisition of typographical expertise. . . . He was, as the Nurse in *Romeo* puts it, 'a man of wax' " (178); "New Light on Compositor E of the Shakespeare First Folio," *The Library*, 6th ser., 2.2 (1980): 156–78. Cf. Cairncross: "That Compositor E was the type of man he was is a mixed blessing. His inefficiency is unfortunate; but his strong imitative tendency, which has so effectively concealed his presence and caused such confusion, may yield valuable results" ("Compositors E and F," 395–96). (On this discourse, see p. 400, n. 8)
6. Since Hinman finds E only in the Tragedies, he would resist these statements. My point is that the very flexibility and malleability of E's spellings make it possible, by Hinman's own logic, to find the impressionable E almost *anywhere* (I: 213n2). While disputing some of Hinman's findings, Cairncross has, by Hinman's methods, found "uneqivocal" evidence of E's "presence" in the Comedies and in the page in question ("Compositors E and F," 378–80).

ances" in order to suggest that it may be based on a notion of essential individuality that is more at home in the mid-twentieth century than in the seventeenth.[7] But this evidence may at least serve to remind us of knowledges available in other forms and sources: first, that the texts we now associate with the name Shakespeare were collaborative creations at a number of points in their production,[8] second, that the system that produced these texts in the printing house was organized around adult/apprentice relations in a way that closely resembles the organization of the acting company that produced these plays and in which Shakespeare himself participated as actor and writer on a daily basis; and third, that such relations are themselves (in a way I have only gestured toward here) legible within a discourse circulating in the play and elsewhere that used the name *Ganymede* in a homoerotically charged fashion—a fashion that often existed *alongside* the possibility of what we now call "heterosexual" marriage.[9] We might read, as an example of such relations, this entry from the will of Augustine Phillips, a sharer in the King's Men—a will in which Phillips' wife Anne is also named executrix:

> Item, I give to Samuel Gilborne, my late apprentice, the sum of forty shillings, and my mouse-colored velvet hose, and a white taffeta doublet, a black taffeta suit, my purple cloak, sword and dagger, and my bass viol.[1]

While I would not argue that an all-male collaborative process is always homoerotic or always produces a homoerotic text, I think we also can't ignore that the process by which this play was first performed *and* published is informed by discourses, rehearsals, and practices of homoeroticism prominent in early modern English culture. Many of these questions disappear—the cultural history that literally unfolds from the Folio pages disintegrates—when editions fail to conserve the words (and, in a way I haven't had space to argue for here, the actual material *form*) of the only text we have of this

---

7. For a brilliant and highly detailed critique of printing-house study (and Hinman's findings) on evidentiary and logical grounds, see D. F. McKenzie, "Printers of the Mind: Some Notes on Bibliographical Theories and Printing-House Practices," *Studies in Bibliography* 22 (1969): 1–75. On the embeddedness of compositorial study in twentieth-century epistemology, see p. 400, n. 8.

8. On the collaborative theatre, see G. E. Bentley, *The Profession of Dramatist in Shakespeare's Time 1590–1642* (Princeton: Princeton University Press, 1971); Stephen Orgel, "What is a Text?" in *Staging the Renaissance: Reinterpretations of Elizabethan and Jacobean Drama*, ed. David Scott Kastan and Peter Stallybrass (New York: Routledge, 1991), 83–87; Jeffrey Masten, "Beaumont and/or Fletcher: Collaboration and the Interpretation of Renaissance Drama," *ELH* 59 (1992): 337–56.

9. Thus, to continue the argument on p. 400, n. 6: unlike Kuhn, I think that there is significant traffic between, on the one hand, the conditions of the play's production and printing as registered in contemporary discourses, and, on the other, the discourse of the play itself, however "unreal" it might seem.

1. Quoted in Bentley 19–20.

play.[2] Editing that attempts to "reclaim what Shakespeare meant" has often left us unable to determine what Renaissance culture meant, and means. Without necessarily knowing whose hand is whose, we need a conservative editorial practice that will keep open the possibility of "ioyn[ing] his hand with his, / Whose heart within his bosome is." And, as you've no doubt guessed by now, I'm hoping that such a conservative practice will ultimately put into play meanings that are, in complicated ways, radical.

ROBERT N. WATSON

[Likenesses: Jaques and the Deer][†]

* * *

Editors beginning with Theobald have often emended Duke Senior's "Here feel we not the penalty of Adam" (2.1.5, Folio) to "Here feel we *but* the penalty of Adam." On this textual crux rests the play's most persistent question: can we redeem ourselves by returning to nature, or are we cursed if we abide there? The emendation makes sense: Duke Senior clearly *does* feel the pain of nature's enmity. But other editors resist the change, for two structurally similar reasons: first, they believe that the Duke may be saying that the pain doesn't bother him because it is a good, honest, primal, outdoorsy pain, and, second, they believe that they should stick to the original reading unless the sense absolutely forbids it. The defenders of the Folio's "not" are thus like the Duke Senior they thereby preserve: they are willing to endure some discomfort for the sake of recovering what seems like the true, original, rough-hewn experience, whether of nature or of Shakespeare.

I favor the original "not," but principally for its ironic value: it signals how deeply this displaced court is in denial. What follows from Duke Senior and his lords proves that the penalty of Adam is fully in force; as the words suggest, Arden resembles Eden, but is not Eden, and the difference between likeness and identity will haunt

2. On this, see Margreta de Grazia and Peter Stallybrass, "The Materiality of the Shake-spearean Text," *Shakespeare Quarterly* 44 (1993): 255–83; and D. F. McKenzie, *What's Past is Prologue: The Bibliographical Society and the History of the Book*, Bibliographical Society Centenary Lecture, July 14, 1992 (Hearthstone Publications, 1993). This is perhaps the place to point out the problematic class politics of my calling for a research and teaching practice based on early, rare editions, while doing research and teaching at Harvard University, where there is easy access to such materials. The emergence and proliferation of inexpensive facsimiles, the Short Title Catalogue collection in micro-film, and, eventually, electronic facsimiles, may at least begin to address this issue.
† From Robert N. Watson, *Back to Nature: The Green and the Real in the Late Renaissance* (Philadelphia: University of Pennsylvania Press, 2006), pp. 80–84. Reprinted by permission of University of Pennsylvania Press.

all the play's similes, facsimiles included. The Duke here boasts how happily his displaced court has escaped "painted pomp" and given itself over completely to an authentic experience of nature. He then proves himself a liar at almost every word. The wind isn't "chiding," it has no "fang" to "bite" with, and it certainly isn't a "counsellor" seeking to "persuade" (2.1.6–11). By the time this ostentatiously alliterative speech ends six lines later, the anthropomorphizing—a pastoral symptom since the originary moment of the genre, the first line of Theocritus's first idyll—has become epidemic: the Duke is finding "tongues in trees, books in the running brooks, / Sermons in stones, and good in every thing" (2.1.16–17).[1]

Amiens, putting the most amiable face on this, praises the Duke's ability to "translate" his experience of untamed nature into "so sweet a style" (2.1.19–20). In classical and Renaissance rhetoric, *translatio* was the term for metaphor, as *similitudo* was for comparison; etymologically, "to translate" is "to carry across." Farmers regularly used "stiles" to cross into animal compounds, and the Duke's translation across the human-animal boundary threatens to produce an ass-headed monster, as it does when Bottom is "translated" in the forest of *A Midsummer Night's Dream* (3.1.119); Jaques will soon assert that to flee to nature, as Duke Senior has, is to "turn ass" (2.5.51). This, we shall see, is the pot's critique of the kettle. But what makes the Duke asinine is his assumption that he can cross this border, into the non-human, so easily. Toward Mother Nature as toward Lady Fortune, the Senecan stoicism the Duke praises is a kind of epistemological aggression, as the free mind subjects everything to itself, itself to nothing.

"Come, shall we go and kill us venison?" the Duke then asks, regretting this necessary violence against the "native burghers of this desert city" (2.1.21, 23). Again he is presuming, not only anthropomorphically, but (more subtly) anthropocentrically: "desert" defines the place by human abandonment, and the deer are not "venison"—animals hunted for game, or (more often) their edible flesh—until his need and aggression make them so.[2] Even before

---

1. George Gascoigne offered Queen Elizabeth a similar kind of dominion in his pageant for her visit to Kenilworth: "The winds resound your worth,/the rockes record your name:/These hills, these dales, these woods, these waves,/these fields pronounce your fame." Terry Comito, *The Idea of the Garden in the Renaissance*. New Brunswick, N.J.: Rutgers University Press, 1978, p. 18, quoting *The Works of George Gascoigne*.
2. Ferdinand de Saussure, *Course in General Linguistics*. Ed. Charles Bally, Albert Sechehaye, and Albert Riedlinger. Trans. Roy Harris. London: Duckworth, 1983, p. 114, uses quite a similar example to demonstrate the problems of verbal designation generally: "The French word *mouton* may have the same meaning as the English word *sheep*; but it does not have the same value. There are various reasons for this, but in part the fact that the English word for the meat of this animal, as prepared and served for a meal, is not *sheep* but *mutton*." On the similarly revealing (though more consciously ironic) characterization of the deer as "burghers" (or, according to Jaques at line 55, "citizens"), cf. William Browne, *Britannia's Pastorals* (1613–16) on "forest citizens" (1.1.510); on the

the hunt begins, they are already no longer their animal selves, already a product for consumption by the human mouth, through the presumption of the human mind. Things are named by our need for them. As Martin Heidegger observed, a threatened humanity "postures as lord of the earth. In this way the illusion comes to prevail that everything man encounters exists only insofar as it is his construct . . . it seems as though man everywhere and always encounters only himself."[3]

That this perceptual crime against nature is distinct from the more perceptible one becomes clear in Jaques's reaction. The lord who reports that reaction is himself incapable of turning off the anthropomorphic switch that generates antique peeping roots, brawling brooks, and a poor "sequestered" stag in a "leathern coat" (this resembles the Duke's slip: "leather" generally meant skin prepared for use by tanning rather than that on a living animal) who has been hurt by "the hunter's aim" (a revealingly solipsistic metonymy for an arrow). When Duke Senior asks, "But what said Jaques? / Did he not moralize this spectacle?" the lord replies, "O yes, into a thousand similes" (2.1.43–45). Capturing the deer is certainly more brutal, but captioning its picture may be no less appropriative. Which has done more insidious violence to pristine nature as a collectivity, during its long siege by humanity: shooting it with arrows or shattering it into similes? The answer may not be obvious, but the question brings Shakespearean drama into the active field of ecocriticism in a duly ambivalent way, without blunting the literary works into tools of facile social advocacy. Shakespeare sustains the moral tension by evoking at once the myth of the English greenwood, associated with the peaceful co-existence of the classes in local communities, and the myth of the hunt, which (though communal in German culture) was generally associated in England with abusive central authority.[4] The ethical quality of human relations thus implicates the human relationship to other animals.

But deep-ecology movements, which attempt to abjure the human perspective and expiate even seemingly benign human interventions, are very different from popular or reform environmentalism, which tends (like Jaques here) toward sentimental identification with particular lovely creatures rather than anything arduously philosoph-

---

notion of wilderness as "desert," cf. J. N[orden], *The Surveyors Dialogue* (1607); cited by Keith Thomas, *Man and the Natural World: Changing Attitudes in England, 1500–1800*. New York: Pantheon, 1983, p. 194. The anthropocentric aspect of "desert" has a Latin parallel in the proximity of *nemus* (grove) and *nemo* (no one).

3. Heidegger, "The Question Concerning Technology"; quoted by Jonathan Bate, *The Song of the Earth*. London: Picador, 2000, p. 68.

4. Simon Schama, *Landscape and Memory*. New York: Vintage, 1995, p. 140, discusses the conflicting ethical valences of greenwood and hunt in English culture.

ical (like Jaques later).[5] Though the deer-hunt scenes offer some emotional aid and comfort to the animal rights movement, the play as a whole undercuts that endorsement by demonstrating that such pervasive anthropomorphizing sentiments may invade and constrain the animal world more insidiously than sporadic open warfare—just as a Petrarchan worshipper can cause a woman more deep and protracted misery than a loudmouthed misogynist transient.

Jaques's projection of his own social complaints onto this animal (2.1.46–59) is interesting characterologically; what is interesting philosophically is the parallel suggestion that he could not cease to do so even if he were a sincere nature-lover—indeed, that he becomes all the more invasive the more he tries to be sympathetic.[6] The "bankrupt" but fashionably "velvet" deer, abandoned by companions "full of the pasture," does not need Jaques's tears, any more than the stream needs those of the deer (2.1.46–49). Jaques concludes (the lord reports) that Duke Senior's court

> Are mere usurpers, tyrants, and what's worse,
> To fright the animals and to kill them up
> In their assigned and native dwelling place.
> *Duke Senior:* And did you leave him in this contemplation?
> *Second Lord:* We did, my lord, weeping and commenting
> Upon the sobbing deer.
>
> (2.1.61–66)

Jaques's position, leaning over the stream with this deer, signals the narcissistic self-involvement of his claim to care for an other (a signal confirmed by the joke at 3.2.285–90 about Jaques seeing his own reflection in the stream as he looks for a fool). He calls the hunters "usurpers," but comparisons between human beings and other creatures, and projections of qualities across that boundary, are themselves, according to George Puttenham, "common usurpations."[7] Jaques has inserted himself in the place of the deer as

5. Compare Montaigne's "Of Cruelty," in Michel de Montaigne, *The Complete Essays of Montaigne*. Trans. Donald M. Frame. Stanford: Stanford University Press, 1948, p. 316, which reports that the tears of the despairing hunted stag "always seemed to me a very unpleasant spectacle," but then pushes the question from this emotional swamp into broader philosophical territory. The introduction to Andrew Dobson, *Green Political Thought*. 3rd ed. London: Routledge, 2000, uses the term "ecologism" (itself divisible into maximalist and minimalist approaches) for something like the deep-ecology alternative to mere reformist environmentalism.
6. Cf. Raymond Williams's distinction, in *The Country and the City*, New York: Oxford University Press, 1973, p. 134, between Gilbert White's technical observation of nature and Romantic observation: White's "close observation and description is of a separated object, another creature. It is at the opposite pole from the human separation of Wordsworth and Clare: a separation that is mediated by a projection of personal feeling into a subjectively particularised and objectively generalised Nature." Jaques is clearly drawn to the Romantic pole.
7. George Puttenham, *The Arte of English Poesie*. 1589. Ed. Gladys Doidge Willcock and Alice Walker. 1936. Rpt. Cambridge: Cambridge University Press, 1970, p. 243.

assiduously, and arguably as uselessly or even tyrannically, as the hunter who will later have the hide of the deer placed over his skin and the horns of the deer placed on his head (4.2.10–11).[8] We may indeed weep—I don't mean to belittle the empathetic impulse here—but we are always commenting as well. As his name may imply (a "jakes" was a privy or outhouse), Jaques is, to put it politely, rather full of pasture himself.

Still, this empathetic impulse may help explain Jaques's eventual decision to "put on a religious life" and to try to learn from "these convertites" such as Duke Frederick who have left their former selves behind (5.4.181–85)—a decision that seems to shock Jaques's comrades and the play's editors alike. As others arrive from court into the forest and rediscover themselves, Jaques takes the next step, toward rediscovering something beyond himself. The quest for transcendence, for sorrowful thought and absolute truth and self-overcoming, inevitably looks like folly in a comic context. Jaques's maunderings about the deer may sound quite different, however, if one hears in them a new translation of the exiled speaker of Psalm 42, who had once enjoyed singing and feasting with his comrades, but for lack of divine certainty has fallen into a melancholy, like that of a hart fleeing to the water. Jaques had been "a libertine / As sensual as the brutish sting itself" (2.7.65–66);[9] and one analogue that may have been on Shakespeare's mind here is the medieval figure of St. Hubert, who once held "a prominent position among the gay courtiers . . . a worldling and a lover of pleasure." When "The tyrannical conduct of Ebroin caused a general emigration of the nobles and others," Hubert joined it, until one day,

> As he was pursuing a magnificent stag, the animal turned and, as the pious legend narrates, he was astounded at perceiving a crucifix between its antlers, while he heard a voice saying: "Hubert, unless thou turnest to the Lord, and leadest an holy life, thou shalt quickly go down into hell." Hubert dismounted, prostrated himself and said, "Lord, what wouldst Thou have me do?" He received the answer, "Go and seek Lambert, and he will instruct you." Accordingly, he . . . renounced all his honors and his military rank, and gave up his birthright to the Duchy of Aquitaine to his younger brother.

Eventually St. Hubert went seeking converts "in the fastnesses of the forest of Ardennes."[1]

8. For the feasting Jaques to acquire a "fair round belly with good capon lin'd" (2.7.154) is a subtler version of the same transaction—one that hunting-averse carnivores must contrive to overlook.
9. When Francis Quarles responds to Psalm 42 in his 1635 *Emblemes*, he stresses that lust is the force hunting and threatening to destroy this hart.
1. *The Catholic Encyclopedia*. Ed. Charles G. Herbermann et al. 15 vols. London: Robert Applegate, 1910, 7:507.

Like so many before him, and like Duke Frederick shortly after, Jaques is inspired by the wilderness to seek more absolute truth, to leave behind his likes.[2] Like the speaker of the psalm, Jaques abandons his "sensual" self (2.7.66) and averts his eyes from the facile matchings by waiting them out in Duke Senior's "abandon'd cave" (5.4.196): "from the vulgar, civil and ordinary man he was, he becomes as free as a deer, and an inhabitant of the wilderness . . . in the unpretentious rooms of the cavernous mountains, where he contemplates . . . free of ordinary lusts, and converses mostly freely with the divinity."[3] This is not, however, a modern rhapsody on the conversion of Jaques, but instead Giordano Bruno's commentary on the transformation of Actaeon[4]—the classical archetype of the man who saw too much, the hunter who forfeited language, and therefore community, and therefore life, because he gazed (rashly, desirously) on a divine form in a woodland stream.

* * *

GABRIEL EGAN

Food and Biological Nature [in] *As You Like It*[†]

For his encyclopaedic *Historie of Four-Footed Beasts* published in 1607, Edward Topsell borrowed heavily from Konrad Gesner's Latin *Historia Animalium* published in Zurich (1551–8), even to the extent of taking an explanatory epistle that justified the project of zoology, as his discipline was later to be known. Because animals are part of the same creation as ourselves, Gesner condemned those who think animals beneath their concern:

> But if any man be so Barbarous, as to thinke that the beasts and such other creatures, cannot affoord him any subiect woorthy

---

2. Cf. Schama, *Landscape and Memory*, p. 152: "Obliged by Robin to spend the night in the forest, the sheriff is stripped of his clothes like St. Francis at the moment of his spiritual rebirth, and garbed instead in Lincoln green, the cloth of the arboreal cloister, as if he were a novice preparing for his vows." See also Schama, p. 551: "Pursuing a stag, St. Louis had been thrown and was only rescued from certain death at the hands of robbers by a timely call on a hunting horn. . . . A more emphatically correctional apparition suddenly loomed up in front of Henry IV in the huge, black, and forbidding form of the phantom 'Grand Veneur' . . . bellowing to the startled king, Amendez-vous [Reform yourself]."
3. Giordano Bruno, *The Heroic Frenzies*, pp. 224–25; quoted by Leonard Barkan in his excellent "Diana and Actaeon: The Myth as Synthesis." *English Literary Renaissance* 10 (1980): 317–59, p. 344.
4. In classical myth, Actaeon was a hunter who came upon naked Diana, goddess of the hunt, in the forest and dared to gaze at her. She became so incensed at the intrusion that she turned him into a stag and he was killed by his own hounds. According to Renaissance philosopher Giordano Bruno, the story was to be interpreted as an allegory of the search for divine beauty and perfection [*Editor*].
† From Gabriel Egan, *Green Shakespeare: From Ecopolitics to Ecocriticism* (London: Routledge, 2006), pp. 92–107. Reprinted by permission.

of his contempaltion [*sic*], then let him thinke so of himselfe
likewise; for what ignoble basenesse is there in bloode, flesh,
bones, vaines, and such like? Doth not the body of man consist
thereof? And then how abhominable art thou to thy selfe, that
doest not rather looke into these which are so neere of kinde
vnto thee?

(Topsell 1607, ¶3v).

Topsell's spelling of 'abhominable' (for 'abominable') was the period's standard and reflects the mistaken belief that the word derived
from the Latin phrase *ab homine*, meaning away from man and
thus beastly (OED abominable, *a.* and *adv.*). Gesner's point, of
course, is that humans and animals are not so far apart in physical
nature, being made of the same stuff and also linked together in
the Great Chain of Being that runs through

the heauenly spirits and degrees of Angels and celestiall
bodies . . . the mindes of men . . . and from men to other
creatures that haue life or sence, as to plants and inanimate
bodyes, so as the inferiors do alwaies so compose themselues
to the imitation of their superiours, euen as their shaddowes
and resemblaunces.

(Topsell 1607, ¶4r)

It is easy to see what trouble this idea might lead to, and Gesner
was quick to qualify his likening of the soul that suffused every
part of the human body to the divine essence suffused through all
creation. Whereas the soul suffered if any part of the human body
was hurt, the divine essence 'is so communicated to creatures, as
it neither is any part or matter, or forme of them; nor yet can be
affected by any thing the creature suffereth, nor yet included in the
creature'. To placate any reader baffled by this apparent contradiction regarding the suffering of animals and their closeness to
human nature, Gesner sighed 'truely these thinges surpasse all the
wit of man' (Topsell 1607, ¶4r).

Gesner's interest in animals here bears upon his Protestant religious orthodoxy (he was a typical product of the Swiss Reformation
of 1522–3) and specifically the conviction that the divine presence
in the sacrament of the Mass was attributable to omnipresence
rather than a transformation of matter enacted by a priest. If Christ-
the-man is everywhere, cruelty to animals is something like a repetition of the crucifixion. Gesner's rhetoric urgently backpedals when
it seems to imply that the suffering of animals entails divine suffering, and he argues that consideration of the 'neather and backer
partes of God', the meaner corners of his Creation, leads us by
'Prickes and Spurres' to the higher matters. These terms from the
urging on of animals take Gesner into a standard biblical justifica-

tion for human domination of the animal kingdom, from Genesis 1.25–6: 'dominion over the fish of the sea, and over the fowl of the air, and over the cattle . . . and over every creeping thing'. This was a justification close to Topsell's heart too: the previous year he completed and saw into print Henry Holland's *The Historie of Adam* (London, 1606) that used this dominion over the animals to illustrate the perfect state of prelapsarian humankind (Holland, sigs. A3V—B1r). Although the standard justification was often repeated in the period, the ways in which humans were like animals were apparent to all and just which forms of domination were reasonable and humane was a matter of considerable difference of opinion. One notable exploration of the question is Shakespeare's *As You Like It*.

The play begins with a man who complains of being treated like an animal:

> [ORLANDO]   For my part, he keeps me rusticall at home—or, to speak more properly, stays me here at home unkept; for call you that keeping for a gentleman of my birth, that differs not from the stalling of an ox? His horses are bred better, for besides that they are fair with their feeding, they are taught their manège, and to that end riders dearly hired. But I, his brother, gain nothing under him but growth, for the which his animals on his dunghills are as much bound to him as I. Besides this nothing that he so plentifully gives me, the something that nature gave me his countenance seems to take from me. He lets me feed with his hinds, bars me the place of a brother, and as much as in him lies, mines my gentility with my education.
>
> (*As You Like It* 1.1.6–19)

Appropriately enough for a play about modern approximations of Eden, this opening complaint is addressed to an Adam. It is not clear from what Orlando says that he thinks himself essentially different from an animal (and hence mistreated to be kept like one): horses are 'bred better' while he only grows, and that from eating with 'hinds', which editors almost universally gloss as meaning farmhands or servants although in this context the sense of female deer is clearly also active. Rather, it sounds as though Orlando fears actually becoming an animal because of his education, as though culture, not nature, will determine this. As Erica Fudge argues, in the Renaissance the humanist privileging of humankind had not fully taken hold, and a man might be thought capable of descending to the level of a dog by his behaviour.[1] For us, of course,

---

1. Erica Fudge, 'How a Man Differs from a Dog', *History Today* 53.6 (2003): 38–44.

the work of Charles Darwin indissolubly links humankind to the animals (which is why it was so abhorrent to a certain strand of nineteenth-century humanist thinking), and we should always remember that for Shakespeare's contemporaries the 'beastilisation of humanity' as Fudge so aptly calls it[2] was always possible. When the villain of the situation enters, Orlando acknowledges his superiority but only inasmuch as society (specifically, the custom of primogeniture) makes him so:

OLIVER   Know you before whom [you stand], sir?

ORLANDO   Ay, better than him I am before knows me. I know you are my eldest brother, and in the gentle condition of blood you should so know me. The courtesy of nations allows you my better, in that you are the first-born; but the same tradition takes not away my blood, were there twenty brothers betwixt us. I have as much of my father in me as you, albeit I confess your coming before me is nearer to his reverence.

(*As You Like It* 1.1.40–8)

It need not be like this. In one of his most optimistic happy endings, Shakespeare dramatized another pair of brothers deciding to let nature (their absolute physical equality) teach their humanity and to ignore this custom: '[DROMIO OF EPHESUS] let's go hand in hand, not one before another' (*The Comedy of Errors* 5.1.430). Once Orlando leaves, Oliver swears to do some of the brother-keeping that Orlando complains is neglected: 'Begin you to grow upon me? I will physic your rankness' (1.1.81–2). This is a horticultural image of Orlando as a plant choking Oliver, just as Prospero thinks of his brother Antonio as 'The ivy which had hid my princely trunk | And sucked my verdure out on 't' (*The Tempest* 1.2.86–7). But as Alan Brissenden observes, Oliver's use of the word 'physic' suggests not only horticulture but also surgery,[3] which two domains Shakespeare allowed to overlap in a celebrated image of careful gardening: 'We at time of year | Do wound the bark, the skin of our fruit trees, | Lest, being over-proud in sap and blood, | With too much riches it confound itself' (*Richard 2* 3.4.59–61).

The central structural contrast of the play is, of course, between the sophistication and corruption of the court, where the entire first act is set, and the innocence and honesty of the country where almost all the remainder of the play is set. After the Fall there could be no hope of attaining a true natural paradise, but one might hope to recover something like it by returning to places that had not

---

2. Erica Fudge, *Perceiving Animals: Humans and Beasts in Early Modern English Culture.* Basingstoke: Macmillan, 2000.
3. Alan Brissenden, ed., *As You Like It.* The Oxford Shakespeare. Oxford: Oxford University Press, 1993, 1.1.82n.

changed much over time. This sense of returning to a former, better state of things is clearly set up by the wrestler:

> CHARLES   They say he is already in the forest of Ardenne, and a many merry men with him; and there they live like the old Robin Hood of England. They say many young gentlemen flock to him every day, and fleet the time carelessly, as they did in the golden world.
>
> (*As You Like It* 1.1.109–13)

Belief in a falling off since the golden age, a descent into corrupted sophistication, is apparent across early modern poetry and prose, and as Andrew Wear points out, 'The idea that fresh air, fresh food and freedom to move were good for pigs (and for men and women)' links the modern Green movement with these writers.[4] The pigs enter the debate via Thomas Fuller's assertion that those running wild in Hampshire produce the best bacon because they eat the ready supply of fallen acorns, which were 'mens meats in the Golden, Hog's food in this Iron Age' (Wear, p. 145). As Wear shows, the countryside was widely (and, statistics confirm, rightly) thought to be a healthier place to live than the city, and going there was a means to recover something of the physical vigour of prelapsarian humankind. Linking the physical and spiritual aspects, Holland's history of Adam completed by Topsell argued that religious correctness was also a means to the same end, as encapsulated in its subtitle: *The Four-Fold State of Man, Well Formed in his Creation, Deformed in his Corruption, Reformed in Grace, and Perfected in Glory.*

That the countryside itself is the cause of the goodness of those who dwell in it is strongly suggested by the play's startling transformations of Oliver and Duke Ferdinand when they leave the court to enter the Forest of Ardenne. The only explanation offered for the latter's initially mean behaviour is Le Beau's 'The Duke is humorous' (1.2.256), which diction, Brissenden notes, appears at this point in the source but also alludes to the fashionable dramatic genre of humours comedy begun by George Chapman's *A Humorous Day's Mirth* at the Rose theatre in 1597. In a brilliant analysis of this fashion, Martin Wiggins shows that Shakespeare absorbed the new style and made it his own[5], and indeed raw statistics confirm this picture. The words 'humour' and 'humourous' flood into Shakespeare's dramatic dialogue at the end of the sixteenth century. Taken in chronological order of composition, the word-counts are 8

---

4. Andrew Wear, 'Making Sense of Health and the Environment in Early Modern England'. In *Medicine in Society: Historical Essays*, ed. Andrew Ware. Cambridge, Cambridge University Press, 1992, pp. 119–47. Quotation is from p. 146.
5. Martin Wiggins, *Shakespeare and the Drama of His Time.* Oxford Shakespeare Topics. Oxford: Oxford University Press, 2000, pp. 64–78.

in *1 Henry 4* (1596–7), 25 in *The Merry Wives of Windsor* (1597–8), 13 in *Henry 5* (1598–9), 9 in *Julius Caesar* (1599), and 8 in *As You Like It* (1599–1600), compared to a background average of 3 or 4 uses in each of his other plays.

The term 'humour' comes from classical medicine (primarily, the work of Galen of Pergamum, 129—*c*.216 CE) and refers to the effect upon personality of the predominance of one of the four fluids of the human body—bile (= choler), blood, melancholy (= black bile), and phlegm—which ought to be in a dynamic equilibrium. The comedy of humours differed from what went before in its concern with human agency, originating in bodily chemistry, above all else, and its relative neglect of plot. As Wiggins puts it, 'the events remain tightly under human control, created not by chance, still less by any supernatural force, but by the machinations, not always benevolent, of particular characters' (Wiggins, p. 72). In having no supernatural agency at work, this kind of comedy lacks the macrocosmic/microcosmic correspondence that [exists] in *Macbeth*, where the natural world reacts to human behaviour. Instead, it has a concern for equilibrium centred on the human body, which reacts to external factors (including environment and diet) and which as a complex dynamic system can be brought back into order. This is essentially another kind of macrocosmic/microcosmic correspondence and one in which the body, not the cosmos, is responsive. Once the body is back in balance the social world is consequentially adjusted: the usurping brothers spontaneously restore what they took.

As Gail Kern Paster reminds us, the Galenic humoral model of human biology and psychology is utterly materialist. Not for its adherents the intangible mysteries of mental energy that Freud later tried to model, rather human thoughts and feelings are essentially a matter of hydraulics:

> For the early moderns, emotions flood the body not metaphorically but literally, as the humors course through the bloodstream carrying choler, melancholy, blood, and phlegm to the parts and as the animal spirits move like lightning from brain to muscle, from muscle to brain.[6]

A corollary of this view is an inherent link between the macrocosm and the microcosm, although Paster avoids these unfashionable terms, leaving them out of her highly detailed index. Nonetheless, they are central to her argument:

> to understand the early modern passions as embodying a historically particular kind of self-experience requires seeing the

6. Gail Kern Paster, *Humoring the Body: Emotions and the Shakespearean Stage*. Chicago: University of Chicago Press, 2004, p. 14.

passions and the body that houses them in ecological terms—
that is, in terms of that body's reciprocal relations to the
world. . . . The link between the inner and outer is often
described in the language of the qualities, since the forces of
cold, hot, moist, and dry not only determine an individual subject's characteristic humors and behaviors but also describe
the characteristic behaviors of other living things—animate
and inanimate.

(Paster, p. 19)

A ready way to influence one's fluid balance was diet, and belief
that particular foods had particular humoral effects is evident
throughout sixteenth-century printed dietaries.[7] Thus to gloss Duke
Senior's question to his men 'Come, shall we go and kill us venison?'
(2.1.21), Brissenden is quite right to invoke contemporary beliefs
about this meat promoting melancholy (2.1.21n). As a fluid, melancholy itself is no bad thing, and one ought to promote its internal
production when deficient. On the other hand, if one has too much
melancholy then one ought to suppress its generation. Balance of
the humoral levels is all, and one's dietary choices informed by
knowledge of one's present state enable the body to exploit negative
feedback to finetune the hydraulic system.

The pervasive classical mythology of the play, however, permits
characters to ponder others' bodily systems and other principles of
feedback and energy renewal. The collocation of the following
remarks in the wrestling scene strongly suggests a particular classical mythological context:

CHARLES   Come, where is this young gallant that is so desirous to lie with his mother earth?

[. . .]

ROSALIND (*to Orlando*)   Now Hercules be thy speed, young man!
(*As You Like It* 1.2.188–98)

This talk of lying with the Earth, wrestling, and Hercules evokes
the encounter with Antaeus: 'Being forced to wrestle with him,
Hercules hugged him, lifted him aloft, broke and killed him; for
when he touched the earth so it was that he waxed stronger, wherefore some said that he was a son of Earth'.[8] In Greek wrestling the
object was to repeatedly throw one's opponent to the ground[9], but
rather than defeating Antaeus such a fall only renews his energy.

7. Joan Fitzpatrick, *Food in Shakespeare*. Aldershot: Ashgate, 2005.
8. Apollodorus, *The Library*. Ed. and trans. George Frazer. Loeb Classical Library. London: Heinemann, 1921. Vol. 1, Books 1–3.9, 223 (2.5.11).
9. Simon Hornblower and Antony Spawforth, ed., *The Oxford Classical Dictionary*. 3rd
   ed. Oxford: Clarendon Press, 1996, 'wrestling.'

This positive-feedback loop—the snowball gathering momentum kind—must be broken by inverting the game's rules and holding him away from the source of his power. The point of this classical allusion is that mortals generally do not benefit from such positive feedback of strength, and that ordinary processes of adjustment and balance are the keys to human physical fitness.

Orlando's defeat of Charles has a hint of supernatural wonder about it, but is essentially mundane. A powerful animal can kill a man, and likewise a man can kill an animal. Orlando is strong, but Adam's warning 'This is no place, this house is but a butchery. | Abhor it, fear it, do not enter it' (2.3.28–9) reminds us of Orlando's opening complaint about being beastilized. Once in the forest, Orlando characterizes the relationship between men and beasts there as fairly evenly matched: 'If this uncouth forest yield anything savage I will either be food for it or bring it for food to thee' (2.6.6–7). This is the 'him or me' character of unmediated nature, and it runs counter to the understanding of the forest as a place where humans can recover their natural dominance over animals. Just as individual living creatures are out to kill and eat one another, so with humankind: in the forest the essential equality of animals and humans is reasserted. On the other hand, scene 2.6 is played on a stage that still contains the banquet laid out at the end of the previous scene, which will succour Orlando and Adam in the next. This suggests that human culture overcomes natural forces, as does culturedness in the sense of refined and gentle behaviour: 'ORLANDO Speak you so gently? Pardon me, I pray you. | I thought that all things had been savage here' (2.7.106–7). He assumed the countryside would be wild but in fact it is peaceful, but only because the good courtiers have brought with them their good manners. However, to agree to Orlando's interpretation would be premature: the play holds culture and nature in tension and refuses to confirm the triumph of either.

Orlando has no sooner carried off Adam than Duke Senior enters with his lords and makes explicit what is at stake: 'I think he [Jaques] be transformed into a beast, | For I can nowhere find him like a man' (2.7.1–2). The transformations at work here go both ways: venison makes a man melancholy and melancholy makes a man like a beast. Duke Senior's qualms about hunting venison were not so much about the violence itself as the proprieties of place:

> [DUKE SENIOR]
> And yet it irks me the poor dappled fools,
> Being native burghers of this desert city,
> Should in their own confines with forkèd heads
> Have their round haunches gored.
> (As You Like It 2.1.22–5)

According to the First Lord's description, Jaques's response to the spectacle of a wounded stag crying into a brook made the same distinction about where (rather than whether) animals should be killed, but first comes a description of utter pathos:

> [FIRST LORD]   . . . a poor sequestered stag
> That from the hunter's aim had ta'en a hurt
> Did come to languish. And indeed, my lord,
> The wretched animal heaved forth such groans
> That their discharge did stretch his leathern coat
> Almost to bursting, and the big round tears
> Coursed one another down his innocent nose
> In piteous chase. And thus the hairy fool,
> Much markèd of the melancholy Jaques,
> Stood on th' extremest verge of the swift brook,
> Augmenting it with tears.
> (*As You Like It* 2.1.33–43)

In its diction of 'Coursed' and 'chase', the touching image of the animal's big tears rolling down its face carries a fractal (that is, self-similar) miniature representation of the chase that led to its predicament, and his leathern 'coat' painfully anticipates what will become of his skin if his body falls into human hands. Even this, however, is framed within language that suggests the town rather than the country. The animal is 'sequestered' in the sense of cut off from his fellows, but also perhaps (and anticipating Jaques's financial metaphors) in the legal sense of a debtor's wealth being seized to pay creditors[1].

Once Jaques begins to 'moralize this spectacle' (2.1.44), the language is almost entirely urban:

> [FIRST LORD]
> First, for his weeping into the needless stream;
> 'Poor deer,' quoth he, 'thou mak'st a testament
> As worldlings do, giving thy sum of more
> To that which had too much.' Then being there alone,
> Left and abandoned of his velvet friend,
> ''Tis right,' quoth he, 'thus misery doth part
> The flux of company.' Anon a careless herd
> Full of the pasture jumps along by him
> And never stays to greet him. 'Ay,' quoth Jaques,
> 'Sweep on, you fat and greasy citizens,
> 'Tis just the fashion. Wherefore should you look
> Upon that poor and broken bankrupt there?'

---

1. *Oxford English Dictionary*. 'sequester' *v*. 3.

Thus most invectively he pierceth through
The body of the country, city, court,
Yea, and of this our life, swearing that we
Are mere usurpers, tyrants, and what's worse,
To fright the animals and to kill them up
In their assigned and native dwelling place.
                              (*As You Like It* 2.1.46–63)

This propriety of place does not bear close scrutiny, for it sounds as though Duke Senior and Jaques agree that animals who confine themselves to the countryside should be safe, which would imply that the ones in the city's abattoirs merely wandered there by mistake and, being where they do not belong, came to deserve their fate. Yet even this fragile distinction between country and city is threatened by Jaques's urban diction that suggests he cannot apprehend the countryside other than through his courtly mind. The dying creature is, in adding water to water, making a pointless will ('testament') as humans do, and the herd that goes by without regarding their fellow are like prosperous citizens that disdain the company of one in financial difficulty ('broken bankrupt'). This is a keen sort of irony: only by putting the event into urban terms can Jaques stir his emotions about it. Or, to be more generous and give credence to the First Lord's interpretation, Jaques equally pierces the natural and the human worlds by showing that they are essentially alike: human society is not so different from animal society.

There is more going on with Jaques and the stag beyond this moralizing, however. Winifred Schleiner draws attention to the contemporary belief that the tear of a stag (the *lapis bezoar*) was itself medicinal to the melancholic[2], so that as Carol Falvo Heffernan points out there is an irony in Jaques foregoing the relief from his condition that is right in front of him[3]. Human melancholics such as Jaques, and animal ones such as stags, were supposed to be drawn to water because of their dryness, and hence the animal's 'augmenting' of the stream with its tears is also an ironic failure to correct the bodily hydraulics. A melancholic should conserve rather than give up its moisture where the addition is negligible, hence the 'needless[ness]' of the stream.

And yet there might also be a kind of self-regulation at work here, perceptible if we recall that humoral theory precedes the mind/body split of Cartesian dualism: Elizabethans observed no sharp distinction between emotional drives and the bodily hydraulics. Indeed,

---

2. Winfred Schleiner, 'Jaques and the Melancholy Stag'. *English Language Notes* 17 (1980): 175–79.
3. Carol Falvo Heffernan, *The Melancholy Muse: Chaucer, Shakespeare, and Early Medicine*. Duquesne Studies: Language and Literature Series, 19. Pittsburgh: Duquesne University Press, 1995, p. 107.

our notion of bodily causation of mental states is itself anachronistic here: 'Melancholia is black bile. That's what it means. . . . black bile doesn't just cause melancholy; melancholy somehow resides in it'[4]. If Jaques got melancholic from eating too much stag (or indeed hare or rabbit, according to contemporary wisdom) then what follows might be his body's self-correction of this imbalance. By generating his emotional state of sympathy for the stag, his bodily appetites are altered (he swears off meat) and so the proper balance can be restored. If, as seems likely, the 'ab[h]ominable' (4.1.6), man-avoiding Jaques seeks Duke Frederick at the close of the play in order to emulate his religious isolation, the monastic life (from the Greek *mono-* meaning alone) will include vegetarianism that will cure his melancholy.

We tend to think of the green-world plays such as *As You Like It* in terms of plant and landscape imagery but in fact our relations with animals are its central subject. That it seems otherwise is probably because the country world is first evoked in terms of plants and landscape ('tongues in trees, books in the running brooks, | Sermons in stones' 2.1.16–17) and the country songs are predominantly about these things ('Under the greenwood tree' 2.5.1, 'unto the green holly' 2.7.181, 191, 'o'er the green cornfield . . . acres of the rye . . . life was but a flower' 5.3.17–29). The final song signals the closing return to the urban with its repetition of every town' (5.4.141, 144). Yet all this talk of plants and landscape is confined to the characters' verbal descriptions of where they are; when they come to talk of their own affairs and what matters to them, nature is animal rather than vegetable. The accelerated pairings up of lovers towards the close release fresh possibilities in this regard, and given more lovers to mock besides herself and Orlando, Rosalind launches on a fresh stream of animal denigration, likening Celia and Oliver's instantaneous reciprocation to 'the fight of two rams' (5.2.29–30) and the general exclamations of love of Phoebe, Silvius, and Orlando to 'the howling of Irish wolves against the moon' (5.2.104–5).

The likening of humankind to animals runs throughout the play: 'ROSALIND [I am as native] As the coney that you see dwell where she is kindled' (3.2.329–30) and '[ROSALIND] boys and women are for the most part cattle of this colour' (3.2.398–9). The animal metaphors run alongside a minor stream of man-as-plant imagery such as Rosalind's 'I'll graft it [the tree] with you [Touchstone]' (3.2.115) and Celia's 'I found him [Orlando] under a tree, like a dropped acorn' (3.2.229–30). Even with the human-as-plant metaphors, the point is our vulnerability to being consumed, like a medlar fruit or an acorn

---

4. Charles Taylor, *Sources of the Self: The Making of Modern Identity*. Cambridge: Harvard University Press, 1989, pp. 188–89.

taken up by one of Fuller's Hampshire hogs. This vulnerability to predation had since classical mythology provided a ready analogy for relations of love: '[CELIA] He was furnished like a hunter— | ROSALIND O ominous—he comes to kill my heart' (3.2.240–1). The common Elizabethan pun on hart/heart provides the connection between the idealized and romantic and the mundane and bodily, and Rosalind's supposed cure for love is a shock to the bodily system:

> [ROSALIND] . . . grieve, be effeminate, changeable, longing and liking, proud, fantastical, apish, shallow, inconstant, full of tears, full of smiles; for every passion something, and for no passion truly anything, as boys and women are for the most part cattle of this colour—would now like him, now loathe him; then entertain him, then forswear him; now weep for him, then spit at him, that I drave my suitor from his mad humour of love to a living humour of madness, which was to forswear the full stream of the world and to live in a nook merely rnonastic. And thus I cured him, and this way will I take upon me to wash your liver as clean as a sound sheep's heart, that there shall not be one spot of love in 't.
>
> (As You Like It 3.2.395–408)

For all that it replaces one malady (love) with another (madness), this presumably imagined cure is of a piece with descriptions of humoral balance elsewhere in the play and it has the outcome— retirement into religious solitude—that the arch-villain Duke Frederick chooses for himself at the close.

Aside from Duke Frederick, who becomes 'abhominable' in the contemporary sense of 'apart from man', the visitors to the forest return at the end of the play to the courtly lives that they earlier claimed to have found inferior to country life. To the duke's eulogy about 'this life more sweet | Than that of painted pomp' (2.1.2–3), Amiens responds 'I would not change it' (2.1.18), meaning the new life for any other. And yet he does change it at the end of the play. Agnes Latham warns us not to read this as satire:

> Life in Arden is natural and happy and wholesome and all good men flourish there. One after another the refugees from the world's unkindness arrive drooping and the forest revives them. . . . At the end of the play the company return refreshed and invigorated to take up their ordinary duties, after what has been a life-enhancing and not a self-deluding interlude. The fact that they return so promptly and so cheerfully is what validates their experience.[5]

---

5. Agnes Latham, ed., As You Like It. Arden Shakespeare. London: Methuen, 1975, p. lix.

This sense of a trip to the forest as an invigorating tonic—much like a walk in the countryside in Jonathan Bate's account of Romantic poetry[6]—can only be sustained by ignoring the play's considerable power to disrupt our sense of country and city as separate domains. More simply, this reading is made possible only by mistaking exile for vacation.

As Jane Kingsley-Smith observes, exile and pastoralism already had a long-standing literary association when Shakespeare came to write *As You Like It*, yet there are 'points of conflict' in the association, most notably because the classical versions tended to show men banished from their farms while Renaissance pastoralists often 'are exiles from court' banished *to* the countryside. The latter direction exemplified the continued resonance of the idea that human beings 'belong in a garden rather than in a city' and hence that, paradoxically, in banishment the exile comes home[7]. (Taken at its widest, the Christian story of paradise lost and regained is, of course, precisely of this structure.) In Shakespeare's time the familiar dramatic expression of this city/country distinction was the so-called city comedy in which innocents from the countryside brought their naivety to the town. Shakespeare produced no city comedies, but in *As You Like It* he engages with the genre's conventions by reversal: courtiers bring their urban ideas to the countryside and find that aspects of city life have preceded them there. The financial depredation that we hear in Jaques's responses to the dying animal—and perhaps also in Duke Senior's confirmation of having 'seen better days' (2.7.120)—is already a feature of the countryside, hence Corin's inability to succour the exiles in 2.4. Rather than conforming to the pastoral stereotype of the self-sufficient and idling keeper of sheep, Corin is a daily labourer ('shepherd to another man' 2.4.77) and can resume his occupation only when the aristocrats buy his master's farm. Of this countryside reality the duke's party seem entirely unaware. No one appears to be growing crops in the world of *As You Like It*; the rustics are all descendants of murdered Abel rather than murderer Cain.

To follow the biblical correspondences for a moment, we can observe that the story of Noah makes a strong distinction between the plant world, which is not rescued in the ark, and the animal kingdom, which is. The plant world, it seems, survives on its own and indeed its capacity to self-regenerate is an index of the water's abating: when a dove returns with an olive leaf, Noah knows that it is safe to leave the ark (Genesis 8.1). The story of the flood is a kind

---

6. Jonathan Bate, *Romantic Ecology: Wordsworth and the Environmental Tradition*. London: Routledge, 1991.
7. Jane Kingsley-Smith, *Shakespeare's Drama of Exile*. Palgrave Shakespeare Studies. Basingstoke: Palgrave Macmillan, 2003, pp. 108–09.

of exile and return that the play mirrors in the flight and return of its groups of main characters, and the two-by-two marches of unclean animals admitted by Noah is, as Jaques observes ('another flood toward' 5.4.35), mirrored in the final scene's pairing of couples. Jaques's allusion to the biblical flood is relevant for the play's various investigations of the natural, because it confirmed human beings' dominion over the animals:

> And the fear of you and the dread of you shall be upon every beast of the earth, and upon every fowl of the air, upon all that moveth upon the earth, and upon all the fishes of the sea; into your hand are they delivered. Every moving thing that liveth shall be meat for you; even as the green herb have I given you all things.
>
> (Genesis 9.2–3)

If the trip into the forest apparently awoke disquiet about human/ animal relations, the analogy of the flood should allow the courtiers to return newly invigorated (as Latham would have us believe) with a sense of the rightness of human dominance of animals.

However, before this renewal of dominion over animals, God apparently also relented regarding Adam's cursed agrarian labour. For the original sin God had said 'cursed is the ground for thy sake; in sorrow shalt thou eat of it all the days of thy life; Thorns also and thistles shall it bring forth to thee; and thou shalt eat the herb of the field' (Genesis 3.17–18), but after the flood

> the LORD said in his heart, I will not again curse the ground any more for man's sake; for the imagination of man's heart is evil from his youth; neither will I again smite any more every thing living, as I have done. While the earth remaineth, seed-time and harvest, and cold and heat, and summer and winter, and day and night shall not cease.
>
> (Genesis 8.21–2)

Whereas the attitude to animals is simply confirmed, the position regarding cultivation seems like a reversal. And indeed, Noah becomes a husbandman and plants a vineyard (whence wine), which epitomizes the re-entry of pleasure into the world (Genesis 9.20).

Any contrast of the agrarian and the pastoral lives in Western literature necessarily draws upon the story of Cain and Abel, which mythologizes the triumph of farming. Once human beings became mostly crop-planters rather than hunters, hunting became a recreational activity, especially for the wealthy. The exile of the courtiers in *As You Like It* bringing with it the necessity to hunt is, in that sense, also a forced return to an earlier form of production and what was formerly the height of aristocratic leisure must be done to survive. As You Like It is concerned with the moral correctness of hunting itself. What links our time with Shakespeare's is a sense that our relationships with animals are a part of what we consider to be a healthy lifestyle. We, like them, worry about how far it is justifiable to make animals suffer for our ends, how far we may treat them as merely instruments. In pondering those relations, we must remember that difference of scale is not difference of kind, for Isabella makes the entirely plausible claim that 'the poor beetle that we tread upon | In corporal sufferance finds a pang as great | As when a giant dies' (Measure for Measure 3.1.77–9).

* * *

MICHAEL JAMIESON

As You Like It: Performance and Reception[†]

Come the millennium As You Like It[1] will be some four hundred years old, so that an essay of this length on the ways it has been performed and how it has been received must be selective. Three broad movements in its performance history can be discerned. First comes a long, blank period from 1600 to 1723 when (a) there is no hard evidence that the play was ever performed in Shakespeare's lifetime, and (b) in the much more fully documented years from 1660 there is every indication that the old comedy was totally ignored in the playhouses of London and the provinces. Next comes a span, ending in the 1890s, when versions of As You Like It were performed with increasing frequency in the English-speaking theatres of Britain and North America, most memorably by star actresses who were applauded in the great role of Rosalind but who often had to appear under the restrictive, even resentful régime of male managers—especially when these gentlemen were themselves leading actors.

[†] From Michael Jamieson, "As You Like It: Performance and Reception" in Edward Tomarken, ed., As You Like It from 1600 to the Present: Critical Essays (New York: Garland, 1997), pp. 623–46.

1. Much information about the performance-history and the treatment of the text on the stage can be found in The New Variorum Edition of As You Like It by Richard Knowles (New York: The Modern Language Association of America, 1977). Full of details about old theatrical customs and traditions is Arthur Colby Sprague, Shakespeare and the Actors: The Stage Business in His Plays, 1660–1905 (Cambridge, MA: Harvard U Press, 1945). Sprague was coauthor with J. C. Trewin of a book which stands as a sequel, Shakespeare's Plays Today: Some Customs and Conventions of the Stage (London: Sidgwick and Jackson, 1970). Two surveys of Shakespearean production are Robert Speaight, Shakespearian Performance (London: Collins, 1973) and Dennis Kennedy, Looking at Shakespeare: A Visual History of Twentieth-Century Performance (Cambridge: Cambridge U Press, 1993). Both authors take an admirably international outlook and their books are splendidly illustrated. In discussing productions from 1952 onwards I have drawn on my own experience—sadly Anglophone—as a playgoer.

This era saw Shakespeare consolidated as England's national poet, and towards its end, especially in London and New York, technological and cultural changes allowed theatrical productions to be much more spectacular and scenic so that the imagination of playgoers and journalists was sometimes focussed on the visual contribution of the managers and the scene-painters. From the mid-nineties onwards the situation is bewildering and complex. As You Like It may not have exercised the Western imagination in quite the same way as Hamlet or King Lear, but the proliferation of performances in schools and colleges, the establishment of institutions in England and North America dedicated mainly to the staging of Shakespeare, the international advent of the director as the authoritative interpreter of theatrical texts, and the impact of radio, film, TV and video all contributed to the regular presentation of this once neglected romantic comedy. Actresses (and on occasion actors) still aspire to play Rosalind; and especially since World War I there have been innovative or conceptual interpretations often in foreign translations. There have also been curious lacunae. Two marvellous English actresses (Dame Ellen Terry, Dame Judi Dench) never played Rosalind, and, amongst British directors generally regarded as notable Shakespeareans, at least five have never directed the play: William Poel, Harley Granville Barker, Tyrone Guthrie, Peter Brook and Peter Hall. The list of foreign directors who never did an As You Like It would be much longer.

As often with Elizabethan and Jacobean texts there is no record of the first performance of As You Like It which most scholars assume was first acted around 1600, perhaps at the recently erected Globe Playhouse on Bankside—to which Jaques' set speech "All the world's a stage" may stand as a precise metatheatrical allusion. A comedy based so closely on the much-reprinted pastoral romance Rosalind (1590) is likely to have proved as popular with audiences as Thomas Lodge's prose narrative already had become with readers. Touchstone, like Jaques, is a Shakespearean invention; and it is possible that the part was created to accommodate the skills of the company's new clown, Robert Armin. That Shakespeare himself played old Adam is a Stratford tradition recorded as a faint local memory as late as 1774. Deductions made from the Folio text have greater interest. The unknown youth who first played Rosalind must have been a talented and resourceful performer.[2] Not only does the heroine dominate and even control the action, but this is the longest woman's part Shakespeare ever wrote (736 lines as

---

2. See Michael Jamieson, "Shakespeare's Celibate Stage: The Problem of Accommodation to the Boy-Actors" in G. E. Bentley, ed., The Seventeenth-Century Stage: A Collection of Critical Essays (Chicago & London: The University of Chicago Press, 1968), 70–93.

against Orlando's 321). Furthermore, this is the only script in the canon in which the boy-actor speaks the epilogue. Another tradition about *As You Like It* was recorded as late as 1865. William Cory, poet, scholar and Eton master, wrote in his journal of a visit to Wilton House

> The house (Lady Herbert said) is full of interest: . . . we have a letter, never printed, from Lady Pembroke to her son, telling him to bring James I from Salisbury to see *As You Like It*; 'we have the man Shakespeare with us.'[3]

Cory never saw the alleged letter, nor could it be produced for E. K. Chambers in 1898.[4] However, a document first transcribed by Peter Cunningham in 1842 does record a payment to the company for a single performance at Court on 2 December 1603. In this time of plague the Court is known to have been at Wilton from around 20 October to 12 December 1603 and the King did visit Salisbury. Nothing supports the idea that the play paid for was *As You Like It*, or even by Shakespeare, but scholars of a romantic bent like to fancy a performance—possibly out of doors—of a comedy which celebrates the sylvan pleasures of the hunt to which King James was passionately devoted.

When the playhouses were reopened in 1660 those middle comedies of Shakespeare which centre on disguise, love and courtship were not revived. Dramatic historians have variously conjectured that *As You Like It* was lacking in downright comic power or was too fresh and clean for the jaded appetites of Restoration rakes. A major reason for the neglect may well be that its male characters did not offer much scope to Restoration actors. The comedy first emerges from obscurity as *Love in a Forest*, an adaptation by Charles Johnson acted at Drury Lane in January 1723. This "improvement" was explained in a prologue:

> In Honour to his Name, and this learn'd Age,
> Once more your much lov'd SHAKESPEAR treads the Stage.
> Another Work from that great Hand appears,
> His Ore's refin'd, but not impar'd by *Years*.

And later:

> Forgive our modern Author's Honest Zeal,
> He hath attempted boldly, if not well:

3. Quoted from the edition by F. W. Cornish in the New Variorum *As You Like It*, 633.
4. E.K. Chambers, *William Shakespeare: A Study of Facts and Problems* 2 vols. (Oxford: Clarendon Press, 1930), vol. 2, 239.

Believe, he only does with Pain and Care,
Presume to weed the beautiful Parterre.[5]

Johnson's weeding of the Shakespearean garden was ruthlessly correct: his excisions include Touchstone and all the shepherds and shepherdesses, with Bottom and his mechanicals brought in at the close to act "Pyramus and Thisbe" to the restored Duke. The adaptation was played for only six nights. The part of Jaques, acted by Colley Cibber, was built up by transforming the First Lord's report in II.i. into a recollection by Jaques himself. This long remained a theatrical tradition.

On 20 December 1740 As You Like It was billed at Drury Lane as "Not Acted these Forty Years" (over a hundred being more likely). There was a strong cast and three of Shakespeare's songs were given new settings by Thomas Arne. The Rosalind was Hannah Pritchard, then twenty-nine, who got off to a bad start. In those more boisterous days, when the auditorium remained illuminated, a performer's "points" were applauded. It was only when Pritchard, given an unbecoming gown by the management, reached the line "Take the cork out of thy mouth that I may drink thy tidings" that she was applauded loudly for her spirited delivery. The performance not only brought her to the top of her profession but created a vogue for other Shakespearean comedies. It was acted twenty-eight times in the season, and Francis Hayman's painting of the wrestling scene, which is now in the Tate Gallery, probably depicts Pritchard (better gowned) as Rosalind with Kitty Clive and Celia.[6]

Pritchard's Rosalind was soon challenged by others, notably the more alluring Peg Woffington, who had earlier made an impact in what were called "breeches parts." From the Restoration onwards actresses had been encouraged to expose themselves to the male gaze, and one of the ways they could be sexually provocative was to reveal their ankles and legs in the roles of rakes and gallants. Rosalind (pace Jan Kott[7]) is not really a breeches part, since the actress does not have to play a man but a girl masquerading as one. Some of the notable later players of Rosalind/Ganymede had previously excelled in such parts. In the neo-classical era tragic and comic roles, especially female ones, were sharply differentiated. Yet the great Sarah Siddons was determined to essay Rosalind. When she did so at Drury Lane in 1785, she muffled herself up as Ganymede, concealing her limbs, and was ridiculed in the press. In the years 1787 to 1814 the

5. Quoted in Michael Dobson, The Making of the National Poet: Shakespeare, Adaptation and Authorship, 1660–1769 (Oxford: Clarendon Press, 1992), 131–2.
6. See Anthony Vaughan, Born to Please: Hannah Pritchard, Actress, 1711–1768 (London: The Society for Theatre Research, 1979), 18–20 and pl 2.
7. Jan Kott, "The Gender of Rosalind," Interpretations: Shakespeare, Buchner, Gautier (Evanston, Ill.: Northwestern U Press, 1992), 39 n 13.

unsurpassable Rosalind was the enchanting Mrs Jordan, a mischievous, infectious player with a voice which reminded Siddons' brother, J. P. Kemble, of a phrase in Sterne: "like the natural notes of some sweet melody which drops from it whether it will or no."[8] She played Rosalind for twenty-seven years at Covent Garden, at Drury Lane and in the provinces. She played her in sickness and in health, often in the advanced stages of pregnancy. For Little Pickle (as the much-loved Dora was called after one of her breeches parts) lived openly with the Duke of Clarence, the future King William IV, and bore him ten FitzClarences, first cousins to the legitimate Victoria, who duly succeeded their father as sovereign. In the years before her widowhood, Queen Victoria was a great playgoer and several times quizzed Lord Melbourne about Dora Jordan, on one occasion when they were contemplating the memorial statue by Chantrey. The royal diary records:

> "She was beautifully formed," Lord M said, "her legs and feet were beautifully formed, as this statue is; and she used to be fond of acting in men's clothes; she used to act . . . Rosalind in *As You Like It*"; "a lovely play," said Lord M, "the prettiest play in the world; and her acting in that was quite beautiful." "She had a beautiful enunciation," he added. She was an Irish girl.[9]

* * *

From the 1780s onwards * * * *As You Like It* was increasingly liked; *Much Ado* had half as many performances; *Twelfth Night* about two thirds. It was first done in New York in 1786 and was more frequently performed there than in London. The acting text was by tradition heavily cut. Among the customary deletions were: Jaques' parody of Amiens' song and the exiled Duke's recollection of Jaques' libertinism; Sir Oliver Martext's appearance; Rosalind's exchange with Jaques; the epiphany of Hymen. Subsequent Bowdlerian excisions concentrated on seeming indelicacies. Cuts reduced running time, but they were sometimes necessitated by such interpolations as songs from other plays. Mrs Jordan was not the only Ganymede to tease Orlando by singing "Cuckoo" from *Love's Labour's Lost*. Stage custom also dictated certain details of costume and stage business. The low comedian playing Touchstone tended to commandeer some of Le Beau's lines in the wrestling scene and often fussily supervised the removal of the insensate Charles.

The presentation of *As You Like It* by William Charles Macready in October 1842 at Drury Lane, then under his management, must

8. William Robson, *The Old Playgoer* (London, 1845; repr. with intro by Robert Gittings, London: Centaur Press, 1969), 141.
9. Quoted by George Rowell, *Queen Victoria at the Theatre* (London: Paul Elek, 1978).

rank as the first which gave one man's vision of the play.[1] For a start Macready had restored much of the Folio text and the players had been thoroughly rehearsed. Great attention and much expense had been given to the scene-painting, which was by Charles Marshall. The fair-copy of the prompt-book has an enthusiastic note: "the most wonderfully perfect representation of Court and pastoral life was witnessed on the English stage." There were ten settings, mostly backcloths, but two scenes exploited the full depth of the Drury Lane stage, the wrestling bout and the finale. A surviving drawing shows the former: the painted backcloth depicts a French château with a forested landscape while in front, centre stage, on a terrace is the wrestling space. There were seventy-three supers (or extras) in this spectacle.

* * *

Macready himself played Jaques in what he later regarded as the favourite among his splendid revivals. He came to regret that he had cast the lively and beautiful comic actress, Louise Nisbett (later Lady Boothby), as Rosalind, for she played the part in the old hoyden tradition, which was not quite to Victorian taste. Subsequently Rosalind was played by the cooler, more elegant Helen Faucit (later Lady Martin), who in retirement wrote several essays on "Shakespeare's Female Characters by One Who Has Impersonated Them." When, in 1843, Macready gave up the management of Drury Lane, the Queen commanded a performance of *As You Like It* and an afterpiece, rather to his displeasure, for The Eminent Tragedian would have preferred to appear in a greater role. Again the royal diary is revealing:

> Macready acted the part of Jacques and pronounced the famous speech about the Ages beautifully but what surprised me most of all was the really beautiful acting of Miss H. Faucit as "Rosalind." She looked pretty in male attire and was lively and "naive".[2]

Macready's production remained a landmark, but actresses continued to covet the role of Rosalind. Charlotte Cushman, the American actress who liked taking men's parts in Shakespeare, played Rosalind rather broadly in London in 1845 and often in New York between 1849 and 1857. Helena Modjeska, whose frail, lady-like Rosalind spoke with Polish inflections, regularly acted coast-to-

---

1. The account of Macready's production draws on Alan Downer, *The Eminent Tragedian, William Charles Macready* (Cambridge, Mass.: Harvard U Press, 1966), 215–6, 223, 243–4, 251, and on Charles H. Shattuck's *Mr Macready Produces As You Like It: a Prompt-book Study* (Urbana, IL: Illinois Phi Mu, 1962).
2. *Queen Victoria at the Theatre.*

coast. Playing opposite her was one of the few men ever to have made much of Orlando, the virile and muscular Maurice Barrymore— founder of a theatrical dynasty—who sparred with a professional prize-fighter as Charles the Wrestler. Hermann Vezin, the American actor and elocutionist, virtually appropriated the role of Jaques in London between 1875 and 1900.

From 1871 to 1902 the most distinguished theatre in London was the Lyceum under Henry Irving, whose charming leading lady, Ellen Terry, was the best-loved actress since Jordan and the highest paid woman in England. But, though she played opposite him in nine sumptuous Shakespearean revivals, Terry was never allowed to play Rosalind. When one of Irving's advisers urged that she must get to play Rosalind while in her prime, the actor-manager (who had been Silvius and Orlando in his long apprentice years) was not enthusiastic about taking on Touchstone.[3]

Terry must have had mixed feelings when she heard rumours of a surprising As You Like It which, for a few summer afternoons in 1884 and 1885 united the worlds of high society and of the Aesthetic Movement in a woodland glade in Surrey.[4] Lady Archibald Campbell, a high priestess of aestheticism, who had been painted by Whistler and published by Wilde, had recently done a portrait of the beautiful American actress, Eleanor Calhoun, as Rosalind, using as background the wood of Coombe Warren, the Duke of Cambridge's country estate near Kingston-upon-Thames. She now invited E. W. Godwin, the architect and designer, to supervise an open-air charity performance of the forest scenes in As You Like It. * * * The acting area was a grove of lime trees with views stretching beyond. It faced a raked stand draped in sage-green, with chairs for three hundred spectators. A green curtain was strung between two trees and lowered into a hidden trench by two foresters to signal the start of the performance. A slain stag was carried in the distance in the hunting scene and deer and goats grazed on the fringes of the action. The experiment was so successful that an extra performance was attended by the Prince of Wales and there was much discussion in the journals about the amazing naturalism of the performance which had made some spectators feel like eavesdroppers.

The gentlemanly actor-managers continued the attempt to cram a convincing Arden within the picture-frames of their West End playhouses. When John Hare and W. H. Kendal collaborated on a production at the civilised St James's Theatre in 1885 the setting included real grass, real ferns, a real waterfall—and Hermann Vezin

---

3. The adviser in 1882 was Squire Bancroft, the first actor to be knighted after Irving. See *The Bancrofts: Recollections of Sixty Years* (London: John Murray, 1909), 326–7.
4. This section is based on "Aesthetic Theatre: The Career of E. W. Godwin" in John Stokes, *Resistible Theatres: Enterprise and experiment in the late nineteenth century* (London: Paul Elek, 1972), 31–68.

as Jaques. The master of this mode of presentation, which involved a good deal of textual rearrangement and interpolation of songs and business, was the American impresario Augustin Daly, who managed theatres named after him in both New York and London. Although purists objected to the "Dalyised" approach, everyone applauded his leading lady, the spirited, red-headed Irishwoman, Ada Rehan, one of the great Rosalinds of all time. Daly died in 1899 and Rehan's withdrawal from her triumphant career suggested to some that he had been Svengali to her Trilby. In 1897 she brought a company to play *As You Like It* out of doors one afternoon at Stratford, but rain drove the players into the new Shakespeare Memorial Theatre, which would later become the centre of the Shakespeare Industry.

By the turn of the century a bewildering amount of scholarly, cultural and institutional attention was being focussed on the staging of Shakespeare, though on the whole *As You Like It* was conventionally treated. William Poel, who pioneered a return to Elizabethan modes of presentation, never directed the comedy.

* * * It was left to Nigel Playfair, who had acted for Poel and Barker, to release *As You Like It* from dreary stage traditions and to animate it with all the resources of modern design.[5] The Memorial Theatre had been closed for the last years of the war and in 1919 Playfair was invited to bring a guest company to the April festivities in *As You Like It*. His actors played a very full text, speaking briskly and lightly. The highly intelligent Athene Seyler played Rosalind with wit and verve and Playfair himself was Touchstone. But the revelation (and—to Benson's loyal followers—the horror) was the designs. Playfair, with a limited budget, had engaged the brilliant young illustrator Claud Lovat Fraser, whose bright, boldly-coloured costumes and sharply stylised settings were based on fourteenth century French missals. They had the clarity of illustrations for children's books. What shocked Stratfordians most, however, was the Londoner's failure to observe an immemorial local tradition. As far back as 1879, when *As You Like It* graced the first festival, H. S. Lucy of Charlecote Park had shot and presented a stag from the very estate on which Shakespeare was supposedly apprehended for poaching deer. That day the trophy of the chase was slowly borne across the stage by the Lucy retainers with their dogs. The stag was stuffed and was carried on-stage—progressively moth-eaten—in all subsequent performances of *As You Like It*. Fraser's designs were thought by some to be subversively Cubist. They had the same brightness of colour and boldness of line that had excited comment

---

5. Sir Nigel Playfair gave witty accounts of his *As You Like It* in two works of reminiscence, *The Story of the Lyric Theatre Hammersmith* (London: Chatto and Windus, 1925), and *Hammersmith Hoy* (London: Faber & Faber, London, 1930), 203–7, the former of which contains designs by Fraser reproduced in colour and black and white.

in Barker's productions; the ultimate influence was probably the stunning *decors* brought to London in Diaghilev's Russian ballets.

* * *

In the twenties and thirties at Stratford and the Old Vic, *As You Like It* was given frequent, fairly conventional revivals. Fabia Drake made a big local reputation as a spirited Rosalind at Stratford, where the seasons now ran for five weeks, first in 1930 and then in 1932, when the new Memorial Theatre was opened. The Vic, with its much longer seasons and its responsive audience of locals, students and dedicated playgoers, was the greater nursery of talent, and its productions got reviewed in the national press. Even the established actress Edith Evans volunteered to work south of the river to stretch herself in a range of Shakespearean parts, including Rosalind in 1926. The Vic also made stars. The radiant and lyrical Peggy Ashcroft, then twenty-five, did her first Rosalind there in 1932 when she was sketched by Sickert putting the chain around Orlando's neck. She was trounced by the reigning drama critic, James Agate, for "taking away the poetry, the depth of feeling and what I should like to call the lineage of the part."[6]

Edith Evans's later Rosalind sheds light on Agate's phrase. She was invited for a season of three plays in 1936 by the brilliant, occasionally maverick director, Tyrone Guthrie, who was determined to improve production values at the Old Vic. There was a problem. Evans wanted to play Rosalind for the last time. Guthrie was blunt: at forty-nine she was too old. He assigned the direction to the actress and teacher of drama, Esmé Church, who in partnership with the designer, Mollie MacEwen decided on pastoral settings *a la* Watteau. Michael Redgrave, then twenty-eight, was Orlando. Evans triumphed by sheer force of will and by her remarkable vocal technique. Never conventionally beautiful, she had the capacity to assume glamour on stage, and she came back to Rosalind after playing some of the witty, independent women of Restoration comedy, including Millamant. She brought wit, style and impeccable timing to speaking the marvellous cadences of Shakespeare's prose. Her performance may have been given added radiance by the fact (disclosed much later in a biography) that she and her young leading man had enjoyed what Dame Edith in old age referred to as "my five-minute love."[7] Reviewing the production for *The Manchester Guardian*, Alan Dent noted that it seemed October in this Arden,

6. *Brief Chronicles: A Survey of the Plays of Shakespeare and the Elizabethans in Actual Performances* (London: Jonathan Cape, 1943), 60–61.
7. Bryan Forbes, *Ned's Girl: The Authorised Biography of Dame Edith Evans* (London: Elm Tree Books/Hamish Hamilton, 1977), 183–8. See also James Forsyth, *Tyrone Guthrie: A Biography* (London: Hamish Hamilton, 1976), 153, 157.

but found the Rosalind "a Meredithian lady rich in mind." Praising
the wit and romance of Evans's performance he concluded: "in the
end the audience is made one Orlando."[8] The production transferred to the West End where within two years Edith Evans first
played her definitive Lady Bracknell.[9]

Two notions of Rosalind seemed to co-exist in the thirties: the
Congrevian or Meredithian witty woman and the *gamine*—
Millamant and Peter Pan. Several actresses who acted Rosalind,
especially on the greensward of the Open Air Theatre in Regent's
Park, also played the Boy Who Did Not Wish to Grow Up. Almost
contemporaneous with Evans's performance was the refugee Dr
Paul Czinner's lavish Anglo-American film of 1936, conceived as a
vehicle for his internationally famous wife, Elisabeth Bergner. The
Viennese star had played Rosalind in German at Zürich in 1920
and at Berlin a couple of years later under the great Max Reinhardt.
The film tended to be reviewed as a film version of Shakespeare
rather than as a movie in its own right. The palace of Duke Frederick recalled the set for an Astaire-Rogers dance routine and the
studio artificiality of the forest was made especially noticeable by
the presence of bleating sheep and grazing deer.[1] Although Laurence Olivier, who had decided Orlando was a bit mad, made a
good impression, Bergner herself—tiny and elfish and given to turning somersaults—was judged to be too cloying, too arch, too coy;
and her palpably thirties make-up tempted one journalist to dub
the film "Lost in the Forest of Elizabeth Arden." Nor did Bergner's
foreign accent make Rosalind's cadenced prose intelligible to film-
goers. The dialogue, over which her great fan Sir James Barrie was
consulted, was pruned of all sexual innuendoes and the running
time was cut to 97 minutes. William Walton composed his first
Shakespearean score for this film, which now has an archival fascination in that several British actors of the old school are preserved
on celluloid and on the sound-track. Henry Ainley (born 1879),
playing the exiled Duke, had been a dashingly handsome Orlando
in 1902. Leon Quartermaine (born 1876) was especially praised for
his measured delivery of "All the world's a stage."

Foreign productions often had a freshness and freedom stem-
ming from the fact that directors were not bound by precedent.
* * * The most amazing production of the comedy in the immediately post-war years was the *Rosalinda* staged in Rome in 1948 by
Luchino Visconti, who envisaged it as "a fantasy, a dream, a fairy-

---

8. Alan Dent, *Prelude and Studies* (London: Macmillan, 1942), 111–2.
9. A much older character from Oscar Wilde's *The Importance of Being Earnest* [Editor].
1. James Agate, *Around Cinemas* (London: Horne & Van Thal, 1946), 173–7.

tale verging on ballet."[2] Accordingly he secured designs from Salvador Dali. Although their production was later dismissed, sight unseen, as a half-hearted attempt at a surrealist staging, the truth was more complex and more intellectually valid, for Dali and Visconti took as their starting-point the extraordinary and mysterious *boschetto* at Bomarzo, a cryptically allegorical grove created around 1560 by an aristocratic humanist and filled with gnomic inscriptions and grotesque sculptures. Dali designed two emblematic rococo backcloths—one Court, one Forest—and costumes of extraordinary richness and elaborateness. On the stage were two elephants bearing obelisks like Bernini's sculptures and a Palladian temple which opened into four sections. The music was by Shakespeare's English contemporaries. Visconti's usual leading lady Rita Morelli was Rosalind, the darkly handsome Vittorio Gassman played Orlando, and a young Roman called Marcello Mastrionni made his début as one of Jaques' foresters.

* * *

Things were perhaps tamer in the English-speaking theatre. Katharine Hepburn appeared as Rosalind at the Cort Theatre in New York in 1950 and later made a hugely successful coast-to-coast tour of the States. This was a lavishly spectacular production by The Theatre Guild, with an imported English director and designer, Michael Benthall and James Bailey, and several London actors. Brooks Atkinson in *The New York Times* complained about the "heavily accented" and "singularly busy" direction, which was:

> . . . equipped with bird songs, owl hoots, a snow-storm, garlanded processionals, wood smoke, choruses, a fine chamber orchestra, and . . . spiced with several episodes of egregious horse-play.

The scholarly stage-historian Arthur Colby Sprague was annoyed by the cuts, transpositions and additions, and by the fact that "the cuckoo and the owl songs from *Love's Labour's Lost* were thrust in for good measure just as they used to be in Victorian times."[3] But, of course, the whole *raison d'etre* of the production was the sprightly star's return to the theatre from Hollywood in her first classical rôle. Several iconic photographs show Hepburn seated against a tree trunk stretching her shapely legs in what look like sheer nylon

2. Visconti's production is briefly described by Monica Stirling in *A Screen of Time: A Study of Luchino Visconti* (New York: Harcourt Brace Jovanovich, 1976), 81–2, and Gaia Servadio in *Luchino Visconti: A Biography* (London: Weidenfeld & Nicolson, 1982), 120, 235.

3. Arthur Colby Sprague and J. C. Trewin, *Shakespeare's Plays Today: Some Customs and Conventions of the Stage* (London: Sidgwick and Jackson, 1970), 79. Sprague quoted Brooks Atkinson, but did not even mention Katharine Hepburn.

tights. Benthall duly returned to London where he was director of the Old Vic between 1953 and 1961 when he supervised the staging of all the plays in the First Folio, often with such emerging stars as Richard Burton, John Neville and Claire Bloom; but in 1955 and 1958, when *As You Like It* was revived, he delegated the actual direction to others. The high level of casting is indicated by the fact that in 1958 Barbara Jefford's tall and well spoken Rosalind was supported by Maggie Smith as Celia, Judi Dench as Phebe and Moyra Fraser as Audrey.

Some reviewers and academics preferred productions of Shakespeare which did not carry the imprint of strong directorial interpretation. Professor Dame Helen Gardner claimed that in the fifties when Glen Byam Shaw was directing at Stratford no-one spoke of Byam Shaw's *As You Like It* but of Peggy Ashcroft's "heavenly Rosalind."⁴

* * * Byam Shaw mounted his third version in 1957, when Dame Peggy Ashcroft, nearing fifty, played her last Rosalind with blazing sincerity and romantic feeling, though she complained in a letter to her mentor George Rylands, the Shakespearean don and director: "Rosalind is a wonderful girl but I wish she didn't talk *quite* so much."⁵

Stratford audiences saw a landmark *As You Like It* in 1961—a radiant production by Michael Elliott for the reorganised Royal Shakespeare Company which made a star of Vanessa Redgrave, daughter of Dame Edith's Orlando. This marked the happiest coming together of director, designer and player. Richard Negri's memorable set was dominated by a vast tree and the whole sloping stage was carpeted in green. Sombre in the early scenes, the stage came alive later with dappled sunshine in the Forest. This was probably the first occasion when most reviewers mentioned the lighting, some even naming the lighting designer, Richard Pilbrow. The magic was Redgrave's. More than common tall, she played Ganymede barefoot, with a working-man's cap pulled down over her eyes. When she finally came running round the great tree in her wedding dress, the audience gasped. Max Adrian may have been the first actor to tinge the sardonic Jaques' melancholy with homosexual desire. The interpretation was totally humanist: Corin haltingly recited Hymen's lines. Redgrave repeated her Stratford triumph at the Aldwych in London and the production was redirected on film for BBC TV which took 138 minutes. Peter Hall, head of the RSC, recalled in his memoirs taking a reluctant play-

4. Helen Gardner, "Shakespeare in the Director's Theatre," chap. 3 of *In Defence of the Imagination* (Oxford: Clarendon Press, 1982), 67.
5. Michael Billington, *Peggy Ashcroft* (London: John Murray, 1988), 170.

goer Jean Renoir to the theatre and placing him for a few minutes at the back of the stalls:

> After a short time I took his arm to show him the way out, but he resisted and stayed, his eyes alight. On stage was a girl like a rush of sunlight. He was watching the twenty-four year old Vanessa Redgrave play Rosalind, her first unqualified triumph.[6]

The Redgrave/Elliott inhibited successors. It seemed to encapsulate that view of Shakespearean comedy put forward by Northrop Frye and C. L. Barber. But in the late sixties theatre people began to think of Arden less as The Green World or The Great Good Place and more as some sort of metaphor for the alternative lifestyle of youth culture and the flower people. A precursor seems to have been Word Baker's modern-dress revival at Stratford, Connecticut, in which Kim Hunter played Rosalind; Orlando was barefoot and in overalls and Sir Oliver Martext was a bicycling vicar. Peter Dews' production at the Birmingham Rep in 1967 with a young cast including Brian Cox as Orlando was graced with Carnaby Street costumes and pop music.

Even before this flower-power As You Like It had briefly transferred to the Vaudeville in London, John Dexter, a brilliant and acerbic Associate Director of the National Theatre, then still at the Old Vic, had been working for over a year on an up-to-date and all-male version with music by Donovan, the folk singer. But the National Theatre's director Laurence Olivier, soon to be made a Life Peer, unexpectedly vetoed the project, fearing public hostility to a drag show.[7] He offered Rosalind to one of the National's leading ladies, Maggie Smith, whose dazzling success in the company had not entirely pleased him.[8] Then in 1971 he suddenly entrusted an all-male production to a safer pair of hands, Clifford Williams, a director with a strongly visual sense on loan from the RSC. Dexter's project was influenced by Jan Kott's essay 'Shakespeare's Bitter Arcadia', especially as regards notions of sexuality and homo-eroticism explored through the concept of the original boy-actor playing the woman Rosalind disguised as the youth Ganymede. Though Kott was copiously quoted in the National Theatre programme, Williams added a note distancing himself from such problematic theories. The intellectual basis of his dazzlingly successful production was perhaps a little fuzzy. (Olivier was reported as having wondered aloud at rehearsals whether the men playing women should perhaps wear

---

6. Peter Hall, *Making an Exhibition of Myself* (London: Sinclair-Stevenson, 1993), 123–4.
7. John Elsom and Nicholas Tomalin, *The History of the National Theatre* (London: Jonathan Cape, 1978), 195–6.
8. Michael Coveney, *Maggie Smith: A Bright Particular Star* (London: Victor Gollancz, 1992), 130.

false bosoms and shave their legs.) Ralph Koltai designed an almost abstract set which could have been used for other plays. In the Forest scenes Plexiglass tubes and cloud-shaped transparencies descended to suggest trees and foliage; kaleidoscopic lighting enhanced the dappled shadows; and Marc Wilkinson's pop-style music seemed almost to emanate from the abstract tubes. The mood was celebratory and festive, and the players, most of whom had been together for several seasons, formed a marvellous *ensemble*.

* * *

The very success of this controversial all-male production provoked strong reactions from other directors. The earliest was the production in 1973 at Stratford by the young Buzz Goodbody, the first woman to be given a permanent directorial appointment at the RSC, hitherto a male oligarchy. A feminist and a Communist, she strove to reclaim the text for women. * * * Trevor Nunn's production in [the RSC's] main house in 1977 turned the comedy, especially in its last act, into a sort of baroque opera with arias for Celia and Orlando and with Hymen descending in a throne of two-dimensional clouds. Terry Hands' production in 1980 was a direct response to his boss's operatic interpretation. For it Farrah designed a monochromatic Jacobean court that was mechanically transformed into a forest in which, as Spring moved into Summer, the pine trees seemed to sprout foliage. Suzanne Fleetwood was a tall and resilient Rosalind; and Sinead Cusack was an observant, rather alarmed Celia. John Bowe, the tough and likeable Orlando, later wrote that Farrah's Arden reminded him of scenes he had imagined when reading *Lord of the Rings*.[9] Terry Hands had indeed returned the action to The Green World.

* * *

The most ambitious and costly *As You Like It* of the century must have been the great German director Peter Stein's seminal production for the Schaubühne in West Berlin.[1] * * * The audience [of] over 300 had first to assemble as promenaders in a long, high hall. The actors in elaborate Elizabethan costumes sat immobile on various platforms; once the play began the early scenes were juxtaposed almost cinematically. The wrestling match was the climax of the first part with a professional wrestler in the non-speaking part of Charles. Then came a chase to the Forest in which the specta-

---

9. In Philip Brockbank, ed., *Players of Shakespeare: Essays in Shakespearean Performance by Twelve Players with the RSC*, 1 (Cambridge: Cambridge U Press, 1985), 67–76.
1. There is an extended description and analysis of this whole enterprise in Michael Patterson's *Peter Stein: Germany's Leading Theatre Director* (Cambridge: Cambridge U Press, 1981), chapter 7.

tors had to follow the actors. They proceeded single-file through a tunnel to a second, bigger space in which Arden had been recreated in almost realistic detail—a pool, tree-trunks, a cottage, a farm, catwalks. The audience sat on three sides while on the fringes of the action various denizens of the Forest wandered: Robin Hood, Robinson Crusoe, a hermit, a witch.

* * *

By the time John Dexter was invited in 1979 to stage *As You Like It* at the National Theatre that organisation had moved to its new complex of three playhouses on the South Bank. Dexter was allocated the huge, awkward saucer of the Olivier stage and he used it as simply as possible to focus attention on the activities taking place on the white raked stage of the court and the green one of the forest. The production emphasised the back-breaking labour of harvesting in the opening scene. Dexter, now more influenced by *The Golden Bough* than by *Shakespeare Our Contemporary*, discovered (or imposed) a savage cruelty in Arden. A young man, naked to the waist and blooded from the chase, was paraded in the hunting scene. Later he turned out to be William and eventually he spoke for a pagan Hymen. The costume designs were richly Elizabethan, and Sara Kestleman as the disguised Rosalind looked as if she had stepped from a miniature by Hilliard. Simon Callow, who was cast, rather against type, as a stubby and endearing Orlando, later wrote in *Being An Actor* (1984) of the dictatorial, bullying methods of the director and said he gave Dexter's performance of Orlando not his own. Michael Bryant as Jaques spoke the famous speech while peeling and eating an apple. After the first night Sir Peter Hall, who had succeeded Olivier as supremo of the National Theatre, dictated a note for his diary:

> . . . slightly slow, slightly tense, but you feel the whole of the Elizabethan mind laid out before you. I have seen the play better performed but never better directed.[2]

He was disappointed that the London reviewers found the three hours the play took too long. What would they have made of Stein's production, rumours of which must have influenced Dexter?

Five British productions in three different media revealed varying degrees of political or directorial interpretation. The BBC TV/Time-Life *As You Like It* (150 minutes), seen on video in innumerable classrooms, remains a monument to the lost cause of canonical Shakespeare. Shot in colour on location in and around Glamis Castle in Scotland in 1978, it never quite reconciles the stylistic

2. John Goodwin, ed., *Peter Hall's Diaries* (London: Hamish Hamilton, 1983), 455.

clash between the real settings in formal gardens and woodlands and the theatrical-looking, rather picture-book medieval costumes.[3] There are good performances by Helen Mirren as Rosalind and Richard Pasco as Jaques. Adrian Noble's much more considered stage production for the RSC in 1985 encouraged the leading actresses (Juliet Stevenson as Rosalind; Fiona Shaw as a distinctly taller Celia) to take a feminist approach to their sisterly relationship.[4] The design by Bob Crowley—considerably simplified at the Barbican in 1986—presented an Arden which was not a specific location but an almost dream-like or Jungian space for self-discovery. When Fiona Shaw proceeded to play Rosalind herself in a production by Tim Albery at the Old Vic in 1989 she looked marvellously androgynous as Ganymede. The court scenes were played against heavy metal walls which later opened to reveal an immense, fairly realistic Arden which was yet some sort of imaginary world. At Stratford in the same year for John Caird's rather superficial production with the RSC the over-ingenious designer Ultz set the court scenes in a thirties corridor—a direct architectural reference to the foyer of the Shakespeare Theatre. The wooden floor was ripped up in a protracted scene by the exiled Duke's henchmen to reveal green turf underneath. Later Rosalind, played by the tiny Sophie Thompson, timidly opened the doors in the back wall to reveal a threatening Arden beyond. All these three stage productions seemed to envisage the Forest as an alternative through-the-looking-glass world. Very different was Christine Edzard's film (1992; 114 minutes) which was conceived as a State of the Nation commentary. There was a deliberate disjunction between the Elizabethan text and the up-to-the-minute social context. The Duke's court was an echoing municipal office peopled by executives, while Arden was a blighted urban wasteland near the Thames inhabited by drop-outs. On film Andrew Tierney was able to play both Orlando and his brother Charles; he carried an aerosol can with which he sprayed the love-poems on walls as graffiti. Audrey kept a mobile snack-bar. The film, however, never caught on and was quickly withdrawn from general release. Deconstruction pleased not the multitude.

No other production of As You Like It can have been seen by more people in more cities with more acclaim than Cheek by Jowl's between 1991 and 1995. This radical and innovative group, founded

3. The text, illustrated with production photographs in colour and black and white was published (London: BBC Publications, 1978). It is divided into 28 scenes which stress location and time of day, e.g. "SCENE 10. *Exterior. A Pine Wood in the Forest of Arden. Day*" or "SCENE II. *Exterior. A Grove of Yew Trees in the Forest of Arden. Day.*" This is close to the old editorial *"Another part of the Forest."*
4. Shaw and Stevenson wrote of their collaborative project in Russell Jackson and Robert Smallwood, eds., *Players of Shakespeare* 2 (Cambridge: Cambridge U Press, 1988), 55–71. Alan Rickman, the young and sardonic Jaques, also contributed, 73–80.

in 1981 by the director Declan Donnellan and his partner the designer Nick Ormerod, began by playing one-night stands and developed into an exciting venture, touring internationally under the auspices of the British Council. The company is committed to integrated casting and it recruits versatile players with physical, vocal and musical skills. Productions are visually resourceful but conceived to be stageable in playing-spaces of all shapes and sizes. Music, always by Paddy Cunneen, is performed live by members of the company. Their *As You Like It* which opened in July 1991 had the first professional all-male cast since 1967. Donnellan confessed later that during the early rehearsals four actresses were on the pay-roll, in case the performers could not avoid what he called the mysogynies of camp.[5] He was much more aware than Clifford Williams of the problematics of an all-male staging; and many in his audiences must have been familiar with current theories about sexuality and gender—Marjorie Garber's *Vested Interests: Cross-Dressing and Cultural Anxiety* was published late in 1991. The adaptable basic set was of white canvas. Fourteen actors trooped in wearing black pants, white collarless shirts, and braces. Jaques, played by a black actor Joe Dixon, spoke the first lines of "All the world's a stage." At "And all the men *and women* merely players" two men (soon to be Rosalind and Celia) stepped aside. Seconds later the play began. There was no attempt at illusion. Lighting was brilliant and bright. The actors in the one scene usually entered before those in the previous scene had left; sometimes they froze onstage until their next scene, with marvellous, almost cinematic effects of irony or parallelism. The playing was spirited with extraordinarily creative doubling—not just Duke Frederick and his brother played by one actor but Charles the Wrestler/Jaques, Adam/Phebe, Le Beau/Corin. Amiens was Hymen in the masque. Rosalind was dazzlingly played by Adrian Lester, a young black Londoner of six-foot two, clearly never a French princess but always a male actor. Rosalind's character by some alchemy became more feminine once Lester was doubly disguised as Ganymede, with a straw hat pulled over a headscarf. Tom Hollander, recently down from Cambridge, played Celia in his own long curly hair. Green streamers descended to suggest the Forest, largely created by lighting. The whole production built up to a final scene of dizzying ambiguities, and the conclusion was extraordinarily joyous and celebratory. Jaques was overtly gay, but rescued from solitariness with a kiss from Amiens. Cheek by Jowl printed on the programme a list of the places this production played at in 1991/92, which reads like a litany: Adelaide, Belfast, Brasilia, Breda, Bury St. Edmunds, Buxton, Cambridge, Coventry, Deny, Dublin, Farnham,

5. Interview with Dominic Cavendish, *The Independent* 4 January 1995, 21.

Hammersmith, Luxembourg, Madrid, New York, Recife, Rio de Janeiro, Rotterdam, São Paulo, Stratford-upon-Avon, Tokyo, Wellington, Winchester, Worthing and York.

In September 1994 Cheek by Jowl joyously recreated this production. Adrian Lester was irreplaceable; David Hobbs once more played both Dukes; and Peter Needham again came very close to ad-libbing as Touchstone. Some of the newcomers were challenged by different doubling: Paul Kissaum was Charles/Corin; Rhasan Stone was Amiens/William; and Richard Cant, originally a double-jointed, skinny Audrey added an aged, doddery automaton of an Adam. The new version was as remarkable as the old and toured for five months: Barcelona, Brooklyn, Bucharest, Craiova, Düsseldorf, Jerusalem, Manchester, Moscow, Norwich, Paris, Pilsen, Princeton, St. Petersburg, Sofia and Tel Aviv. Finally the company played for three weeks early in 1995 to full houses at the Albery in London. The most magical moment came when, during the final music-making and dancing, the house lights came up and Adrian Lester stepped forward, removing his head-dress, to speak the epilogue. The Albery was formerly called the New Theatre. Possibly a few elderly playgoers could recall Edith Evans speaking those very words there almost sixty years ago from the same stage-position. All the world, after all, *is* a stage.

ROBERT SMALLWOOD

[Royal Shakespeare Company Stagings of the Final Scene][†]

> Meantime forget this new-fall'n dignity,
> And fall into our rustic revelry.
> Play music, and you brides and bridegrooms all,
> With measure heap'd in joy, to th' measures fall.
> (5.4.175–8)

With the exception of Duke Frederick, who is elsewhere in the forest taking religious instruction—unless he is present in the person of his alter ego Duke Senior—virtually the whole cast of *As You Like It* will be on stage for its final scene. Frederick's anonymous courtiers will almost certainly be there in their normally doubled roles as Duke Senior's anonymous forest lords; those of Frederick's followers whose names we know, Le Beau and Charles the wrestler, may have managed to get home early, but even they have occasion-

---

† Robert Smallwood, *Shakespeare at Stratford: As You Like It* (London: Arden Shakespeare, 2003), pp. 189–214.

ally been there among the defectors from the corrupt régime who 'flock' to the rightful ruler (1.1.117). William is often brought on to take part in the pageant, and when a director is determined to outdo the dramatist in multiplication of couples 'coming to the ark' (5.4.36) has even been given a partner in the dance to replace his recently lost love, Audrey. It is impossible to do the scene with fewer than a dozen actors and all the Stratford productions considered in this book have used more, some many more. Even so large a stage as that of the Royal Shakespeare Theatre—large in terms of depth, at least, though narrowed by its inexorable proscenium arch— will seem crowded unless such numbers are carefully choreographed. On occasions, indeed, they have been choreographed with the express intention of achieving a sense of crowdedness, of an exuberant community bursting with life and energy. The scene includes a dance involving at least four couples, but quite possibly everyone on stage; the notable entrance of a new character, called Jaques, completing the trio of de Boys brothers, and the notable exit of an old character, also called Jaques, threatening the fun; it includes a protracted story from Touchstone about the seven stages of the lie, told twice to cover a big costume change for Rosalind and Celia; and, most significantly, not to say notoriously and ominously, it includes the arrival of Hymen, the god who 'peoples every town' (5.4.142). It is a scene that offers a major challenge to directors.

In an interview with me for the programme of his 1996 Stratford production, Steven Pimlott had this to say about the arrival of Hymen:

> The main issue, obviously, is whether this is a god, or a bit of dressing up. The Folio's 'Enter Hymen' is unambiguous, though some later editors change this to such things as 'Enter a masquer dressed as Hymen' (which is a very different matter) and there is a stage tradition for a recognisable Corin (or even Adam) to present the part. I think one has to take the Folio at its word and see this as a theophany: the god comes to earth, as in several of Shakespeare's late plays. Hymen is the final manifestation of Arden's magic.

Pimlott's response to that manifestation of magic will be considered later. His presentation here of the issue in principle is admirably clear and challenging. His programme duly lists the name of Hymen and gives the name of the player of the role. Of the twelve other post-war Stratford programmes for *As You Like It* five do the same and seven omit any mention of the character. (Curiously, Agnes Latham's Arden edition of the play, from which the quotations in this book are drawn, also omits Hymen from its list of *Dramatis Personae*, though he is given an entrance, in unamended

Folio form, at 5.4.106.) There is, as Pimlott says, a stage tradition for Corin to 'present' the part of Hymen. This is not, one needs to make clear, a matter of role-doubling, of the actor who appeared earlier in the evening as Corin now giving us his Hymen performance, but of a recognizable, if dressed up, Corin speaking Hymen's part in whatever version of a rural accent we heard from him earlier—sometimes with a strong suggestion that, like Viola, he 'took great pains to study it'.

Rather surprisingly, the 'Corin solution' has been adopted in only three of the post-war Stratford productions of *As You Like It*, those of 1961, 1980 and 1992, though it was also used in the 1968 revival of the 1967 production. In 2000 Gregory Doran played a minor variation on it by having Adam speak Hymen's lines, a resuscitation of Orlando's old servant to late prominence that (surely not altogether coincidentally) was a conspicuous reversal of the decision of his fellow RSC associate director Steven Pimlott in the preceding Stratford production to kill Adam off before the interval. In one production, that of 1952, Hymen was simply cut. In the remaining eight (those of 1946, 1957, 1967, 1973, 1977, 1985, 1989 and 1996) there was some sort of an appearance for Hymen, unexplained at least initially, though this has more often been tongue-in-cheek than a real attempt to present a theophany. How have these different choices worked, in the context of the final scene as a whole, in this sequence of thirteen productions of *As You Like It*?

The reviewers were silent about the final scene in Herbert Prentice's production in 1946, but the promptbook reveals how the episode was handled. It has the name 'Hymen' deleted from the entry at 5.4.106. 'Corin' was substituted but there was clearly a change of mind and it was erased and, at the scene's initial entry, the name Amiens was replaced by 'First Lord'. The final idea emerges after the singing of 'Wedding is great Juno's crown' (140–5): 'Hymen rushes up ramp [at the rear of the stage]; revealed as Amiens; gen[eral] laugh'. Dudley Jones's Amiens, then, the singer in the company, played Hymen, presumably at Rosalind's request; the promptbook calls for a lute accompaniment for his first speech, which was thus doubtless sung. This is the only production so to 'cast' Hymen (for whom there is no listing in the programme) and the only one to use the rather engaging idea of postponing the revelation of his identity until after his magical work has been done.

In 1952, as already mentioned, Glen Byam Shaw simply cut Hymen altogether. Rosalind had also been cut from earlier in the scene (5.4.5–25), so that her first line became 'To you I give myself, for I am yours' (115). Both of Hymen's speeches, and the wedding hymn, are marked in the promptbook for omission. Angus McBean's photograph (Figure 1—posed, of course, but no doubt reproducing

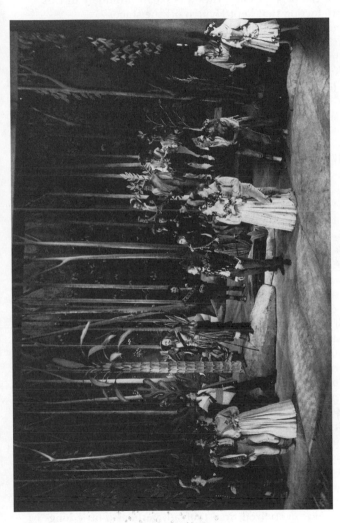

Figure 1 The final scene in Glen Byam Shaw's first Stratford production: Jaques (Michael Hordern) pauses, about to leave, on the mound beside the palm tree; the newly arrived Jaques replacement, Jaques de Boys (Jerome Willis), is below him to his right and Duke Senior (Jack Gwillim) below him to his left, in front of the 'pool'. Corin (Mervyn Blake, with musical assistants) is to the rear right (in 'Home Guard' headgear), looking as if he has just been playing Hymen, though that role had in fact been cut. The four couples (from left to right Celia and Oliver, Rosalind and Orlando, Audrey and Touchstone, and Phebe and Silvius) stand poised for the final dance. (5.4, 1952). Angus McBean © Royal Shakespeare Company.

the stage picture) shows the four couples paired ready for the final dancing and Mervyn Blake's Corin (with his allegedly Home Guard hat) standing at the rear with attendant musicians looking for all the world as though he has just enacted the god of marriage. But if we may trust the promptbook, this was (again uniquely in this sequence) a production that kept Hymen off the stage.

The only comment on this final scene in the reviews provides that very considerable rarity, a notice for the actor of the awkward little role of Jaques de Boys, who has to wait three hours to utter just one speech, a speech packed with highly surprising, yet vital, information. Jerome Willis, we learn, fulfilled the requirements of the role 'with any amount of aplomb' (*Sketch*).* The tribute is apposite, for if we are not wholly convinced that the young man believes absolutely in every syllable of his remarkable story, it is hard to conceive how anyone else in the theatre (on the stage or in the auditorium) will believe it either.

When Byam Shaw returned to the play in 1957 he had changed his mind about Hymen. The programme includes the role and assigns it to Gordon Wright, an actor whose name is not listed against any other part and who was thus presumably making his first appearance of the evening. He entered 'in a farm wain' (*Liv. Post*), with Corin, William and the pages as accompanying musicians (see Figure 2). The critic for the *Birmingham Mail* hated the fact that Hymen 'spoke from a decorated cart', and the photograph certainly seems to capture a certain incongruity in the appearance of Hymen, crowned and robed like a classical god, and the rural humbleness of his mode of transport. The incongruity seems to have been deliberate: to Muriel St Clare Byrne, Hymen was 'patently one of Rosalind's rural neighbours', who had been recruited for a simple bit of rustic mummery and drawn in on a little bright blue cart'. Rosalind, Celia and Touchstone, she thought, had 'knocked those verses off overnight' (*SQ*, 482), and although J.C. Trewin enjoyed the 'beautiful serenity' of the music for the wedding hymn (*Birm. Post*), it is clear (as Byrne remarked) that the event was presented more in the manner of the pageant of the worthies at the end of *Love's Labour's Lost* than as any attempt at theophanic masque.

The chorus of critical delight for Stratford's 1961 *As You Like It* continued, for the most part, right through to include the final scene, though there were isolated voices of doubt about the finale: the *Stage* referred to 'a stylized final tableau, perhaps a little long-drawn-out' and the *Stratford-upon-Avon Herald* thought it 'a shaky moment' when Corin came in as Hymen 'capped in a sort of war bonnet' while 'the forest lords with torches process to a chant not

---

*All reviews are listed by year in Reviews Cited, pp. 461–62 [*Editor*].

Figure 2 The final dance in Glen Byam Shaw's second Stratford production: Jaques has already left, but Hymen (Gordon Wright), in his little blue cart, with musical support from the pages (left), William (Toby Robertson, centre) and Corin (Donald Eccles, right), is still there. Duke Senior (Antony Brown, understudying Cyril Luckham) stands rear centre behind Peggy Ashcroft's Rosalind, with Richard Johnson's Orlando to her left. The other three couples are disposed in two groups of three, Silvius, Touchstone and Audrey to the left and Oliver, Phebe and Celia to the right. The abstract delicacy of Motley's set contrasts with their more naturalistic designs for the preceding production. (5.4, 1957). Angus McBean © Royal Shakespeare Company.

far removed from some ritual hymn of the Blackfeet tribe.' For most reviewers, however, Michael Elliott's response to the challenge of this final scene was a triumph, and something of its theatrical appeal is still discernible in the version made for television. It was presented as an evening scene. The promptbook has an elaborate plan (irreverently labelled 'Entry of the Gladiators') for a procession of eleven chanting forest lords. They carried flaming torches wreathed with roses and wound slowly in from the shadows, preceding two pages in white, then Corin, robed and crowned as Hymen. On the television film he speaks Hymen's lines carefully, with huge earnestness.

Then came Rosalind and Celia. Bernard Levin's report of Vanessa Redgrave's reappearance is perhaps the most rapturous account of any moment in any production of *As You Like It* in the many hundreds of reviews that research for this book has obliged me to read:

> like the arm which held Excalibur, clothed in white samite, mystic wonderful and her sunny locks hang on her temples like the golden fleece . . . If the word enchantment has any meaning it is here.
>
> (*D. Express*)

Many reviewers comment on the powerful effect of this moment (though none quite so ecstatically as this). Two others must speak for all: 'she is the embodiment of feminine radiance, fascination, and tenderness' (*Morn. Adv.*) and the spotlight in which she stands 'is superfluous: she could illuminate a universe' (*Bristol E. Post*, reviewing the Aldwych transfer). Whether Figure 3, which captures the moment, will convince the reader that these eulogies were justified is, as always, a question of taste.

After the princesses' entrance the four couples, 'seeming to awake slowly, as if in a dream' (*Birm. Post*), walked between two rows of torchbearers and were received by Hymen standing at the top of the aisle they formed like a priest at the altar. Jaques de Boys brought, along with his news of Frederick's conversion, the ducal coronet hidden beneath his cloak and presented it to Duke Senior on the line 'His crown bequeathing to his banish'd brother' (5.4.162). The Duke crowned himself and all knelt to him. The withdrawal of Max Adrian's remarkable Jaques—or so it is on the television film, anyway—was firm, sad, immovable: 'To see no pastime, I' (194) is said without the accusatory sneer that some performers of the role find in it, but is clear, absolute, utterly incontrovertible. His departure reminded Robert Speaight of 'Marcel Proust retiring to a monastery' (*SQ*, 434). The final dance, to music in the Elizabethan style that had been used throughout the production, was 'one of the loveliest

Figure 3 The entry of Rosalind (Vanessa Redgrave, left) and Celia (Rosalind Knight) to a stage framed by torch-bearing forest lords Oliver (David Buck) and Orlando (Ian Bannen) are in the left foreground, with Russell Hunter's Corin, playing Hymen, in front of them; in the right foreground are Jill'Dixon's Phebe, Redmond Phillips's Duke Senior, Peter McEnery's Silvius and Patsy Byrne's Audrey. The moment received an extraordinarily enthusiastic critical response. (5.4, 1961). Angus McBean © Royal Shakespeare Company.

dances ever planned for a Shakespeare play' (*Morn. Adv.*), sedate, a little wistful (the solitariness of the Duke is conspicuous in the film) and very much at the 'courtly' end of the spectrum of directorial choices in this series of productions, though during it the 'elephantine flirtatiousness' of Patsy Byrne's Audrey still delighted one reviewer (*Middles. E. Gaz.*).

At the end of David Jones's 1967 production John Higgins felt 'as the counterfeit faces are removed and forgiveness dominates, a rare feeling of humanity running through the theatre, as it does through a memorable last act of *Figaro*' (*FT*, reviewing the Aldwych transfer). The part of Hymen was listed in the programme, with the name of John Kaye against it; he is (presumably deliberately) not mentioned among the actors playing court or forest lords, though he had, in fact, been used to 'swell a scene or two' earlier. He came in slowly, escorting Rosalind and Celia, without special effects or machinery. He wore buskins for additional height, a full-length panelled gown, a tall crown of twigs with a half mask attached, and in his right hand he carried a flaming torch. Interestingly, although the costume and torch returned in the revival of the production the following year, it was now the Corin of Richard Moore who filled the role, theophany thus giving place to amateur theatricals. The promptbook reveals that the 'wedlock hymn' (and the line referring to it—5.4.136, 140–5) was cut, that each couple in turn knelt to Hymen, and that he remained on stage, presiding over events, until after the final dance.

In the world of denim jeans and rock music of Buzz Goodbody's 1973 *As You Like It* the final scene was obviously much more of a candidate for party treatment than for classical theophany. Michael Ensign, an actor whose name does not appear elsewhere in the programme, was nevertheless listed there against the role of Hymen and made a solemn entrance in a long, whitish, caped gown, looking vaguely monk-like and accompanied by a little procession of attendant forest lords carrying lanterns. There was no attempt to 'explain' this manifestation, which audiences presumably took as some sort of spiritual rite in the little hippy commune that Arden seemed to have become in this production. Jean Fuzier and Jean-Marie Maguin, lamenting the fact that the rest of the production seemed 'biased against poetry,' remarked on the striking effect of Hymen's speaking of his verse, finding it 'all too brief and . . . surprisingly out of place' (*Cahiers Elis.*). The promptbook makes it clear that at the end of his second speech, the first three lines of which were cut (5.4.124–64), Hymen moved to his 'marriage position' and that 'masquers' danced down stage and rose petals fell during the wedding hymn. This dance, complete with 'just married' signs and garlands for the participants, quickly became 'a rave-up to rock music' (*S. Telegraph*), a 'jazz festival finale . . . with confetti fluttering from the roof' (*Listener*) while 'grinning supers threw confetti into the house' (*Observer*). After all this, remarked Peter Thomson, 'the unfortunate actor of Jaques de Boys must have felt even more like an unrequested encore' (SS, 149). Amid all the boisterousness two moments stood out: 'Rosalind's "I am yours" [116] to David Suchet's tender Orlando brought an uneven evening to a noble end' (*D. Telegraph*); and the exit of Richard Pasco's Jaques created a moment of chill in the proceedings, 'as if a cloud were passing over the sunlit world of Arden' (*Guardian*). Peter Thomson was struck by the same moment: 'having watched the modern frenzy of the wedding', he writes, Jaques 'spat out "so to your pleasures" [191] disconcertingly. It was only with some difficulty that Duke Senior recovered sufficient poise to restart the dance' (SS, 150). These are the first reviews to mention Jaques's exit in any postwar Stratford production of *As You Like It*. They come just a year after the publication of Anne Barton's seminal essay on the ending of the play, with its description of the exit of Jaques casting a 'tremor' over the proceedings, 'a tremor which guarantees the vitality of the moment itself but which also prefigures its imminent destruction'.[1]

The constant inclination of Trevor Nunn's 1977 *As You Like It* to turn into a baroque opera allowed him to treat the arrival of Hymen as an event in a seventeenth-century court masque—that form of entertainment so elusive for twentieth-century audiences to which the goddesses in *The Tempest* partly belong and to which this scene of *As You Like It* perhaps alludes. Hymen had, in fact, already appeared, in an added preludial trio with Art and Nature; his reappearance at the end was treated with all the arch theatrical self-consciousness with which the production abounded, and the episode was clearly more of a piece with the rest of the evening than is often the case. Just after Graham Crowden's very identifiable Le Beau (the last of this production's defectors from Frederick's court) had been welcomed to the forest community, the little cart, on which Corin and company had arrived, was removed. It had provided an affectionately mocking allusion to the play's recent Stratford performance history and a splendidly misleading prelude to the arrival of Hymen—for on this occasion he was anything but cart-borne. There was a clap of thunder and down he came from the flies on a puffy white cloud. It opened to present him seated under a rainbow, singing a pastiche Purcellian aria adapted (with repeats but no real additions) from the text, while the princesses made their

1. Anne Barton, "*As You Like It* and *Twelfth Night*: Shakespeare's Sense of an Ending." In *Shakesperian Comedy*, ed. Malcolm Bradbury and David Palmer. Stratford-upon-Avon Studies 14. London, 1972, 160–80, p. 691.

Figure 4 In imitation of seventeenth-century masque form, Hymen (Michael Follis) descends in a rainbow on a cloud singing his lines in Purcellian operatic style. His attendants, and the lovers, assemble in deference below. (5.4, 1977). Joe Cocks Studio Collection © Shakespeare Birthplace Trust.

entrances below on terra firma (see Figure 4). 'Rosalind has, presumably, contrived this with real, not pretended, magic', wrote B.A. Young (*FT*), but Roger Warren didn't enjoy its tongue-in-cheek tone and thought that Hymen's 'undifferentiated outpouring . . . with an enormous sheepdoggy wobble' was 'rightly derided by the audience' (*SS*, 146). The exit of Jaques again drew comment: 'his final decision to leave the woodland merrymaking shocks . . . after his having taken a full part in the preceding song-and-dance sequences' (*Morn. Star*). From a singing, cloud-borne Hymen, fully credited in the programme, the pendulum swung back again in 1980. The god of marriage lost his billing to a Corin back in a cart. John Bowe, Orlando in the production, describes the moment:

> And so with the stage adorned with colourful blossom and foliage a cart appears, pulled by the forest lords, chariot-style. On board are Corin, commandeered to play Hymen in this pageant (with terrible verse supplied), Celia, and Rosalind, dressed as a girl again. All is resolved and all presumably live happily ever after . . . To celebrate the cast dance and sing. It's a sort of fertility dance, rather like a Morris dance on the local village green; the audience clap to the beat.[2]

Bowe's judgement of the quality of Hymen's verse was no doubt affected by its treatment: Michael Billington describes Corin's 'lighting up a particularly pungent briar pipe' for the occasion (*Guardian*), though Rosalind still kissed him for his delivery of what one felt sure were her lines. Hands's version of this scene must rank as one of its more boisterously energetic Stratford treatments, 'a pagan love-in and fertility feast involving the cast as a whole' (*New States.*), 'a pagan romp of corn dollies and ancient country gods' (*S. Mercury*). Inevitably its noise and energy and attempted inclusiveness left some unincluded: 'a bewilderingly kitsch version of standard Stratford endings' sniffed Jeremy Treglown (*TLS*); Charles Spencer, on the other hand, found it 'near impossible to keep a smile off the face or a sentimental tear out of the eye' (*New Stand.*, reviewing the Aldwych transfer).

Into this turmoil of exuberance Michael Siberry's fresh-faced and eager Jaques de Boys came rushing with his good news; a dozen years later the same actor would walk out from the same scene in the role of *the* Jaques. The exit of Derek Godfrey's Jaques in 1980 made only a minor dent in the proceedings; Touchstone and Audrey defied his gloomy prognostications about their future with an energetic cuddle.

If the 'tremor' (to repeat Anne Barton's term) of Jaques's exit in 1980 registered little on the Richter scale of critical attention, that

---

2. John Bowe, "Orlando in *As You Like It*." In *Players of Shakespeare 1*, ed. Philip Brockbank. Cambridge, 1989, 67–76, pp. 74–75.

of Alan Rickman's Jaques in 1985 dominated reviewers' comments on
the final scene. This was partly due to the physical prominence he
was given in the preceding moments, silhouetted against the evening sky between the upstage mirror and grandfather clock for the
entrance of Jaques de Boys, who fainted from exhaustion after deliv-
ering his extraordinary news. Revived and reunited with his brothers,
Jaques de Boys was joined by Rickman's Jaques, with his questions
about the newcomer's strange story. Both wore black, the only persons on stage so clothed: two Jaqueses, two Jacks, one to join the
dance, one to walk out of it. Jaques (senior) then stood downstage to
deliver his blessings on each of the couples, rejected contemptuously
the Duke's plea to him to stay, and on 'To see no pastime, I' (5.4.194)
ran upstage, forcing a passage through the assembly, and stepped
through the mirror frame. Its glass came up after him, clonking
gently into the upper frame as he sneered the words 'abandon'd cave'
(195); just as the Duke gathered himself together and was about to
reinstate the dancing, the grandfather clock resumed its ticking.
Jaques 'the fastidious depressive departs through the pier glass, out
of one exile into the next' wrote Michael Ratcliffe in the *Observer*;
Nicholas Shrimpton saw it slightly more positively: 'Jaques steps
through the mirror, abandoning cynicism for curiosity about the
religious life' (*TES*). It was a striking theatrical moment, precisely
balancing the moment when the same mirror had opened to let
Duke Frederick through to become Duke Senior.

The 1985 production was also notable for providing the only invisible Hymen in a sequence of thirteen productions. Apart from Glen
Byam Shaw's cutting it altogether in 1952, every other post-war
Stratford director has offered an actor in the role; Adrian Noble tried
a lighting effect. From a large, flickering, reddish disc over a temporarily darkened stage Hymen's words seemed to emanate, though
an echo effect made their origin difficult to locate. The voice was
unmistakably that of Griffith Jones, who had earlier appeared as Sir
Oliver Martext. In a production in which the doubling of the Dukes
was crucially significant, it was impossible not to connect the successful marriage celebrant of the final scene with his failed priestly
counterpart earlier. Rosalind and Celia came in beneath the moon
and the hymn to Hymen was sung by all four couples standing in a
line holding candles, the great parachute silk that had once been the
snows of Arden now suspended above the stage like an enormous
bridal veil (see Figure 5). Eric Sams thought it worked 'quite well'
and added 'only in such a dream world could Hymen ever appear to
be a denouement' (*TLS*). Nicholas Shrimpton, more grudgingly, felt
that it was striving 'for a sense of magical reconciliation that it
doesn't quite achieve' (*TES*). The Rosalind and Celia of the production describe the moment for themselves (and the changes to it when
the production moved to London):

Figure 5   Beneath the billowing silk sheet that earlier covered Arden in snow and has now become a gigantic bridal veil over the stage, the lovers, holding candles, line up (from left to right Silvius, Phebe, Orlando, Rosalind, Celia, Oliver, Audrey, Touchstone) to sing 'Wedding is great Juno's crown'. Hymen had spoken as a disembodied voice from a flickering point in the great disc visible upstage in the right of the photograph, the only non-human presentation of the god in this series of productions. (5.4.140, 1985). Joe Cocks Studio Collection © Shakespeare Birthplace Trust.

In Stratford Hymen had been represented as a flickering silhouette on a lighted screen, placed upstage, obliging the actors to turn away from the audience to perceive him—this both threw the focus onto an unlikely manifestation which threatened the audience's capacity to believe in what was going on, and deprived them of the characters' responses to the deity and his dictates. In London Hymen became a mere beam of light whose source was *behind* the audience, so that the actors beheld him facing out front. In this way the audience was able to focus not on the god, but on the faces of those whose futures he is deciding.[3]

3. Fiona Shaw and Juliet Stevenson, "Celia and Rosalind in *As You Like It.*" In *Players of Shakespeare 2*, ed. Russell Jackson and Robert Smallwood. Cambridge, 1988, 55–72, p. 70.

The only *As You Like It* director at post-war Stratford to take the same basically theophanic approach to Hymen as his immediate predecessor was John Caird in 1989. His was a jovial giant of a Hymen, played by Andrew Tansey, the last of a trio of roles that had been preceded by Charles the wrestler and William. To the sound of Ilona Sekacz's 'measured, jangling anthem' (*FT*), he strode down the stage in a bright green suit, a child on his shoulders and two others in attendance. Rosalind and Celia followed as his speech forbidding confusion boomed out. Recalling that her Rosalind had no real idea what was going to happen as she made her appointment (at the end of 5.2) with Orlando, Silvius and Phebe, Sophie Thompson describes Rosalind's surprise at

> the arrival from the back of the stage of a figure out of William Blake, a strong man in a green costume with an angel perched on his back, leading two children by the hand. It happens because of faith, belief, magic. Rosalind didn't think when she went rushing off saying she will 'make these doubts all even' (V.iv.25) that she was going to get Hymen ready for his entrance . . . It was the end of human control, as though something else had taken over . . . I didn't really want to know where Hymen had come from, but I was very glad he had come.[4]

Was this figure, one wondered, some version of the 'Green Man' of the Forest and, if so, what was the significance of his making his exit down the central aisle of the stalls? The production had begun with the stalls providing the only way onto or off the stage, but a route had been smashed through to the woodland playing space. The presiding forest god's final exit back into the audience's world was clearly making another of the director's metatheatrical points. After many doubts and grumbles about the production, John Gross confessed himself finally won over: 'By the end of the evening, as the masque of Hymen slips perfectly into place, it has achieved a magic that you would have thought quite beyond it at the beginning' (*S. Telegraph*).

Still to come, though, was the highly symbolic exit of Hugh Ross's exquisitely elegant Jaques. His blessings on the lovers crisply delivered and the Duke's plea that he should remain suavely dismissed, he strode upstage to a door we had not noticed in the rear wall, opened it, paused a moment, silhouetted in a strong back light, and then strode through. The moment vividly recalled Rosalind's opening of the great door to break the clock and escape into Arden—and to give us our play. But Jaques's door closed sharply behind him: the next play this observer of the world's stage was

4. Sophie Thompson, "Rosalind (and Celia) in *As You Like It.*" In *Players of Shakespeare 3*, ed. Russell Jackson and Robert Smallwood. Cambridge, 1993, 77–86, pp. 84–85.

going to see, a most curious study of a converted duke, was to be a private show. Through the door he went and there was a pause as the stage seemed momentarily in darkness. Then up came the lights and an all-inclusive communal dance began, the state of undress—half the forest lords were in shorts and underpants—contrasting sharply with the buttoned-up formality of the evening's opening sequence on the dance-floor forestage.

Corin was back in the role of Hymen in 1992 with as simple an entrance as the god has had in this sequence of productions. Robed, and with a crown of leaves, he simply walked on over the little rustic bridge with Rosalind and Celia on either hand in white wedding dresses. The big effect was left to the music, an elaborate choral number for the wedding hymn that Garry O'Connor thought 'outpastiches Andrew Lloyd Webber' (*Plays & P.*) and Charles Spencer felt created 'a wonderful sense of reconciliation' (*D. Telegraph*)—how remarkably instructive it is to observe the gulf in responses that the same theatrical moment can produce. Jaques's exit was less dramatic than in some recent productions, that distinctive rasping note in Michael Siberry's voice taking on a flatter, sadder tone as he declared himself 'for other than for dancing measures' (5.4.192). His downstage exit (in the sharpest contrast to his predecessor's flamboyant upstage departure) took him out, however, through the stalls, as though his withdrawal from the festivity was into our world. After it we watched the wreaths and high spirits of the final dance just a little more from the outside than would otherwise have been the case.

Steven Pimlott's version of Hymen in 1996 was one of the more notable in the history of the play on the Stratford stage. For the first time the god of marriage was played by a woman, a middle-aged woman who came onto the stage from the stalls wearing a black Marks and Spencer's trouser suit of the sort to be seen at suburban cocktail parties (see Figure 6). In a production dressed in Elizabethan costume this led many playgoers and several reviewers to suppose that a member of the audience must have taken a wrong turning, or suffered some sort of blackout—until, in a homely northern accent, she began to speak Hymen's blessings on the lovers. The ideas behind the moment were expounded by Pimlott in a lecture he gave as part of that year's Shakespeare Birthday celebrations and I paraphrase them here: if gods come from beyond the play's world, then can that not be well suggested by bringing into a play set in the Elizabethan period a figure from a later century; if a theatre performance derives its imaginative power from the audience's willingness to commit to its fiction, then what is more appropriate than to bring in the play's figure of ultimate power from the audience; and if this is primarily a play about a young woman in

Figure 6   A female Hymen (Doreen Andrew on left), having arrived on stage from the stalls in a modern trouser suit, contrasts surprisingly (and for some it proved to be bewilderingly) with the Elizabethan costumes of Liam Cunningham's Orlando (left), Niamh Cusack's Rosalind and Robert Demeger's Duke Senior. (5.4, 1996). Malcolm Davies Collection © Shakespeare Birthplace Trust.

love, then does it not make sense to end it with the blessing of an older woman who may be supposed to have experienced love, marriage, motherhood and grandmotherhood? The persuasiveness of these ideas in the lecture room translated unfortunately (for most watchers of the production, anyway) into a moment of bathos in the theatre. The problem derived from one's fear that something had gone wrong, causing a momentary loss of belief in the theatrical event itself. When the production moved to the Barbican the episode was changed and Hymen's lines were spoken by a woman in Elizabethan costume who made an entrance from the stage, not from the auditorium.

Many reviewers grumbled about the presentation of Hymen— and several thought too that the attempted Elizabethan chorcography of the final dance was simply clumsy ('the worst choreography of the lovers' dance I have yet witnessed in this house' snapped the *Birmingham Post*). Michael Billington was a notable exception, however, and his response is an interesting example of a reviewer perceiving something of the spirit of a production where others saw only its surface. One of Pimlott's 'best touches' he thought, was to make Hymen 'a sensible middle-aged lady in a black trouser suit. It is typical of the intelligence of this production: if these multiple, often patched-up couplings are to survive, you feel it will only be through the beneficence of enlightened womanhood' (*Guardian*).

Also unique in the final scene of the 1996 production was a little gift from Touchstone to the departing Jaques. The blessings on the lovers were spoken with the self-confident authority this Jaques had evinced all evening, and in response to the meanness of his prognostications for his and Audrey's future Touchstone intoned a hollow, deathly 'ha . . . ha' and dropped a skull into Jaques's hands. In his interview for the programme Pimlott refers more than once to Jaques as a 'death's-head' and remarks disapprovingly of his having become 'a Hamlet figure in some recent versions of the play'. Jaques, he says, must be old—and the text offers evidence for that (5.1.3), though few directors have felt bound to observe it—and Touchstone young; if Jaques has any affinities with Hamlet, therefore 'it is a Hamlet who lived on into old age' (1996 programme). And so, before the dancing began and everyone took their partners, Touchstone, the play's Yorick, gave its ageing Hamlet a skull to keep him company as he stalked off in search of the converted Duke.

In the embroidered, colourful world of Stratford's 2000 *As You Like It* such a moment would have been inconceivable. Cut-out festoons of flowers had come down from the flies at the end of 'It was a lover and his lass' (5.3.37) and the stage for the final scene was awash with colour, not at all to the taste of Charles Spencer, who thought it 'a Disneyland technicolour nightmare' (*D. Telegraph*). Audreys over the years at Stratford have been caught in various thoughtlessly undignified moments when admonished by Touchstone to bear their bodies 'more seeming' (5.4.68)—adjusting sleeves or bra straps, showing slightly too much cleavage, sitting, or lolling, a little too nonchalantly, staring too interestedly at the young men. It seemed a measure of this production's over-anxiety and exaggeration that its Audrey was so astonished by the brave new world of dukes and lords that she stood gawping in blank amazement, gradually hoisting the hem of her skirt and revealing her undergarments—it seemed unconsciously rather than in any overt sexual invitation, though the promptbook refers to her 'flirting'; either way, it is a curious 'Stratford first' to have to record.

There were other Stratford firsts about the scene, though the flower-decorated, fluffy-cloud-painted cart that brought in Hymen was scarcely one of them. That Peter Copley's ancient Adam was speaking Hymen's lines was an innovation, however, in a half-century of productions, and his hesitant care in getting them right seemed to suggest the difficulty Rosalind must have had in teaching them to him. The wedding hymn, in the production's usual smoochy jazz style, seemed ill at ease, as so much of the music had, with the

faux-naïf of the setting. After it we saw Phebe weeping at the loss of
her love for Ganymede; and then Jaques de Boys arrived in the dark
court costume that we hadn't seen since the beginning of the evening. He was the first Jaques de Boys since 1961 to bring on the
ducal coronet, which he carried in a large box. Duke Senior held it
aloft on 'our returned fortune' (5.4.173), but the production then
scored another first for this history when he decided not to put it on
but handed it, rather nonchalantly, to one of his followers and determined to 'forget this new-fall'n dignity' (175). Thirteen productions
on, and seconds from the end of the play, and Shakespeare's text is
still yielding interesting innovatory choices to directors. It is the
pleasure of such moments of discovery that illuminates the 'harmless drudgery' of gathering information for a performance history
such as this.

There was nothing actually innovatory about the departure of
Declan Conlon's rather subdued Jaques, but it was unusual in its
mildness. He was quietly interested in his namesake's story, kindly
in his farewells to the lovers and genuinely affectionate in his leave-
taking with the Duke. The Duke's plea that he should 'stay, Jaques,
stay' (5.4.193) was positively forlorn in its urgency, but Jaques's
response, though profoundly gentle, was not to be gainsaid. And, as
so often, the 'tremor' was felt, and it took a few seconds for the
Duke to find the will to set the dances going. William was there,
and with a new partner (yet another rarity), and the lovers' dance,
brief and simple, ended with a kiss between each couple before
Alexandra Gilbreath stepped down to the forestage to address the
audience in her epilogue.

Epilogues are comparatively rare in Shakespeare's plays and
where they occur are usually spoken by some sort of framing chorus-
figure (as in *Henry V* and *Pericles*). Rosalind is the only female
character in a Shakespeare play to be given the responsibility of an
epilogue—as is immediately clear from the way she begins: 'It is
not the fashion to see the lady the epilogue; but it is no more
unhandsome than to see the lord the prologue' (5.4.198–200). A joke
was made of that in 1989 when the dancing stopped and Orlando
stepped forward as if about to address the audience—just as he had
done at the beginning, when Orlando's speech to Adam had been
treated very much as 'the lord the prologue'. But he could only manage a little inarticulate sound of embarrassment that brought Sophie
Thompson's Rosalind to his rescue; she kissed him in reassurance
before taking over the task.

For all that the epilogue to *As You Like It* makes clear that it was
very precisely created for the boy actor who had just played Rosalind, it has always been played in post-war Stratford productions,
and nearly always left uncut. Just twice, the promptbooks reveal,

there were changes to the words 'If I were a woman' (5.4.214–15): in 1973 they were deleted and in 1992 they were altered to 'As I am a woman'. Apart from that, and the removal of the reference to the lord as the prologue in 1946, the epilogue has always been given in full and unchanged.

Comment on its treatment by reviewers is sadly rare, the imminence of that first-night rush from the theatre to phone in copy for the morning edition perhaps taking minds off these closing moments. J.C. Trewin, though, clearly took a special interest in it and nearly always managed to pay its speaker a compliment. In 1957, for example, he wrote that he would 'long remember Peggy Ashcroft's delivery of the Epilogue before the house assured her of its affection and loyalty' (Birm. Post); and elsewhere he referred to her 'glowing charm' in the speech (Illus. Lon. News). The falling cadences of the epilogue's prose, ending in the gracious request to be bidden farewell, do have an extraordinary way of 'conjuring' (5.4.208) affection from the house. Ruth Lodge, whom several reviewers in 1946 had felt was not, on the first night, as at home in the role as they hoped she would later become, was described as giving, in her epilogue, 'a glimpse of what she can do when she comes out into the open' (Evesham J.), and Margaret Leighton, in 1952, made sure that we 'miss not a syllable of the Epilogue, so often a scamper' (Trewin again, in the Lady). Vanessa Redgrave, in 1961, 'sent shivers down the spine' (Guardian) and Eileen Atkins, after all the rock-band high jinks of the final dance in 1973, stilled the audience wonderfully for the epilogue when, 'with the house lights up, as they should be' (Observer), she was 'Rosalind's very self' (Trewin once more, Birm. Post). Kate Nelligan, in 1977, had seemed to Trewin a little too 'calculated' in her spontaneity at times during the evening but in her epilogue she was 'in complete repose . . . much her happiest passage' (Birm. Post), and Frank Marcus felt that Nelligan's epilogue 'touches our hearts' (S. Telegraph). Susan Fleetwood, stepping out from the high-voltage energies of the dance in 1980, seemed to her Orlando to be speaking to 'a sea of smiling, happy faces. I think they've had a good time' (Bowe, 75).

Reviewers' silence on the epilogue in 1985 and 1989 is replaced by actors' comment. Both Juliet Stevenson and Sophie Thompson clearly worried about how to deal with this moment and in Stevenson's case it was changed between Stratford and London:

> In Stratford the dance had lulled the play to its close and the dancers remained on stage for Rosalind's closing address to the audience. We came to realize that this created problems for the audience, who did not know whether the characters were staying in Arden or not, or who, exactly, was talking to them in the epilogue. In London the dance culminated in a

moment of still suspension, as the characters took in the Arden they were about to leave . . . They then exited, through the moon-shaped hole in the backdrop, which both told the story more clearly and laid emphasis on the fantastical nature of the whole event. With Rosalind alone on stage, the epilogue then clearly became a separate event.   (Shaw and Stevenson, 71)

More simply, Sophie Thompson describes her Orlando's failure to speak the epilogue and her needing to take over:

I liked that because it made you remember him at the beginning of the play, unable to put his feelings about Rosalind into words. I liked the fact that here you saw a bit of their being 'together'—Mrs helping Mr in a rather 'social' situation.

(Thompson, 85)

She then goes on to describe how she always began the speech as if she were making it up as she went along, but that when she got to 'My way is to conjure you' (5.4.208) that idea disappeared and 'it somehow changed and reminded us of the magic we'd seen'. She goes on to use the Epilogue as a way of looking into the future, offering a hopeful vision of the marriage of Rosalind and Orlando: 'They understand now that love isn't all romance, and that you have to work at it every single day' (Thompson, 85).

Whether one discerns such prognostications in the Epilogue or not, Thompson's response to the energy and buoyancy of its prose, to what she calls its 'magic', is something that many Rosalinds have evinced. Samantha Bond conveyed it vividly in 1992 as she was caught, almost unawares, in a downstage spotlight while the rest of the cast sat watching her from the forest slope of the stage. Niamh Cusack, too, in 1996, responded joyously to the Epilogue's challenge as she engaged the audience, all 'energy and shrewdness' (*Independent*), with an openness and sparkle that even survive on the archival video. And in the last of this sequence of productions, Alexandra Gilbreath's Rosalind, stepping forward from her embroidered Arden, found in the Epilogue the emotional directness, the wit and vivacity, and the grace, that are the play's gift to the player of Rosalind. As the 2000 season was drawing towards its close, there was much discussion in Stratford of the possibility of a new theatre to replace the 1932 building, and one found oneself wondering, as one watched this thirteenth in the extraordinarily various, and distinguished, sequence with which this book has been concerned, how many more Rosalinds there might be, before a new building came along, who would stand at the front of that stage and secure, with that Epilogue, 'the affection and loyalty of the house'.

Reviews Cited
[by production year]

Unless otherwise stated in the text, all references are to reviews of the original production, not the transfer or revival.

1946

Evesham Journal, 8 June 1946

1952

Lady, 15 May 1952, J.C. Trewin
Sketch, undated cutting in RSC theatre records collection

1957

Birmingham Mail, 3 April 1957
Birmingham Post, 3 April 1957, J.C. T[rewin]
Illustrated London News, 13 April 1957, J.C. Trewin
Shakespeare Quarterly, 8 (1957), 480–2, Muriel St Clare Byrne

1961

Birmingham Post, 5 July 1961, J.C. Trewin
Daily Express, 5 July 1961, Bernard Levin
Guardian, 6 July 1961, Gerard Fay
Middlesbrough Evening Gazette, 5 July 1961
Morning Advertiser, 10 July 1961, Geoffrey Tarran
Shakespeare Quarterly, 12 (1961), 432–4, Robert Speaight
Stratford-upon-Avon Herald, 7 July 1961, Edmund Gardner

ALDWYCH TRANSFER (1962)

Bristol Evening Post, 11 January 1962

ALDWYCH TRANSFER (1967)

Financial Times, 20 July 1967, John Higgins

1973

Birmingham Post, 14 June 1973, J.C. Trewin
Cahiers Elisabéthains, 4 (1973), 51–2, Jean Fuzier and Jean-Marie
   Maguin
Daily Telegraph, 13 June 1973, John Barber
Guardian, 13 June 1973, Michael Billington
Listener, 21 June 1973, John Elsom

Observer, 17 June 1973, Robert Cushman
Shakespeare Survey 27 (1974), 149–50, Peter Thomson
Sunday Telegraph, 17 June 1973, Frank Marcus

1977

Financial Times, 8 September 1977, B.A. Young
Morning Star, 15 September 1977, Gordon Parsons
Shakespeare Survey 31 (1978), 146–7, Roger Warren

1980

Guardian, 5 April 1980, Michael Billington
New Statesman, 11 April 1980, Benedict Nightingale
Sunday Mercury, 6 April 1980
Times Literary Supplement, 18 April 1980, Jeremy Treglown

ALDWYCH TRANSFER (1981)

New Standard, 23 July 1981, Charles Spencer

1985

Observer, 28 April 1985, Michael Ratcliffe
Times Educational Supplement, 10 May 1985, Nicholas Shrimpton
Times Literary Supplement, 3 May 1985, Eric Sams

1989

Financial Times, 15 September 1989, Michael Coveney
Sunday Telegraph, 17 September 1989, John Gross

1992

Daily Telegraph, 24 April 1992, Charles Spencer
Plays and Players, June 1992, Garry O'Connor

1996

Birmingham Post, 27 April 1996, Richard Edmonds
Guardian, 30 April 1996, Michael Billington
Independent, 27 April 1996, Robert Hanks

2000

Daily Telegraph, 27 March 2000, Charles Spencer

Selected Bibliography

• indicates a work included or excerpted in this Norton Critical Edition.

ECOCRITICISM AND RELATED BACKGROUND MATERIALS

• Bastard, Thomas. *Chrestoloros: Seven Books of Epigrams.* London, 1598.
• Benjamin, Walter. *One-Way Street and Other Writings.* Trans. Edmund Jephcott and Kingsley Shorter. London: NLB, 1979.
  Bray, Alan. *Homosexuality in Renaissance England.* 1982; rpt. New York: Columbia University Press, 1995.
  Buell, Lawrence. *The Future of Environmental Criticism: Environmental Crisis and Literary Imagination.* Oxford, Blackwell, 2005.
• Burt, Richard, and John Michael Archer, eds. *Enclosure Acts: Sexuality, Property, and Culture in Early Modern England.* Ithaca: Cornell University Press, 1994. Contains Carroll essay.
  Derrida, Jacques. *The Animal That Therefore I Am.* Ed. Marie-Louise Mallet and trans. David Wills. New York: Fordham University Press, 2008.
  Fleming, Juliet. *Graffiti and the Writing Arts of Early Modern England.* Philadelphia: University of Pennsylvania Press, 2001.
• Fudge, Erica. *Animal.* London: Reaktion Books, 2002.
  Fudge, Erica, Ruth Gilbert, and Susan Wiseman, eds. *At the Borders of the Human: Beasts, Bodies, and Natural Philosophy in the Early Modern Period.* London: Palgrave Macmillan, 1999.
• Gascoigne, George. *The Noble Art of Venery or Hunting.* London, 1611
• Glotfelty, Cheryll, and Harold Fromm, eds. *The Ecocriticism Reader: Landmarks in Literary Ecology.* Athens: University of Georgia Press, 1996. Contains Meeker essay.
  Loomba, Ania, and Jonathan Burton, eds. *Race in Early Modern England: A Documentary Companion.* New York: Palgrave Macmillan, 2007.
  Mazel, David, ed. *A Century of Early Ecocriticism.* Athens and London: University of Georgia Press, 2001.
• Montaigne, Michel de. *Essays.* Trans. John Florio. London, 1613.
  Moore, John. *A Target For Tillage.* London, 1613. Tract on enclosure, pro and con.
• More, Sir Thomas. *Utopia.* 1516; trans. Gilbert Burnet. London, 1684.
  Oliver, Kelly. *Animal Lessons: How They Teach Us to Be Human.* New York: Columbia University Press, 2009.
• Pace, Richard. *De fructu qui ex doctrina percipitur.* Ed. and trans. Frank Manley and Richard S. Sylvester. New York: Renaissance Society of America, 1967.
• Prynne, William. *Histriomastix.* London, 1633.
  Skipp, Victor. *Crisis and Development: An Ecological Case Study of the Forest of Arden 1570–1674.* London: Cambridge University Press, 1978.
• Thomas, Keith. *Man and the Natural World: Changing Attitudes in England, 1500–1800.* London: Penguin, 1983.
  Underdown, David. *Revel, Riot, and Rebellion: Popular Politics and Culture in England 1603–1660.* Oxford: Clarendon Press, 1985.

GENERAL INTRODUCTIONS TO SHAKESPEARE

Bullough, Geoffrey, ed. *Narrative and Dramatic Sources of Shakespeare, Volume Two: The Comedies, 1597–1603.* London: Routledge and Kegan Paul; New York: Columbia University Press, 1968.

De Grazia, Margreta, and Stanley Wells, eds. *The Cambridge Companion to Shakespeare.* Cambridge: Cambridge University Press, 2001.

Dobson, Michael, and Stanley Wells, eds. *The Oxford Companion to Shakespeare.* Oxford: Oxford University Press, 2001.

Greenblatt, Stephen. *Will in the World: How Shakespeare Became Shakespeare.* New York: Norton, 2004. Biography.

Gurr, Andrew, and Mariko Ichikawa. *Staging in Shakespeare's Theatres.* Oxford: Oxford University Press, 2000.

Hodgdon, Barbara, and William B. Worthen, eds. *A Companion to Shakespeare and Performance.* Oxford: Blackwell, 2005, pp. 564–87.

McDonald, Ross, ed. *The Bedford Companion to Shakespeare: An Introduction with Documents.* Boston: Bedford/St. Martin's, 2002.

• Shapiro, James. *A Year in the Life of William Shakespeare: 1599.* New York and London: HarperCollins, 2005.

Wells, Stanley, ed., *Shakespeare: A Bibliographical Guide.* 1973; 2nd ed. New York: Oxford University Press, 1990.

EDITIONS AND COLLECTIONS OF ESSAYS ON *AS YOU LIKE IT*

Bloom, Harold, ed. *Major Literary Characters: Rosalind.* New York: Chelsea House, 1995.

• Bloom, Harold, ed. *William Shakespeare's As You Like It.* New York: Chelsea House, 1988. Contains Colie essay.

Furness, Horace Howard, ed. *A New Variorum Edition of Shakespeare: As You Like It.* 1890; rpt. Philadelphia: J. B. Lippincott, 1918. Good for nineteenth-century opinion.

Halio, Jay L., ed. *Twentieth Century Interpretations of As You Like It.* Englewood Cliffs, N.J.: Prentice-Hall, 1968.

Knowles, Richard, ed. *A New Variorum Edition of Shakespeare: As You Like It.* New York: Modern Language Association, 1977.

Lynch, Stephen J. *As You Like It: A Guide to the Play.* Greenwood Guides to Shakespeare. Westport, Conn.: Greenwood Press, 2003.

Soule, Leslie Wade. *The Shakespeare Handbooks: As You Like It. A Guide to the Text and Its Theatrical Life.* Basingstoke: Palgrave Macmillan, 2005.

• Tomarken, Edward, ed. *As You Like It from 1600 to the Present: Critical Essays.* Garland Reference Library of the Humanities, vol. 1662. New York: Garland, 1997. Includes 130 pp. of reviews of stage performances. Contains Jamieson essay.

OTHER CRITICAL AND HISTORICAL STUDIES OF THE PLAY

Barber, C. L. *Shakespeare's Festive Comedy: A Study of Dramatic Form and Its Relation to Social Custom.* 1959; rpt. Cleveland: Meridian Books, 1963.

Barnaby, Andrew. "The Political Conscious of Shakespeare's *As You Like It.*" *SEL: Studies in English Literature* 36.2 (1996): 373–95.

• Barton, Anne. *Essays, Mostly Shakespearean.* Cambridge: Cambridge University Press, 1994.

Bate, Jonathan. *The Genius of Shakespeare.* New York: Oxford University Press, 1998.

Bednarz, James P. *Shakespeare and the Poets' War.* New York: Columbia University Press, 2001.

Belsey, Catherine. "Disrupting Sexual Difference: Meaning and Gender in the Comedies." In *Alternative Shakespeares*. Ed. John Drakakis. 2nd ed. London: Routledge, 2002, pp. 170–94.

Berry, Edward. "Rosalynde and Rosalind." *Shakespeare Quarterly* 31 (1980): 42–52.

Boehrer, Bruce. *Shakespeare among the Animals: Nature and Society in the Drama of Early Modern England*. Basingstoke: Palgrave Macmillan, 2002.

Bulman, James C. "Bringing Cheek by Jowl's *As You Like It* Out of the Closet: The Politics of Gay Theater." *Shakespeare Bulletin* 22.3 (2004): 31–46.

Bulman, James C. "Queering the Audience: All-Male Casts in Recent Productions of Shakespeare." In *A Companion to Shakespeare and Performance*. Ed Barbara Hodgdon and William B. Worthen. Oxford: Blackwell, 2005, pp. 564–87.

Chakravorty, Swapan. "Translating Arden: Shakespeare's Rhetorical Place in *As You Like It*." In *Shakespeare and the Mediterranean: The Selected Proceedings of the International Shakespeare Association World Congress, Valencia, 2001*, ed. Tom Clayton, Susan Brock, and Vicente Forés. Newark: University of Delaware Press, 2004.

• Chedgzoy, Kate, ed. *Shakespeare, Feminism and Gender*. New Casebooks. Basingstoke: Palgrave, 2001. Contains Traub essay.

Cirillo, Albert R. "*As You Like It*: Pastoralism Gone Awry." *ELH* 38.1 (1971): 19–30.

Doran, Madeleine. *Endeavors of Art: A Study of Form in Elizabethan Drama*. Binghamton: Vail-Ballou Press, 1954.

• Dowden, Edward. *Shakespere: A Critical Study of His Mind and Art*. London: Henry S. King, 1875.

• Dusinberre, Juliet. "Pancakes and a Date for *As You Like It*." *Shakespeare Quarterly* 54.4 (2003): 371–405.

Dusinberre, Juliet. "Rival Poets in the Forest of Arden." *Shakespeare Jahrbuch* 139 (2003): 71–83.

Eccles, Mark. *Shakespeare in Warwickshire*. Madison: University of Wisconsin Press, 1961.

• Egan, Gabriel. *Green Shakespeare: From Ecopolitics to Ecocriticism*. London: Routledge, 2006.

• Gajowski, Evelyn, ed. *Re-Visions of Shakespeare: Essays in Honor of Robert Ornstein*. Newark: University of Delaware Press, 2004. Contains Woodbridge essay.

• Garber, Marjorie, Paul B. Franklin, and Rebecca L. Walkowitz, eds. *Field Work: Sites in Literary and Cultural Studies*. New York: Routledge, 1996. Contains Masten essay.

Garber, Marjorie. *Shakespeare after All*. 2004; rpt. New York: Anchor, 2005.

• Garber, Marjorie. *Vested Interests: Cross-Dressing and Cultural Anxiety*. London: Routledge, 1997.

Greenblatt, Stephen. *Shakespearean Negotiations: The Circulation of Social Energy in Renaissance England*. Berkeley: University of California Press, 1988.

Halio, Jay L. "'No Clock in the Forest': Time in *As You Like It*." *SEL: Studies in English Literature 1500–1900* 2.2 (1962): 197–207.

• Hazlitt, William. *Lectures on the Dramatic Literature of the Age of Shakespeare* (New York: Derby & Jackson, 1860), pp. 198–201.

• Howard, Jean E. "Crossdressing, the Theatre, and Gender Struggle in Early Modern England." *Shakespeare Quarterly* 39.4 (1988): 418–40.

Hopkins, Lisa. "Orlando and the Golden World: The Old World and the New in *As You Like It*." *Early Modern Literary Studies* 8.2 (2002): <http://purl.oclc.org./emls/08-2/hopkgold.htm>.

Hunt, Maurice A. *Shakespeare's As You Like It: Late Elizabethan Culture and Literary Representation*. New York: Palgrave Macmillan, 2008.

• Jameson, Mrs. Anna. *The Heroines of Shakespeare: Their Moral, Poetical and Historical Characteristics*. 1832; rpt. Philadelphia: John E. Potter, 1898.

Jankowski, Theodora A. *Pure Resistance: Queer Virginity in Early Modern English Drama*. Philadelphia: University of Pennsylvania Press, 2000.

Jones, William. "William Shakespeare as William in *As You Like It*." *Shakespeare Quarterly* 11 (1960): 228–31.

Kinney, Clare R. "Feigning Female Faining: Spenser, Lodge, Shakespeare and Rosalind." *Modern Philology* 95.3 (1998): 291–315.

Laroque, François. *Shakespeare's Festive World*. Trans. Janet Lloyd. Cambridge: Cambridge University Press, 1993.

Leggatt, Alexander. *Shakepeare's Comedy of Love*. London: Methuen, 1974.

• Lenz, Carolyn Ruth Swift, Gayle Greene, and Carol Thomas Neely, eds. *The Woman's Part: Feminist Criticism of Shakespeare*. Urbana: University of Illinois Press, 1983. Contains Park essay.

Lewis, Cynthia. "Horns, the Dream-work, and Female Potency in *As You Like It*." *South Atlantic Review* 66.4 (2001): 45–69.

• Lodge, Thomas. *Rosalynde*. Ed. W. W. Greg. London: Chatto and Windus, 1907.

Marcus, Leah S. *Puzzling Shakespeare: Local Reading and Its Discontents*. Berkeley: University of California Press, 1988. Includes material on Elizabeth I and cross-dressed heroines.

• Marshall, Cynthia. "The Doubled Jaques and Constructions of Negation in *As You Like It*." *Shakespeare Quarterly* 49.4 (1998): 375–92.

Marshall, Cynthia. "Wrestling as Play and Game in *As You Like It*." *SEL: Studies in English Literature, 1500–1900* 33.2 (1993): 265–87.

• Montrose, Louis Adrian. "'The Place of a Brother' in *As You Like It*: Social Process and Comic Form." *Shakespeare Quarterly* 32.1 (1981): 28–54.

Nevo, Ruth. *Comic Transformations in Shakespeare*. London: Methuen, 1980.

O'Dair, Sharon. *Class, Critics, and Shakespeare: Bottom Lines on the Culture Wars*. Ann Arbor: University of Michigan Press, 2000.

Orgel, Stephen. "Nobody's Perfect: Or Why Did the English Stage Take Boys for Women?" *South Atlantic Quarterly* 88.1 (1989): 7–29.

Palmer, D. J. "Art and Nature in *As You Like It*." *Philological Quarterly* 49 (1970): 30–40.

Rackin, Phyllis. "Androgyny, Mimesis, and the Marriage of the Boy Heroine on the English Renaissance Stage." *PMLA* 102.1 (1987): 29–41.

Ronk, Martha. "Locating the Visual in *As You Like It*." *Shakespeare Quarterly* 52.2 (2001): 255–76.

Rose, Mary Beth. "Where Are the Mothers in Shakespeare? Options for Gender Representation in the English Renaissance." *Shakespeare Quarterly* 42:3 (1991): 291–314.

Rowan, Jamin C. "Ideas about Nature: An Ecocentric Look at *As You Like It*." *The Upstart Crow* 21 (2001): 15–26.

• Shannon, Laurie. *Sovereign Amity: Figures of Friendship in Shakespearean Contexts*. Chicago: University of Chicago Press, 2002.

Shepherd, Simon. *Amazons and Warrior Women: Varieties of Feminism in Seventeenth-century Drama*. Brighton: Harvester, 1981.

• Smallwood, Robert. *Shakespeare at Stratford: As You Like It*. London: Arden Shakespeare, 2003.

Smith, Bruce R. *Homosexual Desire in Shakespeare's England: A Cultural Poetics*. Chicago: University of Chicago Press, 1991.

Strout, Nathaniel. "*As You Like It, Rosalynde*, and Mutuality." *SEL: Studies in English Literature* 41.2 (2001): 277–95.

Tiffany, Grace. "'That Reason Wonder May Diminish': *As You Like It*, Androgyny, and the Theater Wars." *Huntington Library Quarterly* 57.3 (1994): 213–39.

Traub, Valerie. *Desire and Anxiety: Circulations of Sexuality in Shakespearean Drama*. London: Routledge, 1992.

Tvordi, Jessica. "Female Alliance and the Construction of Homoeroticism in *As You Like It* and *Twelfth Night*." In *Maids and Mistresses, Cousins and Queens:*